SUBJECTIVE WELL-BEING AND LIFE SATISFACTION

D0782042

The quality of people's relationships with and interactions with other people are major influences on their feelings of well-being and their evaluations of life satisfaction. The goal of this volume is to offer scholarly summaries of theory and research on topics at the frontier of the study of these *social psychological* influences—both interpersonal and intrapersonal—on subjective well-being and life satisfaction. The chapters cover a variety of types of relationships (e.g., romantic relationships, friendships, online relationships) as well as a variety of types of interactions with others (e.g., forgiveness, gratitude, helping behavior, self-presentation). Also included are chapters on broader social issues such as materialism, sexual identity and orientation, aging, spirituality, and meaning in life.

Subjective Well-Being and Life Satisfaction provides a rich and focused resource for graduate students, upper-level undergraduate students, and researchers in positive psychology and social psychology, as well as social neuroscientists, mental health researchers, clinical and counselling psychologists, and anyone interested in the science of well-being.

James E. Maddux is University Professor Emeritus in the Department of Psychology and Senior Scholar at the Center for the Advancement of Well-Being at George Mason University in Fairfax, Virginia. He is a Fellow of the American Psychological Association and the Association for Psychological Science.

Frontiers of Social Psychology

Series Editors:
Arie W. Kruglanski, University of Maryland at College Park
Joseph P. Forgas, University of New South Wales

Frontiers of Social Psychology is a series of domain-specific handbooks. Each volume provides readers with an overview of the most recent theoretical, methodological, and practical developments in a substantive area of social psychology, in greater depth than is possible in general social psychology handbooks. The editors and contributors are all internationally renowned scholars whose work is at the cutting edge of research.

Scholarly, yet accessible, the volumes in the *Frontiers* series are an essential resource for senior undergraduates, postgraduates, researchers, and practitioners and are suitable as texts in advanced courses in specific subareas of social psychology.

Published Titles

Subjective Well-Being and Life Satisfaction
James E. Maddux

Positive Psychology
Dana S. Dunn

The Politics of Social Psychology
Crawford & Jussim

Computational Social Psychology
Vallacher, Read, & Nowak

Group Processes
Levine

Ostracism, Exclusion, and Rejection
Williams & Nida

Political Psychology
Krosnick, Chiang, and Stark

Aggression and Violence
Brad J. Bushman

Social Neuroscience
Harmon-Jones & Inzlicht

For continually updated information about published and forthcoming titles in the *Frontiers of Social Psychology* series, please visit: **www.routledge.com/ psychology/series/FSP**

SUBJECTIVE WELL-BEING AND LIFE SATISFACTION

Edited by
James E. Maddux

Taylor & Francis Group

NEW YORK AND LONDON

First published 2018
by Routledge
711 Third Avenue, New York, NY 10017

and by Routledge
2 Park Square, Milton Park, Abingdon, Oxon, OX14 4RN

Routledge is an imprint of the Taylor & Francis Group, an informa business

Library of Congress Cataloging-in-Publication Data
DataNames: Maddux, James E., editor.
Title: Subjective well-being and life satisfaction / edited by James E. Maddux.
Description: 1 Edition. | New York : Routledge, 2018. |
Series: Frontiers of social psychology | Includes bibliographical references
and index.
Identifiers: LCCN 2017039596 | ISBN 9781138282070 (hb : alk. paper) |
ISBN 9781138282087 (pb : alk. paper) | ISBN 9781351231879 (eb)
Subjects: LCSH: Well-being. | Happiness. | Emotions. |
Interpersonal relations.
Classification: LCC BF575.H27 S833 2018 | DDC 152.1/886—dc23
LC record available at https://lccn.loc.gov/2017039596

ISBN: 978-1-138-28207-0 (hbk)
ISBN: 978-1-138-28208-7 (pbk)
ISBN: 978-1-351-23187-9 (ebk)

Typeset in Bembo
by Apex CoVantage, LLC

CONTENTS

Contributors   *viii*

PART I
Foundational Issues   **1**

1 Subjective Well-Being and Life Satisfaction: An Introduction
   to Conceptions, Theories, and Measures   3
   James E. Maddux

2 Social Neuroscience of Subjective Well-Being and
   Life Satisfaction   32
   Alex W. daSilva and Todd F. Heatherton

3 Cultural Differences in Subjective Well-Being: How and Why
   William Tov and Ze Ling Serene Nai   50

PART II
Interpersonal Influences   **75**

4 Intimate Relations, Subjective Well-Being, and Health Behavior:
   Insights From a Dyadic Perspective   77
   Chloe O. Huelsnitz, Alexander J. Rothman, and
   Jeffry A. Simpson

5   The Role of Friendships in Well-Being   103
    Beverley Fehr and Cheryl Harasymchuk

6   Leave Well Enough Alone? The Costs and Benefits
    of Solitude   129
    Robert J. Coplan, John M. Zelenski, and Julie C. Bowker

7   Forgiveness   148
    Everett L. Worthington, Jr., Brandon J. Griffin,
    and Caitlin Provencher

8   Humility   168
    Everett L. Worthington, Jr., Don E. Davis, Joshua N. Hook,
    and Caitlin Provencher

9   Helping and Well-Being: A Motivational Perspective   184
    David A. Lishner and Eric L. Stocks

10 Gratitude   210
    Philip C. Watkins and Daniel Scheibe

11 Social Comparison Processes   230
    Pieternel Dijkstra and Abraham P. Buunk

12 Social Media Use and Well-Being   253
    Jung-Hyun Kim

13 The Social Psychology of Employee Well-Being:
    A Needs-Based Perspective   272
    Nathan A. Bowling

PART III
Intrapersonal and Self-Related Influences   **291**

14 Meaning in Life in Context   293
    Samantha J. Heintzelman

15 The Impact of a Materialistic Value Orientation on
    Well-Being   311
    Helga Dittmar and Megan Hurst

16 Religion, Spirituality, and Well-Being   337
    Joshua A. Wilt, Nick Stauner, and Julie J. Exline

17 Self-Presentation and Subjective Well-Being   355
    James M. Tyler, Katherine E. Adams, and Peter Kearns

18 Self-Awareness, Hypo-Egoicism, and Psychological
    Well-Being   392
    Mark R. Leary

19 Sexual Orientation and Well-Being   409
    Adam W. Fingerhut

20 Motives, Goals, and Well-Being Throughout the Lifespan   432
    Jutta Heckhausen and Joseph S. Kay

PART IV
**Strategies for Enhancing Subjective Well-Being and
Life Satisfaction**   **449**

21 Positive Activity Interventions to Enhance Well-Being:
    Looking Through a Social Psychological Lens   451
    Julia Revord, Lisa C. Walsh, and Sonja Lyubomirsky

Index   *473*

CONTRIBUTORS

Katherine E. Adams, Purdue University, USA

Julie C. Bowker, University at Buffalo, The State University of New York, USA

Nathan A. Bowling, Wright State University, USA

Abraham P. Buunk, University of Groningen, The Netherlands

Robert J. Coplan, Carleton University, Canada

Alex W. daSilva, Dartmouth College, USA

Don E. Davis, Georgia State University, USA

Pieternel Dijkstra, University of Groningen, The Netherlands

Helga Dittmar, University of Sussex, United Kingdom

Julie J. Exline, Case Western Reserve University, USA

Beverley Fehr, University of Winnipeg, Canada

Adam W. Fingerhut, Loyola Marymount University, USA

Brandon J. Griffin, Veterans Administration Medical Center, San Francisco, CA, USA

Cheryl Harasymchuk, Carleton University, Canada

Todd F. Heatherton, Dartmouth College, USA

Jutta Heckhausen, University of California-Irvine, USA

Samantha J. Heintzelman, University of Virginia, USA

Joshua N. Hook, University of North Texas, USA

Chloe O. Huelsnitz, University of Minnesota, USA

Megan Hurst, University of Sussex, United Kingdom

Joseph S. Kay, University of California-Irvine, USA

Peter Kearns, Purdue University, USA

Jung-Hyun Kim, Sogang University, South Korea

Mark R. Leary, Duke University, USA

David A. Lishner, University of Wisconsin Oshkosh, USA

Sonja Lyubomirsky, University of California-Riverside, USA

Ze Ling Serene Nai, Singapore Management University, Singapore

Caitlin Provencher, Virginia Commonwealth University, USA

Julia Revord, University of California-Riverside, USA

Alexander J. Rothman, University of Minnesota, USA

Daniel Scheibe, Eastern Washington University, USA

Jeffry A. Simpson, University of Minnesota, USA

Nick Stauner, Case Western Reserve University, USA

Eric L. Stocks, University of Texas at Tyler, USA

William Tov, Singapore Management University, Singapore

James M. Tyler, Purdue University, USA

Lisa C. Walsh, University of California-Riverside, USA

Philip C. Watkins, Eastern Washington University, USA

Joshua A. Wilt, Case Western Reserve University, USA

Everett L. Worthington, Jr., Virginia Commonwealth University, USA

John M. Zelenski, Carleton University, Canada

PART I

Foundational Issues

1

SUBJECTIVE WELL-BEING AND LIFE SATISFACTION

An Introduction to Conceptions, Theories, and Measures

James E. Maddux

The author is grateful to Michael Bombardier and Shiva Hassanzadeh-Behbaha for helpful comments and suggestions on an earlier version of this chapter.

It is a truth (almost) universally acknowledged that the vast majority of the people on this earth prefer more happiness to less happiness and prefer lives with which they are more often satisfied than dissatisfied. Although some have questioned the value of happiness and life satisfaction and the wisdom of people who value it or study it (e.g., Pérez-Álvarez, 2016), being happy and satisfied with one's life is of great importance to the vast majority of people all over the world (Diener & Oishi, 2000). This alone makes happiness and life satisfaction—typically referred to collectively as *subjective well-being*—worthy subjects of study by social scientists. One does not have to believe that happiness and life satisfaction are the most important things in life to believe that they are important enough to be worth studying and understanding.

A good working definition of subjective well-being is "the experience of joy, contentment, or positive well-being, combined with a sense that one's life is good, meaningful, and worthwhile" (Lyubomirsky, 2013, p. 32). The study of subjective well-being is

> the scientific analysis of how people evaluate their lives—both at the moment and for longer periods such as for the past year [including] people's emotional reactions to events, their moods, and judgments they form about their life satisfaction, fulfillment, and satisfaction with domains such as marriage and work.
> *(Diener, Oishi, & Lucas, 2003, p. 404)*

Subjective well-being (SWB) is a psychological construct concerned not with what people have or what happens to them but with how they *think* about and *feel* about what they have and what happens to them. The study of subjective well-being makes a distinction between the *objective* conditions of someone's life and that person's *subjective* evaluations of and feelings about his or her life. Plenty of relatively rich, healthy people are miserable, and plenty of relatively poor or unhealthy people lead lives of meaning and joy. Average SWB is greater in some relatively poor countries than in some relatively rich countries (Myers, 2000). In addition, as rich nations have become richer over the past several decades (as measured by *per capita* gross domestic product), the average SWB of their citizens has, in general, not increased (Myers, 2000). While acknowledging the importance of *objective* economic well-being (as typically defined by economists), this book focuses on *subjective* well-being—what people think about and how they feel about their lives and how they feel as they go about their lives. (See Angner, 2010, for a more detailed discussion of this distinction.)

It feels good to be happy and satisfied with life, but enhancing people's sense of well-being and life satisfaction is not simply about making them feel better; enhancing subjective well-being has practical value. People with greater subjective well-being are more successful in many life domains, and their success is at least partly due to their greater sense of well-being. They are more social, altruistic, and active; they like themselves and other people better, have stronger bodies and immune systems, and have better conflict resolution skills (Lyubomirsky, King, & Diener, 2005). Higher SWB promotes creative thinking (Eid & Larsen, 2008). People with higher SWB are likely to earn more money (Diener & Biswas-Diener, 2008). They generally experience greater physical health than and live longer than people with lower SWB (Diener, Pressman, Hunter, & Delgadillo-Chase, 2017). They are less vulnerable to catching the common cold, and when they do, they report few symptoms and show fewer objective signs of illness (Cohen, Doyle, Turner, Alper, & Skoner, 2003 in Diener & Biswas-Diener, 2008). In a variety of practical ways, being relatively happy and relatively satisfied with one's life is better than being unhappy and dissatisfied.

The study of SWB is of interest to more people than just psychologists. Economists and policy makers have become increasingly concerned with measures of SWB in addition to traditional objective measures such as standard of living (typically expressed in such statistics as a nation's *per capita* gross domestic product or average income). Some economists link the importance of these objective measures to their impact on SWB. For example, economist Andrew Oswald has stated that "[t]he relevance of economic performance is that it may be a means to an end . . . the enrichment of mankind's feeling of well-being" (Oswald, 1997, p. 1815, quoted in Angner, 2016).

Interest in SWB goes beyond an interest in the SWB of individuals. In the field of education, a "positive education" movement is well under way that is concerned with enhancing the well-being of all members of the education community and includes efforts in primary and secondary schools and universities

(Furlong, Gilman, & Huebner, 2014; Harward, 2016). Organizational and employee well-being are of growing concern and interest in the fields of management and industrial/organizational psychology (e.g., Linley & Harrington, 2013; Youssef & Luthans, 2011). In 2000 Diener (2000) proposed an index for measuring a *nation's* SWB. The notion of "gross national happiness" originated in Bhutan in 1972 and is now incorporated in that government's economic and development planning. Concern for citizens' SWB has made its way into the constitutions of several nations, including Japan, South Korea, Ecuador, and Bolivia. The United Nations released its first annual *World Happiness Report* in 2011. In 2013, Santa Monica, California, became the first city in the United States to officially make its citizens' SWB a priority by launching its Well-Being Project (https://wellbeing. smgov.net). The Organization for Economic Cooperation and Development (OECD) has endorsed the use of measures of SWB as indicators of economic and social progress (OECD, 2013), as has France's Commission on the Measurement of Economic Performance and Social Progress (Diener & Diener, 2017). The United Arab Emirates has a Minister of State for Happiness (Diener & Diener, 2017), and Ecuador has a Minister of Good Living (Diener & Diener, 2017). The United States' Office of the Surgeon General's has launched an initiative to enhance SWB among the American people (Diener & Diener, 2017). The United Nations recently passed a resolution stating that the happiness of citizens should be a goal of governments (Diener & Diener, 2017). Economists and psychologists alike have endorsed the use of measures of SWB in guiding public policy (e.g., Oswald, 1997; Kahneman, 1999; Diener & Seligman, 2004; Dolan & Metcalf, 2012).

The scientific study of SWB is at least 90 years old. These early studies were largely concerned with marital satisfaction and included Hamilton's *A Research in Marriage* (1929), Sailer's *Happiness Self-Estimates of Young Men* (1931), Terman's *Psychological Factors in Marital Happiness* (1938), Burgess and Cottrell's *Predicting Success or Failure in Marriage* (1939), and Hart's *Chart for Happiness* (1940) (Angner, 2016). One of the most important early works was Cantril's *The Pattern of Human Concerns* (1965), which presented the "Cantril ladder" measure of SWB now used in surveys for the United Nation's annual *World Happiness Report* (Helliwell, Layard, & Sachs, 2017). The first major journal review article on SWB was published in 1967 (Wilson, 1967). Other major contributions to the study of SWB include Campbell, Converse, and Rodgers, *The Quality of American Life* (1976) and Andrews and Withey's book *Social Indicators of Well-Being: Americans' Perceptions of Life Quality* (1976). Diener's landmark *American Psychologist* article on SWB was published in 1984. Veenhoven published an independent review of research on SWB that same year (Veenhoven, 1984).

In the 1960s and 1970s, sociologists and quality of life researchers were studying the influence of demographic factors such as income and marriage on SWB (e.g., Bradburn, 1969; Andrews & Withey, 1976; Campbell et al., 1976; Diener et al., 2003). Some mental health researchers advocated extending the definition of mental health beyond the absence of symptoms of psychopathology to also include the presence of happiness and life satisfaction (e.g., Jahoda, 1958; Diener et al., 2003). For several decades social psychologists have studied the personalities, beliefs, and behaviors of happier and unhappier people and people who are more satisfied or less satisfied with their lives (e.g., Wessman & Ricks, 1966; Diener et al., 2003; Brickman & Campbell, 1971; Parducci, 1995; Lyubomirsky, 2001). This book offers a summary of theory and research on the *social psychological factors* (including to some extent personality factors) that influence subjective well-being and life satisfaction.

Understanding the theory and research discussed in the chapters of this book will be enhanced by an understanding of some basic issues in the study of SWB. The goal of this chapter, therefore, is to provide an overview of some of the most important issues in the scientific study of subjective well-being and life satisfaction that will provide the reader with a set of philosophical, conceptual, and methodological tools for evaluating the material in the remaining chapters. This chapter does *not* provide a discussion and critique of every important issue in the study of well-being and life satisfaction, nor does it provide an exhaustive discussion of any of them. Such discussions can be found in any number of the sources referred to in the chapter. The four sections to follow are concerned with (1) conceptions of SWB, (2) theories of SWB, (3) common strategies for measuring SWB, and (4) basic problems in the measurement of SWB.

Conceptions of Subjective Well-Being

As noted previously, SWB is a *psychological construct* concerned with what people think about and how they feel about their lives. Research on psychological constructs requires clear *conceptions* of the constructs and clear *theories* of the constructs. Conceptions of constructs are concerned with how they are defined and measured. Theories of constructs are concerned with explaining and predicting how the phenomena described by the constructs develop and change. Clear and concise conceptions of psychological phenomena must precede theories of them because we have to know *what* we are trying to explain or predict—and how we are going to measure it—before we can conduct research to try to explain or predict it. Clear and concise conceptions of psychological constructs are essential because unless different studies of a psychological construct employ the same or equivalent measures based on the same or equivalent conceptions, comparing findings across studies can be difficult or impossible, and the progress of the science concerned with that phenomena will be hobbled. For example, the field of psychopathology makes a distinction between conceptions of psychopathology and theories of psychopathology (Maddux, Gosselin, & Winstead, 2016). We need to have relatively clear conceptions (definitions) of psychopathologies before we can empirically evaluate theories of how those psychopathologies develop and how they might be changed (Maddux et al., 2016). Likewise, we need a clear and concise conception of SWB before we can conduct research to test theories of how SWB develops and how it can be changed.

Unfortunately, one of the continuing problems with research on SWB is lack of consensus on the conception and measurement of SWB. The major ongoing debate concerns the distinction between *hedonic* conceptions (and measures) of SWB and *eudaimonic* conceptions (and measures) of SWB. Although sometimes labeled as *theories* of SWB, these are not theories of how SWB develops and how it can be changed but simply different conceptions of SWB that lead to different ways of measuring it. This debate has both scientific aspects and moral and ethical aspects.

In *hedonic* (or hedonistic) conceptions, SWB is defined by the balance of pleasant and enjoyable versus unpleasant events in a person's life (Haybron, 2008). A "good life" is one in which there is more pleasure and enjoyment than pain and suffering, regardless of the sources of these events and experiences. The individual's moral attributes, values, virtues, goals, achievements, and contributions to other people and society are largely irrelevant. What matters is to what extent the person enjoys his or her life, generally feels good as opposed to bad, experiences pleasure as opposed to pain and discomfort, and is satisfied versus dissatisfied with his or her life. In hedonic conceptions, the individual is the sole judge of his or her happiness and life satisfaction. The opinions of other people (including philosophers and psychologists) as to whether the person is leading a "good" or "meaningful" life are irrelevant.

Theorists and researchers generally agree on the conception and measurement of hedonic well-being. The conception of hedonic well-being most commonly employed in research is Diener's (1984) *tripartite structure* consisting of measures of positive affect, negative affect, and life satisfaction. A person with high SWB experiences more positive affect than negative affect and is relatively satisfied with his or her life. The vast majority of other theorists and researchers have provided conceptions and measures of hedonic well-being that essentially include these same components or minor variations of them (Huta & Waterman, 2014). Because most of the measures commonly used in research do not actually measure the experience of pleasure or pain, they do not fully capture a hedonic (or hedonistic) conception of well-being as traditionally defined by philosophers, but they are nonetheless referred to as hedonic measures (Disabato et al., 2015).

Eudaimonic conceptions of well-being emphasize the idea that "we flourish by fully exercising our human capacities" (Haybron, 2008, pp. 25–26). This conception can be traced back to Aristotle's *Nichomachean Ethics*, written in 350 BC, in which he used the term *eudaimonia* to refer primarily to the idea that a "good life" involves "achieving the best that is within us, each according to his or her unique talents and capacities" (Ruini & Ryff, 2016, pp. 153–154) or "a life conditioned upon self-truth and personal responsibility" (Ruini & Ryff, 2016). In this conception, well-being is determined not by the quality of one's sensual and emotional experiences but by the extent to which one is living up to one's potential;

making progress toward attaining one's valued goals; and living a life of meaning, purpose, and virtue. In this way, eudaimonic conceptions strive to "capture core aspects of what it means to be human" (Ryff, 2014, p. 23). (See Haybron, 2008; Kashdan, Biswas-Diener, & King, 2008; Ryan & Deci, 2001; and Ryff, 2014, for more detailed discussions of the distinctions between hedonic and eudaimonic well-being.)

Translating the concept of eudaimonic well-being from philosophy to psychology has been problematic due to a lack of consensus among eudaimonia researchers on how to define it and measure it (Biswas-Diener et al., 2009, p. 209; Kashdan et al., 2008). A recent review of the research on eudaimonic well-being reported 11 different conceptions involving various combinations of 12 basic components (Huta & Waterman, 2014). For example, Ryff's (1989, 2014) model proposes six components: self-acceptance, positive relations with others, personal growth, purpose in life, environmental mastery, and autonomy. Keyes' (2006) model proposes the same six as Ryff but adds five components of social well-being: acceptance, actualization, contribution, coherence, and integration. Ryan and Deci's model (Ryan et al., 2013) focuses mainly on the three components of autonomy, competence, and relatedness but includes several others that overlap with the Ryff and Keyes models. The *nested model* (Henriques, Kleinman, & Asselin, 2014) proposes four domains of well-being; subjective (happiness and life satisfaction); health and functioning domain (biological and psychological); environmental (both material and social environments); and values and ideology domain (the moral and ethical perspective of an external observer and evaluator). The *PERMA model* Seligman (2011) offers five components: positive emotions, engagement, meaning, positive relationships, and accomplishment. (Additional conceptions can be found in Huta & Waterman, 2014.) Among the many measures for eudaimonic well-being that have been proposed, Ryff's model has been the subject of the most empirical research regarding both its psychometric properties and its predictive utility (Ryff, 2014).

Hedonic and Eudaimonic Conceptions and Measures: Empirical Evidence

Research on the distinction between hedonic and eudaimonic conceptions and measures of well-being suggests that they are strongly related.

For example, a study conducted at three different sites found correlations between a measure of the hedonic enjoyment of life events and a measure of feelings of personal expressiveness of those events (eudaimonia) of .87, .85, and .83 respectively (Waterman, Schwartz, & Conti, 2008). In addition, participants in the study rated 88% of the activities associated with personal expressiveness as also high on hedonic enjoyment and rated almost 61% of the activities rated as high on hedonic enjoyment as also high on personal expressiveness. However, the measures had different relationships with other measures such as intrinsic motivation, self-determination, self-realization of values, and importance, suggesting that people can conceptually distinguish somewhat between feelings of enjoyment and feelings of personal expressiveness even though the measures of these experiences are highly correlated. (For similar results, see Waterman, 1993.)

Another study with a large national sample in the United States found correlations at two different points in time of .63 and .70 between a measure of happiness (e.g., "In general, I consider myself happy".) and a measure of life meaningfulness (a key eudaimonic concept; e.g., "In general, I consider my life to be meaningful".) (Baumeister, Vohs, Aaker, & Garbinsky, 2013). As in the study noted above, the result of this study suggest that people can distinguish between being happy and having lives that are meaningful. For example, feeling that life is relatively easy or difficult was more strongly related to happiness than to meaningfulness. Monetary scarcity was more detrimental to happiness than to meaningfulness. Thinking about the past and the future predicted greater meaningfulness but less happiness. People rated happiness as more short-lived and fleeting than meaningfulness. Both happiness and meaningfulness were related to social connectedness, but happiness was more closely related to the benefits that one receives from others, while meaningfulness was more closely related to the benefits that one bestows on others. Cultural identity was more closely related to meaningfulness than to happiness. Finally, activities concerned with personal expressiveness were more closely related to meaningfulness than to happiness. A study using both traditional surveys and open-ended questions found that people could distinguish among feeling happy, being satisfied with life, and having a life that is meaningful and that happiness ratings were considerably more closely related to life satisfaction ratings than were rating of meaningfulness (Delle Fave, Brdar, Freire, Vella-Brodrick, & Wissing, 2011).

Various studies have found correlations ranging from .76 to .92 between hedonic and eudaimonic measures of SWB (Keyes, Shmotkin, & Ryff, 2002; Gallagher, Lopez, & Preacher, 2009; Linley, Maltby, Wood, Osborne, & Hurling, 2009; Fredrickson et al., 2013). A recent study with a large international sample failed to support a meaningful empirical distinction between hedonic versus eudaimonic measures of SWB (Disabato, Goodman, Kashdan, Short, & Jarden, 2016). In keeping with much previous research, this study assessed so-called hedonic SWB using Diener's (1984) tripartite model (positive affect, negative affect, and life satisfaction) and eudaimonic SWB using Ryff's (1989) Scales of Psychological Well-Being. The latent correlation between the two sets of measures was .96, well exceeding most thresholds for concluding that two instruments are measuring essentially the same construct (Disabato et al., 2015). In addition, in contrast to the study noted previously, this study found few differences between the correlations of the Diener and Ryff measures and other related measures, providing additional evidence that the measures are tapping the same construct.

A recent review of research on various definitions of both eudaimonic well-being and hedonic well-being and the description of a complicated scheme for categorizing them (Huta & Waterman, 2014) exemplifies the futility of continuing to attempt to find clear distinctions between different "types" of subjective well-being. Despite the traditional philosophical distinction between hedonic and eudaimonic conceptions of SWB, much research strongly suggests that contemporary *measures* of hedonic SWB and contemporary *measures* of eudaimonic SWB (or one or more aspects of it) are measuring the same broad construct, regardless of what we decide to call it. Other research suggests that they are closely related but that people can and do make distinctions between them. Perhaps the most reasonable conclusion to draw from these studies is that measures of so-called hedonic well-being (happiness, positive emotions, life satisfaction) and so-called eudaimonic well-being (personal expressiveness, meaningfulness) reflect a single higher-order factor with multiple lower-order factors (Ryan & Deci, 2001; Disabato et al., 2015). One can also view aspects of eudaimonic well-being such as engaging in personally expressive behaviors and finding meaning in life as "pathways" to happiness and life satisfaction (Disabato et al., 2015), but that still does not mean they are different "types" of well-being.

Which Conception Is "Better"?

Many discussions of the distinctions between hedonic and eudaimonic SWB implicitly or explicitly assume that there is a "moral hierarchy" for distinguishing different "types" of subjective well-being (Kashdan et al., 2008) and that eudaimonic well-being is more morally valid, ethical, virtuous, or "authentic" than hedonic well-being (e.g., Annas, 2002; Haybron, 2001; Nozick, 1974; Waterman, 2007; Seligman, 2002, 2011; Kristjánsson, 2010; Ryff, 2017). At times, advocates of eudaimonic well-being seem to be suggesting that "the Good Life is an experience reserved for individuals who have attained some transcendence from everyday life" (Kashdan et al., 2008, p. 227).

Debates over which conception of SWB is morally and ethically superior are as inevitable as debates over politics and religion because conceptions of SWB, like conceptions of almost all psychological phenomena, are not scientific constructions but *social constructions* (Fried, 2017). Social constructionism is concerned with "examining ways in which people understand the world, the social and political processes that influence how people define words and explain events, and the implications of these definitions and explanations" (Muehlenhard & Kimes, 1999, p. 234; see also Gergen, 1985). Social constructions are based on values and moral and ethical principles, and science cannot prove that one set of values and moral and ethical principles is more correct than another. Therefore, the definitions of social constructions are not *revealed* or *discovered* by the methods of science but are *negotiated* among and *produced* by the people and institutions of society who have an interest in their definitions (Fried, 2017). Universal or "true" definitions of psychological constructs do not exist, and debates over their definitions involve not scientific research but beliefs about the way the world works (or should work), the difference between right and wrong and good and bad, and, in the case of SWB, what *should* make life worth living and how people *should* live their lives.

Research on the influence of culture on conceptions of SWB and related notions provides ample evidence for the socially constructed nature of conceptions of SWB. Cultures differ in their conceptions of SWB and the value they place on SWB. For example, people in Eastern (mainly East Asian) cultures are more likely to equate SWB with the experience of low-arousal emotions such as contentment, peace, and tranquility rather than the more high-arousal emotions of happiness and joy that are more highly valued in Western cultures (Joshanloo, 2014; Cordaro, Brackett, Glass, & Anderson, 2016, p. 222). Western and individualist cultures also value pride and self-satisfaction more highly than Eastern and collectivist cultures do (Eid & Diener, 2001; Diener & Diener, 1995; Diener et al., 2003, p. 415). In Eastern conceptions of SWB, self-transcendence is more important than the self-enhancement that is more characteristic of Western conceptions of SWB, harmony is more highly valued than mastery, and valuing suffering is more important than avoiding suffering (Joshanloo, 2014). In addition, life satisfaction is more strongly related to autonomy, feelings of meaning, and personal growth in Western cultures than in Eastern ones (Diener, Diener, & Diener, 1995 in Eid & Larsen, 2008).

SWB in collectivist cultures is more closely tied to contributions to family and group than to the enjoyment of individual achievements (Diener & Biswas-Diener, 2008, p. 134; Oishi & Diener, 2001). Among Koreans, the word most frequently associated with "happiness" is "family", while among Americans it is "smile" (Shin, Suh, Oem, & Kim, 2017). Koreans also associate "happiness" with social words more than Americans do and are more likely than Americans to associate "happiness" with "family" than with "friends" (Shin et al., 2017).

The differences between Eastern and Western conceptions of SWB—and the differences among conceptions of SWB within the Western tradition itself— cannot be reconciled by research. Just as scientific research cannot prove that one political ideology, religion, or culture is better than another, it cannot prove that one conception of SWB is more or less correct, more or less ethical or moral, or more or less authentic than another. Research cannot tell us whether conceiving of and measuring SWB as a combination of positive affect, negative affect, and life satisfaction (a "hedonic" conception) is more or less correct, true, moral, virtuous, or authentic than conceiving of and measuring SWB as any combination of positive affect, negative affect, life satisfaction, meaningfulness of one's life, attainment of valued goals, the quality of one's relationships, autonomy, and other factors (a "eudaimonic" conception). Research cannot tell us whether a life of "meaning" and "purpose" is more ethical, moral, virtuous, or authentic than a life that is simply filled with good times, pleasure, and positive feelings. Therefore, discussions about the correct or proper way to define SWB and related notions are not scientific discussions; they are always philosophical, ethical, and moral discussions.

This is not to say that they are not important discussions but only that they are not scientific discussions (Disabato et al., 2015; Nettle, 2005) because the correctness of ethical and moral principles cannot be determined through research. As strongly as I may believe that a "life worth living" should be a life of meaning, purpose, and striving to fulfill one's potential, I cannot design a study to test that belief. The basic problem here is that some researchers are trying to use science to do something that science simply cannot do.

Theories of Subjective Well-Being

Although research cannot support or refute conceptions of SWB, it can support or refute theories of SWB because theories (at least good ones) make predictions about the relation between one variable and another or the effect of one variable on another. The two basic types of theories of SWB about which we have considerable research are *life circumstance theories* (also referred to as bottom-up theories) and *dispositional/construal theories* (also referred to as top-down and construal theories).

Life Circumstance Theories

Life circumstance theories propose that SWB is mainly the result of the number of a person's positive and negative life circumstances—both day-to-day life experiences (major and minor) and favorable or unfavorable demographic factors such as socioeconomic status, education, and physical health (Lyubomirsky & Dickerhoof, 2010). From this perspective, people who were born into advantageous circumstances and to whom good things happen more often than bad things will have greater SWB than less advantaged, less fortunate people. In addition, life circumstance theories propose that overall SWB and life satisfaction are the result of satisfaction with a variety of life domains (work, family, etc.) in which positive and negative events, experiences, and emotions may occur.

Some research supports life circumstance theories. For example, a recent longitudinal study of members of athletic teams found that the effect of satisfaction with the team on life satisfaction over time was stronger than the effect of life satisfaction on team satisfaction (Chen, Wu, Lin, & Ye, 2017). In addition, marital satisfaction predicts life satisfaction, but not vice versa (Lance, Lautenschlager, Sloan, & Varca, 1989), and satisfaction with housing, financial situation, and social life predicts overall life satisfaction, but not vice versa (Scherpenzeel & Saris, 1996). Life circumstance theories are also supported by research on the effects of employment, satisfaction with employment, and loss of employment on SWB and mental health (Blustein, 2008). Finally, both positive and negative changes in domain-specific satisfaction predict change in life satisfaction, and as the degree of dissatisfaction with a specific domain increases, so does its influence on life satisfaction (Engle & Bless, 2017). Weighing in against life circumstance theories, however, is the accumulated research that suggests that only about 10% of population-wide differences in SWB can be accounted for by differences among people in their experiences of positive and negative life events (Lyubomirsky & Dickerhoof, 2010). Research also suggests that the SWB *set point* to which people typically return following increases in SWB from positive life events and decreases in SWB following negative life events can be altered by seriously aversive life events such as unemployment or serious disability (Fujita & Diener, 2005; Lucas, 2007; Lucas, Clark, Georgellis, & Diener, 2004), thus providing some support for a life circumstance theory. Research indicating that frequency and quality of sexual activity predict subsequently assessed SWB (while SWB does not predict sexual activity) also supports a life circumstance approach (Kashdan, Goodman, Stiksma, Milius, & McKnight, 2017).

Dispositional/Construal Theories

Dispositional theories propose that SWB primarily results not from life circumstances themselves but from biological or temperamental factors that influence behaviors and cognitions—such as interpretations and appraisals of life circumstances and events—that, in turn, influence SWB (Lyubomirsky & Dickerhoof, 2010, p. 230). Because evidence is strong for genetic influences on predispositions in the way people perceive positive and negative life events (Wessels, Zimmermann, & Leising, 2016), dispositional theories are also *construal theories* because they propose that cognitive construals (beliefs, perceptions, and interpretations) of life events and circumstances mediate the effect of biological or temperamental factors on SWB (Lyubomirsky, 2001).

Supporting dispositional/construal theories is research suggesting that *genetic predisposition* may account for as much as 50% of the differences among people in their current SWB and as much as 80% of long-term differences (i.e., over a period of 10 years) (Lykken & Tellegen, 1996). In addition, monozygotic (identical) twins who are raised apart are more similar in SWB than are dizygotic (fraternal) twins who are raised together (Lykken, 1999). Genetics also strongly influences the establishment of a SWB *set point* to which a person usually returns following a rise or fall in SWB that can result from positive or negative life events, accounting for perhaps 80% of the long-term stability of SWB (Steel, Schmidt, & Shultz, 2008). The stability of SWB also increases with age (Anusic & Schimmack, 2016).

Dispositional/construal theories are also supported by considerable research on the heritability of personality (e.g., Vukasović & Bratko, 2015; Wessels et al., 2016) and the strong relationship between personality and mental health and well-being (Strickhouser, Zell, & Krizan, 2017). Most of this research has been conducted on the so-called Big 5 personality traits: neuroticism, extraversion, agreeableness, conscientiousness, and openness to experience (Steel et al., 2008). The strongest personality trait predictors of SWB are neuroticism and extraversion. Agreeableness, conscientious, and openness to experience are less powerful predictors.

Neuroticism is the general disposition to experience negative emotions such as anxiety and depression, so it is not surprising that people higher in neuroticism generally report lower SWB than those who are lower in neuroticism (Diener et al., 1999; Strickhouser et al., 2017; Steel et al., 2008). People higher in neuroticism are more likely to interpret neutral life events in negative ways and to experience anxiety and depression in reaction to negative life events (Steel et al., 2008). Negative life events actually happen more often to people higher in neuroticism, perhaps because people higher in neuroticism may make poor decisions while depressed or anxious that lead to undesirable consequences (Headley & Wearing, 1989; cited in Nettle, 2005) Neuroticism appears to be a better predictor of negative affect than of positive affect (Costa & McCrae, 1980; DeNeve & Cooper, 1998).

Extraversion is strongly associated with SWB; more extraverted (socially outgoing) people generally report greater SWB than more introverted (solitary) people (Diener et al., 1999; Steel et al., 2008). Because SWB appears to be influenced by the *frequency* of positive emotions rather than their *intensity* (Larsen & Diener, 1985), extraversion may influence SWB because extraverted people have a lower threshold for the activation of positive emotions (Eid & Larsen, 2008). In addition, more extraverted people engage in more social interactions, which are associated with greater SWB regardless of degree of extraversion or introversion (Steel et al., 2008). Extraversion may be a better predictor of positive affect than of negative affect (Costa & McCrae, 1980; DeNeve & Cooper, 1998; Strickhouser et al., 2017).

People high in *agreeableness* (congenial, easy to get along with, considerate) usually report greater SWB than people lower in agreeableness (DeNeve & Cooper, 1998), possibly because they are more likely to promote harmony in relationships and less likely to promote conflict. Highly *conscientiousness* people (organized, dependable, responsible, persistent) report greater SWB than less conscientious people, probably because they are generally more persistent in striving toward meaningful goals, have greater social connectedness, and are more physically active, all of which are associated with greater SWB (Friedman & Kern, 2014; Strickhouser et al., 2017). Lower conscientiousness (impulsiveness) is associated with poorer delay of gratification and greater procrastination, both of which can lead to a range of negative consequences (Steel et al., 2008). *Openness to experience* (e.g., preference for variety, intellectual curiosity) has a modest relationship with SWB but one that is weaker than those of the other four Big 5 traits (Steel et al., 2008).

SWB may also be influenced by how much one's behavior is consistent with one's personality predispositions. For example, for agreeableness and neuroticism, engaging in trait-congruent behavior is associated with greater positive affect, while engaging trait-incongruent behaviors is associated with greater negative affect (Moskowitz & Coté, 1995; Côté & Moskowitz, 2000).

Further evidence for the dispositional component of dispositional/construal theories comes from *social neuroscience* research, which combines work in the neurosciences, social sciences, and cognitive sciences to explain how the brain computes and facilitates social interactions and processes (Chapter 2). Two key assumptions of social neuroscience are that humans are a fundamentally social species and that sociality and well-being are closely linked. Social neuroscience research has demonstrated that being an effective member of a social group depends largely on the ability to infer the mental states of others; detect social threats; and regulate thought, behavior, and emotion and that the brain's *default network* (consisting of the medial prefrontal cortex, posterior cingulate cortex, medial temporal lobes, and portions of parietal cortex) is crucial to the exercise of these abilities. Research also has shown that connections between certain areas of the default network and the brain's reward regions contribute to positive feelings about the self (see Chapter 2).

Support for the dispositional component also can be found in the research on *enduring mental health* that shows that a small minority of people (perhaps 17%) go through life without ever experiencing a formally diagnosable mental disorder (Schaefer et al., 2017). These never-diagnosed people are not generally higher in socioeconomic status than diagnosed people, nor do they report significantly better physical health or have higher intelligence. The differences, instead, appear to be in temperament, personality, and a family history of relatively few mental health problems, all of which have high heritability factors.

Finally, the dispositional component is supported by research on *heart-rate variability*, which is influenced by the vagal nerve in the gut and has strong genetic determinants. High levels of heart-rate variability are associated with, for example, extraversion, agreeableness, and stability of positive affect (Sloan et al., 2016), all of which are good predictors of SWB.

Evolutionary theories of SWB are variations of dispositional/construal theories that propose that some evolved human tendencies move people toward greater SWB but that others make it difficult for people to attain and sustain SWB (Buss, 2000; Nettle, 2005). SWB-enhancing needs include the needs for strong mating bonds, friendship, kinship, and cooperation with others (Buss, 2000). Other evolved tendencies, however, make SWB difficult to attain and sustain. Humans evolved in environments where material resources were always scarce and where status was strongly associated with reproductive success. Therefore, the human brain has been programmed to keep humans striving for status and prestige, such as through the acquisition of material goods (Nettle, 2005). Unfortunately, the pursuit and acquisition of material goods not only does not enhance SWB but actually diminishes it (Chapter 15). Because of this programming, people continually ignore information about what actually does and does not enhance their SWB. Other evolved barriers to SWB that have been proposed by evolutionary theorists include the differences between ancestral and modern environments (e.g., urbanization, mass communication) that can lead to subjective distress, the frequently adaptive nature of subjective distress (e.g., fear, anger, jealousy, competitive urges) that function to benefit one person at the expense of others, the fact that pain from loss is more keenly felt than is the pleasure of a comparable gain (Buss, 2000).

A final evolutionary consideration is the ability of people to quickly adapt to new circumstances (Buss, 2000). With respect to subjective well-being, this adaptation process is referred to as the *hedonic treadmill* (Brickman & Campbell, 1971; Diener, Lucas, & Scollon, 2006), which refers to the tendency of people to return to their particular baseline of subjective well-being following increases or decreases in positive or negative life events, respectively. The problem for subjective well-being seekers is that new pleasures and positive life events may cause a short burst of enhanced SWB but will soon lose their luster as people get used to them and return to their baseline SWB. This process can lead people to seek out even more and bigger pleasures in the quest for enhanced SWB. The hedonic treadmill is at the heart of the negative relationship between materialistic values and SWB (see Chapter 15). (See Diener et al., 2006, for a discussion of ways in which the hedonic treadmill may not be quite as problematic as previously believed.)

One should not conclude from the above research and theory that a biological predisposition toward certain kinds of appraisals and construals means that patterns of appraisals and construals are "fixed" by biology. Instead, a more reasonable conclusion is that biology may establish for any individual a general range within which he or she functions that can nonetheless be powerfully influenced by environmental influences.

The above research provides strong support for the influence on SWB of inherited dispositions to view or construe the world, the self, and other people in certain ways and respond emotionally to life events in certain ways, which then influence SWB. Support for the direct influence of these construals on SWB comes from research on (among other phenomena) social comparison processes (Chapter 11); meaning and purpose in life (Chapter 14); spirituality and religiosity (Chapter 16); self-presentation (Chapter 17); self-awareness and self-preoccupation (Chapter 18); self-determination (Chapter 13); motivations for helping others (Chapter 9); goals and goal attainment (Chapter 20); and cultural influences on SWB (Chapter 3). Because later chapters of this book discuss these topics in detail, they will not be discussed here.

Combining Life Circumstance and Dispositional/ Construal Theories

Both life circumstance and dispositional/construal theories of SWB have merit and are best viewed as complementary rather than mutually exclusive. For example, the results of cross-sectional and longitudinal studies that examined the relation of objective measures of health and a person's subjective evaluations of health to SWB indicate that both objective life circumstances and personality measures (dispositions) influence SWB and that these effects are mediated by people's interpretation or construal of life events and circumstances, including their objective health, which influence SWB not directly but only indirectly through subjective evaluations of health (Brief, Butcher, George, & Link, 1993).

Additional support for combining both approaches comes from another longitudinal study showing that physical health, daily hassles, world assumptions, and constructive thinking all directly influence SWB, supporting both life circumstance theories (health, hassles) and dispositional/construal theories (assumptions, thinking) (Feist, Bodner, Jacobs, Miles, & Tan, 1995). In addition, SWB may directly influence world assumptions, constructive thinking, physical health, and reports of daily hassles, thus supporting dispositional/construal theories (Feist et al., 1995). Thus, it appears that overall life satisfaction is partly the result of life circumstances and events but also partly the result of general disposition or temperament, which influences perceptions of specific life domains (Feist et al., 1995). Finally, certain evolved human characteristics may either facilitate or impede the attainment of subjective well-being by influencing the strategies that people may use to attain subjective well-being.

Measuring Subjective Well-Being: Common Strategies and Measures

Despite the difficulties inherent in developing measures of subjective well-being and related constructs, many such measures have indeed been developed. Some scales measure only the affective components of SWB, some measure only the life satisfaction components, and some measure both components. Others scales assess several or more components that are usually viewed as eudaimonic aspects of well-being. Measures that are primarily affective, especially those that assess more or less "in-the-moment" affect—can be viewed as measures of *experienced well-being*, while measures of life satisfaction, because they require the evaluation of life events and experiences over relatively long periods of time, can be viewed as measures of *evaluated well-being* (Kahneman & Riis, 2005). A thorough review and critique of the dozens of published scales purporting to measure some aspect of SWB is beyond the scope of this chapter. (Additional related scales can be found in Simmons & Lehman, 2013.)

Tripartite Model of Hedonic SWB

The most well-researched conception and measure of hedonic SWB is the tripartite model described previously, which views SWB as consisting of positive affect, negative affect, and life satisfaction, which can be both *general* (satisfaction with life overall) and *domain-specific* (satisfaction with specific domains of life such as work and relationships) (Busseri & Sadava, 2011, pp. 299–300). Measures of life and domain satisfaction are *cognitive* measures based on evaluations of and beliefs about one's life, while measures of positive and negative affect are, of course, *affective* or emotional measures, concerned with how often people experience pleasant and unpleasant feelings (Schimmack, 2008, p. 97). Positive and negative affect are not independent, but the correlations between them are usually weak to moderate, are separable experiences, and can occur at the same time (Bradburn & Caplovitz, 1965; Diener & Emmons, 1984; Lucas, Diener, & Suh, 1996; Pavot, 2008; Schimmack, 2008).

Relationships Among Components of the Tripartite Model

A review of factor analytic research has suggested five different patterns or configurations of the relationships among life satisfaction, positive affect, and negative affect (Busseri & Sadava, 2011). In the *separate components model*, the study of SWB is simply a research domain that does not imply any causal connections among the three components even though the correlations among them may sometimes be strong. In the *hierarchical construct model*, SWB is a higher-order latent factor that produces the correlations among its three lower-order components. In the *causal system model*, SWB is a network of relations in which positive affect and negative affect are independent influences on life satisfaction because people use how they feel (the balance of positive and negative emotions) when thinking about life satisfaction. In the *composite model*, SWB is a combination of positive affect, negative affect, and life satisfaction, and it is necessary to assess all three components when assessing SWB. In the *configuration model*, the configurations of positive affect, negative affect, and life satisfaction can be different for different people and, therefore, one structure might not be applicable to everyone (Busseri & Sadava, 2011, p. 300). Because three of the five models involve all three of the major components of subjective well-being, it is probably best to assess all three components when assessing SWB (Busseri & Sadava, 2011).

Relationship Between Overall Life Satisfaction and Domain-Specific Satisfaction

The relationship between overall life satisfaction and domain-specific satisfaction is both *bottom-up* and *top-down* (Schimmack, 2008). In a *bottom-up* relationship, people first develop satisfaction with specific life and domains and then formulate an overall life satisfaction from these domain satisfactions. In a *top-down* relationship, people first develop a sense of overall life satisfaction that then leads them to positively or negatively evaluate specific life domains (Schimmack, 2008, p. 98). The causal direction matters because only the bottom-up model suggests that overall life satisfaction can be improved by improving satisfaction with specific important life domains and by changing one's life circumstances and events (Schimmack, 2008, p. 99).

Research on the role of personality in SWB supports a top-down relationship between overall life satisfaction and domain-specific satisfaction. Research showing strong and systematic correlations among rating of domain satisfaction also supports a top-down relationship (Schimmack, 2008). Supporting a bottom-up relationship, however, is research showing that *domain importance* influences the relationship between domain satisfaction and life satisfaction, that objective domain characteristics seem to influence life satisfaction, and that people typically think about important life domains when they think about life satisfaction (Schimmack, 2008, p. 99). In addition, as noted previously, both positive and negative changes in domain-specific satisfaction predict change in life satisfaction, and as the degree of dissatisfaction with a specific domain increases, so does its influence on life satisfaction (Engle & Bless, 2017). Top-down and bottom-up processes may operate over time in a feedback loop such that an increase in satisfaction with a specific domain leads to an increase in overall life satisfaction, which then leads a person to view other domains of life more favorably (Andrews & Withey, 1976, cited in Schimmack, 2008).

Measures of Affect and Happiness

The most commonly used measure of affect is the *Positive and Negative Affective Schedule* (PANAS; Watson, Clark, & Tellegen, 1988), which includes 10 positive affect adjectives (e.g., interested, enthusiastic, inspired) and 10 negative affect adjectives (e.g., distress, upset, afraid), all rated on a 5-point scale. The time frame can be adjusted from at the present moment to within the past year. The PANAS has good reliability and validity (Watson et al., 1988; Pavot, 2008). Although the PANAS and most other measures of affect assume that positive and negative affect fall on different dimensions, that assumption has recently been called into question (Mattek, Wolford, & Whalen, 2017).

The *Affect Balance Scale*, also known as the *Bradburn Scale of Psychological Well-Being* (Bradburn, 1969) consists of 10 items (5 positive affect, 5 negative affect) about the respondent's affective experiences over the past several weeks. A "balance" score is obtained by subtracting the negative affect score from the positive affect score (Pavot, 2008). The *Affectometer 2* (Kamman & Flett, 1983) expands the Affective Balance Scale to 40 items, with 4 items each devoted to ten aspects of SWB: confluence, optimism, self-esteem, self-efficacy, social support, social interest, freedom, energy, cheerfulness, and thought clarity. It has high internal consistency and is a good predictor of other measures of SWB (Kamman & Flett, 1983; Pavot, 2008).

The *Fordyce Happiness Measure* (FHM; Fordyce, 1977, 1988) consists of a single 11-point happiness item and three items that ask respondents to estimate the percentage of time that they are happy, unhappy, or neutral. The developer considers the happiness item to be a measure of intensity and the percentage items to be a measure of frequency. The scale takes about a minute to complete. Test-retest reliability is very good and has good convergent validity with other more lengthy scales (Fordyce, 1988).

In the *experience sampling method* (ESM), individuals carry a palm computer and are cued regularly to report on their thoughts and emotions throughout the day. Because data is collected in "real time" and over a period of time, ESM helps to reduce the impact of some of the problems with surveys such as memory distortions and situational effects at the time a survey is completed (Schwarz & Strack, 1999). ESM data correlates moderately to strongly with self-report surveys (Sandvik, Diener, & Seidlitz, 1993; Pavot, 2008), although the amount of data generated can be difficult to summarize and interpret (Scollon, Kim-Prieto, & Diener, 2003; Pavot, 2008; see also Kahneman & Krueger, 2006). Experience sampling methods might provide more information about SWB in "real time" (Eid & Larsen, 2008, p. 5).

In the *day reconstruction method* (DRM; Kahneman, Krueger, Schkade, Schwarz, & Stone, 2004), respondents are asked to reconstruct their experiences and activities during the preceding day, using techniques intended to minimize memory bias (Kahneman et al., 2004). These responses create a record of both the amount of time spent on various activities and the effects of the experiences on the respondent while he or she was engaged in each activity. The results of the DRM are similar to the ESM but it is more efficient and flexible and less disruptive of the respondent's daily life (Pavot, 2008; see also Kahneman & Krueger, 2006; Kahneman et al., 2004; Kahneman & Krueger, 2006). DRM data are moderately correlated with self-report surveys (Kahneman et al., 2004; Pavot, 2008).

The *U-index* (U = unpleasant or undesirable) (Kahneman & Krueger, 2006) measures the proportion of time the respondent spends in a pleasant or unpleasant state. Episodes are classified as pleasant or unpleasant depending on whether the respondent experiences either positive or negative affect most strongly in that episode (Krueger, 2009, p. 3).

Informant reports consist of ratings of an individual's SWB obtained from family members, friends, coworkers, and others who are familiar with the individual. Informant reports correlate well with self-reports of SWB (Pavot, Diener, Colvin, & Sandvik, 1991; Pavot, 2008). Ratings of *facial expressions* from photographs or video recordings also correlate well with self-reports SWB (Pavot, 2008).

Measures of Life Satisfaction

The *Satisfaction with Life Scale* (SWLS; Diener, Emmons, Larsen, & Griffin, 1985) contains 5 items assessing overall life satisfaction. It has good internal consistency and test-retest reliability (Pavot & Diener, 1993b). It contains no items that assess affect (Pavot, 2008). It is one of the most frequently used scales in SWB research, with citations of the original article well into the multiple thousands.

The *Temporal Satisfaction with Life Scale* (TSWLS; Pavot, Diener, & Suh, 1998) is a 15-item version of the Satisfaction with Life Scale with each of the five items of the SWLS reworded to assess past, present, or expected future life satisfaction. It has the same good psychometric characteristics as the SWLS (Pavot et al., 1998; Pavot, 2008).

Cantril's ladder (Cantril, 1965) is a single-item measure that asks the respondent to rate how good his or her life is on a ladder-like figure with 11 rungs, where the top rung (10) represents the best possible life and the bottom rung (0) the worst possible life. It contains no items assessing affect. As noted previously, this scale is used in the United Nations' annual *World Happiness Report* (Helliwell et al., 2017).

The *Multidimensional Students' Life Satisfaction Scale* (MSLSS; Huebner, 1994) is a 40-item scale for assessing the life satisfaction of preadolescents and includes factors pertaining to satisfaction with self, friends, family, school, and living environment. A brief version of the MSLSS has been shown to be useful with high school students (Seligson, Huebner, & Valois, 2003; Pavot, 2008).

The *Life Satisfaction Scale* was designed for older adults (Neugarten, Havighurst, & Tobin, 1961). Similar scales include the *Life Satisfaction Index A*, the *Life Satisfaction Index B*, and the *Life Satisfaction Rating*. These are all multidimensional scales that assess qualities such as zest, fortitude, self-concept, mood, and congruence between desired and achieved goals (Pavot, 2008).

Measures of Eudaimonic Well-Being

The *Scales of Psychological Well-Being* (SPWB; Ryff, 1989) consists of 89 items rated *strongly disagree* (1) to *strongly agree* (6). It contains 6 subscales with 14 items each: self-acceptance, positive relations with others, autonomy, environmental mastery, purpose in life, and personal growth. Ryff (1989) reports that the scale has good construct validity, internal consistency, and test-retest reliability (Crouch, Mack, Wilson, & Kwan, 2017; Ryff, 2014). The SPWB is correlated highly with briefer measures of the three basic dimensions of SWB of life satisfaction, positive affect, and negative affect (Feist et al., 1995). The SPWB is one of the most frequently used scales in SWB research (Crouch et al., 2017). (See Ryff, 2014, for a summary of research on this measure.)

The *Oxford Happiness Inventory* (OHI; Argyle, Martin, & Lu, 1995) and its revision, the *Oxford Happiness Questionnaire* (Hills & Argyle, 2002) are 29-item scales that include items that assess both emotional experiences and life satisfaction. Items assess energy level, optimism, perceived control of life, perceived health, social interest, perceived congruence between desired goals and actual achievements, and a general sense of happiness and life satisfaction. The OHI is a good predictor of other measures of emotions and life satisfaction and has good test-retest reliability and internal consistency (Pavot, 2008, pp. 129–130). It has been criticized for failing to differentiate SWB from predictors, correlates, and consequences of SWB (Kashdan, 2004).

Other eudaimonic measures that have been used less frequently in research include the *Personally Expressive Activities Questionnaire* (Waterman, 1993), the *Questionnaire for Eudaimonic Well-Being* (Waterman et al., 2010), and the *Mental Health Continuum* (Keyes, 2006). (See Huta & Waterman, 2014, for more information.)

Problems in the Measurement of SWB

Lack of a Common Measurement Protocol

As noted previously, a long-standing problem in SWB research has been the lack of a consensus on how to define and measure SWB, which has resulted in difficulty comparing and summarizing results across studies (Diener & Seligman, 2004; Pavot, 2008). As noted previously, some researchers have recommended that all three major components of the tripartite "hedonic" model of SWB should be measured in research (Busseri & Sadava, 2011; Pavot, 2008). However, a very high percentage of studies assess only one or two of these components (Diener & Seligman, 2004; Pavot, 2008). This makes it difficult to compare results across studies and limits the generalizability of the findings of many studies (Pavot, 2008). In addition, as noted previously, the different conceptions and measures of eudaimonic well-being also make comparisons across studies of eudaimonic well-being difficult (Huta & Waterman, 2014). Finally, there is the problem of how to integrate findings from studies using "hedonic" measures of SWB with those using "eudaimonic" measures.

Overreliance on Self-Report Measures

The vast majority of measures of SWB ask people what they think and feel. Even indirect measures such as asking other people to rate the SWB of a target person rely on self-report measures to assess their validity. A question raised frequently concerns whether people can accurately evaluate and honestly report their level of SWB. How do we know that people who say they are happy are actually happy? And to what extent are people's reports of SWB influenced by biases, temporary situational factors, and temporary moods? (Schwarz & Clore, 1983; Schwarz & Strack, 1999). These questions, of course, apply not only to the study of SWB but to the study of almost every psychological phenomena because "psychology is centrally about mental states" and "[t]here is no better way to gauge someone's positive experiences, life satisfaction, self-determination, and meaning in life than to directly ask about them" (Kashdan et al., 2008, p. 220). In addition, the influence of contextual factors and response style on self-reports seems small (Pavot & Diener, 1993a; Schimmack, Böckenholt, & Reisenzein, 2002; Eid & Diener, 2004; Schimmack & Oishi, 2005; Pavot, 2008). As Gilbert (2006) noted: "The attentive person's honest, real-time report is an imperfect approximation of her subjective experience, but is it the only game in town" (p. 70).

Overreliance on Correlational Studies

Most studies of SWB are cross-sectional correlational studies in which measures of SWB (or one or more of its components) and measures of other constructs of interest are given at one point in time via questionnaires (Pavot, 2008). One limitation of these studies is the possible influence of transient mood states and other contextual factors on people's reports of SWB (Schwarz & Strack, 1999). Although the effects of transient mood and context seem small (Pavot & Diener, 1993a; Eid & Diener, 2004; Schimmack & Oishi, 2005; Yap et al., 2016), they should be avoided if possible, but cannot be avoided with correlational studies (Pavot, 2008, p. 134). A second limitation of correlational studies is that they cannot be used to determine the direction of causality among the variables examined (Pavot, 2008).

Reification

A final problem with measures of SWB is that of *reification*, in which an abstract idea and the instruments used to measure it are assumed to represent an actual entity (Angner, 2013). In SWB research, reification consists of confusing the abstract concept represented by measures of SWB with actual happiness "in the sense of the word that moral significance and normative import . . . as it is used in the non-scientific literature" (Angner, 2013, p. 240). Certainly *something* is being measured by the commonly used measures of SWB, and these measures do predict other related measures of interest, but construct validation alone cannot demonstrate "that the underlying construct has anything to do with 'happiness' as the term is used in philosophical or pre-scientific literature" (Angner, 2013, p. 240). The biggest danger posed by trait reification is that it can lead researchers to exaggerate the importance of their results, which can lead to bad science and bad public policy (Angner, 2013). All measures of psychological constructs are vulnerable to problems of reification, but measures of SWB may be even more vulnerable than most because of the ease with which SWB is measured and the ease with which social scientists seem to draw conclusions from such measures (Angner, 2013).

Summary

Interest in subjective well-being and life satisfaction goes back thousands of years and research on subjective well-being goes back at least 90 years. Much of this research has been concerned with correlates and predictors of SWB, which is the focus of the remaining chapters of this book. Much research has also been concerned with differentiating different types of SWB—specifically the distinction between hedonic well-being and eudaimonic well-being. This research shows that people can distinguish between activities and experiences that are more or less "meaningful" and "personally expressive" and those that are more or less enjoyable but that measures of "eudaimonic" well-being and measures of "hedonic" well-being are so highly correlated that they appear to be measuring the same construct. Research on theories of SWB strongly supports dispositional/construals theories that posit that SWB is primarily the result of inherited and learned predispositions to perceive and interpret life events in certain ways over life circumstance theories that propose that SWB is primarily the result of life events and life circumstances not mediated by interpretations of them. Among the problems with measuring subjective well-being and life satisfaction are lack of agreement on the conception of SWB (e.g., hedonic versus eudaimonic), an almost exclusive reliance on self-report measures, overreliance on correlational studies, a lack of consensus on how to measure SWB regardless of conception, and the tendency to reify scores on measures of SWB. The remaining chapters in this book are concerned primarily with the influence of construals (beliefs, attitudes, perceptions) on subjective well-being and life satisfaction, in most cases defined and measured in ways that are more consistent with so-called hedonic well-being than with so-called eudaimonic well-being.

References

Andrews, F. M., & Withey, S. B. (1976). *Social indicators of well-being: Americans' perception of life quality*. New York, NY: Plenum Press.

Angner, E. (2010). Subjective well-being. *The Journal of Socio-Economics, 39*(3), 361–368.

Angner, E. (2013). Is it possible to measure happiness? The argument from measurability. *European Journal for Philosophy of Science, 3*(2), 221–240.

Angner, E. (2016). *A course in behavioral economics* (2nd ed.). London, England: Palgrave Macmillan.

Annas, J. (2002). Should virtue make you happy? *Apeiron, 35*(4), 1–20.

Anusic, I., & Schimmack, U. (2016). Stability and change of personality traits, self-esteem, and well-being: Introducing the meta-analytic stability and change model of retest correlations. *Journal of Personality and Social Psychology, 110*(5), 766–781.

Argyle, M., Martin, M., & Lu, L. (1995). Testing for stress and happiness: The role of social and cognitive factors. In C. D. Spielberger & I. G. Sarason (Eds.), *Stress and emotion* (Vol. 15, pp. 173–187). Washington, DC: Taylor & Francis.

Baumeister, R. F., Vohs, K. D., Aaker, J. L., & Garbinsky, E. N. (2013). Some key differences between a happy life and a meaningful life. *The Journal of Positive Psychology, 8*(6), 505–516.

Biswas-Diener, R., Kashdan, T. B., & King, L. A. (2009). Two traditions of happiness research, not two distinct types of happiness. *The Journal of Positive Psychology, 4*(3), 208–211.

Blustein, D. L. (2008). The role of work in psychological health and well-being: A conceptual, historical, and public policy perspective. *American Psychologist, 63*(4), 228–240.

Bradburn, N. M. (1969). *The structure of psychological well-being*. Chicago, IL: Aldine Publishing Company.

Bradburn, N. M., & Caplovitz, D. (1965). *Reports on happiness*. Chicago, IL: Aldine.

Brickman, P., & Campbell, D. T. (1971). Hedonic relativism and planning the good society. In M. Appley (Ed.), *Adaptation-level theory* (pp. 287–305). New York, NY: Academic Press.

Brief, A. P., Butcher, A. H., George, J. M., & Link, K. E. (1993). Integrating bottom-up and top-down theories of subjective well-being: The case of health. *Journal of Personality and Social Psychology, 64*(4), 646–653.

Buss, D. M. (2000). The evolution of happiness. *American Psychologist, 55*(1), 15–23.

Busseri, M. A., & Sadava, S. W. (2011). A review of the tripartite structure of subjective well-being: Implications for conceptualization, operationalization, analysis, and synthesis. *Personality and Social Psychology Review, 15*(3), 290–314.

Campbell, A., Converse, P. E., & Rodgers, W. L. (1976). *The quality of American life: Perceptions, evaluations, and satisfactions.* New York, NY: Russell Sage Foundation.

Cantril, H. (1965). *The pattern of human concerns.* New Brunswick, NJ: Rutgers University Press.

Chen, L. H., Wu, C. H., Lin, S. H., & Ye, Y. C. (2017). Top-down or button-up? The reciprocal longitudinal relationship between athletes' team satisfaction and life satisfaction. *Sport, Exercise, and Performance Psychology.* Advance online publication. http://psycnet. apa.org/doi/10.1037/spy0000086

Cohen, S., Doyle, W. J., Turner, R. B., Alper, C. M., & Skoner, D. P. (2003). Emotional style and susceptibility to the common cold. *Psychosomatic Medicine, 65*, 652–657.

Cordaro, D. T., Brackett, M., Glass, L., & Anderson, C. L. (2016). Contentment: Perceived completeness across cultures and traditions. *Review of General Psychology, 20*(3), 221–235.

Costa, P. T., & McCrae, R. R. (1980). Influence of extraversion and neuroticism on subjective well-being: Happy and unhappy people. *Journal of Personality and Social Psychology, 38*(4), 668–678.

Côté, S., & Moskowitz, D. S. (1998). On the dynamic covariation between interpersonal behavior and affect: Prediction from neuroticism, extraversion, and agreeableness. *Journal of Personality and Social Psychology, 75*(4), 1032–1046.

Crouch, M. K., Mack, D. E., Wilson, P. M., & Kwan, M. Y. W. (2017). Variability of coefficient alpha: An empirical investigation of the Scales of Psychological Well-Being. *Review of General Psychology, 21*, 255–268.

Delle Fave, A., Brdar, I., Freire, T., Vella-Brodrick, D., & Wissing, M. P. (2011). The eudaimonic and hedonic components of happiness: Qualitative and quantitive findings. *Social Indicators Research, 100*(2), 185–207.

DeNeve, K. M., & Cooper, H. (1998). The happy personality: A meta-analysis of 137 personality traits and subjective well-being. *Psychological Bulletin, 124*(2), 197–229.

Diener, E. (1984). Subjective well-being. *Psychological Bulletin, 95*, 542–575.

Diener, E. (2000). Subjective well-being: The science of happiness and a proposal for a national index. *American Psychologist, 55*(1), 34–43.

Diener, E., & Biswas-Diener, R. (2008). *Happiness: Unlocking the mysteries of psychological wealth.* Malden, MA: Wiley/Blackwell.

Diener, E., & Diener, M. (1995). Cross-cultural correlates of life satisfaction and self-esteem. *Journal of Personality and Social Psychology, 68*, 653–663.

Diener, E., & Diener, C. (2017, April). Governments testing well-being initiatives. *APS Observer, 30*(4). Retrieved from www.psychologicalscience.org/observer/governments-testing-well-being-initiatives

Diener, E., Diener, M., & Diener, C. (1995). Factors predicting the subjective well-being of nations. *Journal of Personality and Social Psychology, 69*, 851–864.

Diener, E., & Emmons, R. A. (1984). The independence of positive and negative affect. *Journal of Personality and Social Psychology, 47*, 105–117.

Diener, E., Lucas, R., & Scollon, C. N. (2006). Beyond the hedonic treadmill: Revising the adaptation theory of well-being. *American Psychologist, 61*, 305–314.

Diener, E., & Oishi, S. (2000). Money and happiness: Income and subjective well-being across nations. In E. Diener & E. M. Suh (Eds.), *Culture and subjective well-being* (pp. 185–218). Cambridge, MA: MIT Press.

Diener, E., Oishi, S., & Lucas, R. E. (2003). Personality, culture, and subjective well-being: Emotional and cognitive evaluations of life. *Annual Review of Psychology, 54*(1), 403–425.

Diener, E., Pressman, S. D., Hunter, J., & Delgadillo-Chase, D. (2017). If, why, and when subjective well-being influences health, and future needed research. *Applied Psychology: Health and Well-Being, 9*, 133–167.

Diener, E., & Seligman, M. E. P. (2004). Beyond money: Toward an economy of well-being. *Psychological Science in the Public Interest, 5*, 1–31.

Diener, E., Suh, E. M., Lucas, R. E., & Smith, H. L. (1999). Subjective well-being: Three decades of progress. *Psychological Bulletin, 125*, 276–302.

Diener, E. D., Emmons, R. A., Larsen, R. J., & Griffin, S. (1985). The Satisfaction with Life Scale. *Journal of Personality Assessment, 49*(1), 71–75.

Disabato, D. J., Goodman, F. R., Kashdan, T. B., Short, J. L., & Jarden, A. (2015). Different types of well-being? A cross-cultural examination of hedonic and eudaimonic well-being. *Psychological Assessment, 28*, 471–482.

Dolan, P., & Metcalfe, R. (2012). Measuring subjective well-being: Recommendations on measures for use by national governments. *Journal of Social Policy, 41*(2), 409–427.

Eid, M., & Diener, E. (2001). Norms for experiencing emotions in different cultures: Inter- and intranational differences. *Journal of Personality and Social Psychology, 81*, 869–885.

Eid, M., & Diener, E. (2004). Global judgments of subjective well-being: Situational variability and long-term stability. *Social Indicators Research, 65*, 245–277.

Eid, M., & Larsen, R. J. (Eds.). (2008). *The science of subjective well-being.* New York, NY: Guilford Press.

Engle, J., & Bless, H. (2017). The more negative the more impact: Evidence from nationally represented data on the relation between domain satisfactions and general life satisfaction. *Social Psychology, 48*, 148–159.

Feist, G. J., Bodner, T. E., Jacobs, J. F., Miles, M., & Tan, V. (1995). Integrating top-down and bottom-up structural models of subjective well-being: A longitudinal investigation. *Journal of Personality and Social Psychology, 68*(1), 138–150.

Fordyce, M. W. (1977). Development of a program to increase personal happiness. *Journal of Counseling Psychology, 24*(6), 511–521.

Fordyce, M. W. (1988). A review of research on the happiness measures: A sixty second index of happiness and mental health. *Social Indicators Research, 20*(4), 355–381.

Fredrickson, B. L., Grewen, K. M., Coffey, K. A., Algoe, S. B., Firestine, A. M., Arevalo, J. M., . . . Cole, S. W. (2013). A functional genomic perspective on human well-being. *Proceedings of the National Academy of Sciences, 110*(33), 13684–13689.

Fried, E. I. (2017). What are psychological constructs? On the nature and statistical modelling of emotions, intelligence, personality traits and mental disorders. *Health Psychology Review, 11*(2), 130–134.

Friedman, H. S., & Kern, M. L. (2014). Personality, well-being, and health. *Annual Review of Psychology, 65*, 719–742.

Fujita, F., & Diener, E. (2005). Life satisfaction set-point: Stability and change. *Journal of Personality and Social Psychology, 88*, 158–164.

Furlong, M. J., Gilman, R., & Huebner, E. S. (Eds.). (2014). *Handbook of positive psychology in schools* (2nd ed.). New York, NY: Routledge.

Gallagher, M. W., Lopez, S. J., & Preacher, K. J. (2009). The hierarchical structure of well-being. *Journal of Personality, 77*(4), 1025–1050.

Gergen, K. J. (1985). The social constructionist movement in modern psychology. *American Psychologist, 40*(3), 266–275.

Gilbert, D. (2006). *Stumbling on happiness.* New York, NY: Knopf.

Harward, D. W. (Ed.). (2016). *Well-being and higher education: A strategy for change and the realization of education's greater purposes.* Washington, DC: Bringing Theory to Practice.

Haybron, D. M. (2001). Happiness and pleasure. *Philosophy and Phenomenological Research, 62*(3), 501–528.

Haybron, D. M. (2008). Happiness, the self and human flourishing. *Utilitas, 20*(1), 21–49.

Headley, B., & Wearing, A. (1989). Personality, life events and subjective well-being: Toward a dynamic equilibrium model. *Journal of Personality and Social Psychology, 57,* 731–739.

Helliwell, J., Layard, R., & Sachs, J. (2017). *World happiness report 2017.* New York: Sustainable Development Solutions Network.

Henriques, G., Kleinman, K., & Asselin, C. (2014). The Nested Model of well-being: A unified approach. *Review of General Psychology, 18*(1), 7–18.

Hills, P., & Argyle, M. (2002). The Oxford Happiness Questionnaire: A compact scale for the measurement of psychological well-being. *Personality and Individual Differences, 33*(7), 1073–1082.

Huebner, E. S. (1994). Preliminary development and validation of a multidimensional life satisfaction scale for children. *Psychological Assessment, 6*(2), 149–158.

Huta, V., & Waterman, A. S. (2014). Eudaimonia and its distinction from hedonia: Developing a classification and terminology for understanding conceptual and operational definitions. *Journal of Happiness Studies, 15*(6), 1425–1456.

Jahoda, M. (1958). *Current concepts of positive mental health.* New York, NY: Basic Books, Inc.

Joshanloo, M. (2014). Eastern conceptualizations of happiness: Fundamental differences with western views. *Journal of Happiness Studies, 15*(2), 475–493.

Kahneman, D. (1999). Objective happiness. In D. Kahneman, E. Diener, & N. Schwarz (Eds.), *Well-being: The foundations of hedonic psychology* (pp. 3–25). New York, NY: Russell Sage Foundation.

Kahneman, D., & Krueger, A. B. (2006). Developments in the measurement of subjective well-being. *The Journal of Economic Perspectives, 20*(1), 3–24.

Kahneman, D., Krueger, A. B., Schkade, D. A., Schwarz, N., & Stone, A. A. (2004). A survey method for characterizing daily life experience: The day reconstruction method. *Science, 306*(5702), 1776–1780.

Kahneman, D., & Riis, J. (2005). Living, and thinking about it: Two perspectives on life. In F. A. Huppert, N. Baylis, & B. Kaverne (Eds.), *The science of well-being* (pp. 285–306). New York: Oxford University Press.

Kammann, R., & Flett, R. (1983). Affectometer 2: A scale to measure current level of general happiness. *Australian Journal of Psychology, 35*(2), 259–265.

Kashdan, T. B. (2004). The assessment of subjective well-being (issues raised by the Oxford Happiness Questionnaire). *Personality and Individual Differences, 36*(5), 1225–1232.

Kashdan, T. B., Biswas-Diener, R., & King, L. A. (2008). Reconsidering happiness: The costs of distinguishing between hedonics and eudaimonia. *The Journal of Positive Psychology, 3*(4), 219–233.

Kashdan, T. B., Goodman, F. R., Stiksma, M., Milius, C. R., & McKnight, P. E. (2017). Sexuality leads to boosts in mood and meaning in life with no evidence for the reverse direction: A daily diary investigation. *Emotion.* Advance online publication. http://psycnet.apa.org/doi/10.1037/emo0000324

Keyes, C. L. (2006). Subjective well-being in mental health and human development research worldwide: An introduction. *Social Indicators Research, 77*(1), 1–10.

Keyes, C. L. M., Shmotkin, D., & Ryff, C. D. (2002). Optimizing well-being: The empirical encounter of two traditions. *Journal of Personality and Social Psychology, 82*(6), 1007–1022.

Kristjánsson, K. (2010). Positive psychology, happiness, and virtue: The troublesome conceptual issues. *Review of General Psychology, 14*(4), 296–310.

Krueger, A. B. (Ed.). (2009). *Measuring the subjective well-being of nations: National accounts of time use and well-being.* Chicago, IL: University of Chicago Press.

Lance, C. E., Lautenschlager, G. J., Sloan, C. E., & Varca, P. E. (1989). A comparison between bottom—up, top—down, and bidirectional models of relationships between global and life facet satisfaction. *Journal of Personality, 57*(3), 601–624.

Larsen, R. J., & Diener, E. (1985). A multitrait-multimethod examination of affect structure: Hedonic level and emotional intensity. *Personality and Individual Differences, 6,* 631–636.

Linley, P. A., & Harrington, S. (Eds.). (2013). *The Oxford handbook of positive psychology and work.* New York: Oxford University Press.

Linley, P. A., Maltby, J., Wood, A. M., Osborne, G., & Hurling, R. (2009). Measuring happiness: The higher order factor structure of subjective and psychological well-being measures. *Personality and Individual Differences, 47*(8), 878–884.

Lucas, R. E. (2007a). Adaptation and the set-point model of subjective well-being: Does happiness change after major life events? *Current Directions in Psychological Science, 16*(2), 75–79.

Lucas, R. E. (2007b). Long-term disability is associated with lasting changes in subjective well-being: Evidence from two nationally representative longitudinal studies. *Journal of Personality and Social Psychology, 92*(4), 717–730.

Lucas, R. E., Clark, A. E., Georgellis, Y., & Diener, E. (2004). Unemployment alters the set-point for life satisfaction. *Psychological Science, 15,* 8–13.

Lucas, R. E., Diener, E., & Suh, E. (1996). Discriminant validity of well-being measures. *Journal of Personality and Social Psychology, 71,* 616–628.

Lykken, D. (1999). *Happiness: What studies on twins show us about nature, nurture, and the happiness set-point.* New York, NY: Golden Books.

Lykken, D., & Tellegen, A. (1996). Happiness is a stochastic phenomenon. *Psychological Science, 7*(3), 186–189.

Lyubomirsky, S. (2001). Why are some people happier than others? The role of cognitive and motivational processes in well-being. *American Psychologist, 56*(3), 239–249.

Lyubomirsky, S. (2013). *The myths of happiness: What should make you happy, but doesn't, what shouldn't make you happy, but does.* New York, NY: Penguin Press.

Lyubomirsky, S., & Dickerhoof, R. (2010). A construal approach to increasing happiness. In J. E. Maddux & J. Tangney (Eds.), *Social psychological foundations of clinical psychology* (pp. 229–244). New York: Guilford Press.

Lyubomirsky, S., King, L., & Diener, E. (2005). The benefits of frequent positive affect: Does happiness lead to success? *Psychological Bulletin, 131*(6), 803–855.

Maddux, J. E., Gosselin, J. T., & Winstead, B. A. (2016). Conceptions of psychopathology: A social constructionist perspective. In J. E. Maddux & B. A. Winstead (Eds.), *Psychopathology: Foundations for a contemporary understanding* (4th ed., pp. 3–17). New York, NY: Routledge.

Mattek, A. M., Wolford, G. L., & Whalen, P. J. (2017). A mathematical model captures the structure of subjective affect. *Perspectives on Psychological Science, 12*(3), 508–526.

Moskowitz, D. S., & Coté, S. (1995). Do interpersonal traits predict affect? A comparison of three models. *Journal of Personality and Social Psychology, 69*(5), 915–924.

Muehlenhard, C. L., & Kimes, L. A. (1999). The social construction of violence: The case of sexual and domestic violence. *Personality and Social Psychology Review, 3*(3), 234–245.

Myers, D. G. (2000). The funds, friends, and faith of happy people. *American Psychologist, 55,* 56–57.

Nettle, D. (2005). *Happiness: The science behind your smile.* New York, NY: Oxford University Press.

Neugarten, B. L., Havighurst, R. J., & Tobin, S. S. (1961). The measurement of life satisfaction. *Journal of Gerontology, 16,* 134–143.

Nozick, R. (1974). *Anarchy, state, and utopia.* New York, NY: Basic Books.

Oishi, S., & Diener, E. (2001). Goals, culture, and subjective well-being. *Personality and Social Psychology Bulletin, 27,* 1674–1682.

Organization for Economic Cooperation and Development. (2013). Retrieved from www.oecd.org/unitedstates/

Oswald, A. J. (1997). Happiness and economic performance. *Economic Journal, 107,* 1815–1831.

Parducci, A. (1995). *Happiness, pleasure, and judgment: The contextual theory and its applications.* Hillsdale, NJ: Lawrence Erlbaum Associates.

Pavot, W. (2008). The assessment of subjective well-being: Successes and shortfalls. In M. Eid & R. J. Larsen (Eds.), *The science of subjective well-being* (pp. 124–140). New York, NY: Guilford.

Pavot, W., & Diener, E. (1993a). The affective and cognitive context of self-reported measures of subjective well-being. *Social Indicators Research, 28,* 1–20.

Pavot, W., & Diener, E. (1993b). Review of the satisfaction with life scale. *Psychological Assessment, 5,* 164–172.

Pavot, W., Diener, E., & Suh, E. (1998). The temporal Satisfaction with Life Scale. *Journal of Personality Assessment, 70*(2), 340–354.

Pavot, W., Diener, E. D., Colvin, C. R., & Sandvik, E. (1991). Further validation of the Satisfaction with Life Scale: Evidence for the cross-method convergence of well-being measures. *Journal of Personality Assessment, 57*(1), 149–161.

Pérez-Álvarez, M. (2016). The science of happiness: As felicitous as it is fallacious. *Journal of Theoretical and Philosophical Psychology, 36*(1), 1–19.

Ruini, C., & Ryff, C. D. (2016). Using eudaimonic well-being to improve lives. In A. M. Wood & J. Johnson (Eds.), *The Wiley handbook of positive clinical psychology* (pp. 153–166). New York: Wiley.

Ryan, R. M., & Deci, E. L. (2001). On happiness and human potentials: A review of research on hedonic and eudaimonic well-being. *Annual Review of Psychology, 52*(1), 141–166.

Ryff, C. D. (1989). Happiness is everything, or is it? Explorations on the meaning of psychological well-being. *Journal of Personality and Social Psychology, 57*(6), 1069–1081.

Ryff, C. D. (2014). Psychological well-being revisited: Advances in the science and practice of eudaimonia. *Psychotherapy and Psychosomatics, 83*(1), 10–28.

Ryff, C. D. (2017). Eudaimonic well-being, inequality, and health: Recent findings and future directions. *International Review of Economics, 64*(2), 159–178.

Sandvik, E., Diener, E., & Seidlitz, L. (1993). Subjective well-being: The convergence and stability of self-report and non-self-report measures. *Journal of Personality, 61*(3), 317–342.

Schaefer, J. D., Caspi, A., Belsky, D. W., Harrington, H., Houts, R., Horwood, L. J., . . . Moffitt, T. E. (2017). Enduring mental health: Prevalence and prediction. *Journal of Abnormal Psychology, 126*(2), 212–224.

Scherpenzeel, A., & Saris, W. (1996). Causal direction in a model of life satisfaction: The top-down/bottom-up controversy. *Social Indicators Research, 38*(2), 161–180.

Schimmack, U. (2008). The structure of subjective well-being. In M. Eid & R. J. Larsen (Eds.), *The science of subjective wellbeing* (pp. 97–123). New York, NY: Guilford.

Schimmack, U., Böckenholt, U., & Reisenzein, R. (2002). Response styles in affect ratings: Making a mountain out of a molehill. *Journal of Personality Assessment, 78*(3), 461–483.

Schimmack, U., & Oishi, S. (2005). The influence of chronically and temporarily accessible information on life satisfaction judgments. *Journal of Personality and Social Psychology, 89*(3), 395–406.

Schwarz, N., & Clore, G. L. (1983). Mood, misattribution, and judgments of well-being: Informative and directive functions of affective states. *Journal of Personality and Social Psychology, 45*(3), 513–523.

Schwarz, N., & Strack, F. (1999). Reports of subjective well-being: Judgmental processes and their methodological implications. In D. Kahneman, E. Diener, & N. Schwarz (Eds.), *Well-being: The foundations of hedonic psychology* (pp. 61–84). New York, NY: Russell Sage.

Scollon, C. N., Kim-Prieto, C., & Diener, E. (2003). Experience sampling: Promises and pitfalls, strengths and weaknesses. *Journal of Happiness Studies, 4*(1), 5–34.

Seligman, M. E. P. (2002). *Authentic happiness: Using the new positive psychology to realize your potential for lasting fulfillment.* New York, NY: Free Press.

Seligman, M. E. P. (2011). *Flourish: A visionary new understanding of happiness and well-being.* New York, NY: Free Press.

Seligson, J. L., Huebner, E. S., & Valois, R. F. (2003). Preliminary validation of the brief multidimensional students' life satisfaction scale (BMSLSS). *Social Indicators Research, 61*(2), 121–145.

Shin, J., Suh, E. M., Oem, K., & Kim, H. S. (2017). What does "happiness" prompt in your mind? Culture, word choice, and experienced happiness. *Journal of Happiness Studies.* https://doi.org/10.1007/s10902-016-9836-8

Simmons, C. A., & Lehmann, P. (2013). *Tools for strengths-based assessment and evaluation.* New York, NY: Springer.

Sloan, R. P., Schwarz, E., McKinley, P. S., Weinstein, M., Love, G., Ryff, C., . . . Seeman, T. (2016). Vagally-mediated heart rate variability and indices of well-being: Results of a nationally representative study. *Health Psychology, 36*(1), 73–81.

Steel, P., Schmidt, J., & Shultz, J. (2008). Refining the relationship between personality and subjective well-being. *Psychological Bulletin, 134*(1), 138–161.

Strickhouser, J. E., Zell, E., & Krizan, Z. (2017). Does personality predict health and well-being? A metasynthesis. *Health Psychology, 36*(8), 797–810.

Veenhoven, R. (1984). *Conditions of happiness.* Netherlands: Springer Netherlands.

Vukasović, T., & Bratko, D. (2015). Heritability of personality: A meta-analysis of behavior genetic studies. *Psychological Bulletin, 141*(4), 769–785.

Waterman, A. S. (1993). Two conceptions of happiness: Contrasts of personal expressiveness (eudaimonia) and hedonic enjoyment. *Journal of Personality and Social Psychology, 64*(4), 678–691.

Waterman, A. S. (2007). On the importance of distinguishing hedonia and eudaimonia when considering the hedonic treadmill. *American Psychologist, 62,* 612–613.

Waterman, A. S., Schwartz, S. J., & Conti, R. (2008). The implications of two conceptions of happiness (hedonic enjoyment and eudaimonia) for the understanding of intrinsic motivation. *Journal of Happiness Studies, 9*(1), 41–79.

Waterman, A. S., Schwartz, S. J., Zamboanga, B. L., Ravert, R. D., Williams, M. K., Bede Agocha, V., . . . Brent Donnellan, M. (2010). The Questionnaire for Eudaimonic Well-Being: Psychometric properties, demographic comparisons, and evidence of validity. *The Journal of Positive Psychology*, *5*(1), 41–61.

Watson, D., Clark, L. A., & Tellegen, A. (1988). Development and validation of brief measures of positive and negative affect: The PANAS scales. *Journal of Personality and Social Psychology*, *54*, 1063–1070.

Wessels, N. M., Zimmermann, J., & Leising, D. (2016). Toward a shared understanding of important consequences of personality. *Review of General Psychology*, *20*(4), 426–436.

Wessman, A. E., & Ricks, D. F. (1966). *Mood and personality*. Oxford, England: Holt, Rinehart, & Winston.

Wilson, W. R. (1967). Correlates of avowed happiness. *Psychological Bulletin*, *67*(4), 294–306.

Yap, S. C. Y., Wortman, J., Anusic, I., Baker, S. G., Scherer, L. D., Donnellan, M. B., & Lucas, R. E. (2016). The effect of mood on judgments of subjective well-being: Nine tests of the judgment model. *Journal of Personality and Social Psychology*. Advance online publication. http://psycnet.apa.org/doi/10.1037/pspp0000115

Youssef, C. M., & Luthans, F. (2011). Positive psychological capital in the workplace: Where we are and where we need to go. In K. M. Sheldon, T. B. Kashdan, & M. E. Steger (Eds.), *Designing positive psychology: Taking stock and moving forward* (pp. 351–364). New York: Oxford University Press.

2

SOCIAL NEUROSCIENCE OF SUBJECTIVE WELL-BEING AND LIFE SATISFACTION

Alex W. daSilva and Todd F. Heatherton

Social neuroscience seeks to explain how the brain computes and facilitates social interactions and processes (Cacioppo, Berntson, & Decety, 2010), combining and elaborating upon work in the neurosciences, social sciences, and cognitive sciences (Cacioppo, 2002; Heatherton, 2011). A key assumption of this field is that humans are fundamentally a social species; as such, sociality and well-being are closely linked. Humans have a fundamental need to belong (Baumeister & Leary, 1995), such that social connections are as important to survival as food and water. Accordingly, much of the research in social neuroscience has examined how people think about themselves and others in social contexts as well as how such thoughts influence well-being (Davidson & McEwen, 2012). This chapter considers how findings from social neuroscience inform the understanding of psychological well-being.

Supporting human social nature is the neocortex—the outermost and most evolutionarily recent layer of our brain. Broadly speaking, the neocortex is crucial to a wide variety of complex cognitive functions, including language, conscious thought, social cognition, emotion regulation, and sensory perception. Evolutionary theory proposes that pair bonding, a strong affinity between partners of a species potentially leading to offspring or lifelong bonding, and paternal nurturing drove the development of this higher-order, specialized brain tissue (Dunbar, 2009). Researchers have proposed that the mechanisms supporting pair bonding also generalize and extend to the formation of larger social groups (Dunbar, 2009). Supporting that notion is research showing that anthropoid primates exhibit a unique correlation between social group size and the size of neocortex; specifically, neocortex volume increases in a linear fashion with social group size (Dunbar & Shultz, 2007). However, what truly sets humans apart from other primates is not brain size but rather brain connectivity; specifically, the complex and intricate connections of a specialized part of neocortex, the prefrontal cortex (Schoenemann, Sheehan, & Glotzer, 2005). Humans are endowed with a brain that facilitates social interaction, in other words, a "social brain". This social brain allows us to navigate the complex communal world in which we live, steering us away from committing faux pas towards the goal of obtaining positive, meaningful social interaction and acceptance.

Past theorists (e.g., Heatherton, 2011; Mitchell & Heatherton, 2009) have identified key brain regions likely comprising the social brain and elaborated upon how these regions contribute to social functioning. In this chapter, we examine how those brain regions contribute to well-being. Similar to others (e.g., Ryff & Keyes, 1995), we define key aspects of well-being as possessing a positive self-view supported by positive and healthy social relationships. Well-being also implies the absence of psychopathology that might otherwise compromise the capacity for flourishing in life (Keyes, 2007). Including the absence of psychopathology in the definition of well-being allows us to illustrate the consequences of dysfunction among neural areas and circuits we identify as important in our definition of well-being. Specifically, in this chapter we explore the functions associated with key regions of the social brain, noting that these regions support feelings of self-positivity and assist in making sense of others in the world around us. Because group/social acceptance is crucial to our species, we will also examine how social rejection and loneliness are represented neurologically and how individual differences in psychological constructs such as self-esteem and rumination may predispose individuals to certain types of psychopathology, particularly, depression. A brief review of the primary methods used by social neuroscientists will help the reader better understand the research on how the components of the social brain support well-being.

The Methods of Social Neuroscience

Since the emergence of social neuroscience, the traditional approach to measurement has been the use of electroencephalography (EEG) and functional neuroimaging (fMRI) to assess brain function related to social processes. EEG measures electrical activity in the brain and is most often used because of its excellent temporal resolution. It helps to identify the timing of neural events that reflect psychological processes. EEG has provided insights into how different activation patterns and frequency bands relate to internalized attention, positivity, and well-being (Aftanas & Golocheikine, 2001; Urry et al., 2004) Unfortunately, EEG has poor spatial resolution and therefore is less useful for understanding localization of brain function.

To assess localization of brain function, most research has used fMRI, which measures brain activity by detecting changes associated with blood flow. When a neural region activates in response to a stimulus, blood flow to the region increases as nutrients and oxygen are delivered. The most common form of fMRI uses the blood-oxygen level dependent contrast (BOLD), which allows researchers to measure the ratio of oxygenated to deoxygenated hemoglobin. Indeed, this methodology has furthered our understanding of complex social processes such as empathy (Fan, Duncan, Greck, & Northoff, 2011); social pain (Eisenberger, Lieberman, & Williams, 2003); cooperation (Rilling et al., 2002); and stereotyping (Contreras, Banaji, & Mitchell, 2011) among many others. Essentially, fMRI is able to identify brain regions whose activity is correlated with mental states or behavior. As methods have evolved, researchers in social neuroscience have sought to use brain activity to predict behavioral outcomes relevant to well-being, such as frequency of social behavior (Powers, Chavez, & Heatherton, 2016) and engaging in healthful behaviors (Falk, Berkman, Whalen, & Lieberman, 2011). Likewise, brain activity can predict real-world future weight gain, eating behavior, and sexual activity (Lopez, Hofmann, Wagner, Kelley, & Heatherton, 2014; Demos, Heatherton, & Kelley, 2012).

A recent trend is the examination of how different brain areas work together to processes information and a growing recognition that brain regions do not work in isolation but that mental states involve the coordinated activity of many regions. At the heart of measuring neural networks is *functional connectivity*—the ways in which the activity of brain regions tends to be correlated—and *structural connectivity*—the extent to which regions are connected physically. Functional connectivity can be examined with *psychophysiological interaction* (PPI) and *resting-state functional connectivity* (rsfMRI). PPI is a measure of event-related functional connectivity allowing researchers to examine the correlation of activity in two distinct brain regions during a task. That is, which areas of the brain are active at the same time when someone performs a specific task? By contrast, rsfMRI measures correlations between spatially distinct regions of cerebral cortex in the absence of a task (Lowe, Mock, & Sorenson, 1998). The person in the scanner simply stares at a fixation cross-hair on the screen while functional imaging takes place. The aim of this approach is to determine networks of brain regions demonstrating synchronous activity at rest; that is, regions of the brain that activate and de-activate together. The premise is that these resting state network connections develop over time and reflect an enduring history of co-activation/de-activation. Such networks roughly support the Hebbian idea that neurons that fire together, wire together. Researchers can examine individual differences within these networks, such as the strength of the connections within a given network, for meaningful information about development, behavior, and psychopathology.

Structural connectivity examines the physical connections between brain regions. It is most commonly assessed through *diffusion tensor imaging* (DTI), which assesses white matter integrity (the strength of axonal connections) by taking advantage of the fact that water molecules are always in motion and that they diffuse differently along different types of neural tissue. White matter reflects the myelin insulation of axons that transmit information across networks. In white matter tracts, water diffuses along the same direction as the actual white matter fibers and myelin. Various statistical approaches allow inferences to be made about connectivity strength of white matter tracts. Successful implementation of these connectivity based techniques has allowed social neuroscience researchers to better understand enduring trait constructs such as self-esteem (Chavez & Heatherton, 2014) and the big five personality traits (Xu & Potenza, 2012), as well as elucidating neural abnormalities in disorders marked by social impairment such as autism spectrum disorders (Von Dem Hagen, Stoyanova, Baron-Cohen & Calder, 2012) and social anxiety disorder (Liao et al., 2010).

Identifying the Networks

Research using resting state functional connectivity approaches has identified several distinct networks (Yeo et al., 2011). One of these, called the *default network*, plays an especially prominent role in well-being (Figure 2.1). The default network is maximally active at rest. That is, when a person is lying in the scanner without an external task, activity within this network is very high. Several theorists believe that the default network is involved in various aspects of self-reflection (about self and others) and internal mentation. Whenever a person is asked to perform a task, irrespective of task type, the default networks shows a reduction in activity.

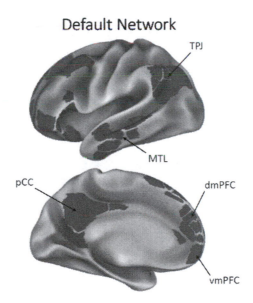

Default Network

FIGURE 2.1 The Default Network

Note: The regions above comprise the default network, a network of brain regions vital to well-being that allow us to reflect on ourselves, others, and the world around us. (TPJ = temporoparietal junction, MTL = medial temporal lobe, pCC = posterior cingulate cortex, dmPFC = dorsomedial prefrontal cortex, vmPFC = vetromedial prefrontal cortex.)

The default network is composed of several brain areas that have independently identified as involved in processing information with respect to selves or others, including the medial prefrontal cortex (mPFC), posterior cingulate cortex (pCC), medial temporal lobe (MTL), and portions of parietal cortex (Buckner, Andrews-Hanna, & Schacter, 2008). Dysfunction within this network is associated with a wide range of psychological disorders including: depressive disorders (Hamilton, Farmer, Fogelman, & Gotlib, 2015; Nejad, Fossati, & Lemogne, 2013; Sheline et al., 2009); anxiety disorders (Zhao et al., 2007); other types of psychopathology such as schizophrenia and bipolar disorder (Ongur et al., 2010; Calhoun et al., 2012); and autism spectrum disorders (Weng et al., 2010) in addition to being linked to abnormalities in aging (Greicius, Srivastava, Reiss, & Menon, 2004).

Andrews-Hanna and colleagues found that different aspects of the default network seemed particularly important for different psychological processes (Andrews-Hanna, Reidler, Sepulcre, Poulin, & Buckner, 2010). The mPFC and posterior cingulate cortex are activated when information is self-relevant or moti-vationally salient; thus, these regions demonstrate preferential activation for tasks like remembering autobiographical events (Summerfield, Hassabis, & Maguire, 2009); self-reflection (Kelley et al., 2002); and evaluating highly salient informa-tion such as an immediate reward (McClure, Laibson, Loewenstein, & Cohen, 2004). The medial temporal lobe contains the hippocampus and its surround-ing structures and plays a prominent role in memory construction and retrieval. It also plays an active role in the ability to simulate potential future happenings (Andrews-Hanna et al., 2010). Along with the temporoparietal junction (TPJ), a more dorsal region of mPFC, dorsomedial prefrontal cortex (dmPFC), plays an integral part in our understanding of the external world and in using our own thoughts, experiences, and emotions to better understand others and the world around us. Broadly, the default network is an indispensable network of regions that allows us to reflect on ourselves and understand the world around us.

The Social Brain and Well-Being

As noted earlier, well-being includes possession of a positive self-view supported by positive, healthy social relationships (Ryff & Keyes, 1995). In others words, well-being requires a functioning social brain. But, what does the brain need to do to allow it to be social? Given the fundamental need to belong, a social brain system needs to monitor signs of social inclusion or exclusion and alter behavior to forestall rejection or resolve other social problems (Heatherton, 2011; Mitchell & Heatherton, 2009). Such a system requires four components, each of which is likely to have a discrete neural signature. First, people need *self-knowledge*—to be aware of their behavior so as to gauge it against societal or group norms. Thus, having a self serves an adaptive function for group living. Second, people need to understand how others are reacting to their behavior so as to predict how others will respond to them. In other words they need *"theory of mind,"* the capacity to attribute mental states to others. This implies the need for a third mechanism, one that *detects threat*, especially in complex situations. Finally, there needs to be a *self-regulatory* mechanism for resolving discrepancies between self-knowledge and social expectations or norms, thereby motivating behavior to resolve any conflict that exists. We will briefly consider the neuroscience basis of each of these, focusing on findings most relevant to well-being.

Neuroscience of the Self

At the heart of any framework surrounding well-being is the notion of self—how the self is personally evaluated, grows, develops, and is viewed by others; thus, it is important to understand how the "self" is represented in the brain. Klein and Loftus (1993) remark, "If there is one subject where we are all experts, it is ourselves". We form attitudes about ourselves through a process known as self-perception; through self-perception, we come to understand our personalities by way of memories and by observing our own behaviors (Bem, 1972). Indeed, this notion and sense of "self" is central to, and, what makes us distinct as humans. (See also Chapter 18.) One can think of a sense of self as encompassing things such as memory, coconscious awareness, somatosensory experience, and the cognizance that one is initiating and executing their volitional actions in the world; a sense of self is unique and separates us from others (Heatherton et al., 2006). The self's neural representation lies within the default network, specifically the medial prefrontal cortex (mPFC). The mPFC can be thought of as a site critical for the convergence of multiple information streams from other brain regions—in other words, a hub where information is integrated, interpreted, and unified. This process is ongoing and assists in not only the construction of a sense self but also in the maintenance of a coherent sense of self.

The first study to examine how self-relevant processing was represented in the brain used positron emission tomography (PET) and a paradigm in which participants performed a trait judgment of themselves along with other cognitive tasks. Craik and Colleagues (1999) observed a relative increase in activity within the mPFC for self-referential processing compared to other cognitive judgments. Recognizing the limits of PET, Kelley et al. (2002) used fMRI with a relatively large sample size. They found that mPFC and posterior cingulate cortex (pCC) displayed an increase in activity when people were making trait judgments about the self relative to trait judgments about a familiar other. This preferential activation for self-relevant material within the mPFC and posterior cingulate cortex also holds up across multiple presentation domains. The finding that distinct cortex, mPFC, underlies self-related processing is one of the most well replicated findings within social neuroscience, having been corroborated by dozens of studies and multiple meta-analyses (Wagner, Haxby, & Heatherton, 2012; Northoff et al., 2006; Denny, Kober, Wager, & Ochsner, 2012; van der Meer, Costafreda, Aleman, & David, 2010).

Self Affect

One important property of selves is that their owners have feelings about them. That is, love them or hate them, those who possess a self have an affective response to however they conceive of themselves. Overall, our self-evaluations tend to be positively biased (Baumeister, Tice, & Hutton, 1989) and we tend to overemphasize our positive attributes (Taylor & Brown, 1988). Given the inherent positivity, we should expect to see neural overlap in brain areas associated with self and positivity. Indeed, the portion of mPFC most commonly activated during self-related tasks is also frequently activated in various reward-related tasks (Haber & Knutson, 2010; Wagner et al., 2012). Likewise, tasks involving the self frequently activate reward centers in the brain such as the ventral striatum (VS) (Northoff & Hayes, 2011). However, we cannot infer a common neural representation of reward and self just because tasks involving reward and self-processing activate similar areas in the brain. A recent study used a computational approach employing machine learning algorithms (used to classify things into categories) to show that mPFC brain activity related to self-referential thought could be decoded by a model created from activation patterns produced by positive compared to negative images (Chavez, Heatherton, & Wagner, 2016). That is, using computational methods, a statistical pattern classifier trained to distinguish positive from negative images (using brain activity) could independently classify whether people were answering questions about themselves or another person. The brain activity of the representation of self and positivity overlap.

Although neural and behavioral evidence support a link between self and positivity, having positive thoughts about oneself is not uniform across people; for example, low self-esteem is associated with diminished amounts of positive affect (Baumeister, Campbell, Krueger, & Vohs, 2003). Recent connectivity based imaging work by Heatherton and colleagues has demonstrated that connectivity between the ventral striatum (an area of the brain involved in reward) and mPFC may give rise to differential feelings of self-worth, both for the long and short term. Specifically, measures of structural (DTI) and functional (PPI) connectivity were used to examine connectivity reflected in both long-term, trait and momentary, state self-esteem (Chavez & Heatherton, 2014). The DTI *structural* results revealed increased connectivity between mPFC and ventral striatum for those high in trait self-esteem, reflecting a stronger, enduring connection between areas associated with self and reward. By contrast, during a trait judgment task, the researchers found increased *functional connectivity* between the same mPFC and ventral striatum regions of interest. That is, ventral striatum and mPFC activated in tandem when participants high in state self-esteem made positive self-relevant judgments reflecting current feelings of self-esteem. This pattern indicates that neural connections incorporating information about self and reward may give rise to feelings of self-worth and feelings of positive well-being. In a separate study, structural connectivity between mPFC and ventral striatum predicted changes in self-esteem over an 8-month period (Chavez & Heatherton, 2016). Specifically, greater white matter connectivity at the beginning of the study predicted higher levels of self-esteem at the end of the study. Essentially, the rich get richer. Those whose brains possess the most robust pathways between self and reward gain more self-esteem over time.

Understanding both behavioral and neural markers associated with self-worth is important because those low in self-esteem are at higher risk for developing psychological disorders such as anxiety or depression, which are threats to well-being (Sowislo & Orth, 2013). Low self-esteem and depression are far from orthogonal constructs as they are frequently highly correlated in cross-sectional studies. In a longitudinal study, Orth and colleagues illustrated that low self-esteem serves as a risk factor for depression in that low self-esteem predicted subsequent levels of depression whereas depression did not predict ensuing levels of self-esteem (Orth, Robins, & Roberts, 2008)—a finding replicated recently in another large sample (Rieger, Göllner, Trautwein, & Roberts, 2016). A recent meta-analysis of 77 depression studies corroborates the notion that low self-esteem contributes to depression (Sowislo & Orth, 2013).

Rumination

Rumination is a coping strategy for negative moods characterized by self-reflection and a repetitive and passive focus on one's negative emotions (Nolen-Hoeksema, 1987). Rumination also plays a role in the relationship between low self-esteem and depression as researchers have found that rumination partially mediates the effect of low self-esteem in an 8-month longitudinal study (Kuster, Orth, & Meier, 2012). Complications with rumination emerge when people begin to think about the causes and consequences of a problem without taking action to remedy their current situations and spend time thinking about how unmotivated and badly they feel (e.g., "I just want to stay in bed all day", "What's wrong with me—why can't I get out of bed?", "I'll never get any work done if I don't get out of bed") (Nolen-Hoeksema, Morrow, & Fredrickson, 1993).

A great deal of research shows that rumination plays a variety of roles in relation to depression, such as the onset of depressive episode and intensity of depressive symptoms (Treynor, Gonzalez, & Nolen-Hoeksema, 2003). More recent work has further elucidated the role rumination plays with respect to well-being, confirming the relationship between rumination and onset of a depressive episode and shedding light on the notion that rumination is related to many disorders beyond depression including anxiety, binge drinking, binge eating, and self-harm (Nolen-Hoeksema, Wisco, & Lyubomirsky, 2008).

When considering rumination and the brain, an obvious candidate as a site of dysfunction is the mPFC due to the inherent self-reflective nature of rumination. Indeed, a recent literature review of depression, rumination, and self-referential processing noted atypical activity in the mPFC among both depressed and non-depressed ruminators (Nejad et al., 2013). Within a depressed population, researchers have also observed hyper-connectivity between regions of the default network and the subgenual prefrontal cortex—an area frequently described as involved with the processing of negative affective information and a target site for deep brain stimulation for depression treatment. This finding may suggest an abnormal integrating of self-referential and affective information (Hamilton et al., 2015). Abnormalities have also been observed in areas associated with memory formation and retrieval. For example, the medial temporal lobe (MTL)—which is also part of the default network, has shown increased activation among non-depressed ruminators at rest perhaps reflecting an increase in internally directed thoughts (Piguet et al., 2014). Further work has even suggested that discrete activity patterns in the hippocampus (which is part of the medial temporal lobe) may be linked to distinct dimensions of rumination (Mandell, Siegle, Shutt, Feldmiller, & Thase, 2014). Thus, rumination, in the presence or absence of depression, is associated with atypical functioning in several regions of the default network.

Neuroscience of Mentalizing

Mentalizing refers to the ability to read and make inferences about the mental states of other people (Gallagher & Frith, 2003). This ability, particularly making inferences about another's current emotional state, is crucial for healthy social relations (Heatherton & Krendl, 2009), and is thus critical to well-being. Without the capacity to mentalize, people would not feel guilty after making a comment that would knowingly hurt the feelings of a friend or feel embarrassed after entering a quiet lecture and letting the door slam loudly behind. Mentalizing allows us to empathize, cooperate, and interpret the behavior of others (Mitchell & Heatherton, 2009). Inferring what others are thinking is a complicated task, largely because we don't have access to another's thoughts. Fortunately, we always have access to a readily available substitute: ourselves. *Simulation* involves using our own thoughts and experiences to advise ourselves about the feelings and intentions of others.

Simulation contains at least two distinct forms: (1) *mirroring*, which is a mediated response from observers as they experience the same mental state as another, and (2) *self-projection*, in which observers imagine themselves in the same situation as another (Waytz & Mitchell, 2011). Mirroring is useful but limited. Experiencing the same emotion or imitating an action of another gives us little information about the underlying intentions behind an action or the cause of an emotion (Frith & Frith, 2006). Self-projection, however, allows people to consider alternatives to events in the immediate environment, such as projecting oneself to an alternative perspective and reading off accompanying thoughts and feelings to conceive what others are thinking (Buckner & Carroll, 2007).

Brain imaging studies demonstrate that the mPFC is involved in thinking about others. Hence, the mPFC is involved both in thinking about self and others. But, these patterns of activity can be distinguished. Research shows that mPFC activity during self-processing and rumination tends to occur in a more ventral region (lower in the brain) than in relation to mentalizing. A meta-analysis of studies using logistic regression on mPFC coordinates from studies examining self and other judgments found a dorsal/ventral gradient (from higher in the mPFC to lower down in the mPFC) where self-judgments displayed a greater probability of activating ventral regions of mPFC, and other-judgments showed a greater probability of activating dorsal regions of mPFC. In simple terms, the region of mPFC activated by thinking about others is slightly above the mPFC region involved in thinking about self. The authors conclude that ventral mPFC is associated with self-related thoughts while the dorsal mPFC is associated with making judgments about the external world (Denny et al., 2012). Their conclusion is consistent with other meta-analyses examining self/other processing such as Wagner and colleagues (2012) who concluded that ventral mPFC is implicated in self-referential cognition where dorsal mPFC is associated with impression formation and inferring the mental states of others.

The mPFC activity observed for mentalizing can be modulated by the degree of perceived similarity between the observer and target person. For example, Mitchell and colleagues found that mentalizing about a fictitious person who possessed sociopolitical beliefs and opinions similar to those of the observer increased activity in ventral mPFC in individuals, whereas mentalizing about a dissimilar person engaged the dorsal mPFC (Mitchell, Macrae, & Banaji, 2006); additional work substantiates this ventral (similar other)/dorsal (dissimilar other) division (Jenkins, MaCrae, & Mitchell, 2008). Thus, when appropriate, we use ourselves as a proxy to gauge the mental states of other people; but this only works for people similar to us. A large body of brain imaging research also suggests that, in addition to the mPFC, the temporoparietal junction (TPJ) and lateral temporal cortex play a pivotal role in inferring the mental states of others (Amodio & Frith, 2006; Saxe, 2006).

Researchers are now examining mentalizing abilities, or rather, lack thereof in psychological disorders. In depressed patients, deficits within the perspective-taking domain are commonly observed during second-order reasoning tasks, when people are asked to consider what other people are thinking others (Cusi, Nazarov, MacQueen, & McKinnon, 2013; Wolkenstein, Schönenberg, Schirm, & Hautzinger, 2011). Perhaps a poor understanding of social situations contributes to and/or exacerbates depressive symptoms. Along those lines, a study found that 58% of depressed patients with second-ordering reasoning deficits relapsed into another episode of major depression compared to 7% of patients without mentalizing deficits (Inoue, Yamada, & Kanba, 2006).

Neuroscience of Threat Detection and Social Belonging

Given the importance of creating and maintaining relationships for well-being, people ought to possess some sort of neural mechanism to monitor their status within their group. The *anterior cingulate cortex* (ACC), traditionally associated with detecting threats of social exclusion, is one such region (Heatherton, 2011). However, different types of social rejection or acceptance may lead to increased activity in different regions of ACC. For instance, one team found that being ostracized was associated with activity in dorsal ACC (Eisenberger et al., 2003) whereas another study found that social acceptance or rejection was associated with activity in more ventral regions of ACC extending anteriorly into medial prefrontal cortex (Somerville, Heatherton, & Kelley, 2006). Dorsal regions of ACC are involved in pain perception, leading some researchers to speculate that social and physical pain share a common neural mechanism. Woo and colleagues (2014) found a network of brain regions, including ventral areas of the prefrontal cortex, that responded to feelings of social rejection induced by having participants view images of a recent ex-romantic partner. This pattern of activity elicited by an ex-romantic partner was quantitatively different from neural activity evoked by the physical pain produced by heat (Woo et al., 2014). These findings add credence to the proposition that a unique neural pattern is associated with social pain compared to more physical pain (Cacioppo et al., 2013).

Failure to form social relationships with others threatens health and well-being (Baumeister & Leary, 1995) and leads to feelings of loneliness. Loneliness refers to feeling distressed about the quantity or, more perhaps more importantly, the quality of one's social relationships (Peplau & Perlman, 1982). Loneliness is associated with a host of psychological difficulties, cognitive deficiencies, sleeping problems, abnormal physiological function, irregularities in the neuroendocrine system, and improper immune functioning (for a review see Hawkley & Cacioppo, 2010). A recent meta-analysis found that the influence of loneliness on mortality was comparable to a host of other recognized risks for mortality identified by the US Department of Health and Human Services including, but not limited to obesity, substance abuse, immunization, injury and violence, and access to health care (Holt-Lunstad, Smith, Baker, Harris, & Stephenson, 2015). This relationship between loneliness and mortality captures the social essences of our species.

Research on the neuroscience of loneliness emerged within the past decade. A defining mark of loneliness is deriving little pleasure from social interactions. By contrast, in most instances, those who are not lonely find social interaction rewarding. Some of the first work examining the neural mechanisms associated with loneliness examined the reward system. Cacioppo and colleagues (2009) found that, compared to non-lonely participants, lonely individuals displayed a different pattern of activity in ventral striatum when viewing positive social images compared to positive nonsocial images (everyday objects) (Cacioppo, Norris, Decety, Monteleone, & Nusbaum, 2009). Specifically, those low in self-reported loneliness showed increased activity in the ventral striatum when shown pictures of positive social images compared to positive nonsocial images while those high in loneliness showed the exact opposite pattern of activation; namely, increased ventral striatum activity to positive images of objects compared to positive social images. In addition, the researchers noted dissimilar patterns of activation in the dmPFC, a region important in the processing of information about other people. That is, dmPFC activity of those low in self-reported loneliness was higher when they were viewing positive social stimuli relative to those high in self-reported loneliness, possibly capturing tendencies of those high in loneliness to maintain psychological distance from others.

An interesting effect also occurs in dmPFC when individuals rejected by their peers observe social scenes. Specifically, activity in dmPFC among socially excluded individuals increases linearly with valence such that it is highest for positive social scenes and lowest for negative social scenes, suggesting that socially excluded individuals prefer to mentalize about positive social information (Powers, Wagner, Norris, & Heatherton, 2013). Collectively, loneliness is characterized by differences within the default network and reward regions (Cacioppo, Capitanio, & Cacioppo, 2014).

Neuroscience of Self-Regulation

Critical to the creation and maintenance of social relationships is the ability to self-regulate. The urge to be rude, dishonest, or lie are feelings all people probably have at times, but they must be tempered to maintain group status. Social emotions serve to keep our behavior within the boundaries of social norms (Beer, 2007) and thus aid in promoting self-regulation (Heatherton, 2011). That is, feelings of shame, guilt, or embarrassment help guide people to performing socially acceptable behaviors and resisting performing socially unacceptable behaviors. In turn, the capacity for self-regulation allows people to control emotions, thoughts, and behaviors to achieve well-being. Heatherton and Wagner (2011) put forth an overarching framework to explain the cognitive neuroscience of self-regulation. The model proposes that successful self-regulation relies on top-down control from regions of the prefrontal cortex over subcortical structures involved with emotion and reward processing. It also proposes that the relative balance between cortical and subcortical activity can either support or undermine self-regulation (Lopez et al., 2017).

Although successful self-regulation is associated with well-being, the ability to regulate emotions is particularly relevant to well-being. Emotion regulation has implications not only for social functioning (keeping your temper in check while meeting with your boss) but also directly for mental health outcomes (the inability to regulate negative affect in depression). Two types of emotion regulation have been identified: *explicit regulation* (an effortful response) and *implicit regulation* (an automatic response). Successful explicit regulation seems to involve lateral regions of prefrontal cortex while successful implicit regulation seems to involve the mPFC/ventral anterior cingulate (Etkin, Büchel, & Gross, 2015).

The ability to reframe a negative experience in a neutral or even positive light is crucial to maintaining a positive sense of self. Reappraisal is an explicit regulation strategy characterized by reexamining an adverse event in unemotional terms

(Gross, 2002). Because it is an explicit emotion regulation strategy, the neural correlates of successful reappraisal involve successful top-down control; that is, increased lateral prefrontal control regions over subcortical structures, in particular, the amygdalae (Ochsner, Bunge, Gross, & Gabrieli, 2002). The inability to regulate negative experiences and emotions are defining features of depression; indeed, depressed individuals have trouble modifying negative emotions and engage in less effective emotion regulation techniques than non-depressed individuals (Berking & Wupperman, 2012). Brain imaging studies of depressed individuals have identified abnormalities in prefrontal regulatory circuitry required for successful emotion regulation during the reappraisal of negative images, perhaps indicating that these areas are "working" in an inefficient fashion when attempting to regulate (Johnstone, Reekum, Urry, Kalin, & Davidson, 2007).

Summary

Given the social nature of our species, human well-being is closely tied to healthy social functioning. Social neuroscience research has demonstrated several key features of what it takes to be an effective group member: a sense of self; the ability to infer the mental states of others; mechanisms to detect social threats; and the capacity to regulate thought, behavior, and emotion. Research within the past two decades has identified the default network as pivotal to supporting the aforementioned facets of sociality. Consisting of the medial prefrontal cortex, posterior cingulate cortex, medial temporal lobes, and portions of parietal cortex, the default network promotes many of the processes that promote positive well-being. In addition, research has demonstrated that connectivity between certain areas of the default network and brain reward regions contribute to positive feelings about the self. Although much of the research so far has focused on aspects of ill-being such as social rejection, loneliness, and depression, future work in social neuroscience may help to identify the brain mechanisms that help people thrive.

References

Aftanas, L., & Golocheikine, S. (2001). Human anterior and frontal midline theta and lower alpha reflect emotionally positive state and internalized attention: High-resolution EEG investigation of meditation. *Neuroscience Letters, 310*(1), 57–60.

Amodio, D. M., & Frith, C. D. (2006). Meeting of minds: The medial frontal cortex and social cognition. *Nature Reviews Neuroscience, 7*(4), 268–277.

Andrews-Hanna, J. R., Reidler, J. S., Sepulcre, J., Poulin, R., & Buckner, R. L. (2010). Functional-anatomic fractionation of the Brains Default Network. *Neuron, 65*(4), 550–562.

Baumeister, R. F., Campbell, J. D., Krueger, J. I., & Vohs, K. D. (2003). Does high self-esteem cause better performance, interpersonal success, happiness, or healthier lifestyles? *Psychological Science in the Public Interest, 4*(1), 1–44.

Baumeister, R. F., & Leary, M. R. (1995). The need to belong: Desire for interpersonal attachments as a fundamental human motivation. *Psychological Bulletin, 117*(3), 497–529.

Baumeister, R. F., Tice, D. M., & Hutton, D. G. (1989). Self-presentational motivations and personality differences in self-esteem. *Journal of Personality, 57*(3), 547–579.

Beer, J. S. (2007). Neural systems for self-conscious emotions and their underlying appraisals. In J. L. Tracy, R. W. Robins, & J. P. Tangney (Eds.), *The self-conscious emotions: Theory and research* (pp. 53–67). New York: Guilford.

Bem, D. J. (1972). Self-perception theory. In L. Berkowitz (Ed.), *Advances in experimental social psychology* (Vol. 6, pp. 1–62). New York: Academic Press.

Berking, M., & Wupperman, P. (2012). Emotion regulation and mental health. *Current Opinion in Psychiatry, 25*(2), 128–134.

Buckner, R. L., Andrews-Hanna, J. R., & Schacter, D. L. (2008). The Brains Default Network. *Annals of the New York Academy of Sciences, 1124*(1), 1–38.

Buckner, R. L., & Carroll, D. C. (2007). Self-projection and the brain. *Trends in Cognitive Sciences, 11*(2), 49–57.

Cacioppo, J. T. (2002). *Foundations in social neuroscience.* Cambridge, MA: MIT Press.

Cacioppo, J. T., Berntson, G. G., & Decety, J. (2010). Social neuroscience and its relationship to social psychology. *Social Cognition, 28*(6), 675–685.

Cacioppo, J. T., Norris, C. J., Decety, J., Monteleone, G., & Nusbaum, H. (2009). In the eye of the beholder: Individual differences in perceived social isolation predict regional brain activation to social stimuli. *Journal of Cognitive Neuroscience, 21*(1), 83–92.

Cacioppo, S., Capitanio, J. P., & Cacioppo, J. T. (2014). Toward a neurology of loneliness. *Psychological Bulletin, 140*(6), 1464–1504.

Cacioppo, S., Frum, C., Asp, E., Weiss, R. M., Lewis, J. W., & Cacioppo, J. T. (2013). A quantitative meta-analysis of functional imaging studies of social rejection. *Scientific Reports, 3*(1), 1–3.

Calhoun, V. D., Sui, J., Kiehl, K., Turner, J., Allen, E., & Pearlson, G. (2012). Exploring the psychosis functional connectome: Aberrant intrinsic networks in schizophrenia and bipolar disorder. *Frontiers in Psychiatry, 2*, 1–13.

Chavez, R. S., & Heatherton, T. F. (2014). Multimodal frontostriatal connectivity underlies individual differences in self-esteem. *Social Cognitive and Affective Neuroscience, 10*(3), 364–370.

Chavez, R. S., & Heatherton, T. F. (2016). Structural integrity of frontostriatal connections predicts longitudinal changes in self-esteem. *Social Neuroscience, 12*(3), 280–286.

Chavez, R. S., Heatherton, T. F., & Wagner, D. D. (2016). Neural population decoding reveals the intrinsic positivity of the self. *Cerebral Cortex*, 1–8.

Contreras, J. M., Banaji, M. R., & Mitchell, J. P. (2011). Dissociable neural correlates of stereotypes and other forms of semantic knowledge. *Social Cognitive and Affective Neuroscience, 7*(7), 764–770.

Craik, F. I., Moroz, T. M., Moscovitch, M., Stuss, D. T., Winocur, G., Tulving, E., & Kapur, S. (1999). In search of the self: A positron emission tomography study. *Psychological Science, 10*(1), 26–34.

Cusi, A. M., Nazarov, A., MacQueen, G. M., & McKinnon, M. C. (2013). Theory of mind deficits in patients with mild symptoms of major depressive disorder. *Psychiatry Research, 210*(2), 672–674.

Davidson, R. J., & McEwen, B. S. (2012). Social influences on neuroplasticity: Stress and interventions to promote well-being. *Nature Neuroscience, 15*(5), 689–695.

Demos, K. E., Heatherton, T. F., & Kelley, W. M. (2012). Individual differences in nucleus accumbens activity to food and sexual images predict weight gain and sexual behavior. *Journal of Neuroscience, 32*(16), 5549–5552.

Denny, B. T., Kober, H., Wager, T. D., & Ochsner, K. N. (2012). A meta-analysis of functional neuroimaging studies of self- and other judgments reveals a spatial gradient for mentalizing in medial prefrontal cortex. *Journal of Cognitive Neuroscience, 24*(8), 1742–1752.

Dunbar, R. I. (2009). The social brain hypothesis and its implications for social evolution. *Annals of Human Biology, 36*(5), 562–572.

Dunbar, R. I., & Shultz, S. (2007). Evolution in the social brain. *Science, 317*, 1344–1347.

Eisenberger, N. I., Lieberman, M. D., & Williams, K. D. (2003). Does rejection hurt? An fMRI study of social exclusion. *Science, 302*, 290–292.

Etkin, A., Büchel, C., & Gross, J. J. (2015). The neural bases of emotion regulation. *Nature Reviews Neuroscience, 16*(11), 693–700.

Falk, E. B., Berkman, E. T., Whalen, D., & Lieberman, M. D. (2011). Neural activity during health messaging predicts reductions in smoking above and beyond self-report. *Health Psychology, 30*(2), 177–185.

Fan, Y., Duncan, N. W., Greck, M. D., & Northoff, G. (2011). Is there a core neural network in empathy? An fMRI based quantitative meta-analysis. *Neuroscience & Biobehavioral Reviews, 35*(3), 903–911.

Frith, C. D., & Frith, U. (2006). The neural basis of mentalizing. *Neuron, 50*(4), 531–534.

Gallagher, H. L., & Frith, C. D. (2003). Functional imaging of "theory of mind". *Trends in Cognitive Sciences, 7*(2), 77–83.

Greicius, M. D., Srivastava, G., Reiss, A. L., & Menon, V. (2004). Default-mode network activity distinguishes Alzheimers disease from healthy aging: Evidence from functional MRI. *Proceedings of the National Academy of Sciences, 101*(13), 4637–4642.

Gross, J. J. (2002). Emotion regulation: Affective, cognitive, and social consequences. *Psychophysiology, 39*(3), 281–291.

Haber, S. N., & Knutson, B. (2010). The reward circuit: Linking primate anatomy and human imaging. *Neuropsychopharmacology, 35*(1), 4–26.

Hamilton, J. P., Farmer, M., Fogelman, P., & Gotlib, I. H. (2015). Depressive rumination, the default-mode network, and the dark matter of clinical neuroscience. *Biological Psychiatry, 78*(4), 224–230.

Hawkley, L. C., & Cacioppo, J. T. (2010). Loneliness matters: A theoretical and empirical review of consequences and mechanisms. *Annals of Behavioral Medicine, 40*(2), 218–227.

Heatherton, T. F. (2011). Neuroscience of self and self-regulation. *Annual Review of Psychology, 62*, 363–390.

Heatherton, T. F., & Krendl, A. C. (2009). Social emotions: Neuroimaging. In L. Squire (Ed.), *Encyclopedia of neuroscience* (Vol. 9, pp. 35–39). Oxford: Academic Press.

Heatherton, T. F., & Wagner, D. D. (2011). Cognitive neuroscience of self-regulation failure. *Trends in Cognitive Sciences, 15*(3), 132–139.

Heatherton, T. F., Wyland, C. L., Macrae, C. N., Demos, K. E., Denny, B. T., & Kelley, W. M. (2006). Medial prefrontal activity differentiates self from close others. *Social Cognitive and Affective Neuroscience, 1*(1), 18–25.

Holt-Lunstad, J., Smith, T. B., Baker, M., Harris, T., & Stephenson, D. (2015). Loneliness and social isolation as risk factors for mortality. *Perspectives on Psychological Science, 10*(2), 227–237.

Inoue, Y., Yamada, K., & Kanba, S. (2006). Deficit in theory of mind is a risk for relapse of major depression. *Journal of Affective Disorders, 95*(1–3), 125–127.

Jenkins, A. C., Macrae, C. N., & Mitchell, J. P. (2008). Repetition suppression of ventromedial prefrontal activity during judgments of self and others. *Proceedings of the National Academy of Sciences, 105*(11), 4507–4512.

Johnstone, T., Reekum, C. M., Urry, H. L., Kalin, N. H., & Davidson, R. J. (2007). Failure to regulate: Counterproductive recruitment of top-down prefrontal-subcortical circuitry in major depression. *Journal of Neuroscience*, 27(33), 8877–8884.

Kelley, W. M., Macrae, C. N., Wyland, C. L., Caglar, S., Inati, S., & Heatherton, T. F. (2002). Finding the self? An event-related fMRI study. *Journal of Cognitive Neuroscience*, 14(5), 785–794.

Keyes, C. L. (2007). Promoting and protecting mental health as flourishing: A complementary strategy for improving national mental health. *American Psychologist*, 62(2), 95–108.

Klein, S. B., & Loftus, J. (1993). The mental representation of trait and autobiographical knowledge about the self. In T. K. Srull & R. S. Wyer Jr. (Eds.), *The mental representation of trait and autobiographical knowledge about the self: Advances in social cognition* (pp. 1–49). Hillsdale, NJ: Lawrence Erlbaum Associates, Inc.

Kuster, F., Orth, U., & Meier, L. L. (2012). Rumination mediates the prospective effect of low self-esteem on depression. *Personality and Social Psychology Bulletin*, 38(6), 747–759.

Liao, W., Chen, H., Feng, Y., Mantini, D., Gentili, C., Pan, Z., . . . Zhang, W. (2010). Selective aberrant functional connectivity of resting state networks in social anxiety disorder. *NeuroImage*, 52(4), 1549–1558.

Lopez, R. B., Chen, P. A., Huckins, J. F., Hofmann, W., Kelley, W. M., & Heatherton, T. F. (2017). A balance of activity in brain control and reward systems predicts self-regulatory outcomes. *Social Cognitive and Affective Neuroscience*, 12(5), 832–838.

Lopez, R. B., Hofmann, W., Wagner, D. D., Kelley, W. M., & Heatherton, T. F. (2014). Neural predictors of giving in to temptation in daily life. *Psychological Science*, 25(7), 1337–1344.

Lowe, M., Mock, B., & Sorenson, J. (1998). Functional connectivity in single and multislice echoplanar imaging using resting-state fluctuations. *NeuroImage*, 7(2), 119–132.

Mandell, D., Siegle, G. J., Shutt, L., Feldmiller, J., & Thase, M. E. (2014). Neural substrates of trait ruminations in depression. *Journal of Abnormal Psychology*, 123(1), 35–48.

McClure, S. M., Laibson, D. I., Loewenstein, G., & Cohen, J. D. (2004). Separate neural systems value immediate and delayed monetary rewards. *Science*, 306(5695), 503–507.

Mitchell, J. P., & Heatherton, T. F. (2009). Components of a social brain. In M. S. Gazzaniga (Ed.), *Cognitive neurosciences IV* (4th ed., pp. 951–958). Cambridge, MA: MIT Press.

Mitchell, J. P., Macrae, C. N., & Banaji, M. R. (2006). Dissociable medial prefrontal contributions to judgments of similar and dissimilar others. *Neuron*, 50(4), 655–663.

Nejad, A. B., Fossati, P., & Lemogne, C. (2013). Self-referential processing, rumination, and cortical midline structures in major depression. *Frontiers in Human Neuroscience*, 7, 1–9.

Nolen-Hoeksema, S. (1987). Sex differences in unipolar depression: Evidence and theory. *Psychological Bulletin*, 101(2), 259–282.

Nolen-Hoeksema, S., Morrow, J., & Fredrickson, B. L. (1993). Response styles and the duration of episodes of depressed mood. *Journal of Abnormal Psychology*, 102(1), 20–28.

Nolen-Hoeksema, S., Wisco, B. E., & Lyubomirsky, S. (2008). Rethinking rumination. *Perspectives on Psychological Science*, 3, 400–424.

Northoff, G., & Hayes, D. J. (2011). Is our self nothing but reward? *Biological Psychiatry*, 69(11), 1019–1025.

Northoff, G., Heinzel, A., Greck, M. D., Bermpohl, F., Dobrowolny, H., & Panksepp, J. (2006). Self-referential processing in our brain: A meta-analysis of imaging studies on the self. *NeuroImage*, 31(1), 440–457.

Ochsner, K. N., Bunge, S. A., Gross, J. J., & Gabrieli, J. D. (2002). Rethinking feelings: An fMRI study of the cognitive regulation of emotion. *Journal of Cognitive Neuroscience*, 14(8), 1215–1229.

Ongur, D., Lundy, M., Greenhouse, I., Shinn, A. K., Menon, V., Cohen, B. M., & Renshaw, P. F. (2010). Default mode network abnormalities in bipolar disorder and schizophrenia. *Psychiatry Research: Neuroimaging, 183*(1), 59–68.

Orth, U., Robins, R. W., & Roberts, B. W. (2008). Low self-esteem prospectively predicts depression in adolescence and young adulthood. *Journal of Personality and Social Psychology, 95*(3), 695–708.

Peplau, L. A., & Perlman, D. (Eds.). (1982). *Loneliness: A sourcebook of current theory, research, and therapy.* New York, NY: Wiley.

Piguet, C., Desseilles, M., Sterpenich, V., Cojan, Y., Bertschy, G., & Vuilleumier, P. (2014). Neural substrates of rumination tendency in non-depressed individuals. *Biological Psychology, 103*, 195–202.

Powers, K. E., Chavez, R. S., & Heatherton, T. F. (2016). Individual differences in response of dorsomedial prefrontal cortex predict daily social behavior. *Social Cognitive and Affective Neuroscience, 11*(1), 121–126.

Powers, K. E., Wagner, D. D., Norris, C. J., & Heatherton, T. F. (2013). Socially excluded individuals fail to recruit medial prefrontal cortex for negative social scenes. *Social Cognitive and Affective Neuroscience, 8*(2), 151–157.

Rieger, S., Göllner, R., Trautwein, U., & Roberts, B. W. (2016). Low self-esteem prospectively predicts depression in the transition to young adulthood: A replication of Orth, Robins, and Roberts (2008). *Journal of Personality and Social Psychology, 110*(1), e16–e22.

Rilling, J. K., Gutman, D. A., Zeh, T. R., Pagnoni, G., Berns, G. S., & Kilts, C. D. (2002). A neural basis for social cooperation. *Neuron, 35*(2), 395–405.

Ryff, C. D., & Keyes, C. L. (1995). The structure of psychological well-being revisited. *Journal of Personality and Social Psychology, 69*(4), 719–727.

Saxe, R. (2006). Uniquely human social cognition. *Current Opinion in Neurobiology, 16*(2), 235–239.

Schoenemann, P. T., Sheehan, M. J., & Glotzer, L. D. (2005). Prefrontal white matter volume is disproportionately larger in humans than in other primates. *Nature Neuroscience, 8*(2), 242–252.

Sheline, Y. I., Barch, D. M., Price, J. L., Rundle, M. M., Vaishnavi, S. N., Snyder, A. Z., . . . Raichle, M. E. (2009). The default mode network and self-referential processes in depression. *Proceedings of the National Academy of Sciences, 106*(6), 1942–1947.

Somerville, L. H., Heatherton, T. F., & Kelley, W. M. (2006). Anterior cingulate cortex responds differentially to expectancy violation and social rejection. *Nature Neuroscience, 9*(8), 1007–1008.

Sowislo, J. F., & Orth, U. (2013). Does low self-esteem predict depression and anxiety? A meta-analysis of longitudinal studies. *Psychological Bulletin, 139*(1), 213–240.

Summerfield, J. J., Hassabis, D., & Maguire, E. A. (2009). Cortical midline involvement in autobiographical memory. *NeuroImage, 44*(3), 1188–1200.

Taylor, S. E., & Brown, J. D. (1988). Illusion and well-being: A social psychological perspective on mental health. *Psychological Bulletin, 103*(2), 193–210.

Treynor, W., Gonzalez, R., & Nolen-Hoeksema, S. (2003). Rumination reconsidered: A psychometric analysis. *Cognitive Therapy and Research, 27*, 247–259.

Urry, H. L., Nitschke, J. B., Dolski, I., Jackson, D. C., Dalton, K. M., Mueller, C. J., . . . Davidson, R. J. (2004). Making a life worth living: Neural correlates of well-being. *Psychological Science, 15*(6), 367–372.

Van Der Meer, L., Costafreda, S., Aleman, A., & David, A. S. (2010). Self-reflection and the brain: A theoretical review and meta-analysis of neuroimaging studies with implications for schizophrenia. *Neuroscience & Biobehavioral Reviews, 34*(6), 935–946.

Von Dem Hagen, E. A., Stoyanova, R. S., Baron-Cohen, S., & Calder, A. J. (2012). Reduced functional connectivity within and between "social" resting state networks in autism spectrum conditions. *Social Cognitive and Affective Neuroscience*, *8*(6), 694–701.

Wagner, D. D., Haxby, J. V., & Heatherton, T. F. (2012). The representation of self and person knowledge in the medial prefrontal cortex. *Wiley Interdisciplinary Reviews: Cognitive Science*, *3*(4), 451–470.

Waytz, A., & Mitchell, J. P. (2011). Two mechanisms for simulating other minds: Dissociations between mirroring and self-projection. *Current Directions in Psychological Science*, *20*, 197–200.

Weng, S., Wiggins, J. L., Peltier, S. J., Carrasco, M., Risi, S., Lord, C., & Monk, C. S. (2010). Alterations of resting state functional connectivity in the default network in adolescents with autism spectrum disorders. *Brain Research*, *1313*, 202–214.

Wolkenstein, L., Schönenberg, M., Schirm, E., & Hautzinger, M. (2011). I can see what you feel, but I can't deal with it: Impaired theory of mind in depression. *Journal of Affective Disorders*, *132*(1–2), 104–111.

Woo, C., Koban, L., Kross, E., Lindquist, M. A., Banich, M. T., Ruzic, L., . . . Wager, T. D. (2014). Separate neural representations for physical pain and social rejection. *Nature Communications*, *5*, 5380.

Xu, J., & Potenza, M. N. (2012). White matter integrity and five-factor personality measures in healthy adults. *NeuroImage*, *59*(1), 800–807.

Yeo, B. T., Krienen, F. M., Sepulcre, J., Sabuncu, M. R., Lashkari, D., Hollinshead, M., . . . Buckner, R. L. (2011). The organization of the human cerebral cortex estimated by intrinsic functional connectivity. *Journal of Neurophysiology*, *106*(3), 1125–1165.

Zhao, X., Wang, P., Li, C., Hu, Z., Xi, Q., Wu, W., & Tang, X. (2007). Altered default mode network activity in patient with anxiety disorders: An fMRI study. *European Journal of Radiology*, *63*(3), 373–378.

3

CULTURAL DIFFERENCES IN SUBJECTIVE WELL-BEING

How and Why

William Tov and Ze Ling Serene Nai[1]

Nearly every year, it seems, rankings of the "happiest" countries are updated, released, and publicized. Although these rankings fluctuate from year to year, some of the highest levels of well-being are consistently observed in Northern Europe and some of the lowest in Africa (e.g., Helliwell, Layard, & Sachs, 2017). Why do societies differ in well-being? The contrast between Northern Europe and Africa draws attention to the importance of economic development and sociopolitical stability. Indeed, societies that are characterized by greater wealth and social stability have higher average levels of life satisfaction than those faring less well on these factors (Stevenson & Wolfers, 2008; Tov, Diener, Ng, Kesebir, & Harter, 2009). Broad socioeconomic factors such as per capita gross domestic product (GDP), life expectancy, and perceived corruption collectively account for 20% to 75% of the variance in national well-being depending on the measure used (Helliwell, Huang, & Wang, 2017). Levels of well-being are higher in economically developed nations in part because people are better able to meet basic needs for food, comfort, and security (Diener, Ng, Harter, & Arora, 2010). Citizens in wealthy countries also tend to experience greater freedom of choice and expression (Inglehart, Foa, Peterson, & Welzel, 2008; Tov & Diener, 2008). Nevertheless, a considerable proportion of variance in national well-being remains unaccounted for by socioeconomic development. This is not surprising considering that societies differ on a host of other variables such as climate, geography, population density, as well as cultural values, beliefs, and practices.

In this chapter, we examine cultural differences in well-being and review the work that has been done to account for these differences. To ask how culture influences well-being is distinct from asking how economic development or climate influences well-being. Severe poverty and harsh climates can reduce well-being by making it difficult for people to meet basic needs (Fischer & van de Vliert, 2011).

In contrast, the effect of culture on well-being needs to be understood in the context of a system of values, beliefs, and practices that tend to be organized around certain themes (e.g., individualism); it requires an understanding of the shared logic that underlies people's assumptions, perceptions, and inclinations to feel and behave a certain way. Although we distinguish cultural variables from economic and ecological variables, we also agree that they shape and mutually influence each other in significant ways (Cohen, 2001; Fiske, Kitayama, Markus, & Nisbett, 1998; Inglehart, 1997). For example, increasing societal wealth may alter one's dependence on kinship ties, enabling a more individualistic culture to emerge (Triandis, 1989). However, a cultural analysis of well-being may often require observations and theoretical tools that differ from a strictly economic analysis of well-being. It forces us to consider factors beyond basic needs that shape happiness and life satisfaction around the world. As governments and international organizations develop indicators of well-being to inform public policy (Diener & Tov, 2012; Organisation for Economic Co-operation and Development, 2017), the influence of cultural values and beliefs on people's well-being—including their understanding of what constitutes happiness and satisfaction—should be carefully studied and factored into the interpretation of self-reported well-being (National Research Council, 2013), as well as the design of policies and interventions aimed at improving well-being. For example, the efforts of North American school systems to promote the self-esteem of students (Heine, Lehman, Markus, & Kitayama, 1999) assume a particular view of the healthy, well-adjusted person that may not be shared in other cultures. We will begin by defining what we mean by the terms *well-being* and *culture*. Then we discuss in what sense cultures differ in well-being (i.e., *how* do cultures differ). We also consider the factors that mediate cultural differences in well-being (i.e., *why* do cultures differ). Because the question of *how* cultures differ in well-being has been addressed previously (Tov & Diener, 2007, 2013; Scollon & Tov, 2012), we review this area selectively and devote more discussion to the question of *why* cultures differ. Much of our review reflects the existing body of research, which is dominated by comparisons of Westerners (i.e., people of European or North American cultural heritage) with Easterners (i.e., people of Asian—especially East Asian cultural heritage). Very few studies have examined respondents from other world regions (e.g., Latin America, Africa, the Middle East)—at least not to the degree that East-West differences have been investigated. We later discuss the limitations that this underrepresentation may have for our understanding of how culture shapes well-being. We also discuss future directions that are needed to advance the field of culture and well-being.

Subjective Well-Being

We conceptualize well-being within the paradigm of *subjective* well-being (SWB; Diener, 1984; Diener, Suh, Lucas, & Smith, 1999), which refers to the various ways that people evaluate and experience their lives in a positive manner. A person with high levels of SWB would ideally experience (1) positive emotions frequently, (2) negative emotions infrequently, and (3) evaluate their life as a whole as very satisfying. Thus SWB entails affective experiences as well as cognitive judgments (life satisfaction or life evaluation). Although the three components of SWB are typically correlated with each other, they are known to have distinct correlates (Tay & Diener, 2011). Thus how cultures differ in SWB may depend on which component is considered. (See Chapter 1 for a more detailed discussion.)

Culture and Possible Mediators of Cultural Differences in Well-Being

We define *culture* as a system or pattern of beliefs, values, and practices shared and socially transmitted among people in a relatively enduring context (Markus & Kitayama, 2010; Triandis, 1994). Because "context" can be conceptualized in different ways (e.g., home versus work, city, nation, or world region), and people typically operate in multiple contexts, a single individual can be influenced by multiple systems and subsystems of culture. Thus it is possible to speak of individuals who are "bicultural", whose thoughts, feelings, and behavior may shift depending on the cultural context or cultural knowledge that is most salient to them at a particular moment (Hong, Morris, Chiu, & Benet-Martinez, 2000). Because cultural influences on psychological processes are not fixed, scholars have admonished against equating culture with whole groups of people (Markus & Kitayama, 2010). Although this point is well taken, much research has relied on comparisons between different groups (e.g., Easterners versus Westerners) to test the hypothesized effects of culture on well-being. Such studies need not imply that the effects of culture are fixed; instead, group differences can be viewed as differences in central tendencies (average levels of behavior) while allowing for both interindividual and *intra*individual variability among people in the same cultural group. Group comparisons should not be the only tool employed by cultural psychologists; nevertheless, they can be extremely informative especially when potential mediators are measured and tested. Four types of constructs have been studied as mediators of cultural differences in well-being.

Individualist-Collectivist Values

Triandis (1994, 1995, 2001) conceptualized *individualism* and *collectivism* as two major cultural patterns ("syndromes") that differ in the extent to which the individual (versus one's in-group) serves as the primary reference for thought, feelings, and behavior. Individualist cultures emphasize personal goals over in-group goals; behavior is based primarily on one's personal attitudes and preferences. Collectivist cultures emphasize in-group goals over personal goals; behavior is based primarily on in-group norms. Triandis (2001) suggested that child-rearing practices tend to support the dominant cultural syndrome. Individualist cultures emphasize independence, exploration, creativity, and self-reliance. Collectivist cultures emphasize conformity, obedience, security, and reliability. Cross-cultural psychologists have usually measured individualist and collectivist *values* as opposed to norms and practices (but see House, Hanges, Javidan, Dorfman, & Gupta, 2004). For example, participants might rate how important it is to have freedom in how they approach their jobs (Hofstede, 2001). Individualist values tend to be endorsed more strongly in North America, Western Europe, and Northern Europe; collectivist values tend to be endorsed more strongly in Asia, Latin America, and Africa (Diener & Diener, 1995; Hofstede, 2001; House et al., 2004).

Self-Construal

Cultures differ in the aspects of the self that are most salient to the individual (Triandis, 1989). For example, Markus and Kitayama (1991) proposed that Western cultures cultivate an *independent self-construal* that views the self as an autonomous entity, distinct and separable from others. The independent self consists of a unique configuration of personal attributes that is stable across situations. In contrast, many non-Western cultures cultivate an *interdependent self-construal* that views the self as an entity that is fundamentally connected to others and contextually embedded. The interdependent self is organized with reference to how others in a relationship are thinking, feeling, and behaving; it consists of multiple configurations of personal attributes that shift according social roles. The distinction between independent and interdependent self-construals has obvious parallels with individualism-collectivism (Brewer & Chen, 2007; Triandis & Gelfand, 1998). However, not all scholars view them as synonymous terms (Fiske et al., 1998; Vignoles et al., 2016). Therefore, we consider self-construals separately from individualist and collectivist values.

Relational Beliefs

A few studies have tested beliefs about one's relationship with others as mediators of cultural differences in well-being. These include the extent to which one is fulfilling parental expectations or feels responsible for the happiness of others. Although such beliefs might be taken as indicators of collectivism there are different varieties of collectivism such as horizontal and vertical collectivism (Triandis & Gelfand, 1998); in-group collectivism (House et al., 2004); and relational collectivism (Brewer & Chen, 2007). The relational beliefs that have been studied thus far in culture and well-being research might reflect one or more of these forms of collectivism. Alternatively they might be specific to a particular cultural area (East Asia but not Latin America). We consider these beliefs separately from collectivist values and interdependent self-construal.

Dialectical Beliefs

Naïve dialecticism refers to lay beliefs about change and contradiction (Peng & Nisbett, 1999; Spencer-Rodgers, Williams, & Peng, 2010). High levels of dialectical thinking are characterized by the belief that the universe is not static but constantly in flux, alternating between opposite states (e.g., hot becomes cold). This understanding encourages a greater tolerance for contradiction—an acceptance of the idea that objects, events, and states of being often consist of opposing elements. If happiness often turns into sadness (and vice versa), then it makes sense that a person could be described as *both* happy and sad. A growing body of research suggests that people of East Asian cultural heritage tend to hold dialectical beliefs more strongly than those of Western cultural heritage (Spencer-Rodgers et al., 2010). The origin of such differences may be rooted in distinct philosophical traditions. Eastern philosophies such as Taoism stress the mutual dependence of contrasting states: "Thus Something and Nothing produce each other; The difficult and the easy complement each other" (Lao Tzu, 1963, II, 5–6). In contrast, Western philosophers such as Aristotle emphasized the law of noncontradiction—that "A is B" and "A is not B" cannot both be true (Peng & Nisbett, 1999). Beliefs about change and contradiction may influence how positive and negative emotions are experienced in different cultures.

Cultural Differences in SWB

Cultures can differ in SWB in three ways. First, cultures differ in how strongly the components of SWB (positive affect, negative affect, and life satisfaction) correlate with each other; we refer to this as differences in structure (see also Chapter 1). Second, cultures differ in mean levels of SWB such that some societies are "happier" than others. Third, cultures differ in the correlates of well-being with certain factors covarying more strongly in one cultural context versus another.

The Structure of SWB

Past research emphasized the independence of positive affect (PA) and negative affect (NA; Bradburn, 1969; Watson, Clark, & Tellegen, 1988), suggesting that the experience of PA and NA were unrelated. However, inconsistent relations between PA and NA could be due to differences in how affect is measured. Self-report affect scales vary in their response formats (Russell & Carroll, 1999). Some scales measure how *often* emotions are felt (frequency); others measure how *strongly* they are felt (intensity). Correlations between PA and NA are also weakened by measurement error. When these factors are taken into account, measures of PA and NA tend to be inversely related (Barrett & Russell, 1998; Green, Goldman, & Salovey, 1993) especially when frequency rather than the intensity is measured (Diener, Larsen, Levine, & Emmons, 1985).

Nevertheless, the inverse relation between PA and NA varies across nations (Schimmack, Oishi, & Diener, 2002), indicating that the degree to which emotional experiences are uniformly positive or negative may depend on cultural context. The correlation between PA and NA tends to be *less* negative among Easterners than Westerners, suggesting that the former tend to experience mixtures of positive and negative emotions to a greater degree. A similar pattern has been observed *within* bicultural Asian Canadians in an experience sampling study (Perunovic, Heller, & Rafaeli, 2007). When Asian Canadians recently spoke an Asian language or identified with an Asian culture, their momentary feelings of PA were less correlated with their feelings of NA. However, when they recently spoke a non-Asian language or identified with a Western culture, PA and NA were more inversely correlated. That Asian Canadians' language use and identity can fluctuate across situations may reflect the different cultural contexts they experience (e.g., with family versus at school) on a daily basis.

Cultural differences in the relation between PA and NA may be influenced by levels of individualism-collectivism. Western cultures tend to be more individualistic, and the negative correlation between PA and NA is stronger in individualist (versus collectivist) nations (Schimmack et al., 2002). In the case of the United States, a history of voluntary settlement by Europeans in America may have shaped a culture in which independence and self-reliance are strongly valued (Kitayama, Ishii, Imada, Takemura, & Ramaswamy, 2006; Sims, Tsai, Jiang, Wang, Fung, & Zhang, 2015). Settlers to a new frontier may be self-selected. That is, people with certain values, personality traits, or genetic predispositions may be more inclined to leave their homelands to pursue a better life elsewhere. Alternatively, the harsh frontier environment itself may foster individualistic behavior—putting a premium on self-protection and self-reliance (Kitayama et al., 2006).

Whether the attributes of settlers are self-selected or shaped by environment, the tendency to maximize PA and minimize NA may have been functional in such circumstances—helping settlers to endure, explore, and transform the wild terrain to suit their needs. Sims et al. (2015) proposed that the cultural legacy of voluntary settlement by European settlers influenced the emotion regulation strategies of their American descendants. In contrast, East Asians—at least those without such a cultural history (see Kitayama et al., 2006)—may not share the goal of maximizing PA as it has the potential to be socially disruptive to one's in-group. East Asians may instead be more tolerant of negative experiences, especially if it preserves social harmony. Thus, European Americans may exhibit a stronger desire to maximize PA and minimize NA compared with East Asians, which in turn should result in a stronger inverse relation between PA and NA. In support of this hypothesis, Sims et al. (2015) showed first that European American students endorsed individualist (versus collectivist) values more strongly than Chinese students from Hong Kong and the mainland. Second, individualist values were associated with a greater desire to experience higher levels of PA relative to NA.

Third, cultural differences in the PA-NA correlation were significantly accounted for by the desire to maximize PA and minimize NA. Thus, PA and NA tend to be experienced as opposing states in European American students in part because individualist values may encourage the maximization of PA (and minimization of NA), which in turn influences how they regulate and pursue emotional experiences. Among Chinese students, the desire to maximize PA/minimize NA may conflict with collectivist values. With less motivation to up-regulate PA and down-regulate NA, Chinese students may experience a greater mixture of emotions in daily life.

One problem with the voluntary settlement theory is that it does not explain why, on average, PA and NA are inversely related in individualistic countries *other than* the US Moreover, even after controlling for individualism-collectivism, PA-NA correlations were still weaker in Asian countries (Schimmack et al., 2002), suggesting that other elements of culture may be involved. For example, in a successful situation, Japanese participants reported more mixed emotions than European American participants (Miyamoto, Uchida, & Ellsworth, 2010). This difference was partly mediated by a greater sense of responsibility for the feelings of others on the part of Japanese participants. For the latter group, success was often accompanied by feelings of happiness but also fear of troubling others. Dialectical beliefs may also account for cultural differences in mixed affective experiences. Stronger dialecticism among East Asians may lead them to seek balance between PA and NA, or at the very least tolerate feelings of NA along with PA over a period of time. Consistent with this hypothesis, Chinese students reported a greater tendency to experience a mixture of PA and NA than European American students (Spencer-Rodgers et al., 2010), and this difference was mediated by differences in dialectical beliefs.

In addition to cultural differences in the correlation between PA and NA, there are also cultural differences in the extent to which emotions are associated with life satisfaction (LS). Compared with collectivist cultures, individualist cultures place more emphasis on internal feelings, attitudes, and preferences as guides for action and decision-making (Triandis, 1995). As a result, affective experiences correlate more strongly with judgments of LS in individualist cultures (Suh, Diener, Oishi, & Triandis, 1998). In contrast, people in collectivist cultures considered both their feelings and the normative desirability of LS in their society. If high levels of LS are undesirable in one's society, those in collectivist cultures may not report high LS despite frequent feelings of PA.

Mean Levels of SWB

In most societies around the world—except those marred by extreme poverty and social instability—people report levels of well-being that are slightly above neutral, implying that most people are at least mildly "happy" (Diener & Diener, 1996). Still, there is considerable cultural variation in average levels of SWB. East Asians often report lower levels of SWB than Westerners (for a review, see Tov & Diener, 2007). These differences have been attributed to individualism–collectivism. Individualist countries tend to report higher levels of SWB than collectivist countries even after controlling for national wealth (Diener, Diener & Diener, 1995; Fischer & Boer, 2011). However, the exact process by which individualistic values influence mean levels of SWB remains unclear. Fischer and Boer (2011) suggested that individualist cultures promote and facilitate greater autonomy for people to pursue their personal goals. Individualist countries offer greater protection for the rights and liberties of their citizens (Diener et al., 1995). Although greater autonomy and freedom are associated with higher levels of well-being (Helliwell et al., 2017; Inglehart et al., 2008; Tay & Diener, 2011), researchers have not formally tested the extent to which these constructs mediate the relation between individualism and SWB.

A closely related view is that self-construals may promote or limit the experience and expression of SWB. Again, it seems autonomy may be a mechanism through which this occurs. Those with an independent self-construal might feel free to express their internal attitudes and feelings or pursue their personal interests. In contrast, those with an interdependent self-construal may feel more restricted because they are often be guided by a consideration for the reaction of others (Markus & Kitayama, 1991). Whereas those with an independent self-construal might feel free to express their internal attitudes and feelings or pursue their personal interests, those with an interdependent self-construal may feel more restricted. Compared with US participants, for instance, Taiwanese participants tended to rate their self-worth as more contingent on the approval of others (Liu, Chiu, & Chang, 2017). This contingency partially mediated the cultural difference in SWB: Taiwanese who were more sensitive to others' approval reported lower levels of well-being.

Oishi and Sullivan (2005) did not examine self-construals per se—but they asked students to rate the extent to which their parents had specific expectations for their academic and social development. Compared with European American students, (1) Asian American students reported that their parents had more specific expectations; (2) the more specific expectations were, the less likely students felt they were fulfilling them; and (3) lower perceived fulfillment was associated with lower LS. In other words, the specificity of parental expectations and their perceived fulfillment mediated cultural differences in life satisfaction.

Dialectical beliefs may also influence average levels of well-being. Ng and Hynie (2016) reasoned that a potential cost of holding contradictory beliefs is that everyday decisions may be more difficult to make. Indecision may have negative effects on SWB because more effort is expended on making the decision and even after it is made, one is less likely to be satisfied. Ng and Hynie provided support for this hypothesis in a study of East Asian and European Canadians. The former reported higher levels of dialecticism and chronic indecisiveness, and lower levels of LS. Importantly, the indirect effect from culture to dialecticism to indecisiveness to LS was significant. In other words, East Asian Canadians were less satisfied than European Canadians in part because their greater tolerance for contradiction may impede the confidence with which they make decisions in daily life. Dialectical beliefs might also influence whether people attempt to increase (up-regulate) or decrease (down-regulate) the frequency, intensity, or duration of certain emotions. Miyamoto and Ma (2011) examined dialectical beliefs about positive emotions (e.g., whether something bad might happen if one continued to feel happy). Asian students endorsed dialectical beliefs more than European American students; these beliefs in turn were associated with a greater tendency to *dampen* rather than savor PA. In another study, students rated their emotions twice: just after learning their grade on an exam and again the following day. Among those who did well on the exam, European Americans maintained their PA the next day to a greater extent than Asians, and this difference was partially mediated by dialectical beliefs. Thus, Asian students' greater dialecticism resulted in a larger drop in PA the next day. This finding suggests that dialecticism fosters cultural differences in emotion regulation strategies, which may then create differences in average levels of PA. It also offers some insight into why the experience of PA and NA tends to be less polarized among Easterners than Westerners (see "The Structure of SWB").

Correlates of SWB

Several studies have reported cultural differences in the correlates of SWB. Examples include self-esteem, relationship harmony, self-consistency, and emotion regulation.

Self-Esteem

Though self-esteem is generally associated with greater SWB (Diener et al., 1999), the magnitude of this relation varies across cultures. Correlations between self-esteem and LS tend to be larger in Western samples than in East Asian samples (Kwan, Bond, & Singelis, 1997; Park & Huebner, 2005). Various explanations have been offered. Westerners tend to possess an independent self-construal in which unique traits and abilities are defining elements of the self (Heine et al., 1999; Kwan et al., 1997; Markus & Kitayama, 1991). In contrast, East Asians tend to possess an interdependent self-construal in which social roles and obligations are more salient than individual attributes. More broadly, Westerners may endorse individualist values such as self-reliance and self-actualization (Triandis, 1995). Personal accomplishments are important, and measures of individualism correlate with valuing achievement (Oishi, Schimmack, Diener, & Suh, 1998). Thus, self-esteem should be highly desirable in individualist cultures as an indicator that one has successfully distinguished oneself from others. Indeed, when individualism is specifically examined (instead of East-West regional differences), self-esteem and

LS correlate more strongly in individualist than in collectivist societies (Diener & Diener, 1995; Oishi, Diener, Lucas, & Suh, 1999).

Relationship Harmony

Several studies have found that relationship harmony and attaining goals that made close others happy were more consistently associated with SWB for Asians and Asian Americans than for European Americans (Kang, Shaver, Sue, Min, & Jing, 2003; Kwan et al., 1997; Oishi & Diener, 2001). These findings are consistent with the idea that Asian cultures tend to value collectivism or promote an interdependent self-construal. Harmonious relationships are critical in a culture in which one is dependent on and prioritizes the needs of one's in-group. However, the previous studies did not test whether collectivist values or interdependent self-construals *mediated* cultural differences in the effect of relationship harmony on SWB. It would be valuable to conduct such tests. A larger cross-national study did *not* find, for example, that satisfaction with family had a greater impact on LS in collectivist (versus individualist) countries (Diener & Diener, 1995).

Self-Consistency

Another correlate of SWB that may be culturally dependent is self-consistency. For example, a person who is equally kind to friends, family, and strangers is more self-consistent than one who is only kind to friends. Self-consistency was a much stronger predictor of SWB for US participants (absolute rs = .27 to .50) than for Korean participants (absolute rs < .22; Suh, 2002). These differences might reflect different cultural goals and affordances. For example, individualist cultures encourage and enable consistency by valuing the needs and interest of the individual. Collectivist cultures, on the other hand, prioritize the needs and interest of one's in-group. Because the in-group can shift in salience (e.g., friends, family, work colleagues; Triandis, 1995), adaptability rather than consistency may be valued more in collectivist cultures. Self-consistency also implies that the self as a unique, stable configuration of attributes (i.e., an independent self) has been successfully achieved. Such consistency may be of less importance in cultures that view the self as contextualized and organized by one's relationships (i.e., an interdependent self; Markus & Kitayama, 1991). Yet another possible factor is dialectical beliefs. Consistency may be less of a mandate in dialectical cultures that cultivate a view of the world as constantly changing and alternating between opposing states. English and Chen (2007) showed that dialectical beliefs were associated with less consistency. These beliefs also mediated differences between Asian American and European Americans in self-consistency. To date, however, it is unknown whether dialecticism (or individualism or self-construals) *account for* cultural differences in the effects of self-consistency on SWB. Moreover, although Easterners tend to be less consistent across relationships, they tend to be as consistent as Westerners *within* their relationships (English &

Chen, 2007; Koh, Scollon, & Wirtz, 2014). How within-relationship consistency affects SWB across cultures remains to be investigated.

Emotion Regulation

How emotions are chronically regulated may have implications for SWB. The tendency to reappraise events in a more positive or less negative manner is positively associated with LS, whereas the tendency to suppress emotional expression is negatively associated with LS (Gross & John, 2003). However, the negative effects of emotional suppression may not generalize across culture. For example, suppression tends to be associated with depression and NA among European Americans but not among people of Eastern cultural heritage (Butler, Lee, & Gross, 2007; Cheung & Park, 2010; Su, Lee, & Oishi, 2013). Because Easterners tend to construe the self as interdependent, they may be relatively more inclined than Westerners to consider the reaction of others prior to a course of action. For example, when Japanese and American participants watched a stressful film with an experimenter present, Japanese participants tended to smile more than Americans (Ekman, 1999). No cultural difference was observed when participants watched the film alone: Both groups expressed negative emotion, suggesting that Japanese may have been masking their negative emotions when the experimenter was present. The controlled expression of emotion may facilitate the goals of an interdependent self (e.g., maintaining social harmony) and therefore, be less detrimental to well-being. Cheung and Park (2010) did find that suppression was weakly associated with depression among people with an interdependent self-construal; however they did not examine whether this mediated the ethnic difference they observed between Asian Americans and European Americans. Su et al. (2013) observed that the tendency to suppress positive disengaged emotions (e.g., pride, feelings of superiority) was associated with greater depression among European American but not Chinese Singaporean participants. Moreover, the moderating effect of culture was mediated by independent self-construal. In both groups, an independent self-construal was associated with lower levels of depression. However, European Americans who suppressed feelings of pride and superiority construed the self as less independent. In contrast, suppression was unrelated to independent self-construal among Chinese Singaporeans. These results suggest that, for Americans, feelings of pride may signal to the self that one has successfully distinguished oneself from others in a positive way. The suppression of pride and feelings of superiority removes this signal to the self, leading European Americans to construe themselves as less independent.

Additional Issues, Limitations, and Future Directions

Culture and well-being research has grown greatly since the seminal paper by Diener and Diener (1995). Despite this growth, we must acknowledge some limitations in the existing body of research. Some of these could be viewed as challenges faced by the broader fields of cultural and cross-cultural psychology (Triandis, 2007; Fiske et al., 1998).

Measurement Issues

Cross-cultural research is challenging for many reasons—not least of which is ensuring equivalence of measurement. When scales are translated into different languages, there is a risk that the meaning of an item is altered. Very often, translated measures are back-translated into the original language to check that meaning has been retained (Brislin, 1970). A failure to back-translate may have contributed to the finding that Tanzania ranked 2nd out of 70 countries on happiness but 70th on life satisfaction in the World Values Survey (Tov & Au, 2013). Technical notes suggested problems with the Kiswahili translation of *happiness*. The World Values Survey also measures happiness and life satisfaction using single items, which can intensify the impact of problematic translations. Vittersø, Røysamb, and Diener (2002) examined responses to the five-item Satisfaction with Life Scale across 41 nations. In most countries, item responses were strongly intercorrelated suggesting that the concept of life satisfaction may be similarly understood across cultures. However, responses were less consistent in poorer countries—which could reflect a lack of familiarity with responding to survey items.

Response styles are another potential threat to the validity of cross-cultural comparisons. Chen, Lee, and Stevenson (1995) observed a tendency for East Asian participants to select the midpoint of the scale, whereas North American participants were more likely to give extreme responses (i.e., select the endpoints). However, this pattern has not been consistently observed on measures of well-being (Diener, Suh, Smith, & Shao, 1995). Furthermore, adjustments for response styles do not seem to alter cross-cultural comparisons drastically (e.g., Chen et al., 1995; Tsai, Knutson, & Fung, 2006; but see Schimmack, Oishi, & Diener, 2005). If a person tends to give high (or low) ratings across items, this effect might be removed by ipsatizing item responses (subtracting the person's mean response from each item response). Tsai et al. (2006) found that cultural differences between Hong Kong Chinese and European Americans were largely consistent whether raw scores or ipsatized scores were compared.

Factor analytic methods can be used to evaluate the equivalence of measures across cultures. If responses to five items measuring LS are strongly correlated with each other, a factor analysis should reveal that the items all "load" onto a single factor. That is, the items have so much in common with each other that they probably measure the same construct. People who are truly satisfied with life should agree with items such as "I am satisfied with life" and "The conditions of my life are excellent" (Diener et al., 1985). A factor thus represents the underlying construct (e.g., life satisfaction) that influences responses to the items; and the item loading represents how much an item correlates with or is influenced by that underlying construct. If the satisfied people neither agree nor disagree with an item such as "I often feel cheerful", its loading on the LS factor will be lower than items that they *do* agree with. This would suggest that the cheerfulness item may be measuring something other than life satisfaction.

In cross-cultural research, multigroup confirmatory factor analysis (CFA) can be used to evaluate different levels of measurement invariance (Chen, 2008; Cheung & Rensvold, 2000). This approach essentially involves a comparison of the factor analytic results across two or more groups. Configural invariance is established when items intended to measure the same construct (e.g., LS) load onto the same factor in each cultural group studied. If five of the LS items load onto the same factor in the US, but only two of the items load together in China, this might suggest that the scale is not measuring the same construct in both cultures. That said, configural invariance has been established across many nations for scales measuring LS (Lucas & Diener, 2008; Vittersø et al., 2002); PA; and NA (Kuppens, Ceulemans, Timmerman, Diener, & Kim-Prieto, 2006; Lucas & Diener, 2008).

A higher level of invariance (*metric invariance*) exists when items not only load onto the same factors across cultures, but their loadings also are equivalent in *magnitude*. An item like "The conditions of my life are excellent" might load significantly with other LS items onto a common factor among both Easterners and Westerners, but the loading could be stronger for one group than the other. Although such an item informs us of how satisfied people are in both groups, a stronger loading among Westerners than Easterners, for example, might suggest that LS is based more heavily on the conditions of one's life among the former than the latter.

A still higher level of invariance (*scalar invariance*) exists when items have equivalent points of origin or intercepts. How a person rates the LS items (i.e., their observed responses) should reflect how satisfied with life they really are (i.e., their latent or true level of LS). Ideally, an Easterner and a Westerner who are equally satisfied with life (i.e., their latent LS is equivalent) should give the same ratings on the LS items. However, cultural norms such as modesty or self-criticism (Heine et al., 1999; Kim, Chiu, Peng, Cai, & Tov, 2010; Oishi, 2006) may lead Easterners to give *lower* ratings than Westerners even when they are equally satisfied with life. The item might still distinguish Easterners and Westerners who are satisfied versus dissatisfied with life, but the item intercepts would be lower for Easterners. Thus an Easterner and a Westerner might both be extremely satisfied, but the Easterner rates her LS as "5" and the Westerner as "7" on a 7-point scale. Both may be slightly dissatisfied with life, but the Easterner rates her LS a "2" and the Westerner a "4". In other words, cultural differences in the item intercepts but not the item loadings indicate a bias that is uniform across levels of latent LS.[2]

Different levels of invariance may affect the validity of cross-cultural comparisons in different ways (Chen, 2008). If items measuring self-esteem load more strongly onto a common factor among Westerners than Easterners (lack of metric invariance), this could inflate the slope of self-esteem on LS in the former relative to the latter. If item responses overestimate the true level of LS in Western samples, but underestimate it in Eastern samples (lack of scalar invariance), this could artificially inflate mean differences between the two groups. As the use of advanced psychometric methods in cross-cultural research increases, the measurement invariance of scales measuring culture or SWB should be investigated more closely. It remains to be seen whether previously reported cultural differences in mean levels and correlates of SWB still hold when measurement equivalence is verified.

Identifying the Mechanisms Underlying Cultural Differences in SWB

Matsumoto and Yoo (2006) discussed the progression of cross-cultural research from early observations of group differences in behavior to the measurement of cultural dimensions (e.g., individualism-collectivism) along which countries could be discriminated. The next phase of cross-cultural research should involve studies that link the major dimensions or elements of culture to group differences in behavior. In other words, there is a need for studies that identify the "active cultural ingredients" (Matsumoto & Yoo, 2006) or mediators underlying group differences in psychological processes. As we reviewed earlier, a number of researchers have identified mediators of cultural differences in SWB structure and mean levels. Notwithstanding these important contributions, more work is needed on several fronts.

First, few studies have identified mediators of cultural differences in the *correlates* of SWB. Though Eastern and Western samples differ in the extent to which self-esteem, self-consistency, relationship harmony, and emotional suppression correlate with SWB, the cultural processes accounting for these differences are not well understood and deserve more attention. What are needed are tests of *mediated moderation*—showing that the moderating effect of cultural group operates through its effect on another variable. For example, research has suggested that (1) self-esteem has a stronger effect on SWB in Western (versus Eastern) samples because (2) individualist cultures place more value on positive self-worth and (3) Western countries score higher on individualism (Diener & Diener, 1995; Kwan et al., 1997; Oishi et al., 1999; Park & Huebner, 2005). What awaits is a formal test of mediation to investigate whether the East-West group difference is accounted for by differences in individualism (see Yuki, Sato, Takemura, & Oishi, 2013, for a closely related analysis). If the difference is fully accounted for by variation in individualism, the next step might be to identify the specific aspects of individualism (e.g., self-reliance, uniqueness, self-expression, etc.; Vignoles et al., 2016) that moderate the effects of self-esteem. If the difference is not fully accounted for, then factors other than individualistic values should be considered.

Second, although some researchers have evoked individualism and self-construals as explanations for cultural differences in SWB, they have not always measured these constructs directly and tested whether they mediate cultural differences in the hypothesized manner (for exceptions, see Liu et al., 2017; Sims et al., 2015; Su et al., 2013). In the case of East-West comparisons, this is a critical point because these cultures vary on other types of values, beliefs, and practices. We have noted how dialectical beliefs also mediate cultural differences in the structure and mean levels of SWB (Miyamoto & Ma, 2011; Miyamoto et al., 2010; Ng & Hynie, 2016; Spencer-Rodgers et al., 2010). It may be that values, self-construals, and dialectical beliefs each account for some differences but not others. This could be learned from studies that assess some or all of these constructs, enabling their mediating effects to be compared.

Third, other elements of culture can be investigated as mediators. For instance, the types of emotions that people desire to feel (ideal affect) vary across cultures. Whereas European Americans tend to desire high-arousal PA (e.g., enthusiasm), Hong Kong Chinese tend to desire low-arousal PA (e.g., calm; Tsai et al., 2006). Cultural differences in ideal affect (i.e., what people want to feel) may underlie differences in actual affect (i.e., the emotions people actually feel) by influencing the way people regulate their emotions. This is suggested by Miyamoto and Ma's (2011) study in which prolonged happiness was less desirable among Asian students than European American students, and those who held such beliefs experienced PA for a shorter duration after doing well on an exam. Moreover, discrepancies between ideal and actual PA may be associated with depression in culturally distinct ways. For European Americans, discrepancies in actual versus ideal high-arousal PA but not low-arousal PA predicted depression; for Hong Kong Chinese, the reverse pattern was observed (Tsai et al., 2006). The emotions people *want* to feel may be shaped by their goals and values (Tsai, Miao, Seppala, Fung, & Yeung, 2007). People who value power, for example, desire to feel anger and pride (Tamir et al., 2016). The latter emotions may be helpful when confronting others or asserting oneself—both of which support the goal of maintaining one's position over others. Thus, ideal affect may mediate the relation between values and actual affective experience (as well as SWB more generally).

We have largely focused on values, self-construals, and beliefs. Nevertheless, cultural practices—the way people *actually* behave and interact in a society—may also mediate group differences in SWB. For example, child-rearing practices emphasize self-enhancement in the US but self-criticism in Japan (Heine et al., 1999). Whereas European American mothers may try to cultivate their child's self-esteem, Japanese mothers may draw attention to their child's shortcomings. These different practices may be related to individualism-collectivism, but not entirely. It is not clear, for instance, that self-criticism is a fundamental aspect of all collectivist cultures (see next section). Differences in self-enhancement and self-criticism may explain the tendency for European American participants to base their weekly satisfaction on their *best* day of the week, whereas Japanese participants base it on their *worst* day of the week (Oishi, 2002). This hypothesis remains to be tested.

Moving Beyond East-West Differences

As evident from our review, research on cultural differences in SWB draws heavily from comparisons of Easterners and Westerners. Tov and Au (2013) examined the representation of nations in the World Database of Happiness (Veenhoven, n.d.)—the most comprehensive collection of survey data on well-being. Almost 70% of the data come from European and North American nations, and 15% from Asian nations. Though we certainly need more well-being studies in Asia (the region encompasses a wide swath from the Middle East to East Asia), the proportion of data from Latin America (9%) and Africa (6%) is even less. By comparison, 61% of the world population lives in the Asian region, 14% in Africa, and 9% in Latin America (Tov & Au, 2013). Thus the Asian and African regions are underrepresented in the current database on well-being. This imbalance reflects the longer history of population surveys conducted in the West.

Expanding research outside of the East-West axis will critically advance theory on culture and well-being. Researchers draw heavily on constructs such as individualism-collectivism or independent-interdependent self-construals to develop hypotheses about how culture influences well-being. Western cultures are typically viewed as individualist and promoting an independent self-construal. The remaining regions of the world are presumably collectivist and interdependent. However, there is tremendous diversity in the "non-Western" world. For example, although Latin America and Asia are thought to promote collectivist values and interdependent self-construals (Hofstede, 2001; Markus & Kitayama, 1991; Triandis, 1995), average levels of SWB in many Latin American countries are higher than they are in Asia (Helliwell et al., 2017). Clearly there are important differences among Asian, Latin American, and African cultures, both within and between regions. A recent cross-national study revealed *several* distinct aspects of independence and interdependence that were measured by self-construal scales (Vignoles et al., 2016). African, Asian, and Latin American samples were similar in their emphasis on receptiveness to others. Nonetheless, relative to the other two groups, African samples emphasized self-interest more, whereas Latin American samples emphasized self-expression and uniqueness more. How these varieties of independence-interdependence influence the structure, mean levels, and the correlates of well-being in Africa and Latin America would enrich our understanding of how culture shapes well-being. It is also important to acknowledge that a great deal of diversity exists *within* African, Latin American, and Asian countries—each with unique histories (e.g., colonization, political transformations) and unique mixtures of indigenous and immigrant populations.

Operationalizing Culture

Cross-cultural researchers (e.g., Hofstede, 2001; Triandis, 1995) have noted that cultural dimensions such as individualism-collectivism are meant to be descriptions of societies rather than individuals. This distinction may apply to the concept of culture more generally as a *system* of shared beliefs, values, and practices. Yet, cross-cultural psychologists often measure cultural values and self-construals by administering scales to individuals. Are researchers studying "culture" or are they studying individuals with specific values and beliefs?

The meaning of a construct measured at the individual level may not be equivalent to one measured at the societal level. For instance, in one study, individuals who endorsed collectivist values reported higher levels of well-being (Bettencourt & Dorr, 1997). In contrast, collectivist *nations* often yield lower levels of SWB than individualist nations (Diener et al., 1995; Fischer & Boer, 2011). Such discrepancies do not necessarily imply that individual-level measures of culture are useless. They simply suggest that the equivalence of measures across levels of analysis should be empirically scrutinized and not just assumed. Other studies have observed higher levels of SWB among *individuals* who possess an independent self-construal or individualistic values (Benet-Martínez & Karakitapoğlu-Aygün, 2003; Su et al., 2013), consistent with the nation-level findings. Occasional discrepancies could be due to variations in the specific measures of cultural orientation employed. Some scales may emphasize certain aspects of independence/interdependence and de-emphasize other aspects (Vignoles et al., 2016). Our review has focused on the self-endorsement of cultural values and beliefs. However, other approaches are worth acknowledging. Instead of asking participants to rate their personal values and beliefs, they could be asked to rate the *perceived cultural importance* of various values, beliefs, and norms in their society (Wan, Chiu, Tam, Lee, Lau, & Peng, 2007). The perceived *congruence* between the values of the individual and those of his or her society may enhance SWB beyond personal endorsement. Supporting this idea, extraverted individuals are happier if they live in extraverted countries (i.e., societies characterized by high mean levels of extraversion; Fulmer et al., 2010).

Other scholars have suggested that cultural differences may not always manifest in the values that people consciously endorse. Markus and Kitayama (2010) noted that the expression of cultural values and beliefs may be more tacit than is typically appreciated. An alternative to operationalizing culture through self-report measures might be to code cultural products such as books, movies, and newspapers for distinctive features and themes. Oishi, Graham, Kesebir, and Galinha (2013) examined the definition of happiness in dictionaries from 30 nations. In the majority of nations (80%), happiness was defined as luck or fortune. However, SWB was higher in countries that defined happiness not as luck but as state of pleasure, satisfaction, or contentment. The authors suggested that, in countries where happiness is *not* viewed as luck, people may assume it is a state attainable through personal actions and decision-making.

Finally, we have not said much about the influence of religion on SWB. If culture is a system of shared beliefs, values, and practices, then it seems that religions qualify as a form of culture (Cohen, 2009). Religiosity is associated with greater SWB—in part because religious individuals tend to report higher levels of social support and purpose in life (Diener, Tay, & Myers, 2011). Religious groups also differ in their beliefs about the world (Safdar, Lewis, Greenglass, & Daneshpour, 2009), and worldviews such *social cynicism* and *reward for application* are associated with LS (Chen et al., 2016). More directly, religious teachings may influence the type of emotions people want to feel. Relative to Christian Americans, Buddhist Americans value low-arousal PA more and high-arousal PA less (Tsai, Miao, & Seppala, 2007); these differences are independent of ethnicity. In addition, a content analysis of English-language self-help books published in the US revealed that Buddhist books emphasized low-arousal PA more than Christian books, whereas the reverse was observed for high-arousal PA. This study reinforces the potential utility of studying cultural products.

Conclusion

Cultural values and beliefs influence SWB by shaping the structure and inter-relationships among PA, NA, and LS; mean levels of SWB; and the correlates of SWB across cultural contexts. Since our last review (Tov & Diener, 2007), there have been many promising developments and directions in studies of culture and well-being. Advanced statistical methods to evaluate measurement equivalence have become more popular; future applications to scales measuring culture and SWB could alter some of the cultural differences we have noted above. Researchers are also asking important questions about the mechanisms underlying cultural differences in SWB. Some mediators that have already been examined are dialectical beliefs, individualist-collectivist values, and self-construals. However, more research in this area is needed. Specific aspects of individualism or self-construals should be measured and tested. There has also been an increase in cross-national collaborations (e.g., Saucier et al., 2015), and with this, we hope, more comparative studies of culture and SWB that involve Latin American and African countries. Finally, alternative ways of operationalizing culture (e.g., cultural practices, perceived cultural importance, cultural products, religious beliefs, worldviews) can expand our understanding of how culture influences SWB.

Notes

1 Correspondence concerning this article should be sent to William Tov, School of Social Sciences, Singapore Management University, 90 Stamford Road, Level 4, Singapore 178903, Republic of Singapore. Email: williamtov@smu.edu.sg.
2 In actuality, we cannot observe a person's true or latent level of life satisfaction, we can only improve our estimate of it by improving the reliability and validity of items in the scale. Suppose an LS scale possesses high test-retest reliability and is validated by showing

high correlations between self-reported LS and informant reported LS (e.g., close others rating how satisfied they think the respondent is). This LS scale will provide a better estimate of a person's true level of LS than a scale with poorer reliability and validity evidence. Such a scale might then be used as a standard to evaluate other scales and items.

References

Barrett, F. L., & Russell, J. A. (1998). Independence and bipolarity in the structure of current affect. *Journal of Personality and Social Psychology, 74,* 967–984.

Benet-Martínez, V., & Karakitapoğlu-Aygün, Z. (2003). The interplay of cultural syndromes and personality in predicting life satisfaction comparing Asian Americans and European Americans. *Journal of Cross-Cultural Psychology, 34,* 38–60.

Bettencourt, B. A., & Dorr, N. (1997). Collective self-esteem as a mediator of the relationship between allocentrism and subjective well-being. *Personality and Social Psychology Bulletin, 23,* 955–964.

Bradburn, N. M. (1969). *The structure of psychological well-being.* Chicago, IL: Aldine Publishing Co.

Brewer, M. B., & Chen, Y. R. (2007). Where (who) are collectives in collectivism? Toward conceptual clarification of individualism and collectivism. *Psychological Review, 114,* 133–151.

Brislin, R. W. (1970). Back-translation for cross-cultural research. *Journal of Cross-Cultural Psychology, 1,* 185–216.

Butler, E. A., Lee, T. L., & Gross, J. J. (2007). Emotion regulation and culture: Are the social consequences of emotion suppression culture-specific? *Emotion, 7,* 30–48.

Chen, C., Lee, S. Y., & Stevenson, H. W. (1995). Response style and cross-cultural comparisons of rating scales among East Asian and North American students. *Psychological Science, 6,* 170–175.

Chen, F. F. (2008). What happens if we compare chopsticks with forks? The impact of making inappropriate comparisons in cross-cultural research. *Journal of Personality and Social Psychology, 95,* 1005–1018.

Chen, S. X., Lam, B. P., Wu, W. H., Ng, J. K., Buchtel, E. E., Guan, Y., & Deng, H. (2016). Do people's world views matter? The why and how. *Journal of Personality and Social Psychology, 110,* 743–765.

Cheung, G. W., & Rensvold, R. B. (2000). Assessing extreme and acquiescence response sets in cross-cultural research using structural equations modeling. *Journal of Cross-Cultural Psychology, 31,* 187–212.

Cheung, R. Y., & Park, I. J. (2010). Anger suppression, interdependent self-construal, and depression among Asian American and European American college students. *Cultural Diversity and Ethnic Minority Psychology, 16,* 517–525.

Cohen, A. D. (2009). Many forms of culture. *American Psychologist, 64,* 194–204.

Cohen, D. (2001). Cultural variation: Considerations and implications. *Psychological Bulletin, 127,* 451–471.

Diener, E. (1984). Subjective well-being. *Psychological Bulletin, 95,* 542–575.

Diener, E., & Diener, C. (1996). Most people are happy. *Psychological Science, 7,* 1181–1185.

Diener, E., & Diener, M. (1995). Cross-cultural correlates of life satisfaction and self-esteem. *Journal of Personality and Social Psychology, 68,* 653–663.

Diener, E., Diener, M., & Diener, C. (1995). Factors predicting the subjective well-being of nations. *Journal of Personality and Social Psychology, 69,* 851–864.

Diener, E., Emmons, R. A., Larsen, R. J., & Griffin, S. (1985). The Satisfaction With Life Scale. *Journal of Personality Assessment, 49,* 71–75.

Diener, E., Larsen, R. J., Levine, S., & Emmons, R. A. (1985). Intensity and frequency: Dimensions underlying positive and negative affect. *Journal of Personality and Social Psychology, 48,* 1253–1265.

Diener, E., Ng, W., Harter, J., & Arora, R. (2010). Wealth and happiness across the world: Material prosperity predicts life evaluation, whereas psychosocial prosperity predicts positive feeling. *Journal of Personality and Social Psychology, 99,* 52–61.

Diener, E., Suh, E. M., Lucas, R. E., & Smith, H. L. (1999). Subjective well-being: Three decades of progress. *Psychological Bulletin, 125,* 276–302.

Diener, E., Suh, E. M., Smith, H., & Shao, L. (1995). National differences in reported subjective well-being: Why do they occur? *Social Indicators Research, 34,* 7–32.

Diener, E., Tay, L., & Myers, D. G. (2011). The religion paradox: If religion makes people happy, why are so many dropping out? *Journal of Personality and Social Psychology, 101,* 1278–1290.

Diener, E., & Tov, W. (2012). National accounts of well-being. In K. C. Land, A. C. Michalos, & M. J. Sirgy (Eds.), *Handbook of social indicators and quality of life research* (pp. 137–156). New York, NY: Springer.

Ekman, P. (1999). Facial expressions. In T. Dalgleish & M. J. Power (Eds.), *Handbook of cognition and emotion* (pp. 301–320). Chichester, UK: John Wiley & Sons.

English, T., & Chen, S. (2007). Culture and self-concept stability: Consistency across and within contexts among Asian Americans and European Americans. *Journal of Personality and Social Psychology, 93,* 478–490.

Fischer, R., & Boer, D. (2011). What is more important for national well-being: Money or autonomy? A meta-analysis of well-being, burnout, and anxiety across 63 societies. *Journal of Personality and Social Psychology, 101,* 164–184.

Fischer, R., & Van de Vliert, E. (2011). Does climate undermine subjective well-being? A 58-nation study. *Personality and Social Psychology Bulletin, 37,* 1031–1041.

Fiske, A. P., Kitayama, S., Markus, H. R., & Nisbett, R. E. (1998). The cultural matrix of social psychology. In D. Gilbert, S. Fiske, & G. Lindzey (Eds.), *The handbook of social psychology* (Vol. 2, pp. 915–981). New York, NY: Oxford University Press.

Fulmer, C. A., Gelfand, M. J., Kruglanski, A. W., Kim-Prieto, C., Diener, E., Pierro, A., & Higgins, E. T. (2010). On "feeling right" in cultural contexts: How person-culture match affects self-esteem and subjective well-being. *Psychological Science, 21,* 1563–1569.

Green, D. P., Goldman, S. L., & Salovey, P. (1993). Measurement error masks bipolarity in affect ratings. *Journal of Personality and Social Psychology, 64,* 1029–1041.

Gross, J. J., & John, O. P. (2003). Individual differences in two emotion regulation processes: Implications for affect, relationships, and well-being. *Journal of Personality and Social Psychology, 85,* 348–362.

Heine, S. J., Lehman, D. R., Markus, H. R., & Kitayama, S. (1999). Is there a universal need for positive self-regard? *Psychological Review, 106,* 766–794.

Helliwell, J. F., Huang, H., & Wang, S. (2017). Social foundations of world happiness. In J. F. Helliwell, R. Layard, & J. D. Sachs (Eds.), *World happiness report 2017* (pp. 8–47). New York, NY: Sustainable Development Solutions Network.

Helliwell, J. F., Layard, R., & Sachs, J. D. (2017). Overview. In J. F. Helliwell, H. Huang, & S. Wang (Eds.), *World happiness report 2017* (pp. 2–7). New York, NY: Sustainable Development Solutions Network.

Hofstede, G. (2001). *Culture's consequences: Comparing values, behaviors, institutions, and organizations across nations* (2nd ed.). Thousand Oaks, CA: Sage.

Hong, Y.-Y., Morris, M. W., Chiu, C.-Y., & Benet-Martinez, V. (2000). Multicultural minds: A dynamic constructivist approach to culture and cognition. *American Psychologist, 55,* 709–720.

House, R. J., Hanges, P. J., Javidan, M., Dorfman, P. W., & Gupta, V. (2004). *Culture, leadership, and organizations: The GLOBE study of 62 societies.* Thousand Oaks, CA: Sage Publications.

Inglehart, R. (1997). Modernization, postmodernization and changing perceptions of risk. *International Review of Sociology, 7,* 449–459.

Inglehart, R., Foa, R., Peterson, C., & Welzel, C. (2008). Development, freedom, and rising happiness: A global perspective (1981–2007). *Perspectives on Psychological Science, 3,* 264–285.

Kang, S.-M., Shaver, P. R., Sue, S., Min, K.-H., & Jing, H. (2003). Culture-specific patterns in the prediction of life satisfaction: Roles of emotion, relationship quality, and self-esteem. *Personality and Social Psychology Bulletin, 29,* 1596–1608.

Kim, Y.-H., Chiu, C.-Y., Peng, S., Cai, H., & Tov, W. (2010). Explaining East-West differences in the likelihood of making favorable self-evaluations: The role of evaluation apprehension and directness of expression. *Journal of Cross-Cultural Psychology, 41*(1), 62–75. https://doi.org/10.1177/0022022109348921

Kitayama, S., Ishii, K., Imada, T., Takemura, K., & Ramaswamy, J. (2006). Voluntary settlement and the spirit of independence: Evidence from Japan's "northern frontier". *Journal of Personality and Social Psychology, 91*(3), 369–384.

Koh, S., Scollon, C. N., & Wirtz, D. (2014). The role of social relationships and culture in the cognitive representation of emotions. *Cognition and Emotion, 28,* 507–519.

Kuppens, P., Ceulemans, E., Timmerman, M. E., Diener, E., & Kim-Prieto, C. (2006). Universal intracultural and intercultural dimensions of the recalled frequency of emotional experience. *Journal of Cross-Cultural Psychology, 37,* 491–515.

Kwan, V. S. Y., Bond, M. H., & Singelis, T. M. (1997). Pancultural explanations for life satisfaction: Adding relationship harmony to self-esteem. *Journal of Personality and Social Psychology, 73,* 1038–1051.

Lao Tzu. (1963). *Tao te ching* (D. C. Lau, Trans.). London, England: Penguin Books.

Liu, C.-H., Chiu, Y.-H. C., & Chang, J.-H. (2017). Why do Easterners have lower well-being than Westerners? The role of others' approval contingencies of self-worth in the cross-cultural differences in subjective well-being. *Journal of Cross-Cultural Psychology, 48,* 217–224.

Lucas, R. E., & Diener, E. (2008). Can we learn about national differences in happiness from individual responses? A multilevel approach. In F. J. R. van de Vijver, D. A. van Hemert, & Y. H. Poortinga (Eds.), *Multilevel analysis of individuals and cultures* (pp. 223–248). New York, NY: Taylor & Francis.

Markus, H. R., & Kitayama, S. (1991). Culture and the self: Implications for cognition, emotion, and motivation. *Psychological Review, 98,* 224–253.

Markus, H. R., & Kitayama, S. (2010). Cultures and selves: A cycle of mutual constitution. *Perspectives on Psychological Science, 5,* 420–430.

Matsumoto, D. (2006). Are cultural differences in emotion regulation mediated by personality traits? *Journal of Cross-Cultural Psychology, 37,* 421–437.

Matsumoto, D., & Yoo, S. H. (2006). Toward a new generation of cross-cultural research. *Perspectives on Psychological Science, 1,* 234–250.

Miyamoto, Y., & Ma, X. (2011). Dampening or savoring positive emotions: A dialectical cultural script guides emotion regulation. *Emotion, 11*, 1346–1357.

Miyamoto, Y., Uchida, Y., & Ellsworth, P. C. (2010). Culture and mixed emotions: Co-occurrence of positive and negative emotions in Japan and the United States. *Emotion, 10*, 404–415.

National Research Council. (2013). *Subjective well-being: Measuring happiness, suffering, and other dimensions of experience.* Washington, DC: National Academies Press.

Ng, A. H., & Hynie, M. (2016). Naïve dialecticism and indecisiveness: Mediating mechanism and downstream consequences. *Journal of Cross-Cultural Psychology, 47*, 263–276.

Oishi, S. (2002). The experiencing and remembering of well-being: A cross-cultural analysis. *Personality and Social Psychology Bulletin, 28*, 1398–1406.

Oishi, S. (2006). The concept of life satisfaction across cultures: An IRT analysis. *Journal of Research in Personality, 40*, 411–423.

Oishi, S., & Diener, E. (2001). Re-examining the general positivity model of subjective well-being: The discrepancy between specific and global domain satisfaction. *Journal of Personality, 69*, 641–666.

Oishi, S., Diener, E. F., Lucas, R. E., & Suh, E. M. (1999). Cross-cultural variations in predictors of life satisfaction: Perspectives from needs and values. *Personality and Social Psychology Bulletin, 25*, 980–990.

Oishi, S., Graham, J., Kesebir, S., & Galinha, I. C. (2013). Concepts of happiness across time and cultures. *Personality and Social Psychology Bulletin, 39*, 559–577.

Oishi, S., Schimmack, U., Diener, E., & Suh, E. M. (1998). The measurement of values and individualism-collectivism. *Personality and Social Psychology Bulletin, 24*, 1177–1189.

Oishi, S., & Sullivan, H. W. (2005). The mediating role of parental expectations in culture and well-being. *Journal of Personality, 73*, 1267–1294.

Organisation for Economic Co-Operation and Development. (2017). *Better life initiative: Measuring well-being and progress.* Retrieved from www.oecd.org/statistics/better-life-initiative.htm

Park, N., & Huebner, E. S. (2005). A cross-cultural study of the levels and correlates of life satisfaction among adolescents. *Journal of Cross-Cultural Psychology, 36*, 444–456.

Peng, K., & Nisbett, R. E. (1999). Culture, dialectics, and reasoning about contradiction. *American Psychologist, 54*, 741–754.

Perunovic, E. W. Q., Heller, D., & Rafaeli, E. (2007). Within-person changes in the structure of emotion: The role of cultural identification and language. *Psychological Science, 18*, 607–613.

Russell, J. A., & Carroll, J. M. (1999). On the bipolarity of positive and negative affect. *Psychological Bulletin, 125*, 3–30.

Safdar, S., Lewis, J. R., Greenglass, E., & Daneshpour, M. (2009). An examination of proactive coping and social beliefs among Christians and Muslims. In K. Leung & M. H. Bond (Eds.), *Psychological aspects of social axioms* (pp. 177–196). New York, NY: Springer.

Saucier, G., Kenner, J. S., Iurino, K., Bou Malham, P., Chen, Z., Thalmayer, A. G., . . . Altschul, C. (2015). Cross-cultural differences in a global "survey of world views". *Journal of Cross-Cultural Psychology, 46*, 53–70.

Schimmack, U., Oishi, S., & Diener, E. (2002). Cultural influences on the relation between pleasant emotions and unpleasant emotions: Asian dialectic philosophies or individualism-collectivism? *Cognition & Emotion, 16*, 705–719.

Schimmack, U., Oishi, S., & Diener, E. (2005). Individualism: A valid and important dimension of cultural differences between nations. *Personality and Social Psychology Review, 9*, 17–31.

Scollon, C. N., & Tov, W. (2012). Cultural similarities and differences in the conceptualization of emotion. In P. A. Wilson (Ed.), *Łódź studies in language, vol. 27: Dynamicity in emotion concepts* (pp. 235–252). Frankfurt, Germany: Peter Lang.

Sims, T., Tsai, J. L., Jiang, D., Wang, Y., Fung, H. H., & Zhang, X. (2015). Wanting to maximize the positive and minimize the negative: Implications for mixed affective experience in American and Chinese contexts. *Journal of Personality and Social Psychology, 109,* 292–315.

Spencer-Rodgers, J., Peng, K., & Wang, L. (2010). Dialecticism and the co-occurrence of positive and negative emotions across cultures. *Journal of Cross-Cultural Psychology, 41,* 109–115.

Spencer-Rodgers, J., Williams, M. J., & Peng, K. (2010). Cultural differences in expectations of change and tolerance for contradiction: A decade of empirical research. *Personality and Social Psychology Review, 14,* 296–312.

Stevenson, B., & Wolfers, J. (2008). Economic growth and subjective well-being: Reassessing the Easterlin paradox. *Brookings Papers on Economic Activity,* Spring, 1–87.

Su, J. C., Lee, R. M., & Oishi, S. (2013). The role of culture and self-construal in the link between expressive suppression and depressive symptoms. *Journal of Cross-Cultural Psychology, 44,* 316–331.

Suh, E. M. (2002). Culture, identity consistency, and subjective well-being. *Journal of Personality and Social Psychology, 83,* 1378–1391.

Suh, E. M., Diener, E., Oishi, S., & Triandis, H. C. (1998). The shifting basis of life satisfaction judgments across cultures: Emotions versus norms. *Journal of Personality and Social Psychology, 74,* 482–493.

Tamir, M., Schwartz, S. H., Cieciuch, J., Riediger, M., Torres, C., Scollon, C., . . . Vishkin, A. (2016). Desired emotions across cultures: A value-based account. *Journal of Personality and Social Psychology, 111,* 67–82.

Tay, L., & Diener, E. (2011). Needs and subjective well-being around the world. *Journal of Personality and Social Psychology, 101,* 354–365.

Tov, W., & Au, E. W. M. (2013). Comparing well-being across nations: Conceptual and empirical issues. In I. Boniwell, S. David, & A. Conley (Eds.), *Oxford handbook of happiness* (pp. 448–464). Oxford, UK: Oxford University Press.

Tov, W., & Diener, E. (2007). Culture and subjective well-being. In S. Kitayama & D. Cohen (Eds.), *Handbook of cultural psychology* (pp. 691–713). New York, NY: Guilford.

Tov, W., & Diener, E. (2008). The well-being of nations: Linking together trust, cooperation, and democracy. In B. A. Sullivan, M. Snyder, & J. L. Sullivan (Eds.), *Cooperation: The political psychology of effective human interaction* (pp. 323–342). Malden, MA: Blackwell.

Tov, W., & Diener, E. (2013). Subjective well-being. In K. D. Keith (Ed.), *Encyclopedia of crosscultural psychology* (pp. 1239–1245). Hoboken, NJ: John Wiley & Sons.

Tov, W., Diener, E., Ng, W., Kesebir, P., & Harter, J. (2009). The social and economic context of peace and happiness. In R. S. Wyer, C.-Y. Chiu, & Y.-Y. Hong (Eds.), *Understanding culture: Theory, research and application* (pp. 239–258). New York: Psychology Press.

Triandis, H. C. (1989). The self and social-behavior in differing cultural contexts. *Psychological Review, 96,* 506–520.

Triandis, H. C. (1994). Major cultural syndromes and emotion. In S. Kitayama & H. R. Markus (Eds.), *Emotion and culture: Empirical studies of mutual influence* (pp. 285–308). Washington, DC: American Psychological Association.

Triandis, H. C. (1995). *Individualism and collectivism.* Boulder, CO: Westview Press.

Triandis, H. C. (2001). Individualism-collectivism and personality. *Journal of Personality, 69,* 907–924.

Triandis, H. C. (2007). Culture and psychology: A history of the study of their relationship. In S. Kitayama & D. Cohen (Eds.), *Handbook of cultural psychology* (Vol. 17, pp. 59–76). New York, NY, US: Guilford press.

Triandis, H. C., & Gelfand, M. J. (1998). Converging measurement of horizontal and vertical individualism and collectivism. *Journal of Personality and Social Psychology, 74,* 118–128.

Tsai, J. L., Knutson, B., & Fung, H. H. (2006). Cultural variation in affect valuation. *Journal of Personality and Social Psychology, 90,* 288–307.

Tsai, J. L., Miao, F. F., & Seppala, E. (2007). Good feelings in Christianity and Buddhism: Religious differences in ideal affect. *Personality and Social Psychology Bulletin, 33,* 409–421.

Tsai, J. L., Miao, F. F., Seppala, E., Fung, H. H., & Yeung, D. Y. (2007). Influence and adjustment goals: Sources of cultural differences in ideal affect. *Journal of Personality and Social Psychology, 92,* 1102–1117.

Veenhoven, R. (n.d.). *World database of happiness.* Retrieved from http://worlddatabaseofhappiness.eur.nl/

Vignoles, V. L., Owe, E., Becker, M., Smith, P. B., Easterbrook, M. J., Brown, R., . . . Bond, M. H. (2016). Beyond the "east—west" dichotomy: Global variation in cultural models of selfhood. *Journal of Experimental Psychology: General, 145,* 966–1000.

Vittersø, J., Røysamb, E., & Diener, E. (2002). The concept of life satisfaction across cultures: Exploring its diverse meaning and relation to economic wealth. In E. Gullone & R. Cummins (Eds.), *Social indicators research book series: The universality of subjective well-being indicators* (pp. 81–103). Dordrecht, Netherlands: Kluwer Academic Publishers.

Wan, C., Chiu, C. Y., Tam, K., Lee, S., Lau, I. Y., & Peng, S. (2007). Perceived cultural importance and actual self-importance of values in cultural identification. *Journal of Personality and Social Psychology, 92,* 337–354.

Watson, D., Clark, L. A., & Tellegen, A. (1988). Development and validation of brief measures of positive and negative affect: The PANAS scales. *Journal of Personality and Social Psychology, 54,* 1063–1070.

Yuki, M., Sato, K., Takemura, K., & Oishi, S. (2013). Social ecology moderates the association between self-esteem and happiness. *Journal of Experimental Social Psychology, 49,* 741–746.

PART II
Interpersonal Influences

4

INTIMATE RELATIONS, SUBJECTIVE WELL-BEING, AND HEALTH BEHAVIOR

Insights From a Dyadic Perspective

Chloe O. Huelsnitz, Alexander J. Rothman, and Jeffry A. Simpson

How Do Individuals Influence Their Partner's Health Behavior? Insights From a Dyadic Perspective

Imagine a couple, Adam and Maggie, who are involved in a highly satisfying, committed relationship. Although Adam and Maggie had different beliefs and behaviors regarding their own health at the start of their relationship, after several years together, many of their beliefs and behaviors have converged. Adam's and Maggie's overall health and well-being is now better than it was when they first met. According to a growing body of research (e.g., Robles, Slatcher, Trombello, & McGinn, 2014), Adam and Maggie's story is not atypical. However, despite the overarching finding that better relationships are associated with better well-being and health outcomes in partners across time, we still do not really understand *how* relationships promote better health and well-being. How do Maggie and Adam affect each other over time in ways that result in better outcomes for each of them?

Most theorists agree that interpersonal relationships can and do affect general well-being (e.g., Diener & Chan, 2011; Ryan & Deci, 2001). General well-being, however, is affected by a wide array of different outcomes. Some researchers, for instance, have focused on subjective well-being (SWB; also known as hedonic well-being; Diener, 1984), which is assessed by measures of general happiness, life satisfaction, the presence of positive affect, and/or the absence of negative affect (Diener & Chan, 2011). Other researchers have examined psychological well-being (PWB; Ryff & Singer, 1998, 2000), which is tapped by measures such as self-acceptance, positive relationships with others, autonomy, purpose, self-efficacy, and personal growth (Ryff, 1989). Many investigators assess both subjective and psychological well-being when trying to estimate an individual's general well-being (e.g., Kamp Dush & Amato, 2005; Proulx, Helms, & Buehler, 2007).

Even though physical health is often not formally mentioned in definitions of psychological or subjective well-being, a growing number of researchers have also assessed general well-being using measures of physical health (e.g., Karademas & Giannousi, 2013). In fact, there is mounting evidence that health outcomes may be both a cause and a consequence of general well-being. Boehm and Kubzansky (2012), for example, have found that positive psychological well-being protects people from cardiovascular disease, independent of traditional risk factors such as high blood pressure or high inflammation. It is likely the case that there are bi-directional links between well-being and physical health, such that physical health status can also predict well-being. Given that sickness is often associated with discomfort or pain, having health problems may lead individuals to experience greater negative affect and lower self-efficacy (Ryan & Deci, 2001).

Over the past few decades, a sizable body of research has confirmed that individuals who have higher-quality relationships with their friends, family, and romantic partners typically report higher levels of well-being (Horwitz, White, & Howell-White, 1996); live longer (Holt-Lunstad, Smith, & Layton, 2010); have fewer health problems (Burman & Margolin, 1992); and have better function-ing immune systems (e.g., Cohen, Doyle, Skoner, Rabin, & Gwaltney, 1997; Lutgendorf et al., 2005). Among the different relationships that individuals have, romantic relationships are unique in terms of the potential impact they can exert on both dyad members spanning very long periods of time (Kelley et al., 1983). Consistent with this claim, married people report having higher well-being over time (e.g., Gove, Hughes, & Style, 1983; Kamp Dush & Amato, 2005; Lee, Sec-combe, & Shehan, 1991; Waite, 1995) and experience significantly lower mortality rates compared to unmarried men and women as a group (Rendall, Weden, Favreault, & Waldron, 2011).

The benefits of close relationships on health and well-being, however, are not attributable to marital status per se (Holt-Lunstad, Birmingham, & Jones, 2008; Kamp Dush & Amato, 2005). Rather, it is the satisfaction, partner responsiveness, commitment, and support derived from involvement in high-quality romantic relationships that most strongly predict better well-being and health outcomes. Increases in marital quality across time are associated with both decreases in physical illness (Wickrama, Lorenz, Conger, & Elder, 1997) and increases in well-being (Proulx et al., 2007). Moreover, marital strain accelerates the decline in self-rated health that typically occurs as people age (Umberson, Williams, Powers, Liu, & Needham, 2006). In a recent meta-analysis of 126 studies involving 72,000 individuals, Robles and colleagues (2014) found that better marital quality also forecasts lower risk of mortality. Thus, merely being in a romantic relationship is not what drives better health and well-being outcomes; it is being in a *high-quality* romantic relationship that is most beneficial.

Given the reciprocal relation between well-being and health, close relation-ships—especially their quality—could play a key role in helping us better understand how to improve people's overall well-being via better health outcomes. We already know that close relationships and the actions of each partner are associated with markers of general well-being, but we know less about how they affect health outcomes in particular. As several recent reviews have confirmed (e.g., Martire, Schulz, Helgeson, Small, & Saghafi, 2010; Pietromonaco, Uchino, & Schetter, 2013), most prior research examining romantic relationships and health has measured the beliefs, behaviors, and outcomes of just one person in a relationship. Fortunately, researchers are beginning to adopt a dyadic approach (e.g., Howland et al., 2016), taking into account the characteristics of both dyad members to isolate the effects that partners might have on an individual's (i.e., an actor's) health-relevant beliefs, behaviors, and outcomes.

The aims of the current chapter, therefore, are threefold: (1) to review prior *dyadic research* that has examined the processes through which romantic partners and relationships affect physical health outcomes; (2) to more carefully delineate how individuals in a romantic relationship affect each other's health behavior, which in turn may affect their health outcomes; and (3) to examine the personal, relational, and situational factors that might affect the way in which relationship partners affect each other's health-relevant behavior.

Dyadic Models of Romantic Relationships and Health

In order to capture the effect of dyadic processes on an individual's health outcomes, research must be designed and analyzed in a way that incorporates the characteristics of both the individual (i.e., the actor) and his/her partner (i.e., the partner) on the actor's health outcomes. Early research on romantic relationships and health examined associations from only the actor's perspective (i.e., "What does Adam think of Maggie and his relationship with her?"). Recently, some investigators have developed dyadic models of health, which consider not only the actor's perspective, but the partner's perspective as well (e.g., Lewis, Gladstone, Schmal, & Darbes, 2006; Pietromonaco et al., 2013). Unlike in studies that assess differences between and within individuals, general dyadic models, such as the Actor-Partner Interdependence Model (APIM; Kenny, Kashy, & Cook, 2006), assess differences between and within couples while accounting for the noninde-pendence in actor and partner responses. Dyadic models allow researchers to test when an individual's behavior is guided by his or her *own* beliefs and when an individual's behavior is affected by his or her *partner's* beliefs. Figure 4.1 depicts a general dyadic model indicating how characteristics of the actor (e.g., Adam) and his partner (e.g., Maggie) might affect each other's health-relevant outcomes. *Health* is defined as morbidity (the incidence and frequency of illness and disease) and mortality (the length of lifespan and cause of death). In addition, characteristics of the relationship in which the actor and partner are involved, such as its length or level of satisfaction, may affect each person's health-relevant outcomes.

Why is it important to model the unique effect of the partner (or the relationship) in dyadic models of health? If only the characteristics of the actor are

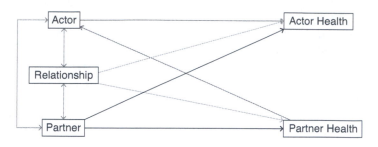

FIGURE 4.1 Dyadic Model Depicting the Mutual Influence Between the Actor, Relationship, and Partner on the Actor's and Partner's Health

considered in the link leading to the actor's health, such associations may contain variance that actually is associated with the partner or the relationship. For example, if only Adam's perceptions are measured and he perceives that Maggie has no effect on his health (even if she does), it may appear as though Adam's beliefs about his health are the sole predictors of his health outcomes. A dyadic approach enables researchers to address this issue and examine the extent to which Maggie affects Adam's health, statistically controlling for Adam's own effect on his health.

Some research has examined associations between the actor, partner, and relationship on the actor and partner's health dyadically, usually without testing for or assuming the processes underlying these associations. In other words, although some research has documented that partners do affect an actor's health, research has not identified the processes through which this occurs. The dyadic effects shown in Figure 4.1 suggest the potential impact of the relationship and the partner on the actor's health. Note that each person in the dyad is both an actor and a partner; "actor" denotes the individual whose outcomes are being examined, whereas "partner" denotes the individual whose effect is being examined. Thus, when examining the effect of Maggie on Adam's health, Maggie is the partner and Adam is the actor. Alternatively, when examining the effect of Adam on Maggie's health, Maggie is the actor and Adam is the partner. In the following sections, we review research on the effect of the partner on the actor's health and the effect of the relationship on the actor's health.

Partner Characteristics → Actor Health

To date, research testing the pathways shown in Figure 4.1 has focused on whether psychological characteristics of the partner (e.g., his/her personality traits) predict the actor's physical health (e.g., reports of health problems). The majority of these studies involve couples in which one person has been diagnosed with a chronic illness or health condition and the other person is a caregiver or potential source of support. For example, among women undergoing treatment for breast cancer, their romantic partner's level of anxiety predicts women's degree of physical fatigue (Segrin, Badger, Dorros, Meek, & Lopez, 2007). Research conducted with other diagnosed partner/undiagnosed partner dyads has found that aspects of well-being, such as the partner's depression (Chung, Moser, Lennie, & Rayens, 2009; Dorros, Card, Segrin, & Badger, 2010); psychological distress (Kim et al., 2008); and perceived stigma of the health condition (Liu, Xu, Lin, Shi, & Chen, 2013) predict poorer reports of physical quality of life[1] in the actor. In contrast, actors report better physical health if they have a partner who is confident s/he can help the actor manage the health condition (Vellone et al., 2013), or is higher in spirituality (Kim et al., 2011), conscientiousness (Roberts, Smith, Jackson, & Edmonds, 2009), or optimism (Kim, Chopik, & Smith, 2014). Although these studies provide evidence that the partner affects the actor's health outcomes, they do not examine actor-level processes that explicate *how* the partner affects the actor's health, which we address in more detail below.

Relationship → Actor Health

To what extent do features of the relationship predict an actor's health outcomes? In dyadic models, relationship predictors incorporate both the actor's and the partner's responses on relationship-relevant variables, which can be objective or subjective. For example, marital status and relationship length are objective relationship-relevant variables because their values are the same, regardless of whether the actor or partner does the reporting. Since these constructs are objective aspects of the relationship, the observed associations between them and health outcomes (e.g., the association between marital status and health; Rendall et al., 2011) ought to be the same in both dyadic and non-dyadic research.

However, dyadic models should provide unique insights into the effects of subjective, emergent relationship variables, derived from perceptions of the actor and/or the partner. For example, Barr and Simons (2014) assessed the actor's perception of the partner's hostility and the partner's perception of his/her own hostility and found that their averaged hostility score predicted poorer self-rated health for both individuals. They also measured the actor's relationship satisfaction and the partner's relationship satisfaction and found that the averaged score predicted better physical health.

Researchers have also used the extent of agreement or disagreement between the actor's and partner's responses to determine whether differences between actor and partner perceptions predict health outcomes. For example, dissimilarity in psychological stress between cancer survivors and their spouses predicts the spouses' (but not the cancer survivor's) quality of physical health (Kim et al., 2008). Merz and colleagues (2011) found that differences between actor and partner perceptions of how much the actor was affected by his/her symptoms of prostate cancer predicted lower physical quality of life in actors (i.e., the cancer patients).

Processes Underlying the Effects of Romantic Relationships on Health

In light of the fact that many romantic relationships last for long periods of time and romantic partners frequently live together, romantic partners have the capacity to exert considerable impact on one another's health outcomes. Consistent with this logic, married couples show concordance across a variety of biological, psychological, and behavioral outcomes, including blood pressure (Al-Kandari, Crews, & Poirier, 2002); cholesterol (Barrett-Connor, Suarez, & Criqui, 1982); depression (e.g., Siegel, Bradley, Gallo, & Kasl, 2004); eating patterns (Bove, Sobal, & Rauschenbach, 2003); alcohol consumption (Graham & Braun, 1999; Stimpson, Masel, Rudkin, & Peek, 2006); and smoking behavior (Stimpson et al., 2006). This concordance is not completely explained by the initial similarities that attract individuals to one another (i.e., assortative mating), nor by shared environments (see Meyler, Stimpson, & Peek, 2007, for a review of health concordance within couples). This evidence suggests that some form of influence must be occurring between relationship partners.

Health researchers have proposed three distinct routes through which partners can affect an actor's health outcomes: (1) biological processes (e.g., inducing changes in the actor's hormonal profile); (2) psychological processes (e.g., inducing changes in the actor's attitudes, beliefs, and/or feelings); and (3) behavioral processes (e.g., inducing changes in the actor's health behaviors) (Kiecolt-Glaser & Newton, 2001; Pietromonaco, Uchino, & Schetter, 2014; Slatcher & Selcuk, 2017). Figure 4.2 illustrates how the actor, relationship, and partner might affect the actor's health outcomes via the actor's biological, psychological, and behavioral processes. To date, research has focused predominantly on how characteristics of the *actor* lead to biological, psychological, and behavioral processes within the actor, which in turn affect the actor's health (Umberson & Montez, 2010). However, there is a growing literature on how characteristics of the relationship and the partner may also affect each of these processes enroute to predicting the actor's health outcomes.

Biological processes, which include physiological variables, are known to predict immediate and/or long-term health outcomes, such as those implicated in allostatic and restorative processes (see Robles et al., 2014, for a detailed review of biological processes linking relationships and health). *Psychological processes* include affective processes, social-cognitive processes (e.g., appraisal), and attitudes/beliefs. *Behavioral processes* involve behavioral choices and habits that may affect health outcomes. Such behaviors can be health promoting, such as eating a balanced diet or engaging in physical activity, or health-compromising, such as smoking.

In Figure 4.2, the double-sided arrows represent mutual effects between the actor, partner, and relationship, as well as between actor biological, psychological, and behavioral processes. Although the partner's health does not appear in the model, it is assumed that the partner, relationship, and actor also affect the partner's health via the same mechanisms.

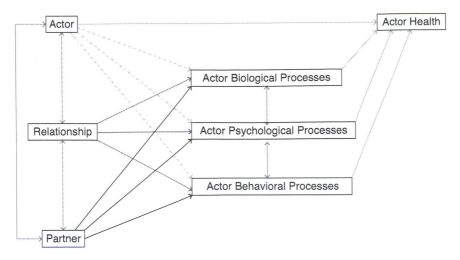

FIGURE 4.2 A Model Showing How the Actor, Relationship, and Partner Affect the Actor's Health Through Biological, Psychological, and Behavioral Processes

In the next two sections, we briefly review research showing that characteristics of the partner and/or relationship can affect the actor's biological and psychological processes. However, because behavioral processes are an understudied pathway in the link between relationships and health (Robles et al., 2014), our primary focus will be to delineate how characteristics of the partner and relationship can affect the actor's behavioral processes. In doing so, we not only review the empirical literature regarding this pathway, but also identify opportunities for additional empirical and theoretical work.

Actor Biological Processes

Of the three processes featured in Figure 4.2, biological processes have received the most empirical attention to date (see Robles & Kiecolt-Glaser, 2003; Robles et al., 2014; Kiecolt-Glaser, Gouin, & Hantsoo, 2010). Within this domain, research has focused on: (1) allostatic processes, which are "acute changes in stress-related hormones and immune measures" (Robles et al., 2014, p. 4) that are activated by environmental challenges, and (2) restorative processes, which return the individual back to his/her original state before facing further environmental challenges (Robles & Carroll, 2011). Over time, the repeated activation of allostatic processes, such as cardiovascular reactivity, can erode multiple biological systems (Robles & Carroll, 2011) that trigger long-term health problems (Robles & Kiecolt-Glaser, 2003). Restorative processes, such as sleep and wound healing, return the individual to homeostasis once environmental challenges have ceased and, thus, are complementary to allostatic processes (Robles & Carroll, 2011).

Features of romantic relationships can affect both allostatic and restorative processes. For example, marital quality is associated with lower cardiovascular reactivity during relationship conflict, lower cortisol reactivity during couple interactions, and better immune system functioning, all of which are allostatic processes associated with the long-term quality of physical health (see Robles et al., 2014). Moreover, couples that display greater hostility during their interactions experience slower wound healing and higher inflammation (Kiecolt-Glaser et al., 2005). Slower wound healing prolongs the allostatic processes that combat infection and impedes an individual's return to homeostasis (Robles & Carroll, 2011; Singer & Clark, 1999), and greater inflammation predicts earlier death in older adults (Ershler & Keller, 2000; Kiecolt-Glaser et al., 2010).

Some research indicates that certain characteristics of the partner are also related to allostatic and restorative processes in the actor. For example, individuals who have insecurely attached romantic partners show increased hypothalamic–pituitary–adrenal (HPA) reactivity (an allostatic process) in response to relationship conflict compared to those who have securely attached partners (Powers, Pietromonaco, Gunlicks, & Sayer, 2006). Moreover, individuals' perceptions of their partners, such as how responsive they perceive their partners to be, predict restorative processes, such as the quality of sleep (e.g., Selcuk, Stanton, Slatcher, & Ong, 2017).

In sum, although research has not tested all of the biological processes linking actor, partner, and relationship characteristics to actor health outcomes, the strong connections between actor/partner/relationship characteristics and allostatic and restorative processes and between these processes and health indicate that this may be a central route through which relationship partners affect each other's health outcomes.

Actor Psychological Processes

Psychological processes have also been hypothesized to mediate the effects of romantic relationships on health. Such processes encompass a wide array of variables, such as social-cognitive processes, affective processes, and indicators of psychopathology and mental health (Pietromonaco et al., 2014; Robles et al., 2014; Uchino, 2006). Most prior research has focused on mental health (Robles et al., 2014). Given that depression and other mental health problems predict various diseases (Prince et al., 2007), these psychological characteristics most likely serve as key intervening processes that connect the effects of partners and relationships with actor health outcomes. For example, individuals whose partners are hostile or disagreeable are more likely to report depressive symptoms (cf. Marshall, Simpson, & Rholes, 2015), which may lead them to engage in unhealthy behaviors and have poorer health outcomes over time. In addition, psychological processes are related to biological processes, such as immune functioning (Kiecolt-Glaser, McGuire, Robles, & Glaser, 2002). The bi-directional arrows between psychological processes and behavioral processes and between psychological processes and biological processes shown in Figure 4.2 denote these interrelationships.

Research has revealed that, among couples in which the actor is undergoing cardiac rehabilitation, having a partner who engages in more health-related supportive behaviors (e.g., listening to the spouse's concerns about protecting his/her health, encouraging the spouse to make healthy choices) predicts improvements in the actor's mental health (Franks et al., 2006). Conversely, having a partner who engages in more controlling behaviors (e.g., reminding the spouse to take care of his/her health) predicts decreases in the actor's mental health. For dyads in which the actor is diagnosed with a health condition, the partner's perceptions of the controllability of the actor's health condition predicts increases in the actor's depressive symptoms (Karademas & Giannousi, 2013). For dyads in which the actor is a caregiver for a sick partner, the frequency of the partner's illness symptoms (Ayotte, Yang, & Jones, 2010) and deteriorations in the partner's health (Pruchno, Wilson-Genderson, & Cartwright, 2009) both predict increases in the actor's depressive symptoms.

Another way in which the partner and relationship may affect the actor's health is through affective and attributional processes. Beyond depression and other mental health symptoms, affective and attributional processes mediate the association between relationship variables and health (Robles et al., 2014). For example, Laurent and Powers (2006) found that individuals who blame their partners for their negative behaviors during a stressful interaction have higher cortisol levels (for men) and slower rates of cortisol recovery (for women). In addition, couples that are more distressed exhibit more negative affect during interactions with each other (Heyman, 2001). Negative affect, in turn, is related to biological processes such as greater cardiovascular reactivity, which has deleterious consequences for long-term health (Robles & Kiecolt-Glaser, 2003).

The partner and relationship may also impact the actor's health through changes in the actor's thoughts and feelings regarding certain health-relevant behaviors. Traditional models of health behavior have identified a broad array of psychological states that inform and guide people's behavioral decisions (see Conner & Norman, 2005; Rothman & Salovey, 2007; Sheeran, Klein, & Rothman, 2017). For example, the Theory of Planned Behavior (TPB; Ajzen, 1985) posits that the actor's attitudes (i.e., his/her positivity about a behavior), subjective norms (i.e., perceived social pressures regarding a behavior), and perceived behavioral control (i.e., one's perceived ability to successfully engage in a behavior) predict the actor's intentions, which subsequently predict his/her behavior. Health research examining the effect of attitude, norms, and self-efficacy constructs has found that these psychological characteristics reliably predict an array of health behaviors, although some constructs are stronger predictors than others (McEachan et al., 2016; Sheeran et al., 2017).

When conceptualized within an interpersonal, dyadic approach, the psychological states identified in models such as the TPB may affect not only one's own intentions and behavior, but also the intentions and behavior of one's partner. For example, a partner's attitudes, subjective norms, and perceived behavioral control regarding his/her *own* eating might predict the actor's behavioral intentions and/or behavior. Testing this premise, Howland and colleagues (2016) examined the relative influence of both actor and partner beliefs on intentions to exercise.

Above and beyond the actor's attitudes, norms, and perceived behavioral control, they found that the *partner's* perceived behavioral control of his/her own exercise predicted the actor's exercise intentions. This finding illustrates the potential value of including the partner's beliefs when modeling the actor's beliefs and behaviors. However, the precise manner in which the partner's beliefs affect the actor remains unclear. It could be that the partner's beliefs influence the actor through the partner's own exercise behaviors or through the partner's statements or expressions about exercise. We return to this broader issue below.

Actor Behavioral Processes

Behavioral processes have received less attention than psychological or biological processes in research on relationships and health outcomes (Robles et al., 2014). Nevertheless, the behavioral choices that individuals make on a daily basis should have a substantial effect on their quality of life, general well-being, and long-term health prospects. Indeed, in the United States, chronic diseases are the main cause of death and health behaviors such as tobacco use, poor diet, and physical inactivity represent the most prominent risk factors for chronic diseases (Bauer, Briss, Goodman, & Bowman, 2014). Why and *how* do romantic partners affect each other's health behaviors?

There are several reasons to believe that partners should affect actors' health behavior. One reason is that romantic partners typically share living spaces and social environments that afford the opportunity to engage in healthy or unhealthy behaviors. Romantic partners are likely to share decisions about eating, substance use, sexual practices, and exercise. When they move in together, partners also have the opportunity to form routines regarding sleeping, oral hygiene, cooking, and other joint activities. Following cultural shifts during the past few decades, cohabitation is no longer restricted to marital relationships. According to the National Center for Health Statistics, 48% of women interviewed between 2006 and 2010 reported pre-marital cohabitation with a partner (Copen, Daniels, & Mosher, 2012).

Another reason to anticipate that partners affect actors' health behaviors is romantic partners often are invested in each other's good long-term outcomes. As interdependence increases and "me" becomes "we", partners have a vested interest in the actor's health behaviors because the actor's health outcomes may ultimately affect the partner. In the short term, the actor's unhealthy behaviors could make it more difficult for the partner to pursue his/her own health goals. In the long term, the actor's unhealthy behaviors could result in health problems, meaning that the partner might need to become a caregiver. Romantic partners also care deeply about one another in most cases and often want what is best for each other. Thus, the partner not only has an opportunity to affect the actor via their shared environment, but also the motivation to promote the actor's health and overall well-being by influencing the actor's behaviors.

Even though partners should affect actors' health behaviors, research has not delineated the specific ways in which partners can and do affect or change such behaviors. For example, it is unclear whether partners intentionally try to change the actor's health behavior using specific strategies or tactics, or whether the partner unintentionally affects the actor's health behavior by modeling certain practices through her or his own health behavior. It is also unclear whether the process through which partners affect the actor's behavior rely on initial changes in the actor's beliefs. Given that the health behaviors that individuals in relationships engage in on a daily basis might exert a substantial effect on their long-term health, it is important to understand *how* partners affect actor's behavioral processes.

Dyadic Model of Partner Influence

In order to conceptualize the different ways in which a romantic partner can affect the actor's health behavior, we have developed a dyadic model of partner influence that depicts several distinct pathways (see Figure 4.3). The model illustrates how the partner's health beliefs with respect to both him/herself and his/her partner (i.e., the actor) might affect measures of the actor's psychological and behavioral processes, which in turn may affect the actor's health outcomes. In what follows, we discuss what is currently known about these different pathways. First, we delineate how the partner might influence the actor's psychological processes (i.e., beliefs about his/her health) through enacting influence strategies and/or through the partner's own engagement in certain health behaviors. *Influence strategies* are behaviors enacted by the partner with the intended goal of changing the actor's behavior to be consistent with the partner's beliefs regarding the actor or regarding

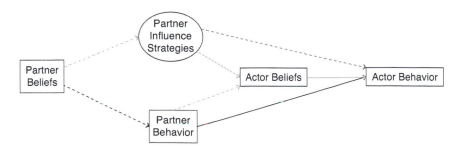

FIGURE 4.3 A Dyadic Model of Partner Influence Illustrating Distinct Pathways Through Which a Partner's Beliefs Can Influence an Actor's Health Behavior

what the actor should do. Second, we delineate how the partner might influence the actor's behavioral processes (i.e., his/her health behaviors) through enacting influence strategies and/or through the partner's own enactment of certain health behaviors.

Partner Influence Through Actor's Psychological Processes

How does the partner affect the actor's psychological processes, such as the actor's beliefs about his/her own health behavior? Returning to Maggie and Adam, Maggie's beliefs about her behavior may predict her own health behavior, which, in turn, might elicit changes in Adam's beliefs about his own behavior (partner beliefs → partner behavior → actor beliefs). Maggie's beliefs about Adam's health could also lead her to engage in strategies designed explicitly to change Adam's beliefs (partner beliefs → partner influence strategies → actor beliefs). In both pathways, Adam's beliefs should then predict his health-relevant behavior.

Partner Beliefs → Partner Behavior → Actor Beliefs

The first route from the partner's health beliefs to the actor's beliefs may occur through the partner's own health behavior. This route has two sub-paths: (1) how partner health beliefs predict the partner's health behavior and (2) how the partner's health behavior predicts the actor's health beliefs.

Partner Beliefs → Partner Behavior

This initial step in the partner influence process is predicated on core assumptions that have guided intrapersonally focused research on health behavior (Conner & Norman, 2005), so we touch on it just briefly. There is abundant evidence that people's health beliefs shape their own health behavior (e.g., McEachan et al., 2016; Sheeran et al., 2016). In a recent meta-analysis of studies examining associations between individuals' beliefs and health intentions and behaviors, McEachan and colleagues (2016) found medium-sized correlations between attitudes and intentions and health behavior and small- to medium-sized correlations between norms and autonomy (a facet of perceived behavioral control) predicting health behavior. Similarly, in another recent meta-analysis of studies that experimentally changed partner beliefs, Sheeran and colleagues (2016) found that experimentally manipulated changes in attitudes, norms, and self-efficacy led to medium-sized changes in intention and small- to medium-sized changes in behavior.

Partner Behavior → Actor Beliefs

There are several ways in which a partner could affect an actor's beliefs about a given health issue. Imagine that Maggie has specific beliefs about her own healthy eating (e.g., "It is important for me to eat healthy foods, and I want to eat healthier") as well as beliefs about Adam's healthy eating (e.g., "It is important for Adam to eat healthy foods, and I want Adam to eat healthier"). Maggie's beliefs about her own healthy eating could motivate her to enact behaviors consistent with those beliefs, such as eating more vegetables at dinnertime and commenting on how delicious they are. Adam may then observe Maggie enjoying vegetables every evening and begin to think more positively about healthy foods.

At least one dyadic study has investigated the role of partner communication with respect to this particular pathway. Manne, Kashy, Weinberg, Boscarino, and Bowen (2012) recruited couples in which both members were non-adherent with certain cancer screening guidelines and assessed their self-perceived risk of colorectal cancer, the perceived benefits and barriers to screening, their screening intentions, and the frequency with which they talked about screening. The partner's perceived cancer risk predicted him/her discussing cancer screening with the actor more frequently, which in turn predicted increases in the actor's screening intention. Interestingly, partners who thought more about the implications of their screening behavior for the relationship were also more likely to discuss screening with their spouse. One limitation of this study is that the investigators did not assess the extent to which the partner discussed screening because of his/her beliefs about the spouse. In other words, it is unclear whether the partner discussed screening because of beliefs about his or her own health or because of the partner's beliefs about his/her *spouse's* health.

Partner Beliefs → Partner Influence Strategies → Actor Beliefs

A second route from the partner's health beliefs to the actor's beliefs may occur through the partner's use of influence strategies. This route is broken down into two sub-paths: (1) how partner health beliefs predict the partner's use of influence strategies and (2) how the partner's influence strategies affect the actor's health beliefs.

Partner Beliefs → Partner Influence Strategies

Maggie's beliefs about Adam's eating could also motivate her to use specific influence strategies designed to change Adam's beliefs about healthy eating. Research has identified several dimensions and categories that reflect the different influence strategies relationship partners can use to influence each other's health behaviors.

To date, most dyadic research has examined social influence at the level of social control and social support (e.g., Burkert, Knoll, Luszczynska, & Gralla, 2012; Franks et al., 2006; Franks, Wendorf, Gonzalez, & Ketterer, 2004; Hong et al., 2005). *Social control* typically is conceptualized as interpersonal interactions characterized by constraint, regulation, and influence (Franks et al., 2004; Lewis & Butterfield, 2007). For example, reminding the actor to protect his/her health or trying to influence the actor's healthy choices fall under the umbrella of social control. *Social support*, on the other hand, is conceptualized as the emotional and instrumental assistance that relationship partners give to each other (Lewis & Rook, 1999). An example is listening to the actor's concerns about his/her health, encouraging the actor to make healthier choices, or taking action to protect the actor's health (Franks et al., 2004). In general, both social control and social support from relationship partners tends to be beneficial for health outcomes, although these effects are often moderated by the specific influence strategies that partners enact to control or support the individual (Craddock, vanDellen, Novak, & Ranby, 2015; Uchino, 2006).

Several influence strategies that involve social control or social support have been studied in romantic relationships. Informed by previous social influence research, Lewis, Butterfield, Darbes, and Johnston-Brooks (2004) identified three dimensions on which these strategies differ: positive—negative, bilateral—unilateral, and direct—indirect (see also Lewis & Butterfield, 2007). *Positive strategies* involve the use of rational logic, modeling, and positive reinforcement (e.g., complimenting the partner). *Negative strategies* involve attempts at inducing negative emotions in the actor by expressing negative emotions (e.g., making the actor feel guilty). *Bilateral strategies* reflect reciprocal actions of "give-and-take" between partners (e.g., bargaining with the actor). *Unilateral strategies* involve one-sided attempts to get the actor to change (e.g., stating how important the behavior change is). *Direct strategies* center on addressing the health behavior straightforwardly (e.g., asking the actor to change the behavior). Finally, *indirect strategies* reflect roundabout attempts to get the actor to change his/her behavior (e.g., hinting about positive behavior change). One example of an indirect strategy is *invisible influence*, which entails support intentionally provided by the partner that is not perceived by the actor (e.g., Bolger, Zuckerman, & Kessler, 2000; Girme, Overall, & Simpson, 2013; Howland & Simpson, 2010). The positive—negative and direct—indirect dimensions are consistent with distinctions made in research on communication in relationships (e.g., Overall, Fletcher, Simpson, & Sibley, 2009), whereas the distinction between bilateral—unilateral strategies is consistent with research on power and relationship satisfaction (Aida & Falbo, 1991).

Partner beliefs do predict the partner's enactment of specific influence strategies. Butterfield and Lewis (2002), for instance, found that, when partners are motivated to influence the actor and feel capable of influencing the actor, they are more likely to try to influence the actor using various influence strategies. Specifically, the partner's desire for the actor to change positively predicts greater use of positive, negative, direct, indirect, and unilateral strategies. The partner's perception that change will be difficult positively predicts the use of more negative and indirect strategies. In addition, the more helpless the partner feels when trying to induce change in the actor predicts less frequent use of bilateral strategies and more frequent use of negative ones (Butterfield & Lewis, 2002).

In a study investigating influence in same-sex relationships, Lewis et al. (2006) interviewed each member of the couple about the kinds of health behaviors they try to change in their partner, the influence strategies they use to change their partner's behaviors, and their motivations for enacting certain strategies. The most frequently cited reasons (motives) for enacting influence strategies included family history, age/maturity, being HIV-positive, and relationship quality (e.g., wanting to spend more time together). Although Lewis and colleagues (2006) did not assess whether different motivations predicted the use of *specific* influence strategies, couples in their study were more likely to use positive social control strategies than negative social ones.

Partner Influence Strategies → Actor Beliefs

To date, research has not determined whether the partner's enactment of certain influence strategies predicts changes in the actor's beliefs as investigators have focused on whether influence strategies predict changes in the actor's behavior. However, the partner's use of influence strategies should be a central route through which the partner's health beliefs impact the actor's health beliefs. Research in other relationship domains has confirmed that some influence strategies are more effective than others in changing the actor's beliefs (e.g., Overall et al., 2009). For example, direct influence strategies may be more effective than indirect ones because direct strategies involve straightforwardly communicating about the belief. Positive direct influence strategies may be especially effective because, when the partner expresses positive emotions and frames an influence strategy in a positive way, the actor should be less resistant to persuasion (Overall et al., 2009). When a health issue is particularly severe, negative direct influence strategies are more effective over time, although uncomfortable in the short term (Overall et al., 2009). The reason for this delayed benefit is that negative direct strategies often provide information that partners may not enjoying hearing, but need to know in order to eventually change their behavior or view their health differently.

By invoking the relationship, bilateral strategies can also be an effective way to change the actor's health beliefs. Individuals in close romantic relationships experience cognitive interdependence as they include their partner in their own sense of self (Aron, Aron, Tudor, & Nelson, 1991) and perceive themselves less as individuals and more as a unit (Agnew, Van Lange, Rusbult, & Langston, 1998). When individuals consider the effects of their health behavior on their romantic partners, they may re-evaluate their health beliefs. This process, known as *transformation of motivation*, leads individuals to behave in ways that are best for their partner and their relationship instead of themselves (Agnew et al., 1998). One promising avenue for future research is to determine whether individuals who experience more interdependence are more likely to use bilateral influence strategies and whether bilateral influence strategies are more effective in changing actor beliefs than other kinds of influence strategies.

Partner Influence on Actor's Behavior

How does the partner affect the actor's behavior? Returning to Maggie and Adam, Maggie's beliefs should predict her own health behavior, which then might evoke changes in Adam's health behavior (partner beliefs → partner behavior → actor behavior). Maggie's beliefs about Adam's health could also motivate her to engage in strategies intended to change Adam's behaviors (partner beliefs → partner influence strategies → actor behaviors). In both pathways, partner health beliefs might affect actor health behavior without necessarily altering actor beliefs.

Partner Beliefs → Partner Behavior → Actor Behavior

The first route from the partner's health beliefs to the actor's behavior is through the partner's behavior. This route contains two sub-paths: (1) how partner health beliefs predict the partner's own health behaviors and (2) how the partner's health behaviors predict the actor's health behaviors. Since we have already discussed how partner health beliefs predict the partner's own health behavior, we focus on the second sub-path.

Partner Behavior → Actor Behavior

There are two ways in which the partner's own health behaviors could affect the actor's health behaviors: (1) modeling the desired health behavior and (2) changing the local environment. To the extent that Maggie's beliefs about healthy eating lead her to engage in healthier eating, her modeling of healthy eating behavior could yield changes in Adam's behavior, regardless of whether that was Maggie's original intent. In a review of research on how modeling affects eating behavior, Cruwys, Bevelander, and Hermans (2015) found that people not only use others' eating as a guide for their own eating, but this behavioral response is motivated partially by affiliation goals. Thus, romantic partners may model one another's behavior just because they want to affiliate, without necessarily altering their beliefs about the importance of healthy eating.

Maggie's desire to behave in line with her beliefs about healthy eating could also motivate her to change her immediate environment in ways that support healthier eating. For example, Maggie might keep junk food out of the house, choose restaurants that have healthier options when she and Adam eat out, and pack healthy snacks when the two are traveling together. Adam may thus be more inclined to eat healthier simply because his environment affords the opportunity, not because he has changed his beliefs. All of these behaviors are based on Maggie's beliefs about the importance of her own healthy eating, yet they result in Adam eating more healthfully.

Despite clear evidence that romantic partners are concordant on many health behaviors (Meyler et al., 2007), only a few studies have tested whether concordance is due to the fact that people form relationships with similar others (i.e., assortative mating) or whether partners influence the actor's health beliefs and behaviors via modeling, environmental affordances, or the enactment of influence strategies. Although there is evidence for initial similarities in health behaviors due to assortative mating (e.g., Bove et al., 2003; Jackson, Steptoe, & Wardle, 2015), there is also evidence of behavior change due to the effect of partners. In one longitudinal study, when the partner changed to a healthier behavior, the actor was also more likely to make a positive health behavior change than if the partner did not make a healthy behavior change (Jackson et al., 2015). However, the reasons for the actor's health behavior changes were not assessed in these studies. Additional research needs to determine the extent to which the partner's behavioral modeling versus the use of influence strategies affect concordance rates across different health behaviors enacted by romantic partners.

Partner Beliefs → Influence Strategies → Actor Behavior

The second route from the partner's health beliefs to the actor's health behavior is through the partner's use of influence strategies. This route has two sub-paths: (1) how partner health beliefs predict the partner's use of influence strategies and (2) how the partner's influence strategies predict the actor's health behavior. Since we have already discussed how partner health beliefs predict the partner's use of influence strategies, we will focus on the second sub-path.

Influence Strategies → Actor Behavior

Several studies have tested the impact that partner influence strategies have on the actor's behavior. Prior studies have focused primarily on the effectiveness of different influence strategies in changing actor behavior, and little if any research has examined whether influence strategies also elicit changes in actor's beliefs.

Franks and colleagues (2006) investigated whether the partner's provision of health-related social support and social control predicted health behavior among patients undergoing cardiac rehabilitation. Partner's reports of the amount of social support they gave during or soon after cardiac rehabilitation predicted more health-promoting behaviors by actors 6 months later. In contrast, partner's reports of their amount of social control predicted decreases in health-promoting behaviors in actors over time.

Social support that is specific to a given health behavior may be especially effective in influencing actors' behavior. To test this premise, Burkert et al. (2012) assessed the role of the partner in predicting pelvic-floor exercises in prostate-cancer patients following radical prostatectomy. They found that partner reports of providing more pelvic-floor exercise-specific support predicted more frequent pelvic-floor exercises by actors. Not surprisingly, partner reports of engaging in more social control negatively predicted actors' pelvic-floor exercise. In addition,

Darbes and Lewis (2005) found that partners who received higher levels of HIV-specific social support from each other engaged in less HIV risk behavior, both at baseline and 6 months later.

Lewis and Butterfield (2007) also investigated the effect of social control strategies on health-promoting behaviors. In this study, each spouse identified the health behaviors that she/he was attempting to influence the actor (their mate) to change. Each spouse was then interviewed about the social control situations, his/her own attempts to influence the spouse's behavior, and his/her behavioral reactions to the partner's influence attempts. The partner's use of more frequent positive, direct, and bilateral social control strategies predicted more health-promoting behavioral reactions in the actor (i.e., how much the actor changed his/her behavior in the direction the partner wanted). When partners used these strategies more frequently, actors were more likely to respond to the influence attempt by doing what their spouses wanted or changing their behavior to align it with what their spouses wanted.

Future Research Directions and Considerations

In this chapter, we have enumerated several different ways in which partner beliefs can affect the actor's psychological and behavioral processes linked to the actor's long-term health outcomes, which is one important component contributing to general well-being. Although several sub-paths of the dyadic model of partner influence shown in Figure 4.3 have been investigated, all of the pathways need to be tested together to more fully understand how partner beliefs affect actor health outcomes.

To properly test the pathways in the model, investigators need to design studies that: (1) are longitudinal; (2) assess partner and actor reasons for engaging in certain health behaviors and influence strategies; and (3) consider potential moderators within the model, such as features of the actor, the relationship, and the health behavior in question. Partners have many opportunities to affect each other's health beliefs and behavior starting early in the relationship, so sometimes influence effects may have occurred *before* they are measured in studies. For example, Maggie might have affected Adam's eating behavior when they first started living and grocery shopping together. In such cases, one may not detect partner effects because the partner has already changed the actor. Changes in actor's beliefs may also have occurred *after* behavior change. For example, Adam might be engaging in healthier eating without believing that it is important, but, over time, his beliefs might eventually shift following his behavior change (e.g., "I must like healthy foods because I eat them all the time"). Study designs need to differentiate between these two types of effects.

As reviewed in this chapter, several studies have examined sub-paths within the different routes from partner beliefs to actor behavior in the model. However, future research needs to assess the beliefs and behavior of *both* the partner and the actor to fully examine these paths and understand exactly how partners affect actors. For example, Manne and colleagues (2012) found that the partner's perceived cancer risk predicted the degree to which he discussed cancer screening with the actor (his wife). However, because Manne and colleagues did not measure the motivations for discussing cancer screening, we do not know whether men did so because of their beliefs about their own cancer risk, because of their beliefs about the actor's possible cancer risk, or both. To understand whether the partner is actively trying to influence the actor or whether the partner is merely engaging in a specific behavior because of his/her own beliefs, it is essential to understand the motivations and reasons underlying the behavior.

With regard to the specific behavior, it is also important to determine whether and the extent to which the current romantic partner is the sole source of social "influence" on the actor. Are there other social partners that also affect the actor's health behaviors? The actor's friends may be especially important to consider for behaviors such as eating (Howland, Hunger, & Mann, 2012). Individuals are more likely to model the eating behavior of people who are similar to them and/or with whom they are trying to affiliate (Cruwys et al., 2015). If so, friends may be more likely to affect an individual's eating behavior than other social partners do, perhaps including the current romantic partner. Finally, it is also important to emphasize the recursive nature of the associations in the model. For example, the actor's health ought to influence the partner's relationship satisfaction (e.g., Zhou et al., 2011), which is likely to feed back into the model as a moderator on the effectiveness of the partner's influence strategies, and so on. In addition, given the reciprocal associations between partners over time, it also is important to factor in time with respect to the behavior and relationship (e.g., when did the behavior start, when did partner influence begin, when did changes in relationship satisfaction occur over time).

Implications of the Dyadic Model of Partner Influence for Well-Being

In addition to properly testing the paths of the model, it is also important for future research to consider consequences of partner influence for other aspects of well-being, such as self-efficacy and positive affect. For example, research on invisible influence shows that whereas providing direct, visible support to the partner can reduce their autonomy and self-efficacy, providing indirect, invisible support can boost self-efficacy (Howland & Simpson, 2010). Thus, some types of influence strategies may be more likely to benefit aspects of well-being beyond physical health. Influence strategies that are able to boost aspects of subjective and psychological well-being may be more effective in promoting lasting change in an individual's health behavior.

Another factor implicated in most paths of the dyadic model of partner influence is motivation. In order for influence to occur, partners must be motivated to either try to influence the actor (partner beliefs ➔ partner influence strategies) or to engage in health behaviors for their own sake (partner beliefs ➔ partner behavior). In addition, actors must be motivated to change their own health behavior in order for the changes to stick. Motivation on both the part of the actor and partner could be intrinsic or extrinsic in nature (Ryan & Deci, 2000). Research shows that intrinsic motivation (engaging in a behavior because of the positive feelings resulting from the behavior itself; Ryan & Deci, 2000) is linked to both well-being and long-term positive health outcomes (Kasser & Ryan, 1996; Ng et al., 2012). Extrinsic rewards generally decrease intrinsic motivation (Deci, Koestner, & Ryan, 1999).

If Maggie is motivated to influence Adam because of the positive feelings she derives from trying to support Adam (i.e., intrinsic motivation); Maggie may be more likely to use influence strategies that are positive (rather than negative); and Maggie also may be more willing to continue trying to support Adam over time. With regard to the actor, if Adam is motivated to engage in the behavior in order to receive praise from Maggie or to avoid criticism from Maggie (i.e., extrinsic motivation), he may be less likely to maintain the health behavior change over time. Ultimately, it is important to consider the effects of dyadic influence on well-being, as different effects of the partner's influence on the actor's self-efficacy or motivation could determine whether the change in health behavior will be fleeting or permanent. This example also illustrates the value of adopting a dyadic perspective, as the motivation of both the partner and actor are important determinants of long-term behavioral change.

Conclusion

Research has established that romantic relationships predict important long-term health and well-being outcomes (Holt-Lunstad et al., 2010; Kiecolt-Glaser & Newton, 2001; Rendall et al., 2011). Building on this foundation, researchers have started to investigate how features of the actor, the partner, and their relationship affect the health of actors via biological, psychological, and behavioral processes (Kiecolt-Glaser et al., 2010; Robles et al., 2014; Uchino, 2006; Uchino, Cacioppo, & Kiecolt-Glaser, 1996). Although research has shown that partners do affect each other's health outcomes, we still need to better understand the *processes* through which partner influence occurs within relationships in order to inform future research on how the partner may be "harnessed" to improve individuals' health and well-being outcomes.

Note

1 Given that most research reviewed in this chapter measures physical quality of life subjectively, "physical quality of life" refers to subjective measures of physical quality of life unless otherwise noted.

References

Agnew, C. R., Van Lange, P. A., Rusbult, C. E., & Langston, C. A. (1998). Cognitive inter-dependence: Commitment and the mental representation of close relationships. *Journal of Personality and Social Psychology, 74*, 939–954.

Aida, Y., & Falbo, T. (1991). Relationships between marital satisfaction, resources, and power strategies. *Sex Roles, 24*, 43–56.

Ajzen, I. (1985). From intentions to actions: A theory of planned behavior. In J. Kuhl & J. Beckmann (Eds.), *Action-control: From cognition to behavior* (pp. 11–39). Heidelberg, Germany: Springer. http://dx.doi.org/10.1007/978-3-642-69746-3_2

Al-Kandari, Y., Crews, D. E., & Poirier, F. E. (2002). Length of marriage and its effect on spousal concordance in Kuwait. *American Journal of Human Biology, 14*, 1–8. doi: 10.1002/ajhb.1137

Aron, A., Aron, E. N., Tudor, M., & Nelson, G. (1991). Close relationships as including other in the self. *Journal of Personality and Social Psychology, 60*, 241–253. http://dx.doi.org/10.1037/0022-3514.60.2.241

Ayotte, B. J., Yang, F. M., & Jones, R. N. (2010). Physical health and depression: A dyadic study of chronic health conditions and depressive symptomatology in older adult couples. *Journal of Gerontology: Psychological Sciences, 65B*, 438–448. doi: 10.1093/geronb/gbq033

Barr, A. B., & Simons, R. L. (2014). A dyadic analysis of relationships and health: Does couple-level context condition partner effects? *Journal of Family Psychology, 28*, 448–59. https://doi.org/10.1037/a0037310

Barrett-Connor, E., Suarez, L., & Criqui, M. H. (1982). Spouse concordance of plasma cholesterol and triglyceride. *Journal of Chronic Diseases, 35*, 333–340.

Bauer, U. E., Briss, P. A., Goodman, R. A., & Bowman, B. A. (2014). Prevention of chronic disease in the 21st century: Elimination of the leading preventable causes of premature death and disability in the USA. *The Lancet, 384*, 45–52.

Boehm, J. K., & Kubzansky, L. D. (2012). The heart's content: The association between positive psychological well-being and cardiovascular health. *Psychological Bulletin, 138*, 655–691. doi: 10.1037/a0027448

Bolger, N., Zuckerman, A., & Kessler, R. C. (2000). Invisible support and adjustment to stress. *Journal of Personality and Social Psychology, 79*, 953–961.

Bove, C. F., Sobal, J., & Rauschenbach, B. S. (2003). Food choices among newly married couples: Convergence, conflict, individualism, and projects. *Appetite, 40*, 25–41.

Burkert, S., Knoll, N., Luszczynska, A., & Gralla, O. (2012). The interplay of dyadic and individual planning of pelvic-floor exercise in prostate-cancer patients following radical prostatectomy. *Journal of Behavioral Medicine, 35*, 305–317. https://doi.org/10.1007/s10865-012-9416-2

Burman, B., & Margolin, G. (1992). Analysis of the association between marital relation-ships and health problems: An interactional perspective. *Psychological Bulletin, 112*, 39–63. https://doi.org/10.1037/0033-2909.112.1.39

Butterfield, R. M., & Lewis, M. A. (2002). Health-related social influence: A social ecologi-cal perspective on tactic use. *Journal of Social and Personal Relationships, 19*, 505–526.

Chung, M. L., Moser, D. K., Lennie, T. A., & Rayens, M. K. (2009). The effects of depressive symptoms and anxiety on quality of life in patients with heart failure and their spouses: Testing dyadic dynamics using Actor-Partner Interdependence Model. *Journal of Psycho-somatic Research, 67*, 39–35. doi: 10.1016/j.jpsychores.2009.01.009

Cohen, S., Doyle, W. J., Skoner, D. P., Rabin, B. S., & Gwaltney, J. M. (1997). Social ties and susceptibility to the common cold. *Journal of the American Medical Association, 277*, 1940–1944.

Conner, M., & Norman, P. (2005). *Predicting and changing health behavior: Research and practice with social cognition models* (3rd ed.). Berkshire, England: McGraw-Hill.

Copen, C. E., Daniels, K., & Mosher, W. D. (2012). First marriages in the United States: Data from the 2006–2010 national survey of family growth. *National Health Statistics Reports, 64*, 1–22.

Craddock, E., van Dellen, M. R., Novak, S. A., & Ranby, K. W. (2015). Influence in relationships: A meta-analysis on health-related social control. *Basic and Applied Social Psychology, 37*, 118–130. doi: 10.1080/01973533.2015.1011271

Cruwys, T., Bevelander, K. E., & Hermans, R. C. J. (2015). Social modeling of eating: A review of when and why social influence affects food intake and choice. *Appetite, 86*, 3–18. http://dx.doi.org/10.1016/j.appet.2014.08.035

Darbes, L. A., & Lewis, M. A. (2005). HIV-specific social support predicts less sexual risk behavior in male couples. *Health Psychology, 24*, 617–622. doi: 10.1037/0278-6133.24.6.617

Deci, E. L., Koestner, R., & Ryan, R. M. (1999). A meta-analytic review of experiments examining the effects of extrinsic rewards on intrinsic motivation. *Psychological Bulletin, 125*, 627–668.

Diener, E. (1984). Subjective well-being. *Psychological Bulletin, 95*, 542–575.

Diener, E., & Chan, M. Y. (2011). Happy people live longer: Subjective well-being contributes to health and longevity. *Applied Psychology, 3*, 1–43.

Dorros, S. M., Card, N. A., Segrin, C., & Badger, T. A. (2010). Interdependence in women with breast cancer and their partners: An inter-individual model of distress. *Journal of Consulting Clinical Psychology, 78*, 121–125. doi: 10.1037/a0017724

Ershler, W., & Keller, E. (2000). Age-associated increased interleukin-6 gene expression, late-life diseases, and frailty. *Annual Review of Medicine, 51*, 245–270.

Franks, M. M., Stephens, M. A. P., Rook, K. S., Franklin, B. A., Keteyian, S. J., & Artinian, N. T. (2006). Spouses' provision of health-related support and control to patients participating in cardiac rehabilitation. *Journal of Family Psychology, 20*, 311–318. https://doi.org/10.1037/0893-3200.20.2.311

Franks, M. M., Wendorf, C. A., Gonzalez, R., & Ketterer, M. (2004). Aid and influence: Health-promoting exchanges of older married partners. *Journal of Social and Personal Relationships, 21*, 431–445. https://doi.org/10.1177/0265407504044839

Girme, Y. U., Overall, N. C., & Simpson, J. A. (2013). When visibility matters. *Personality and Social Psychology Bulletin, 39*, 1441–1454. https://doi.org/10.1177/0146167213497802

Gove, W. R., Hughes, M., & Style, C. B. (1983). Does marriage have positive effects on the psychological well-being of the individual? *Journal of Health and Social Behavior, 24*, 122–131.

Graham, K., & Braun, K. (1999). Concordance of use of alcohol and other substances among older adult couples. *Addictive Behaviors, 24*, 839–856.

Heyman, R. E. (2001). Observation of couple conflicts: Clinical assessment applications, stubborn truths, and shaky foundations. *Psychological Assessment, 13*, 5–35.

Holt-Lunstad, J., Birmingham, W., & Jones, B. Q. (2008). Is there something unique about marriage? The relative impact of marital status, relationship quality, and network social support on ambulatory blood pressure and mental health. *Annals of Behavioral Medicine, 35*, 239–244. https://doi.org/10.1007/s12160-008-9018-y

Holt-Lunstad, J., Smith, T. B., & Layton, J. B. (2010). Social relationships and mortality risk: A meta-analytic review. *PLoS Medicine, 7*, e1000316. https://doi.org/10.1371/journal.pmed.1000316

Hong, T., Franks, M., Gonzalez, R., Keteyian, S., Franklin, B., & Artinian, N. (2005). A dyadic investigation of exercise support between cardiac patients and their spouses. *Health Psychology*, *24*, 430–434. https://doi.org/10.1037/0278-6133.24.4.430

Horwitz, A. V., White, H. R., & Howell-White, S. (1996). Becoming married and mental health: A longitudinal study of a cohort of young adults. *Journal of Marriage and Family*, *58*, 895–907.

Howland, M., Farrell, A. K., Simpson, J. A., Rothman, A. J., Burns, R. J., Fillo, J., & Wlaschin, J. (2016). Relational effects on physical activity: A dyadic approach to the theory of planned behavior. *Health Psychology*, *35*, 733–741. https://doi.org/10.1037/hea0000334

Howland, M., Hunger, J. M., & Mann, T. (2012). Friends don't let friends eat cookies: Effects of restrictive eating norms on consumption among friends. *Appetite*, *59*, 505–509.

Howland, M., & Simpson, J. A. (2010). Getting in under the radar: A dyadic view of invisible support. *Psychological Science*, *21*, 1878–1885. https://doi.org/10.1177/0956797610388817

Jackson, S. E., Steptoe, A., & Wardle, J. (2015). The influence of partner's behavior on health behavior change: The English longitudinal study of ageing. *JAMA Internal Medicine*, *175*, 385–392.

Kamp Dush, C. M., & Amato, P. R. (2005). Consequences of relationship status and quality for subjective well-being. *Journal of Social and Personal Relationships*, *22*, 607–627.

Karademas, E. C., & Giannousi, Z. (2013). Representations of control and psychological symptoms in couples dealing with cancer: A dyadic-regulation approach. *Psychology and Health*, *28*, 67–83. doi: 10.1080/08870446.2012.713954

Kasser, T., & Ryan, R. M. (1996). Further examining the American dream: Differential correlates of intrinsic and extrinsic goals. *Personality and Social Psychology Bulletin*, *22*, 280–287.

Kelley, H. H., Berscheid, E., Christensen, A., Harvey, J. H., Huston, T. L., Levinger, G., . . . Peterson, D. R. (1983). Analyzing close relationships. In H. H. Kelley, E. Berscheid, A. Christensen, J. H. Harvey, T. L. Huston, G. Levinger, . . . D. R. Peterson (Eds.), *Close relationships* (pp. 67–92). New York, NY: Freeman.

Kenny, D. A., Kashy, D. A., & Cook, W. L. (2006). *Dyadic data analysis*. New York, NY: Guilford Press.

Kiecolt-Glaser, J. K., Gouin, J., & Hantsoo, L. (2010). Close relationships, inflammation, and health. *Neuroscience Biobehavior Review*, *35*, 33–38. doi: 10.1016/j.neubiorev.2009.09.003

Kiecolt-Glaser, J. K., Loving, T. J., Stowell, J. R., Malarkey, W. B., Lemeshow, S., Dickinson, S. L., & Glaser, R. (2005). Hostile marital interactions, proinflammatory cytokine production, and wound healing. *Archives of General Psychiatry*, *62*, 1377–1384.

Kiecolt-Glaser, J. K., McGuire, L., Robles, T. F., & Glaser, R. (2002). Psychoneuroimmunology: Psychological influences on immune function and health. *Journal of Consulting and Clinical Psychology*, *70*, 537–547. doi: 10.1037//0022-006X.70.3.537

Kiecolt-Glaser, J. K., & Newton, T. L. (2001). Marriage and health: His and hers. *Psychological Bulletin*, *127*, 472–503. doi: 10.1037//0033-2909.127.4.472

Kim, E. S., Chopik, W. J., & Smith, J. (2014). Are people healthier if their partners are more optimistic? The dyadic effect of optimism on health among older adults. *Journal of Psychosomatic Research*, *76*, 447–453. doi: 10.1016/j.jpsychores.2014.03.104

Kim, Y., Carver, C. S., Spillers, R. L., Crammer, C., & Zhou, E. S. (2011). Individual and dyadic relations between spiritual well-being and quality of life among cancer survivors and their spousal caregivers. *Psycho-Oncology*, *20*, 762–770.

Kim, Y., Kashy, D. A., Wellisch, D. K., Spillers, R. L., Kaw, C. K., & Smith, T. G. (2008). Quality of life of couples dealing with cancer: Dyadic and individual adjustment among breast and prostate cancer survivors and their spousal caregivers. *Annals of Behavioral Medicine, 35,* 230–238. doi: 10.1007/s12160-008-9026-y

Laurent, H. K., & Powers, S. I. (2006). Social-cognitive predictors of hypothalamic-pituitary-adrenal reactivity to interpersonal conflict in emerging adult couples. *Journal of Social and Personal Relationships, 23,* 703–720. doi: 10.1177/0265407506065991

Lee, G. R., Seccombe, K., & Shehan, C. L. (1991). Marital status and personal happiness: An analysis of trend data. *Journal of Marriage and Family, 53,* 839–844.

Lewis, M. A., & Butterfield, R. M. (2007). Social control in marital relationships: Effect of one's partner on health behaviors. *Journal of Applied Social Psychology, 37,* 298–319. https://doi.org/10.1111/j.0021-9029.2007.00161.x

Lewis, M. A., Butterfield, R. M., Darbes, L. A., & Johnston-Brooks, C. (2004). The conceptualization and assessment of health-related social control. *Journal of Social and Personal Relationships, 21,* 669–687. https://doi.org/10.1177/0265407504045893

Lewis, M. A., Gladstone, E., Schmal, S., & Darbes, L. A. (2006). Health-related social control and relationship interdependence among gay couples. *Health Education Research, 21,* 488–500.

Lewis, M. A., McBride, C. M., Pollak, K. I., Puleo, E., Butterfield, R. M., & Emmons, K. M. (2006). Understanding health behavior change among couples: An interdependence and communal coping approach. *Social Science and Medicine, 62,* 1369–1380. https://doi.org/10.1016/j.socscimed.2005.08.006

Lewis, M. A., & Rook, K. S. (1999). Social control in personal relationships: Impact on health behaviors and psychological distress. *Health Psychology, 18,* 63–71. https://doi.org/10.1037/0278-6133.18.1.63

Liu, H., Xu, Y., Lin, X., Shi, J., & Chen, S. (2013). Associations between perceived HIV stigma and quality of life at the dyadic level: The Actor-Partner Interdependence Model. *PLoS One, 8,* e55680. doi: 10.1371/journal.pone.0055680

Lutgendorf, S. K., Sood, A. K., Anderson, B., McGinn, S., Maiseri, H., Dao, M., . . . Lubaroff, D. M. (2005). Social support, psychological distress, and natural killer cell activity in ovarian cancer. *Journal of Clinical Oncology, 23,* 7105–7113.

Manne, S., Kashy, D., Weinberg, D. S., Boscarino, J. A., & Bowen, D. J. (2012). Using the interdependence model to understand spousal influence on colorectal cancer screening intentions: A structural equation model. *Annals of Behavioral Medicine, 43,* 320–329.

Marshall, E., Simpson, J. A., & Rholes, W. S. (2015). Personality, communication, and depressive symptoms across the transition to parenthood: A dyadic longitudinal investigation. *European Journal of Personality, 29,* 216–234. doi: 10.1002/per.1980

Martire, L. M., Schulz, R., Helgeson, V. S., Small, B. J., & Saghafi, E. M. (2010). Review and meta-analysis of couple-oriented interventions for chronic illness. *Annals of Behavioral Medicine, 40,* 325–342. https://doi.org/10.1007/s12160-010-9216-2

McEachan, R., Taylor, N., Harrison, R., Lawton, R., Gardner, P., & Conner, M. (2016). Meta-analysis of the reasoned action approach (RAA) to understanding health behaviors. *Annals of Behavioral Medicine, 50,* 592–612. doi: 10.1007/s12160-016-9798-4

Merz, E. Malcarne, V., Ko, C. M., Sadler, M., Kwack, L., Varni, J. W., & Sadler, G. R. (2011). Dyadic concordance among prostate cancer patients and their partners and health-related quality of life: Does it matter? *Psychological Health, 26,* 651–666. doi: 10.1080/08870441003721251

Meyler, D., Stimpson, J. P., & Peek, M. K. (2007). Health concordance within couples: A systematic review. *Social Science and Medicine, 64,* 2297–2310. https://doi.org/10.1016/j.socscimed.2007.02.007

Ng, J., Ntoumanis, N., Thogersen-Ntoumani, E. C., Deci, E. L., Ryan, R. M., Duda, J. L., & Williams, G. C. (2012). Self-determination theory applied to health contexts: A meta-analysis. *Perspectives on Psychological Science, 7*, 325–340.

Overall, N. C., Fletcher, G. J., Simpson, J. A., & Sibley, C. G. (2009). Regulating partners in intimate relationships: The costs and benefits of different communication strategies. *Journal of Personality and Social Psychology, 96*, 620–639.

Pietromonaco, P. R., Uchino, B., & Schetter, C. D. (2013). Attachment theory for health and disease. *Health Psychology, 32*, 499–513. https://doi.org/10.1037/a0029349

Powers, S. I., Pietromonaco, P. R., Gunlicks, M., & Sayer, A. (2006). Dating couples' attachment styles and patterns of cortisol reactivity and recovery in response to a relationship conflict. *Journal of Personality and Social Psychology, 90*, 613–628. https://doi.org/10.1037/0022-3514.90.4.613

Prince, M., Patel, V., Saxena, S., Maj, M., Maselko, J., Phillips, M. R., & Rahman, A. (2007). No health without mental health. *The Lancet, 370*, 859–877.

Proulx, C. M., Helms, H. M., & Buehler, C. (2007). Marital quality and personal well-being: A meta-analysis. *Journal of Marriage and Family, 69*, 576–593.

Pruchno, R., Wilson-Genderson, M., & Cartwright, F. (2009). Self-rated health and depressive symptoms in patients with end-stage renal disease and their spouses: A longitudinal dyadic analysis of late-life marriages. *The Journals of Gerontology Series B: Psychological Sciences and Social Sciences, 64B*, 212–221. https://doi.org/10.1093/geronb/gbp006

Rendall, M. S., Weden, M. M., Favreault, M. M., & Waldron, H. (2011). The protective effect of marriage for survival: A review and update. *Demography, 48*, 481–506. https://doi.org/10.1007/s13524-011-0032-5

Roberts, B. W., Smith, J., Jackson, J. J., & Edmonds, G. (2009). Compensatory conscientiousness and health in older couples. *Psychological Science, 20*, 553–559. https://doi.org/10.1111/j.1467-9280.2009.02339.x

Robles, T. F., & Carroll, J. E. (2011). Restorative biological processes and health. *Social and Personality Psychology Compass, 5*, 518–537.

Robles, T. F., & Kiecolt-Glaser, J. K. (2003). The physiology of marriage: Pathways to health. *Physiology and Behavior, 79*, 409–416.

Robles, T. F., Slatcher, R. B., Trombello, J. M., & McGinn, M. M. (2014). Marital quality and health: A meta-analytic review. *Psychological Bulletin, 140*, 140–187.

Rothman, A. J., & Salovey, P. (2007). The reciprocal relation between principles and practice: Social psychology and health behavior. In A. W. Kruglanski & E. T. Higgins (Eds.), *Social psychology: Handbook of basic principles* (2nd ed., pp. 826–849). New York, NY: Guilford Press.

Ryan, R. M., & Deci, E. L. (2000). Self-determination theory and the facilitation of intrinsic motivation, social development, and well-being. *American Psychologist, 55*, 68–78.

Ryan, R. M., & Deci, E. L. (2001). On happiness and human potentials: A review of research on hedonic and eudaimonic well-being. *Annual Review of Psychology, 52*, 141–166.

Ryff, C. D. (1989). Happiness is everything, or is it? Explorations on the meaning of psychological well-being. *Journal of Personality and Social Psychology, 57*, 1069–1081.

Ryff, C. D., & Singer, B. (1998). The contours of positive human health. *Psychological Inquiry, 9*, 1–28.

Ryff, C. D., & Singer, B. (2000). Interpersonal flourishing: A positive health agenda for the new millennium. *Personality and Social Psychology Review, 4*, 30–44.

Segrin, C., Badger, T., Dorros, S. M., Meek, P., & Lopez, A. M. (2007). Interdependent anxiety and psychological distress in women with breast cancer and their partners. *Psychooncology, 16*, 634–643. doi: 10.1002/pon.1111

Selcuk, E., Stanton, S. C., Slatcher, R. B., & Ong, A. D. (2017). Perceived partner responsiveness predicts better sleep quality through lower anxiety. *Social Psychological and Personality Science, 8*, 83–92.

Sheeran, P., Klein, W. M., & Rothman, A. J. (2017). Health behavior change: Moving from observation to intervention. *Annual Review of Psychology, 68*, 573–600.

Sheeran, P., Maki, A., Montanaro, E., Avishai-Yitshak, A., Bryan, A., Klein, W. M. P., . . . Rothman, A. J. (2016). The impact of changing attitudes, norms, and self-efficacy on health-related intentions and behavior: A meta-analysis. *Health Psychology, 35*, 1178–1188.

Siegel, M. J., Bradley, E. H., Gallo, W. T., & Kasl, S. V. (2004). The effect of spousal mental and physical health on husbands' and wives' depressive symptoms among older adults: Longitudinal evidence from the health and retirement survey. *Journal of Aging and Health, 16*, 398–425.

Singer, A. J., & Clark, R. A. F. (1999). Cutaneous wound healing. *New England Journal of Medicine, 341*, 738–746.

Slatcher, R., & Selcuk, E. (2017). A social psychological perspective on the links between close relationships and health. *Current Directions in Psychological Science, 26*, 16–21. https://doi.org/10.1177/0963721416667444

Stimpson, J. P., Masel, M. C., Rudkin, L., & Peek, M. K. (2006). Shared health behaviors among older, Mexican American spouses. *American Journal of Health Behavior, 30*, 495–502.

Uchino, B. N. (2006). Social support and health: A review of physiological processes potentially underlying links to disease outcomes. *Journal of Behavioral Medicine, 29*, 377–387. https://doi.org/10.1007/s10865-006-9056-5

Uchino, B. N., Cacioppo, J. T., & Kiecolt-Glaser, J. K. (1996). The relationship between social support and physiological processes: A review with emphasis on underlying mechanisms and implications for health. *Psychological Bulletin, 119*, 488–531. https://doi.org/10.1037/0033-2909.119.3.488

Umberson, D., & Montez, J. K. J. (2010). Social relationships and health: A flashpoint for health policy. *Journal of Health and Social Behavior, 51*, 1–16. https://doi.org/10.1177/0022146510383501.Social

Umberson, D., Williams, K., Powers, D. A., Liu, H., & Needham, B. (2006). You make me sick: Marital quality and health over the life course. *Journal of Health and Social Behavior, 47*, 1–6.

Vellone, E., Chung, M. L., Cocchieri, A., Rocco, G., Alvaro, R., & Riegel, B. (2013). Effects of self-care on quality of life in adults with heart failure and their spousal caregivers: Testing dyadic dynamics using the Actor-Partner Interdependence Model. *Journal of Family Nursing, 20*, 120–141. https://doi.org/10.1177/1074840713510205

Waite, L. J. (1994). Does marriage matter? *Demography, 32*, 483–507.

Wickrama, K. A. S., Lorenz, F. O., Conger, R. D., & Elder, G. H. (1997). Marital quality and physical illness: A latent growth curve analysis. *Journal of Marriage and Family, 59*, 143–55.

Zhou, E. S., Kim, Y., Rasheed, M., Benedict, C., Bustillo, N. E., Soloway, M., . . . Penedo, F. J. (2011). Marital satisfaction of advanced prostate cancer survivors and their spousal caregivers: The dyadic effects of physical and mental health. *Psychooncology, 20*, 1352–1357. doi:10.1002/pon.1855

5

THE ROLE OF FRIENDSHIPS IN WELL-BEING

Beverley Fehr and Cheryl Harasymchuk

> *Friendship is unnecessary, like philosophy, like art. . . . It has no survival value; rather it is one of those things which give value to survival.*
>
> —C. S. Lewis

Satisfying, fulfilling relationships play a major role in people's physical and emotional well-being (e.g., Berscheid & Reis, 1998; Uchino, 2004). Close relationships even affect longevity. For example, a recent study found that happily married people who underwent bypass surgery were 2.5 times more likely to be alive 15 years later than their unmarried counterparts. Marital satisfaction was even more critical than marital status—those who were happily married were 3.2 times more likely to be alive than those who were unhappily married (King & Reis, 2012). However, not everyone can draw on the resource of a happy marriage. Demographic data show that the number of people who are married is declining, at least in the Western world (Eurostat, 2017). This demographic shift and other social changes (e.g., increases in divorce, single-parent families) have led to a greater reliance on friends for intimacy and support (e.g., Dykstra, 1995; Hartup & Stevens, 1997). Thus, the cultivation of close, satisfying friendships may be more important now than ever before.

The goal of this chapter is to review and integrate research on the importance of friendships to well-being, with a focus on adults. We begin with the question "What is a friend?" This question has been answered in the popular media, by laypeople, and by social scientists. We present these answers and point out common threads. In the social sciences, friendships have been defined at the macro level (e.g., analyses of composition of friendship networks) and at the micro level (e.g., delineations of the features or characteristics of friendship relationships). Some scholars have conceptualized friendship in terms of the rules that friends are expected to follow and in terms of the expectations and standards that are held for this kind of relationship. We review these areas of research, as well as research on variations in conceptions of friendship as a function of individual differences (e.g., gender, sexual identity) and culture. We end this section with a discussion of whether social media (e.g., Facebook) has changed the definition of this kind of relationship.

In the second half of the chapter, we focus on the role of friendships in contributing to well-being. First, we ask, "What makes for a satisfying friendship?" and review research that addresses this issue. Next, we document the importance of friendship in promoting physical and psychological well-being. As shall be seen, there is solid scientific evidence to support C. S. Lewis's assertion that friends bring value to survival. It also shall be seen that evidence runs counter to his assertion that friends are not necessary for survival.

What Is a Friend?

Popular entertainers and scholars alike have attempted to define what it means to be a friend. For instance, in popular music, a friend is "somebody to lean on" (Bill Withers, "Lean on me", 1972), to be grateful for (Andrew Gold, "Thank you for being a friend", 1978), to support (Carole King, "You've got a friend", 1971), and protect in hard times (Paul Simon, "Bridge over troubled waters", 1970). Thus, at least in these examples, the theme of social support is paramount. A friend is someone who will be there for you—someone who can be counted on when, to use the words of Carole King, you are "down and troubled and you need a helping hand" ("You've got a friend").

In the realm of social science, scholars across disciplines have offered an array of definitions and conceptualizations of friendship (e.g., Fehr, 1996; Vernon, 2010). As will be seen, these include macro-level approaches that focus on properties of friendship in a larger social world and micro-level approaches that focus on the qualities of the relationship that people have with their friends (e.g., openness, support, assistance).

Macro-Level Definitions of Friendship

For some scholars, defining a friend involves considering the larger context, that is, the social network in which people are embedded. Social networks (whether offline or online) are comprised of the people in one's life (e.g., family, romantic partners, neighbors, co-workers, Facebook friends, teammates). Friends are thus one component (albeit an important component) of a larger network. In fact, people's social networks are predominantly populated by friends. For example, Fischer (1982a) examined the social networks of large samples of adults living in various regions of northern California. The respondents considered 58% of the people in their social network to be friends. Nearly half (23%) if these were considered to be friends exclusively, whereas 35% had an additional relationship with the respondent such as co-worker, neighbor, or kin. In an analysis of the social ties of college students and elderly adults, Green and colleagues found that friends comprised the lion's share of the social network for both groups. Specifically, in college students' networks, 57% of were designated as friends, 29% as family, and 14% as other (e.g., acquaintances). Percentages were similar among elderly adults: 60% friends, 23% family, and 17% other (Green, Richardson, Lago, & Schatten-Jones, 2001).

Social scientists who study friendship from a macro approach examine the patterns of networks (e.g., through visual displays that represent people and their connections), the structure of the networks, and their impact on community engagement (Knoke & Yang, 2008; Scott, 2017; Wasserman & Faust, 1994). From this perspective, the definition of friendship depends on the function the relationship serves within the network. Thus, friendships can be classified into types (e.g., acquaintance, fun friend, Facebook friend, close best friend; Fehr, 1996; Spencer & Paul, 2006). Friendships also have been classified in terms of the **strength of the social tie** (Granovetter, 1973; Oishi & Kesebir, 2012). Strength is determined by the "amount of time, the emotional intensity, the intimacy (mutual confiding), and the reciprocal services which characterize the tie" (Granovetter, 1973, p. 1361). Close or best friends are referred to as strong ties in the network, whereas Facebook friends or acquaintances would be considered weak ties. Although more common in children's friendship research, adult friendships have also been defined in terms of the rank order of "top friends" in the friendship network (DeScioli, Kurzban, Koch, & Liben-Nowell, 2011).

Macro-level perspectives on friendship also focus on various aspects of the friendship network (e.g., size, composition). A common way of describing a friendship network is in terms of its **size** (e.g., Wrzus, Hänel, Wagner, & Neyer, 2013). Scholars employ several methods to assess the size of friendship networks including guided interviews (e.g., Terhell, van Groenou, & Van Tilburg, 2007), questionnaires (e.g., Levy-Storms & Lubben, 2006), and free recall methods (e.g., Binder, Roberts, & Sutcliffe, 2012; Brewer & Webster, 1999). It is common for assessments of network size to include questions about the frequency of contact (i.e., how active the friendship is) and the quality of those interactions. For instance, network size questionnaires might include questions about the number of friends the respondent feels close to, the number that can be called upon for help, and the number of friends with whom the respondent can discuss private matters (e.g., Green et al., 2001; Lubben & Gironda, 2003).

Another way to define the friendship network is in terms of its **composition**. Network composition has been assessed numerous ways including racial or ethnic diversity (e.g., Hendrickson, Rosen, & Aune, 2011; Reynolds, 2007) and attitudinal congruence (e.g., Visser & Mirabile, 2004).

Friendship networks also have been classified into different types or styles. For example, based on her analysis of the friendship networks of elderly people, Matthews (2000) identified three distinct styles as a function of number of friends, duration of friendship and closeness. People classified as having a *discerning friendship style* had a few very close friends to whom they were deeply committed. These friendships were long lasting, considered irreplaceable, and clearly differed from acquaintanceships. Those with an *independent friendship style* avoided establishing close or enduring friendship ties, but rather preferred having a few people in their network with whom they could engage in friendly interactions. These social ties tended to be based on circumstantial factors. People with an *acquisitive friendship style* were motivated to continue establishing new friendships. Their social networks included both long-standing close friendships as well as peripheral acquaintanceships.

In follow-up research, Miche, Huxhold, and Stevens (2013) found evidence that the acquisitive style could be subdivided into two categories, labeled *selectively acquisitive* and *unconditionally acquisitive*. The former category consisted of people who had a large number of friends, but showed evidence of selectivity in terms of the friends who were retained (retention was generally based on closeness). The latter category consisted of people who had the largest number of friends; both close and more distant ties were retained.

In sum, in macro-level approaches, friends are viewed as part of a larger network of social ties. Friendships are classified as different types based on the function and the strength of ties. The structure of the friend network is examined in terms of several variables including size and composition. In these analyses, the emphasis is placed on the entire network of friends (i.e., the "friendship landscape", rather than one particular friendship). As discussed next, friendships also are frequently defined at the micro-level where the emphasis is on the properties or characteristics of the relationship.

Micro-Level Definitions of Friendship

According to Allan (1989):

> "[F]riend" is not just categorical label, like "colleague" or "cousin", indicating the social position of each individual relative to the other. Rather it is a relational term which signifies something about the quality and character of the relationship involved.
>
> *(p. 16)*

Relational definitions of friendship can be divided into top-down approaches in which relationship scientists (experts) elucidate the meaning of friendship and bottom-up approaches wherein laypeople are asked to define the meaning of this concept.

Experts' Definitions of Friendship

A common approach to defining friendship is to specify properties or characteristics of this kind of relationship. Fehr (1996) reviewed scholars' definitions of friendships (see Table 1.2, p. 7) and concluded that these definitions could be summarized as: Friendship is "a voluntary, personal relationship, typically providing intimacy and assistance, in which two parties like one another and seek each other's company" (p. 7). Similar definitions have been offered in more recent literature. For example, in a research program by Demir and colleagues, participants are provided with the following definition: "A friend is someone who you enjoy doing things together with, count on to support you when you need it, provide support when he/she needs it, talk about your everyday life, problems, concerns, ideas, and intimate thoughts" (Demir, Özdemir, & Weitekamp, 2007, p. 250).

Other social scientists have conceptualized friendships in terms of the functions they serve. For example, Mendelson and colleagues defined friendship in terms of six **functions**: stimulating companionship, help, intimacy, reliable alliance, emotional security, and self-validation (Mendelson & Aboud, 1999; Mendelson & Kay, 2003). Stimulating companionship refers to spending time together and engaging in enjoyable and exciting activities. Help is defined as providing practical assistance, guidance, and information. Intimacy is conceptualized as self-disclosure, acceptance, and being sensitive to the friend's needs. Reliable alliance is defined as loyalty and the assurance that one can count on one's friend. Emotional security is defined as the comfort a friend provides in novel or threatening situations. Finally, self-validation refers to a friend as encouraging, reassuring, and helping one maintain a positive self-image. Companionship, help, intimacy, and reliable alliance align with other definitions offered in the literature (see Fehr, 1996). Self-validation and emotional security are less commonly represented.

One notable feature of friendships is that they are voluntary relationships; people choose and establish their friendship ties (unlike ties with family, co-workers or neighbors). People can also terminate those friendships with few social sanctions (unlike marriages, for example, which have far-reaching legal and social network consequences when they begin and end). In fact, friendship has been described as *the* most voluntary relationship (see Fehr, 1996). Despite this voluntariness, people hold expectations for the kinds of behaviors that they expect from their friends and well as rules and standards that they apply to the behavior of friends. According to Henderson and Argyle (1986), "rules provide the framework in which the relationship is given stability, by regulating potential sources of conflict that might disrupt the relationship" (p. 266). In a landmark program of research, Argyle and Henderson (1984) examined the rules of friendship in Britain, Italy, Japan, and Hong Kong. Participants in these studies were presented with 43 rules of friendship and were asked to rate each in terms of importance. Six rules were considered most important: standing up for a friend in his/her absence, sharing news of success, showing emotional support, trusting and confiding in each other, volunteering to help in a time of need, and striving to be pleasurable company. Friendship rules fell into four general categories: rules about sustaining or signaling intimacy (e.g., self-disclosure, expression of anger or anxiety, trust); rules about the proper exchange of rewards (e.g., repaying debts, emotional support, and volunteering help); rules regulating potential dyadic conflict (e.g., teasing and respecting privacy); and rules regulating potential sources of third party conflict (e.g., jealousy, tolerance of each other's friends).

Other scholars have defined friendship in terms of **ideal standards** or **expectations** (Clark & Ayers, 1993; Hall, 2011, 2012; La Gaipa, 1977). Based on a meta-analysis of friendship articles published between 1971 and 2009, Hall (2011) identified four key friendship expectations: symmetrical reciprocity (e.g., loyalty, genuineness, trust); communion (emotional support, self-disclosure, intimacy, empathic understanding); solidarity (sharing activities, companionship, spending time together); and agency (what a friend can offer in terms of resources, status, rewards). In a subsequent analysis, Hall (2012) split the solidarity category into expectations of enjoyment and similarity and added instrumental aid to the list.

Laypeople's Definitions of Friendship

Fischer (1982b) commented that people use the term *friend* "loosely and often" (p. 298). A number of researchers also have explored what lay people have in mind when they use this term (e.g., Adams, Blieszner, & De Vries, 2000; Bell, 1981; Fischer, 1982b; Hays, 1984; Weiss & Lowenthal, 1975; see Fehr, 1996, for a review). For instance, Crawford (1977) asked middle-aged people living in Britain to define close friends by asking them to complete the sentence, "A close friend is someone . . .". The responses in order of frequency were:

• I can trust
• I can call on for help
• I can go out with
• I see often
• who comes into my home
• I've known for a long time
• whose company I enjoy

In a study along the same lines, Sapadin (1988) asked professionals in three major US cities to complete the sentence, "A friend is someone . . .". The most frequent responses were the following:

• with whom you are intimate
• you can trust
• you can depend on
• with whom you share things

- who accepts you
- with whom you have a caring relationship
- with whom you are close
- you enjoy

More recently, Policarpo (2015) asked people in Portugal, ranging in age from 18 to 96 years, to answer two questions: "To you, what is a good friend?" and "To you, what is an intimate friend?" The three most frequently listed responses to the first question were: presence (being there for the other in good times and bad); unconditional support (being an effective support when needed, being able to count on the friend); and trust (someone you can rely on). When asked to define an intimate friendship, the three most frequent responses were: self-disclosure, trust, and family (e.g., he's like a brother to me). Based on a cluster analysis of these responses, Policarpo (2015) delineated a four-fold typology of the meaning of friendship: family-oriented (conceptualizing friendships as family), trust-oriented (regarding trust as the most important feature of friendships), self-oriented (conceptualization of friendship in terms of self-disclosure and unconditional support), and presence-oriented (being there for one other is of utmost importance).

Finally, Fehr (2004) examined the meaning of an intimate friendship by assessing people to describe the kinds of interactions or patterns of relating that are indicative of intimacy in same-sex friendships. More specifically, she proposed that lay people have knowledge of the kinds of patterns of relating that are prototypical of intimacy in a friendship along with knowledge of patterns of relating that are less likely to promote intimacy. A series of studies conducted with university students and a middle-aged community sample in Canada found that interaction patterns pertaining to responsive disclosure (e.g., "If I need to talk, my friend will listen"); emotional support (e.g., "If I'm sad or depressed, my friend will cheer me up"); loyalty, caring, and the like were considered prototypical of intimacy. Interaction patterns pertaining to practical support (e.g., "If I need money, my friend will lend it to me"); doing activities together (e.g., "If I want to have fun, my friend will go out with me"); and spending time together (e.g., "If I just want to do nothing, my friend will be fine with that") were considered nonprototypical.

In summary, there is not a single, clear, agreed-upon definition of friendship. However, there are striking commonalities in scholars' definitions and in the conceptions of friendship held by laypeople. Regardless of whether one is considering features or characteristics of friendship, friendship functions, or rules and expectations, several themes stand out. Perhaps the most salient feature is the provision of social support, especially emotional support ("being there" for a friend in good times and bad; offering comfort during difficult times). This theme is prominent in popular songs, experts' conceptions and in lay conceptions of friendship. Another theme that stands out is self-disclosure. A friend is someone with whom you can share personal, intimate information with the confidence that he or she will listen and be responsive. A friend is also someone you can trust and rely on, someone who is loyal, who cares, who accepts you as you are, and who is committed to the relationship. A friend is also a source of enjoyable companionship, which includes engaging in activities together but also simply spending time together in one another's presence ("hanging out"). One aspect of friendship that is not in the spotlight but is highlighted by a few scholars is that friends are a source of self-validation or self-affirmation, meaning that friends help one to maintain a positive image of oneself.

Definitions of Friendship as a Function of Sex and Gender, Culture, and Online Context

Relationship scientists have been interested not only in defining friendship, but also in examining how definitions vary as a function of sexuality and gender, including gender of participants, gender composition of the friendship (same-sex or cross-sex), and sexual orientation or identity. (Research also has examined age-related differences in conceptions of friendship but given our focus on adult friendships, that research is not reviewed here.) Cultural differences in conceptions of friendship have received some research attention as well. Recently, social scientists have begun to examine how the context (offline versus online) shapes conceptions of friendship.

Gender, Sexuality, and Sexual Identity

Do women and men differ in their views of friendship? Here the evidence is mixed. Policarpo (2015) found that, when defining a good friend, women were more likely than men to mention presence (being there) and trust, with no gender difference found for support. When responses were aggregated into four clusters (family-oriented, trust-oriented, self-oriented, and presence-oriented), women and men did not differ significantly. Similarly, Fehr (2004) did not find significant gender differences in participants' perceptions of the kinds of interactions that are indicative of an intimate friendship. Wrzus et al. (2013) also did not obtain gender effects when defining friendships in terms of network size.

In contrast, Adams et al. (2000) found that women were more likely to define friendship in affective terms (e.g., caring, compatibility), whereas men were more likely to define friendship in terms of what they termed "proxy measures", such as frequency of contact or duration of the friendship. Women also typically rate their same-sex friends as fulfilling the functions of friendship (e.g., providing stimulating companionship, intimacy, self-validation) than do men (Johnson, 2016; Mendelson & Aboud, 1999). Similarly, in research on friendship rules, intimate disclosure and more emotional support are rated higher by women than men (Argyle & Henderson, 1984). In Hall's (2011) meta-analysis of sex differences in friendship expectations, women held higher friendship expectations, overall, than did men. When analyzed in terms of the four categories of expectations, women assigned higher ratings to symmetrical reciprocity (e.g., loyalty, genuineness, trust) and communion (e.g., emotional support, self-disclosure, intimacy). Men rated agency (i.e., what a friend can offer in terms of resources, status, rewards) significantly higher than did women.

Scholars also have examined whether the meaning of friendship varies as a function of gender composition of the friend pair. Elkins and Peterson (1993) predicted that women would describe their same-sex friendships more positively than would men. They asked participants to rate same- and cross-sex actual and ideal friendships in terms ten dimensions (e.g., liking, self-disclosure, security, self-affirmation, utility value). For both actual and ideal friendships, men rated same-sex friends significantly lower in terms of these qualities compared to the other three groups (i.e., women in same-sex friendships, women and men in cross-sex friendships).

In terms of friendship functions or benefits, Mendelson and Kay (2003) found that women were rated as fulfilling the six friendship functions (e.g., stimulating companionship, self-validation, reliable alliance) to a greater extent in same-sex than in cross-sex friendships. In contrast, Johnson (2016) found that both women and men rated same-sex friendships higher in terms of friendship functions than cross-sex friendships.

Recently, friendship researchers have been chastised for their "heterosexist bias" (e.g., Pearl, 2006; Logan, 2013). Indeed, the vast majority of friendship studies are focused on the friendships of heterosexual women and men (most often their same-sex friendships; to a much lesser extent, but still present in the research literature, the friendships that heterosexual women and men have with each other (i.e., cross-sex friendships)). There has been a call for research on definitions of friendship and friendship networks of gay men and lesbian women and people of differing sexual identities.

Julien, Chartrand, and Bégin (1999) compared the networks of couples in lesbian, gay and heterosexual (marital) relationships. They found that gay and lesbian couples had a larger social network and shared more friendship ties than heterosexual couples. The authors point out that same-sex couples cannot count on institutional and familial support for their relationships and therefore may cultivate a larger network of other social ties. In a study of the friendship networks of lesbians, Logan (2013) found that these women had sex-segregated friendship networks (i.e., their friendship networks consisted primarily of women). More specifically, 89% of the participants reported that most of their friends were women (57% reported that most of their friends were lesbian). Male friends tended to be gay. She comments that:

> Heterosexual women, by and large, are funneled into mixed-sex networks via heterosexual partnership and motherhood. Single heterosexual women also network within mixed-sex peer and dating groups. Lesbians do not need to interact with men in order to secure a partner; therefore, entering sex-integrated social networks is not necessary for finding partnerships.
>
> *(Logan, 2013, p. 1511)*

There also is evidence that friendship networks of gay men and lesbians are more likely to include former romantic partners than is the case for heterosexual women and men (e.g., Allan, 2008; Weinstock & Rothblum, 1996; Weston, 1991). According to Hall (2011, 2012), "the bonds between former [lesbian] lovers often glue extended families of friends together" (p. 242).

In a treatise on the meaning of friendship for bisexual women, Pearl (2006) commented that bisexual women do not "neatly draw a line between their friendships and sexual relationships" (p. 119). The main finding extracted from interview data was that bisexual women find it difficult to establish friendship networks because they are stigmatized by both heterosexuals and homosexuals as being over-sexed or sexually confused. As a result, bisexual women often do not reveal their sexual identity to others for fears of being rejected. According to the respondents' accounts, these fears are often confirmed.

Finally, Wentland and Reissing (2011, 2014) argued that it is important to differentiate between different kinds of casual sex relationships, including whether or not the relationship is a friendship. They conducted a study on the meaning of one-night stands, booty calls, fuck buddies, and friends with benefits; only in the latter category is the relationship defined as a friendship.

In summary, a number of studies have addressed the issue of whether heterosexual women and men view friendship differently. Here the findings are mixed, such that some studies do not find gender differences whereas other studies do. When gender differences are found, they are consistently in the direction of women valuing friendships, particularly their same-sex friendships, more than men do (in terms of their affective quality, the functions they fulfill, they support provide, and so on). Women also hold higher expectations for friendships than do men. The one exception is that men hold higher expectations of agency (the status and resources that a friend can provide). More recently research is examining the meaning of friendship for non-heterosexual people (e.g., gay men, lesbian women, bisexual women). The findings so far show that the friendship networks of these groups differ from each other and from those of heterosexual women and men.

Culture

Most research on the meaning of friendship has been conducted in North America. Argyle and Henderson (1984) were among the first to examine how the meaning of friendship differs as a function of culture. As mentioned earlier, in their landmark paper, they gathered data on friendship rules in Britain, Japan, Italy, and Hong Kong. They focused on the rules that all four country samples shared; however, there were significant cultural differences as well. For example, people in the United Kingdom endorsed the highest number of friendship rules (21 of 43), followed by Hong Kong (21), then Italy (19), and finally Japan (5). When a factor analysis of the 43 rules was conducted, 11 factors emerged. Cultural differences were found for 7 of these factors. However, there was not a clear explanation for differences that emerged.

In Argyle and Henderson's research, one might have expected that participants from individualistic cultures (Britain) might have endorsed different rules than participants from more collectivistic cultures (Italy, Hong Kong, Japan). That was not the case. However, differences between individualist and collectivist cultures have been found in other studies. For example, Malikiosi-Loizos and Anderson (1999) hypothesized that friendship networks would be smaller but more reciprocal in collectivist cultures than in individualist cultures. This hypothesis was tested in samples of university students in Greece and the United States. Results supported predictions. Similarly, Adams and Plaut (2003) found that people in Ghana, West Africa, had smaller friendship networks than people in the United States. They also found that Ghanaian participants would report greater caution about friendships because of the embeddedness of relationships in that culture (i.e., greater implications for the group if there is conflict; less mobility and therefore fewer opportunities to seek new friendships if existing friendships dissolve). They also found that Ghanaians emphasized practical assistance when describing friendships whereas Americans were more likely to emphasize intimacy and emotional support. The authors point out that the greater poverty in West Africa, relative to the United States, can explain Ghanaian's greater emphasis on material support.

Finally, Reynolds (2007) examined the friendship networks of Caribbean young people living in Britain. The majority of participants indicated that their three best or closest friends shared their own ethnic background. These friends were seen as providing more social capital (trust, reciprocity, emotional support, community, and identity) than their cross-ethnic friends.

Online Friendships

The advent of social media sites such as Facebook has generated renewed interest in the question of "What is a friend?" Certainly, standard definitions that have existed in the pre-social media era (e.g., in terms of closeness, provision of social support, trust) would not seem to apply when people have hundreds or even thousands of Facebook "friends". In one study, for example, 42% of participants (an online community sample) reported that they had more than 300 Facebook friends; 11% reported over 1,000. Only a very small minority of these people were also face-to-face friends with the respondents (Lima, Marques, Muiños, & Camilo, 2017).

According to Valkenburg and Peter (2011), there are two competing views on how friendships have been altered by increased online communication and social media sites. One perspective is that the meaning of quality friendships is being diluted and replaced with superficial interactions (displacement hypothesis); the other perspective is that social media sites and online communication enhance the quantity and quality of interactions (stimulation hypothesis). (So far there seems to be more support for the stimulation hypothesis, although the evidence is mixed.) Other scholars have pointed out that the meaning of friendship has not changed as a result of social media sites, but rather that the term friend (as in Facebook friends) is being conflated with weaker social ties such as acquaintances (e.g., Amichai-Hamburger, Kingsbury, & Schneider, 2013; boyd & Ellison, 2007). Still others have argued that social media sites have changed how people initiate friendships, rather than their actual meaning (di Gennaro & Dutton, 2007; see also Chapter 12).

Just as in offline friendships, there are rules that govern what it means to be a friend on social media sites. For example, Bryant and Marmo (2012) examined the rules associated with Facebook friendships. In this study, participants reported on close friends, casual friends, or acquaintances. Examples of the most frequently listed rules from a larger list of 36 included: "I should expect a response from this person if I post on his/her profile."; "I should NOT say anything disrespectful about this person on Facebook."; "I should consider how a post might negatively impact this person's relationships.". The rules were classified into five categories: communication channels (the number of modes in which Facebook communication takes place, such as private vs. public); deception and control (i.e., controlling a friend's profile access); relational maintenance; negative consequences for the self; and negative consequences for a friend. Rules also differed as a function of friendship type. For example, communicating via multiple channels was considered more acceptable for close friends, followed by casual friends and then acquaintances. Acquaintances were expected, more than the other friendship types, to comply with rules concerning deception and the friend's profile access. (The authors suggest that people are more likely to feel they can trust closer friends not to be deceptive.) Interestingly, image maintenance (e.g., a friend not posting negative information about oneself) was paramount in these rules but is not a major focus in face-to-face friendships. (An exception is Mendelson and Aboud's (1999) work on friendship functions in which helping the other maintain a positive image is one of six friendship functions.)

Some researchers have compared the features or characteristics of online and offline friendships. For instance, in a study conducted in Hong Kong, Chan and Cheng (2004) examined whether variables such as interdependence, breadth and depth of self-disclosure, understanding, commitment, and network convergence differed depending on whether a friendship was online or offline. Participants were asked rate an online and an offline friend terms of these features and to report on the duration of involvement. Online friendships were rated lower on all of these qualities than offline friendships. When comparisons were made in terms of duration, both types of friends were rated higher as duration increased. Differences between online and offline friendships were greatest from the initiation to the one-year stage. After that, the differences in the two kinds of friendships diminished.

In sum, the research so far does not offer a conclusive picture of how definitions of friendship vary as a function of whether they are online or offline. One issue is that people seem to apply the term "friend" more indiscriminately in online than offline contexts (people do not claim to have hundreds or thousands of face-to-face friends). In addition, little is known about the composition and structure of online friendship networks. What is known is that there some differences in how these types of friendship are conceptualized. Online friendships have rules that are specific to that medium. There also is evidence that online friendships are rated lower in terms of friendship qualities such self-disclosure, understanding, commitment, and the like, although these differences lessen with the duration of the friendship. Clearly, more research is needed in order to fully understand similarities and differences in conceptions of online versus face-to-face friendships.

The Role of Friendships in Well-Being

There are two key issues that have captured the attention of friendship researchers: "What makes for a satisfying friendship?" and "What role does friendship play in predicting overall well-being?" To answer the first question, scholars have examined individual-level variables (e.g., age, gender, personality); social variables (e.g., quantity of social interactions); and cognitive variables (e.g., friendship expectations) as well as the functions, benefits, or rewards of the relationship. To answer the second question, scholars have examined macro- and micro-level variables. The most common approach has been to correlate measures of friendship quality with measures of well-being (satisfaction with life). Mediators of the relation between friendship quality and satisfaction with life also have been tested.

What Makes for a Satisfying Friendship?

Social scientists have addressed the issue of what makes for a satisfying friendship from a number of different angles. We begin with an examination of individual difference variables.

Individual-Level Factors

In a large-scale study examining predictors of friendship satisfaction, Gillespie, Lever, Frederick, and Royce (2015) found that demographic variables such as education, income, and marital status were insignificant or weak predictors of friendship satisfaction (assessed with a one-item face-valid measure). After controlling for these variables, age was a significant predictor (such that older adults were more satisfied with their friendships than younger adults). The study did not find gender differences in friendship satisfaction. Further, both women and men reported greater satisfaction with their same-sex friendships than their cross-sex friendships.

Personality factors also have been studied. Demir and Weitekamp (2007) tested links between the Big Five personality traits and friendship quality. Extraversion, conscientiousness, and agreeableness were positively correlated with friendship quality; openness and neuroticism were not related to the quality of friendships. In a study of first-year college students, Pressman and colleagues (2005) examined the relation between social network size (defined as the people who are most important and closest to you) and four personality traits (extraversion, neuroticism, self-esteem, and hostility). Only extraversion was correlated with network size, such that people high on this trait reported a greater number of social ties. Brissette, Scheier, and Carver (2002) examined the link between dispositional optimism and size of friendship networks among students entering college. Optimism was correlated with network size after the first 2 weeks of college, but did not predict increases in network size over the course of the first semester.

Social Variables

In an impressive longitudinal study, Carmichael, Reis, and Duberstein (2015) had participants report on their daily interactions at ages 20, 30, and 50 (using the Rochester Interaction Record, Reis & Wheeler, 1991). When the participants were 50 years of age, the researchers also measured various outcomes, including friendship quality (measured with an intimacy scale and a closeness scale). The *quantity* of social interactions at age 20 predicted friendship quality at age 50 (controlling for age 30). The *quality* of social interactions at age 20 predicted the quality of interactions at age 30, which, in turn, predicted friendship quality at age 50.

Cognitive Variables

In other research, scholars have studied the link between friendship satisfaction and cognitive variables, including the standards and expectations that people hold for friendships (i.e., what you expect from your friends); ideals (i.e., what you want in an ideal friendship); and prototypes (i.e., your knowledge of what a friendship is). To assess friendship standards, Hall, Larson, and Watts (2011) asked participants to imagine the perfect, same-sex friend and then rate that ideal friendship in terms of four friendship maintenance behaviors identified by Oswald, Clark, and Kelly (2004): positivity (e.g., behaviors that make the friendship enjoyable and rewarding); interaction (e.g., doing activities together); openness (e.g., self-disclosure); and support (e.g., emotional support). Next, participants engaged in a 5-day diary study in which they reported on interactions with a same-sex best, close, and casual friend (e.g., purpose of interaction, goals met) and rated the extent to which the friendship met their expectations that day. On the last day, a measure of friendship satisfaction was administered. Not surprisingly, participants were most satisfied with their best friendship, followed by their close friendship, with the lowest satisfaction reported in casual friendships. Women set higher standards for their ideal friendship than did men, but there was no gender difference in fulfillment of expectations on a daily basis nor in ratings of friendship satisfaction. High ideal standards predicted higher fulfillment of friendship expectations on a daily basis for women but not for men. For men, the relationship between ideal standards and having expectations met was curvilinear (men with the lowest and with the highest ideals reported that daily interactions with their friend did not meet their expectations; men in the "middle" (those with medium ideals) reported that their expectations were fulfilled in daily interactions with their friend). Finally, daily fulfillment of friendship expectations was associated with increased friendship satisfaction (as assessed on the last day).

In conceptually similar research, Demir and Orthel (2011) examined the role of discrepancies between ideal and ideal friendships in predicting the quality of best friendships. Both women and men rated their ideal friendship higher in quality than their actual friendship. However, in this study, women reported higher actual and ideal friendship quality than did men. As hypothesized, the discrepancy between ideal and actual friendships was negatively correlated with friendship quality and happiness for both women and men.

In more recent research, Fehr and Harasymchuk (in press) developed a prototype-matching model of friendship satisfaction. This research was based research by Fehr (2004) (discussed earlier) delineating the kinds of interactions that people regard as indicative of intimacy in a same-sex friendship. Fehr and Harasymchuk posited that, when evaluating the quality of their friendships, people assess the extent to which their friendship matches the prototype of intimacy. They predicted and found that the extent to which people rated their friendship as characterized by prototypical patterns of relating (e.g., "If I want to talk, my friend will listen") was strongly correlated with friendship satisfaction; embodiment of nonprototypical interaction patterns (e.g., "If I want to have fun, my friend will go out with me") was less strongly associated with friendship quality. Thus, there is evidence that the extent to which a friendship matches one's ideals or matches the prototype of intimacy, the greater the satisfaction with that friendship.

Functions, Benefits, and Rewards

Mendelson and Aboud (1999) administered the McGill Friendship Questionnaire-Friend's Functions (Companionship, Help, Reliable Alliance, Emotional Security, Self-Validation; Mendelson & Aboud, 1999) to young people in their late teens and early adulthood, along with the McGill Friendship Questionnaire—Respondent's Affection (a measure of positive feelings and satisfaction in a friendship). Participants also reported on the level of their friendship (ranging from acquaintance to best friend). The fulfillment of friendship functions predicted affection (positive feelings and satisfaction) regardless of the level of friendship. Similar findings were obtained in a subsequent study using these measures with same- and cross-sex friendship pairs (Mendelson & Kay, 2003).

In another study examining predictors of friendship satisfaction, Deci, La Guardia, Moller, Scheiner, and Ryan (2006) predicted that autonomy support (defined as understanding the other's perspective and being responsive by allowing the other to make independent choices and take initiatives) from a close friend would predict benefits such as need satisfaction and friendship quality. Further, they expected that friends would show evidence of reciprocity. In their first study, the researchers administered the Friendship Autonomy Support Questionnaire to same- and cross-sex close friend pairs along with measures of psychological need satisfaction and four indices of friendship quality (emotional reliance, attachment security, dyadic adjustment, and closeness). Perceived autonomy support was positively correlated with need satisfaction and the indices of relationship quality. Female-female dyads perceived higher perceived higher autonomy support than the other friend pairs. Male-male dyads scored significantly lower on emotional reliance and attachment security than the other friend types. Evidence of mutuality was found for autonomy support received from the friend and for the indices of relationship quality (i.e., one friend's score was positively correlated with other friend's scores on these measures; Deci et al., 2006).

In a follow-up study, Deci et al. (2006) administered the same measures as in Study 1 as well as a measure of autonomy support provided to the friend, the experience of positive and negative emotions and additional measures of friendship quality. Male-male dyads scored lower than the other friendship pairs on nearly all of the measures. Receiving autonomy support was correlated positively with the other variables (except for the expected negative correlation with negative affect) at both the individual and dyadic levels. Providing autonomy support predicted higher need satisfaction and relationship quality. Mutuality was evident for autonomy support provided, relationship satisfaction, and the experience of negative emotions.

In sum, there are many predictors of friendship satisfaction. These include extraversion, quantity of social interactions, having expectations and ideals met, and the receipt of benefits such as companionship, intimacy, support, and the like. Thus, qualities of the individual and of the dyadic relationship play a role.

The Role of Friendships in Predicting Health, Happiness, and Life Satisfaction

There is considerable research on the benefit of close relationships for psychological and physical health (e.g., Berscheid & Reis, 1998; Myers, 2004; Uchino, 2004). In most of this research, respondents are asked about close ties, which could include friends, partners, or family members) or are specifically asked about family ties and/or partners (typically spouses). Thus, when friendships are included, they typically have been "lumped in" with other close ties. However, in the past decade, researchers have begun to consider that satisfying friendships also might contribute to life satisfaction and physical and mental well-being. This could be colloquially summed up as "happy with friends; happy with life". As shall be seen, there is considerable support for the idea that satisfying friendships are an important ingredient in well-being. Friendship researchers also have sought to determine mediators of the link between satisfying friendships and satisfaction with life.

Satisfaction With Life/Subjective Well-Being

In most of the research on the link between friendship satisfaction and well-being, the latter construct is assessed with the Subjective Well-Being Scale (e.g., "Overall, how satisfied are you with your life nowadays?"; Diener, 1994) or the Satisfaction with Life Scale (e.g., "I am satisfied with my life."; Diener, Emmons, Larsen, & Griffin, 1985). A consistent finding in these studies is that friendship satisfaction is correlated with overall life satisfaction. For example, Gillespie et al. (2014) reported correlation of .49 for men and .40 for women between friendship satisfaction and life satisfaction in a sample of more than 25,000 adults recruited via NBCNews.com. These relations remained significant when controlling for other variables (e.g., demographic, satisfaction with job, health status).

In a decade-long program of research by Demir and colleagues, friendship quality has been assessed using the McGill Friendship Questionnaire-Friendship Functions (Mendelson & Aboud, 1999). As mentioned earlier, this scale measures six functions that are served by friendships (Companionship, Help, Reliable Alliance, Emotional Security, and Self-Validation); the extent to which a given friendship fulfills these functions is correlated with friendship satisfaction (see section on Friendship Satisfaction). However, in the studies by Demir and colleagues, this scale is taken as an index of friendship quality (scores on the six friendship function subscales are combined). A major focus of this work has been to examine the link between friendship quality and happiness. In these studies, conducted with American university students, correlations between friendship quality and life satisfaction (happiness) generally fall in the range of $r = .18$ to .25. We include this research in this section because in many of these studies, happiness is measured using standard well-being scales (Satisfaction with Life Scale (Diener et al., 1985); Subjective Happiness Scale (Lyubomirsky & Lepper, 1999)) as well as direct reports of happiness (specifically, the PANAS (Positive and Negative Affect Schedule); Watson, Clark, & Tellegen, 1988), with happiness scores being derived by subtracting the negative affect composite score from the positive affect composite. In some studies, happiness assessed in this way was combined with the well-being scales. (See Chapter 1 for a discussion of various strategies for measuring subjective well-being.)

In one of the early studies in this series, Demir and Weitekamp (2007) found that, as expected, friendship quality and happiness were positively correlated in best friendships. (Conflict in the friendship was negatively correlated with happiness.) A regression analysis found that friendship quality predicted happiness above and beyond personality (Big Five traits). In another study, Demir et al. (2007) compared the quality of best friends, first closest and second closest friendships as predictors of happiness. Only quality of the best friend relationship was a significant predictor.

In subsequent studies, Demir and colleagues explored mediators of the friendship quality-happiness relation. Demir and Özdemir (2010) found that basic need satisfaction mediated the relation between friendship quality and happiness (in a sample of best friends). In a second study, the authors asked participants to name their best friend and their first and second close friends. Need satisfaction mediated the relation between quality and happiness for all friendship types. Other significant mediators of the friendship quality-happiness relation found in this research (generally focused on best friendships) include perceived mattering (i.e., the perception that you are important to your friend and make a difference in his or her life; Demir, Özen, Doğan, Bilyk, & Tyrell, 2011) and personal sense of uniqueness (feeling that one's special or unique qualities are appreciated; Demir, Şimşek, & Procsal, 2013). Thus, there is strong evidence that friendship quality (as assessed in terms of friendship functions such as emotional security and companionship) is strongly correlated with personal happiness. Moreover, there is evidence that this relation is mediated by need satisfaction, perceived mattering and personal uniqueness. The evidence suggests that these relations do not vary by gender.

Van der Horst and Coffé (2012) examined the relation between friendship network characteristics (number of friends, heterogeneity of friendship network, and frequency of contact) as predictors of well-being (assessed with single items measuring happiness, life satisfaction, job or main activity satisfaction, financial satisfaction and health satisfaction) using data from the General Society Survey of Canada (2003). Further, they predicted that the link between the friendship variables and well-being would be mediated by type of contact (face-to-face, telephone, email/internet) and benefits of friendships (more social trust, less stress, better health, and more social support; assessed with single items). The results indicated that having more friends, higher frequency of contact and lower friendship heterogeneity predicted three of the four friendship benefits (social trust, stress, and health). Frequency of contact and number of friends, as well as heterogeneity of the friendship network increased the probability of receiving social support. As predicted, these benefits predicted higher levels of well-being.

In a large-scale American study, Oishi and Kesebir (2012) asked participants to list their very close, close, and distant friends. Based on their responses, participants' networks were classified as deep and narrow (a few very close friends) versus broad and shallow (a large number of weaker ties). Having deep, narrow friendship networks was associated with greater subjective well-being and more positive affect (than having broad, shallow networks) for people who were residentially stable and who lived in economically poorer areas (compared to those who were residentially mobile and rich, were residentially mobile and poor, or were residentially stable and rich). The authors suggest that residential stability allows one to invest in deeper friendships. Deeper friendships also are advantageous for people living in poverty because it increases the probability that they will receive help.

Health Outcomes

There is mounting evidence that having friendships, particularly close, satisfying friendships, predicts self-reported physical and mental health. Although they did not specifically focus on friendships, Carmichael et al. (2015) found that the quantity and quality of social interactions at ages 20 and 30 predicted positive psychological outcomes (assessed by combining measures of loneliness, depression and well-being) at age 50.

Elkins and Peterson (1993) had participants rate ideal and actual same- and cross-sex friends along ten dimensions (e.g., declaration of liking, self-disclosure, salience of emotional expression, self-affirmation) and a measure of dysphoria (created by combining scores on the Satisfaction with Life Scale with scores on depression and self-esteem scales). Generally, ideal friendships were rated higher on these dimensions than actual friendships. Actual and ideal friendships were rated lowest by men in same-sex friendships (ratings of the other three friendship types did not differ significantly from one another). However, discrepancies between actual and ideal ratings did not differ as a function of gender or friendship type. In addition, discrepancies (i.e., one's actual friendship falling short of one's ideals) were correlated with dysphoria for both women and men in both same- and cross-sex friendships.

The bulk of the research on the relation between friendships and mental and physical health has focused on friendship network factors rather than on qualities of the friendship. Research by Miche et al. (2013) on friendship styles (see earlier section on the "Macro-Level Definitions of Friendships") found that having an independent style (i.e., avoiding close friendships) was associated with poorer self-reported health. The authors suggest that, when people are in poor health, they turn away from friends. (As discussed later, it is also the case that impoverished friendship networks predict poor health.)

Larger friendship networks generally are associated with better physical and mental health. For example, a study of more than 7,000 middle-aged adults in Britain found that having a smaller friendship network at age 42 predicted poorer psychological well-being at age 50 (Cable, Bartley, Chandola, & Sacker, 2012). In a study focused on physical health, Pressman et al. (2005) examined the role of social network size (defined as the people who are most important or closest to you) and loneliness in the development of antibodies to an influenza vaccine. Small networks and loneliness were significant, independent predictors of antibody development. However, neither loneliness nor having a small social network were associated with engagement in health-promoting behaviors.

Several other researchers have examined the relation between friendship networks and loneliness (the latter is often divided into social loneliness (the absence of social ties) and emotional loneliness (the absence of a few close ties)). Green and colleagues (2001) found that size of social networks was correlated with lower social loneliness among young people (college students) but not among the elderly. Social network size was not associated with emotional loneliness in either age group (Green et al., 2001). In research along the same lines, Binder and colleagues (2012) found that the number of friendship ties that people considered to be significant (i.e., close, but not closest friends) was associated with lower social and emotional loneliness. However, the number of core ties (closest friendships) was not related to social loneliness and, unexpectedly, was positively correlated with emotional loneliness (Binder et al., 2012). Finally, a study of international university students found that having a higher ratio of friends from one's own country in the friendship network was associated with greater satisfaction, contentment and less homesickness (Hendrickson et al., 2011).

Turning to physical health, in a large-scale study of more than 2,000 cancer patients, Lewis and Martinez (2014) found that the number of social ties (defined for participants as the number of close friends, either relatives or non-relatives) was associated with the pro-health behavior of seeking cancer-related information. This relation was mediated by communication efficacy (i.e., the participant's confidence that he or she had the skills to engage in effective communication or information seeking behavior).

Thanakwang and Soonthorndhada (2011) assessed the friendship networks (number of friends, number who can be called upon for help, support, and discuss private matters) among nearly 500 elderly people (ages 60–103 years) in Thailand. Friendship networks predicted self-reported health behaviors (e.g., physical functioning, cognitive functioning, spiritual health). This relation was mediated by health-promoting behaviors from friends, such as encouragement to exercise, eat healthy foods, and manage stress.

In an analysis of data gathered as part of the Longitudinal Study on Aging, Sabin (1993) examined predictors of mortality rates (4 years after the initial data collection) in a sample of people ages 70 and over. Interestingly, in this study, contact with family and kin was not associated with reduced mortality. Instead, what the authors terms "socioexpressive" variables were the strongest predictors. This cluster included contact with friends and neighbors, volunteer work, and regular attendance at religious services. Within this category, church attendance was the strongest predictor of reduced mortality, followed by involvement in volunteerism, and then contact with friends. The authors point out that all of the socioexpressive variables are voluntary in nature and presumably provide people with interest and enjoyment in live. They speculate that familial relationships might take the form of instrumental help which may be less influential in promoting longevity.

Turning to comparisons of online and offline friendships, Helliwell and Huang (2013) compared the effects of the number of offline versus Facebook friends on levels of well-being (measured with questions about life satisfaction and happiness) in a large sample of Canadian respondents. The number of face-to-face friends was positively associated with well-being. This was not the case for Facebook friends. In fact, there was some evidence that having more Facebook friends was negatively associated with well-being. Lima et al. (2017) followed up on this research with two large community samples in Portugal. They found that both the quantity and quality of face-to-face friendships was correlated with self-reported physical health, mental health, and subjective well-being. These relations were mediated by bonding (e.g., social support, social trust) and social capital (e.g., social interaction, social integration). (The former was a more powerful mediator than the latter.) These studies did not find a relation between Facebook friendships and health and well-being. In fact, having Facebook friends was negatively associated with bonding (feeling that there are people in your life who you can trust and count on for support). The authors conclude that:

> This study shows that this "digitalization" of our lives should not replace the value of promoting and keeping offline friendships. Face-to-face friends, with whom we interact in physical settings or through a variety of means, and with whom we can establish caring and close relationships, are fundamental for our health and well-being.
>
> *(p. 10)*

Thus, there is compelling evidence that having a large number of friends contributes to a happy, fulfilling, healthy life. This seems especially true when those friendships are close and satisfying. (See Chapter 12 for a discussion of research on online relationships and health and well-being.) Because studies on the link between friendships and well-being are correlational, they cannot determine causal relationships. The assumption is that friendships contribute to health and well-being, but it is also likely that health and well-being influence the formation and maintenance of friendships. For example, as noted earlier, Miche et al. (2013) interpreted the negative correlation between health and an independent friendship style as indicating that people pull away from their friends when they are in poor health.

Conclusion

Friendship often has been described as the "neglected relationship", given the focus on romantic and familial relationships in the close relationships literature (see Fehr, 1996). However, as this chapter has shown, there is a wealth of information on how people conceptualize and define friendships, both in terms of network variables and relational variables. There is also an impressive body of research on predictors of friendship satisfaction and the role of friendships in physical and psychological well-being. Although more research is needed, findings amassed so far are compelling. Thus, it no longer seems accurate to describe friendship as a neglected relationship. What has been neglected, however, is research on non-heterosexual kinds of friendship and how these kinds of friendships play a role in well-being. Additional research also is required before it will be clear whether online friendships make significant contributions to, or detract from, well-being. What can be said with certainty is that social science research does not support C. S. Lewis's assertion that friendships have no survival value. However, there is resounding support for his assertion that friends bring value to survival.

References

Adams, R. G., Blieszner, R., & De Vries, B. (2000). Definitions of friendship in the third age: Age, gender, and study location effects. *Journal of Aging Studies, 14*(1), 117–133.

Adams, R. G., & Plaut, V. C. (2003). The cultural grounding of personal relationship: Friendship in North American and West African worlds. *Personal Relationships, 10*(3), 333–347.

Allan, G. (1989). *Friendship*. Harvester Wheatsheaf: London.

Allan, G. (2008). Flexibility, friendship, and family. *Personal Relationships, 15*(1), 1–16.

Amichai-Hamburger, Y., Kingsbury, M., & Schneider, B. H. (2013). Friendship: An old concept with a new meaning? *Computers in Human Behavior, 29*(1), 33–39.

Argyle, M., & Henderson, M. (1984). The rules of friendship. *Journal of Social and Personal Relationships, 1*(2), 211–237.

Bell, R. R. (1981). Friendships of women and of men. *Psychology of Women Quarterly, 5*(3), 402–417.

Berscheid, E., & Reis, H. T. (1998). Attraction and close relationships. In D. T. Gilbert, S. T. Fiske, G. Lindzey, (Eds.), *The handbook of social psychology* (Vols. 1–2, 4th ed., pp. 193–281). New York, NY, US: McGraw-Hill.

Binder, J. F., Roberts, S. G., & Sutcliffe, A. G. (2012). Closeness, loneliness, support: Core ties and significant ties in personal communities. *Social Networks, 34*(2), 206–214.

boyd, D. M., & Ellison, N. B. (2007). Social network sites: Definition, history, and scholarship. *Journal of Computer-Mediated Communication, 13*(1), 210–230.

Brewer, D. D., & Webster, C. M. (1999). Forgetting of friends and its effects on measuring friendship networks. *Social Networks, 21*(4), 361–373.

Brissette, I., Scheier, M. F., & Carver, C. S. (2002). The role of optimism in social network development, coping, and psychological adjustment during a life transition. *Journal of Personality and Social Psychology, 82*(1), 102.

Bryant, E. M., & Marmo, J. (2012). The rules of Facebook friendship: A two-stage examination of interaction rules in close, casual, and acquaintance friendships. *Journal of Social and Personal Relationships, 29*(8), 1013–1035.

Cable, N., Bartley, M., Chandola, T., & Sacker, A. (2012). Friends are equally important to men and women, but family matters more for men's well-being. *Journal of Epidemiology and Community Health, 67*, 166–171.

Carmichael, C. L., Reis, H. T., & Duberstein, P. R. (2015). In your 20s it's quantity, in your 30s it's quality: The prognostic value of social activity across 30 years of adulthood. *Psychology and Aging, 30*(1), 95.

CDC/National Center for Health Statistics. (2015, November 23). *National marriage and divorce rate trends*. Retrieved from www.cdc.gov/nchs/nvss/marriage_divorce_tables.htm

Chan, D. K. S., & Cheng, G. H. L. (2004). A comparison of offline and online friendship qualities at different stages of relationship development. *Journal of Social and Personal Relationships*, *21*(3), 305–320.

Clark, M. L., & Ayers, M. (1993). Friendship expectations and friendship evaluations: Reciprocity and gender effects. *Youth & Society*, *24*(3), 299–313.

Crawford, M. (1977). What is a friend. *New Society*, *42*(785), 116–117.

Deci, E. L., La Guardia, J. G., Moller, A. C., Scheiner, M. J., & Ryan, R. M. (2006). On the benefits of giving as well as receiving autonomy support: Mutuality in close friendships. *Personality and Social Psychology Bulletin*, *32*(3), 313–327.

Demir, M., & Orthel, H. (2011). Friendship, real: Ideal discrepancies, and well-being: Gender differences in college students. *Journal of Psychology*, *145*(3), 173–193.

Demir, M., & Özdemir, M. (2010). Friendship, need satisfaction and happiness. *Journal of Happiness Studies*, *11*(2), 243–259.

Demir, M., Özdemir, M., & Weitekamp, L. A. (2007). Looking to happy tomorrows with friends: Best and close friendships as predict happiness. *Journal of Happiness Studies*, *8*, 243–271.

Demir, M., Özen, A., Doğan, A., Bilyk, N. A., & Tyrell, F. A. (2011). I matter to my friend, therefore I am happy: Friendship, mattering, and happiness. *Journal of Happiness Studies*, *12*(6), 983–1005.

Demir, M., Şimşek, Ö. F., & Procsal, A. D. (2013). I am so happy cause my best friend makes me feel unique: Friendship, personal sense of uniqueness and happiness. *Journal of Happiness Studies*, *14*(4), 1201–1224.

Demir, M., & Weitekamp, L. A. (2007). I am so happy' cause today I found my friend: Friendship and personality as predictors of happiness. *Journal of Happiness Studies*, *8*(2), 181–211.

DeScioli, P., Kurzban, R., Koch, E. N., & Liben-Nowell, D. (2011). Best friends: Alliances, friend ranking, and the MySpace social network. *Perspectives on Psychological Science*, *6*(1), 6–8.

Diener, E. (1994). Assessing subjective well-being: Progress and opportunities. *Social Indicators Research*, *31*(2), 103–157.

Diener, E. D., Emmons, R. A., Larsen, R. J., & Griffin, S. (1985). The satisfaction with life scale. *Journal of Personality Assessment*, *49*(1), 71–75.

di Gennaro, C., & Dutton, W. H. (2007). Reconfiguring friendships: Social relationships and the Internet. *Information, Communication & Society*, *10*(5), 591–618.

Dykstra, P. A. (1995). Loneliness among the never and formerly married: The importance of supportive friendships and a desire for independence. *Journals of Gerontology Series B: Psychological Sciences and Social Sciences*, *50*(5), S321–S329.

Elkins, L. E., & Peterson, C. (1993). Gender differences in best friendships. *Sex Roles*, *29*(7), 497–508.

Eurostat. (2017, June 2). *Marriage and divorce statistics*. Retrieved from http://ec.europa.eu/eurostat/statistics-xplained/index.php/Marriage_and_divorce_statistics

Fehr, B. (1996). *Friendship processes* (Vol. 12). London: Sage.

Fehr, B. (2004). Intimacy expectations in same-sex friendships: A prototype interaction pattern model. *Journal of Personality and Social Psychology*, *86*(2), 265.

Fehr, B., & Harasymchuk, C. (2017). A prototype-matching model of satisfaction in same-sex friendships. *Personal Relationships*.

Fischer, C. S. (1982a). *To dwell among friends: Personal networks in town and city*. Chicago: University of Chicago Press.

Fischer, C. S. (1982b). What do we mean by "friend"? An inductive study. *Social Networks*, *3*(4), 287–306.

Gillespie, B. J., Lever, J., Frederick, D., & Royce, T. (2015). Close adult friendships, gender, and the life cycle. *Journal of Social and Personal Relationships*, *32*(6), 709–736. General Society Survey of Canada. Retrieved from www23.statcan.gc.ca/imdb/p2SV.pl?Function=getSurvey&Id=5509

Gold, A. (1978). Thank you for being a friend. On *All this and heaven too* [record]. United States: Asylum Records.

Granovetter, M. S. (1973). The strength of weak ties. *American Journal of Sociology*, *78*(6), 1360–1380.

Green, L. R., Richardson, D. S., Lago, T., & Schatten-Jones, E. C. (2001). Network correlates of social and emotional loneliness in young and older adults. *Personality and Social Psychology Bulletin*, *27*(3), 281–288.

Hall, J. A. (2011). Sex differences in friendship expectations: A meta-analysis. *Journal of Social and Personal Relationships*, *28*(6), 723–747.

Hall, J. A. (2012). Friendship standards: The dimensions of ideal expectations. *Journal of Social and Personal Relationships*, *29*(7), 884–907.

Hall, J. A., Larson, K. A., & Watts, A. (2011). Satisfying friendship maintenance expectations: The role of friendship standards and biological sex. *Human Communication Research*, *37*(4), 529–552.

Hartup, W. W., & Stevens, N. (1997). Friendships and adaptations in the life course. *Psychological Bulletin*, *121*, 355–370.

Hays, R. B. (1984). The development and maintenance of friendship. *Journal of Social and Personal Relationships*, *1*(1), 75–98.

Helliwell, J., & Huang, H. (2013). Comparing the happiness effects or real and on-line friends. *PLoS ONE*, *8*, e72754. doi: 10.1371/journal.pone.0072754

Henderson, M., & Argyle, M. (1986). The informal rules of working relationships. *Journal of Organizational Behavior*, *7*, 259–275.

Hendrickson, B., Rosen, D., & Aune, R. K. (2011). An analysis of friendship networks, social connectedness, homesickness, and satisfaction levels of international students. *International Journal of Intercultural Relations*, *35*(3), 281–295.

Johnson, A. (2016). *The nature of friendship: How attraction and friendship benefits compare in same- and cross-sex friendships* (Unpublished honors thesis). University of Winnipeg, Winnipeg, Canada.

Julien, D., Chartrand, E., & Bégin, J. (1999). Social networks, structural interdependence, and conjugal adjustment in heterosexual, gay, and lesbian couples. *Journal of Marriage and Family*, *61*(2), 516–530.

King, C. (1971). You've got a friend. On *Tapestry* [record]. United States: Ode—A&M.

King, K. B., & Reis, H. T. (2012). Marriage and long-term survival after coronary artery bypass grafting. *Health Psychology*, *31*(1), 55.

Knoke, D., & Yang, S. (2008). *Social network analysis* (Vol. 154, 2nd ed.). Thousand Oaks, CA: Sage.

La Gaipa, J. J. (1977). Testing a multidimensional approach to friendship. In S. Duck (Ed.), *Theory and practice in interpersonal attraction* (pp. 249–270). London: Academic Press.

Levy-Storms, L., & Lubben, J. E. (2006). Network composition and health behaviors among older Samoan women. *Journal of Aging and Health*, *18*(6), 814–836.

Lewis, N., & Martinez, L. S. (2014). Does the number of cancer patients' close social ties affect cancer-related information seeking through communication efficacy? Testing a mediation model. *Journal of Health Communication*, *19*(9), 1076–1097.

Lima, M. L., Marques, S., Muiños, G., & Camilo, C. (2017). All you need is Facebook friends? Associations between online and face-to-face friendships and health. *Frontiers in Psychology, 8*(68).

Logan, L. S. (2013). Status homophily, sexual identity, and lesbian social ties. *Journal of Homosexuality, 60*(10), 1494–1519.

Lubben, J., & Gironda, M. (2003). Centrality of social ties to the health and well-being of older adults. In B. Berkman & L. Harootyan (Eds.), *Social work and health care in an aging society* (pp. 319–350). New York: Springer.

Lyubomirsky, S., & Lepper, H. S. (1999). A measure of subjective happiness: Preliminary reliability and construct validation. *Social Indicators Research, 46*(2), 137–155.

Malikiosi-Loizos, M., & Anderson, L. R. (1999). Accessible friendships, inclusive friendships, reciprocated friendships as related to social and emotional loneliness in Greece and the USA. *European Psychologist, 4*(3), 165.

Matthews, S. H. (2000). Friendship styles. In J. F. Gubrium & J. A. Holstein (Eds.), *Aging and everyday life* (pp. 155–194). Malden, MA: Blackwell.

Mayer, A., & Puller, S. L. (2008). The old boy (and girl) network: Social network formation on university campuses. *Journal of Public Economics, 92*(1), 329–347.

Mendelson, M. J., & Aboud, F. E. (1999). Measuring friendship quality in late adolescents and young adults: McGill friendship questionnaires. *Canadian Journal of Behavioural Science, 31*(2), 130–132.

Mendelson, M. J., & Kay, A. C. (2003). Positive feelings in friendship: Does imbalance in the relationship matter? *Journal of Social and Personal Relationships, 20*(1), 101–116.

Miche, M., Huxhold, O., & Stevens, N. L. (2013). A latent class analysis of friendship network types and their predictors in the second half of life. *Journals of Gerontology Series B: Psychological Sciences and Social Sciences, 68*(4), 644–652.

Myers, D. G. (2004). Human connections and the good life: Balancing individuality and community in public policy. In P. A. Axley & S. Joseph (Eds.), *Positive psychology in practice* (pp. 641–657). Hoboken, NJ: Wiley.

Oishi, S., & Kesebir, S. (2012). Optimal social-networking strategy is a function of socioeconomic conditions. *Psychological Science, 23*(12), 1542–1548.

Oswald, D. L., Clark, E. M., & Kelly, C. M. (2004). Friendship maintenance: An analysis of individual and dyad behaviors. *Journal of Social and Clinical Psychology, 23*(3), 413–441.

Pearl, M. L. (2006). Relating the personal experiences of bisexual women to the friendship literature. *Journal of Bisexuality, 6*(3), 115–127.

Policarpo, V. (2015). What is a friend? An exploratory typology of the meanings of friendship. *Social Sciences, 4*(1), 171–191.

Pressman, S. D., Cohen, S., Miller, G. E., Barkin, A., Rabin, B. S., & Treanor, J. J. (2005). Loneliness, social network size, and immune response to influenza vaccination in college freshmen. *Health Psychology, 24*(3), 297.

Reis, H. T., & Wheeler, L. (1991). Studying social interaction with the Rochester Interaction Record. *Advances in Experimental Social Psychology, 24*, 269–318.

Reynolds, T. (2007). Friendship networks, social capital and ethnic identity: Researching the perspectives of Caribbean young people in Britain. *Journal of Youth Studies, 10*(4), 383–398.

Sabin, E. P. (1993). Social relationships and mortality among the elderly. *Journal of Applied Gerontology, 12*(1), 44–60.

Sapadin, L. A. (1988). Friendship and gender: Perspectives of professional men and women. *Journal of Social and Personal Relationships, 5*(4), 387–403.

Scott, J. (2017). *Social network analysis* (4th ed.). Thousand Oaks, CA: Sage.

Simon, P. (1970). Bridge over troubled water. On *Simon & Garfunkel's Bridge over troubled water* [record]. United States: Columbia Records.

Spencer, L., & Paul, R. (2006). *Rethinking friendship: Hidden solidarities today*. Princeton, NJ: Princeton University Press.

Terhell, E. L., van Groenou, M. I. B., & Van Tilburg, T. (2007). Network contact changes in early and later postseparation years. *Social Networks, 29*(1), 11–24.

Thanakwang, K., & Soonthorndhada, K. (2011). Mechanisms by which social support networks influence healthy aging among Thai community-dwelling elderly. *Journal of Aging and Health, 23*, 1352–1378.

Uchino, B. N. (2004). *Social support and physical health: Understanding the health consequences of relationships*. New Haven, CT: Yale University Press.

Valkenburg, P. M., & Peter, J. (2011). Online communication among adolescents: An integrated model of its attraction, opportunities, and risks. *Journal of Adolescent Health, 48*(2), 121–127.

Van der Horst, M., & Coffé, H. (2012). How friendship network characteristics influence subjective well-being. *Social Indicators Research, 107*(3), 509–529.

Vernon, M. (2010). *The meaning of friendship*. New York: Palgrave Macmillan.

Visser, P. S., & Mirabile, R. R. (2004). Attitudes in the social context: The impact of social network composition on individual-level attitude strength. *Journal of Personality and Social Psychology, 87*(6), 779.

Wasserman, S., & Faust, K. (1994). *Social network analysis: Methods and applications* (Vol. 8). Cambridge: Cambridge University Press.

Watson, D., Clark, L. A., & Tellegen, A. (1988). Development and validation of brief measures of positive and negative affect: The PANAS scales. *Journal of Personality and Social Psychology, 54*(6), 1063–1070.

Weinstock, J. S., & Rothblum, E. D. (1996). What we can be together: Contemplating lesbians' friendships. In J. S. Weinstock & E. D. Rothblum (Eds.), *Lesbian friendships: For ourselves and each other* (pp. 3–30). New York, NY: New York University Press.

Weiss, L., & Lowenthal, M. F. (1975). Life-course perspectives on friendship. In L. Weiss & M. F. Lowenthal (Eds.), *Four stages of life* (pp. 48–61). San Francisco, CA: Jossey-Bass.

Wentland, J. J., & Reissing, E. D. (2011). Taking casual sex not too casually: Exploring definitions of casual sexual relationships. *Canadian Journal of Human Sexuality, 20*, 75–91.

Wentland, J. J., & Reissing, E. (2014). Casual sexual relationships: Identifying definitions for one night stands, booty calls, fuck buddies, and friends with benefits. *Canadian Journal of Human Sexuality, 23*(3), 167–177.

Weston, K. (1991). *Families we choose: Lesbians, gays, kinship*. New York: Columbia University Press.

Withers, B. (1972). Lean on me. On *Still Bill* [record]. Los Angeles: Sussex.

Wrzus, C., Hänel, M., Wagner, J., & Neyer, F. J. (2013). Social network changes and life events across the life span: A meta-analysis. *Psychological Bulletin, 139*(1), 53–80.

6

LEAVE WELL ENOUGH ALONE? THE COSTS AND BENEFITS OF SOLITUDE

Robert J. Coplan, John M. Zelenski, and Julie C. Bowker

Solitude is a normative human experience throughout the lifespan. The average time spent alone during waking hours displays an increasing trajectory across development, from about 15% in childhood, up to 30% in adulthood, and peaking at almost 50% among older adults (Larson, 1990). However, despite the ubiquitous nature of solitary experiences, being alone is often portrayed in Western society as a less than desirable state. Indeed, the notion that solitude has negative consequences for well-being could be considered *archetypal*, with a history that can be traced back thousands of years (Genesis 2:18, "And the LORD God said 'It is not good for the man to be alone.'").

The potential costs of solitude for well-being are underscored in contemporary psychological theories that emphasize the basic necessity of social affiliation (Baumeister & Leary, 1995) and the damaging effects of loneliness (Hawkley & Cacioppo, 2010). In support of this perspective, growing evidence suggests that the simple act of engaging in social interactions makes us happier (Epley & Schroeder, 2014). In contrast, excessive time spent alone has been linked with a wide range of social, emotional, and psychological difficulties across the lifespan (Coplan & Bowker, 2014).

Notwithstanding, there is also a long history of theoretical arguments espousing the potential benefits of solitude (e.g., Maslow, 1968; Merton, 1958; Storr, 1988; Winnicott, 1958). Such approaches highlight the importance of spending time alone for self-exploration and self-reflection (Goossens, 2014); creativity (Csikszentmihalyi, 1996); or stress reduction and self-renewal (Korpela & Staats, 2014). Time alone may be a particularly welcome respite for individuals with certain personality traits such as introversion (e.g., Hill & Argyle, 2001). However, despite these (often fervent) arguments, surprisingly little empirical research has demonstrated the positive impacts of solitude (Long & Averill, 2003).

In this chapter, we review theory and research pertaining to the links between solitude and well-being. We begin with an overview of the conceptual and methodological approaches to the psychological study of solitude. This is followed by a brief summary of the evidence demonstrating the various potential costs of spending excessive time alone. We then closely examine the supposition that solitude can also serve beneficial functions, including some promising areas worthy of future investigation. Our goal is to begin to untangle the so-called *paradox of solitude* (Galanaki, 2015; Larson, 1999). Although spending time alone is believed to serve self-enhancing functions, solitude is often experienced as undesirable and painful.

Are We Alone? Conceptual and Methodological Approaches

Given the ubiquitous nature of the experience of solitude, we might expect an extensive empirical literature directly examining the psychological costs and benefits of spending time alone. However, the relation between solitude and other psychological constructs has most often been studied *indirectly* (Coplan & Bowker, 2014). Moreover, one might also assume that solitude would be a relatively concrete construct to operationalize and assess (e.g., the state of being physically separated from others). However, we have found that there is considerable variation in how being alone is conceptualized and measured.

For example, Wilson and colleagues (2014) employed a very strict definition of solitude, characterized by both by a physical separation from others, as well as the lack of any accompanying activities. In a series of studies, participants were placed in a closed room by themselves for 15 minutes and instructed not to engage in any other contemporaneous activities (i.e., to spend the time "entertaining themselves with their thoughts", p. 75). Of note, participating college students sitting alone for 15 minutes under these circumstances overwhelmingly reported that they did not enjoy this experience! By way of contrast, other researchers ask participants to engage in a specific activity while in solitude, such as a taking walk alone in an arboretum (Berman, Jonides, & Kaplan, 2008). Notwithstanding, these conceptualizations of solitude share a common approach that considers the impact of momentary experiences of being alone (i.e., solitude as a *state*).

Time spent alone can also be considered and assessed as it regularly occurs over the course of peoples' daily routines and experiences (i.e., solitude as a *trait*). This is typically done via self-report, including diary reports and experience sampling, consolidated to represent *typical* behaviors. For example, Leary, Herbst, and McCrary (2003) instructed participants to retrospectively report the number of times over the last month that they participated in several different activities "by themselves" (p. 63) (see also Burger, 1995). Similarly, Chua and Koestner (2008) had participants describe the "percentage of waking time they spent in solitude per day" (p. 646). Using an experience sampling approach, Larson and Csikszentmihalyi (1978) used pagers to randomly signal adolescents to report if they were "alone, with friends or acquaintances, with strangers, other" (p. 680). More recently, van Roekel, Scholte, Engels, Goossens, and Verhagen (2015) utilized a smart phone app to conduct momentary assessments of whether participants were "alone or with others" (p. 912). Of note, in most (if not all) of these studies, participants were not provided with specific definitions of what was meant by terms such as *alone* or *by yourself.*

Finally, observational studies of children's and adolescents' typical social behaviors in naturalistic settings have also focused on the causes and consequences of *playing alone* in the presence of peers (see Coplan & Ooi, 2014). For example, Coplan, Ooi, & Rose-Krasnor (2015) observed elementary school-aged children on the playground during recess and lunch on multiple occasions over a 3-week period. *Solitary play* was coded when the "child is playing alone, typically at a distance of more than 3 feet from other children, and paying little or no attention to the group" (p. 634). In this context, peer interaction was clearly the norm, as children were observed to spend, on average, less than 10% of their time "alone" in the playground.

In all of these studies, solitude is generally conceived of as a *physical* separation from others. However, differences in operationalization and methodologies make it very difficult to compare results across studies. Moreover, many researchers view solitude as a broader phenomenon that encompasses more than just one's proximity to others. These ideas can be traced historically to philosophers such as Michel de Montaigne (1965), who in the 16th century described solitude as a state of natural personal experience that could be accomplished both alone and in the company of others. From this perspective, being alone refers to a *self-perceived* separation from others (Larson, 1990). For example, it is not uncommon for individuals to report feeling alone and lonely despite being in the physical presence of family or peers (van Roekel et al., 2015). In contrast, perceived social connectedness can reduce feelings of aloneness and loneliness among elderly individuals who live alone (Wethington & Pillemer, 2014). Coplan and Bowker (2017) describe this distinction as conceiving solitude as a *state of mind* rather than a *state of being.*

The notion of solitude as physical separation from others is also challenged by the rapidly changing contemporary technologies related to computer-mediated communication and social networking. Over 25 years ago, Larson (1990) foreshadowed such issues when he asserted that individuals watching television or listening to music by themselves should be considered alone (whereas individuals talking on the phone should not) because there are no demands or expectations for social responsiveness. Today, someone can be physically isolated from others but be in the *virtual* presence of thousands of other individuals, for example, while engaging in social interactions within the digital realm of multi-player on-line games (Quandt & Kröger, 2014). In addition, expectations that we must respond to electronic communications in real time on our smart phones can interrupt otherwise solitary activities (Kushlev, Proulx, & Dunn, 2016).

Another consideration relevant to our understanding of the potential consequences of solitude refers to peoples' putative *reasons* for spending time alone
(Coplan, Ooi, & Nocita, 2015). For example, Long, Seburn, Averill, and More
(2003) asked people about a range of reasons for solitude and found that three factors were most prominent. One reason was clearly unpleasant, labeled loneliness,
whereas the other two were both neutral to pleasant: inner directed (self-discovery,
inner peace) and outer directed (transcendent spirituality and intimacy—feeling
close though physically separated).

Researchers also emphasize the difference between internal and external
sources of solitude (Rubin & Mills, 1988). For example, solitude may be externally
imposed on people via social processes that force individuals to be alone because
they are rejected and ostracized by others. Not surprisingly, being actively isolated
by one's peers can cause substantive and long-lasting damage to psychological
health and well-being (Rubin, Bukowski, & Bowker, 2015; Williams & Nida,
2011). Alternatively, people can seek solitude because of internal factors such as
motivations, cognitions, and emotions. In the developmental psychology literature,
this process is referred to as *social withdrawal*, whereby individuals remove themselves from opportunities for social interactions in order to spend more time alone
(Rubin, Coplan, & Bowker, 2009).

However, a further set of distinctions can also be made. For example, some
individuals withdraw into solitude because they are seeking to avoid social situations. This may be because social interaction is a cause of social stress (e.g., *social
anxiety*, Hofmann, 2007) or because they fail to derive pleasure from social experiences (e.g., *social anhedonia*, Silvia & Kwapil, 2011). In such cases, it is difficult to
separate the potential negative implications of solitude from the potential negative implications of being anxious or depressed. Nevertheless, in such instances,
being alone can lead to increased loneliness, worry, and depression, which in turn
can to greater social withdrawal (Brown, Silvia, Myin-Germeys, & Kwapil, 2007).
Such avoidance of social situations also may evoke negative reactions from peers—
initiating a transactional process whereby social withdrawal and social ostracism
reinforce each other over time—further amplifying negative outcomes (Rubin
et al., 2009).

In contrast, some individuals seek solitude not to avoid social situations, but
because spending time alone tends to be a positive experience for them. This
motivation has been referred to in the extant literature as *preference for solitude*
(Burger, 1995), *affinity for aloneness* (Goossens, 2014), and *solitropic orientation*
(Leary et al., 2003), as is typically associated with personality traits such as introversion (Hill & Argyle, 2001) and (low) sociability (Cheek & Buss, 1981). It is
this *type* of solitude that is most often characterized as having an impact on well-
being that is either positive (Long & Averill, 2003) or, at worst, benign (Coplan
et al., 2015). However, spending too much time in solitude for *any reason* may
come at a cost.

The Benefits of Social Interaction

Perhaps the strongest set of arguments espousing the costs of solitude derives from theory and research on the benefits of *getting along well with others* for our well-being. Of note, these broad approaches do not typically invoke a direct causal link between solitude and ill-being. Instead, the focus is more on what people may be *missing out on* if they spend too much time alone. In this regard, we consider two exemplars of the benefits of social interaction across the lifespan.

The Importance of Peers

Considerable empirical evidence indicates that peer interactions are necessary for the development of children's social and cognitive skills and a healthy sense of self and others (Piaget, 1932; Rubin et al., 2015; Sullivan, 1953). For example, research shows that peers provide a unique social context to learn about interpersonal conflict and compromise and to develop negotiation as well as perspective-taking skills. By extension, children who interact less frequently with their peers may forego important learning opportunities and experiences that foster psychological health and well-being (Rubin et al., 2009). An underlying assumption that emerged from this area of research is that children and adolescents who seek solitude must be doing so because of some form of duress (e.g., negative experiences in the peer group, social anxiety).

Considerable empirical evidence documenting the costs of solitude has emerged in the study of childhood social withdrawal. As described earlier, social withdrawal refers to the process whereby children remove themselves from opportunities to engage socially with peers (Rubin et al., 2009). Throughout childhood and adolescence, social withdrawal is concurrently and predictively associated with a wide range of socio-emotional and psychological difficulties, particularly in terms of anxiety, depressive symptoms, and loneliness (e.g., Rubin, Chen, McDougall, Bowker, & McKinnon, 1995). Socially withdrawn children also struggle in their social interactions with peers, and are more likely than their more sociable counterparts to experience rejection, exclusion, and victimization (Gazelle & Ladd, 2003; Rubin, Wojslawowicz, Rose-Krasnor, Booth-LaForce, & Burgess, 2006). Taken together, this research has identified social withdrawal as one of the strongest risk factors for developmental psychopathology (Deater-Deckard, 2001; Rubin et al., 2009).

However, the vast majority of studies of childhood social withdrawal do not directly assess time spent alone, instead, focusing on different motivational and emotional contributions to socially withdrawn behaviors. For example, shy and socially anxious youth often withdraw from peers due to social fears and socio-evaluation concerns (Crozier, 1995). As we mentioned earlier, it is difficult to separate the impact on well-being of these negative feelings from the impact of the solitary behaviors that may accompany them. However, Coplan et al. (2013) recently reported that the childhood shyness (assessed as a self-reported personality trait) was uniquely associated with indices of socio-emotional difficulties even after controlling for observed socially withdrawn behaviors at school. In contrast, evidence suggests that children who choose to spend more time alone because they like it experience comparatively few psychosocial difficulties (e.g., Coplan, Prakash, O'Neil, & Armer, 2004). Some have argued that such *unsociable* children may face fewer negative social and emotional consequences (compared to their shy counterparts) because they are not actively rebutting social invitations from peers—and may thus engage in *just enough* social interaction to reap its positive benefits (Bowker & Raja, 2011).

Nevertheless, regardless of its underlying reasons, solitude-seeking behaviors during childhood and adolescence may elicit negative responses from others and thereby contribute to psychological distress associated with social withdrawal because these behaviors are judged by others to be atypical and in sharp contrast to social norms and expectations for social interactions and relationship and group involvement (Chen, 2010). Indeed, negative psychosocial costs of social withdrawal during childhood and adolescence have been found not only in the aforementioned studies conducted in Western societies, such as the United States and Canada (e.g., Rubin et al., 1995), but also in studies in non-Western societies, including China (Chen, Cen, Li, & He, 2005); India (Bowker & Raja, 2011); and Turkey (Bayram Özdemir, Cheah, & Coplan, 2015). This supports the notion that the need to socially engage with peers may be universal.

Happier Together

Also contrary to the research on the costs of solitude is theory and research suggesting that social interaction is typically pleasant and likely essential to psychological health. For example, among the short list of widely purported universal basic needs is the need to belong (Baumeister & Leary, 1995) or the need for relatedness (Ryan & Deci, 2000). People who meet these needs and feel close to others typically thrive, whereas loneliness and ostracism are (almost by definition) unpleasant and linked with poor health and maladaptive behaviors (Holt-Lunstad, Smith, Baker, Harris, & Stephenson, 2015; Williams & Nida, 2011). The universal importance of social connection is further underscored in taxonomies of values. In contrast to basic needs, values are, by definition, good, even while allowing for individual and cultural differences in their priority. For example, benevolence and universalism (i.e., social justice/equality) (Bardi & Schwartz, 2003); care and loyalty (Graham et al., 2011); humanity; and justice virtues (Peterson & Seligman, 2004) all underscore the importance of positive interpersonal relationships. Some theorists view positive social relationships as hallmarks of psychological health (Ryff, 1989), and people who are dispositionally sociable report higher levels of well-being across many indicators (Steel, Schmidt, & Shultz, 2008).

It may be that our close relationships *stick with us* psychologically, so that intermittent moments of solitude do not threaten the benefits that these relationships provide. For example, according to attachment theory, secure attachments are associated with increased comfort and confidence in taking risks and exploring (Feeney & Collins, 2014). The mental model of a secure base eases the need for support seeking, potentially facilitating productive moments of solitude. Being alone need not disrupt a general sense of connection. For example, experience sampling studies suggest that telling close others about the positive experiences we had without them can further boost positive moods (Gable, Reis, Impett, & Asher, 2004).

Beyond our close relationships, the moments we spend with others, especially in conversation, seem better on average than the moments we spend alone. For example, moments of fun are experienced as more fun if other people are present; this is especially true with close others, but also with strangers (Reis, O'Keefe, & Lane, 2016). In contrast, a study using the day reconstruction time sampling method found that people rated the periods when they were alone as least positive, even compared to paid work (including talking with clients and bosses), housework, and similar to the notoriously unpleasant commuting (Kahneman, Krueger, Schkade, Schwarz, & Stone, 2004). In another study using experience sampling, it was found that periods of solitude were associated with lower momentary positive affect and higher momentary negative affect (along with elevated cortisol levels—a common physiological indicator of stress) (Matias Nicolson, & Freire, 2011).

Most of these studies are correlational, so causal direction is ambiguous. In addition, positive moods may facilitate and negative moods may inhibit the desire to socialize (Whelan & Zelenski, 2012). Nonetheless, experimental manipulations support both causal directions. For example, being randomly assigned to chat with strangers on public transportation, in the psychology lab, or to a barista are all associated with more positive emotions than doing the same activities without engaging in social interaction (Epley & Schroeder, 2014; Sandstrom & Dunn, 2013; Zelenski et al., 2013), and this is true of dispositional introverts and extraverts alike. Moreover, people tend to underestimate how enjoyable socializing with non-close others will be.

Of course, social interactions can also carry some risks of aversive experiences (e.g., conflict, anxiety, shame, exclusion, and others), but overall, being with others appears to be a generally pleasant and important experience. To the extent that a good life is the sum of many good moments (see Fleeson, 2001), social engagement seems key to a good life. Yet, despite the strength of evidence for the positive benefits of socializing, it remains possible to have too much of a good thing. As with other basic pleasures, such as food or sex, constant engagement is not ideal. For example, although extensive bouts of social interaction are associated with immediate gains in positive moods, they may also carry the delayed cost of later exhaustion (Leikas & Ilmarinen, 2017).

Making the Case(s) for the Benefits of Solitude

If we accept the conclusion that social interaction is beneficial for people's well-being, a logical extension could be that solitude is *not*. However, as mentioned previously, it has also long been argued that solitude can serve *positive* functions (e.g., de Montaigne, 1965). Moreover, the supposition that time spent alone can have concrete benefits for our health and well-being remains prevalent in contemporary popular essays (e.g., Achor, 2010; Cain, 2012). However, direct empirical evidence of the specific and unique benefits of solitude remains elusive (Coplan & Bowker, 2014). In the following sections, we take a closer look at (in our view) the two most common assertions regarding the potential benefits of solitude.

Solitude Is Restorative

Perhaps the most prevalent positive portrayal of solitude is as a *restorative haven* (Long et al., 2003). There are many potential explanations for this characterization. For example, simply doing things with other people may increase the intensity of people's experiences. This idea can be traced back to Zajonc's (1965) idea of *social facilitation*, and has recently re-emerged in slightly different forms. Shteynberg (2015) has proposed *shared attention* as a mechanism that often operates when we are doing things with other people. Manipulating alone versus shared activities produced more intense moods, stronger motivations, better memory, and more extreme judgments. For example, tasting pleasant or unpleasant chocolates with an experimenter produced better and worse ratings of flavor, respectively, than did tasting alone (Boothby, Clark, & Bargh, 2014). Extrapolating from these findings, it can be postulated that being alone would serve to *reduce* the intensity of our emotional experiences. There is at least some initial preliminary support for this notion. Nguyen, Ryan, and Deci (2017) observed decreases in high-arousal emotions (both pleasant and unpleasant) when participants spent time in solitude.

Other less direct evidence can be found in the experiences and activities that we may engage in when alone. For example, solitude and restoration are commonly linked in the context of *nature*. People identify nature as a frequent place to experience the more positive forms of solitude (e.g., spirituality, inner peace, self-discovery; Long et al., 2003). Overall, people rate time spent in, and even images of, natural environments as more pleasant than built or urban environments (MacKerron & Mourato, 2013; McMahan & Estes, 2015). Other potential benefits of being in nature include improved physical health (e.g., lower blood pressure, lower cholesterol; see Maller, Townsend, Pryor, Brown, & St Leger, 2005) and psychological well-being (e.g., mindfulness, vitality, reduced stress; see Capaldi, Passmore, Nisbet, Zelenski, & Dopko, 2015).

According to *attention restoration theory* (Kaplan, 1995), periods of sustained, focused attention and environments that demand attentional resources (e.g., making your way down a busy street) eventually produce fatigue and irritability. To recover, people require environments that allow for a break and more *soft fascina-tion*, or for attention to wander more naturally. Intense social interaction likely falls into the category of fatiguing activities, rather than restorative, and solitude the opposite. Yet most research on this topic has focused on natural environments and the soft fascination they provide. For example, one study fatigued people with a difficult cognitive task and then had them take a walk (alone) either through the city or through an arboretum (Berman et al., 2008). The walks in nature produced better performance on a directed attention task following the walks.

Much of this research does not focus on solitary experiences in nature *per se*, particularly as an explicit comparison with nature experiences in the company of others. That said, a careful review of the research showed that many instances of the beneficial effects of being in nature were found with solitary participants (Korpela & Staats, 2014). Moreover, there are some studies of *perceived* restor-ativeness (i.e., based on self-reports, as opposed to direct tests of attention and other cognitive tasks) where researchers have tried to identify the most beneficial features of being in nature by asking about or experimentally manipulating the presence of other people in natural environments. However, the findings are com-plex and depend on the location, state of fatigue, and other factors (Korpela & Staats, 2014). One the one hand, being with others in nature, especially close oth-ers, can alleviate safety concerns and provide an opportunity to share experiences, such as a cute creature or beautiful plant. On the other hand, the presence of oth-ers can distract from the experience of nature and thwart attention restoration by creating attentional demands (e.g., Staats & Hartig, 2004; Staats, Van Gemerden, & Hartig, 2010). Although studies in nature do not provide ironclad evidence for the specific and unique benefits of solitude, they do offer many reasons to think the combination of nature and solitude is often restorative and a potential source of psychological well-being.

Solitude May Be Particularly Good for Introverts

Another common assertion is that some people may be more prone than others to experience benefits in solitude. For example, from a self-determination theory perspective (Ryan & Deci, 2000), we would expect people who are autonomously motivated to spend time alone to benefit from such experiences more so than those who feel that they are forced to spend time alone. In support of this notion, Chua and Koestner (2008) reported that time spent alone was associated with negative outcomes among participants with lower autonomous motivation for solitude but not among those with higher autonomous motivation. Similarly, Leung (2015) found that as compared to their more sociable counterparts, indi-viduals with a higher general preference for solitude perceived spending time alone engaged with digital media (i.e., using a tablet) as more stress-reducing. These findings underscore the idea that the benefits of solitude may be affected by individual differences such as social motivations.

Personality may also matter. For example, *introversion* correlates positively with both self-reported preferences for solitude and actual time spent alone (Zelenski, Sobocko, & Whelan, 2014). Introverts also report lower subjective well-being than extraverts (Steel et al., 2008). This raises the question of whether solitude is beneficial for introverts or may in fact be making them unhappy. Considerable theory and research has attempted to unpack the ambiguous correlations. For example, Little (2016) articulated his notion of restorative niches with a personal story about once hiding in the bathroom after he completed delivering an exuberant public lecture. According to Little (2008), people may act out of character to pursue important goals; these efforts are productive and rewarding but also necessitate some recovery afterwards. From this perspective, solitude would be assumed to represent as a restorative niche for introverts (i.e., required after behaving in extraverted ways).

Although this notion has intuitive appeal, data have not really been supportive. Overall, nearly everyone ultimately reports enjoying moments of extraverted behavior, and there is little evidence of consequent fatigue or other costs for introverts (Fleeson & Gallagher, 2009; Zelenski, Santoro, & Whelan, 2012). However, as we mentioned previously, even in the case of socializing, it may be possible for people to experience too much of a good thing. Leikas and Ilmarinen (2017) recently conducted an experience sampling study tracking sociable and extraverted behavior in daily life. In the moment (i.e., while it was occurring), socializing was associated with pleasant moods (as in previous studies). However, 3 hours after intense social interactions, both extraverts and introverts tended to report more fatigue. It may be, therefore, that *everyone* benefits from some recovery time in solitude following social interactions. This remains a question for future research.

Still unanswered is the question of whether introverts' greater time in solitude specifically diminishes or enhances their subjective well-being. On one hand, extraverted behavior produces positive emotions, which may explain why extraverts are generally happier than introverts (Wilt, Noftle, Fleeson, & Spain, 2012). However, extraverted *behavior* is more than just socializing, as it can also encompass novelty seeking, higher activity level, and the pursuit of adventure. For example, one can *act* extraverted on a solo mountain bike run. Studies that track social activity more specifically find that it accounts for less of the link between extraversion and positive emotions (Lucas, Le, & Dyrenforth, 2008). Indeed, researchers do not widely consider the causal core of extraversion to be the propensity to socialize. Rather, the manifestation of sociability among extraverts is more typically viewed as a consequence of a more general reward sensitivity (Carver, Sutton, & Scheier, 2000). When the socialness and pleasantness of activities is carefully parsed, extraverts are more likely to choose things that are pleasant rather than social (Lucas & Diener, 2001).

Overall, extraverts seem to have a higher baseline of positive affect and are more attuned to pursuing rewards. In addition, extraverts report more happiness than introverts across contexts, even when they are alone (Pavot, Diener, & Fujita, 1990).

Thus, although introverts might be able to boost their moods in the moment with more outgoing behavior (like extraverts), there is not clear evidence to suggest that the chronic differences in well-being between introverts and extraverts are specifically accounted for by co-occurring differences of their experiences of solitude.

A Call to Action: Promising Places to Further Explore the Benefits of Solitude

As we have seen, there is little direct empirical evidence in support of even the most common assertions regarding the benefits of solitude. In this section, we briefly outline some potentially promising areas of future research that may help to provide additional (and more compelling) evidence.

Alone Across the Lifespan

One idea worthy of future exploration is the possibility that the benefits of solitude differ at different points in our development. For example, it has been argued that solitary play in early childhood promotes concentration, mastery, and autonomy (Katz & Buchholz, 1999), whereas time alone in adolescence facilitates identity formation (Goossens, 2014) and reduces stress (Larson, 1990). A developmental approach also suggests that time in solitude could prove particularly useful for coping with major life role transitions at different states of adulthood (e.g., getting married, becoming a parent). For example, the transition to motherhood appears to be especially challenging to the psychological health of many women (Lee & Gramotnev, 2007). However, researchers have suggested that this is not only to due to feelings of aloneness and lack of perceived support (among other factors), but also perhaps to the *lack* of solitude and *me-time* (Barclay, Everitt, Rogan, Schmied, & Wyllie, 1997; Bialeschki & Michener, 1994). Thus, some solitary time could prove helpful for new mothers (and likely fathers too).

Alone in the Now

Future investigations should also more carefully consider the benefits of solitary experiences involving *mindfulness* and *meditation* (Salmon & Matarese, 2014). A growing body of research supports the efficacy of mindful-based interventions (which promote a sense of psychological solitude and meditation) for individuals with internalizing problems (e.g., anxiety, depression), substance-use disorders, and physical illnesses such as cancer (e.g., Cash et al., 2015; Tamagawa, Speca, Stephen, & Carlson, 2015). There is also growing evidence to suggest that mindfulness interventions produce benefits in non-clinical populations (e.g., Davidson et al., 2003). One reason why these interventions are likely helpful across many contexts is because they help to reduce stress. Indeed, some evidence also supports the utility of mindfulness-based programs in *preventing* psychological problems and building resilience in individuals of all ages (Greenberg & Harris, 2012). Additional work is needed to support the beneficial outcomes of such programs and to better undercover the specific mechanisms of influence.

Creatively Alone

A longstanding notion is that solitude is essential for the enhancement of creativity (e.g., Thoreau, 1854). For example, Csikszentmihalyi (1996) argued that spending time alone in practice is a requirement the optimal development of musical and artistic skills. Long and Averill (2003) stated that "the link between creativity and solitude is so ubiquitous that it has become almost a cliché: the scientist alone in a laboratory, the writer in a cabin in the woods, or the painter in a bare studio" (p. 25). Despite this broad assertion, experimental evidence of the specific benefits of solitude for creativity remains scarce, although recent empirical work demonstrates the value of solitude in the creation of original ideas and the solving of complex problems. For example, Korde and Paulus (2017) compared the effects of different combinations and orders of social conditions (alone vs. group) on the efficiency of ideation (i.e., brainstorming). Results indicated that people in a *hybrid* condition that alternated solitary and group brainstorming sessions generated the most new ideas. The authors suggested that generating ideas with others may help people generate ideas later when they are alone.

Alone in Our (Final) Thoughts

Solitude has a long history of philosophical speculation and theory—but a comparatively short history of empirical study. As research examining the psychological implications of solitude for well-being continues moves forward, there are a number of unresolved issues and questions that merit increased attention.

First, the study of solitude would benefit immensely from a more clearly delineated conceptual framework (i.e., definitions, nomenclature, underlying mechanism) to guide research questions and methodologies. In this regard, the notion of *perceived* solitude (Larson, 1990) seems increasingly relevant in contemporary society where being physical separated from others no longer implies a lack of social connectedness. Indeed, Larson's (1990) original conceptualization of solitude draws upon specific aspects of *impression management theory* (e.g., Goffman, 1971), which suggests that the boundaries of being alone and with others are defined by expectations for social communication (e.g., greetings and salutations). This approach also seems applicable to *virtual* contexts and can thus provide a broad framework for bringing the study of solitude into the digital age. Importantly, subjectively perceiving oneself as being alone may turn out to be a critical prerequisite for individuals to experience the potential benefits of solitude. But by extension, a *false* sense of solitude (i.e., when interruptions can and do break it frequently) may also serve to reduce any positive effects.

This leads us to a seemingly critical unanswered question in understanding the links between solitude and well-being is: What is the *active ingredient* of solitude? Through experimental manipulation, we could directly compare the effects of various *components* of solitude experiences (e.g., physical separation from others, freedom from external distractions, privacy, perceived removal of social demands, etc.). Relatedly, do different behaviors or activities (e.g., being in nature, meditating, surfing the net, etc.) impact our well-being differently when we engage in them alone versus with others?

Another potentially important issue is the effect of *dosage* (i.e., frequency of solitude). Larson (1990) found that adolescents who spend a moderate amount time in solitude reported lower levels of psychological distress relative to adolescents who experienced the least or the most time alone. This suggests that the link between solitude and well-being might follow the Yerkes-Dodson law (Yerkes & Dodson, 1908), which dictates that performance increases with levels of arousal— but only to a certain point. It can be further speculated that, although there may be wide variation among individuals in terms of *optimal* levels of solitude, at least some solitude is probably good for everyone. Indeed, among adolescents, *aversion to aloneness* has been negatively associated with self-esteem and positively associated with depression (Teppers, Luyckx, Vanhalst, Klimstra, & Goossens, 2014).

To further complicate matters, the active ingredients of solitude and the impact of dosage may vary not only across periods of development but also across cultures. Despite the apparent universality of the need to belong, there are wide cultural differences in attitudes, beliefs, and values about characteristics, behaviors, and constructs related to solitude (Chen, 2010). For example, preferring to play alone at school may be viewed benignly in Western cultures because it is viewed as an expression of personal choice and individualism, independence, and self-reliance (e.g., Coplan et al., 2015). In contrast, the same behavior in mainland China has been demonstrated to evoke rebuke (e.g., Liu et al., 2015), perhaps because it is considered as violating cultural expectations regarding group cohesion and collectivism.

Moving forward, we would speculate that the effects of solitude on our well-being might be best thought of as similar to spending time in direct *sunlight*. Regularly experiencing at least some sunlight is probably good for all of us (e.g., source of vitamin D), and particularly important to the well-being of some of us (e.g., Seasonal Affective Disorder). There are individual differences in the optimal time that we should spend in the sun (e.g., some people get sunburned more easily than others), but chronic overexposure puts all of us at increased risk for substantive long-term negative consequences (e.g., melanoma).

References

Achor, S. (2010). *The happiness advantage: The seven principles of positive psychology that fuel success and performance at work.* New York: Crown Publishers.

Barclay, L., Everitt, L., Rogan, F., Schmied, V., & Wyllie, A. (1997). Becoming a mother—an analysis of women's experience of early motherhood. *Journal of Advanced Nursing, 25,* 719–728.

Bardi, A., & Schwartz, S. H. (2003). Values and behavior: Strength and structure of relations. *Personality and Social Psychology Bulletin, 29,* 1207–1220.

Baumeister, R. F., & Leary, M. R. (1995). The need to belong: Desire for interpersonal attachments as a fundamental human motivation. *Psychological Bulletin, 117,* 497–529.

Bayram Özdemir, S., Cheah, C. S., & Coplan, R. J. (2015). Conceptualization and assessment of multiple forms of social withdrawal in Turkey. *Social Development, 24,* 142–165.

Berman, M. G., Jonides, J., & Kaplan, S. (2008). The cognitive benefits of interacting with nature. *Psychological Science, 19,* 1207–1212.

Bialeschki, M. D., & Michener, S. (1994). Re-entering leisure: Transition within the role of motherhood. *Journal of Leisure Research, 26,* 57.

Boothby, E. J., Clark, M. S., & Bargh, J. A. (2014). Shared experiences are amplified. *Psychological Science, 25,* 2209–2216.

Bowker, J. C., & Raja, R. (2011). Social withdrawal subtypes during early adolescence in India. *Journal of Abnormal Child Psychology, 39*(2), 201–212.

Brown, L. H., Silvia, P. J., Myin-Germeys, I., & Kwapil, T. R. (2007). When the need to belong goes wrong: The expression of social anhedonia and social anxiety in daily life. *Psychological Science, 18,* 778–782.

Burger, J. M. (1995). Individual differences in preference for solitude. *Journal of Research in Personality, 29,* 85–108.

Cain, S. (2012). *Quiet: The power of introverts in a world that can't stop talking.* New York: Crown Publishers.

Capaldi, C. A., Passmore, H. A., Nisbet, E. K., Zelenski, J. M., & Dopko, R. L. (2015). Flourishing in nature: A review of the benefits of connecting with nature and its application as a wellbeing intervention. *International Journal of Wellbeing, 5,* 1–16.

Carver, C. S., Sutton, S. K., & Scheier, M. F. (2000). Action, emotion, and personality: Emerging conceptual integration. *Personality and Social Psychology Bulletin, 26,* 741–751.

Cash, E., Salmon, P., Weissbecker, I., Rebholz, W. N., Bayley-Veloso, R., Zimmaro, L. A., Floyd, A., Dedert, E., & Sephton, S. E. (2015). Mindfulness meditation alleviates fibromyalgia symptoms in women: Results from a randomized clinical trial. *Annuals of Behavioral Medicine, 49,* 319–330. doi: 10.1007/s12160-014-9665-0

Cheek, J. M., & Buss, H. A. (1981). Shyness and sociability. *Journal of Personality and Social Psychology, 41,* 330–339.

Chen, X. (2010). Shyness-inhibition in childhood and adolescence: A cross-cultural perspective. In K. H. Rubin & R. J. Coplan (Eds.), *The development of shyness and social withdrawal* (pp. 213–235). New York: Guilford.

Chen, X., Cen, G., Li, D., & He, Y. (2005). Social functioning and adjustment in Chinese children: The imprint of historical time. *Child Development, 76,* 182–195.

Chua, S. N., & Koestner, R. (2008). A self-determination theory perspective on the role of autonomy in solitary behavior. *The Journal of Social Psychology, 148,* 645–648.

Coplan, R. J., & Bowker, J. C. (2014). *The handbook of solitude: Psychological perspectives on social isolation, social withdrawal, and being alone.* New York: Wiley-Blackwell.

Coplan, R. J., & Bowker, J. C. (2017). Should we be left alone? Psychological perspectives on the implications of seeking solitude. In I. Bergmann & S. Hippler (Eds.), *Cultures of solitude: Loneliness—limitation—liberation* (pp. 287–302). Bern: Peter Lang.

Coplan, R. J., & Ooi, L. L. (2014). The causes and consequences of playing alone in childhood. In R. Coplan & J. C. Bowker (Eds.), *The handbook of solitude: Psychological perspectives on social isolation, social withdrawal, and the experience of being alone* (pp. 111–128). New York: Wiley-Blackwell.

Coplan, R. J., Ooi, L. L., & Nocita, G. (2015). When one is company and two is a crowd: Why some children prefer solitude. *Child Development Perspectives, 9*, 133–137.

Coplan, R. J., Ooi, L. L., & Rose-Krasnor, L. (2015). Naturalistic observations of schoolyard social participation: Marker variables for socio-emotional functioning in early adolescence. *Journal of Early Adolescence, 35*, 628–650.

Coplan, R. J., Prakash, K., O'Neil, K., & Armer, M. (2004). Do you "want" to play? Distinguishing between conflicted shyness and social disinterest in early childhood. *Developmental Psychology, 40*(2), 244.

Coplan, R. J., Rose-Krasnor, L., Weeks, M., Kingsbury, A., Kingsbury, M., & Bullock, A. (2013). Alone is a crowd: Social motivations, social withdrawal, and socio-emotional functioning in later childhood. *Developmental Psychology, 49*, 861–875.

Crozier, W. (1995). Shyness and self-esteem in middle childhood. *British Journal of Educational Psychology, 65*(1), 85–95.

Csikszentmihalyi, M. (1996). *Creativity: Flow and the psychology of discovery and invention.* New York: Harper Collins.

Davidson, R. J., Kabat-Zinn, J., Schumacher, J., Rosenkranz, M., Muller, D., Santorelli, S. F., . . . Sheridan, J. F. (2003). Alterations in brain and immune function produced by mindfulness meditation. *Psychosomatic Medicine, 65*, 564–570.

Deater-Deckard, K. (2001). Annotation: Recent research examining the role of peer relationships in the development of psychopathology. *Journal of Child Psychology and Psychiatry, 42*, 565–579.

Epley, N., & Schroeder, J. (2014). Mistakenly seeking solitude. *Journal of Experimental Psychology: General, 143*, 1980–1999.

Feeney, B. C., & Collins, N. L. (2014). A new look at social support: A theoretical perspective on thriving through relationships. *Personality and Social Psychology Review, 19*, 113–147.

Fleeson, W. (2001). Toward a structure-and process-integrated view of personality: Traits as density distributions of states. *Journal of Personality and Social Psychology, 80*, 1011–1027.

Fleeson, W., & Gallagher, P. (2009). The implications of Big Five standing for the distribution of trait manifestation in behavior: Fifteen experience-sampling studies and a meta-analysis. *Journal of Personality and Social Psychology, 97*, 1097–1114.

Gable, S. L., Reis, H. T., Impett, E. A., & Asher, E. R. (2004). What do you do when things go right? The intrapersonal and interpersonal benefits of sharing positive events. *Journal of Personality and Social Psychology, 87*, 228–245.

Galanaki, E. P. (2015). Solitude as a state of positive aloneness in childhood and adolescence. In C. J. Kowalski, J. P. Cangemi, & A. Rokach (Eds.), *Loneliness in life: Education, business, and society* (pp. 168–190). Dubuque, IA: McGraw Hill.

Gazelle, H., & Ladd, G. W. (2003). Anxious solitude and peer exclusion: A diathesis-stress model of internalizing trajectories in childhood. *Child Development, 74*, 257–278.

Goffman, E. (1971). *Relations in public: Microstudies of the public order.* New York: Harper and Row.

Goossens, L. (2014). Affinity for aloneness and preference for solitude in childhood: Linking two research traditions. In R. J. Coplan & J. Bowker (Eds.), *The handbook of solitude:*

Psychological perspectives on social isolation, social withdrawal, and being alone (pp. 150–166). New York: Wiley-Blackwell.

Graham, J., Nosek, B. A., Haidt, J., Iyer, R., Koleva, S., & Ditto, P. H. (2011). Mapping the moral domain. *Journal of Personality and Social Psychology, 101,* 366–385.

Greenberg, M. T., & Harris, A. R. (2012). Nurturing mindfulness in children and youth: Current state of research. *Child Development Perspectives, 6*(2), 161–166.

Hawkley, L. S., & Cacioppo, J. T. (2010). Loneliness matters: A theoretical and empirical review of consequences and mechanisms. *Annals of Behavioral Medicine, 40,* 218–227.

Hills, P., & Argyle, M. (2001). Happiness, introversion-extraversion and happy introverts. *Personality and Individual Differences, 30,* 595–608.

Hofmann, S. G. (2007). Cognitive factors that maintain social anxiety disorder: A comprehensive model and its treatment implications. *Cognitive Behavior Therapy, 36,* 193–209.

Holt-Lunstad, J., Smith, T. B., Baker, M., Harris, T., & Stephenson, D. (2015). Loneliness and social isolation as risk factors for mortality a meta-analytic review. *Perspectives on Psychological Science, 10,* 227–237.

Kahneman, D., Krueger, A. B., Schkade, D. A., Schwarz, N., & Stone, A. A. (2004). A survey method for characterizing daily life experience: The day reconstruction method. *Science, 306,* 1776–1780.

Kaplan, S. (1995). The restorative benefits of nature: Toward an integrative framework. *Journal of Environmental Psychology, 15,* 169–182.

Katz, J. C., & Buchholz, E. S. (1999). "I did it myself": The necessity of solo play for preschoolers. *Early Child Development and Care, 155,* 39–50.

Korde, R., & Paulus, P. B. (2017). Alternating individual and group idea generation: Finding elusive certainty. *Journal of Experimental Social Psychology, 70,* 177–190.

Korpela, K., & Staats, H. (2014). The restorative qualities of being alone with nature. In R. J. Coplan & J. C. Bowker (Eds.), *The handbook of solitude: Psychological perspectives on social isolation, social withdrawal, and being alone* (pp. 351–367). Chichester, UK: Wiley-Blackwell.

Kushlev, K., Proulx, J., & Dunn, E. W. (2016, May). Silence your phones: Smartphone notifications increase inattention and hyperactivity symptoms. In *Proceedings of the 2016 CHI Conference on Human Factors in Computing Systems* (pp. 1011–1020). New York: ACM.

Larson, R. W. (1990). The solitary side of life: An examination of the time people spend alone from childhood to old age. *Developmental Review, 10,* 155–183.

Larson, R. W. (1999). The uses of loneliness in adolescence. In K. J. Rotenberg & S. Hymel (Eds.), *Loneliness in childhood and adolescence* (pp. 244–262). New York, NY: Cambridge University Press.

Larson, R. W., & Csikszentmihalyi, M. (1978). Experiential correlates of time alone in adolescence. *Journal of Personality, 46,* 677–693.

Leary, M. R., Herbst, K. C., & McCrary, F. (2003). Finding pleasure in solitary activities: Desire for aloneness or disinterest in social contact? *Personality and Individual Differences, 35,* 59–68.

Lee, C., & Gramotnev, H. (2007). Life transitions and mental health in a national cohort of young Australian women. *Developmental Psychology, 43,* 877.

Leikas, S., & Ilmarinen, V. J. (2017). Happy now, tired later? Extraverted and conscientious behavior are related to immediate mood gains, but to later fatigue. *Journal of Personality, 85,* 603–615.

Leung, L. (2015). Using tablet in solitude for stress reduction: An examination of desire for aloneness, leisure boredom, tablet activities, and location of use. *Computers in Human Behavior, 48*, 382–391.

Little, B. R. (2008). Personal projects and free traits: Personality and motivation reconsidered. *Social and Personality Psychology Compass, 2*, 1235–1254.

Little, B. R. (2016). *Brian Little: Who are you really? The puzzle of personality.* Retrieved from www.ted.com/talks/brian_little_who_are_you_really_the_puzzle_of_personality

Liu, J., Chen, X., Coplan, R. J., Ding, X., Zarbatany, L., & Ellis, W. (2015). Shyness and unsociability and their relations with adjustment in Chinese and Canadian children. *Journal of Cross-Cultural Psychology, 46*, 371–386.

Long, C. R., & Averill, J. R. (2003). Solitude: An exploration of benefits of being alone. *Journal for the Theory of Social Behavior, 33*, 21–44.

Long, C. R., Seburn, M., Averill, J. R., & More, T. A. (2003). Solitude experiences: Varieties, settings, and individual differences. *Personality and Social Psychology Bulletin, 29*, 578–583.

Lucas, R. E., & Diener, E. (2001). Understanding extraverts' enjoyment of social situations: The importance of pleasantness. *Journal of Personality and Social Psychology, 81*, 343–356.

Lucas, R. E., Le, K., & Dyrenforth, P. S. (2008). Explaining the extraversion/ positive affect: Sociability cannot account for extraverts' greater happiness. *Journal of Personality, 76*, 385–414.

MacKerron, G., & Mourato, S. (2013). Happiness is greater in natural environments. *Global Environmental Change, 23*, 992–1000.

Maller, C., Townsend, M., Pryor, A., Brown, P., & St Leger, L. (2005). Healthy nature healthy people: Contact with nature as an upstream health promotion intervention for populations. *Health Promotion International, 21*, 45–54.

Maslow, A. H. (1968). *Toward a psychology of being.* New York: Van Nostrand.

Matias, G. P., Nicolson, N. A., & Freire, T. (2011). Solitude and cortisol: Associations with state and trait affect in daily life. *Biological Psychology, 86*, 314–319.

McMahan, E. A., & Estes, D. (2015). The effect of contact with natural environments on positive and negative affect: A meta-analysis. *The Journal of Positive Psychology, 10*, 507–519.

Merton, T. (1958). *Thoughts in solitude.* New York: Farrar, Straus, and Giroux.

Montaigne, M. (1965). Of solitude. In D. M. Frame (Trans.), *The complete essays of Michel de Montaigne* (pp. 174–183). Stanford, CA: Stanford University Press.

Nguyen, T. T., Ryan, R. M., & Deci, E. L. (2017, January). *Differentiated effects of solitude on affect activation and affect valence.* Poster presented at the Society for Personality and Social Psychology, San Antonio, TX.

Pavot, W., Diener, E., & Fujita, F. (1990). Extraversion and happiness. *Personality and Individual Differences, 11*(12), 1299–1306.

Peterson, C., & Seligman, M. E. P. (2004). *Character strengths and virtues: A handbook and classification.* Oxford: Oxford University Press and American Psychological Association.

Piaget, J. (1932). *The Moral Judgment of the Child.* New York: Harcourt, Brace Jovanovich.

Quandt, T., & Kröger, S. (2014). *Multiplayer: The social aspects of digital gaming.* New York: Routledge.

Reis, H. T., O'Keefe, S. D., & Lane, R. D. (2016). Fun is more fun when others are involved. *The Journal of Positive Psychology, 11*, 547–557.

Rubin, K. H., Bukowski, W. M., & Bowker, J. C. (2015). Children in peer groups. In R. M. Lerner (Series Ed.), M. H. Bornstein & T. Leventhal (Vol. Eds.), *Handbook of child psychology and developmental science, vol. 4: Ecological settings and processes in developmental systems* (7th ed., pp. 175–222). New York: Wiley-Blackwell.

Rubin, K. H., Chen, X., McDougall, P., Bowker, A., & McKinnon, J. (1995). The waterloo longitudinal project: Predicting internalizing and externalizing problems in adolescence. *Development and Psychopathology, 7*(4), 751–764.

Rubin, K. H., Coplan, R. J., & Bowker, J. C. (2009). Social withdrawal in childhood. *The Annual Review of Psychology, 60*, 141–171.

Rubin, K. H., & Mills, R. S. (1988). The many faces of social isolation in childhood. *Journal of Consulting and Clinical Psychology, 56*, 916–924.

Rubin, K. H., Wojslawowicz, J. C., Rose-Krasnor, L., Booth-LaForce, C., & Burgess, K. B. (2006). The best friendships of shy/withdrawn children: Prevalence, stability, and relationship quality. *Journal of Abnormal Child Psychology, 34*(2), 139–153.

Ryan, R. M., & Deci, E. L. (2000). Self-determination theory and the facilitation of intrinsic motivation, social development, and well-being. *American Psychologist, 55*, 68–78.

Ryff, C. D. (1989). Happiness is everything, or is it? Explorations on the meaning of psychological well-being. *Journal of Personality and Social Psychology, 57*, 1069–1081.

Salmon, P., & Matarese, S. (2014). Mindfulness meditation: Seeking solitude in community. In R. J. Coplan & J. C. Bowker (Eds.), *The handbook of solitude: Psychological perspectives on social isolation, social withdrawal, and being alone* (pp. 335–350). New York: Wiley-Blackwell.

Sandstrom, G. M., & Dunn, E. W. (2013). Is efficiency overrated? Minimal social interactions lead to belonging and positive affect. *Social Psychological and Personality Science, 5*, 437–442.

Shteynberg, G. (2015). Shared attention. *Perspectives on Psychological Science, 10*(5), 579–590.

Silvia, P. J., & Kwapil, T. R. (2011). Aberrant asociality: How individual differences in social anhedonia illuminate the need to belong. *Journal of Personality, 79*, 1315–1332.

Staats, H., & Hartig, T. (2004). Alone or with a friend: A social context for psychological restoration and environmental preferences. *Journal of Environmental Psychology, 24*, 199–211.

Staats, H., Van Gemerden, E., & Hartig, T. (2010). Preference for restorative situations: Interactive effects of attentional state, activity-in-environment, and social context. *Leisure Sciences, 32*, 401–417.

Steel, P., Schmidt, J., & Shultz, J. (2008). Refining the relationship between personality and subjective well-being. *Psychological Bulletin, 134*, 138–161.

Storr, A. (1988). *Solitude: A return to the self.* New York: Free Press.

Sullivan, H. S. (1953). *The interpersonal theory of psychiatry.* New York, NY: Norton.

Tamagawa, R., Speca, M., Stephen, J. E., & Carlson, L. (2015). Predictors and effects of class attendance and home practice of yoga and meditation among breast cancer survivors in a mindfulness-based cancer recovery program. *Mindfulness, 6*, 1201–2010.

Teppers, E., Luyckx, K., Vanhalst, J., Klimstra, T., & Goossens, L. (2014). Attitudes towards aloneness during adolescence: A person-centered approach. *Infant and Child Development, 23*, 239–248.

Thoreau, H. D. (1854). *Walden; or, life in the woods.* Boston: Ticknor & Fields.

Van Roekel, E., Scholte, R., Engels, R., Goossens, L., & Verhagen, M. (2015). Loneliness in the daily lives of adolescents: An experience sampling study examining the effects of social contexts. *Journal of Early Adolescence, 35*, 905–930.

Wethington, E., & Pillemer, K. (2014). Social isolation among older people. In R. Coplan & J. C. Bowker (Eds.), *The handbook of solitude: Psychological perspectives on social isolation, social withdrawal, and the experience of being alone* (pp. 242–259). New York: Wiley-Blackwell.

Whelan, D. C., & Zelenski, J. M. (2012). Experimental evidence that positive moods cause sociability. *Social Psychological and Personality Science, 3,* 430–437.

Williams, K. D., & Nida, S. A. (2011). Ostracism: Consequences and coping. *Current Directions in Psychological Science, 20,* 71–75.

Wilson, T. D., Reinhard, D. A., Westgate, E. C., Gilbert, D. T., Ellerbeck, N., Hahn, C., . . . Shaked, A. (2014). Just think: The challenges of the disengaged mind. *Science, 345,* 75–77.

Wilt, J., Noftle, E. E., Fleeson, W., & Spain, J. S. (2012). The dynamic role of personality states in mediating the relationship between extraversion and positive affect. *Journal of Personality, 80,* 1205–1236.

Winnicott, D. W. (1958). The capacity to be alone. In D. W. Winnicott (Ed.), *The maturational processes and the facilitating environment* (pp. 29–36). London: Kamac Books.

Yerkes, R. M., & Dodson, J. D. (1908). The relation of strength of stimulus to rapidity of habit-formation. *Journal of Comparative Neurology and Psychology, 18,* 459–482.

Zajonc, R. B. (1965). Social facilitation. *Science, 149,* 269–274.

Zelenski, J. M., Santoro, M. S., & Whelan, D. C. (2012). Would introverts be better off if they acted more like extraverts? Exploring emotional and cognitive consequences of counterdispositional behavior. *Emotion, 12,* 290–303.

Zelenski, J. M., Sobocko, K., & Whelan, D. C. (2014). Introversion, solitude, and subjective well-being. In R. J. Coplan & J. C. Bowker (Eds.), *The Handbook of solitude: Psychological perspectives on social isolation, social withdrawal, and being alone* (pp. 184–201). New York: Wiley-Blackwell.

Zelenski, J. M., Whelan, D. C., Nealis, L. J., Besner, C. M., Santoro, M. S., & Wynn, J. E. (2013). Personality and affective forecasting: Trait introverts underpredict the hedonic benefits of acting extraverted. *Journal of Personality and Social Psychology, 104,* 1092–1108.

7

FORGIVENESS

*Everett L. Worthington, Jr., Brandon J. Griffin,
and Caitlin Provencher*

Forgiveness is one of many strategies that people use to cope with an inevitable experience of being either a victim or perpetrator of an offense. It is intuitive that forgiveness ought to be related to well-being. When people harbor condemning negative emotions toward others or themselves, well-being is compromised. It is not surprising, then, to find that forgiveness has been experimentally related to well-being. For example, forgiveness is related to both physical and mental health (Toussaint, Worthington, & Williams, 2015); interpersonal functioning (Riek & Mania, 2012); and religious/spiritual well-being (Davis et al., 2014). We will not summarize research that duplicates these more focused examinations. Rather, we examine these findings through several theoretical lenses, connecting the empirical study of forgiveness to ongoing theoretical dialogues within the broader discourse of psychological science.

In the current chapter, we attempt to (1) conceptualize well-being; (2) define forgiveness; (3) consider theories of forgiveness and their relationship to well-being, illustrating theoretical speculations with empirical research; (4) evaluate support for theories and identify unanswered questions in studying forgiveness and its relationship to well-being from each perspective; and (5) discuss research on interventions to promote forgiveness to provide speculation about why explicit forgiveness interventions have been shown to promote well-being.

Understanding Well-Being

Two approaches dominate the study of well-being. One conceptualizes well-being as *hedonic*; the other as *eudaimonic*. Distinctions have been hotly debated. They have been respectively characterized as leading to an empty versus full life (Peterson, Park, & Seligman, 2005); as being related to subjective (Diener, 1984) versus objective well-being (Ryan & Deci, 2000, 2001; Ryan, Huta, & Deci, 2008); as being self-focused versus self and other focused (Ryff, 2014); and as being self-oriented versus virtue-oriented (Huta & Ryan, 2010). While these conceptualizations have been helpful in directing research on well-being, theoretical distinctions have begun to give way in the face of a failure to generate empirical support differentiating between the *hedonic* and *eudaimonic* well-being (Disabato, Goodman, Kashdan, Short, & Jarden, 2016; Kashdan, Biswas-Diener, & King, 2008).

Psychologists have defined *hedonia* as how satisfying one evaluates his or her life or how happy one is with life. The most used model of hedonic well-being is Diener's (1984) model, which conceptualizes well-being as consisting of life satisfaction and balance between positive and negative affect (for a review, see Busseri & Sadava, 2011). Conversely, to date, there is no single agreed-upon theory or methodological approach to studying *eudaimonia*. Eudaimonia connotes something for the good of an individual and others, according to its source in Aristotelian ethics. Moving from definition to empirical operationalization, eudaimonic models of well-being focus on a generally positive way of being, typically including personal meaning and growth even in hardship, which is distinct from transient states of happiness (Ryff, 2014).

Empirical Research on Differences

Despite the definitional debates, scholars have found virtually no discriminant validity between *hedonia* and *eudaimonia*. In fact, six recent studies examine *hedonia* and *eudaimonia* by comparing Diener's (1984) tripartite model of hedonic subjective well-being with Ryff's eudaimonic psychological well-being model. Results revealed that *hedonia* and *eudaimonia* are typically correlated strongly, with bivariate associations ranging from .76 to .92 between measures purporting to assess hedonic and *eudaimonic* well-being (Keyes, Shmotkin, & Ryff, 2002; Gallagher, Lopez, & Preacher, 2009, Study 2; Linley, Maltby, Wood, Osborne, & Hurling, 2009; Gallagher et al., 2009, Study 1; Fredrickson et al., 2013; Disabato et al., 2016). It is probably safe to conclude that existing psychometric studies of the well-being models of *hedonia* and *eudaimonia* are only slightly different. Making distinctions might only be useful in certain contexts, such as with specific samples or salient outcomes.

Correlates of Hedonic and Eudaimonic Well-Being

We can see, for example, how models might overlap if we look at correlates of *hedonic* and *eudaimonic* well-being. Good mental health is related to subjective happiness as well as to persistent hope, meaning-making, or other-orientation. However, differences might be observed among individuals whose life situation is characterized by hardship and adversity, setting the occasion for possible fluctuations or stability in well-being over time depending on one's *hedonic* or *eudaimonic* orientation. Longitudinal investigation is required to study well-being over time to expose differences, rather than correlational designs that have typically been used. Also, we suggest that an orientation toward others that is characteristic of *eudaimonic* well-being might play more of a role in outcomes that extend beyond the individual, such as interpersonal functioning, in comparison *hedonic* well-being that is primarily self-oriented. Again, methodological sophistication such as the use of Actor-Partner Interdependence Modeling would be needed to provide nuanced exploration of the theorized differences between *hedonic* and *eudaimonic* well-being. In studying forgiveness—an individual experience occurring in interpersonal context, and one that is not always associated with happiness—we prefer a *eudaimonic* view of well-being, but we acknowledge this to be a personal preference conditioned by our subject matter rather than some judgment based on the weight of objective evidence.

Understanding Forgiveness

When people experience injustices, they evaluate of how much injustice has occurred, and as subsequent events happen (such as related offenses, court rulings, apologies, and restitution) people adjust their injustice gap (see Davis et al., 2016; Worthington, 2006). The *injustice gap* is the difference between the way a person would like an injustice resolved and the current assessment of injustice. Although justice is a social and societal process, not necessarily directly affecting forgiveness, the internal perception of justice affects one's likelihood of forgiving. Large injustice gaps are hard to forgive. They elicit attempts to reduce the injustice gap—i.e., seeing justice done, turning the issue over to God, etc. When an injustice gap persists, usually aided by rumination, so do distressing emotions such as resentment, bitterness, hostility, hate, anger, and anxiety (i.e., *unforgiveness*). Forgiveness is usually needed to reduce unforgiveness.

What Forgiveness Is

Early scientific writing on forgiveness treated it as a complex yet unitary experience (Enright & the Human Development Study Group, 1996; McCullough, Pargament, & Thoresen, 2000; Worthington, 1998). More recently, however, it has become clear that there are two types of forgiveness. One process is making a *decision to forgive* (Davis et al., 2015), which is a behavioral intention to treat an offender with respect. The offended person does not forget the offense but makes a decision to attempt to act differently towards the offender to the extent that it is safe and prudent to do so. The second type of forgiveness, referred to as *emotional forgiveness*, is an emotional transformation by which negative, condemning emotions are reduced and possibly replaced by positive, affirming emotions. Negative unforgiving emotions are gradually reduced by juxtaposing positive emotions (i.e., empathy, sympathy, compassion, or love) against them resulting in a lessening of net negativity. Complete emotional forgiveness, then, might be characterized by reaching neutral emotion (or equal intensity of negative and positive emotions) in the case of forgiving a stranger or person with whom one does not intend or care to interact in the future. The person experiencing complete forgiveness of an offender they do not intend to interact with in the future would be settled and not motivated to continue efforts at emotional replacement. But with continuing and valued relationships, usually people are not content to stop at emotional neutrality or balance of positive and negative emotions. For instance, if one's spouse offended one, emotional forgiveness would move the person toward less negativity, but one would not feel completely forgiving if one simply felt nothing toward the person who is valued and a continuing relationship partner. Complete forgiveness might require attempting to keep adding experiences of compassion or love until a net positive emotional valence was experienced. That is, complete forgiveness eliminates all negative emotion and leaves one feeling some positive emotional reaction to the valued person. Exline, Worthington, Hill, and McCullough (2003) first identified these related but distinct types of forgiveness. There is not unanimous acceptance of this perspective among scientists investigating forgiveness, but it is likely the dominant perspective. Ultimately, as has been well-established in the literature, forgiveness is related to well-being in domains including physical, psychological, relational, and religious/spiritual functioning—but decisional forgiveness affects different aspects as does emotional forgiveness (Worthington, 2006).

What Forgiveness Is Not

In establishing a precise definition of forgiveness, it is important to consider how forgiveness differs from alternative ways in which an individual might respond to wrongdoing or injustice. Forgiveness is often confused with other concepts. Forgiveness is not forgetting. If one has forgotten an offense, there is no need to forgive. It is also not forbearing, which is refusing to respond to an offense, usually for the good of group harmony. Forgiveness is not excusing, condoning, or justifying the offense. It is not reconciling with the other person; reconciliation requires two people working together to restore trust in a ruptured relationship. Nor is forgiving saying, "I forgive you", which could be said for manipulation rather than as a true expression of one's inner decision to forgive or emotional forgiveness.

The Intersection of Forgiveness and Well-Being

This section examines basic social psychological processes that contribute to various types of well-being—physical well-being, psychological well-being, relational well-being, and spiritual well-being. Our goal in this section is not to re-review the recently reviewed vast literatures we mentioned earlier but to describe findings illustrating some mechanisms by which the forgiveness-well-being relationship might be established.

Forgiveness and Physical Well-Being

Hill, Heffernan, and Allemand (2015) reviewed studies in the areas of global well-being (i.e., life satisfaction and happiness), romantic relationship well-being, and family well-being, and they presented a model showing forgiveness linked to health by four mediators (e.g., relationship harmony, relationship mastery and maintenance, adaptive identity development, and self-acceptance and self-worth). In addition, Larkin, Goulet, and Cavanagh (2015) showed that reducing physical stress and concomitant peripheral arousal, improving vagal tone (thus affecting the parasympathetic nervous system), changing baseline levels of cortisol, decreasing the number of cortisol transients, and reducing epinephrine are all associated with positive physical health.

Forgiveness and Psychological Well-Being

Griffin, Worthington, Lavelock, Wade, and Hoyt (2015) examined 54 studies in a decade review since the publication of a prior synthesis (Toussaint & Webb, 2005). They summarized their findings using four propositions. Ten empirical studies supported Proposition 1—that unforgiveness is related to poor mental health. For example, Worthington (2006) suggested that physiological indicators, including brain, hormonal, and sympathetic nervous system activity, and changes in blood chemistry all imply that physical indicators of stress accompany higher unforgiveness toward others. These produce negative emotional and psychological states and over time affect mental health. Twenty-seven studies (Griffin et al., 2015) have related forgiveness and better mental health (Proposition 2). State forgiveness and trait forgivingness—the propensity to be forgiving across time, numerous people, and numerous offenses—both predict fewer psychological symptoms. Forgiveness or forgivingness have been found to be related to less depression, death anxiety, somatic symptoms, state anxiety, stress, trait anger, neuroticism, rumination, fear, hostility, and posttraumatic stress disorder. Forgiveness, though, does not just reduce people's negativity. It is related to life satisfaction, positive affect, optimism, size of social support network, satisfaction with one's support network, vitality, and self-reported health. Although the relationships between forgiveness and many mental health variables are strong, they are based mostly on cross-sectional research. It is impossible to determine whether forgiveness causes better mental health, whether people with greater mental health are more likely to forgive, or whether both are related to some other variable like resilience.

Griffin et al. also reviewed research relating to whether individual differences moderate the impact of forgiveness on mental health (Proposition 3). They identified 14 studies examining moderating effects of age, gender, and motivation to forgive. They reviewed research relating to whether forgiveness affected mental health through psychological states (Proposition 4). Only five studies addressed that proposition. Forgiveness produces less rumination, and that contributes to more positive mental health. Also, forgiveness builds hope, which also improves general mental health. Forgiveness improves self-esteem and reduces negative affect, but self-esteem and negative affect have less clearly been shown to affect mental health.

Forgiveness and Relational Well-Being

Forgiveness Works Through Relationships

When conflict is chronic or frequent in relationships—whether family, couple, occupational, or friendship relationships—the emotion of unforgiveness can occur, usually through rumination, and relationship well-being often suffers (Fincham, Beach, & Davila, 2007). Forgiveness, which increases behavioral intentions to change behaviors (i.e., decisional forgiveness) or reduces rumination and motivations to avenge or avoid (i.e., emotional forgiveness), can promote subjective well-being by reducing the number of conflicts in a relationship. It does so by changing the forgiver's behavioral intentions, emotions, and motivations to keep bringing up old hurts. Thus, old hurts and offenses do not surface as often and intrude into current attempts to resolve differences. Forgiveness might also increase relationship well-being by promoting social support. When people forgive quickly and easily, they tend to garner more support from more people. When partners can forgive, they also are able to promote closer emotional bonds and hence more intimacy. Worthington (2005) has described satisfying couple relationships as being those in which partners can form, maintain, strengthen, and repair, when damaged, close emotional bonds. Forgiveness is a way that such intimate bonds can be repaired when they are damaged by some hurtful or offensive act. Moreover, a person who has not made a decision to forgive and who is holding unforgiving emotions toward an offender might experience greater fluctuations in moment-by-moment relations in any relationship. Thus, the person will likely experience less control in the relationship. Forgiveness is not essential to relationships, but it also is part of reconciliation, which is an evolutionary adaptation that maintains stability in social groups (McCullough, 2008).

Forgiveness and Romantic Relationships

Many studies have examined the relationships between forgiveness and romantic relationship well-being (for a review, see Waldron & Kelley, 2008; and for a meta-analysis, see Reik & Mania, 2012). Forgiveness—making a decision to forgive and perhaps experiencing less unforgiving emotion—both consistently correlate with greater relationship success. Indeed, forgiveness of one's partner correlates with greater romantic relationship satisfaction (e.g., Wieselquist, 2009). Forgiveness appears to influence relationship satisfaction because forgiving individuals put more effort into their relationship and use fewer negative conflict tactics (Braithwaite, Selby, & Fincham, 2011). Forgiveness might also promote trust, which in turn predicts greater satisfaction.

Forgiveness and Occupational Well-Being

Research has documented that forgiveness not only occurs often in the workplace, but it also makes the workplace a more humane place to spend a majority of people's waking hours (for a review, see Fehr & Gelfand, 2012). Barclay and Saldanha (2016) conducted two studies employing guided expressive writing exercises for 1 day (Study 1) or 4 consecutive days (Study 2). They compared non-offense writing as a control to traditional Pennebaker-oriented expressive writing for 20 minutes and two other conditions in which 10 minutes of traditional expressive writing occurred either before or after 10 minutes explicitly writing about forgiveness. They showed that forgiveness in organizations helps transcend the injustice gap and expressive writing helped by allowing people to express negative emotions and move on to forgiveness. Perceived resolution of the conflict mediated the relationship between expressive writing and forgiveness. Most of the research on forgiveness and occupational well-being has not measured individual worker well-being. Instead, it has assumed that forgiveness can enhance the work environment by leading to less lasting negative emotions in victims of workplace injustice and more cooperation among people who inflicted and received transgressions. Prior research thus assumed that forgiveness will have payoffs in individual well-being that parallel the payoffs in organizational emotional climate.

Forgiveness and Spiritual and Religious Well-Being

Davis et al. (2013) conducted an extensive meta-analysis on forgiveness and religious spirituality (R/S). For the relationship between R/S and trait forgivingness, the total number of participants from the 64 samples was 99,177. For the relationship between R/S and state forgiveness, the total number of participants from the 50 samples was 8,932. The effect size for R/S and trait forgivingness was .29, and that between R/S and state forgiveness was .15. The relationship between R/S and state forgiveness was stronger when R/S was measured as a contextual ($r = .31$; e.g., R/S appraisal) rather than dispositional ($r = .10$; e.g., R/S commitment) construct. However, meaningful relationships between R/S variables and forgiveness did not matter what R/S construct was assessed—religiosity, spirituality, intrinsic religiosity, extrinsic religiosity, religious well-being, existential well-being, spiritual searching or doubting, R/S context, and R/S relationship.

For religions that believe in a divine Being, divine forgiveness is feeling forgiven by that Being. For religions and spiritualties in which other objects are treated as Sacred—such as humans, nature, or cosmic transcendence—divine forgiveness is reaching a sense of peace with the Sacred. When people do wrong, many people feel forgiven by God for their particular offenses. Some do not feel so. Toussaint, Williams, Musick, & Everson (2001) initiated the investigation of forgiveness by God through a national sample that supposedly reflected a distribution of ages, social statuses, education as the US population. Since that time, Toussaint and his colleague Webb have continued to study people's sense of forgiveness by God and the predictors of it. They have found that egregiousness of offense, degree of religious commitment, and religious beliefs have contributed to feeling forgiven by God. The importance of divine forgiveness, or forgiveness by God, to different people not surprisingly varies by population and type of problem.

Established Theories of Forgiveness

Three theories have received substantial attention in research on forgiveness and well-being—stress-and-coping theory, the process model of forgiveness, and interdependence theory. McCullough (2008) recently added an evolutionary theory pertaining to social survival.

Stress-and-Coping Theory of Forgiveness

Worthington (2006) and Strelan and Covic (2006) have both advanced stress-and-coping theories of forgiveness using Lazarus (1999) stress-and-coping framework to conceptualize transgressions as stressors. They noted that appraisals of the transgression as potentially or actually threatening triggered stress responses. Stress responses involved upheavals in cognition, behavior, emotion, and physiology, demanding a coping attempt to re-establish homeostasis. This theoretical perspective has been consistently employed to describe the associations of forgiveness with psychological and physical health.

A stress-and-coping theory of forgiveness helps predict physical and psychological reactions to being transgressed. It suggests that chronic or repeated strong stress-reactions affect stress-related physiological processes involving cortisol, blood pressure, heart rate, and other responses associated with the hypothalamus-pituitary-adrenal axis. It suggests also that mental health benefits might accrue to those who forgive, especially if coping attempts are fruitful. In addition, a stress-and-coping theory of forgiveness engages interpersonal and meaning-focused coping strategies. Because it might also incorporate the effects of social support, stress-and-coping theory of forgiveness is currently the most comprehensive theory. The theory does have weaknesses. It does not reliably predict which reactions to being transgressed against will occur. Also, the stress response is an undifferentiated whole-body response. Priority is given to changes in intrapsychic outcomes rather than relational or religious/spiritual responses.

Enright's Process Model of Forgiveness

Enright and Fitzgibbons (2014) suggested that a four-phase repeatable process occurs on the road to forgiving. In the Uncovering phase, the person gains an understanding of the offense and the consequence of the injury to the one's life. In the Decision phase, the person learns about forgiveness and makes a decision to commit to forgiving on the basis of this understanding. Forgiveness is embraced as a choice in which the person must, at a minimum, be willing to forgive. In the Work phase, people seek to attain an empathic understanding of the offender and potential reasons that the offender might have had for his or her offensive or hurtful acts. This helps reframe the offense and offender, seeing the person as a fallible human. In the Deepening phase, people might discover some sense of meaning or ultimate purpose in suffering. They might also feel more connected with others and experience less sadness and more purpose in life.

This is process of forgiving is not descriptive. No experimental data support such a naturally occurring forgiveness process. Rather, the phases occur within Enright and Fitzgibbons' process forgiveness intervention that induces forgiveness in willing people. However, psychotherapy protocols generally intend to lead participants along structured experiences that might induce people to forgive. Thus, process model is more accurately a model of intervention than a descriptive theory of forgiveness as it naturally occurs.

Interdependence Theory of Forgiveness

Thibaut and Kelley's (1959; Kelley & Thibaut, 1978) interpersonal theory of interdependence focuses on a repertoire of behaviors within a dyad and the outcomes (satisfying or dissatisfying) for each partner. It is based on a mutual exchange of rewards and costs, balanced against each partner's expectations. Sometimes outcomes of exchanges are *correspondent*, when partners agree. At other times disagreements create dilemmas such as transgressions, incompatible goals, or difficult communications, which test the relationship. Each partner must choose whether to maximize his or her own well-being or to prioritize the relationship by setting aside strict demands for justice in favor of more reconciliative experiences like apologizing, offering restitution, seeking forgiveness, or forgiving. These dilemmas are also *diagnostic situations* because a partner's transformation of motivation from a naturally self-oriented desire for retaliation (which has been discerned at the gut level through assessment of proprioceptive gut responses) to pursuing such self-interest or not doing so (i.e., by forgiving, accepting, or forbearing) reveals information about the value one's partner holds for the relationship. In diagnostic situations, individuals can act consistently with gut-level self-interest or with relationship-oriented values. Over time in healthy-functioning close relationships, other-oriented motivations may become routine—habits of the heart—and partners might not even think about gut-level self-oriented responses (Righetti, Finkenauer, & Finkel, 2013).

Interdependence theory is focused on interpersonal interactions. Forgiving a target influences the well-being of the forgiver and offender through effects on physical health, mental health, relationships, spirituality, community well-being, and societal well-being (e.g., in-group versus out-group relationships). Each of those has intertwined influences on the others. However, to date, most research on interdependence theory is focused on the end-point of relational well-being, with little focus on the mechanisms of effect. Yet, the theory suggests that, when a partner reliably values the other partner over self-interest, individuals develop *trust*, which often leads to forgiveness. Frequent forgiveness in turn builds trust. This reciprocal relationship builds a beneficial *mutual cyclical growth* (Wieselquist, 2009). Greater attention is needed on how forgiveness might be a mechanism of relational well-being, especially in a dyadic context. Thus, interdependence theory provides a strong framework for exploring the contributions of forgiveness to relational well-being, though exploration is needed of the role of forgiveness as a bidirectional cause and consequence of relational outcomes.

Evolutionary Theory of Forgiveness—Another Interpersonal Approach

McCullough (2008) suggested a distal-cause explanation for forgiveness—evolutionary theory—which has present-day implications in terms of benefits to individuals and their relationships. He argued that evolution resulted in the natural selection of traits in people for experiencing a sense of injustice and urge to punish violators of justice and traits for regulating emotions quickly so that group solidarity could be maintained or restored. In this theory, revenge is adaptive because it punishes transgressors of group norms, which increases the chances of group survival (hence survival of group members). However, if only revenge were at work, social groups would eventually splinter into individuals (assuming that all individuals eventually violate group norms). Thus, forgiveness as a motive was also selected to allow groups to restore social equilibrium and restore the transgressor to good favor within the group. Based on this theory, two variables will affect willingness to forgive: high relationship value and low risk of exploitation (Burnette, McCullough, Van Tongeren, & Davis, 2012). In recent work, McCullough, Pedersen, Tabak, and Carter (2014) found that conciliatory gestures promote forgiveness and reduced anger in individuals because they signal that one is willing (1) to lower one's social status by offering conciliation, showing a value on the relationship, and (2) to lower the victim's risk that the offender will exploit the victim in the future. Thus, McCullough's evolutionary theory suggests that forgiveness should lead to individual well-being and also well-being within relationships and larger social groups.

This research is consistent with de Waal and Pokorny's (2005) theorizing and observational research on reconciliation in primates. While the description of the processes McCullough has documented seems consistent with reconciliation, we might question whether he and his colleagues are describing forgiveness, which depending on one's definition, seems to be more a decision or emotional change than reconciliation, or is describing reconciliation. It appears that McCullough is describing reconciliation and calling it forgiveness because forgiveness is usually defined as an internal motivational, emotional, cognitive, and intentional statement, which non-human primates might not be capable of. Forgiveness, to the extent it is such an internal set of processes involving (as we have defined it) a decision and an emotional transformation, might have had far less time to evolve than has the more behavioral reconciliation. Reconciliation, it has been forcefully argued by de Waal and Pokorny (2005), has evidence supporting its evolutionary origin. We believe that forgiveness might reflect more social and linguistic adaptations than does reconciliation. Thus, McCullough's (2008) argument is more likely an argument for reconciliation in humans than one that is about forgiveness.

Burgeoning Theories of Forgiveness

Three rising theories provide insight into forgiveness and well-being: forgiveness and relational spirituality (Worthington & Sandage, 2015); virtue theory; and exposure theory.

Spirituality and Religion Theory of Relational Forgiveness

Shults and Sandage (2006) described a theory of forgiveness and relational spirituality, and Davis and his colleagues (2008) applied this model within an empirical framework. R*elational* spirituality, which has a long tradition in Christianity, focuses not on the object of devotion (e.g., God), but on the *relationship* between the object and the person and finds spirituality intertwined with each relationship and differing across different relationships (such as relationship with God versus with the church in general versus a specific congregation). Davis et al. described the relationships among the Sacred (S) and each of the victim (V), offender (O), and transgression (T). Worthington and Sandage (2015) summarized numerous studies and theoretical approaches in describing the important effects of different relationships that could exist between the Sacred and the victim (SV), the Sacred and the offender (SO), and the Sacred and the transgression (ST). Worthington and Sandage summarized numerous measures to assess the different aspects of the model (see Appendix; pp. 275–278) and a summary of the research (see summary tables on pp. 84–89 and 100–105). In general, the Sacred-Victim relationship has been described using attachment to God, anger toward God, commitment to

God, satisfaction with one's relationship to God and other ways to describe the SV relationship. More strength (using any of these variety of constructs) in the relationship of the victim to the sacred is related to more likelihood of forgiving. Similarly, the victim perceives the offender's relationship to God as either similar or dissimilar to the victim's own relationship. The more similarly the relationship is perceived to be, the more likely the victim is to forgive the offender.

The theory set out to be perhaps the first comprehensive framework for organizing all of the findings on forgiveness—on physical, psychological, relational, and spiritual health. It is modeled as a pyramid, which has a base looking at three elements—the victim, the offender, and the transgression as well as the relationships among them. The intent was to organize all variables applying to the people, the event, and the interpersonal context. Then, the Sacred (S) was added at the apex of the pyramid, suggesting three other spiritual relationships. However, the theory falls short in two ways. First, like Enright's theory, this theory has been used to date is as a theory of psychotherapy rather than as a broad organizational schema for basic research findings, which was the intention in creating the theory. Second, although religious and spiritual clients are prevalent in psychotherapy, clients who want overtly religious or spiritual treatments are far less frequent and of those clients, a minority wish to deal with forgiveness issues. Thus, the practical utility of the theory is limited. It has wider potential as an organizational system for comprehensively making sense of secular and spiritually oriented research findings, but to date that has not been exploited by basic scientific investigators.

Virtue Theory of Forgiveness

Most people consider forgiveness to be a virtue, and as such, it has been found to be correlated with other virtues such as gratitude, humility, love, sympathy, empathy, altruism, compassion, justice, conscientiousness, and agreeableness (Fehr, Gelfand, & Nag, 2010). Ultimately, all of those virtues are thought to contribute to well-being. Philosophers and theologians have dealt more with moral and spiritual well-being; psychologists have dealt more with physical, psychological, and relational well-being. Virtue theories in the classical sense are not cognitive theories. Rather, classical virtue theory involves glimpsing one's goal, practicing the virtue until it becomes a habit of the heart, meeting challenges (either self- or life-imposed), and ultimately experiencing life satisfaction (see Worthington & Allison, 2018). Rather than learn such virtues from direct teaching or reading, we often learn virtues from a community of people who have established rhythms and rituals that afford opportunities to practice, models to observe, and a community-based narrative to fit into. Virtue theory suggests that many virtues are related and are generated with more input from personality than some other theories advocate (like interpersonal or evolutionary theories). Of course, situations trigger virtuous acts and also can instigate a virtue from lower down in one's virtue hierarchy than one might normally think is likely. So there is a definite interaction between personality and situations.

But there is also an expected interrelationship among the virtues within virtue theory. Many people seek to develop positive characters, and if they are successful, they exhibit many virtues—not just forgiveness—and those virtues tend to contribute to physical, psychological, moral, relational, civic, and spiritual well-being. There are categories of virtues in which the virtues are interrelated. In 2005, Berry et al. identified three categories of virtues: warmth-based virtues (involving love, humility, forgiveness, altruism, and other-oriented virtues), conscientiousness-based virtues (involving self-control, conscientiousness, justice, and other personally and socially responsible virtues), and epistemic-based virtues (involving wisdom, knowledge, learning and other cognitive virtues). In 2015, McGrath analyzed 1,070,549 cases of people completing the VIA Classification and identified a three-virtue model consisting of Caring, Self-Control, and Inquisitiveness, which he proposed as a latent structure for the VIA strengths. In both systems, forgiveness is a lynchpin of the warm, other-focused virtues.

Acting virtuously is not always related to physical health. In fact, we can easily imagine times when doing moral, virtuous acts will not fit in with situations and could cause interpersonal reactions that at a minimum could result in a loss of social support. It might even lead to rejection. Virtue is its own reward, goes an old saying. But if people are rejected socially, that can have both mental health and physical health fallout. Virtue theory seems a strong contribution to spiritual health, and it can contribute positively to aspects of mental health and relational health. But it says nothing about physical health and the likelihood is that, in both relational and mental health, findings will be mixed. At this point, a formal virtue theory has not received enough empirical attention to have a good sense of its contributions and deficits.

Exposure Theory of Forgiveness

Summary

Some evidence has accumulated to suggest that exposure plus time will yield forgiveness. This model has not been articulated in prior writing on forgiveness. The major evidence supporting this theory comes from the intervention research. Wade, Hoyt, Kidwell, and Worthington (2014) meta-analyzed 54 randomized clinical trials. Although most of the studies involved Enright and Fitzgibbons (2014) process model or Worthington's (2006) REACH Forgiveness model, the results were clear: No differences were found across any models of intervention to promote forgiveness and every intervention outperformed control treatments. Regardless of which intervention was considered, the rate of forgiveness was the same—described by a linear increase of about 0.1 standard deviations of increase in forgiveness per hour of sustained therapeutic attention. Exposure might have been responsible for the results that people lessened unforgiveness and forgave. Efficacious models assumed that minimal requirements were met: (1) The model dealt explicitly with forgiveness; (2) defined forgiveness; (3) promoted a sense of empathy for the offender (Fehr et al., 2010); (4) went beyond making a mere decision to forgive and promoted emotional forgiveness (see Baskin & Enright, 2004); and (5) providing engaging exercises that occupied the participant's attention. However, numerous proposed mechanisms (i.e., cognitive, emotional, behavioral, physiological, or environmental manipulations) yield the same essential response. We suggest, that whatever mechanisms interventions seek to promote, other things consistent with an exposure explanation are happening. That is, what is occurring is confrontation with an imagined or recalled inescapable stimulus (i.e., the remembered offense and offender). Thus, forgivers deal with it in ways that match their personal strengths—through emotional replacement, cognitive change, motivational transformation, behavioral programming, or environmental changes.

Note that, although the data we adduced to initiate discussion of exposure theory are derived from an intervention, this is not an intervention theory of how one comes to forgive. It does not depend on a particular sequence of therapeutic maneuvers or stages or phases of a psychotherapist-led intervention. This is evident because the data from all known evidence-based treatments to promote forgiveness, including all theoretical approaches, groups, individual, and couple therapies, and even do-it-yourself workbooks all fall along a common regression relationship. Thus, we suggest that even naturally occurring interventions like (1) conversations with friends, (2) reading forgiveness literature in books or online, or (3) private concentrated efforts to forgive might follow the same exposure dose-effect regression line and might, therefore, generate the same effects on well-being.

Summary of Potential Theoretical Reasons for the Linear Dose-Response Relationship

According to exposure theory, people might forgive for several reasons. First, they might simply become deconditioned to stress-reactions or fatigue the stress-reaction. Second, exposure might provide attentional focus on forgiving that permitted various cognitive activities that foster forgiveness to occur. Third, exposure might give time for other psychological, emotional, cognitive, or behavioral experiences that affect their coping with unforgiveness. Fourth, exposure might involve response prevention, forcing people to think about the offender while preventing avoidance of such thinking and also preventing acting on vengeful cognition. Fifth, exposure might instigate explicit cognition about reducing unforgiveness and their prefrontal cortex activation can potentiate emotional regulation. Sixth, exposure might work as in some models of fear conditioning, like Foa, McNally, and Williams (1996), and like suggested in Worthington (1998). In that conceptualization, extinction occurs because of the creation of new, structures that compete with the original unforgiving structure. The old unforgiving structure and the new, non-pathological structure contain overlapping elements. The same stimuli and responses can activate both structures. Thus, exposure therapy is successful when the new structure is more readily activated. Relapse may occur when the old structure is activated. This is consistent with a rebuttal to the idea of "forgive and forget". This rebuttal suggests that forgiving is not forgetting but is remembering differently. That is, the old (vengeance-oriented or avoidance-oriented) memory exists, but the new (forgiving) memory is more easily called to mind.

Two Types of Exposures

McCullough, Luna, Berry, Tabak, and Bono (2010) have shown experimentally that people who experience hurts or offenses tend to experience a predictable decay in the unforgiveness following a log function (i.e., a power curve)—at least over the first 3 weeks following an offense. They also experience an accompanying delayed but predictable increase in benevolence. McCullough et al. (2010) identified people in their first day after experiencing a transgression. The curve describing the group of forgivers' responses was a sharply decreasing curve, suggesting that, in the first day, sharp decreases in unforgiveness occurred, and with each passing day additional decreases, of less and less magnitude were experienced—on the average. The shape of the decay curve is the same power curve as describes other chaotic processes coming to an equilibrium or stasis. These data support an exposure theory in which people might employ different ways of dealing with their transgressions to facilitate gradual desensitization—but the net result was that exposure resulted in decreases (on the average) of unforgiveness by people in a group. Because the choice among multiple methods of reducing unforgiveness—like forgiving or forbearing, seeking justice, turning it over to God, or acceptance and moving on—is not fixed, the process is essentially chaotic movement toward stasis.

However, clearly not all people's responses follow a power curve describing a decrease in unforgiveness. McCullough et al. (2010) plotted numerous single cases. For some, unforgiveness simply did not decrease. We might hypothesize that these people reacted without changing for several reasons. Some transgressions might have been very damaging, and victims must cope with physical, psychological, relational, or spiritual damage, facing it daily and thus responding to overwhelming cues daily. For others, insufficient exposure might have been available to provide a natural course of forgiveness, especially if others involved in the transgression are inaccessible to the forgiver (e.g., dead, lack of communication technology, avoidance, etc.) or the potential forgiver was prone to denial and thought suppression.

Exposure theory has not been previously described. Our account is a bare-bones summary and needs expansion. It is non-specific in describing the mechanisms by which forgiveness might occur. We mentioned six potential mechanisms:

deconditioning or fatigue to stress-reactions; attentional focus permitting cognitive and emotional coping; giving time for other psychological, emotional, cognitive, or behavioral experiences; response prevention; instigation of explicit cognition and prefrontal cortex activation can potentiate emotional regulation; and emotional deconditioning. The non-specificity in detailing mechanisms is at once the weakness and a potential strength for this theory. Exposure engages individual ways of trying to promote forgiveness and also engages individual mechanisms that connect forgiveness and well-being. For some, exposure to a book about forgiveness (for example) might stimulate better physical well-being through reducing stress or perhaps through improving hope and alleviating depression or perhaps through improving one's relationship with a partner or perhaps through re-energizing a person's spiritual life. The individual is engaged. Psychotherapeutic approaches focus people in need of psychological help due to some impairment from a psychological disorder. But, for the vast majority of people who might want to forgive, no disorder is impairing them and exposure can provide individual motivations to change.

Conclusions From Examining Theories and Findings on Forgiveness and Well-Being

We do not find evidence of an integrative theory of forgiveness and well-being that could provide heuristic insight into all the elements of well-being. The empirical research on forgiveness and well-being is a mature literature. Much of it is organized by outcome variables—physical, psychological, relational, and spiritual variables—and that tends to force use of specific theories with specific outcomes. This mitigates against a comprehensive model of forgiveness and well-being being accepted in the psychological community. Forgiveness enhances the well-being of both victims and perpetrators of wrongdoing. In fact, numerous lines of research have shown forgiveness to be related to physical and psychological well-being as well as relational and spiritual well-being. Research on well-being shows that different aspects of well-being are often related to each other and the earlier-articulated wall of separation between hedonic and *eudaimonic* well-being has seriously crumbled in recent years. Forgiveness, as an other-oriented virtue that tends to reduce interpersonal and intrapersonal experiences of stress, has clearly been related to all four major types of well-being. But, although forgiveness research has accumulated, we noted that a weakness in most forgiveness research is that how the intrapersonal experiences of decisional and emotional forgiveness happen has not been strongly theory driven by some omnibus theory. Rather, stress-and-coping theory seems to best explain forgiveness' effects on physical and psychological well-being (with the exception that Enright and Fitzgibbons' process theory also explains psychological and sometimes physical well-being in psychotherapy patients), interdependence theory and evolutionary theory seem to best explain forgiveness' effects on relational well-being, and Worthington and

Sandage's and virtue theory seem to explain forgiveness' impact on moral and spiritual well-being. We articulated an exposure theory of forgiveness for the first time. We note that it is supported by only indirect data at this point. However, we tentatively suggest that, because our theory posits that exposure is about any focused attempts to forgive, exposure might potentiate each individual's mechanisms both for forgiving and for experiencing physical, psychological, relational, and spiritual well-being—whichever ones and how many ones might be meaningful to the forgiver.

References

Barclay, L. J., & Saldanha, M. F. (2016). Facilitating forgiveness in organizational contexts: Exploring the injustice gap, emotions, and expressive writing interventions. *Journal of Business Ethics, 137*(4), 699–720. http://dx.doi.org/10.1007/s10551-015-2750-x

Baskin, T. W., & Enright, R. D. (2004). Intervention studies in forgiveness: A meta-analysis. *Journal of Counseling and Development, 82,* 79–90.

Braithwaite, S. R., Selby, E. A., & Fincham, F. D. (2011). Forgiveness and relationship satisfaction: Mediating mechanisms. *Journal of Family Psychology, 25,* 551–559.

Burnette, J. L., McCullough, M. E., Van Tongeren, D. R., & Davis, D. E. (2012). Forgiveness results from integrating information about relationship value and exploitation risk. *Personality and Social Psychology Bulletin, 38*(3), 345–356.

Busseri, M. A., & Sadava, S. W. (2011). A review of the tripartite structure of subjective well-being: Implications for conceptualization, operationalization, analysis, and synthesis. *Personality and Social Psychology Review, 15,* 290–314.

Davis, D. E., Hook, J. N., Van Tongeren, D. R., DeBlaere, C., Rice, K. G., & Worthington, E. L., Jr. (2015). Making a decision to forgive. *Journal of Counseling Psychology, 62*(2), 280–288.

Davis, D. E., Hook, J. N., & Worthington, E. L., Jr. (2008). Relational spirituality and forgiveness: The roles of attachment to God, religious coping, and viewing the transgression as a desecration. *Journal of Psychology and Christianity, 27*(4), 293–301.

Davis, D. E., Van Tongeren, D. R., Hook, J. N., Davis, E. B., Worthington, E. L., Jr., & Foxman, S. (2014). Relational spirituality and forgiveness: Appraisals that may hinder forgiveness. *Psychology of Religion and Spirituality, 6*(2), 102–112.

Davis, D. E., Worthington, E. L., Jr., Hook, J. N., & Hill, P. C. (2013). Research on forgiveness and religion/spirituality: A meta-analytic review. *Psychology of Religion and Spirituality, 5*(4), 233–241.

Davis, D. E., Yang, X., DeBlaere, C., McElroy, S. E., Van Tongeren, D. R., Hook, J. N., & Worthington, E. L., Jr. (2016). The injustice gap. *Psychology of Religion and Spirituality, 8*(3), 175–184.

de Waal, F. B. M., & Pokorny, J. J. (2005). Primate questions about the art and science of forgiving. In E. L. Worthington, Jr. (Ed.), *Handbook of forgiveness* (pp. 17–32). New York, NY: Brunner-Routledge.

Diener, E. (1984). Subjective well-being. *Psychological Bulletin, 95,* 542–575.

Disabato, D. J., Goodman, F. R., Kashdan, T. B., Short, J. L., & Jarden, A. (2016). Different types of well-being? A cross-cultural examination of hedonic and eudaimonic well-being. *Psychological Assessment, 28*(5), 471–482.

Enright, R. D., & Fitzgibbons, R. P. (2014). *Forgiveness therapy: An empirical guide for resolving anger and restoring hope.* Washington, DC: American Psychological Association.

Enright, R. D., & The Human Development Study Group. (1996). Counseling within the forgiveness triad: On forgiving, receiving forgiveness and self-forgiveness. *Counseling & Values, 40*(2), 107–127.

Exline, J. J., Worthington, E. L., Jr., Hill, P., & McCullough, M. E. (2003). Forgiveness and justice: A research agenda for social and personality psychology. *Personality and Social Psychology Review, 7*(4), 337–348.

Fehr, R., Gelfand, M. H., & Nag, M. (2010). The road to forgiveness: A meta-analytic synthesis of its situation and dispositional correlates. *Psychological Bulletin, 136*(5), 894–914.

Fehr, R., & Gelfand, M. J. (2012). The forgiving organization: A multilevel model of forgiveness at work. *Academy of Management Review, 37*(4), 664–688.

Fincham, F. D., Beach, S. R., & Davila, J. (2007). Longitudinal relations between forgiveness and conflict resolution in marriage. *Journal of Family Psychology, 21*(3), 542–545.

Foa, E. B., McNally, R. J., & Williams, L. (1996). Mechanisms of change in exposure therapy. In R. M. Rapee (Ed.), *Current controversies in the anxiety disorders* (pp. 329–343). New York, NY: Guilford Press.

Fredrickson, B. L., Grewen, K. M., Coffey, K. A., Algoe, S. B., Firestine, A. M., Arevalo, J. M., . . . Cole, S. W. (2013). A functional genomic perspective on human well-being. *PNAS Proceedings of the National Academy of Sciences of the United States of America, 110*(33), 13684–13689.

Gallagher, M. W., Lopez, S. J., & Preacher, K. J. (2009). The hierarchical structure of well-being. *Journal of Personality, 77*(4), 1025–1050.

Griffin, B. J., Worthington, E. L., Jr., Lavelock, C. R., Wade, N. G., & Hoyt, W. T. (2015). Forgiveness and mental health. In L. L. Toussaint, E. L. Worthington, Jr., & D. R. Williams (Eds.), *Forgiveness and health: Scientific evidence and theories relating forgiveness to better health* (pp. 77–90). New York, NY: Springer.

Hill, P. L., Heffernan, M. E., & Allemand, M. (2015). Forgiveness and subjective well-being: Discussing mechanisms, contexts, and rationales. In L. L. Toussaint, E. L. Worthington, Jr., & D. R. Williams (Eds.), *Forgiveness and health: Scientific evidence and theories relating forgiveness to better health* (pp. 155–169). New York, NY: Springer.

Huta, V., & Ryan, R. M. (2010). Pursuing pleasure or virtue: The differential and overlapping well-being benefits of hedonic and eudaimonic motives. *Journal of Happiness Studies, 11*, 735–762. http://dx.doi.org/10.1007/s10902-009-9171-4

Kashdan, T. B., Biswas-Diener, R., & King, L. A. (2008). Reconsidering happiness: The costs of distinguishing between hedonics and eudaimonia. *The Journal of Positive Psychology, 3*, 219–233. http://dx.doi.org/10.1080/17439760802303044

Kelley, H. H., & Thibaut, J. (1978). *Interpersonal relations: A theory of interdependence.* New York, NY: Wiley.

Keyes, C. L. M., Shmotkin, D., & Ryff, C. D. (2002). Optimizing wellbeing: The empirical encounter of two traditions. *Journal of Personality and Social Psychology, 82*, 1007–1022.

Larkin, K. T., Goulet, C., & Cavanagh, C. (2015). Forgiveness and physiological concomitants and outcomes. In L. L. Toussaint, E. L. Worthington, Jr., & D. R. Williams (Eds.), *Forgiveness and health: Scientific evidence and theories relating forgiveness to better health* (pp. 61–76). New York, NY: Springer.

Lazarus, R. S. (1999). *Stress and emotion: A new synthesis.* New York: Springer.

Linley, P. A., Maltby, J., Wood, A. M., Osborne, G., & Hurling, R. (2009). Measuring happiness: The higher order factor structure of subjective and psychological well-being measures. *Personality and Individual Differences, 47*, 878–884.

McCullough, M. E. (2008). *Beyond revenge: The evolution of forgiveness.* San Francisco: Jossey-Bass.

McCullough, M. E., Luna, L. R., Berry, J. W., Tabak, B. A., & Bono, G. (2010). On the form and function of forgiving: Modeling the time-forgiveness relationship and testing the valuable relationships hypothesis. *Emotion, 10*(3), 358–376.

McCullough, M. E., Pargament, K. I., & Thoresen, C. E. (Eds.). (2000). *Forgiveness: Theory, research, and practice.* New York, NY: Guilford Press.

McCullough, M. E., Pedersen, E. J., Tabak, B. A., & Carter, E. C. (2014). Conciliatory gestures promote forgiveness and reduce anger in humans. *PNAS Proceedings of the National Academy of Sciences of the United States of America, 111*(30), 11211–11216.

McGrath, R. E. (2015). Integrating psychological and cultural perspectives on virtue: The hierarchical structure of character strengths. *The Journal of Positive Psychology, 10*(5), 407–424.

Peterson, C., Park, N., & Seligman, M. E. P. (2005). Orientations to happiness and life satisfaction: The full life versus the empty life. *Journal of Happiness Studies, 6*, 25–41. http://dx.doi.org/10.1007/s10902-004-1278-z

Riek, B. M., & Mania, E. W. (2012). The antecedents and consequences of interpersonal forgiveness: A meta-analytic review. *Personal Relationships, 19*(2), 304–325. doi: 10.1111/j.1475-6811.2011.01363.x

Righetti, F., Finkenauer, C., & Finkel, E. J. (2013). Low self-control promotes the willingness to sacrifice in close relationships. *Psychological Science, 24*, 1533–1540.

Ryan, R. M., & Deci, E. L. (2000). Self-determination theory and the facilitation of intrinsic motivation, social development, and well-being. *American Psychologist, 55*, 68–78. http://dx.doi.org/10.1037/0003-066X.55.1.68

Ryan, R. M., & Deci, E. L. (2001). On happiness and human potentials: A review of research on hedonic and eudaimonic well-being. *Annual Review of Psychology, 52*, 141–166.

Ryan, R. M., Huta, V., & Deci, E. L. (2008). Living well: A self-determination theory perspective on eudaimonia. *Journal of Happiness Studies, 9*, 139–170.

Ryff, C. D. (2014). Psychological well-being revisited: Advances in the science and practice of eudaimonia. *Psychotherapy and Psychosomatics, 83*, 10–28.

Shults, F. L., & Sandage, S. J. (2006). *Transforming spirituality: Integrating theology and psychology.* Grand Rapids, MI: Baker Academic.

Strelan, P., & Covic, T. (2006). A review of forgiveness process models and a coping framework to guide future research. *Journal of Social and Clinical Psychology, 25*, 1059–1085.

Thibaut, J. W., & Kelley, H. H. (1959). *The social psychology of groups.* New York, NY: Wiley.

Toussaint, L. L., & Webb, J. R. (2005). Theoretical and empirical connections between forgiveness, mental health, and well-being. In E. L. Worthington, Jr. (Ed.), *Handbook of forgiveness* (pp. 349–362). New York, NY: Brunner-Routledge.

Toussaint, L. L., Williams, D. R., Musick, M. A., & Everson, S. A. (2001). Forgiveness and health: Age differences in a U.S. probability sample. *Journal of Adult Development, 8*(4), 249–258.

Toussaint, L. L., Worthington, E. L., Jr., & Williams, D. R. (Eds.). (2015). *Forgiveness and health: Scientific evidence and theories relating forgiveness to better health.* Dordrecht: Springer Science Business Media.

Wade, N. G., Hoyt, W. T., Kidwell, J. E. M., & Worthington, E. L., Jr. (2014). Efficacy of psychotherapeutic interventions to promote forgiveness: A meta-analysis. *Journal of Consulting and Clinical Psychology, 82*(1), 154–170.

Waldron, V. R., & Kelley, D. L. (2008). *Communicating forgiveness.* Thousand Oaks, CA: Sage Publications.

Wieselquist, J. (2009). Interpersonal forgiveness, trust, and the investment model of commitment. *Journal of Social and Personal Relationships, 26,* 531–548.

Worthington, E. L., Jr. (1998). The Pyramid Model of Forgiveness: Some interdisciplinary speculations about unforgiveness and the promotion of forgiveness. In E. L. Worthington, Jr. (Ed.), *Dimensions of forgiveness: Psychological research and theological perspectives* (pp. 107–137). Philadelphia, PA: Templeton Foundation Press.

Worthington, E. L., Jr. (Ed.). (2005). *Handbook of forgiveness.* New York, NY: Routledge.

Worthington, E. L., Jr. (2006). *Forgiveness and reconciliation: Theory and application.* New York, NY: Routledge.

Worthington, E. L., Jr., & Allison, S. T. (2018). *Heroic humility: What the science of humility can say to people raised on self-focus.* Washington, DC: American Psychological Association.

Worthington, E. L., Jr., & Sandage, S. J. (2015). *Forgiveness and spirituality in psychotherapy: A relational approach.* Washington, DC: American Psychological Association.

8

HUMILITY

Everett L. Worthington, Jr., Don E. Davis,
Joshua N. Hook, and Caitlin Provencher

Humility and Well-Being

Humility is a relatively new and growing area of scientific study. One reason for the increase in studies examining humility recently has to do with theory and empirical evidence linking humility to well-being. This evidence should accelerate interdisciplinary interest of researchers, practitioners, and the general public and lead to expansion beyond the study of humility. In the current chapter, we first define humility and well-being. Then, we review the extant empirical research linking humility and well-being. Finally, we discuss limitations of the review and areas for future research.

Definitions

What Is Humility?

The link between humility and well-being may seem doubtful to anyone who misunderstands humility as a Casper Milquetoast, wimpy ascension to any demand—reasonable, unreasonable, or even abusive. Researchers have provided much more precise (and positive) definitions of humility. Davis et al. (2010, 2011) define humility as having three components: accurate self-appraisal of strengths and limitations, with a teachable attitude (i.e., an eager willingness to learn ways to strengthen weaknesses and faults); interpersonal modesty; and a warm, other-oriented self-focus. Worthington, Goldstein et al. (2017) found initial evidence for this tripartite definition, in particular the first two components. Worthington, Davis, and Hook (2017) tasked numerous research teams with beginning their chapters presenting reviews of sub-areas of humility by articulating the definition of humility they used in their research. Most definitions of humility involved three parts. First, humility involves an accurate view of self that was neither too positive nor too negative and that recognized strengths but also limitations. Having an accurate view of self does not refer to objective accuracy of self-knowledge—because it is impossible to establish a criterion of what would be true self-knowledge. Rather, an accurate view of oneself refers to, first, reporting what one believes to be true of oneself in one's heart. Teachability and ownership of limitations and weaknesses (Wallace, Chiu, & Owens, 2017) refer to having an attitude that is not defensive about weaknesses but rather seeks input allowing one to correct faults or strengthen weaknesses. Second, humility involves a modest self-presentation— again not so modest that one is falsely modest, nor so bold that one takes every opportunity to recount his or her accomplishments (Davis et al., 2016; cf. Cai et al., 2010). Third, humility involves having a "quiet ego". In other words, a focus on the self was less prominent among humble individuals. However, regarding the quiet ego, researchers diverged into two camps. Some emphasized that a quiet ego occurs when a person focuses beyond themselves, *necessarily* toward others, and toward lifting others up rather than putting them down. Others emphasized that a quiet ego comes through a contemplative spirit, from practices of mindfulness, and from non-responsiveness to provocation. We have preferred the former emphasis because practicing mindfulness or other forms of ego quieting might not necessarily curb self-aggrandizement or self-promotion, but a true orientation to building others up will *necessarily* temper self-promotional tendencies. Numerous studies provide data addressing these different emphases, but neither side has achieved hegemony.

Some researchers have defined and studied particular types of humility. General humility is a judgment by others or self-judgment reflecting humble attitudes and behaviors across situations, relationships, and time. Relational humility is a characteristic of specific relationships, which can vary within a person between relationships. Thus, a person could show high levels of humility within a romantic relationship but act arrogantly as a work supervisor and grovel as a work subordinate. Cultural humility is a type of relational humility reflecting relationships that involve people or groups from different cultures. It indicates respectful treatment of diverse others as individuals yet recognizing that each has aspects of life strongly influenced by culture. Both individual and cultural contexts and influences are worthy of understanding. Intellectual humility refers to one's way of relating to people around intellectual ideas. Religious and political humility were subtypes that were particularly important because of the emotional valence attached to the Sacred and to political philosophies. Spiritual humility is an indication of reverence, awe, and respect in relation to what one treats as Sacred. As we observe in the concluding sections of this chapter, the issue of whether these are really different types of humility or aspects of a single humility is unresolved at this time.

Researchers have also begun to study *state humility*. For example, Kruse, Chancellor, and Lyubomirsky (2017) showed that humility (which is an internal, attitudinal trait or state) differed from modesty, which generally is thought to be behavior that is in line with cultural expectations and that seeks not to offend (or be respectful to) people who hold those expectations. Lyubomirsky and her team of researchers also have shown that awe, gratitude, kindness, and self-affirmation can trigger states of humility that can dominate short-term situations, although it is unclear how long such humble states last and how powerful they are for what kinds of people.

Various instruments that have been developed to assess humility and types of humility. Hill et al.'s (2017) review of assessments of humility included self-reports; single-informant-reports by someone who knows the person; round-robin consensus reports in which people within a group might rate each other on humility and multiple perspectives could be considered simultaneously (Davis et al., 2013; Meagher, Leman, Bias, Latendresse, & Rowatt, 2015); and an implicit associations test (Rowatt, Powers, Targhetta, Comer, Kennedy, & Labouff, 2006). They evaluated the psychometric adequacy of each method of assessment, and they determined that they often triangulated into a near-consensus; however, at times implicit measures (i.e., Rowatt et al., 2006) did not predict self- or other-reports closely. Still undeveloped are physiological bio-markers of humility and behavioral measures of humility.

What Is Well-Being?

Definitions of well-being fall into two major types. Hedonic subjective well-being (SWB), usually defined as a person's overall evaluation of their lives and emotional experiences consisting of life satisfaction, presence of positive affect, and lack of negative affect (Diener, 1984). SWB thus includes broad appraisals, such as life and health satisfaction judgments and specific feelings that reflect how people are reacting to the events in their lives.

Eudaimonic well-being, which some argue is more objective than subjective (even though most measures are self-report), often emphasizes virtue and benefit for others as well as the self (Ryan, Deci & Ryan, 2000; Ryff, 2014; Seligman, 2011). Ryff (1989, 2014) has suggested that eudaimonic well-being consists of six areas of psychological well-being: autonomy, environmental mastery, personal growth, positive relations with others, purpose in life, and self-acceptance. Advocates of hedonic and eudaimonic well-being offer strong conceptual arguments for the correctness of their point of view, but the empirical results tell a different story. A review of six studies comparing Diener's (1984) tripartite model of subjective well-being with Ryff's (2014) psychological well-being model concludes that these debates are more philosophical than empirical and that hedonic and eudaimonic well-being capture the same latent well-being variable and show a similar pattern of correlations with other criterion variables (Chapter 7; see also Chapter 1).

Overview of Chapter

This present chapter does not present a comprehensive review of empirical research on humility. Such reviews can be found in Worthington et al. (in press) and Worthington, Davis and Hook (2017). Instead, our purpose in this chapter is to describe the evidence linking humility to well-being by focusing on four aspects of well-being: (1) religious and spiritual, (2) social or relational, (3) emotional and psychological, and (4) physical. We drew heavily on a recent review chapter (Worthington, Goldstein et al., in press) that evaluated 96 sources, and we added chapters, dissertations, and empirical articles to bring the review current through June 30, 2017. Overall, we added 99 new sources.[1]

Humility and Religious/Spiritual Well-Being

Several lines of evidence suggest that humility may be related to religious/spiritual well-being. First, humility is strongly related to religiousness—regardless of religion. In a theologically focused book chapter, Porter et al. (2017) discussed the role of humility in five major world religions (i.e., Judaism, Christianity, Islam, Buddhism, and Hinduism), all of which considered humility an important virtue. Thus, religious individuals may be more likely to be humble because it aligns with their religious values. Worthington, Goldstein et al.'s (in press) spirituality hypothesis proposes that to the extent that a person has a strong sense of connection to the Sacred, the person will likely have spiritual humility (Davis et al., 2010). To the extent that a person is spiritually humble, the person will be more personally, intellectually, relationally, and culturally humble. Spiritual humility was also found to be related to other types of humility (Davis et al., 2010).

Additional research has supported the hypothesized link between humility and religious/spiritual well-being. First, humility is connected to religiousness, which is in turn related to well-being (McCullough, Hoyt, Larson, Koenig, & Thoresen, 2000). Aghababaei and colleagues (2016) conducted 5 studies using a total of 1,375 participants from Iran, Malaysia, and Poland and found Scores on the Honesty—Humility scale of the HEXACO-PI (Lee & Ashton, 2004) were more highly correlated with religiousness than with scores on variables from the Big Five, though both agreeableness and conscientiousness also were highly related to religiousness. Extraversion was somewhat related to religiousness. The personality characteristics associated with religiousness were relatively consistent across models and measures. Among the reason that religiosity is related to well-being is that religiosity is related to better health practices, more social support, and fewer risky behaviors.

Second, humility might help individuals connect with others who are religiously different, which might reduce negative attitudes, aggressive motives, prejudice, and discrimination. Van Tongeren et al. (2016) reasoned that part of humility is regulating self-enhancing motives in service of others and conducted three studies to evaluate the extent to which humility reduced negative attitudes, behavioral intentions, and behaviors toward religious out-group members. In Study 1, humility about one's religious beliefs was associated with more positive attitudes towards people who adhered to other religions. In Study 2, people imagined that their important beliefs were criticized. Relational and intellectual humility were correlated with less aggressive behavioral intentions toward the person they imagined to have criticized them. In Study 3, people were implicitly primed with humility using a computer-based word-matching task involving humility-related or neutral words. After being criticized, the humility-primed participants gave less hot sauce (a behavioral measure of aggression) to a religious out-group member who criticized their cherished views relative to participants in the neutral prime condition. These studies provide additional evidence that religious and spiritual humility are related to religious and spiritual well-being.

Third, humility might reduce religious conflict. Zhang et al. (in press) examined how (1) intellectual humility about one's religious ideas (i.e., religious humility) and (2) perceptions of others' intellectual humility about the other's religious ideas might affect responses to a religious conflict. They had people describe what happened during a religious conflict in the past. Zhang et al. (in press) had 200 participants complete online questionnaires about their experience during a previous religious conflict. Participants rated their own religious humility (i.e., whether they were humble in sharing ideas regarding the offender's religious beliefs and values); their perceptions about whether the offender might be religiously humble toward the participant's religious beliefs and values; and their own general humility. Next, they reported their forgiveness of the offender following a recalled religious conflict. Both victim religious humility and perceived religious humility of the offender were positively associated with forgiveness, even when controlling for general humility.

Fourth, religious participants might have higher humility, as indicated by less defensiveness and motives toward retaliation after being criticized. Recall is often subject to self-interested and self-enhancing biases (see Van Tongeren & Myers, 2017). In three studies, Van Tongeren, Davis, Hook, Rowatt, and Worthington (2017) examined whether religious people understand humility differently from those not self-identifying as religious. In Study 1, as hypothesized, religious respondents described themselves as more humble than did non-religious respondents. Study 2 involved two community samples and a humility prime to all participants that involved recalling a time of embarrassment and shame. The prime affected people differently depending on their religious affiliation. The experimenters then criticized the participants to provoke an ego-threatening feeling. Religious participants primed with humility reported less likelihood of retaliating. Religious respondents more strongly valued being referred to as humble than did non-religious respondents, which is consistent with belonging to a religion that explicitly values humility (see Porter et al., 2017). As hypothesized, Study 3 found that people primed to recall a time of humility were less defensive than people not so primed. In a main effect of religiousness, religious and non-religious people were equally defensive; however, religious people self-reported more humility than did non-religious people.

Fifth, humility might lead to more experiences of suffering, awe, and elevation (i.e., feelings of higher closeness to the Sacred), which might affect the degree of religious spirituality. Preston and Shin (2016) conducted five studies that found that spiritual experience created a small sense of self and also (somewhat related) a sense of humility before the Sacred. We might think of a small sense of self as being me-focused (e.g., I'm insignificant or I'm unworthy) but a sense of humility is Sacred-focused (e.g., I am more focused on how majestic the Sacred is).

Sixth, people who have low religious humility (e.g., religious devotees, missionaries, jihadists) might lead to a restriction of their religious experiences. Such people often hold their religious beliefs firmly (or even rigidly) and may be very meek and submissive to the sacred but are not open to new religious experiences. But Preston and Shin found that the effect of spiritual experiences led to feelings of awe by creating feelings of a small sense of self and generating a sense of spirituality humility before the Sacred. The effects of spiritual experiences on awe created a sense of a small self and a sense of spiritual humility in people who were religious and people who were not. However, religious people recalled more explicitly religious events and life-and-death events as their sources of spirituality. People who did not identify as religious, however, were more likely to report experiences in nature, peak experiences, science, and yoga/meditation as spiritual experiences.

Seventh, humility might increase connections both with the Sacred and with others. Research has found strong support for a connection between humility and religiousness and spirituality. This was true of both spiritual humility and intellectual humility regarding religious beliefs, values, and practices. First, spiritual humility does not necessarily translate into intellectual humility over religious beliefs, values, and practices (Preston & Shin, 2017). Second, people who are spiritually humble may hold sacred a number of spiritual objects (i.e., God, humanity, nature, or the transcendent). Those who hold religious objects sacred (i.e., God, Scripture, the religious community) likely differ from those who are non-religiously spiritual (i.e., only humanity, nature, or the impersonal transcendent but do not associate these with God).

Humility and Social or Relational Well-Being

People may be drawn to humble people because they admire or simply like to be in relationships with them and therefore wish to become more humble so that others will be socially drawn to them (Worthington et al., 2017). If humility promotes other-oriented motivations and behaviors, then humble people ought to make good relationship partners, and one might want to invest heavily in such relationships in order to increase commitment of both partners. Research supports a number of hypotheses about the social value of humility. Humility tends to strengthens social bonds (*social bond hypothesis*), promotes sacrifice for others (sacrifice-threshold hypothesis), buffers the social wear-and-tear of the competition on the relationships (social oil hypothesis), makes better leaders (humble leader hypothesis), and yields more physically and mentally healthy partners (social health-transmission hypothesis).

The *societal peace hypothesis* proposes that, to the extent that a particular society is composed of more humble citizens, the society is likely to be more socially just (due to the other-orientedness of humility); less combative (due to less offense-taking, more awareness of one's own limitations); more modest (instead of provocatively, presenting one's position); and more valuing of diversity (due to the other-orientedness of humility) (Worthington, Goldstein et al., in press). Numerous studies have supported this hypothesis (for a review, see Davis et al., 2017).

Humility and Other-Oriented Virtues

Humility can promote social well-being by promoting virtuous behavior, especially for those who are other-oriented. Worthington, Goldstein et al. (in press) found that humility was related to altruism, forgiveness, and gratitude. Numerous studies have found positive relationships between humility and virtues. For example, humility is correlated with altruism, compassion, generosity, gratitude, forgiveness, and kindness. In general, humility, which is oriented towards the valuing of other people, seems to be selectively related to other virtues that elevate people and not so much to virtues that are more highly related to conscientiousness or wisdom. In addition, in an intervention study, humility intervention resulted in an increase in trait ratings of patience as well as increased forgiveness (Lavelock et al., 2014).

Humility and Trust

High humility is also related to trust in dyadic relationships and trust in societal institutions. Trust yields peaceful and lower-stress feelings and thus is related to social well-being. For example, Thielmann and Hilbig (2015) examined personality traits within a trust game, which involved making decisions based on trusting that the opponent would live up to stated intentions. Trustworthiness (i.e., actually living up to one's own stated intentions) was predicted by honesty-humility—but not by either positive reciprocity (i.e., responding in kind to the other player's positive actions) or negative reciprocity (i.e., responding to the other player's negative actions with similar subsequent negative actions). All studies revealed consistent support for the honesty-humility's connection to trustworthiness, showing an exclusive link between honesty-humility and trustworthiness, irrespective of the level of prior trust. In contrast, Pfattheicher and Böhm (in press) found that individuals high in honesty-humility showed high levels of trust when people had positive social expectations about the trustworthiness of others. However, people low in honesty-humility did not show trust regardless of whether others were perceived to be trustworthy. When uncertainty in the self was induced, trust went down, especially in those high in honesty-humility. Individuals high in honesty-humility reported reduced trust in others because their own self-doubts decreased their positive social expectations about others. Honesty-humility also predicted trust in the police and self-doubts undermined trust in the police especially for individuals high in honesty-humility. Their research shows that people high in honesty-humility are not unconditionally prosocial.

Humility and Couple Relationships

High humility seems to be helpful in couple relationships, and positive romantic relationships have long been known to contribute to well-being (Kim & McKenry, 2002). For instance, Nonterah and colleagues (2016) followed heterosexual married couples from 3 months prior to childbirth until 21 months after childbirth. Partners who viewed each other as humble reported higher marriage commitment and quality than those not viewing each other as humble. In addition, higher initial levels of stress in couples resulted in couples perceiving their partners as decreasing in humility across the transition. A key limitation of this study was the reliance on self-report measures of humility and stress. Using the same sample, Ripley and colleagues (2016) found that higher levels of relational humility predicted lower levels of stress initially and over time. They suggested that relational humility's other-orientation and prosocial interactional style might elicit more positive social support, which might result in less perceived stress and better support for coping.

Perceived Breaches in Cultural Humility Lead to Decrements in Social Functioning

A related line of work on cultural humility in psychotherapy has examined psychotherapy relationships in which the clients have perceived that their psychotherapist perpetrated (usually unintentional) identity-related offenses (sometimes called *microaggressions*; Hook, Davis, Owen, & DeBlaere, 2017). In a sample of racial/ethnic minority individuals, negative emotions due to an identity-related offense were more extreme if clients perceived their psychotherapist not to be very culturally humble. In addition when clients perceived their psychotherapist to be culturally humble, that in turn predicted better psychotherapy outcomes (Davis et al., 2016). Similarly, another study of racial/ethnic minority clients found that clients who rated their psychotherapists as more culturally humble also reported fewer microaggressions (Hook et al., 2016). In another study of clients at a university counseling center, clients who perceived psychotherapists to have more missed opportunities to explore the clients' salient cultural identities tended to have more negative psychotherapy outcomes, but this relationship was buffered by the degree to which clients saw their therapist as culturally humble.

Humility and Psychological Well-Being

Relatively few studies have explicitly examined the link between humility and psychological well-being. The *virtue and vice hypothesis* suggests that humility is a meta-virtue that pertains to a variety of contexts and is core to other virtues and vices that prioritize the needs of a relationship or group over one's own needs (Worthington, Goldstein et al., in press) However, many virtues are associated with psychological, social, and physical well-being for practitioners of the virtue (e.g., friendship, Chapter 5; forgiveness, Chapter 7; altruism, Chapter 9; gratitude, Chapter 10; meaning and purpose in life, Chapter 14). Worthington, Goldstein et al. found that humility was related to several kinds of virtues, including altruism, forgiveness, gratitude, and self-control. Research has corroborated, but rarely extended (cf. Schwager, Hülsheger, & Lang, 2016), prior findings on humility and virtue. Some research has incorporated designs that allow causal inferences. For example, Tong et al. (2016) conducted four experiments showing that a prime for humility (i.e., recalling humility experiences) enhanced self-control, as evidenced by ability to maintain hand grip pressure, resist eating chocolate, or persevere in a tedious task (Tong et al., 2016).

Several studies have also found a link between humility and vices, specifically the *dark triad traits* (narcissism, Machiavellianism, and psychopathy). For example, a recent meta-analysis of the relationships of the dark triad traits with each other demonstrated a strong relationship between honesty-humility and all three of the dark triad traits (Muris, Merckelbach, Otgaar, & Meijer, 2017).

The *ultimate satisfaction hypothesis* proposes that humility will help people evaluate their life as satisfying, even if they do not rate it as necessarily happier than do others (Worthington, Goldstein et al., in press). For example, several studies have addressed the ultimate satisfaction that comes from acting with humility—usually concerned with meaning or purpose in life. Yu, Chang, and Kim (2016) found that humility predicted meaning in life for Asian American college students but not for European American college students. Zhang et al. (in press) found that individuals with high intellectual humility preserved their sense of belongingness and meaning when engaging in a diverse religious group.

Humility and Physical Well-Being

The *humility-health hypothesis* suggests that humble people are high in agreeableness and conscientiousness (Worthington, Goldstein et al., in press). Agreeableness is related to calmer responses to stressors, thus resulting in fewer stress-related disorders, and conscientiousness is related to better health behaviors, thus making health problems less likely and more effectively dealt with when they occur. A second proposal of the humility-health hypothesis is that high humility is related to better mental health, which is related to physical health. Similarly, as noted previously, high humility is related to better relationships, and better relationships are related to better physical health (see Chapter 4). Only one study supported the hypothesis (Krause, 2012), and it was a national probability sample that examined self-rated health and self-report of humility. One newer study was tangentially related (Tong et al., 2016). Some research had shown that humility is related to self-regulation (Hsu & Chang, 2015), which is an important predictor of physical well-being. Tong et al. (2016) examined humility and self-regulation using a series of four experiments, as we described (above) in the section on psychological well-being. In addition, using a large national sample, Krause, Pargament, Hill, and Ironson (2016) examined whether humility buffered (i.e., protected against) the effects of stressful life events on four measures of well-being: happiness, life satisfaction, depressed affect, and generalized anxiety disorder. They found that humility buffered the negative relationship between stressful life events and all four measures of well-being.

Discussion

Considerable research indicates humility is related to both religious and spiritual well-being and social and relational well-being. Less evidence supports the relationship between humility and psychological well-being. Virtually no research connects humility with physical well-being.

A limitation of the research connecting humility with well-being is that it has, for the most part, examined only direct effects (such as those connecting humility and spirituality, humility and social functioning, etc.). A few articles have identified moderators, and even fewer have tested mediational models. Formal articulations of theories have been lacking to propose mediators between humility and well-being outcomes. This is a big need in the literature.

Potential Mediators Between Humility and Aspects of Well-Being

Humility is likely to affect religious and spiritual well-being through affecting connections with religious or spiritual communities. In addition, humility is highly related to religion, and for religious people, humility will likely be related to fewer health-risky behaviors (i.e., smoking, risk-taking, getting in fights, drinking and drug use) and thus will result in fewer accidents, less involvement in crime or violence, and fewer behavior-mediated health disorders.

Mediators between humility and social well-being include stronger social bonds, better social relationships, less conflict, buffering of negative stress and mood by more social support, and better communication. The primary need is for studies that tests the causal inferences implied by these hypotheses, as well as their possible boundary conditions.

A variety of theories have addressed how humility can promote greater psychological well-being. Potential mechanisms include enhanced emotional functioning; more satisfying social relations; more connection within religious- and spiritually focused communities; less conflict; less anger and rumination; less strain of maintaining a false self-presentation; more teachability, which solicits more aid from others; more emotional satisfaction; and peace from doing a "good" thing like lifting needy others up. Humility's relationship to psychological well-being is mediated by a number of variables. These include social support increased, rumination decreased, religious identification increased, societal connection increased, sense of ultimate satisfaction, or meaning in life increased.

The link between humility and physical well-being is perhaps in greatest need of attention from theorists and researchers. The current evidence for this relationship is weak, but a few mechanisms are worth exploring further. First, humility related to owning human limitations (i.e., being able to admit one's limitations and seek ways to deal with them) may help people cope with severe adversity rather than holding themselves to unrealistic standards and maintaining a belief that one should be finished with grief in a brief period. Second, humility may prevent risky behaviors that harm health or damage relationships, which protect health. Third, humility promotes social bonds, which can enhance health and reduce mortality. These questions remain unanswered.

Key Unresolved Questions in Humility Studies

Many questions about humility remain unresolved. Among those are the following:

1. Most researchers agree that humility involves accurate self-assessment with teachability about one's limitations and that modesty is part of humility (see Davis, McElroy et al., 2016). There is less agreement, however, on the role of the quiet ego and lack of self-focus. Does humility require focus on the elevation and promotion of others in addition to a quiet ego? Or does humility require *only* a quiet ego?

2. Who should define humility? Several researchers have taken a bottom-up approach to defining humility, seeking to determine what lay people understand by the concept. This has some advantages. Self-reports of perceived humility are the raw data of what humility is, and therefore these researchers might argue that determining how people understand humility is crucial to interpreting findings. On the other hand, if experts present an explicit definition of humility, then presumably lay people—even those who might privately disagree with the expert's definition—might use the definition provided and thus make interpretation advantageous relative to averaging lay people's different lay definitions. Wiedman, Cheng, and Tracy (2016) conducted a bottom-up analysis of lay respondents' psychological structure of humility. In five studies ($N = 1,479$) that involve: (1) cluster analysis and categorization of humility-related

words, generated by both lay persons and academic experts; (2) exploratory and confirmatory factor analyses of momentary and dispositional humility experiences; and (3) experimental induction of a momentary humility experience. Across these studies, they found that lay conceptions of humility took two forms—"appreciative" and "self-abasing" humility. *Appreciative humility* is elicited by personal success; involves action tendencies that lift and honor others; and is positively associated with authentic pride, guilt, and prestige-based status. It also conceptually overlaps with gratitude. In contrast, *self-abasing humility* is elicited by personal failure; involves negative self-evaluations; promotes hiding from others' evaluations; and is associated with dispositions such as shame, low self-esteem, and submissiveness. Self-abasing humility might be part of self-condemnation rather than being thought of as a different part of humility. As such, it might be misnamed. This may illustrate the dangers of a bottom-up, non-expert-informed definitional approach. At best, such approaches tell not what a concept is, but what non-experts might conflate with the concept or what it might mean to non-experts in different situations.

3. Are there distinct types of humility—like intellectual, relational, and spiritual humility—or are the different types of humility aspects of a single construct of general humility?

4. Can humility be accurately assessed? Numerous measures exist (see Hill et al., 2017), but under what conditions does each validly assess humility? What criteria should be used to assess the accuracy of an assessment? Can behavioral criteria be developed that would be more definitive than self-report? Physiological? Should triangulation be employed, comparing various self-report instruments with physiological and behavioral indices?

5. Is humility a root virtue related determinatively to a cluster of virtues and of vices? That is, is humility necessary for people to be (for example) altruistic, compassionate, empathic or is low humility necessary if a person is (for example) narcissistic, manipulative, or psychopathic?

6. How are state humility, relational humility, and general (trait) humility related? When is it most useful to consider each type of humility?

7. How does humility change with age and experience? Is suffering necessary to produce humility? Is humility born of suffering different from that born of awe and elevation?

8. What aspects of well-being are most affected by humility?

9. By what mechanisms might humility affect different aspects of well-being?

10. What moderates connections between humility and the aspects of well-being?

11. What interventions might be used to help people who wish to become more humble to most successfully achieve that goal in the briefest time and maintain it longest?

In this chapter, we evaluated the status of research on humility and well-being and concluded that there is strong evidence that humility produces religious and spiritual well-being and social well-being. However, the evidence is modest that humility produces psychological and emotional well-being, and the evidence is almost non-existent for physical well-being. Few mediational mechanisms have been proposed, much less investigated, for these connections. Many important questions still exist in the field.

Note

1 Worthington, Goldstein et al. (in press) reviewed 96 empirical articles on humility published between January 2000 and August 2015. For the present chapter, we expanded our search to include chapters and dissertations, which uncovered 45 additional sources from January 2000 to August 2015. Using the search parameters for articles, dissertations, and chapters published between September 2015 and June 30, 2017, we located 303 additional sources. We grouped these studies into four categories: (1) religious or spiritual well-being (e.g., spiritual★, spiritual health, spiritual well-being, religion, peacefulness); (2) relational or social well-being (e.g., relation★,relational health, satisfaction, commitment, virtues, altruism, compassion, love,); (3) psychological (e.g., depression, anxiety, mental health, resilience, adaptability, anxi★, depress★) and emotional (e.g., emotional health, happiness, gratitude, happ★, mindful★, unhapp★), and subjective (e.g., subjective well-being, eudiamon★) well-being; and (4) physical well-being (e.g., physical health, disease, stress, occupational health, health). Of all of the articles, chapters, and dissertations, we judged 99 articles to be related to humility and well-being.

References

Aghababaei, N., Błachnio, A., Arji, A., Chiniforoushan, M., Tekke, M., & Fazeli Mehrabadi, A. (2016). Honesty—humility and the HEXACO structure of religiosity and well-being. *Current Psychology: A Journal for Diverse Perspectives on Diverse Psychological Issues, 35*(3), 421–426.

Cai, H., Sedikides, C., Gaertner, L., Wang, C., Carvallo, M., Xu, Y., . . . Jackson, L. E. (2010). Tactical self-enhancement in China: Is modesty at the service of self-enhancement in East Asian culture? *Social Psychological and Personality Science, 2*(1), 59–64.

Davis, D. E., Hook, J. N., Worthington, E. L., Jr., Van Tongeren, D. R., Gartner, A. L., & Jennings, D. J., II. (2010). Relational spirituality and forgiveness: Development of the Spiritual Humility Scale (SHS). *Journal of Psychology and Theology, 38,* 91–100.

Davis, D. E., Hook, J. N., Worthington, E. L., Jr., Van Tongeren, D. R., Gartner, A. L., Jennings, D. J. II., & Emmons, R. A. (2011). Relational humility: Conceptualizing and measuring humility as a personality judgment. *Journal of Personality Assessment, 93,* 225–234.

Davis, D. E., McElroy, S. E., Rice, K. G., Choe, E., Westbrook, C., Hook, J. N., . . . Worthington, E. L., Jr. (2016). Is modesty a subdomain of humility? *The Journal of Positive Psychology, 11*(4), 439–446.

Davis, D. E., Placeres, V., Choe, E., DeBlaere, C., Zeyala, D., & Hook, J. N. (2017). Relational humility. In E. L. Worthington, Jr., D. E. Davis, & J. N. Hook (Eds.), *Handbook of humility: Theory, research, and applications* (pp. 105–118). New York, NY: Routledge.

Davis, D. E., Rice, K. G., McElroy, S. E., DeBlaere, C., Choe, E., Van Tongeren, D. R., Hook, J. N. (2016). Distinguishing intellectual humility and general humility. *The Journal of Positive Psychology, 11*(3), 215–224.

Davis, D. E., Worthington, E. L., Jr., Hook, J. N., Emmons, R. A., Hill, P. C., Bollinger, R. A., & Van Tongeren, D. R. (2013). Humility and the development and repair of social bonds: Two longitudinal studies. *Self and Identity, 12,* 58–77.

Deci, E. L., & Ryan, R. M. (2000). The "what" and "why" of goal pursuits: Human needs and self-determination of behavior. *Psychological Inquiry, 11,* 227–268. doi: 10.1207/S15327965PLI1104_01

Diener, E. (1984). Subjective well-being. *Psychological Bulletin, 95,* 542–575. http://dx.doi.org/10.1037/0033-2909.95.3.542

Hill, P. C., Laney, E. K., Edwards, K. J., Wang, D. C., Orme, W. H., Chan, A. C., & Wang, F. L. (2017). A few good measures: Colonel Jessup and humility. In E. L. Worthington, Jr., D. E. Davis, & J. N. Hook (Eds.), *Handbook of humility: Theory, research, and application* (pp. 119–134). New York, NY: Routledge.

Hook, J. N., Davis, D. E., Owen, J., & DeBlaere, C. (2017). *Cultural humility: Engaging diverse identities in therapy.* Washington, DC: American Psychological Association.

Hook, J. N., Farrell, J. E., Davis, D. E., DeBlaere, C., Van Tongeren, D. R., & Utsey, S. O. (2016). Cultural humility and racial microaggressions in counseling. *Journal of Counseling Psychology, 63*(3), 269–277.

Hsu, K.-Y., & Chang, Y.-L. (2015). Effects of effortful control and HEXACO personality traits on adolescents' internalizing and externalizing problem behaviors. *Chinese Journal of Psychology, 57*(1), 1–25.

Kim, H. K., & McKenry, P. C. (2002). The relationship between marriage and psychological well-being A longitudinal analysis. *Journal of Family Issues, 23*(8), 885–911.

Krause, N. (2012). Religious involvement, humility, and change in self-rated health over time. *Journal of Psychology and Theology, 40*(3), 199–210.

Krause, N., Pargament, K. I., Hill, P. C., & Ironson, G. (2016). Humility, stressful life events, and psychological well-being: Findings from the landmark spirituality and health survey. *The Journal of Positive Psychology, 11*(5), 499–510.

Kruse, E., Chancellor, J., & Lyubomirsky, S. (2017). State humility: Measurement, conceptual validation, and intrapersonal processes. *Self and Identity, 16*(4), 399–438.

Lavelock, C. R., Worthington, E. L., Jr., Davis, D. E., Griffin, B. J., Reid, C., Hook, J. N., & Van Tongren, D. R. (2014). The quiet virtue speaks: An intervention to promote humility. *Journal of Psychology and Theology, 42*(1), 99–110.

Lee, K., & Ashton, M. C. (2004). Psychometric properties of the HEXACO personality inventory. *Multivariate Behavioral Research, 39,* 329–358.

McCullough, M. E., Hoyt, W. T., Larson, D. B., Koenig, H. G., & Thoresen, C. (2000). Religious involvement and mortality: A meta-analytic review. *Health Psychology, 19,* 211–222.

Meagher, B. R., Leman, J. C., Bias, J. P., Latendresse, S. J., & Rowatt, W. C. (2015). Contrasting self-report and consensus ratings of intellectual humility and arrogance. *Journal of Research in Personality, 58,* 35–45.

Muris, P., Merckelbach, H., Otgaar, H., & Meijer, E. (2017). The malevolent side of human nature: A meta-analysis and critical review of the literature on the dark triad (narcissism, Machiavellianism, and psychopathy). *Perspectives on Psychological Science 12*(2), 183–204.

Nonterah, C. W., Garthe, R. C., Reid, C. A., Worthington, E. L., Jr., Davis, D. E., Hook, J. N., . . . Griffin, B. J. (2016). The impact of stress on fluctuations in relational humility as couples transition to parenthood. *Personality and Individual Differences, 101,* 276–281.

Pfattheicher, S., & Böhm, R. (in press). Honesty-Humility under threat: Self-uncertainty destroys trust among the nice guys. *Journal of Personality and Social Psychology.* http://dx.doi.org.proxy.library.vcu.edu/10.1037/pspp0000144

Porter, S. L., Rambachan, A., Vélez de Cea, A., Rabinowitz, D., Pardue, S., & Jackson, S. (2017). Religious perspectives on humility. In E. L. Worthington Jr., D. E. Davis, & J. N. Hook (Eds.), *Handbook of humility: Theory, research, and applications* (pp. 47–61). New York, NY: Routledge.

Preston, J. L, & Shin, F. (2017). Spiritual experiences evoke awe through the small self in both religious and non-religious individuals. *Journal of Experimental Social Psychology, 70,* 212–221. http://dx.doi.org.proxy.library.vcu.edu/10.1016/j.jesp.2016.11.006

Ripley, J. S., Garthe, R. C., Perkins, A., Worthington, E. L., Jr., Davis, D. E., Hook, J. N., . . . Eaves, D. (2016). Perceived partner humility predicts subjective stress during transition to parenthood. *Couple and Family Psychology: Research and Practice, 5*(3), 157–167.

Rowatt, W. C., Powers, C., Targhetta, V., Comer, J., Kennedy, S., & Labouff, J. (2006). Development and initial validation of an implicit measure of humility relative to arrogance. *The Journal of Positive Psychology, 1,* 198–211.

Ryff, C. D. (1989). Happiness is everything, or is it? Explorations on the meaning of psychological well-being. *Journal of Personality and Social Psychology, 57,* 1069–1081. http://dx.doi.org/10.1037/0022-3514.57.6.1069

Ryff, C. D. (2014). Psychological well-being revisited: Advances in the science and practice of eudaimonia. *Psychotherapy and Psychosomatics, 83,* 10–28. http://dx.doi.org/10.1159/000353263

Schwager, I. T. L., Hülsheger, U. R., & Lang, J. W. B. (2016). Be aware to be on the square: Mindfulness and counterproductive academic behavior. *Personality and Individual Differences, 93,* 74–79.

Seligman, M. P. (2011). *Flourish.* New York, NY: Atria.

Thielmann, I., & Hilbig, B. E. (2015). The traits one can trust: Dissecting reciprocity and kindness as determinants of trustworthy behavior. *Personality and Social Psychology Bulletin, 41*(11), 1523–1536.

Tong, E. M. W., Tan, K. W. T., Chor, A. A. B., Koh, E. P. S., Lee, J. S. Y., & Tan, R. W. Y. (2016). Humility facilitates higher self-control. *Journal of Experimental Social Psychology, 62,* 30–39.

Van Tongeren, D. R., Davis, D. E., Hook, J. N., Rowatt, W., & Worthington, E. L., Jr. (2017). Religious differences in reporting and expressing humility. *Psychology of Religion and Spirituality,* April 27, 2017, No Pagination Specified. http://dx.doi.org/10.1037/rel0000118

Van Tongeren, D. R., & Myers, D. G. (2017). A social psychological perspective on humility. In E. L. Worthington, Jr., D. E. Davis, & J. N. Hook (Eds.), *Handbook of humility: Theory, research, and application* (pp. 150–164). New York, NY: Routledge.

Van Tongeren, D. R., Stafford, J., Hook, J. N., Green, J. D., Davis, D. E., & Johnson, K. A. (2016). Humility attenuates negative attitudes and behaviors toward religious out-group members. *The Journal of Positive Psychology, 11*(2), 199–208.

Wallace, A. S., Chiu, C. Y. (C.), & Owens, B. P. (2017). Organizational humility and the better functioning business non-profit and religious organizations In E. L. Worthington, Jr., D. E. Davis, & J. N. Hook (Eds.), *Handbook of humility: Theory, research, and application* (pp. 246–259). New York, NY: Routledge.

Watkins, P. (this volume). Gratitude.

Weidman, A. C., Cheng, J. T., & Tracy, J. L. (2016). The psychological structure of humility. *Journal of Personality and Social Psychology,* July 25, 2016, No Pagination Specified. http://dx.doi.org/10.1037/pspp0000112

Worthington, E. L., Jr., Davis, D. E., & Hook, J. N. (Eds.). (2017). *Handbook of humility: Theory, research, and application*. New York, NY: Routledge.

Worthington, E. L., Jr., Goldstein, L., Cork, B., Griffin, B. J., Garthe, R. C., Lavelock, C. R., Davis, D. E., Hook, J. N., & Van Tongeren, D. R. (in press). Humility: A qualitative review of definitions, theory, concept, and research support for seven hypotheses. In L. Edwards and S. Marques (Eds.), S. Lopez (Gen. Ed.), *The Oxford handbook of positive psychology*, 3rd Edition. New York: Oxford University Press and Oxford Handbooks Online, www.oxfordhandbooks.com

Yu, E. A., Chang, E. C., & Kim, J. H. J. (2016). Asian American culturally relevant values as predictors of meaning in life in Asian and European American college students: Evidence for cultural differences? *Asian American Journal of Psychology*, 7(3), 159-166. http://dx.doi.org.proxy.library.vcu.edu/10.1037/aap0000042

Zhang, H., Hook, J. N., Farrell, J. E., Moser, D. K., Van Tongeren, D. R., & Davis D. E. (2016). The effect of religious diversity on religious belonging and meaning: The role of intellectual. *Psychology of Religion and Spirituality*. http://dx.doi.org.proxy.library.vcu.edu/10.1037/rel0000108

9

HELPING AND WELL-BEING

A Motivational Perspective

David A. Lishner and Eric L. Stocks

Helping others is a ubiquitous social behavior in humans. We help kin, friends, acquaintances, strangers, members of other species, and even highly abstract targets such as social groups and the environment. Human helping behavior can range from brief instances of aid that incur little cost to the helper, to extreme forms of assistance that involve costs spanning years, or even decades. Over the past 50 years, social scientists have sought to understand *who* are helped, *how* they are helped, and *why* they are helped (Penner, Dovidio, Piliavin, & Schroeder, 2005). More contemporary research, however, has begun to examine the possibility that helping may also benefit the well-being of the helper him- or herself (Crocker, Canevello, & Brown, 2017; Inagaki & Orehek, 2017). This counterintuitive and intriguing possibility is the focus of the present chapter.

Defining Helping Behavior

Helping behavior refers to any action carried out to improve the welfare of another individual or entity. Other terms synonymous with this definition include *prosocial behavior* and *prosocial action*. Terms such as *parenting, caregiving, volunteerism,* and *giving support* also describe helping behavior, but they typically encompass a relatively limited or special type of helping behavior (helping of children, helping those with chronic needs, or helping behavior facilitated in an organizational or collective context). Moreover, in this chapter, we explicitly avoid using the term *altruism* to define helping behavior or a subclass of helping behavior due to the term's use in research to encompass a variety of evolutionary, behavioral, or motivational phenomena. As it is used here, helping behavior is defined independently of the motivation for engaging in the helping behavior. This distinction is necessary because one may seek to help others for a variety of motivational reasons. As will become clear, the particular motivations that initiate and guide helping behavior are important in understanding the association between helping and helpers' well-being. For this reason it is essential to clearly distinguish between the *act* of helping and the *motivation* for helping.

Defining Well-Being

Well-being is a complex term with multiple meanings. Many consider well-being to be primarily subjective, in that it reflects momentary or global evaluations of satisfaction and happiness in one's current state or life (Diener, Oishi, & Lucas, 2003). These evaluations can be relatively general (e.g., sense of overall satisfaction in life), or specific to certain life domains (e.g., satisfaction with one's marriage or career) or events (e.g., happiness in response to a recent accomplishment). High subjective well-being is usually defined as consisting of high positive affect, high satisfaction, low negative affect, and a sense of vitality and meaning in one's activities, although it is important to treat these as related but conceptually distinct indicators of well-being (Kyeongmo, Lehning, & Sacco, 2016; Lucas, Diener, & Suh, 1996; Ryan & Deci, 2001). Additionally, physical health and functioning often are considered indicators of well-being by those interested in understanding and fostering positive public health outcomes (CDC, 2016; see also Chapter 1).

Given the complexity of well-being, we adopt a relatively broad conceptualization of this construct that encompasses an organism's level of positive physical and psychological functioning both within and across various life domains. When well-being is high, an organism's physical and psychological functioning and experience is positive, robust, and healthy. When well-being is low, an organism's physical and psychological functioning and experience is negative, weak, or compromised. Both physical and psychological functioning can vary along multiple dimensions (e.g., physical mobility, physical strength, psychological alertness, ability to self-regulate). Moreover, one may have compromised functioning along one dimension yet still have high functioning along other dimensions. Given these conceptualizations, we therefore use the term *physical well-being* to describe an organism's degree of functioning along all relevant physical dimensions that apply to a specific life domain or across life domains in general. Similarly, we use the term *psychological well-being* to describe an organisms' degree of functioning along all relevant psychological dimensions that apply to a specific life domain or across life domains in general.

In humans, high levels of physical and psychological well-being give rise to subjective feelings of satisfaction, happiness, competence, and related positive emotions. In contrast, low levels of physical and psychological well-being give rise to subjective feelings of dissatisfaction, distress, incompetence, and related negative emotions. We use the term *subjective well-being* to describe the extent of these feelings. Like physical and psychological well-being, subjective well-being may pertain to functioning within a specific life domain or across life domains in general. Because both physical well-being and psychological well-being give rise to subjective well-being, it does not correspond perfectly to either. For this reason, one may experience relatively high levels of subjective well-being even though one or more dimensions of physical or psychological well-being are low due to high levels on one or more other physical or psychological dimensions of well-being.

Physical, psychological, and subjective well-being also may be considered in terms of stable or temporary states. Although one's general levels of well-being may be relatively stable across time, events may trigger fluctuations in this stability. For example, a person with generally high levels of well-being may experience a temporary decrease in well-being due to a stressful life event or sickness that then reverts back to baseline levels once the event or sickness has passed. Likewise, a series of re-occurring events may produce a systematic shift in one's general levels of well-being. For instance, long-term changes in life status (e.g., divorce, unemployment) or chronic illness may shift ones previously high levels of baseline well-being to lower levels. Given the joint influences of physical well-being and psychological well-being on subjective well-being, variation in physical and psychological well-being across situation or time would be expected to result in corresponding variation in subjective well-being. Ultimately, well-being is probably best conceptualized as a combination of stable and fluctuating variation in the physical and psychological functioning of an organism both within and across different life domains (physical well-being and psychological well-being). Moreover, in humans, this relative degree of functioning manifests proportionally in subjective feelings of satisfaction, happiness, competency, and the like (subjective well-being).

Measuring Well-Being

The complex relation between subjective well-being and the combination of physical and psychological well-being have implications for how well-being is measured or assessed in research. Generally speaking, subjective well-being is easy to assess by use of self-report rating scales. One essentially asks participants how satisfied, positive, or competent they feel at a given moment or in general. However, it can be difficult to determine whether variation in self-report ratings of subjective well-being reflect corresponding variation in physical well-being, psychological well-being, or a combination thereof. Physical and psychological dimensions of well-being can be assessed by using behavioral measures (e.g., degree of physical mobility, longevity, performance on cognitive tasks). Yet, it can be difficult to determine whether variation in measures of physical and psychological well-being directly correspond to variation in subjective well-being. These measurement issues will be important to consider when evaluating research on the association between helping and well-being.

Evidence of a Positive Association Between Helping and Well-Being

Based on these conceptualizations of helping behavior and well-being, we can consider whether empirical evidence of a link between helping and well-being exists. The research addressing this question can be organized into two broad classes of research: (1) studies of helping and its associations with longevity and measures of mental health and (2) studies of experimental induction of helping and its effects on self-report measures of affect and self-evaluation. In the first class of research, measures of longevity more directly assess physical well-being, whereas measures of mental health more directly reflect psychological well-being, subjective well-being, or both. In the second class of research, self-report measures of affect and self-evaluation best reflect subjective well-being.

Helping, Longevity, and Mental Health

One class of evidence supporting the link between helping and well-being comes from research that reports a positive association between helping behavior and both longevity and measures of mental health (Brown & Brown, 2014; Oman, 2007; Piliavin, 2003; Post, 2005; Wilson & Musick, 2000). Perhaps the most impressive findings are those revealing that people who engage in helping activities tend to live longer. This association appears to generalize across multiple types of helping behavior including informal caregiving of spouses, friends, and family members (e.g., Brown, Nesse, Vinokur, & Smith, 2003; Brown et al., 2009; Poulin, Brown, Dillard, & Smith, 2013), as well as more formal volunteer activities directed at providing assistance to those in one's community (e.g., Muscik, Herzog, & House, 1999; Oman, Thoresen, & McMahon, 1999).

In most of this research, reports of helping behavior are used to predict future mortality. Consequently, the prospective aspect of the research permits stronger causal inference to be made (i.e., that helping behavior is a possible causal contributor to longevity). Moreover, many of the more recent studies find evidence of the longitudinal association even after statistically holding constant a variety of potentially confounding variables such as social support, health status, physical functioning, and religious practice that may indirectly account for the helping-longevity association. Evidence also suggests that among volunteers, the positive effect of helping behavior on longevity may be specific to volunteer activities carried out in the service of other-oriented and value-expressive motivations as opposed to self-focused motivations (e.g., desire for self-enhancement, desire to learn about the self or develop skills; Konrath, Fuhrel-Forbis, Lou, & Brown, 2012). One potential limitation of this research is that the studies typically involve caregivers and volunteers who are older adults, a population in which mortality is more variable than in younger individuals. Thus, longevity may make for a more sensitive indicator of physical well-being in older adults than in younger adults.

Helping also predicts mental health (Brown & Brown, 2014; Piliavin, 2003; Post, 2005; Wilson & Musick, 2000). Evidence suggests a positive association between helping and measures of mental health, including global ratings of positive affect, life satisfaction, and self-esteem (e.g., Dulin & Hill, 2003; Dulin, Hill, Anderson, & Rasmussen, 2001; Kahana, Bhatta, Lovegreen Kahana, & Midlarsky, 2013; Martela & Ryan, 2015). Evidence also suggests that helping behavior is inversely associated with indicators of stress and negative affect (e.g., Raposa, Laws, & Ansell, 2016). However, this inverse association is not found in the research as frequently as the positive association noted above (e.g., Dulin & Hill, 2003; Martela & Ryan, 2015). This discrepancy in associations suggests the effect of helping on positive indicators of mental health may be more generalizable than the effect of helping on negative indicators of mental health.

Much like the association between helping and longevity, the positive association between helping and mental health appears to generalize across different types of helping (e.g., Dulin et al., 2001; Kahana et al., 2013; Poulin et al., 2010). Moreover, the age of participants in studies of helping and mental health (e.g., Martela & Ryan, 2015) tends to be broader than the age of participants in helping-longevity research. However, unlike helping-longevity studies, which typically use measures of helping to predict future longevity, helping-mental health research instead tends to use concurrent measurement of helping and mental health (although there are some exceptions; see Wink & Dillon, 2007). This general methodical limitation permits only a weak inference that helping causes better mental health. It may be that people with good mental health are more helpful.

Experimental Induction of Helping

The research on helping, longevity, and mental health provide for a compelling case that helping behavior is associated with well-being. However, evidence of a causal effect of helping on well-being is mostly limited to research in which helping was used to predict future physical well-being as measured by longevity. The research on helping and mental health offers evidence that the association between helping and well-being extends to psychological and subjective well-being, but it does not permit causal conclusions regarding the association because helping and mental health are typically measured concurrently. To address the question of causality, it would be ideal if one could experimentally manipulate helping and then examine its effects on measures of well-being. Fortunately, a third body of work exists, in which researchers experimentally manipulated helping behavior and then measured its effect on measures indicative of subjective well-being.

For example, in a series of studies, Williamson and Clark (1989) found that participants asked by a confederate to assist in cleaning up a mess reported more positive changes in mood compared to those who were given no opportunity to help or those asked to help, but who were situationally constrained from helping.

In another experiment, more positive changes in mood were found when single, male participants were permitted an opportunity to help (versus not help) an ostensible female participant who requested assistance in sorting materials for an upcoming task. These effects, however, were limited to participants who were told that the female participant was romantically available but not when they were told that she was romantically unavailable. Other earlier experimental work has also found effects of manipulated helping on participant mood, but not consistently (e.g., Harris, 1977, who found participants reported higher mood after helping a confederate look for a dropped slip of paper, but not after giving a "lost" confederate directions).

More recent experimental work provides additional evidence of a causal effect of helping on well-being. Research on prosocial spending in which participants are randomly assigned an opportunity or no opportunity to allocate money to those in need (or to recall such instances) suggests that prosocial spending produces feelings of positive affect (Aknin et al., 2013; Dunn, Aknin, & Norton, 2014). This effect is most potent when spending results in producing positive impact (as opposed to no impact) for the recipient or the recipient is a close other. Finally, Gray (2010) found in three studies that those given the opportunity to donate money to charity (versus no opportunity) or to create a story about themselves helping another (versus engaging in work) persevered longer on strength tasks. This finding is particularly notable in that it used a behavioral measure that can be interpreted as assessing physical well-being. A corresponding effect on self-reported positive affect also was found in the three experiments, but was only statistically significant in one of them.

Weinstein and Ryan (2010) proposed that the causal effect of helping behavior on well-being is driven by the satisfaction of psychological needs for competence, relatedness, and autonomy. When helping behavior results in satisfaction of these psychological needs, enhanced positive well-being results. To investigate this explanation, they conducted two experiments in which autonomous (versus controlled) helping was manipulated in two different ways. In one experiment, autonomous helping was manipulated by giving participants choice in how much money to allot between themselves and an ostensible partner they believed was also participating in the study (versus forcing participants to distribute the money in a predetermined manner). In the second experiment, the researcher requested assistance during a break in the study procedure in a manner that suggested the participant had a choice to help (versus had no choice to help). In both studies, helpers who were given no choice in deciding to help reported lower subjective well-being (based on a composite measure that included ratings of positive affect, vitality, and self-esteem) than did those in the autonomous choice conditions. Moreover, these effects were accounted for (mediated) by ratings of the extent to which needs for competence, relatedness, and autonomy were satisfied. In a follow-up experiment, Martela and Ryan (2016) found a similar pattern of findings when comparing those randomly assigned to a condition in which effort on a game resulted in humanitarian donations versus those in a condition in which game effort did not result in humanitarian donations. Subjective well-being (positive affect, vitality, and event meaningfulness) was higher for those in the donation condition than those in the non-donation condition, and the effect was accounted for by self-reported psychological need satisfaction.

Summary

Taken as a whole, research on helping, longevity, and mental health appears consistent with the hypothesis that engaging in helping behavior is positively associated with physical, psychological, and subjective well-being. Moreover, results of studies that involved experimental induction of helping behavior and measurement of states indicative of subjective well-being suggests the association may be causal such that engaging in helping behavior produces higher levels of subjective well-being. However, the experimental findings also provide evidence that the causal effect may depend on who is helped; the impact of the benefit for the recipient; and whether helping makes the helper feel more competent, related, and autonomous.

Evidence of a Negative Association Between Helping and Well-Being

Although most research suggests that helping increases well-being, some research suggests otherwise. Specifically, research on informal caregiving of close others and family members suggests helping is associated with negative outcomes indicative of lower well-being, particularly when the helping involves long-term care of older individuals or those with mental or physical illness (for reviews and meta-analyses, see Baronet, 1999; Pinquart & Sörensen, 2003, 2007; Schulz & Monin, 2012; Schulz & Sherwood, 2008; Vitaliano, Zhang, & Scanlan, 2003; for a reassessment of this research, see Brown & Brown, 2014).

Many of the studies substantiating the claim of a negative association between informal caregiving and well-being are similar in design to the studies of helping, longevity, and mental health discussed previously. Studies of informal caregiving involve measuring the degree of caregiver helping and then using it to predict concurrent or future measures of well-being, usually indicators of lower physical, psychological, or subjective well-being such as stress, negative mental health outcomes, and mortality. According to Brown and Brown (2014), the discrepancy between the results of these studies and studies finding a positive association between helping and well-being is the failure in the former studies to address the influence of confounding variables that cloud the positive association. These confounding variables include pre-existing dispositional and situational differences of participants that predict lower well-being independent of caregiving, yet may co-occur with how the degree of caregiving is measured. For instance, those who are able to offer more care to a disabled family member may be those who have higher physical, psychological, or subjective well-being in general. Failure to hold constant these pre-existing differences in well-being may obscure the positive association between the amount of caregiving offered and well-being. In contrast, many of the studies that find evidence of a positive association typically attempt to statistically or methodologically hold these types of confounding variables constant while evaluating the association between amount of caregiving and degree of well-being.

Even if Brown and Brown (2014) are correct, one additional newer body of research also complicates the issue. This research involves examination of pathological, "irrational" forms of helping behavior, or tendencies to engage in such behavior, that results in negative outcomes for the intended recipients of help or for the individual initiating the help (Oakley, Knafo, Madhavan, & Wilson, 2012). Research on *pathological helping* (usually referred to as "pathological altruism") and its potential negative impacts on the helper suggests that, under certain circumstances, helping is detrimental to one's well-being, even in situations that do not involve informal caregiving of ailing close others. For example, one may engage in helping to foster a false sense of personal goodness or positive self-evaluation (Burton, 2012); maintain a negative co-dependent relationship; or avoid dealing with negative aspects of the self (McGrath & Oakley, 2012; Turvey, 2012). Moreover, excessive helping may lead to burnout, particularly when the suffering of those in need is extreme, difficult to alleviate, or difficult to avoid (e.g., long-term care of family members, repeated exposure to those in need among healthcare professionals; Klimecki & Singer, 2012).

Why Does Helping Increase or Decrease Well-Being? Theoretical Explanations

A number of theories have been advanced to explain why helping increases well-being. Implicit in several of these theories are conditions under which helping would be expected to have little impact on well-being or may even decrease well-being. One explanation for the positive effect of helping on well-being is that helping promotes a shift away from more restrictive internal standards, values, and perspectives that one may use to establish a personal sense of meaning to a broader range of internal standards, values, and perspectives one may use to establish a personal sense of meaning. Helping can, therefore, promote "response shift", which offers the helper more diverse ways of achieving a higher sense of life quality and well-being (Schwartz, 2007).

Others have argued that engaging in purposeful activity that one can initiate and control produces a sense of autonomy and mastery, which in turn increases physical health and happiness, both indicators of well-being (Langer & Rodin, 1976; Rodin & Langer, 1977). Similarly, Weinstein and Ryan (2010) argue that voluntary and successful helping satisfies psychological needs for autonomy, relatedness, and competence, which in turn results in a sense of positive well-being. These perspectives suggest that helping will only increase well-being if it is perceived as voluntary and successful. Involuntary helping or voluntary but unsuccessful helping would not increase well-being.

The extent to which volunteerism fulfills the specific motivations for initiating volunteerism (e.g., to acquire personal growth, to establish relationships with others) is hypothesized to increase feelings of satisfaction (Clary & Snyder, 1999; Clary et al., 1998). Cialdini and colleagues (Baumann, Cialdini, & Kenrick, 1981; Cialdini & Kenrick, 1976) have proposed that individuals in many cultures are socialized to experience mood enhancement when they help others, regardless of the context. As a result, engaging in helping makes them feel good. This socialization results from positive reinforcement for engaging in helping behavior during childhood and adolescence. Crocker et al. (2017) suggest that these and other helping motivations may be classified into one of two general types: *otherish* motivation and *selfish* motivation. They argue that helping driven by otherish motivations is more likely to enhance well-being than helping driven by selfish motivations because such helping results in feeling connected to others in a meaningful way.

Finally, a model that shares some similarity to the categorization scheme advocated by Crocker et al. (2017) was proposed by Brown and colleagues (Brown & Brown, 2014; Brown & Cialdini, 2015). They distinguish between *other-directed* motivation and *self-directed* motivation in seeking to describe the positive and negative impacts of helping on caregivers. However, Brown and colleagues are more specific in describing the evolutionary and motivational aspects of what is meant by other-directed motivation. According to their model, empathic concern, which generates other-directed motivation, increases helping but also has the "side effect" of engaging brain processes involved in the attenuation of stress. However, this benefit is not obtained when helping is produced by self-directed motivational states (e.g., desire for material rewards, desire to avoid unpleasant feelings produced by observing others in need). Thus, helping that is driven by other-directed motivation provides a buffer against the costs of helping such as physical demand and stress, whereas helping driven by self-directed motivation provides no such buffer. Brown and Cialdini (2015) further propose that the other-directed motivation responsible for buffering of stress is an evolved mechanism that has the adaptive function of promoting the fitness of individuals by directing caregiving toward others with whom one has close, interdependent relationships (e.g., offspring, kin, friends). Moreover, even though this other-directed motivational system originally evolved in the context of promoting the welfare of close others, the system can be initiated by non-kin who exhibit the appropriate distress cues or needs. The evolutionary explanation for the origin of this other-directed motivational system is explained by *selective-investment theory* (SIT; Brown & Brown, 2006), but the psychological and biological mechanisms proposed to account for this other-directed motivation also can be accommodated by Batson's (2011) *empathy-altruism model* of altruistic motivation. In contrast to selective-investment theory, the empathy-altruism model proposes the capacity for altruistic care stems from generalization of a mechanism evolved to promote care of young referred to as *selective tenderness and nurturance diffused* (STAND).

Brown and Brown (2014) believe their model can account for the apparent negative association between informal caregiving and well-being. When studies control for pre-existing dispositional and situational sources of stress independent of the degree of caregiving, informal caregiving is found to produce higher well-being. Higher well-being results because informal caregiving is predominantly driven by other-directed motivation, which buffers against stress specific to the caregiving experience.

Motivations for Helping and Their Impact on Well-Being: A Strain-Satisfaction Theoretical Framework

We propose an expansion of the motivational framework offered by Brown and colleagues (Brown & Brown, 2014; Brown & Cialdini, 2015) provides the best available approach for conceptualizing how and when helping will be related to well-being. This expansion entails maintaining the psychological and biological aspects of the stress-buffering, other-directed (altruistic) motivational route while considering a variety of additional motivations that may spur helping. These motivations include self-directed (egoistic) motivations, as well as collective-directed and principle-directed motivations. Moreover, we consider how the success or failure of helping and its costs interact with helping motivations to impact well-being. We believe this *strain-satisfaction framework* can account for apparent empirical discrepancies in the literature as well as provide important implications for theory and application.

It is important to note that unlike the dual motivation model proposed by Brown and colleagues (Brown & Brown, 2014; Brown & Cialdini, 2015), the strain-satisfaction framework concerns only proximate psychological mechanisms involved in the link between helping and well-being. It offers no strong evolutionary claims regarding the origins of the motivations or mechanisms it incorporates. For instance, it can accommodate either the rival SIT or STAND evolutionary accounts for the origin of altruistic motivation described earlier.

The Costs of Helping: Three Types of Helping-Related Strain

According to the strain-satisfaction framework, helping others incurs costs that are in addition to the normal short-term or long-term costs of caring for oneself (e.g., additional expenditure of time and effort). Of course, as Batson (1987, 2011) reminds us, although helping behavior may increase the welfare of another, it often is *egoistic* in that it is motivated by a desire to benefit oneself as an ultimate goal. In contrast to egoism, helping that is *altruistic* is motivated by a desire to benefit another as an ultimate goal. In addition to egoism and altruism, Batson (1994) proposes at least two other broad motivations for helping. These include *collectivism*, which is motivation to benefit a group as an ultimate goal, and *principlism*, which is motivation to uphold a moral principle (e.g., fairness) as an ultimate goal. Although these motivations are distinct, more than one can be salient at a given time. Many of these motivations may occur in combination to produce helping behavior. Nevertheless, even though these motivations produce helping for different reasons, engaging in helping, whatever the reason, produces costs in the form of expenditure of physical and psychological resources.

Expenditure of physical or psychological resources by a helper in the service of helping motivations can produce three potential forms of strain in the helper (cf., Brown & Brown, 2014). The first, which is always present, is *behavioral strain* produced by the act of helping. The magnitude of behavioral strain is proportional to the degree of cost incurred by the act of helping. As the amount, intensity, and duration of helping increase, so does behavioral strain. Although relatively low behavioral strain may produce little negative impact on well-being, once behavioral strain increases beyond a certain threshold, it will produce corresponding decreases in well-being. Moreover, the threshold at which behavioral strain begins to negatively impact well-being will be lower for those dealing with high pre-existing costs in maintaining their own welfare. For a given strain threshold, the impact of behavioral strain produced by helping will be more substantial in instances of intense and enduring helping of those with long-term vulnerability (e.g., children, disabled individuals, the chronically ill) as opposed to single, short-term instances of helping (e.g., helping a friend move, holding the door open for someone).

Achieving motivational goals leads to feelings of satisfaction and higher psychological well-being, whereas failing to achieve goals leads to feelings of dissatisfaction and lower psychological well-being (Ryan & Deci, 2001). This means that, even though engaging in helping will involve some level of behavioral strain, achieving helping motivational goals can still result in increased psychological well-being. As noted previously, Weinstein and Ryan (2010) propose that much of the well-being increase of successful helping stems from feelings of competence, autonomy, and relatedness that are experienced when goals are achieved. Moreover, their research emphasizes the importance of perceived autonomy in choosing to engage in helping as a necessary condition for the corresponding increase in well-being to occur.

In contrast, failing to achieve helping motivation goals can produce *motivational strain*, which includes feelings of dissatisfaction, hopelessness, incompetence, or frustration. Thus, attempting but failing to help results in additional strain above and beyond the behavioral strain incurred in making the helping attempt. Unsuccessful helping typically results in motivational strain, but not always. Some helping motivation goals can be met by simply making a good faith attempt to help another, even if the helping attempt is unsuccessful (see Table 9.2). In such instances, unsuccessful helping would not cause motivational strain because the ultimate goal of helping is still acquired.

A third form of strain is *precipitating strain*. In some instances, the conditions that evoke helping motivation may themselves be a source of strain for the potential helper. For instance, some motivations for helping are directed at reducing aversive arousal experienced when observing the suffering of another or are directed at avoiding anticipated sources of punishment that might occur if one chooses not to help another. These precipitating feelings or perceptions are conditions that produce strain and thus specific types of helping motivation aimed at eliminating the strain. Depending on the nature of the precipitating strain, successful helping or a good faith attempt at helping can reduce or eliminate the precipitating strain. Helping situations in which those in need evoke helping motivations in response to precipitating strain have higher potential to lower well-being because unsuccessful help results in three types of strain: (1) maintenance of the precipitating strain that originally evoked helping motivation, (2) behavioral strain produced by attempting to help, and (3) motivational strain produced by failing to meet helping motivation goals.

Types of Helping Motivations

According the strain–satisfaction framework, the relative increase or decrease in the degree of well-being produced by helping is a joint function of helping-related strain (precipitating, behavioral, motivational) and the extent to which helping results in successfully achieving helping motivation goals. However, the extent to which helping results in successfully achieving helping motivation goals depends on the type of helping motivation. As noted previously, Batson (1994) has identified four general motivations for helping: egoism, altruism, collectivism, and principlism. Of the four, egoism can be viewed as a motivation to increase the welfare of the self. Egoism, however, can be further refined into motives aimed at (1) acquiring rewards for the self, (2) avoiding punishments for the self, (3) avoiding aversive arousal, and (4) a "oneness motivation" aimed at enhancing perceived aspects of the self that overlap with those of another person (Batson, 1987, 2011; Batson et al., 1997; Cialdini et al., 1997; Maner et al., 2002). The rewards and punishments categories can be further divided into social rewards and punishments (e.g., praise, censure) and various personal rewards and punishments (e.g., positive mood, guilt). Table 9.1 lists these different egoistic motivations for helping along with altruistic, collectivistic, and principlistic motivations for helping and the specific ultimate goal associated with each (see also Batson, 2011).

TABLE 9.1 Motivations for Helping and Their Ultimate Goals

Motivation	Ultimate Goal
1. Egoism	Increase the welfare of the self.
Aversive-Arousal Reduction	Reduce aversive arousal produced by the perception of need.
Reward-Seeking	Acquire rewards.
Social Rewards	Acquire socially conveyed awards (e.g., praise, fame, compensation).
Personal Rewards	Acquire personally conveyed awards (e.g., pride, increased self-esteem).
Negative State Relief	Acquire rewards to obtain mood enhancement.
Vicarious Joy	Experience vicarious joy with another whose need has been reduced.
Punishment-Avoiding	Avoid punishments.
Social Punishments	Avoid socially conveyed punishments (e.g., censure, criticism).
Personal Punishments	Avoid personally conveyed punishments (e.g., guilt).
Benefit Aspects of the Self	Benefit perceived personal aspects shared between the self and person in need.
2. Altruism	Increase the welfare of another.
3. Collectivism	Increase the welfare of a group or collective.
4. Principlism	Uphold a moral principle.

Egoistic Motivations for Helping and Well-Being

Egoistic motivation for helping represents the most varied class of potential motivations for helping (see Table 9.1). Although helping can offer a means to achieve the goal corresponding to each class of motivations, helping is not always necessary to obtain the egoistic goal. For instance, two types of egoistic goals listed in Table 9.1—vicarious joy and benefitting aspects of the self—may be obtained by observing a person in need receive assistance from someone else without the observer helping the person directly. Even in instances where egoistic goals can only be met by helping a person in need directly, successful helping may not be required. For example, reward and punishment goals often may be met by making a good faith attempt at helping (e.g., Batson & Weeks, 1996). Reduction of aversive arousal is an egoistic goal that may be met as long as helping (by oneself or someone else) is successful, but it can also be met by escaping or avoiding exposure to the person in need of help (Stocks, Lishner, & Decker, 2009).

Considering reduction of aversive-arousal motivation (see Table 9.1) also illustrates the importance of successful helping in enhancing well-being. When escape from the need situation is impossible, the aversive arousal produced by perceiving another in need might only be reduced by successfully helping the person in need.

Although behavioral strain will be incurred while engaging in helping, if the helping is successful, the precipitating strain will be eliminated and the goal will be obtained. The overall outcome is generally positive and enhances well-being. But if helping is unsuccessful, the precipitating strain of aversive arousal is maintained, behavioral strain is incurred by engaging in helping, and motivational strain is incurred as feelings of dissatisfaction, incompetence, or inadequacy. The overall outcome is negative and reduces well-being. This scenario illustrates how helping success and the type of motivation spurring helping can create the potential for a triple dose of strain.

Social punishment avoidance is another egoistic helping motivation that is typically evoked by states that may be considered forms of precipitating strain (see Table 9.1). In this case, the precipitating strain arises from anticipation of social punishments for not helping. Anticipation of punishments can produce anxiety. The anticipation of social punishments for not helping also may give rise to a negative state of psychological reactance produced by a perceived loss of freedom or choice in deciding whether to assist a person in need. If helping is unsuccessful and the attempt is considered inadequate by those who would administer the punishment, anxiety about punishment is either maintained or negative consequences resulting from the administration of punishment are incurred (precipitating strain). Moreover, motivational strain for failing to achieve the egoistic goal may be incurred. Even if helping is successful, the precipitating strain may linger if the helper believes the social pressure may occur again in a similar context in which a person in need of assistance is encountered. Thus, helping motivated by desire to avoid social punishments is unlikely to produce a net increase in well-being. Desire to reduce negative states that may be experienced when encountering a person in need (e.g., sadness; see Table 9.1) is an additional egoistic motivation that may be prone to a triple dose of strain if helping is unsuccessful but that should result in increased well-being if helping is successful. How successful helping leads to motivational satisfaction and the potential for precipitating strain for various helping motivations is summarized in Table 9.2.

Finally, researchers have proposed a variety of other motivations for helping that will not be discussed here. Examples include motivation to increase self-understanding, skill development, or self-esteem (Clary & Snyder, 1999). Other examples include seeking reciprocal benefit and conforming to social standards (Oarga, Stavrova, & Fetchenhauer, 2015). Although these and others are motivational sources of helping with the potential to impact helper well-being, these motivations can be conceptualized as specific forms of the more general types of egoistic motivations summarized above and in Table 9.1 (e.g., desire to acquire rewards, desire to avoid punishments). This means these more specific motivations would be expected to relate to strain and impact well-being in a manner that corresponds to the more general egoistic motivation category to which they belong.

TABLE 9.2 Motivations for Helping, Helping Success, and Precipitating Strain

Motivation	Must Helper's Attempt Be Successful to Produce Ultimate Goal Satisfaction?	Does Failed Helping Attempt Lead to Maintenance of Precipitating Strain?
1. Egoism		
Aversive-Arousal Reduction	Yes.	Yes (e.g., feelings of personal distress).
Reward-Seeking		
Social Rewards	No, if failed attempt is socially justifiable.	No.
Personal Rewards	No, if failed attempt is personally justifiable.	No.
Negative State Relief	Yes.	Yes (e.g., negative mood, sadness).
Vicarious Joy	Yes.	No.
Punishment-Avoiding		
Social Punishments	No, if failed attempt is socially justifiable.	Yes, if attempt is unjustifiable (e.g., fear of punishment, reactance).
Personal Punishments	No, if failed attempt is personally justifiable.	Yes, if attempt is unjustifiable (e.g., feelings of guilt).
Benefit Aspects of the Self	Yes.	No.
2. Altruism	Yes.	No.
3. Collectivism	Yes.	No.
4. Principlism	No, if principle is re-established.	No.

Altruistic Motivation for Helping and Well-Being

Helping produced by altruistic motivation may be particularly effective at increasing well-being. Like several of the other motivations for helping, unsuccessful altruistic helping would be expected to produce motivational strain because the goal to increase the other's welfare would go unmet. But as noted by Brown and Cialdini (2015; see also Brown & Brown, 2014), the biological-emotional mechanisms responsible for this motivation (what they call other-directed motivation) appears to buffer against stress. Because stress is a component of behavioral strain in helpers, attenuation of stress permits the helper to obtain relatively higher net increases in well-being when helping is successful and relatively lower net decreases in well-being when helping is unsuccessful.

Collectivistic Motivation for Helping and Well-Being

Collectivism is a potential helping motivation somewhat like altruism, in that helping must be successful for an increase in well-being to occur; otherwise, motivational strain is incurred. Also, because the goal of collectivism is to increase the welfare of a group, its potential for precipitating strain is not a countervailing concern when considering the negative impact of failing to meet a collectivist goal on well-being. However, successful collectivist helping may be particularly effective in directly enhancing well-being because it has a wide-ranging impact on the welfare of others. Helping more people may mean more successful helping and thus result in greater well-being.

Principlistic Motivation for Helping and Well-Being

When a person is in need due to the violation of one or more moral principles (e.g., principles of fairness or justice), one may attempt to help a person in need as an instrumental means of re-establishing adherence to the moral principle that has been violated. Like several of the egoistic motivations, principlism does not necessarily require that helping be successful to acquire goal satisfaction. As long as the helping attempt results in the helper re-establishing adherence to the moral principle, the ultimate goal of principlism can be achieved. For example, an attempt to address the harm produced by a violation of a moral principle may not increase the welfare of those previously harmed by the violation, but the attempt may result in implementing procedures that ensure protection against violation of the principle at a future time (e.g., enactment of rules or laws that promote adherence to the principle). Well-being would be increased because of success in re-establishing adherence to the moral principle despite a failure to successfully help the specific person harmed by the initial violation. One could also imagine a scenario in which a helper is able to assist the specific person harmed by the initial moral violation yet fails to successfully re-establish adherence to the principle in question. In such an instance, motivational strain would result despite successful helping. Also, principlism may be evoked in response to a precipitating feeling of moral outrage that a moral principle has been violated (cf., Van de Vyver & Abrams, 2015). If so, it would be important to consider the impact of precipitating strain on well-being in cases where helping is driven by principlism (although this possibility is not included in Table 9.2).

Summary of the Strain-Satisfaction Framework

The strain-satisfaction framework proposes that helping increases well-being to the extent that the ultimate goals of various helping motivations are achieved by the helping act. This effect on positive well-being derives primarily from feelings of personal satisfaction, competency, autonomy, and relatedness that result from successful attainment of helping goals. For many helping motivations, attainment of the helping goal requires that helping increase the welfare of another or others. While attaining the ultimate goals of helping motivations provides a means for increasing well-being, this potential exists along with the countervailing potential that strain linked to the helping act can decrease well-being. Thus, in certain helping situations, successful attainment of helping goals produces an increase in a helper's well-being that exceeds the negative effects on the helper's well-being produced by strain. However, in other helping situations, the strain incurred by helping may overcome the benefits to helpers' well-being and instead result in a net decrease in well-being. Moreover, this interplay between helping strain and successful attainment of helping goals exists over a backdrop of other costs with which a helper must contend to ensure maintenance of his or her own welfare. The interplay between strain and successful attainment of helping motivation goals differs as a function of which helping motivations are responsible for initiating and guiding the helping attempt. Some helping motivations may have a higher potential to produce certain forms of strain than others (aversive-arousal reduction motivation, social-punishment avoidance motivation), whereas others may buffer against certain forms of strain (e.g., altruistic motivation) or enhance well-being in the form of achieving particularly meaningful and impactful helping goals (e.g., collectivistic motivation).

Promoting and Undermining the Effects of Helping on Well-Being

The strain-satisfaction framework suggests a number of implications for understanding empirical work on helping and well-being as well as for identifying factors that can promote or undermine helping effects on well-being. The major advantage of the framework is that it offers an explanation for the empirical discrepancies in the research on helping and well-being. Specifically, it can explain why research on volunteerism and experimental laboratory research usually produce evidence consistent with the hypothesis that helping increases well-being and why research on informal caregiving usually produces mixed evidence. The framework also provides insight into which helping conditions are most likely to increase well-being and which are most likely to decrease well-being. Generally, conditions that maximize successful attainment of helping motivation goals and minimize various forms of strain will increase well-being, and conditions that make attainment of helping motivation goals difficult and offer little buffering of strain will decrease well-being.

Resolving Empirical Discrepancies

As noted previously, the non-experimental research usually produces mixed evidence (Brown & Brown, 2014) regarding the direction of association between helping and well-being. In contrast, the experimental research tends to reveal evidence of a positive association. A closer look at the non-experimental research, however, reveals an important division between studies on volunteerism and well-being and studies on informal caregiving and well-being. Studies on volunteerism generally produce consistent evidence of a positive association between helping and well-being, whereas studies on informal caregiving produce mixed evidence for this association. Moreover, studies of informal caregiving provide evidence for a positive association, but only when studies adequately hold constant confounding variables related to well-being on which study participants possess pre-existing differences (Brown & Brown, 2014).

The strain-satisfaction framework suggests these three general classes of research capture different aspects of the interplay between helping strain and the consequences of helping success. First, volunteerism is a form of helping in which the individual chooses to engage in helping and typically does so through commitment to an organized institution or social program. In other words, those who engage in volunteerism will generally be those who have autonomy in helping others and perceive the costs of maintaining their own welfare are low enough to incur the additional costs of helping. This means the strain threshold at which behavioral strain will produce negative effects on well-being will typically be much higher among volunteers. Moreover, the institution or program through which volunteers channel their helping typically provides resources to ensure that the possibility of successful helping is maximized and that the volunteer experience does not produce undue strain on the helper.

In contrast, informal caregiving is typically forced upon the helper by the long-term need of an individual whose welfare the helper values, irrespective of the current costs the helper faces in maintaining his or her own welfare. For informal caregivers, the strain threshold at which stain will produce negative effects on well-being will typically be lower, and the amount of behavioral strain will be of higher intensity and of longer duration given the type of assistance that is required to address the long-term need. The lack of a formal organizational structure to facilitate the helping behavior and afford buffers against strain means successful helping is less certain. Additionally, the long-term needs informal caregivers face also may be more prone to producing precipitating strain that may be maintained in instances where helping is unsuccessful (e.g., feeling of personal distress, feelings of guilt).

Yet, because informal caregiving typically involves valued others, the potential for altruism (other-directed) motivation and its stress attenuating properties also is high. Thus, a portion of the behavioral strain of meeting altruistic motivation goals in the context of informal caregiving is offset given the nature of the motivation spurring helping. This opposing constellation of forces explains why holding constant pre-existing differences in variables related to well-being besides helping gives rise to a positive association between amount of helping and well-being in the informal caregiving literature. By holding constant confounding pre-existing caregiver differences one is holding constant the behavioral strain threshold, as well as other variables that can result in motivational strain (e.g., low behavioral efficacy), diminish well-being, and, consequently, cloud the countervailing positive association between helping and well-being.

Finally, the evidence of a positive causal association between helping and well-being in experimental research can be attributed to methodological control of different sources of strain. By randomly assigning participants to helping versus non-helping conditions, one holds constant individual differences in the helping strain threshold across experimental condition. Moreover, the type and difficulty of helping is held constant across participants, which controls for levels of precipitating strain, and behavioral strain. By holding strain constant among helpers, the positive association between meeting helping motivation goals and well-being is detectable when comparing experimentally created helpers to non-helpers.

Ways to Promote Helping That Enhances Well-Being

Those who wish to encourage prosocial behavior or physical and mental health, such as leaders of volunteer organizations or health policy advocates, would do well to consider the conditions under which helping increases well-being. In general, the best way to ensure that helping enhances well-being is to combine resources that maximize the success of helping with resources that directly or indirectly reduce the strain of helping.

One direct approach to reducing the strain of helping is to facilitate helpers' ability to obtain their helping goals as efficiently as possible. In other words, the more helping benefit conveyed to beneficiaries of help per unit of resource expended by the helper, the lower his or her behavioral strain. Also, facilitating help with high impact for recipients is perceived as more meaningful and important to helpers and therefore produces more substantive increases in well-being. This idea may be fruitful grounds for future investigation.

In many severe need situations, helping may have a higher likelihood of failing, which will increase helping motivational strain and lower well-being. In these circumstances a direct approach to reducing helping strain may be to re-focus the helper's perception of the need of the recipient of the help. For example, focusing on a need that cannot be met (e.g., death from terminal illness) may produce helping that is relatively unsuccessful (e.g., delay but not avoidance of eventual death); increase motivational strain; and in turn decrease well-being. But focusing on a need that might be met (e.g., reduction of pain) may produce helping that is relatively successful (e.g., increasing comfort) and therefore enhance the well-being of the helper.

The effectiveness of both facilitating the attainment of helper's goals and re-focusing helpers perceptions to different aspects of need depend crucially on the helping motivations active in the potential helper. For instance, a helper motivated to achieve social rewards will not be satisfied if one makes it easier for the helper to assist someone in need but does not facilitate making the helping act public or socially reinforced. Likewise, attempts to re-focus the helper's perception of need away from an aspect of need relevant to the particular motivation spurring the attempt to help (e.g., obtaining personal rewards) to an aspect of need irrelevant to that particular motivation (e.g., obtaining social rewards) will not result in increased well-being, even if helping is successful. The issue of ensuring that successful helping meets the ultimate goals spurring the helping attempt is consistent with work of Clary et al. (1998), who found that volunteer satisfaction was related to whether the volunteer behavior meets the perceived goals of the volunteer's motivations for engaging in volunteer activity. Moreover, research suggests that volunteers are less satisfied when their volunteer activities are directed at meeting multiple goals than when directed at meeting a single goal (Kiviniemi, Snyder, & Omoto, 2002). This finding may be explained in two ways. First, the increase in well-being that results from successful goal attainment for one motivation can be undermined by the decrease in well-being that results from a failure to attain a goal for another motivation. Alternatively, seeking to achieve two goals may lead to increased strain that can decrease well-being.

In contrast to providing resources that minimize helping-related strain directly, it is also possible to assist caregivers minimize strain indirectly by giving them resources that enable them to reduce the costs of maintaining their own welfare. Those who can better care for themselves can better care for others, satisfy helping motivation goals, and in turn increase their well-being. Reducing the costs of maintaining one's own welfare indirectly reduces the potential impact of strain on well-being by raising the threshold at which strain begins to diminish well-being. Indirectly reducing the impact of strain is less important for volunteer caregivers because their initial decision to commit to volunteerism indicates belief that they can incur the strain of helping others (i.e., their perceived strain threshold is relatively high) and because they can choose to reduce their volunteer activities if costs of maintaining their own welfare are for some reason increased. However, informal caregivers or occupational caregivers typically have less choice in deciding to help as a result of uncontrollable life circumstances or job requirements. For this reason, organizations or social programs that provide resources or education to assist caregivers manage personal costs of managing their own welfare enable caregivers to incur higher levels of helping-related strain before negative impacts on well-being accrue.

Threats to Helping That Enhances Well-Being

One of the major threats to well-being that the strain-satisfaction framework might explain is *empathy burnout*, sometimes called *compassion fatigue* or *empathic distress fatigue* (Figley, 2002; Sabo, 2006). Empathy burnout is the experience of chronic high levels of distress or depressive affect produced by continued exposure to the suffering of others, particularly by informal or professional caregivers who cannot avoid contact with the suffering others or caregivers who cannot fully address or eliminate the source of suffering. There is some debate as to whether empathic concern (i.e., feelings of compassion and tenderness) or personal distress (aversive negative feelings) in response to the needs of others is the source of empathic burnout (Klimecki & Singer, 2012). However, because empathic concern and its accompanying altruistic motivation buffers stress, we suggest personal distress and its accompanying aversive-arousal reduction motivation (see Table 9.1) will be the more likely culprit.

The strain–satisfaction framework can explain the causes of empathy burnout. Caregivers who face ongoing exposure to the suffering of others that is severe, chronic, or difficult to eliminate or reduce face high levels of strain and limited achievement of their helping goals. Specifically, in response to the perceived suffering, the caregiver experiences aversive arousal, which motivates action to reduce the aversive arousal (behavioral strain). But because helping is generally unsuccessful at eliminating the suffering, the goal of reducing aversive arousal is not achieved. Consequently, goal frustration (motivational strain) and maintenance of the aversive arousal (precipitating strain) are experienced or maintained at high levels. The person's limited ability to achieve his or her helping goal means that the negative impact on well-being produced by strain outweighs the positive impact produced by limited, if any, goal achievement. This analysis can be applied to any helping motivation for which failure to help might maintain precipitating strain, including the motivation to reduce aversive arousal, the motivation to relieve a negative-state, and both classes of punishment avoidance motivation (see Table 9.1). Thus, according to the strain–satisfaction framework, empathy burnout can be construed as a special case of a larger class of "helping burnout" phenomena, which is a possibility not previously considered in the empathy burnout literature.

One implication of the strain–satisfaction interpretation of helping burnout is that it suggests certain helping motivations produce a lower likelihood that helping will increase well-being due to their link to more numerous forms of helping strain. For this reason, seeking to increase well-being by encouraging these helping motivations (aversive-arousal reduction, negative-state relief, personal and social punishments) should generally be avoided. Instead, altruism, collectivism, and certain egoistic reward-acquisition helping motivations (personal rewards, vicarious joy) offer more promise in promoting helping that will increase well-being. Altruistic helping has the additional advantage of buffering against stress (behavioral strain), and collectivist helping may be a more potent cause of well-being enhancement upon goal achievement. Moreover, personal rewards and vicarious joy are forms of reward-acquisition motivation that are worth encouraging because they are not evoked by anticipation of negative consequences or the experience of negative states and so involve low, if any, precipitating strain. Also, unlike the motivation for acquisition of social rewards, motivations for acquisition of personal rewards and vicarious joy do not require an agent external to the helper to administer these rewards.

One final threat to promoting helping and well-being may be to overemphasize the potential well-being benefits of helping. As Wilson and Musick (2000) note, focusing too much on the benefits of helping to the helper's well-being may lead people to underestimate their ability to manage the strain such helping entails. In other words, overemphasis on well-being benefits of helping may direct people to overestimate their personal strain threshold when deciding to help. Overestimation of the strain threshold may in turn result in them receiving less of an increase, and possibly even a decrease, in well-being in response to helping than what they expected. In addition, overemphasis on the benefits of helping to the well-being of helpers may lead them to focus on the personal rewards of helping. Overemphasis on the personal rewards of helping may in turn undermine other forms of helping motivation that may contribute to more beneficial well-being outcomes when dealing with certain needs or helping situations (cf., Batson, Coke, Jasnoski, & Hanson, 1978; Batson, Fultz, Schoenrade, & Paduano, 1987; Batson, Harris, McCaul, Davis, & Schmidt, 1979).

Conclusion

Does helping increase well-being? The answer based on the empirical findings is affirmative. However, to fully understand when and why helping increases well-being requires a more complicated answer. We suggest conceptualizing the well-being outcome of the helper as a function of the joint influence of (1) the strain incurred by the helping attempt and (2) whether the helper achieves the goals that motivated the initiation of the helping attempt. According to this strain-satisfaction framework, helping will increase well-being only when the positive impact of achieving helping goals outweighs the countervailing negative impact on well-being produced by three forms of helping-related strain. The best way to promote helping that increases well-being is to (1) facilitate the ability of helpers to succeed in the helping attempt, (2) facilitate factors that buffer against strain incurred by helpers produced by the helping attempt, and (3) provide resources that permit the helper to better manage the personal costs of maintaining his or her own welfare. Positive well-being effects of helping may also be increased by discouraging helping motivations evoked by precipitating states that contribute to strain and by encouraging helping motivations that buffer against strain or involve goals that can promote high impact helping of others.

References

Aknin, L. B., Barrington-Leigh, C. P., Dunn, E. W., Helliwell, J. F., Burns, J., Biswas-Diener, R., . . . Ashton-James, C. E. (2013). Prosocial spending and well-being: Cross-cultural evidence for a psychological universal. *Journal of Personality and Social Psychology*, *104*, 635–652.

Baronet, A. M. (1999). Factors associated with caregiver burden in mental illness: A critical review of the research literature. *Clinical Psychology Review*, *19*, 819–841.

Batson, C. D. (1987). Prosocial motivation: Is it ever truly altruistic? In L. Berkowitz (Ed.), *Advances in experimental social psychology* (Vol. 2, pp. 267–299). New York, NY: Academic Press.

Batson, C. D. (1994). Why act for the public good? Four answers. *Personality and Social Psychology Bulletin*, *20*, 603–610.

Batson, C. D. (2006). SIT or STAND? *Psychological Inquiry, 17,* 30–59.

Batson, C. D. (2011). *Altruism in humans.* New York, NY: Oxford University Press.

Batson, C. D., Coke, J. S., Jasnoski, M. L., & Hanson, M. (1979). Buying kindness: Effect of an extrinsic incentive for helping on perceived altruism. *Personality and Social Psychology Bulletin, 4,* 86–91.

Batson, C. D., Fultz, J., Schoenrade, P. A., & Paduano, A. (1987). Critical self-reflection and self-perceived altruism: When self-reward fails. *Journal of Personality and Social Psychology, 53,* 594–602.

Batson, C. D., Harris, C. A., McCaul, K. D., Davis, M., & Schmidt, T. (1979). Compassion or compliance: Alternative dispositional attributions for one's helping behavior. *Social Psychology Quarterly, 42,* 405–409.

Batson, C. D., Sager, K., Garst, E., Kang, M., Rubchinsky, K., & Dawson, K. (1997). Is empathy-induced helping due to self-other merging? *Journal of Personality and Social Psychology, 73,* 495–509.

Batson, C. D., & Weeks, J. L. (1996). Mood effects of unsuccessful helping: Another test of the empathy-altruism hypothesis. *Personality and Social Psychology Bulletin, 22,* 749–758.

Baumann, D. J., Cialdini, R. B., & Kenrick, D. T. (1981). Altruism as hedonism: Helping and self-gratification as equivalent responses. *Journal of Personality and Social Psychology, 40,* 1039–1046.

Brown, R. M., & Brown, S. L. (2014). Informal caregiving: A reappraisal of effects on caregiving. *Social Issues and Policy Review, 8,* 74–102.

Brown, S. L., & Brown, R. M. (2006). Selective investment theory: Recasting the functional significance of close relationships. *Psychological Inquiry, 17,* 1–29.

Brown, S. L., & Cialdini, R. B. (2015). Functional motives and functional consequences of prosocial behavior. In D. Schroeder & W. Graziano (Eds.), *The Oxford handbook of prosocial behavior* (pp. 346–361). New York, NY: Oxford University Press.

Brown, S. L., Nesse, R. M., Vinokur, A. D., & Smith, D. M. (2003). Providing social support may be more beneficial than receiving it: Results from a prospective study of mortality. *Psychological Science, 14,* 320–327.

Brown, S. L., Smith, D. M., Schulz, R., Kabeto, M. U., Ubel, P. A., Poulin, M., . . . Langa, K. M. (2009). Caregiving behavior is associated with decreased mortality risk. *Psychological Science, 20,* 488–494.

Burton, R. A. (2012). Pathological certitude. In B. Oakley, A. Knafo, G. Madhavan, & D. S. Wilson (Eds.), *Pathological altruism* (pp. 131–137). New York: Oxford University Press.

Centers for Disease Control and Prevention. (2016, March). *Well-being concepts.* Retrieved from www.cdc.gov/hrqol/wellbeing.htm

Cialdini, R. B., Brown, S. L., Lewis, P. L., Luce, C., & Neuberg, S. L. (1997). Reinterpreting the empathy-altruism relationship: When one into one equal oneness. *Journal of Personality and Social Psychology, 73,* 481–494.

Cialdini, R. B., & Kenrick, D. T. (1976). Altruism as hedonism: A social development perspective on the relationship of negative mood state and helping. *Journal of Personality and Social Psychology, 34,* 907–914.

Clary, E. G., & Snyder, M. (1999). The motivations to volunteer: Theoretical and practical considerations. *Current Directions in Psychological Science, 8,* 156–159.

Clary, E. G., Snyder, M., Ridge, R. D., Copeland, J., Stukas, A. A., Haugen, J., & Miene, P. (1998). Understanding and assessing the motivations of volunteers: A functional approach. *Journal of Personality and Social Psychology, 74,* 1516–1530.

Crocker, J., Canevello, A., & Brown, A. A. (2017). Social motivation: Costs and benefits of selfishness and otherishness. *Annual Review of Psychology, 68,* 299–325.

Diener, E., Oishi, S., & Lucas, R. E. (2003). Personality, culture, and subjective well-being: Emotional and cognitive evaluations of life. *Annual Review of Psychology, 54*, 403–425.

Dulin, P. L., & Hill, R. D. (2003). Relationships between altruistic activity and positive and negative affect among low-income older adult service providers. *Aging and Mental Health, 7*, 294–299.

Dulin, P. L., Hill, R. D., Anderson, J., & Rasmussen, D. (2001). Altruism as a predictor of life satisfaction in a sample of low-income older adult service providers. *Journal of Mental Health and Aging, 7*, 349–359.

Dunn, E. W., Aknin, L. B., & Norton, M. I. (2014). Prosocial spending and happiness: Using money to benefit others pays off. *Current Directions in Psychological Science, 23*, 41–47.

Figley, C. R. (2002). Compassion fatigue: Psychotherapists' chronic lack of self care. *Journal of Clinical Psychology, 58*, 1433–1441.

Gray, K. (2010). Moral transformation: Good and evil turn the weak into the mighty. *Social Psychological and Personality Science, 1*, 253–258.

Harris, M. B. (1977). Effect of altruism on mood. *The Journal of Social Psychology, 102*, 197–198.

Inagaki, T. K., & Orehek, E. (2017). On the benefits of giving social support: When, why, and how support providers gain by caring for others. *Current Directions in Psychological Science, 26*, 109–113.

Kahana, E., Bhatta, T., Lovegreen, L. D., Kahana, B., & Midlarsky, E. (2013). Altruism, helping, and volunteering: Pathways to well-being in late life. *Journal of Aging and Health, 25*, 159–187.

Kiviniemi, M. T., Snyder, M., & Omoto, A. M. (2002). Too many of a good thing? The effects of multiple motivations on stress, cost, fulfillment, and satisfaction. *Personality and Social Psychology Bulletin, 28*, 732–743.

Klimecki, O., & Singer, T. (2012). Empathic distress fatigue rather than compassion fatigue? Integrating findings from empathy research in psychology and social neuroscience. In B. Oakley, A. Knafo, G. Madhavan, & D. S. Wilson (Eds.), *Pathological altruism* (pp. 368–383). New York: Oxford University Press.

Konrath, S., Fuhrel-Forbis, A., Lou, A., & Brown, S. (2012). Motives for volunteering are associated with mortality risk in older adults. *Health Psychology, 31*, 87–96.

Kyeongmo, K., Lehning, A. J., & Sacco, P. (2016). Assessing the factor structure of well-being in older adults: Findings from the national health and aging trends study. *Aging & Mental Health, 20*, 814–822.

Langer, E. J., & Rodin, J. (1976). The effects of choice and enhanced personal responsibility for the aged: A field experiment in an institutional setting. *Journal of Personality and Social Psychology, 34*, 191–198.

Lucas, R. E., Diener, E., & Suh, E. (1996). Discriminant validity of well-being measures. *Journal of Personality and Social Psychology, 71*, 616–628.

Maner, J. K., Luce, C. L., Neuberg, S. L., Cialdini, R. B., Brown, S., & Sagarin, B. J. (2002). The effects of perspective taking on motivations for helping: Still no evidence for altruism. *Personality and Social Psychology Bulletin, 28*, 1601–1610.

Martela, F., & Ryan, R. M. (2015). The benefits of benevolence: Basic psychological needs, beneficence, and the enhancement of well-being. *Journal of Personality, 84*, 750–764.

Martela, F., & Ryan, R. M. (2016). Prosocial behavior increases well-being and vitality even without contact with the beneficiary: Causal and behavioral evidence. *Motivation and Emotion, 40*, 351–357.

McGrath, M., & Oakley, B. (2012). Codependency and pathological altruism. In B. Oakley, A. Knafo, G. Madhavan, & D. S. Wilson (Eds.), *Pathological altruism* (pp. 49–74). New York: Oxford University Press.

Musick, M. A., Herzog, A. R., & House, J. S. (1999). Volunteering and mortality among older adults: Findings from a national sample. *Journal of Gerontology: Social Sciences, 54B,* S173–S180.

Oakley, B., Knafo, A., Madhavan, G., & Wilson, D. S. (2012). *Pathological altruism.* New York: Oxford University Press.

Oarga, C., Stavrova, O., & Fetchenhauer, D. (2015). When and why is helping others good for well-being? The role of belief in reciprocity and conformity to society's expectations. *European Journal of Social Psychology, 45,* 242–254.

Oman, D. (2007). Does volunteering foster physical health and longevity? In S. G. Post (Ed.), *Altruism and health: Perspectives from empirical research* (pp. 15–32). New York, NY: Oxford University Press.

Oman, D., Thoresen, C. E., & McMahon, K. (1999). Volunteerism and mortality among the community-dwelling elderly. *Journal of Health Psychology, 4,* 301–316.

Penner, L. A., Dovidio, J. F., Piliavin, J. A., & Schroeder, D. A. (2005). Prosocial behavior: Multilevel perspectives. *Annual Review of Psychology, 56,* 365–392.

Piliavin, J. A. (2003). Doing well by doing good: Benefits for the benefactor. In C. L. M. Keyes & J. Haidt (Eds.), *Flourishing: Positive psychology and the life well lived* (pp. 227–247). Washington, DC: American Psychological Association.

Pinquart, M., & Sörensen, S. (2003). Differences between caregivers and non-caregivers in psychological health and physical health: A meta-analysis. *Psychology and Aging, 18,* 250–267.

Pinquart, M., & Sörensen, S. (2007). Correlates of physical health of informal caregivers: A meta-analysis. *Journal of Gerontology: Social Sciences, 62,* 126–137.

Post, S. G. (2005). Altruism, happiness, and health: It's good to be good. *International Journal of Behavioral Medicine, 12,* 66–77.

Poulin, M. J., Brown, S. L., Dillard, A. J., & Smith, D. M. (2013). Giving to others and the association between stress and mortality. *American Journal of Public Health, 103,* 1649–1655.

Poulin, M. J., Brown, S. L., Ubel, P. A., Smith, D. M., Jankovic, A., & Langa, K. M. (2010). Does a helping hand mean a heavy heart? Helping behavior and well-being among spouse caregivers. *Psychology and Aging, 25,* 108–117.

Raposa, E. B., Laws, H. B., & Ansell, E. B. (2016). Prosocial behavior mitigates the negative effects of stress in everyday life. *Clinical Psychological Science, 4,* 691–698.

Rodin, J., & Langer, E. J. (1977). Long-term effects of a control-relevant intervention with the institutionalized aged. *Journal of Personality and Social Psychology, 35,* 897–902.

Ryan, R. M., & Deci, E. L. (2001). On happiness and human potentials: A review of research on hedonic and eudaimonic well-being. *Annual Review of Psychology, 52,* 141–166.

Sabo, B. M. (2006). Compassion fatigue and nursing work: Can we accurately captures the consequences of caring work? *International Journal of Nursing Practice, 12,* 136–142.

Schulz, R., & Monin, J. K. (2012). The costs and benefits of informal caregiving. In S. L. Brown, R. M. Brown, & L. A. Penner (Eds.), *Moving beyond self-interest: Perspectives from evolutionary biology, neuroscience, and the social sciences* (pp. 178–198). New York, NY: Oxford University Press.

Schulz, R., & Sherwood, P. R. (2008). Physical and mental health effects of family caregiving. *American Journal of Nursing, 108,* 23–27.

Schwartz, C. (2007). Altruism and subjective well-being: Conceptual model and empirical support. In S. G. Post (Ed.), *Altruism and health: Perspectives from empirical research* (pp. 33–42). New York, NY: Oxford University Press.

Stocks, E. L., Lishner, D. A., & Decker, S. K. (2009). Altruism or psychological escape: Why does empathy promote prosocial behavior? *European Journal of Social Psychology, 39*, 649–655.

Turvey, B. E. (2012). Pathological altruism: Victims and motivational types. In B. Oakley, A. Knafo, G. Madhavan, & D. S. Wilson (Eds.), *Pathological altruism* (pp. 177–192). New York, NY: Oxford University Press.

Vitaliano, P. P., Zhang, J., & Scanlan, J. M. (2003). Is caregiving hazardous to one's physical health? A meta-analysis. *Psychological Bulletin, 129*, 946–972.

Weinstein, N., & Ryan, R. M. (2010). When helping helps: Autonomous motivation from prosocial behavior and its influence on well-being for the helper and recipient. *Journal of Personality and Social Psychology, 98*, 222–244.

Williamson, G. M., & Clark, M. S. (1989). Providing help and desired relationship type as determinants of changes in moods and self-evaluations. *Journal of Personality and Social Psychology, 56*, 722–734.

Wilson, J., & Musick, M. (2000). The effects of volunteering on the volunteer. *Law and Contemporary Problems, 62*, 141–168.

Wink, P., & Dillon, M. (2007). Do generative adolescents become healthy older adults? In S. G. Post (Ed.), *Altruism and health: Perspectives from empirical research* (pp. 15–32). New York, NY: Oxford University Press.

10

GRATITUDE

Philip C. Watkins and Daniel Scheibe

In 1975—long before the psychology of gratitude was of any interest to researchers—a little-known paper was published that demonstrated the social power of a simple gratitude expression (McGovern, Ditzian, & Taylor, 1975). These researchers arranged a situation where a confederate asked participants to take a painful shock for them. Most participants (75%) agreed to do so, but the confederate then either did nothing, or she simply thanked them for taking the shock. Subsequently the rate at which the participants took additional shocks for the confederate was assessed. Whereas those who were not thanked returned to their pre-request rate, those who were thanked continued to take shocks for the confederates at about three times the rate of those not thanked. In short, one simple "thank you" encouraged participants to continue to help, even though it resulted in a painful cost. Gratitude appears to have significant social benefits.

In this chapter we review the benefits of gratitude to subjective well-being, with particular attention to the social psychological mechanisms of this relationship. After defining gratitude, we review research showing that gratitude is important to subjective well-being. Although it is now clear that gratitude is important to living well, research is lacking concerning the mechanisms of the relationship of gratitude to well-being. One of the most likely ways that gratitude enhances well-being is through supporting social well-being, and much of this chapter will be devoted to describing research that supports this mechanism. Finally, we will summarize the research in this area by explaining Algoe's Find, Remind, and Bind theory of gratitude and our theory of psychological amplification. Our hope is that the reader will not only gain a general understanding of the importance of gratitude to well-being, but that researchers will also be encouraged to engage in needed areas of gratitude research.

Defining Gratitude

Although there are a few unresolved issues regarding the definition of gratitude, there is fairly clear consensus, as long as researchers are clear about which level of analysis they are operating on. We follow Rosenberg's (1998) distinction between gratitude as an emotion and gratitude as an affective trait. Although Rosenberg also makes an important distinction at the level of mood (a more long-term, background emotional state), to date very little work has been directed at gratitude as a mood state (but see McCullough, Tsang, & Emmons, 2004). For this reason we limit our discussion of the definition of gratitude to the levels of emotion and affective trait.

First we define gratitude as an emotional state. Following Emmons (2004), we submit the following definition: People experience the emotion of gratitude when they affirm that something good has happened to them and they recognize that someone else is largely responsible for this benefit (Watkins & McCurrach, in press). This definition invites several points of discussion. First, this definition makes clear that gratitude is the product of a number of simultaneous appraisals, and thus, gratitude is a cognitively imbued emotion. Second, although some gratitude scholars would argue that "someone else" should simply be an outside force, we argue that some personalization of an agent is involved, be that another human, a divine agent, or another force. We also take a broad understanding of "something good"; it may be a specific time and place event, a broader "good" over a longer period of time, or that good may be the perception that the grateful person has escaped something bad (as in the case of surviving a hurricane, cf. Coffman, 1996).

Gratitude as an affective state has usually been measured with a simple self-report procedure using the adjectives "grateful", "thankful", and "appreciative" (the Gratitude Adjectives Scale; McCullough, Emmons, & Tsang, 2002). We often add these adjectives to the Positive and Negative Affect Scales (e.g., Watkins, Uhder, & Pichinevskiy, 2015), and this seems to effectively measure the emotion of gratitude and these adjectives always emerge as a separate factor in the extended Positive and Negative Affect Scales (PANAS-X, McCurrach, Timbrook, & Watkins, 2015).

Gratitude may also be analyzed at the level of affective trait or disposition. People high in trait gratitude experience gratitude easily over a broad range of circumstances. Stated differently, grateful people have a low threshold for gratitude. The six-tem Gratitude Questionnaire (GQ-6) is a unifactoral measure that is probably the most developed and utilized assessment of trait gratitude (McCullough et al., 2002). This questionnaire is easy to use and has excellent psychometrics. Our Gratitude, Resentment, and Appreciation Test (GRAT) has been frequently used in gratitude research and has good psychometric characteristics (Watkins, Woodward, Stone, & Kolts, 2003). Whereas the GQ-6 measures trait gratitude in a fairly straightforward and descriptive fashion, we developed the GRAT based on the theory that the disposition of gratitude was based on three lower-order traits: a sense of abundance, an appreciation of simple pleasures, and an appreciation of others. We developed a shorter measure (GRAT-S; Thomas & Watkins, 2003) that seems to perform as well as the original questionnaire (Diessner & Lewis, 2007; Froh et al., 2011).

The gratitude subscale of the Values in Action Scale (VIA; Peterson & Seligman, 2004) may be useful to researchers who wish to measure and compare gratitude to other strengths. The VIA questionnaire is designed to assess the 24 strengths as defined by the VIA project (Peterson & Seligman, 2004). Although valuable for comparing gratitude to other strengths, if researchers are specifically interested in understanding dispositional gratitude, we recommend using the more well-tested measures described earlier. All of these instruments rely on self-report and as such carry all of the baggage associated with self-report measures. Implicit assessments measure a construct indirectly—e.g., the Implicit Associations Test—and thus avoid many of the problems associated with direct self-report. Although several researchers have unsuccessfully attempted to develop an implicit measure of gratitude, we still believe that an implicit measure of this construct may prove to be valuable.

A final issue concerning the measurement of gratitude is the difference between gratitude and indebtedness. Research now fairly clearly indicates that indebtedness—usually defined as feeling obligated to repay—is sometimes positively correlated with gratitude (e.g., Watkins, Scheer, Ovnicek, & Kolts, 2006), but shows patterns of response to scenarios that are quite distinct from gratitude (Watkins et al., 2006). In addition, trait indebtedness is actually negatively related to both trait gratitude and subjective well-being (Van Gelder, Ruge, Brown, & Watkins, 2007). Some research even suggests that gratitude and indebtedness are more strongly associated in men than women (e.g., Uhder, Watkins, & Ovnicek, 2009), and more research should be directed to gender differences between gratitude and indebtedness. The distinction between gratitude and indebtedness highlights the fact that gratitude is not simply an emotion of reciprocity. In fact, when the norm of reciprocity is made more noticeable to respondents in the context of a gift, gratitude is *less* likely (Watkins et al., 2006). The distinction between gratitude and indebtedness will become more important when we consider the social mechanisms of the relationship of gratitude to well-being. Thus, we also recommend that gratitude researchers include measures of indebtedness in their studies.

Gratitude and Subjective Well-Being

Gratitude is strongly associated with measures of subjective well-being (e.g., McCullough et al., 2002; Watkins et al., 2003), and is often one of the foremost strengths predicting well-being (e.g., Peterson, Ruch, Beermann, Park, & Seligman, 2007). Moreover, a recent multiple regression analysis found that of the 24 VIA strengths, only gratitude and love of learning uniquely predicted well-being after controlling for age and gender (Kaufman, 2015). Stronger evidence of the importance of gratitude to human flourishing comes from several prospective studies that have found that gratitude predicts subsequent increases in subjective well-being (e.g., Wood, Maltby, Gillett, Linley, & Joseph, 2008). The most convincing evidence, however, for the position that gratitude causes enhanced well-being comes from experimental studies. More than 30 true experimental studies that have shown that gratitude increases subjective well-being compared to control conditions (for reviews, see Davis et al., 2016; Watkins, 2014; Watkins & McCurrach, in press; Wood, Froh, & Geraghty, 2010). We will discuss some of these studies in more depth later, but we can confidently conclude that gratitude is important to living well and thus serves as an important foundation for well-being.

How Does Gratitude Promote Well-Being?

Because of the success of gratitude treatments in enhancing well-being, researchers have turned to investigating the mechanisms of this relationship: What are the factors that explain how gratitude promotes well-being? Although there are a number of viable mechanisms to consider (see Watkins, 2014), we believe that cognitive and social mechanisms are the most likely social psychological factors that help us understand how gratitude promotes subjective well-being.

Cognitive Mechanisms of the Gratitude and Well-Being Relationship

Does gratitude promote well-being because it encourages cognitive biases that are conducive to happiness? Although gratitude is viewed as a cognitively imbued emotional state, little research has investigated the cognitive characteristics of gratitude. Recently, we used a "recognition task" borrowed from the *cognitive bias modification* paradigm (Hertel & Mathews, 2011) that taps real-time interpretations of ambiguous situations (Scheibe, Watkins, McCurrach, & Mathews, 2016). After participants read and imagined themselves in a number of different ambiguous benefit scenarios, they were given a "recognition test" that assessed their recognition on items that disambiguate the scenario in either a positive or negative fashion. For example, in one scenario, the respondent is asked to imagine a friend setting the respondent up on a blind date. As with most social benefits, there are a number of ambiguities about this situation. Later, participants are given a "recognition test" that asks respondents to rate how closely the meanings of several statements are to the original scenario. In this example scenario participants were to respond to "Your friend thinks you really need help in getting a date" (a negative disambiguation) and "Your friend believes they genuinely met someone who could make you happier" (a positive disambiguation). Their recognition ratings should be reflective of how they initially interpreted the scenario. After controlling for general positive response bias, we found that trait gratitude was associated with a positive interpretation bias of the scenarios. Others have found similar results with more direct self-report measures (e.g., Wood, Maltby, Stewart, Linley, & Joseph, 2008). Studies also have found memory biases associated with gratitude. For example, in one study, we asked participants to intentionally recall positive and negative memories from their life and also to record positive and negative memory intrusions (Watkins, Grimm, & Kolts, 2004). We found that trait gratitude was associated with a positive bias in both intentional and intrusive autobiographical memory. These findings support the notion that gratitude may create positive cognitive biases that enhance well-being.

Our findings from a recent intervention study lend additional support to the theory that gratitude may promote cognitive processes that enhance well-being (Watkins et al., 2015). In a randomized control trial (RCT), participants were assigned to one of three intervention conditions: memory placebo, pride three-blessings, or gratitude three-blessings. In each treatment participants completed their exercise each day for a week. In the memory placebo condition, participants recalled a different personal semantic memory each day (such as their typical route through their grocery store). In both of the three-blessings treatments, participants were asked to recall "three good things" that had happened to them in the last 48 hours (similar to Seligman, Steen, Park, & Peterson, 2005). In the pride three-blessings condition, we asked our participants to write about how each blessing they recalled made them feel "better than others or better than average", whereas in the gratitude three-blessings treatment we asked them to write about how each blessing made them feel grateful. We included the pride three-blessings comparison condition because we wanted to test the notion that it was actually grateful processing that enhanced well-being, rather than simply recalling positive memories. As predicted, the gratitude three-blessings treatment significantly outperformed the other conditions in enhancing subjective well-being, but notably, this difference was most pronounced in our follow-up assessments. As seen in Figure 10.1, the well-being of those in the gratitude treatment continued to increase after the treatment phase, while the well-being of those in the other conditions did not. Seligman et al. (2005) found a similar pattern of results.

Why did the well-being of those in the gratitude treatment continue to climb after treatment? We believe that the gratitude three-blessings treatment actually modified cognitive processes in a way that promoted their future subjective well-being. We argued that daily recalling positive events and processing them with gratitude: (1) enhanced people's ability to notice and attend to positive events, (2) encouraged them to interpret positive events in a grateful manner, and (3) encouraged individuals to recall grateful memories (Watkins & McCurrach, 2016).

We designed a similar RCT to test these ideas (Watkins, McCurrach, & Timbrook, 2016). Once again, the gratitude treatment outperformed the placebo condition in enhancing well-being, and did so for eudaimonic in addition to hedonic well-being, although we did not see the same pattern of well-being in our follow-up

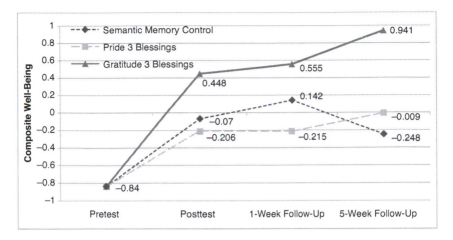

FIGURE 10.1 Impact of Grateful Recounting on Subjective Well-Being

Notes: Adapted from Watkins et al. (2015), published by the *Journal of Positive Psychology*, Taylor & Francis, web site: www.tandfonline.com, used by permission.

assessment. In this study, the well-being of those in the gratitude condition did not continue to climb following treatment. This might be because we only included a 2-week follow-up assessment, and we recommend that future research should use longer follow-up assessments. What was unique about this study is that we used several cognitive bias measures—both interpretation and memory bias—that allowed us to investigate whether these cognitive processes were mediating the impact of the gratitude intervention on well-being. We used the recognition task described earlier to test real-time interpretation biases of benefit scenarios and a recall task for life events from the past week to assess memory bias. Although the gratitude treatment significantly enhanced positive memory bias, it did not impact interpretation bias, and neither of these mediated the impact of the gratitude intervention on well-being. However, gratitude did partially mediate treatment. In other words, the gratitude people experienced in the past week partially explained why the gratitude treatment outperformed the placebo in enhancing well-being.

These results make sense because it is unlikely that asking people to write a sentence or two about how a positive event makes them feel grateful would actually modify habitual interpretation biases. In our view, the results from Scheibe et al. (2016) are consistent with a more reasonable theory that we propose here. In this study, we found that although trait gratitude was moderately correlated with a positive interpretation bias, this bias did not mediate the impact of gratitude on subjective well-being. Conversely, trait gratitude completely mediated the impact of positive benefit interpretation bias on well-being. Thus, the model that emerges is that it is not that gratitude promotes positive interpretation biases but that positive interpretation biases are important to trait gratitude. In other words a fundamental requirement to being a grateful person is that one interprets benefit scenarios in a positive fashion. For example, when people attribute altruistic rather than selfish motives to benefits they receive, this is likely to promote a more grateful disposition. This model suggests that training positive benefit interpretation biases (as has been successfully accomplished in the cognitive bias modification paradigm, Hertel & Mathews, 2011) could promote trait gratitude and may make interventions like grateful recounting more successful.

We propose that the fact that several studies have found that gratitude mediates the effectiveness of grateful recounting exercises is not merely an emotional effect. It is not that participants are briefly experiencing a bit more gratitude while they are counting their blessings, which then causes subjective well-being to continue to increase after treatment. Rather, we propose that grateful recounting causes cognitive changes involved with *appreciation* that promotes both gratitude and subjective well-being over the long term. Following Janoff-Bulman and Berger (2000), we define appreciation as taking note of the positive and increasing the psychological value of the object that appreciation is focused on (for a more thorough discussion of these ideas, see Watkins & Bell, 2017). Thus, just as when a house appreciates it increases in monetary value, when we appreciate something in our life it takes on increased psychological value for us. According to Janoff-Bulman and Berger, increased personal value is largely due to psychological processes related to "specialness". Although appreciation might lead to emotions other than gratitude, we submit that appreciation is a psychological process fundamental to gratitude. In short, we believe that gratitude interventions like grateful recounting enhance long-term well-being by training cognitive processes related to appreciation—noticing and enhancing the personal value of the good. In other words, when people recount their blessings and write about how these things make them feel grateful, this is likely to enhance psychological processes related to appreciation, which in turn should enhance well-being. We believe that further theoretical and empirical exploration of the construct of appreciation is crucial for the science of gratitude to progress (see also Fagley, 2016).

Social Mechanisms of the Gratitude and Well-Being Relationship

Although cognitive mechanisms show some promise for helping us understand how gratitude promotes well-being, currently there is much more evidence in favor of social mechanisms. We do not believe that these two categories of explanations are mutually exclusive; it is easy to see how noticing and appreciating the good that others do for us would enhance social mechanisms of well-being. As has been often emphasized in this book, the perception of social support appears to be important to happiness (Lakey, 2013). Thus, if gratitude enhances our relationships, this could be how it enhances our well-being more generally. This idea is supported by several studies that have found that perceived social support mediates the relationship between gratitude and subjective well-being (e.g., Kong, Ding, & Zhao, 2015; Lin & Yeh, 2014). These studies support the idea that gratitude enhances social well-being, which in turn enhances subjective well-being, but *how* does gratitude enhance social well-being? We first explore the social impact of *experiencing* gratitude, followed by discussing the impact of *expressing* gratitude on relationships. Finally we will examine how experiencing and expressing gratitude might interact to promote social well-being.

The Social Consequences of Experiencing Gratitude

There is much debate about the nature of emotion, but virtually all emotion scholars agree that emotions activate certain thought-action tendencies (Fredrickson, 1998; Frijda, 2007). While not forcing one to perform certain behaviors, emotions prepare us for adaptive (and sometimes maladaptive) thoughts and behaviors. When one is afraid, one feels like running; when one is angry, one feels like fighting. What are the thought-action tendencies of experiencing gratitude? In a nutshell, the thought-action tendencies of gratitude are definitively *prosocial*. When people feel grateful, they tend to think and behave in ways that are advantageous to their social world. For example, in a series of studies, Algoe and Haidt (2009) found strong support for the prosocial action tendencies of gratitude. In one study (Study 1), 74% of the participants who recalled a grateful memory reported positive relationship motivations (e.g., wanting to be closer to someone), whereas only 30% of those who recalled a joy memory did so. Similarly, Tsang (2006) compared the grateful responses to a favor (the gratitude condition) with a similar benefit that participants received by chance. Those in the gratitude condition showed greater helping behavior but not so for the mere benefit condition. Moreover, reports of gratitude predicted more helping behavior whereas indebtedness did not. Thus, Tsang's results suggest that the experience of gratitude does not promote responses that simply adhere to the norm of reciprocity, and as we will see, additional research (to be discussed below) has supported the distinction between gratitude and indebtedness or "feeling obligated to repay".

Perhaps the strongest support for the prosocial consequences of experiencing gratitude comes from a series of studies conducted by Bartlett and DeSteno (2006). They manipulated gratitude by having a confederate apparently repair a participant's computer, which relieved the participant from having to repeat an onerous computer task. Compared to the control condition, those in the gratitude condition spent significantly more time helping their benefactor. Gratitude mediated their results whereas awareness of reciprocity did not. In other words, self-reported gratitude explained why those in the gratitude condition were more likely to help, whereas awareness of reciprocity did not. Moreover, in Study 2, they found that those in the gratitude condition were not only more willing to help their benefactor, but also spent more time helping a another confederate they were not familiar with. These results speak against a simple reciprocity interpretation; the prosocial tendencies of gratitude are not merely an attempt to "repay" the benefactor but extend beyond the benefactor to strangers even when that behavior results in decreased positive affect.

Studies have also investigated more specific prosocial consequences of experiencing gratitude. Research shows that gratitude enhances several relationship-enhancing qualities. Several studies support the idea that gratitude promotes positive interpretations of others (e.g., Wood et al., 2008). Jackson, Lewandowski, Fleury, and Chin (2001) found that, after they experimentally induced gratitude, grateful participants were more likely to attribute positive behaviors to a target person. They also were more likely to make these positive interpretations after a gratitude emotion induction than after a happiness induction. Thus, some evidence supports the theory that experiencing gratitude enhances positive thinking about others, but more research needs to target the cognitive consequences of gratitude.

Gratitude also may promote subjective well-being by enhancing perceived social support. Evidence suggests that, when we feel grateful, we think about how others are supporting us. For example, in a study of breast cancer patients, Algoe and Stanton (2012) found that gratitude in response to benefits from others increased their perceptions of social support (but only for those women low in ambivalence about emotional expression). The mediation studies described earlier (e.g., Kong et al., 2015) also provide support for this idea, As we noted earlier, perceived social support appears to be much more important to happiness than objective indicators of social support (Lakey, 2013). One can receive many benefits from others, but unless this becomes a vital part of one's awareness, one is not likely to feel supported by others. Experiencing gratitude in response to benefits of others should amplify awareness of benefits, thus resulting in increased perception of social support, which should then result in enhanced well-being.

Research also shows that experiencing gratitude promotes the development of new relationships. For example, in a prospective study, Froh, Bono, and Emmons (2010) found that gratitude increased social integration. In other words, gratitude predicted how much the participants felt involved with and a part of their new social group. Using their computer malfunction procedure to induce gratitude, Bartlett, Condon, Cruz, Baumann, and Desteno (2012) found that gratitude promoted social affiliation and social inclusion—even when the inclusion came at a cost. In addition, Algoe, Haidt, and Gable (2008) used a sorority tradition to investigate how gratitude impacts the development of relationships. In this tradition an "older sister" is assigned to a new sorority member and showers her with anonymous gifts for a week. After this period a "revelation" ceremony takes place where the previously anonymous benefactors are revealed to their younger sisters. The younger sisters reported their gratitude for the gifts they received, and gratitude positively predicted relationship development 1 month later. Similarly, in a daily experience sampling study of cohabiting romantic partners, Algoe,

Gable, and Maisel (2010) found that thoughtful benefits resulted in both gratitude and indebtedness in the beneficiary, but that only experiencing gratitude predicted enhanced relationship connectedness and satisfaction. Once again, this result points to the difference between gratitude and indebtedness and supports the idea that gratitude is not merely a reciprocity response. In short, several studies now offer strong support for the theory that gratitude results in relationship building behaviors.

Research suggests that experiencing gratitude not only helps build relationships but also motivates relationship maintenance. Kubacka, Finkenauer, Rusbult, and Keijsers (2011) followed married couples for 4 years after their marriages and found that perceived responsiveness to one's needs from one's spouse prompted gratitude, which motivated relationship maintenance behaviors in the recipient. We will say more about this study later, but not only does this study provide strong evidence that the experience of gratitude promotes relationship maintenance, it also highlights the importance of perceived responsiveness to triggering gratitude (cf. Algoe et al., 2008). One of the primary factors that activates gratitude may be benefits that the recipient perceives are specifically oriented to his or her needs. More strong evidence for the importance of gratitude to relationship maintenance comes from a series of studies conducted by Joel, Gordon, Impett, MacDonald, and Keltner (2013). Two daily experience studies and an experiment provided converging evidence that perceived investment in a romantic relationship promotes gratitude, which then encourages the grateful individual to further invest in the relationship. Thus, behaviors that communicate relationship commitment are likely to enhance a partner's gratitude, which in turn prompts the partner to commit to the relationship. These were relatively young romantic relationships and research with couples who have been together longer would be informative.

One of the most important ways that relationships endure is through cooperation, and several studies have shown that gratitude promotes cooperation. DeSteno, Bartlett, Baumann, Williams, and Dickens (2010) used their computer repair gratitude induction and the "give some dilemma game" to investigate how gratitude might prompt economic cooperation. This game is similar to the prisoner's dilemma, which is often used in social psychological research to investigate self versus communal interest. In addition to manipulating gratitude, the researchers also manipulated whom the participants' thought they would be playing with: either the confederate or a stranger. Even though participants would have benefited most by not giving tokens to their partner, those in the gratitude condition gave significantly more tokens to their partner than did those in the control condition, and mediation analysis showed that increased gratitude explained why those in the gratitude condition gave more tokens. Importantly, this effect was identical for those they knew (their benefactor in the gratitude condition), and for a confederate they had no previous contact with, demonstrating once again that gratitude is not merely a reciprocity response. Several other studies have found that gratitude promotes cooperative behavior. For example Gino and Schweitzer (2008) found that people induced to feel grateful were more likely to accept advice from other participants. Moreover, Jia, Tong, and Lee (2014) found that induced gratitude prompted individuals to be more likely to share the goals of others in their social group, which would also seem to promote cooperation.

People are only likely to cooperate when they trust others in their group, and research shows that gratitude promotes trust in relationships. In a series of studies, Dunn and Schweitzer (2005) showed that incidental gratitude enhanced trust. Research also suggests that secure attachment priming promotes gratitude (Konkler, Nienhuis, Hutchinson, Vance, & Watkins, 2015). Therefore, trust and gratitude may operate in an upward spiral, with gratitude enhancing trust, and trust promoting gratitude. Trust may be one of the most important factors in the binding and maintenance of relationships, and thus, one way that gratitude might promote healthy relationships is by enhancing trust. Although trust is likely to be a prerequisite for gratitude (Solom, Watkins, McCurrach, & Scheibe, 2017), one way that gratitude enhances well-being is by allowing us to trust others, which helps develop and maintain important relationships

Gratitude not only promotes relationship development and maintenance, it also appears to inhibit antisocial thought-action tendencies. For example, Watkins et al. (2006) found that gratitude was negatively associated with antisocial thought-action tendencies. In addition, in five studies, DeWall, Lambert, Pond, Kashdan, & Fincham (2012) found converging evidence that gratitude actually inhibits aggression, further bolstering the idea that gratitude is a prosocial emotion.

We have seen that gratitude is a definitively prosocial emotion: When we experience gratitude, we tend to think and behave in ways that enhance our relationships, and we're more likely to help those around us. *How* is gratitude prosocial? What are the mechanisms that help us understand how gratitude promotes prosocial behavior? One likely mechanism is that experiencing gratitude helps individuals delay gratification. To be effective in one's social world, individuals must be able to resist their immediate urges and accept short-term costs to achieve more long-term social gains. Most research on delay of gratification has been concerned with resisting immediate urges or inhibiting "hot" emotions (emotions that encourage "go" responses). DeSteno (2009), however, has stressed that one may delay gratification by activating other competing hot emotions. His research has found that one such hot emotion that helps people delay gratification is gratitude (DeSteno, Li, Dickens, & Lerner, 2014). It appears that grateful people tend to be patient people (Dickens & DeSteno, 2016), and the ability to be patient and to delay gratification is critical to social competence. Why is the ability to delay gratification so important to relationships? Often, the long-term health of a relationship is dependent on the ability of an individual to delay gratification. For example, marriages cannot be successful unless one is able to resist sexual opportunities when one is away from one's spouse. Everyday communication serves as another example. To effectively communicate in a relationship, one must be willing to listen to the other, which means that one may often have to delay their gratification of saying what one wants to say. Interrupting others is usually a failure to delay gratification. As the sage says on more than one occasion in the Proverbs of the Bible, "The heart of the righteous ponders how to answer, but the mouth of the wicked pours out evil things" (15:28, English Standard Version).

In sum, we have seen that gratitude promotes a number of relationship-enhancing qualities. It enhances positive interpretations of others, promotes the initiation and development of relationships, encourages relationship maintenance, and perhaps most importantly, enhances trust. Gratitude also inhibits antisocial thoughts and actions, and this may be because gratitude allows us to delay gratification, which might be an important factor in social competence.

The Social and Personal Consequences of Expressing Gratitude

We have seen that experiencing gratitude results in a number of desirable prosocial tendencies, but experiencing gratitude is only half of the equation: The *expression* of gratitude is also important. Indeed, to separate experiencing and expressing gratitude into different sections of this chapter might be somewhat misleading. The function of emotions is to prepare us for some adaptive patterns of thinking and behaving, and thus to discuss the experience of gratitude without the expression of gratitude leaves an incomplete picture of gratitude. Gratitude cannot be seen as a gnostic pursuit—only emphasizing the internal personal experience of gratitude—gratitude must be embodied, and that is why a discussion of the expression of gratitude is so crucial. Fortunately, research strongly supports the importance of the expression of gratitude to social well-being In this section, we explore how expressing gratitude to another enhances social well-being.

The first issue is how expressing gratitude affects the one expressing gratitude. As C. S. Lewis was struggling with the function of praise, he wrote (1958, p. 95):

> I think we delight to praise what we enjoy because the praise not merely expresses but completes the enjoyment; it is its appointed consummation. It is not out of compliment that lovers keep on telling one another how beautiful they are; the delight is incomplete until it is expressed.

If we can agree that praise is a form of expressing gratitude, then Lewis has made some provocative claims about the importance of expressing gratitude and how it might impact personal well-being. Lewis suggests that the one providing the praise may actually benefit as much if not more than the person receiving the praise.

This seems to run counter to some approaches in the social sciences to social emotions—that it is all about keeping social balances, that if someone does something for me then I simply obey "The Norm of Reciprocity" and express my gratitude back to them so as to reinforce their benevolence to me (Gouldner, 1960). One turn of positive social reinforcement deserves another, so to speak. But

Lewis's insight suggests that there is something in expressing gratitude that amplifies the joy of receiving a benefit in that expressing gratitude for a favor completes the joy of the benefit. Research generally supports Lewis's claims. For example, in Watkins et al. (2003) people wrote a letter to someone they felt grateful for (Watkins et al., 2003). People who wrote the letter experienced a greater increase in positive affect than those in the control condition (where participants wrote about the layout of their living room).

Even stronger evidence comes from Seligman and colleagues' "gratitude visit" intervention (2005) in which participants wrote a letter to someone they believed they needed to thank and then actually read the letter to the recipient. This intervention has powerful immediate effects on subjective well-being and outperformed all other positive psychology interventions tested by Seligman et al. when well-being was assessed immediately following treatment. The participants' happiness had returned to baseline 3 months after the intervention, but it would seem unreasonable to expect one expression of gratitude to permanently increase one's happiness. Regular intentional expressions of gratitude like this would likely be needed to result in long-term increases in subjective well-being. How frequent these gratitude expressions should be is an important empirical question. It is quite likely that more is not necessarily better with interventions like the "gratitude visit". We are aware of studies that have asked participants to text "gratitude letters" to friends three times per day for several weeks. Interventions like this do not seem to be very effective, probably because they put an unrealistic burden on participants and make the gratitude expression mundane. More research is needed to delineate "best practices" for using the gratitude visit.

Lambert, Clark, Durtschi, Fincham, and Graham (2010) encouraged participants to express gratitude to a friend, once per week for 3 weeks. Following the treatment period, those encouraged to express gratitude reported increased communal strength in their relationship compared to comparison conditions. In another study using the same gratitude expression intervention, Lambert and Fincham (2011) found that those who expressed gratitude to a friend were more likely to report more positive perceptions of their friend and increased comfort sharing relationship concerns. In sum, these studies support the idea that expressing gratitude has personal benefits that indirectly and directly impact well-being.

But how do gratitude expressions impact others? First and foremost, research shows that people like grateful people and particularly dislike ungrateful people. It seems reasonable to assume that grateful people are those who express gratitude frequently (e.g., McCullough et al., 2002), and when asked to identify acquaintances who are grateful and not so grateful, people report that they like their grateful friends far more than their ungrateful friends (Watkins, Martin, & Faulkner, 2003; see also Williams & Bartlett, 2015). When individuals express gratitude towards others it increases the perception of their overall likeability by their peers. As noted previously McGovern et al. (1975), found that even a simple "thank you" was enough to increase a stranger's likeability and tripled the likelihood that the participant would endure physical pain on behalf of the person expressing gratitude. This simple affection for the one expressing gratitude can play out in several ways in interpersonal relationships.

Consistent with McGovern et al. (1975), several studies have shown that gratitude expressions enhance one's social world by increasing prosocial behavior directed toward the expresser. One way that gratitude expression positively impacts the individual receiving the expression is through increased feelings of social worth (Grant & Gino, 2010). Grant and Gino presented four studies showing that expressing gratitude increased prosocial behavior in the one receiving the expression, and the mechanism for this relationship appeared to be via social worth. In other words, these studies supported the theory that, when people receive an expressions of gratitude, this increases their perceived social worth, which in turn makes them more likely to display prosocial behavior (see also Cho & fast, 2012).

Expressing gratitude also improves one's social world by enhancing affiliative behaviors in those receiving the gratitude expression. For example, Williams and Bartlett (2015) found that those receiving a gratitude expression (a written note) were more likely to leave their contact information for the expresser than those not receiving such an expression. Moreover, the mechanism for this effect seemed to be through perceived interpersonal warmth; the more they felt the gratitude expression was a display of friendliness and thoughtfulness on the part of the expresser, the more likely they were to leave their contact information. As will become clear, gratitude expressions do not necessarily enhance relationships unless they communicate interpersonal warmth to the person receiving the gratitude expression.

A powerful way of examining the impact of gratitude expressions is through studying gratitude in romantic relationships. Algoe, Kurtz, and Hilaire (2016) found that receiving expressions of gratitude ("other-praising behavior") was strongly associated with feeling more loved. The recipient's perception of the gratitude expression is crucial when considering positive consequences of gratitude expression (Algoe & Zhaoyand, 2016). If the gratitude expression is viewed as insincere, then the positive effects will be mitigated and possibly reversed (Algoe & Zhaoyand, 2016). Thus, disingenuous gratitude expressions are not likely to be helpful to relationships, and more research is needed on what comprises genuine expressions of gratitude and how these might impact relationships.

The Interaction of Experiencing and Expressing Gratitude in Relationships: A Cycle of Virtue

Research has highlighted the importance of "cycles of virtue" or "upward spirals" in maintaining and enhancing well-being (e.g., Fredrickson & Joiner, 2002; Watkins, 2004). The converse of "vicious cycles" often found in emotional disorders, *upward spirals* describe ways in which positive emotions like gratitude produce consequences that in turn enhance additional positive emotions in a continual

cycle, thus supporting long-term subjective well-being. Experiencing and expressing gratitude both produce a number of prosocial consequences. It is possible,
therefore, that the experience and expression of gratitude act in an upward spiral
between individuals to enhance social well-being. Several studies provide support
for this possibility. For example, Kubacka et al. (2011) conducted a prospective
study with couples married at least 4 years. They found that one of the most common triggers of gratitude for one's spouse was when he or she observed the spouse
engaging in relationship maintenance behaviors. Experiencing this gratitude then
led the recipient of the relationship maintenance to express their gratitude by
engaging in relationship maintenance behaviors themselves, which presumably
should result in more experienced and expressed gratitude in their partner. In a
series of studies, Gordon, Impett, Kogan, Oveis, and Keltner (2012) showed how
gratitude is an important component in a cycle of virtue in romantic relationships. First, when one partner feels appreciated by their partner, he or she is more
likely to appreciate his or her partner, and this in turn produces more relationship
maintenance behaviors. When the other partner sees these attempts at relationship
maintenance, he or she then feels more appreciated by the partner and expresses
his or her appreciation through further commitment and attempts to maintain
the relationship (see also, Algoe et al., 2010; Joel et al., 2013). In sum, expressing
gratitude toward a spouse makes that spouse feel more appreciated, enhances his
or her gratitude toward the other partner, and in turn encourages him or her to
express appreciation to his or her partner, thus completing an upward spiral that is
likely to be important to healthy relationships.

Theories That Explain How Gratitude Promotes Well-Being

We conclude with two complementary theories that help integrate and comprehend the research on how gratitude enhances well-being. We begin with Algoe's
Find, Remind, and Bind theory of how gratitude enhances social well-being (Algoe,
2012). Algoe argues that gratitude enhances relationships through three adaptive functions. First, gratitude helps us *find* new relationships that promote our
well-being. We have seen that grateful people are well liked, and it is likely that
people find it easier to initiate relationships with grateful individuals. Furthermore, we have seen that gratitude promotes affiliative behaviors and thus should
encourage individuals to find new relationships. Second, gratitude *reminds* us of
the individuals who are important to our well-being and thus enhances relationship maintenance. Finally, gratitude helps *bind* relationships. Evidence shows that
gratitude predicts healthy relationship development.

We propose a more general theory of how gratitude promotes well-being
and believe that it is complementary to Algoe's approach. We suggest that gratitude amplifies the good in one's life (Watkins, 2008, 2014). Just as an amplifier
increases the volume of sound going into a microphone, so gratitude amplifies
blessings in one's life. Just as a magnifying glass increases the size of the object

it is focused on, so gratitude magnifies the good that it is focused on. Gratitude increases the signal strength of who and what is good in our life. As convincingly argued by Baumeister, Bratslavsky, Finkenauer, and Vohs (2001), "Bad is stronger than good". They concluded from their review of the research that bad events, bad interactions, bad feedback, and bad memories have more psychological power over us than good. Although one could argue that this principle suggests that we should try to eliminate negative emotional experiences, unpleasant events cannot be avoided. Even though we experience significantly more pleasant than unpleasant events in a typical day, because "bad is stronger than good", it is easy for us to let the bad experiences overshadow the good ones. Therefore, psychological processes that amplify the good should be important to well-being, and this could explain why gratitude has shown such strong relationships with happiness. Gratitude amplifies the good in our ongoing experience, the good we see from our past, the good we see in others, and even the good in ourselves. Although there have been overstatements about the good of gratitude (see Wood et al., 2016), and there are many questions yet to be answered, research clearly supports the proposition that gratitude is important to emotional and social well-being. As Dietrich Bonhoeffer concluded, "In ordinary life we hardly realize that we receive a great deal more than we give, and that it is with gratitude that life becomes rich" (1997, p. 109).

References

Algoe, S. B. (2012). Find, remind, and bind: The functions of gratitude in everyday relationships. *Social and Personality Psychology Compass, 6*, 455–469.

Algoe, S. B., Gable, S. L., & Maisel, N. C. (2010). It's the little things: Everyday gratitude as a booster shot for romantic relationships. *Personal Relationships, 17*, 217–233.

Algoe, S. B., & Haidt, J. (2009). Witnessing excellence in action: The "other-praising" emotions of elevation, gratitude, and admiration. *The Journal of Positive Psychology, 4*, 105–127.

Algoe, S. B., Haidt, J., & Gable, S. L. (2008). Beyond reciprocity: Gratitude and relationships in everyday life. *Emotion, 8*, 425–429.

Algoe, S. B., Kurtz, L. E., & Hilaire, N. M. (2016). Putting the "you" in "thank you": Examining other-praising behavior as the active relational ingredient in expressed gratitude. *Social Psychological and Personality Science, 7*, 658–666.

Algoe, S. B., & Stanton, A. L. (2012). Gratitude when it is needed most: Social functions of gratitude in women with metastatic breast cancer. *Emotion, 12*, 163–168.

Algoe, S. B., & Zhaoyang, R. (2016). Positive psychology in context: Effects of expressing gratitude in ongoing relationships depend on perceptions of enactor responsiveness. *The Journal of Positive Psychology, 11*, 399–415.

Bartlett, M. Y., Condon, P., Cruz, J., Baumann, J., & Desteno, D. (2012). Gratitude: Prompting behaviours that build relationships. *Cognition and Emotion, 26*, 2–13.

Bartlett, M. Y., & DeSteno, D. (2006). Gratitude and prosocial behavior: Helping when it costs you. *Psychological Science, 17*, 319–325.

Baumeister, R. F., Bratslavsky, E., Finkenauer, C., & Vohs, K. D. (2001). Bad is stronger than good. *Review of General Psychology, 5*, 323–370.

Bonhoeffer, D. (1997). *Letters & papers from prison.* New York: Touchstone. Original work published in 1953.

Cho, Y., & Fast, N. J. (2012). Power, defensive denigration, and the assuaging effect of gratitude expression. *Journal of Experimental Social Psychology, 48,* 778–782.

Coffman, S. (1996). Parents' struggles to rebuild family life after Hurricane Andrew. *Issues in Mental Health Nursing, 17,* 353–367.

Davis, D. E., Choe, E., Meyers, J., Wade, N., Varjas, K., Gifford, A., . . . Worthington, E. J. (2016). Thankful for the little things: A meta-analysis of gratitude interventions. *Journal of Counseling Psychology, 63,* 20–31.

DeSteno, D. (2009). Social emotions and intertemporal choice: "Hot" mechanisms for building social and economic capital. *Current Directions In Psychological Science, 18,* 280–284.

DeSteno, D., Bartlett, M. Y., Baumann, J., Williams, L. A., & Dickens, L. (2010). Gratitude as moral sentiment: Emotion-guided cooperation in economic exchange. *Emotion, 10,* 289–293.

DeSteno, D., Li, Y., Dickens, L., & Lerner, J. S. (2014). Gratitude: A tool for reducing economic impatience. *Psychological Science, 25,* 1262–1267.

DeWall, C. N., Lambert, N. M., Pond, R. J., Kashdan, T. B., & Fincham, F. D. (2012). A grateful heart is a nonviolent heart: Cross-sectional, experience sampling, longitudinal, and experimental evidence. *Social Psychological and Personality Science, 3,* 232–240.

Dickens, L., & DeSteno, D. (2016). The grateful are patient: Heightened daily gratitude is associated with attenuated temporal discounting. *Emotion, 16,* 421–425.

Diessner, R., & Lewis, G. (2007). Further validation of the Gratitude, Resentment, and Appreciation Test (GRAT). *The Journal of Social Psychology, 147,* 445–447.

Dunn, J. R., & Schweitzer, M. E. (2005). Feeling and believing: The influence of emotion on trust. *Journal of Personality and Social Psychology, 88,* 736–748.

Emmons, R. A. (2004, July). Gratitude is the best approach to life. In L. Sundarajan (Chair), *Quest for the good life: Problems/promises of positive psychology.* Symposium presented at the Annual Convention of the American Psychological Association, Honolulu, HI.

Fagley, N. S. (2016). The construct of appreciation: It is so much more than gratitude. In D. Carr (Ed.), *Perspectives on gratitude: An interdisciplinary approach* (pp. 70–84). Oxford: Taylor and Francis.

Fredrickson, B. L. (1998). What good are positive emotions? *Review of General Psychology, 2,* 300–319.

Fredrickson, B. L., & Joiner, T. (2002). Positive emotions trigger upward spirals toward emotional well-being. *Psychological Science, 13,* 172–175.

Frijda, N. H. (2007). *The laws of emotion.* Mahwah, NJ, US: Lawrence Erlbaum Associates Publishers.

Froh, J. J., Bono, G., & Emmons, R. (2010). Being grateful is beyond good manners: Gratitude and motivation to contribute to society among early adolescents. *Motivation and Emotion, 34,* 144–157.

Froh, J. J., Fan, J., Emmons, R. A., Bono, G., Huebner, E. S., & Watkins, P. (2011). Measuring gratitude in youth: Assessing the psychometric properties of adult gratitude scales in children and adolescents. *Psychological Assessment, 23,* 311–324.

Gino, F., & Schweitzer, M. E. (2008). Blinded by anger or feeling the love: How emotions influence advice taking. *Journal of Applied Psychology, 93,* 1165–1173.

Gordon, A. M., Impett, E. A., Kogan, A., Oveis, C., & Keltner, D. (2012). To have and to hold: Gratitude promotes relationship maintenance in intimate bonds. *Journal of Personality and Social Psychology, 103,* 257–274.

Gouldner, A. W. (1960). The norm of reciprocity: A preliminary statement. *American Socio-logical Review, 25*, 161–178.

Grant, A. M., & Gino, F. (2010). A little thanks goes a long way: Explaining why gratitude expressions motivate prosocial behavior. *Journal of Personality and Social Psychology, 98*, 946–955.

Hertel, P. T., & Mathews, A. (2011). Cognitive bias modification: Past perspectives, current findings, and future applications. *Perspectives on Psychological Science, 6*, 521–536.

Jackson, L. A., Lewandowski, D. A., Fleury, R. E., & Chin, P. P. (2001). Effects of affect, stereotype consistency and valence of behavior on causal attributions. *The Journal of Social Psychology, 141*, 31–48.

Janoff-Bulman, R., & Berger, A. R. (2000). The other side of trauma: Towards a psychology of appreciation. In J. H. Harvey & E. D. Miller (Eds.), *Loss and trauma: General and close relationship perspectives* (pp. 29–44). Philadelphia: Brunner-Routledge.

Jia, L., Tong, E. W., & Lee, L. N. (2014). Psychological "gel" to bind individuals' goal pur-suit: Gratitude facilitates goal contagion. *Emotion, 14*, 748–760.

Joel, S., Gordon, A. M., Impett, E. A., MacDonald, G., & Keltner, D. (2013). The things you do for me: Perceptions of a romantic partner's investments promote gratitude and commitment. *Personality and Social Psychology Bulletin, 39*, 1333–1345.

Kaufman, S. B. (2015, August 2). *Which character strengths are most predictive of well-being?* [Scientific American blog post]. Retrieved from http://blogs.scientificamerican.com/beautiful-minds/which-character-strengths-are-most-predictive-of-well-being/

Kong, F., Ding, K., & Zhao, J. (2015). The relationships among gratitude, self-esteem, social support and life satisfaction among undergraduate students. *Journal of Happiness Studies, 16*, 477–489.

Konkler, J. G., Nienhuis, A., Hutchinson, D. E., Vance, P., & Watkins, P. C. (2015, May). *Security and gratitude: Secure attachment priming enhances gratitude.* Poster presented to the Annual Convention of the Western Psychological Association, Las Vegas, NV.

Kubacka, K. E., Finkenauer, C., Rusbult, C. E., & Keijsers, L. (2011). Maintaining close relationships: Gratitude as a motivator and a detector of maintenance behavior. *Personal-ity and Social Psychology Bulletin, 37*, 1362–1375.

Lakey, B. (2013). Perceived social support and happiness: The role of personality and rela-tional processes. In S. A. David, I. Boniwell, & A. C. Aters (Eds.), *The Oxford Handbook of Happiness* (pp. 847–859). Oxford, UK: Oxford University Press.

Lambert, N. M., Clark, M. S., Durtschi, J., Fincham, F. D., & Graham, S. M. (2010). Ben-efits of expressing gratitude: Expressing gratitude to a partner changes one's view of the relationship. *Psychological Science, 21*, 574–580.

Lambert, N. M., & Fincham, F. D. (2011). Expressing gratitude to a partner leads to more relationship maintenance behavior. *Emotion, 11*, 52–60.

Lewis, C. S. (1958). *Reflections on the Psalms.* New York: Harcourt, Brace and Co.

Lin, C., & Yeh, Y. (2014). How gratitude influences well-being: A structural equation mod-eling approach. *Social Indicators Research, 118*, 205–217.

McCullough, M. E., Emmons, R. A., & Tsang, J. (2002). The grateful disposition: A conceptual and empirical topography. *Journal of Personality and Social Psychology, 82*, 112–127.

McCullough, M. E., Tsang, J., & Emmons, R. A. (2004). Gratitude in intermediate affective terrain: Links of grateful goods to individual differences and daily emotional experi-ence. *Journal of Personality and Social Psychology, 86*, 295–309.

McCurrach, D., Timbrook, T., & Watkins, P. C. (2015, April). The phenomenology of joy. In P. C. Watkins (Chair), *Joy and gratitude: Exploration of a relationship important to well-being*. Symposium presented at the Annual Convention of the Western Psychological Association, Las Vegas, NV.

McGovern, L. P., Ditzian, J. L., & Taylor, S. P. (1975). The effect of positive reinforcement on helping with cost. *Bulletin of the Psychonomic Society, 5*, 421–423.

Peterson, C., Ruch, W., Beermann, U., Park, N., & Seligman, M. P. (2007). Strengths of character, orientations to happiness, and life satisfaction. *The Journal of Positive Psychology, 2*, 149–156.

Peterson, C., & Seligman, M. E. P. (2004). *Character strengths and virtues: A handbook and classification*. New York: American Psychological Association and Oxford University Press.

Rosenberg, E. (1998). Levels of analysis and the organization of affect. *Review of General Psychology, 2*, 247–270.

Scheibe, D., Watkins, P. C., McCurrach, D., & Mathews, A. (2016, May). *Cognitive characteristics of gratitude*. Poster presented to the Annual Convention of the Association for Psychological Science, Chicago, IL.

Seligman, M. E. P., Steen, T. A., Park, N., & Peterson, C. (2005). Positive psychology progress: Empirical validation of interventions. *American Psychologist, 60*, 410–421.

Solom, S., Watkins, P. C., McCurrach, D., & Scheibe, D. (2017). Thieves of thankfulness: Traits that inhibit gratitude. *Journal of Positive Psychology, 12*, 120–129.

Thomas, M., & Watkins, P. (2003, May). *Measuring the grateful trait: Development of the revised GRAT*. Presentation to the 83rd Annual Convention of the Western Psychological Association, Vancouver, BC, Canada.

Tsang, J. (2006). Gratitude and prosocial behaviour: An experimental test of gratitude. *Cognition and Emotion, 20*, 138–148.

Uhder, J., Watkins, P. C., & Ovnicek, M. (2009, May). *The debt of gratitude is lighter for women than for men*. Poster presented at the 21st Annual Convention of the Association for Psychological Science, San Francisco, CA.

Van Gelder, M., Ruge, L., Brown, A., & Watkins, P. C. (2007, May). *Gratitude and indebtedness are distinct traits: Differential associations with well-being*. Presentation to the Annual Convention of the Western Psychological Association, Vancouver, BC, Canada.

Watkins, P. C. (2004). Gratitude and subjective well-being. In R. A. Emmons & M. E. McCullough (Eds.), *The psychology of gratitude* (pp. 167–192). New York: Oxford University Press.

Watkins, P. C. (2008). Gratitude: The amplifier of blessing. In A. Przepiorka (Ed.), *Closer to emotions II* (pp. 49–62). Lublin, Poland: Publishing House of Catholic University of Lublin.

Watkins, P. C. (2014). *Gratitude and the good life: Toward a psychology of appreciation*. Dordrecht, Netherlands: Springer.

Watkins, P. C., & Bell, J. (2017). Current theories and research in the psychology of gratitude. In M. A. Warren, S. I. Donaldson, (Eds.), *Scientific advances in positive psychology* (pp. 103–129). Santa Barbara, CA: Praeger/ABC-CLIO.

Watkins, P. C., Grimm, D. L., & Kolts, R. (2004). Counting your blessings: Positive memories among grateful persons. *Current Psychology, 23*, 52–67.

Watkins, P. C., Martin, B. D., & Faulkner, G. (2003, May). *Are grateful people happy people? Informant judgments of grateful acquaintances*. Presentation to the 83rd Annual Convention of the Western Psychological Association, Vancouver, BC, Canada.

Watkins, P. C., & McCurrach, D. (2016). Exploring how gratitude trains cognitive processes important to subjective well-being. In D. Carr (Ed.), *Perspectives on gratitude: An interdisciplinary approach* (pp. 27–40). Oxford: Taylor and Francis.

Watkins, P. C., & McCurrach, D. (in press). Progress in the science of gratitude. In S. Lopez, L. Edwards, & S. Marques (Eds.), *The Oxford handbook of positive psychology* (3rd ed.). New York: Oxford.

Watkins, P. C., McCurrach, D., & Timbrook, T. (2016, May). *Grateful recounting impacts eudaimonic more than hedonic well-being.* Poster presented to the Annual Convention of the Association for Psychological Science, Chicago, IL.

Watkins, P. C., Scheer, J., Ovnicek, M., & Kolts, R. (2006). The debt of gratitude: Dissociating gratitude from indebtedness. *Cognition and Emotion, 20,* 217–241.

Watkins, P. C., Uhder, J., & Pichinevskiy, S. (2015). Grateful recounting enhances subjective well-being: The importance of grateful processing. *Journal of Positive Psychology, 2,* 91–98.

Watkins, P. C., Woodward, K., Stone, T., & Kolts, R. D. (2003). Gratitude and happiness: The development of a measure of gratitude and its relationship with subjective well-being. *Social Behavior and Personality, 31,* 431–452.

Williams, L. A., & Bartlett, M. Y. (2015). Warm thanks: Gratitude expression facilitates social affiliation in new relationships via perceived warmth. *Emotion, 15,* 1–5.

Wood, A. M., Emmons, R. A., Algoe, S. B, Froh, J. J., Lambert, N. M., & Watkins, P. C. (2016). A dark side of gratitude? Distinguishing between beneficial gratitude and its harmful impostors for the positive clinical psychology of gratitude and well-being. In A. M. Wood & J. Johnson (Eds.), *The Wiley handbook of positive clinical psychology* (pp. 137–151). Chichester: Wiley.

Wood, A. M., Froh, J. J., & Geraghty, A. W. A. (2010). Gratitude and well-being: A review and theoretical integration. *Clinical Psychology Review, 30,* 890–905.

Wood, A. M., Maltby, J., Gillett, R., Linley, P. A., & Joseph, S. (2008). The role of gratitude in the development of social support, stress, and depression: Two longitudinal studies. *Journal of Research in Personality, 42,* 854–871.

Wood, A. M., Maltby, J., Stewart, N., Linley, P. A., & Joseph, S. (2008). A social-cognitive model of trait and state levels of gratitude. *Emotion, 8,* 281–290.

11

SOCIAL COMPARISON PROCESSES

Pieternel Dijkstra and Abraham P. Buunk

Social comparisons—comparing one's own situation, characteristics, or achievements with those of others—are an essential part of human social life. In particular, the evaluative component of well-being has been long considered to depend on social comparisons. Indeed, one's well-being depends not only on, for instance, the fulfillment of one's needs, but also on how one's own needs fulfillment compares with that of others. Before the midst of the past century, Hyman (1942) noted in a now classic paper that one's assessment of how well off one is on such dimensions as financial position, intellectual capabilities, and physical attractiveness is dependent on the group with whom one compares oneself. A more direct link of social comparisons to well-being came from the well-known American Soldier study (Stouffer, Suchman, Devinney, Star, & Williams, 1949), which showed, among others results, that black soldiers from Northern states reported less satisfaction with their situation than did black soldiers from the South, supposedly because both groups compared themselves with black people outside the army, a reference group that was, at the time, considerably worse off in the South than in the North. The more sociologically oriented work on reference groups that grew out of these early studies (e.g., Singer, 1980) suggested that one's well-being does not depend on one's absolute level of outcomes, but on one's level of outcomes compared to that of others. A recent, albeit somewhat indirect, illustration of this notion comes from more research that showed that, when choosing between having an absolutely larger income or an income that was absolutely less but larger than others' incomes, both men and women chose the greater relative income (Hill & Buss, 2006).

Although theorizing on social comparison can be traced back to classic contributions to social psychology and sociology, including work on the self, adaptation level, and reference groups (Buunk & Gibbons, 2006; Suls & Wheeler, 2000), it was not until Festinger's (1954) classic paper that the term *social comparison* was proposed and a detailed theory on social comparison was outlined. Festinger's original theory on social comparison was restricted to the comparison of abilities and opinions and did not relate social comparisons to well-being, over the past decades. Since that time, however, work on social comparison has undergone numerous transitions and reformulations, and in the process, has developed into a lively, varied, and complex area of research encompassing many different paradigms, approaches, and applications (e.g., Buunk & Gibbons, 2006; Suls & Wheeler, 2000). For example, since Festinger, research has found that, in addition to self-evaluation, individuals often compare themselves with others to improve their skills or abilities (*self-improvement*) and to protect or enhance their self-esteem (*self-enhancement*; e.g., Wills, 1981; Wood, 1989). The current and rather broad concept of social comparison therefore refers to "any process in which individuals relate their own characteristics to those of others" (Buunk & Gibbons, 2000, p. 491) and encompasses comparisons on many different dimensions.

An important consequence of this development is the focus of many social comparison studies on issues directly related to well-being, something that no researcher would have considered during the early years of social comparison research after Festinger's (1954) seminal article. One of the first to link the concept of social comparisons explicitly to well-being was Wills (1981), who argued that *downward social comparisons*—comparisons with less fortunate others—can diminish negative affect and raise people's subjective well-being by reducing stress. Whereas Wills focused on social comparisons under threat, many subsequent studies have analyzed more generally how social comparisons may affect factors that are related to well-being, such as affective responses, self-esteem, and optimism.

The present chapter aims to provide a review of the most important literature regarding the role of social comparison processes with regard to well-being. In so doing, the present chapter may not only contribute to a better understanding of how and why social comparisons are related to well-being, but also provide avenues for interventions aimed at improving well-being by using social comparisons. Before discussing the literature in the domain of social comparisons and well-being, we will first explain the basic theory regarding the different types of social comparisons individuals make.

Types of Social Comparisons

Individuals may engage in different types of social comparisons with others. Individuals may compare themselves with others who are as well off as they are (*lateral* comparisons), with others who are better off (*upward* comparisons), or with others who are worse off (*downward* comparisons). With whom individuals choose to compare themselves depends largely on the motive underlying the comparison. If *self-evaluation* is the dominant motive, individuals usually will compare themselves with others whose condition or circumstances are similar to that of themselves ('the similarity hypothesis'; Festinger, 1954; Suls & Wheeler, 2000). If others' condition or circumstances are too far from one's own, either above or below, it is not possible to estimate one's own condition or circumstances accurately. If *self-improvement* is the dominant motive individuals usually will compare themselves upwards with others who are better off than they are (e.g., Suls & Wheeler, 2000). Observing another person who is better off can reveal information about how to improve and may raise feelings of self-confidence and self-efficacy (e.g., Blanton, Buunk, Gibbons, & Kuyper, 1999). Finally, if *self-enhancement* is the dominant motive, individuals generally compare themselves downwards with others who are worse off than they are themselves (e.g., Suls & Wheeler, 2000). Perceiving oneself as better off through downward comparison boosts self-esteem, reduces anxiety, and generates the positive affect essential for self-enhancement. In contrast, comparing oneself to someone who is better off may deflate the ego and produce negative affect.

The effect of social comparison information depends not only on the direction of the comparison but also on how individuals interpret social comparison information (Buunk, Collins, Taylor, Van Yperen, & Dakof, 1990; Collins, 1996). According to the *identification-contrast model* (Buunk & Ybema, 1997), when evaluating themselves, individuals may *contrast* themselves with a comparison target by focusing on the differences between themselves and the target. Social comparison, however, may also evoke *identification* with a target. In identifying with a target, individuals assume similarity between themselves and the target, feel psychologically close to the target, and often perceive a common fate with the target, viewing the situation of the target as a potential future for themselves (see also Buunk, Zurriaga, & González, 2006). As a consequence, individuals may follow one of four strategies: *upward identification, upward contrast, downward contrast*, or *downward identification* (Van der Zee, Bakker, & Buunk, 2001). In general, when individuals identify with a comparison target, their self-image is enhanced by upward comparisons (upward identification) and lowered by downward comparisons (downward identification). Conversely, when individuals contrast with a comparison target, their self-image is enhanced by downward comparisons (downward contrast) and lowered by upward comparisons (upward contrast).

The identification-contrast model may help understand how and why social comparisons affect well-being and may help interpret the findings from social comparison research reviewed in this chapter. In the remaining part of this chapter, we will review the literature on social comparisons in relation to several indices of well-being, such as positive affect and a positive self-image. Special attention will be paid to well-being in times of adversity. Studying social comparisons in relation to well-being in times of difficulty is important, since especially under circumstances that challenge well-being individuals feel an enhanced need for social comparison. In stressful or uncertain circumstances social comparisons may enhance feelings of security and reduce stress by providing information about how others, in similar situations, are coping and may offer reassurance if one concludes that one is better off than others. In addition, we will discuss several implications of social comparison research that may help develop interventions aimed at raising individuals' well-being.

Positive Affective Responses

According to the *broaden-and-build theory* of positive emotions (Fredrickson, 2006), positive emotions may momentarily broaden people's attention and thinking, enabling them to draw flexibly on higher-level connections and wider-than-usual ranges of perceptions and ideas. In turn, these broadened and flexible outlooks help people to discover and build survival-promoting personal resources, such as self-esteem and improved relations with others, that may be especially relevant for well-being. From the perspective of the broaden-and-build theory, social comparisons may be one of the mechanisms individuals (unconsciously) use to evoke and maintain positive affect.

The identification-contrast model proposes that the direction of comparison (downward versus upward) is not the only factor determining affective outcomes. Consistent with this proposal, many studies have shown that both upward and downward comparisons may evoke positive affect. More specifically, upward comparisons have been found to evoke positive emotions, such as feelings of inspiration (Lockwood, Shaughnessy, Fortune, & Tong, 2012) and hope (e.g., Locock & Brown, 2010). For instance, Lockwood et al. (2012) found that especially during transitions to a novel cultural environment, individuals profit from upward comparisons to those who have experienced a similar transition. These upward comparisons may help reduce uncertainty and may inspire individuals to make appropriate adjustments to their novel environments. Downward comparisons also may evoke positive emotions, such as pride (e.g., Lange & Crusius, 2015) and relief (e.g., Habib et al., 2015). For example, pupils who received information that they were performing much better than classmates experienced more pride than pupils that did not receive this information, especially when this information was accompanied by public social comparison praise by the teacher (Webster, Duval, Gaines & Smith, 2003).

It must be noted, however, that positive emotions induced by social comparisons may also have adverse effects on one's relations with others. For example, expressing pride may lead others to feel envious (Lange & Crusius, 2015). Thus, although outperforming others in itself can be satisfying, in competitive environments outperforming others and experiencing pride may clash with relational goals. In addition to evoking envy in others, outperformers may also experience discomfort when they believe that their superior status poses a threat to the outperformed person (Exline & Lobel, 2001).

The identification-contrast model also proposes that the direction of comparison (downward versus upward) is not the only factor determining affective outcomes. Consistent with this proposal, many studies show that both upward and downward comparisons may also evoke negative affect. For example, several studies have found that upward comparisons evoke or strengthen feelings of shame and embarrassment (e.g., Cheung, Gilbert & Irons, 2004) and that downward comparisons evoke or strengthen feelings of worry and anxiety (e.g., Petersen, Taube, Lehmann, Van den Bergh, & Von Leupoldt, 2012). Studies that explicitly have examined both the direction of the comparison (upward or downward) and the degree to which individuals either contrast or identify with the information they obtain from the social comparison (i.e., the contrast-identification model) generally have shown that upward identification and/or downward contrast evoke positive emotions. For instance, people in intimate relationships show improved mood when identifying upwards with couples that have a more satisfied relationship (Buunk & Ybema, 2003). Likewise, the more students identified with a successful fictitious student (upward comparison target), the less negative affect they experienced (Michinov, 2001).

To better understand the affective outcomes of social comparisons, both Smith (2000) and Buunk, Kuyper, and Van der Zee (2005) further elaborated the contrast-identification model by arguing that social comparisons may evoke specific affective responses depending on three dimensions: (1) The direction of comparison (upward versus downward), (2) the interpretation of social comparison information (contrast versus identification), and (3) the focus of attention (on the consequences for the self versus others; see Table 11.1).

In line with their theoretical model, Buunk et al. (2005) showed that, at least in the classroom, students most frequently made upward identifications with the focus on the self, which lead to feelings of hope that in the future they might

TABLE 11.1 Affective Responses as a Function of Comparison Direction, Interpretation of Social Comparison Information, and Focus of Attention

Comparison Type	Buunk et al. (2005)	Schmitt (2000)
Upward		
Identification		
• Focus on self	Hope	Optimism
• Focus on other	Sympathetic enjoyment	Admiration
Contrast		
• Focus on self	Frustration	Depression/shame
• Focus on other	Resentment	Resentment
Downward		
Identification		
• Focus on self	Worry	Fear/worry
• Focus on other	Compassion	Pity
Contrast		
• Focus on self	Relief	Pride
• Focus on other	Contempt	Contempt/scorn

receive a good grade similar to that of the target they were identifying with. Although few studies have explicitly assessed on what exactly individuals focus their attention during the process of social comparison (self versus other), the models of both Buunk and colleagues and Schmitt explain why and how specific types of social comparisons may lead to different affective responses.

Several studies suggest that that the mood-enhancing pattern of social comparisons (upward identification and downward contrast) may not only improve mood but also, in the long run, enhance feelings of well-being. For instance, nurses who responded with more positive affect to upward comparisons and with less negative affect to downward comparisons, showed a decrease in burnout symptoms 1 year later (Buunk, Zurriaga, & Peiro, 2010). The fact that the consequences of social comparisons have long-term consequences is consistent with the reasoning behind the broaden-and-build theory of positive emotions (Fredrickson, 2006). A likely explanation from this theory is that positive emotions enhance ways of coping that, in the long run, contribute to well-being, such as problem-focused coping. Indeed, Burns and colleagues (2008) showed that positive emotions and well-being-enhancing coping strategies, such as positive reframing, seeking counsel and problem solving, mutually build on one another, creating an upward spiral toward enhanced emotional well-being (see also Fredrickson & Joiner, 2002). Downward contrast and upward identification may serve as important underlying mechanisms that help initiate and maintain this process. Van der Zee and colleagues (2000), for instance, found that cancer patients who identified with others who were doing better and contrasted themselves against others who were doing worse were more likely to engage in well-being-enhancing coping styles, such as reinterpretation-growth, social support, and problem solving. Likewise, Carmona, Buunk, Peiro, Rodriguez, and Bravo (2006) showed that teachers who identified with others who were doing worse (downward identification) and compared themselves with other teachers who were doing better (upward contrast) were more likely to experience burnout and less likely to engage in problem-focused coping, whereas upward identification was negatively related to burnout and positively related to problem-focused coping. Likewise, in sample of fibromyalgia outpatients, Cabrera-Perona, Buunk, Terol-Cantero, Quiles-Marcos, and Martín-Aragón (2017) recently found that as patients contrasted themselves more often with other patients doing better (upward contrast) and identified more often with other patients doing worse (downward identification), they more often engaged in the maladaptive coping strategy of catastrophizing, that is, negative thoughts about and negative expectations of pain.

Positive Self-Image

A positive self-image and high self-esteem are important to well-being (e.g., Nielsen et al., 2016). Individuals with a more positive self-image or a higher self-esteem generally report higher levels of happiness, positive affect, mental health and life satisfaction and lower levels of psychological distress (e.g., Orth, Robins, Meier, & Conger, 2016). Social comparisons can affect self-image and self-esteem in at least two ways. First, individuals may use downward contrast for self-enhancement, in which the self is enhanced by focusing on those things that make them better than others. Second, and more indirectly, upward comparisons may provide individuals with important information for self-improvement, a process also called "social learning" (Bandura, 1962, 1971). In this case self-esteem may be enhanced not because one focuses on how one is superior to others, but because one actually becomes more competent or skilled in both an absolute and relative sense.

As predicted by the identification-contrast model, several studies show that individuals may use social comparisons to self-enhance. For instance, in a study among fourth and fifth graders, the more pupils reported using downward identification and upward contrast, the lower were their perceptions of their scholastic competence, whereas the more pupils reported using upward identification and downward contrast, the higher were their perceptions of their scholastic competence (Boissicat, Pansu, Bouffard, & Cottin, 2012). This study suggests that downward contrast and upward identification are particularly adaptive in school and classroom settings. Downward contrast may help students maintain high self-esteem, while upward identification may help them improve their academic performance (Chung, Schriber, & Robins, 2016; Dijkstra, Kuyper, Buunk, Van der Werf, & Van der Zee, 2008). The important role of downward contrast in educational settings is also corroborated by research on the *big-fish-little-pond effect*—the phenomenon that equally able students have lower academic self-esteem in schools or classes where the average achievement level is higher than in schools or classes where the average achievement level is lower (see Marsh et al., 2008, for a review). Thus, as predicted by the identification-contrast model, academic self-esteem is improved in classes or schools that provide students with ample opportunities for downward contrast, whereas it is lowered in classes or schools that hold little opportunities for such contrast among students. It must be noted that downward comparisons, although they may increase academic self-esteem, are not very helpful with regard to academic performance. In contrast, academic performance is facilitated by upward comparisons, especially in the form of upward identifications, which provide students with useful information that enables them to improve their performances. In other domains, research also shows that individuals self-enhance in line with the principles of the identification-contrast model. For example, a study of social media showed that exposure to downward comparison targets (e.g., targets with a low-activity social network or unhealthy habits) resulted in higher self-esteem than exposure to upward comparison targets (e.g., targets with a high-activity social network or healthy habits; Vogel, Rose, Roberts, & Eckles, 2014).

The studies described previously involve social comparisons to actual social comparison targets, but individuals may also cognitively *construct* such targets.

An important assumption of the identification-contrast model is that individuals have a "wired in" tendency to develop or maintain a positive self-image—or high self-esteem—by attaining a subjective feeling of doing better than others on relevant dimensions. A positive self-concept or a high self-esteem based on such cognitive constructions may generate the positive affect that helps build the resources individuals need to cope with stress; conquer obstacles; and take on life's challenges by facilitating adaptive coping with stressors and life's problems (e.g., Tomaka, Morales-Monks, & Shamaley, 2013) and fostering perseverance and performance (e.g., Sommer & Baumeister, 2002).

The tendency to rate oneself as higher on positive attributes and lower on negative attributes than most other people has been referred to as the *better-than-average (BTA) effect* (e.g., Kuyper, Dijkstra, Buunk, & Van der Werf, 2011), also called illusory superiority (Hoorens, 1995). In studies assessing the BTA effect, individuals usually compare themselves with a relatively ambiguous group of others ('most other people') or an ambiguous comparison target (the "average" or "typical" person) that provides plenty of opportunities to construct or confirm a positive perception of the self. The BTA effect has been observed in a variety of settings. For example, Meyer (1980) found that most people in work settings believed that they performed better than about 75% of others with the same job; very few people considered themselves less than average. In addition, 80% of the higher professionals and managers believed that they belonged to the best 10% of people with the same job as they had. Likewise, in a sample of over 15,000 secondary school students in The Netherlands, Kuyper et al. (2011) found that most children think they are more athletic, likable, attractive, and more capable of and eager to get high grades than most of their classmates. In a similar vein, undergraduate students believe that they are more likely than their peers to use condoms when having sex with someone for the first time (Ross & Bowen, 2010). Of course, the individual's may believe that his or her perception of being better than others is correct. Because it is impossible, however, for the majority of people to be above average, the belief of most people that they are better than average is biased and inaccurate (Kuyper et al., 2011).

In general, one's relationships with others also play a role in the enhancement of the self. As individuals are more attached to others, perceptions of these (close) others may increasingly become part of the self-image. This phenomenon has been referred to as *overlapping selves* (Aron, Aron, Tudor, & Nelson, 1991) and the *interdependent self* (Markus & Kitayama, 1991). As a consequence, individuals may also derive high self-esteem from viewing their close relationships as (overly) positive resulting in an *extended BTA-effect* (e.g., Fowers, Veingrad, & Dominics, 2002; Martz et al., 1998), sometimes also referred to as *relationship superiority* or *positive illusions* (e.g., Buunk, 2001; Dijkstra & Barelds, 2008). For instance, Suls, Lemos, and Stewart (2002) found that undergraduates rated themselves higher on positive traits than the "average" undergraduate, they also rated their friends superior on these traits relative to the "average" undergraduate. Likewise, individuals often perceive the relationship with their partners as superior to the relationships of other people (Buunk, 2001; Buunk & Van Yperen, 1991; Rusbult, Van Lange, Wildschut, Yovetich, & Verette, 2000). This extended BTA-effect generally makes people feel better about their relationships and themselves and may enhance relationship satisfaction. For instance, Buunk (2001) showed that the extent to which individuals viewed their relationship as superior to those of others predicted relationship satisfaction (see also Rusbult et al., 2000). In addition, Buunk and Van Yperen (1991) found the extent to which individuals perceived to derive greater gains from their own marriage compared with similar others to be a significant predictor of relationship satisfaction.

Although self-enhancement by means of social comparisons may lead to a high self-esteem and a positive self-image, comparisons that blatantly favor the self and are communicated publicly are generally not appreciated by others (Hoorens, Pandelaere, Oldersma, & Sedikides, 2012). People who verbalize their self-superiority beliefs to others are seen as arrogant and are thought to view others negatively. Although it contributes to a positive self-image and high self-esteem, the BTA-effect may undermine relations with others when individuals are too explicit about their beliefs concerning their own superiority.

Individuals use social comparisons not only to maintain or enhance their self-image but also to remain optimistic about their future. In general, most people see their own futures as more rosy than those of others. More specifically, most people believe that they are more likely than others to experience positive events in the future and less likely to experience negative events, a phenomenon called *unrealistic optimism*. In the first study of this phenomenon, Weinstein (1980) found that students rated positive events, such as getting a good job offer before graduation or living past 80, as more likely to occur to them than to their classmates. In contrast, students rated negative events, such as having a heart attack before the age of 40 or developing a drinking problem, as less likely to occur to them than to their classmates. Although seeing a positive future may increase feelings of hope, optimism, and satisfaction with life, it also brings risks, especially in the area of health and lifestyle. Unrealistic optimism with regard to one's health can undermine health-promoting practices by decreasing worry (Suls, 2011; Weinstein, 1982). Dillard, McCaul, and Klein (2006), for instance, found that unrealistically optimistic smokers were more likely to endorse beliefs that there is no risk of lung cancer if one smokes only for a few years and that getting lung cancer depends on one's genes. More importantly, unrealistically optimistic smokers were less likely to plan on quitting smoking. Another study found that people who were unrealistically optimistic about avoiding the influenza A virus reported lower intentions to wash their hands and use hand sanitizers (Kim & Niederdeppe, 2013).

In addition to leading to self-enhancement, which leads to high self-esteem and a positive self-image, social comparisons that lead to self-improvement may also fuel high self-esteem and a positive self-image. If self-improvement is the underlying motive, individuals may identify with others who perform better than themselves but who resemble themselves on attributes such as gender and age (e.g., Buunk, Cohen-Schotanus, & Van Nek, 2007; Dijkstra et al., 2008). Consistent with the identification–contrast model, these upward comparisons enable individuals to obtain information about how others are performing that they can then use to improve their own performance, a process called *social learning* (Bandura, 1962, 1971). However, upward comparisons will facilitate learning and self-improvement only if an individual believes that he or she can attain the performance level of the upward comparison target. Only then will individuals identify with and feel inspired by the role model and feel a sense of self-efficacy for the specific task involved (e.g., Huguet, Dumas, Monteil, & Genestoux, 2001). If the individual perceives the difference between the self and the upward comparison target as too large, then the individual may lose hope and feel incapable of reaching performance level of the upward comparison target. In the worst case, they may contrast themselves with the upward comparison target, leading to feelings of distress and inferiority. Therefore, when self-improvement is the leading motive for social comparison, individuals generally prefer to compare themselves with those who are *somewhat* better because these targets enable social learning while having a limited negative effect on self-esteem (Blanton et al., 1999; Dijkstra et al., 2008). If individuals do indeed succeed in improving themselves, both mood and self-esteem may increase. In addition, when comparing the improved self with others, it may become easier to identify with upward comparison targets and make downward contrasts, which may both further increase well-being.

Several recent studies suggest that feelings of envy motivate individuals to self-improve. Envy is the emotion that "occurs when a person lacks another's superior quality, achievement, or possession and either desires it or wishes that the other lacked it" (Parrott & Smith, 1993, p. 906). Envy is thus always evoked by upward social comparisons and accompanied by the goal of reducing the difference between oneself and the superior other. Envy, however, may be either benign or malicious (Van de Ven, Zeelenberg, & Pieters, 2009). Whereas individuals who experience benign envy usually try to improve themselves to reduce the difference with the envied person, individuals who experience malicious envy usually try to reduce the difference with the envied person by derogating him or her. Van de Ven, Zeelenberg, and Pieters (2011) found that feelings of benign envy, but not feelings of admiration or malicious envy, motivate people to improve themselves. They also found that upward social comparisons triggered benign envy and subsequent better performance only when people thought self-improvement was attainable, as noted previously. When participants thought self-improvement was difficult, upward social comparisons merely led to admiration but not to the motivation to improve.

Life Satisfaction and Well-Being in the Face of Adversity

How satisfied individuals are with their lives is based strongly on evaluations of how they are doing compared to others. Boyce, Brown, and Moore (2010), for instance, showed that life satisfaction is related not to absolute income or the position of one's income relative to some wage standard, but to the ranked position of one's income within their reference group (similar in age, educational level, etc.). If individuals conclude that they have a higher income than others in their reference group—implying downward contrast—they are more satisfied with their lives. Consistent with the identification-contrast model, downward contrasts tend to enhance satisfaction with one's own life. Downward contrasts seem to become even more important for well-being when individuals find themselves in uncertain or distressing circumstances or when they are confronted with strenuous life events, such as unemployment, financial strain, or suffering from a severe illness. Under these circumstances, downward contrasts help individuals maintain and enhance well-being and life satisfaction. For instance, in times of economic downturn, downward contrast may become especially important in helping one to remain satisfied about one's income. If individuals make more downward comparisons with workers in lower social groups who earn less, they feel more satisfied with their earning. In contrast, a dissatisfied feeling (that of relative deprivation) is evoked when workers make upward comparisons, especially in times of economic downturn. Feelings of deprivation will therefore be especially prevalent among workers at the lowest income level (Tao, 2015).

Many studies on downward contrast have been conducted among individuals suffering from chronic diseases. Severe illnesses of both self and close others can be regarded as one of the most threatening and stressful events that people may experience during their lives and may severely corrode life satisfaction (Scully, Tosi, & Banning, 2000). As a consequence, when confronted with a severe illness, both of oneself or a close other, individuals often feel an enhanced need to compare themselves with fellow patients in an attempt to restore a sense of well-being and life satisfaction. Under these circumstances, downward contrast can be a an adaptive strategy for enhancing the positive affect that may help build the resources one needs to cope with the stressful circumstances surrounding a severe illness. Wood and colleagues (1985), for instance, found that breast cancer patients made a preponderance of spontaneous downward comparisons. A study of nurses by Buunk Ybema, Gibbons, and Ipenburg (2001) showed that the relations between negative affect and upward comparisons and between positive affect and downward comparisons were strongest for nurses who reported more burnout symptoms. Likewise, Van der Zee et al. (1996) found that cancer patients made more frequent downward comparisons (comparisons with patients who were worse off than them) than did healthy people, a strategy that helped them maintain a level of subjective well-being similar to their healthy counterparts. Blanchard, Blalock, DeVellis, DeVellis, and Johnson (1999) showed that mothers of premature infants made more downward social comparisons to other mothers and their babies, and, as a consequence, made more favorable evaluations of their infants relative to the typical premature baby. More in general, in a review of 23 studies, Tennen, McKee, and Affleck (2000) concluded that downward social comparisons are prominent in populations with serious medical problems, such as patients suffering from rheumatoid arthritis, cancer, and chronic pain, and that these downward comparisons are generally associated with positive adjustment. Upward contrasts, on the other hand, usually are associated with relatively low psychological well-being among individuals with lowered physical well-being. For instance, Buunk, Zurriaga, and González (2006) found that among patients with a spinal cord injury, upward contrast was quite strongly related to negative emotions. Findings were similar among community-dwelling elderly for whom this type of social comparison was accompanied by lower life satisfaction (Frieswijk, Buunk, Steverink, & Slaets, 2004) and among teachers for whom this type of social comparison was related to more burnout symptoms (Carmona et al., 2006). Likewise, Buunk and colleagues (2006) found that among people with spinal cord injuries, upward contrast was related strongly to depression.

Although patients in the early stages of severe medical illnesses, such as cancer, may feel a need for social comparisons with fellow patients, the opposite may be true in advanced stages of a potentially incurable disease, when chances of recovery are limited. In advanced stages of an incurable disease, the need to compare the self with fellow patients will often decrease because it becomes increasingly more difficult to make downward contrasts. In this stage of the disease, comparing the self with fellow patients will often result in upward contrasting comparisons that generate distress. To avoid negative emotions, such patients may ignore social comparison information that emphasizes the severity of their disease relative to other patients and look elsewhere for information that may help them cope with their situation. For example, Morrell and colleagues (2012) found that patients in advanced stages of ovarian cancer (stages III and IV) avoided contact with other ovarian cancer patients and preferred to seek the company of "normal" others and information that facilitated upward identification. Something similar may occur with individuals with chronic diseases such as rheumatoid arthritis (RA). For example, Blalock, Afifi, DeVellis, Holt, and DeVellis (1990) found that nearly 50% of the unprompted social comparisons made by patients involved others not affected by RA. After controlling for differences in physical health status, they found that patients who emphasized their similarity to, rather than their differences from, individuals not affected by RA exhibited better psychological adjustment. Consistent with the identification-contrast model, especially in the case of downward comparison, feelings of negative affect were mediated by identification with the target of the downward comparison (see also DeVellis et al., 1990).

Although upward identifications may also help individuals remain a high sense of well-being, several studies show that a high degree of stress or lowered physical well-being may hinder such upward identifications. For instance, Buunk, Ybema, Gibbons, and Ipenburg (2001) found that among sociotherapists making an upward comparison generated more positive and less negative affect than making a downward comparison. However, those reporting high levels of burnout reported lower levels of positive affect from upward comparisons than did those reporting low levels of burnout. Therefore, people experiencing stress or lowered well-being may benefit more from downward contrast than from upward identification, as discussed earlier in this paragraph.

Individual Differences That Affect the Relation Between Social Comparison and Well-Being

Not everyone seems equally able to use social comparisons to generate positive affect, a positive self-image, and a sense of well-being under difficult circumstances. Several studies show that individuals high in neuroticism tend to identify themselves with others who are worse off (e.g., Buunk, Van der Zee, & Van Yperen, 2001), increasing the likelihood that social comparisons will generate negative affect and lower well-being. Other studies show that individuals high in neuroticism compare themselves more often than those low in neuroticism, both upward and downward, with both types of comparison generating relatively high levels of negative affect (e.g., Van der Zee, Oldersma, Buunk, & Bos, 1998). Similar findings have been reported for low self-esteem, one of the components of neuroticism (e.g., Cramer, Song, & Drent, 2016). As do individuals high in neuroticism, individuals low in self-esteem often interpret both upward and downward comparison information more negatively than individuals high in self-esteem (Buunk et al., 1990). These findings are consistent with the broader research on neuroticism, self-esteem and coping (e.g., Mohiyeddini, Bauer, & Semple, 2015) that shows that individuals characterized by high neuroticism or low self-esteem show relatively inadequate coping strategies in response to stress compared to individuals low in neuroticism respectively high in self-esteem. It seems that, in general, neurotic and low self-esteem individuals find it relatively difficult to profit from the potential positive effects that may result from social comparisons.

Another individual difference that affects the relationship between well-being and social comparisons is *social comparison orientation (SCO)*, which refers to the disposition of to engage more or less frequently in on social comparisons, compare oneself more frequently with others, be interested in information about the thoughts and behaviors of others in similar situations, and be relatively sensitive to social comparisons (Gibbons & Buunk, 1999; Buunk & Gibbons, 2006). Buunk, Zurriaga, Peíró, Nauta, and Gosalvez (2005) showed that employees high in SCO reported more contrast in their social comparisons, that is, they reported more positive affect after downward comparisons and more negative affect after upward comparisons than did those lower in SCO. In addition, a number of studies suggest that SCO may moderate the association between engaging in social comparisons and well-being. In a study of nurses, Buunk and colleagues (2010) found that among individuals with a high SCO, the frequency of comparisons predicted feelings of burnout 9–10 months later. Van der Zee and colleagues (1998) found that cancer patients high in SCO responded with more negative affect to downward comparisons than to upward comparisons. In addition, individuals high in SCO are relatively sensitive to the experience of relative deprivation, that is resentment originating from the belief that one has been deprived more than other of desired and deserved outcomes (see also Callan, Kim, & Matthews, 2015). In a longitudinal study among nurses, Buunk, Zurriaga, Gonzalez-Roma, and Subirats (2003) found that feelings of relative deprivation increased among those nurses high in social comparison orientation who, 10 months earlier, had engaged more often in downward and upward comparisons and had derived both positive and negative feelings from these comparisons. This heightened sense of relative deprivation may lead to higher levels of psychological distress and burnout symptoms, undermining individuals' well-being and ability to cope with stress (e.g., De la Sablonnière, Tougas, De la Sablonnière, & Debrosse, 2012). However, SCO may also, under certain conditions, enhance well-being. For example, Buunk, Groothof, and Siero (2007) found that individuals who were exposed to a comparison target with a very dissatisfying social life evaluated their own social life as better than did participants who were exposed to a comparison target with a very satisfying social life. This was true, however, only for individuals high in SCO, suggesting that individuals high in SCO tend to contrast themselves more to others than individuals low in SCO. Likewise, Buunk, Oldersma, and De Dreu (2001) examined the extent to which relationship satisfaction can be enhanced by making downward contrasts. They found that asking individuals who were dissatisfied with their relationship to think of aspects in which they were better off than other couples resulted in enhanced relationship satisfaction, but only for those high in SCO. A possible explanation for the diverse effects of SCO is that SCO interacts with other situational and individual difference variables, such as the specific dimension or attribute individuals compare themselves on with others, in determining identification or contrast with a comparison target.

In addition, features of the upward and downward comparison targets may affect the relation between social comparison and well-being. For instance, experimental studies in the domain of personal relationships have shown that the extent to which a comparison target puts in effort into the relationship plays a role in the degree to which social comparisons with regard to one's marriage may affect mood. For example, Buunk and Ybema (2003) examined the effects on a woman's mood of a story of either a (1) happily married woman who put a lot of effort in her marriage, (2) a happily married woman who did not put effort in her marriage, (3) an unhappily married woman who put a lot of effort in her marriage, or (4) an unhappily married woman who did not put effort in her marriage. Upward targets evoked more positive mood than downward targets, and women especially tended to identify with the upward high-effort target. However, downward comparisons, although negatively affecting mood, resulted in a more positive evaluation of one's own relationship than did upward comparisons, suggesting that identification effected mood and that contrast effected self-evaluation. The role of both SCO and the extent to which a comparison target puts in effort, this time in overcoming a depression, was examined by Buunk and Brenninkmeijer (2001) among depressed and non-depressed individuals. This study showed that, as non-depressed individuals were higher in SCO a comparison target who overcame his or her depression through active coping (high effort) evoked a relatively positive mood whereas a comparison target who spontaneously overcame his or her depression (low effort) evoked a relatively negative mood. In contrast, as depressed individuals were higher in SCO, the low-effort target evoked a relatively positive mood change, and the high-effort target a relatively negative one. Findings like these are important because educational material that aims to inspire depressed patients by presenting a formerly depressed patient who overcame his or her depression through active coping may have adverse effects for some patients. Because passivity and a lack of energy are important symptoms of depression, some depressed people may feel incapable of active coping. In addition, because of their heightened reactivity to social comparison information, this may have a negative effect on mood especially among those high in SCO.

Social Comparison-Based Interventions That May Increase Well-Being

Interventions that help individuals to make better use of those social comparisons may increase positive affect, positive self-image, and well-being in difficult times and enhance well-being. One target group that may profit from social comparison-based interventions are clients who suffer from low self-esteem or high neuroticism. In general, these individuals find it relatively hard to make the self-enhancing upward identifications and downward contrasts that may provide them with a sense of pride, inspiration, hope, or a positive self-image (Buunk et al., 1990). To help these clients to make upward identifications more frequently, a therapist may first help them identify those targets that they perceive as inspiring role models and whose accomplishments they perceive as attainable. They may then help clients identify *with* these targets by, for instance, asking questions that help clients become more aware of their similarities with the comparison target. Consistent with the theoretical models of both Smith (2000) and Buunk et al. (2005), clients may also generate feelings of hope and optimism by means of upward identifications by focusing their attention on the potential implications of the role model's situation for their own actual or future situation. A therapist can encourage this by asking questions such as "What does this mean for your own situation?" and "How does it feel that the situation of this person is within reach for you as well?". In addition, therapists can help clients suffering from low self-esteem or neuroticism make more effective downward contrasts that enhance self-esteem and that, when focused on the self, may make them feel competent and proud. For example, a therapist could ask a client, to think about aspects about themselves or their situation that are superior to those of others and how focusing on these aspects makes them feel about themselves.

With patients confronted with chronic illnesses, health professionals may encourage them to engage in downward contrasts to enhance well-being and reduce stress, at least when individuals are not yet in the final stages of their disease. For example, health professionals may help patients to identify and think about those aspects of their lives in which they are doing better than fellow patients. Nonetheless, also upward comparisons with fellow patients may be helpful, but only when accompanied by the proper information about their disease and its treatment. For instance, Bennenbroek and colleagues (2003) presented cancer patients with audiotapes of fellow cancer patients talking about different elements of their treatment and disease: either (1) the procedure of the treatment, (2) their emotions about the disease and the treatment, or (3) the way they coped with their disease. This study showed that mood was elevated and self-efficacy increased when patients listened to fellow patients talking about the procedure or coping, but not about their emotions, suggesting that social comparisons regarding the procedure and coping may be useful supplements for patient educational material.

The many studies that have examined social comparison processes have shed a new light on special educational classes and may therefore help create more optimal learning conditions for pupils, especially for pupils ranked at the top and the bottom of their class in terms of achievement. Although intellectually gifted pupils may benefit academically more from special classes than from general classes, their self-esteem may suffer because of the reduced opportunities for downward contrast. For pupils with learning disabilities the opposite seems to true. Pupils who perform at the lower end of the distribution in regular class may profit from special classes for learning disabled pupils because these classes provide them with more opportunities for making downward comparisons while minimizing upward contrasts, which may enhance pupils' self-esteem (e.g., Dijkstra et al., 2008). At the same time, the use of special classes for pupils with learning disabilities may limit the possibilities for the upward identifications that might help pupils improve their performances. Decisions such as whether a specific pupil should attend special or general education therefore seem to depend partly on what the pupil needs most: an improvement in self-esteem or an improvement in performance. For instance, a pupil with a learning disability and fragile self-esteem may be better off in a special classroom than in a general classroom, even though the latter may provide more opportunities for the upward comparisons that might improve performances.

Finally, more in general, with regard to an unhealthy lifestyle, it seems important to tackle the negative effects unrealistic optimism may have on the adoption of preventive health behaviors. This may especially apply to individuals engaged in unhealthy habits, such as smoking and unsafe sex who run a relatively high risk of developing health problems. The challenge for health educators is to present health-related information in way that minimizes unrealistic optimism without compromising the individuals' general optimism about their future. Research suggests several ways to present information about health risks that reduces unrealistic optimism. Weinstein (1983), for instance, found that information about peers' actual risks of developing health problems almost eliminated optimistic biases for these health problems. In addition, Gold and De Sousa (2012) found that for health problems about which individuals are likely to feel concern, framing health information positively rather than negatively (for instance, "having a healthy heart" rather than "becoming ill with heart disease") reduces unrealistic optimism for getting the condition. In addition to providing information about health risks, it is of vital importance to include practical advice regarding how to limit these risks. Providing information about health risks only may evoke feelings of anxiety and fear and increase the chances that individuals will reject the health message (Maloney, Lapinski, & Witte, 2011). By also providing practical advice about how to diminish health risks, individuals may be more likely to both acknowledge health risks and remain optimistic about their future.

Conclusion

Social comparisons strongly affect people's affective responses and mood states, self-image, and perceptions of well-being, especially in times of adversity. The studies reviewed in this chapter provide evidence for the identification-contrast model, which contends that, to experience positive affect, a positive self-image, and enhanced well-being, individuals should identify with similar others who are doing better and contrast with similar others who are doing worse. Consistent with the broaden-and-build theory, these comparisons may not only raise mood and self-esteem in the short run, but also enhance well-being in the long run by facilitating coping strategies that contribute to future well-being. This conclusion is compatible with the evolutionary psychological assumption that social cognition is shaped by human striving for survival and reproductive success (e.g., Seyfarth & Cheney, 2015) and that individuals may use social comparisons to facilitate this striving. By selectively comparing themselves with others, humans maintain or evoke positive affect, positive self-image, and increased subjective well-being that may promote survival and reproduction, especially under conditions of stress when survival and reproductive success are challenged. The identification-contrast model describes how individuals compare themselves in general, but humans also show much individual variability in using social comparisons. Exactly how individuals compare themselves with similar others and what the effects of these comparisons are depends on individual difference variables, such as social comparison orientation, self-esteem, and neuroticism, as well as the characteristics of the comparison target and the situation individuals find themselves in. Research on social comparison theory and well-being provides scholar-practitioners with ample avenues for improving well-being by means of strengthening those social comparisons that contribute to well-being.

References

Aron, A., Aron, E. N., Tudor, M., & Nelson, G. (1991). Close relationships as including other in the self. *Journal of Personality and Social Psychology, 60*(2), 241–253.

Bandura, A. (1962). Social learning through imitation. In M. R. Jones (Ed.), *Nebraska Symposium on Motivation* (pp. 211–274). Oxford, England: University of Nebraska Press.

Bandura, A. (1971). *Social learning theory.* New York: General Learning Press.

Bennenbroek, F. T. C., Buunk, A. P., Stiegelis, H. E., Hagedoorn, M., Sanderman, R., Van den Bergh, A. C. M., & Botke, G. (2003). Audiotaped social comparison information for cancer patients undergoing radiotherapy: Differential effects of procedural, emotional and coping information. *Psycho-Oncology, 12,* 567–579.

Blalock, S. J, Afifi, R. A., DeVellis, B. M., Holt, K., & DeVellis, R. F. (1990). Adjustment to rheumatoid arthritis: The role of social comparison processes. *Health Education Research, 5,* 361–370.

Blanchard, L. W., Blalock, S. J., DeVellis, B. M., DeVellis, R. F., & Johnson, M. R. (1999). Social comparisons among mothers of premature and full-term infants. *Children's Health Care, 28,* 329–348.

Blanton, H., Buunk, B. P., Gibbons, F. X., & Kuyper, H. (1999). When better-than-others compare upward: Choice of comparison other and comparative evaluation as independent predictors of academic performance. *Journal of Personality and Social Psychology, 76,* 420–430.

Boissicat, N., Pansu, P., Bouffard, T., & Cottin, F. (2012). Relation between perceived scholastic competence and social comparison mechanisms among elementary school children. *Social Psychology of Education, 15,* 603–614.

Boyce, C. J., Brown, G. D. A., & Moore, S. C. (2010). Money and happiness: Rank of income, not income, affects life satisfaction. *Psychological Science, 21,* 471–475.

Burns, A. B., Brown, J. S., Sachs-Ericsson, N., Plant, E. A., Curtis, J. T., Fredrickson, B. L., & Joiner, T. E. (2008). Upward spirals of positive emotion and coping: Replication, extension, and initial exploration of neurochemical substrates. *Personality and Individual Differences, 44*(2), 360–370.

Buunk, A. P. (2001). Perceived superiority of one's own relationship and perceived prevalence of happy and unhappy relationships. *British Journal of Social Psychology, 40,* 565–574.

Buunk, A. P., & Brenninkmeijer, V. (2001). When individuals dislike exposure to an actively coping role model: Mood change as related to depression and social comparison orientation. *European Journal of Social Psychology, 31,* 537–548.

Buunk, A. P., Cohen-Schotanus, J., & van Nek, R. H. (2007). Why and how people engage in social comparison while learning social skills in groups. *Group Dynamics: Theory, Research, and Practice, 11*(3), 140–152.

Buunk, A. P., & Gibbons, F. X. (2006). Social comparison orientation: A new perspective on those who do and those who don't compare with others. In S. Guimond (Ed.), *Social comparison and social psychology; understanding cognition, intergroup relations and culture* (pp. 15–33). Cambridge: Cambridge University Press.

Buunk, A. P., Groothof, H. A. K., & Siero, F. W. (2007). Social comparison and satisfaction with one's life. *Journal of Social and Personal Relationship, 24,* 197–206.

Buunk, A. P., Kuyper, H., & Van der Zee, Y. G. (2005). Affective response to social comparison in the classroom. *Basic and Applied Social Psychology, 27,* 229–237.

Buunk, A. P., Oldersma, F. L., & De Dreu, K. W. (2001). Enhancing satisfaction through downward comparison: The role of relational discontent and individual differences in social comparison orientation. *Journal of Experimental Social Psychology, 37*, 452–467.

Buunk, A. P., Van der Zee, K. I., & Van Yperen, N. W. (2001). Neuroticism and social comparison orientation as moderators of affective responses to social comparison at work. *Journal of Personality, 69*, 745–763.

Buunk, A. P., & Van Yperen, N. W. (1991). Referential comparisons, relational comparisons, and exchange orientation: Their relation to marital satisfaction. *Personality and Social Psychology Bulletin, 17*, 709–717.

Buunk, A. P., & Ybema, J. F. (2003). Feeling bad, but satisfied: The effects of upward and downward comparison with other couples upon mood and marital satisfaction. *British Journal of Social Psychology, 42*, 613–628.

Buunk, A. P., Ybema, J. F., Gibbons, F. X., & Ipenburg, M. (2001). The affective consequences of social comparison as related to professional burnout and social comparison orientation. *European Journal of Social Psychology, 31*, 46–55.

Buunk, A. P., Zurriaga, R., & González, P. (2006). Social comparison, coping and depression in people with spinal cord injury. *Psychology & Health, 21*(6), 791–807.

Buunk, A. P., Zurriaga, R., Gonzalez-Roma, V., & Subirats, M. (2003). Engaging in upward and downward comparisons as a determinant of relative deprivation at work: A longitudinal study. *Journal of Vocational Behavior, 62*, 370–388.

Buunk, A. P., Zurriaga, R., & Peiro, J. M. (2010). Social comparison as a predictor of changes in burnout among nurses. *Anxiety, Stress & Coping, 2*, 181–194.

Buunk, A. P., Zurriaga, R., Peiro, J. M., Nauta, A., & Gosalvez, I. (2005). Social comparisons at work as related to a cooperative social climate and to individual differences in social comparison orientation. *Applied Psychology: An International Review, 54*, 61–80.

Buunk, B. P., Collins, R. L., Taylor, S. E., Van Yperen, N. W., & Dakof, G. A. (1990). The affective consequences of social comparison: Either direction has its ups and downs. *Journal of Personality and Social Psychology, 59*(6), 1238–1249.

Buunk, B. P., & Gibbons, F. X. (2000). Toward an enlightenment in social comparison theory: Moving beyond classic and Renaissance approaches. In J. Suls & L. Wheeler (Eds.), *Handbook of social comparison: Theory and research* (pp. 487–499). Dordrecht, Netherlands: Kluwer Academic Publishers.

Buunk, B. P., & Ybema, J. F. (1997). Social comparisons and occupational stress: The identification-contrast model. In B. P. Buunk, F. X. Gibbons, (Eds.), *Health, coping, and well-being: Perspectives from social comparison theory* (pp. 359–388). Mahwah, NJ, US: Lawrence Erlbaum Associates Publishers.

Cabrera-Perona, V., Buunk, A. P., Terol-Cantero, M. C., Quiles-Marcos, Y., & Martín-Aragón, M. (2017). Social comparison processes and catastrophising in fibromyalgia: A path analysis. *Psychology & Health, 32*, 1–20.

Callan, M. J., Kim, H., & Matthews, W. J. (2015). Age differences in social comparison tendency and personal relative deprivation. *Personality and Individual Differences, 87*, 196–199.

Carmona, C., Buunk, A. P., Peiro, J. M., Rodriguez, N. V., & Bravo, M. J. (2006). Do social comparison and coping styles play a role in the development of burnout? Cross-sectional and longitudinal findings. *Journal of Occupational and Organizational Psychology, 79*, 85–99.

Cheung, M. S. P., Gilbert, P., & Irons, C. (2004). An exploration of shame, social rank and rumination in relation to depression. *Personality and Individual Differences, 36*, 1143–1153.

Chung, J., Schriber, R. A., & Robins, R. W. (2016). Positive illusions in the academic context: A longitudinal study of academic self-enhancement in college. *Personality and Social Psychology Bulletin, 42*(10), 1384–1401.

Collins, R. L. (1996). For better or worse: The impact of upward social comparison on self-evaluations. *Psychological Bulletin, 119*(1), 51–69.

Cramer, E. M., Song, H., & Drent, A. M. (2016). Social comparison on Facebook: Motivation, affective consequences, self-esteem, and Facebook fatigue. *Computers in Human Behavior, 64*, 739–746.

De la Sablonnière, R., Tougas, F., De la Sablonnière, E., & Debrosse, R. (2012). Profound organizational change, psychological distress and burnout symptoms: The mediator role of collective relative deprivation. *Group Processes & Intergroup Relations, 15*, 776–790.

DeVellis, R. F., Holt, K., Renner, B. R., Blalock, L. W., Cook, H. L., Klotz, M. L., Mikow, V., & Harring, K. (1990). The relationship of social comparison to rheumatoid arthritis symptoms and affect. *Basic and Applied Social Psychology, 11*, 1–18.

Dijkstra, P., & Barelds, D. P. H. (2008). Positive illusions about one's partner's physical attractiveness. *Body Image, 5*(1), 99–108.

Dijkstra, P., Kuyper, H., Buunk, A. P., Van der Werf, G., & Van der Zee, Y. (2008). Social comparison in the classroom: A review. *Review of Educational Research, 78*, 828–879.

Dillard, A. J., McCaul, K. D., & Klein, W. P. (2006). Unrealistic optimism in smokers: Implications for smoking myth endorsement and self-protective motivation. *Journal of Health Communication, 11*(Suppl1), 93–102.

Exline, J., & Lobel, M. (2001). Private gain, social strain: Do relationship factors shape responses to outperformance? *European Journal of Social Psychology, 31*, 593–607.

Festinger, L. (1954). A theory of social comparison processes. *Human Relations, 7*, 117–140.

Fowers, B. J., Veingrad, M. R., & Dominics, C. (2002). The unbearable lightness of positive illusions: Engaged individuals' explanations of unrealistically positive relationship perceptions. *Journal of Marriage and Family, 64*, 450–460.

Fredrickson, B. L. (2006). The broaden-and-build theory of positive emotions. In M. Csikszentmihalyi & I. S. Csikszentmihalyi (Eds.), *A life worth living: Contributions to positive psychology* (pp. 85–103). New York: Oxford University Press.

Fredrickson, B. L., & Joiner, T. (2002). Positive emotions trigger upward spirals toward emotional well-being. *Psychological Science, 13*, 172–175.

Frieswijk, N., Buunk, A. P., Steverink, N., & Slaets, J. P. (2004). The effect of social comparison information on the life satisfaction of older persons. *Psychology and Aging, 19*, 183–190.

Gibbons, F. X., & Buunk, A. P. (1999). Individual differences in social comparison: Development of a scale of social comparison orientation. *Journal of Personality and Social Psychology, 76*, 129–142.

Gold, R. S., & de Sousa, P. N. (2012). When does event valence affect unrealistic optimism? *Psychology, Health & Medicine, 17*(1), 105–115.

Habib, M., Borst, G., Poirel, N., Houdé, O., Moutier, S., & Cassotti, M. (2015). Socio-emotional context and adolescents' decision making: The experience of regret and relief after social comparison. *Journal of Research on Adolescence, 25*, 81–91.

Hill, S. E., & Buss, D. M. (2006). Envy and positional bias in the evolutionary psychology of management. *Managerial & Decision Economics, 27*(2–3), 131–143.

Hoorens, V. (1995). Self-favoring biases, self-presentation, and the self-other asymmetry in social comparison. *Journal of Personality, 63*, 793–817.

Hoorens, V., Pandelaere, M., Oldersma, F., & Sedikides, C. (2012). The hubris hypothesis: You can self-enhance, but you'd better not show it. *Journal of Personality, 80*(5), 1237–1274.

Huguet, P., Dumas, F., Monteil, J. M., & Genestoux, N. (2001). Social comparison choices in the classroom: Further evidence for students' upward comparison tendency and its beneficial impact on performance. *European Journal of Social Psychology, 31*, 557–578.

Hyman, H. (1942). The psychology of subjective status. *Psychological Bulletin, 39*, 473–474.

Kim, H. K., & Niederdeppe, J. (2013). Exploring optimistic bias and the integrative model of behavioral prediction in the context of a campus influenza outbreak. *Journal of Health Communication, 18*(2), 206–222.

Kuyper, H., Dijkstra, P., Buunk, A. P., & Van der Werf, M. P. (2011). Social comparisons in the classroom: An investigation of the better than average effect among secondary school children. *Journal of School Psychology, 49*, 25–53.

Lange, J., & Crusius, J. (2015). Dispositional envy revisited: Unraveling the motivational dynamics of benign and malicious envy. *Personality and Social Psychology Bulletin, 41*, 284–294.

Lockwood, P., Shaughnessy, S. C., Fortune, J. L., & Tong, M. (2012). Social comparisons in novel situations: Finding inspiration during life transitions. *Personality and Social Psychology Bulletin, 38*, 985–996.

Locock, L., & Brown, J. B. (2010). "All in the same boat"? Patient and carer attitudes to peer support and social comparison in motor neurone disease (MND). *Social Science & Medicine, 71*, 1498–1505.

Maloney, E. K., Lapinski, M. K., & Witte, K. (2011). Fear appeals and persuasion: A review and update of the Extended Parallel Process Model. *Social and Personality Psychology Compass, 5*(4), 206–219.

Markus, H. R., & Kitayama, S. (1991). Culture and the self: Implications for cognition, emotion, and motivation. *Psychological Review, 98*(2), 224–253.

Marsh, H. W., Seaton, M., Trautwein, U., Lüdtke, O., Hau, K. T., O'Mara, A. J. & Craven, R. G. (2008). The big-fish-little-pond-effect stands up to critical scrutiny: Implications for theory, methodology, and future research. *Educational Psychology Review, 20*, 319–350.

Martz, J. M., Verette, J., Arriaga, X. B., Slovik, L. F., Cox, C. L., & Rusbult, C. E. (1998). Positive illusion in close relationships. *Personal Relationships, 5*(2), 159–181.

Meyer, H. H. (1980). Self-appraisal of job performance. *Personnel Psychology, 33*, 291–295.

Michinov, N. (2001). When downward comparison produces negative affect: The sense of control as a moderator. *Social Behavior and Personality, 29*, 427–444.

Mohiyeddini, C., Bauer, S., & Semple, S. (2015). Neuroticism and stress: The role of displacement behavior. *Anxiety, Stress & Coping: An International Journal, 28*, 391–407.

Morrell, B., Jordens, C. F. C., Kerridge, I. H., Harnett, P., Hobbs, K., & Mason, C. (2012). The perils of a vanishing cohort: A study of social comparisons by women with advanced ovarian cancer. *Psycho-Oncology, 21*, 382–391.

Nielsen, L., Stewart-Brown, S., Vinther-Larsen, M., Meilstrup, C., Holstein, B. E., & Koushede, V. (2016). High and low levels of positive mental health: Are there socioeconomic differences among adolescents? *Journal of Public Mental Health, 15*, 37–49.

Orth, U., Robins, R. W., Meier, L. L., & Conger, R. D. (2016). Refining the vulnerability model of low self-esteem and depression: Disentangling the effects of genuine self-esteem and narcissism. *Journal of Personality and Social Psychology, 110*, 133–149.

Parrott, W. G., & Smith, R. H. (1993). Distinguishing the experiences of envy and jealousy. *Journal of Personality and Social Psychology, 64*(6), 906–920.

Petersen, S., Taube, K., Lehmann, K., Van den Bergh, O., & Von Leupoldt, A. (2012). Social comparison and anxious mood in pulmonary rehabilitation: The role of cognitive focus. *British Journal of Health Psychology, 17*, 463–476.

Ross, L. L., & Bowen, A. M. (2010). Sexual decision making for the "better than average" college student. *Journal of American College Health, 59*, 211–216.

Rusbult, C. E., Van Lange, P. A. M., Wildschut, T., Yovetich, N. A., & Verette, J. (2000). Perceived superiority in close relationships: Why it exists and persists. *Journal of Personality and Social Psychology, 79*, 521–545.

Scully, J. A., Tosi, H., & Banning, K. (2000). Life event checklists: Revisiting the Social Readjustment Rating Scale after 30 years. *Educational and Psychological Measurement, 60*(6), 864–876.

Seyfarth, R. M., & Cheney, D. L. (2015). How sociality shapes the brain, behaviour and cognition. *Animal Behaviour, 103*, 187–190.

Singer, E. (1980). Reference groups and social evaluations. In M. Rosenberg & R. H. Turner (Eds.), *Social psychology: Sociological perspectives* (pp. 66–93). New York: Basic Books.

Smith, R. (2000). Assimilative and contrastive reactions to upward and downward social comparisons. In J. Suls & L. Wheeler (Eds.), *Handbook of social comparison: Theory and research* (pp. 173–200). Dordrecht, Netherlands: Kluwer Academic Publishers.

Sommer, K. L., & Baumeister, R. F. (2002). Self-evaluation, persistence, and performance following implicit rejection: The role of trait self-esteem. *Personality and Social Psychology Bulletin, 28*, 926–938.

Stouffer, S. A., Suchman, E. A., Devinney, L. C., Star, S. A., & Williams, R. J. (1949). *The American soldier: Adjustment during army life.* Studies in Social Psychology in World War II, Vol. 1. Oxford, England: Princeton University Press.

Suls, J. (2011). Social comparison processes: Implications for physical health. In H. S. Friedman (Ed.), *The Oxford handbook of health psychology* (pp. 269–280). New York, NY, US: Oxford University Press.

Suls, J., Lemos, K., & Stewart, L. H. (2002). Self-esteem, construal, and comparisons with the self, friends, and peers. *Journal of Personality and Social Psychology, 82*, 252–261.

Suls, J., & Wheeler, L. (2000). *Handbook of social comparison: Theory and research.* Dordrecht, Netherlands: Kluwer Academic Publishers.

Tao, H. (2015). Multiple earnings comparisons and subjective earnings fairness: A cross-country study. *Journal of Behavioral and Experimental Economics, 57*, 45–54.

Tennen, H., McKee, T. E., & Affleck, G. (2000). Social comparison processes in health and illness. In J. Suls & L. Wheeler (Eds.), *Handbook of social comparison: Theory and research* (pp. 443–483). Dordrecht, Netherlands: Kluwer Academic Publishers.

Tomaka, J., Morales-Monks, S., & Shamaley, A. G. (2013). Stress and coping mediate relationships between contingent and global self-esteem and alcohol-related problems among college drinkers. *Stress and Health: Journal of the International Society for the Investigation of Stress, 29*, 205–213.

Van de Ven, N., Zeelenberg, M., & Pieters, R. (2009). Leveling up and down: The experiences of benign and malicious envy. *Emotion, 9*(3), 419–429.

Van de Ven, N., Zeelenberg, M., & Pieters, R. (2011). Why envy outperforms admiration. *Personality and Social Psychology Bulletin, 37*(6), 784–795.

Van der Zee, K. I., Bakker, A. B., & Buunk, A. P. (2001). Burnout and reactions to social comparison information among volunteer caregivers. *Anxiety Stress and Coping, 14*, 391–410.

Van der Zee, K. I., Buunk, A. P., De Ruiter, J. H., Tempelaar, R., Van Sonderen, E., & Sanderman, R. (1996). Social comparison and the subjective well-being of cancer patients. *Basic and Applied Social Psychology, 18*, 453–468.

Van der Zee, K. I., Buunk, B., Sanderman, R., Botke, G., & Van den Bergh, F. (2000). Social comparison and coping with cancer treatment. *Personality and Individual Differences, 28*, 17–34.

Van der Zee, K. I., Oldersma, F., Buunk, A. P., & Bos, D. (1998). Social comparison preferences among cancer patients as related to neuroticism and social comparison orientation. *Journal of Personality and Social Psychology, 75*, 801–810.

Vogel, E. A., Rose, J. P., Roberts, L. R., & Eckles, K. (2014). Social comparison, social media, and self-esteem. *Psychology of Popular Media Culture, 3*, 206–222.

Webster, J. M., Duval, J., Gaines, L. M., & Smith, R. H. (2003). The roles of praise and social comparison information in the experience of pride. *The Journal of Social Psychology, 143*(2), 209–232.

Weinstein, N. D. (1980). Unrealistic optimism about future life events. *Journal of Personality and Social Psychology, 39*(5), 806–820.

Weinstein, N. D. (1982). Unrealistic optimism about susceptibility to health problems. *Journal of Behavioral Medicine, 5*(4), 441–460.

Weinstein, N. D. (1983). Reducing unrealistic optimism about illness susceptibility. *Health Psychology, 2*(1), 11–20.

Wills, T. A. (1981). Downward comparison principles in social psychology. *Psychological Bulletin, 90*(2), 245–271.

Wood, J. V. (1989). Theory and research concerning social comparisons of personal attributes. *Psychological Bulletin, 106*(2), 231–248.

Wood, J. V., Taylor, S. E., & Lichtman, R. R. (1985). Social comparison in adjustment to breast cancer. *Journal of Personality and Social Psychology, 49*, 1169–1183.

12

SOCIAL MEDIA USE AND WELL-BEING

Jung-Hyun Kim

Social media is defined as "forms of electronic communication through which users create online communities to share information, ideas, personal messages, and other content" (Merriam-Webster, 2017). Social media has achieved remarkable growth, especially since 2006 when Facebook was opened to everyone. Although Facebook is now the leading social media, there are more than 200 services available (Wikipedia, 2017), and the number of social media users is estimated to surpass 2.3 billion worldwide as of 2017 and is still growing (Statista, 2017). Such unprecedented penetration rate within such a short period has attracted many researchers, and there has been a fast growing body of studies on social media. As with other media studies, researchers have been focusing on questions such as, "What kinds of people use social media and why do they use them?" and "What are the social and psychological consequences of using social media and which factors determine them?" However, the research findings on psychosocial effects of social media have been inconsistent and controversial. Studies suggest that social media use enhances users' well-being and reduces ill-being (e.g., loneliness), while others indicate that heavy use of social media can exacerbate users' existing problems or even create new ones (e.g., addictive or unregulated use).

Because of the inconsistent research findings and diverse factors contributing to social media's influences on users, this chapter cannot provide a definitive answer to the questions raised above. Rather, the goal of this chapter is to provide a systematic overview of the existing research for a better understanding of where we are and where we might go from here. This chapter's themes tap on the association between users' existing psychosocial characteristics and social media use (A), the effects of social media use on users' well-being (B), and whether users' existing psychosocial issues get improved or worse due to the use of social media (A + B)

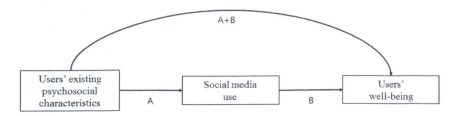

FIGURE 12.1 Three Main Associations in Social Media and Well-Being Research

(see Figure 12.1). Furthermore, this chapter examines the alleged causal associations between users' psychosocial composites and social media use—does social media use lead to users' ill-being, or do the psychosocially challenged rely on social media?

The scope of this chapter is limited to social media, although there is plenty of research on related media including Internet, smartphone, or other computer-mediated communication platforms that can provide help in understanding social media.

Social Media versus Social Network Sites

With SixDegrees.com as the first recognizable social media launched in 1997 (see boyd & Ellison, 2007 for the history of social media), social media was originally designed to enable users "to present themselves, articulate their social networks, and establish or maintain connections with others" (Ellison, Steinfield, & Lampe, 2007, p. 1143). Thus, the most important differences between social media and other online communication platforms are that social media users (1) reveal at least some personal information (in a public or semi-public profile) and (2) present lists of their social networks so that they can observe each other's list of "who knows who" (boyd & Ellison, 2007). boyd and Ellison (2007) have argued that "social network site", not "social networking site", should be a correct term for services such as Facebook because the former emphasizes unique and original functions of social media—enabling users to make their existing social networks visible and maintain them rather than initiating new relationships with strangers online.

According to Google search trend statistics, the term "social media" started to be used more frequently than "social network" in 2011, and this transition might have something to do with the fact that social media giants like Facebook or Twitter began to expand their influences and scopes to the domain of traditional mass media (Veerasamy, 2013). As people started to use it for diverse functions such as information seeking or entertainment beyond its primary purpose of connection and communication, social media started to incorporate publishing functions of traditional mass media (i.e., TV, newspapers, Internet news sites, etc.). Considering its widened range of roles and the popularity of the term surpassing "social network" since 2011, this chapter will stick with "social media".

Who Uses Social Media and Why?

What kinds of people use social media more than others? Research on this topic looks at the associations between people's personalities usually measured by "Big Five" traits of extraversion, agreeableness, openness, conscientiousness and neuroticism (John & Srivastava, 1999), and social media use. People with high levels of extraversion (also similar traits such as sociability and leadership) turn out to use social media a lot (Correa, Hinsley, & de Zúñiga, 2010; Ryan & Xenos, 2011). These findings make sense considering social media's original intent — to make users' existing social networks visible and maintain them. Those who are extraverted have a higher level of communication competence (Wright et al., 2013) and thus have a larger number of both offline and online friends than introverted ones. In addition, one study showed that Facebook users with higher levels of loneliness have smaller numbers of friends and post more about their negative emotional states than those with lower levels of loneliness, which leads to lower levels of satisfaction in social media use (Jin, 2013).

These findings do not mean, however, that extraverted individuals always use social media more than ones who are socially less active. For example, those who are neurotic or anxious use social media as a way to seek support and company, which are not affluent for them offline (Correa et al., 2010). Although extraverted people might use social media as a way to maintain and strengthen their existing social networks, those who are not confident or comfortable in interacting with others rely on social media to compensate for what they lack in social support and relationships. Some studies found that people who experience low self-esteem (Utz & Beukeboom, 2011), loneliness (Skues, Williams, & Wise, 2012; Lee, Noh, & Koo, 2013), or depression (Andalibi, Ozturk, & Forte, 2015) use social media more frequently than those with healthier psychological elements. In addition to using social media more frequently, people who are lonelier or more anxious have stronger emotional attachment to their social media platforms than those who are less lonely or less anxious (Clayton, Osborne, Miller, & Oberie, 2013). Individuals higher in narcissism also use social media more than those lower in narcissism (Ryan & Xenos, 2011). Because "a grandiose sense of self-importance or uniqueness" (Raskin & Terry, 1988, p. 891) is a part of narcissism's composites, people high in narcissism rely on social media for self-promotion (Carpenter, 2012) and disclose more textual and visual information about themselves than people low in narcissism (Liu, Ang, & Lwin, 2016).

Individuals with somewhat unhealthy psychosocial qualities (e.g., loneliness, depression, neuroticism, anxiety, narcissism, low self-esteem, etc.) are likely to have relatively poor communication skills (Jones, 1982) and strong desires to avoid the disapproval of others (Jackson & Ebnet, 2006; Spitzberg & Canary, 1985). Because face-to-face interactions allow few chances to modify what they would say, those with some psychosocial issues may view face-to-face interactions as risky and therefore may not feel comfortable in them (Kim, LaRose, & Peng, 2009). These people do, of course, desire to be connected to and get support from others, and social media interactions, because they are less intimidating than face-to-face interactions (Bian & Leung, 2014; Townsend, 2000), can be very attractive to those who are fearful of failing in face-to-face interactions. For example, one study showed that the more depressed individuals are, the more negative online self-disclosure they engage in as a way to attract social support from their social media friends (Park & Lee, 2016). Another study also found that individuals with poor mental health (e.g., psychological distress or suicidal ideation) are greater users of social media, supporting the association between poor psychosocial elements and social media use (Sampasa-Kanyinga & Lewis, 2015). This study also showed that the majority of participants using social media reported an unmet need for emotional support offline.

Associations between Social Media Use and Well-Being

Positive Associations

In the early era of research and adoption of social media (roughly between 2006 and 2011), researchers paid attention to positive prospects of social media in establishing and maintaining social networks. For example, social media was found to increase "weak ties" (Donath & boyd, 2004), because it does not take much effort to become acquaintances with others and maintain acquaintance status in social media (Boogart, 2006; Kim & Lee, 2011). Weak ties refer to loose connections among individuals who might be able to provide informational support but not emotional support (Granovetter, 1983). On the other hand, "strong ties" mean tightly knit and emotionally close relationships such as family and close friends (Ellison et al., 2007). One of the early studies on social media showed that the more time users spent on social media, the more they became emotionally attached to social media, which eventually increased the number of both weak ties and strong ties (Ellison et al., 2007). This study, however, did not examine whether the intensive use of social media or the increased networks actually improved users' well-being. As the number of social media users increased drastically, researchers began to examine the association between social media use and users' psychosocial well-being.

Well-being in social media research is defined and operationalized in diverse ways, but these can be roughly narrowed down to a few. The first and relatively direct way to measure well-being is to gauge one's subjective perception of happiness (Lyubomirsky & Lepper, 1999) or life satisfaction (Diener, Emmons, Larson, & Griffin, 1985). Another way to measure well-being is to assess the degree to which one's negative psychosocial states (e.g., depression, loneliness, anxiety, and stress) decrease with greater use of social media.

Investigating the association between social media use and users' well-being is not simple because it depends on diverse factors such as users' characteristics (e.g., demographics or personalities) or the ways they use social media. Given that one of the major functions of social media is to connect with others, a group of researchers examined the association between the size of networks (i.e., how many friends are listed in users' social media) and users' well-being.

Social Network Size and Well-Being

A large network size means more opportunities to develop and maintain relationships with others, which was found to have a negative association with depression and anxiety (Wright et al., 2013), while increasing satisfaction with life (Grieve, Indian, Witteveen, Tolan, & Marrington, 2013). One likely explanation for the positive association between social network size and users' well-being is that users perceive a greater amount of social support as the size of their networks increase (Manago, Taylor, & Greenfield, 2012). The augmented happiness might be derived from the exhibition of users' social networks, which provides affirmation of their self-worth (e.g., "I am a worthy person because I have this many friends") (Kim & Lee, 2011). Social media allows users to collect friends and memorabilia from them in the form of wall postings and comments (Toma, 2010), and such tangible evidence of meaningful relationships with others can become a valuable source for self-affirmation. Thus, social media can be a place where people go to repair their damaged ego (Toma & Hancock, 2013) with articulated and displayed proofs of support.

Such "more-friends-more-support" proposition requires further investigation because not all friends listed in social media are likely to be sources of meaningful social support (Nabi, Prestin, & So, 2013). Supporting this idea, one study found that Facebook users maintained close connections with less than 3% of their listed friends (Marlow, 2009). Because people have limited time and resources, the larger the users' social media networks become, the less time and effort they can devote to each friend. Having an extremely large number of social media friends can even give others an impression that listed friends might be simply a large group of passive audience for users who mindlessly expand their networks without putting much effort toward growing meaningful relationships with members of their networks (Kim & Lee, 2011). In that sense, having a large number of social media friends might not always provide greater social support and make users happier.

In response to the above speculation, Kim and Lee (2011) hypothesized a non-linear association between social network size and users' perceived social support (Kim & Lee, 2011). In other words, they predicted that users with too few friends would receive very limited social support, but users with too many friends would not have sufficient time and effort to maintain quality relationships with them either. Kim and Lee (2011) found an inverted U-shaped curve association between the number of Facebook friends and users' perceived social support. This finding suggests that social media friends may serve as a valuable source of social support only up to the point at which users can manage their networks, but too many friends after that point hinder users' perceptions of social support.

Self-Presentation Styles and Well-Being

Another major function of social media is to allow users to present themselves (Ellison et al., 2007), Therefore, how users portray themselves and others' reaction to such portrayals can be important factors influencing their well-being. Social media is a type of computer-mediated communication (CMC) platforms in which interaction and self-presentation are asynchronous, editable, and deprived of nonverbal cues (e.g., gestures, eye contact, and physical appearances). In addition, all the interaction with others can be archived permanently, if not removed, and broadcasted to a large audience (Toma, 2016; Walther, 1996). Thus, social media-based interactions are different from face-to-face interactions that are impromptu (people have little time to refine their messages), evanescent, and delivered to a relatively small audience compared to social media (Toma, 2016). Such characteristics of social media endow people with much more control over how they present themselves to others (Walther, 2007; Zhao, Grasmuck, & Martin, 2008; Tidwell & Walther, 2002). With such control available and a large audience summoned (338 friends per Facebook user on average; Pew Research, 2014), it is natural that people want to present themselves in positive ways to their online friends, even to the point that they craft desirable selves that are different from their real selves.

An interesting twist, however, is that social media users cannot create individuals who are totally disconnected from their real selves because a majority of their social media friends are offline friends who already know the users. Considering both users' capacity to refine their self-presentation and social media's root in offline relationships, theory and research on impression management in CMC (Tidwell & Walther, 2002) and self-presentation in online dating (Gibbs, Ellison, & Heino, 2006) propose two types of self-presentation strategies. One is *positive self-presentation* in which users decide to reveal only socially desirable aspects of themselves (Zhao et al., 2008), the other is *honest self-presentation* in which users choose to present themselves honestly, including their negative features (Gibbs et al., 2006). Both types of self-presentation strategies are positively associated with users' well-being, but the mechanisms underlying those two are different.

A group of studies suggest that social media users can gain self-affirmation from constructing positive profiles or images about themselves (Kim & Lee, 2011; Steele, 1988; Toma, 2010). These findings can be explained by positive illusion theory (Taylor & Brown, 1988) positing that a positively puffed-up perception of self can help people cope with negative or stressful situations that are threatening to their self-worth (Taylor & Armor, 1996). In addition, positive self-presentation in social media can serve as a venue for self-affirmation by boosting self-esteem (Toma, 2013) or soothing a hurt ego (Toma & Hancock, 2013). By presenting self in a positive way to impress and receive affirmation from an audience (social media friends), users can create an optimistic cycle and strengthen positive beliefs about themselves.

On the other hand, honest emotional disclosure can also improve users' psychosocial well-being by serving as a way to express and build intimacy on social media (Manago et al., 2012). Kim and Lee (2011) found that the route from honest self-presentation to enhanced well-being is mediated by users' perceived support from social media friends. Social media friends are likely to provide social support in response to a user's honest self-disclosures and sincere requests for support (e.g., confession of loneliness or depression) (Park & Lee, 2016), and the perception of social support plays a key role in enhancing the user's psychosocial well-being (Kim & Lee, 2011). While showing only polished and positive self enhances well-being via self-affirmation, such affirmation might not be rooted in meaningful social support from social media friends. However, the augmented well-being via honest self-presentation tends to be based on social support as a response to users' truthful disclosure of their difficulties and needs.

Negative Associations

Negative associations between social media use and well-being also depend on various specifics such as types or intensity of use, user characteristics, etc.

Passive Use and Well-Being

One of the core characteristics of social media—allowing users to publish edited or refined public profiles or updates—might have different and opposite effects on well-being depending on whether a user looks at his or her own site or the sites of others. Although positive self-presentation may provide self-affirmation and increase users' self-worth and self-esteem (Toma & Hancock, 2013), the same desirable self-presentation by others might lower observers' well-being. Looking at others' polished and positive updates can leave a user feeling discouraged or depressed based on the assumption that he/she does not measure up to others' wonderful lives (Toma, 2016). That is, engaging in frequent and constant "social-surveillance" would lead users to occupy themselves with upward social comparison processes (Joinson, 2008). An irony is that, although most users are aware of their desire and tendency to put polished images of themselves on their own sites, they may not be aware that everyone else does the same thing (Toma, 2016).

Social surveillance or browsing others' sites without actively posting or reply-ing is called *passive use* of social media (Burke, Marlow, & Lento, 2010). Such passive use leads to negative upward social comparison with others whose self-presentation and postings are usually desirable, which eventually diminishes one's well-being. The social comparison process can elicit negative emotions, such as envy (Lee, Park, & Shablack, 2015) or brooding (Shaw, Timpano, Tran, & Joor-mann, 2015), and may increase social anxiety (Shaw et al., 2015) or depression (Feinstein et al., 2013). This has been referend to as "Facebook depression" (Selfhout, Branje, Delsing, ter Bogt, & Meeus, 2009; Kross et al., 2013). Because Facebook depression is caused by observing others' profiles or postings, those who have more friends (larger networks) and spend more time reading others' updates may experience greater levels of depression (Blease, 2015) or loneliness (Burke et al., 2010). Another aspect to consider in examining the effect of passive use on social media users' well-being is the composition of audience. A group of stud-ies found that those who follow a larger number of strangers are more at risk for negative feelings about selves (Lup, Trub, & Rosenthal, 2015) or false belief that others are happier (Chou & Edge, 2012) than those who follow a smaller number of strangers. Thus, simply having a large network might not necessarily increase social media depression arisen from negative social comparison, because those using social media to keep in touch solely with people they already know are found to be not much at risk for negative consequences (Lup et al., 2015).

Problematic Use and Well-Being

In addition to passive use, excessive use can be another source of problems. Cast-ing a gloomy outlook on users' well-being, excessive or uncontrolled use of social media has been one of the fastest growing domains of research (e.g., Campisi et al., 2012; Chou & Edge, 2012; Karaiskos, Tzavellas, Balta, & Paparrigopoulos, 2010; Satici & Uysal, 2015). Such dysregulated use of social media has been referred to as social media addiction (Uysal, Satici, & Akin, 2013), compulsive use (Wohn & LaRose, 2014), or problematic use (Lee-Won, Herzog, & Park, 2015). Regardless of its name, problematic use of social media share some common characteristics with behavioral addictions, such as pathological gambling, compulsive shopping, or video game addiction (Choliz, 2010). Although it does not involve any chemical or substance, behavioral addiction shows similar symptoms as substance addictions: craving (preoccupation with social media), tolerance (spending more and more time on social media without realizing how time passes), withdrawal (experienc-ing anxiety when not using social media), and feeling that other activities that used to be fun are no longer enjoyable (American Psychiatric Association, 2013).

Problematic use of social media is found to have diverse negative influences on users' well-being, such as decreased academic motivation (Wohn & LaRose, 2014), decreased self-esteem (Denti et al., 2012), depression, anxiety, and insomnia (Koc & Gulyagci, 2013). Furthermore, other studies indicate that problematic use of social media can lead to avoidance of offline social interactions (Cam & Isbulan, 2012), which can eventually lead to increased loneliness (Skues et al., 2012).

Positive or Negative Associations Depending on Communication and Relationship Types

The associations between social media use and users' well-being might not be neatly categorized as aforementioned but may depend on content or formats of interaction via social media. One study showed that adolescents' self-esteem was affected solely by the tone of the feedback received on their profiles: Positive feedback enhanced their self-esteem, while negative feedback decreased it (Valkenburg, Peter, & Schouten, 2006). While this study examined the content of feedback, another study (Burke et al., 2010) examined formats of interaction and found that directed communication was associated with a greater feeling of bonding and lower levels of loneliness. Directed communication refers to interactions between a user and his/her friend in which the user directly identifies a specific friend, such as photo tagging, wall posts, messages, one-on-one chat sessions, and feedback comments on postings. Meanwhile, keeping track of one's friends' updates via "feed", an aggregated stream of friends' posts or news, is associated with reduced feeling of bonding and increased loneliness (Burke et al., 2010).

One of the reasons directed communication would increase the feeling of bonding while reducing loneliness might be concerned with the level of social presence. Social presence is defined as the degree of awareness of another person in an interaction and the consequent appreciation of an interpersonal relationship (Short, Williams, & Christie, 1976; Rice, 1993; Walther, 1992). The more immediate and intimate the interaction is, the greater social presence people perceive from their interaction partners (Argyle & Dean, 1965; Burgoon, Buller, Hale, & deTurck, 1984). If so, pictures are suggested to facilitate more social presence than text, because of the former's richness and vividness in conveying the presence of a communication partner compared to the latter (Sundar, 2008). In support of this idea, one study found that image-based social media such as Snapchat and Instagram decreased users' loneliness and increased subjective well-being, while text-based social media did not (Pittman & Reich, 2016).

In addition to the types of interactions (directed communication vs. feed reading) and the levels of social presence users perceive from postings, with whom users interact and whose postings they read are also found to influence users' well-being. One study showed that users felt happier after reading a positive post by someone close to them and sadder after reading a negative post (Lin & Utz, 2015). This study suggests that simply having direct interaction with others might not increase users' well-being, but rather shows that tie strengths play a significant role in influencing users' affective well-being. The stronger the tie, the more closely users seem to identify with others' emotions and therefore engage in negative upward comparison less and experience a lower level of envy (Lin & Utz, 2015).

Overall, the association between social media use and well-being can be either positive or negative depending on a number of factors such as the size of networks, self-presentation styles, types and intensity of use, content and formats of communication, and the strength of social ties. A few systemic reviews on the effects of social media have listed positive influences such as increased self-esteem, perceived social support, increased social capital, and increased opportunity for self-disclosure, as well as negative influences such as increased possibility of identity theft, privacy invasion, social isolation, social media depression, and cyber-bullying (e.g., O'Keeffe & Clarke-Pearson, 2011; Best, Manktelow, & Taylor, 2014). On the other hand, some research has not found any significant association between social media use and clinical depression (Jelenchick, Eickhoff, & Moreno, 2013) nor an association between social media network size and users' life satisfaction (Lönnqvist & Itkonen, 2014).

Can Social Media Cause Changes in Well-Being?

Although many studies suggest causal relationship between social media use and users' well-being, determining causation with cross-sectional data is difficult. Therefore, researchers have been calling for longitudinal or cross-lagged investigations of the causal association between social media use and users' well-being. There have been some efforts to do this. For example, Kross et al. (2013) asked participants to report their subjective well-being via text messages 5 times a day over the course of 2 weeks and found that participants' Facebook use worsen their life satisfaction. In addition, Yao and Zhong (2014) examined the association between social media use and loneliness over the course of 4 months using a cross-lagged panel study and found that increased use of social media led to higher levels of loneliness, suggesting that online social contacts might not be an effective alternative for offline social interactions in reducing loneliness.

Other researchers have tried to examine causation via experimental studies. For example, Sagioglou and Greitemeyer (2014) asked participants to spend 20 minutes on their own social media accounts and found that their mood became more negative after social media use. Similarly, Brooks (2015) also found that those who spent more time on social media performed lower on the assigned experimental task, as well as showed lower levels of happiness compared to those who spent less time on social media. Verduyn et al. (2015) used both experimental and longitudinal investigation to establish the causality association between passive use of social media and affective well-being. In the experimental study, they found that passive use (i.e., browsing social media without posting or replying to others) led to lower levels of affective well-being of the participants, and also found the same causality association in the 6-day longitudinal investigation.

These studies all support the proposition that heavy use of social media can diminish users' well-being, such as increased loneliness or lower happiness, but not the other way around—that higher levels of loneliness or lower levels of happiness leads to heavier use of social media. It is too early to conclude that heavy use of social media will always lead to psychosocial problems because there has not been sufficient research to validate causality. For example, a diary study investigating the causal association between narcissism and social media use (Walters & Horton, 2015) is a good example of turning the causality relationship around showing that narcissism was a reliable predictor of subsequent Facebook use even after controlling for earlier Facebook use. Furthermore, as mentioned previously, people with psychological issues such as low self-esteem (Utz & Beukeboom, 2011), loneliness (Skues et al., 2012; Lee et al., 2013), and depression (Andalibi et al., 2015) claim to use social media as a way to compensate for their deficient offline relationships, although there are few longitudinal studies proving that psychological issues cause social media use.

Enhancement versus Compensation

The question of whether or not social media actually help the psychosocially distressed or impaired compensate for what they lack requires putting two associations together: The first association is between users' *preceding* psychosocial states (before social media use) and social media use, and the second one is between social media use and users' *subsequent* psychosocial states (after social media use). Thus, this question asks if a user's existing psychosocial problems improve or worsen due to the use of social media.

Two theoretical frameworks can provide some guidelines in answering this important question. The first framework, the *social enhancement model* ("the rich get richer, the poor get poorer" model; Kraut et al., 2002), was developed to explain the effects of the Internet as well as specific media based on the Internet, such as social media. This framework posits that people who have affluent social resources offline would use and benefit more from online services than ones who lack offline social resources. With healthy and strong social support already available and without much to compensate for, the "socially rich" feel comfortable and confident in exploring and developing relationships online. Meanwhile, without much social support and with much to compensate for, the "socially poor" feel anxious and incompetent in exploring and developing relationships online (Han et al., 2012; Kim, 2017).

The *social compensation model* ("the poor get richer" model; McKenna & Bargh, 1998) proposes that people who have insufficient offline social resources will use and benefit more from exploring and building relationships online than will people with sufficient social resources. Because they have relatively few offline relationships, the socially poor might have more time and be more eager to explore and develop relationships online than the socially rich. In addition, with much to compensate for, the socially poor would be active in participating in online activities. In contrast, spending time online would interfere with the existing relationships for the socially rich who are already enjoying satisfactory offline social resources (Han et al., 2012; Kim, 2017).

Few studies have examined the extended associations among one's existing psychosocial problems, social media use, and the subsequent effect of social media use on one's existing psychosocial problems. One study found that lonely people engage in higher levels of self-disclosure via social media than less lonely people, which leads to a large amount of social support from others, followed by users' higher levels of well-being (Lee et al., 2013). The results of this study support the social compensation model (the poor get richer model) by showing lonely people can enhance their well-being via social media use.

However, so far, a larger number of studies support the social enhancement model (the poor get poorer model) rather than the social compensation model. Carpenter's study (2012) found that people high in narcissism use social media for self-promotion, but the narcissistic individuals' sense of entitlement and exploitativeness eventually led them to engage in anti-social behavior in their social media accounts. Ryan et al.'s review (2014) and Lee-Won et al.'s study (2015) also support the social enhancement model by showing that individuals with psychosocial problems (i.e., loneliness, social anxiety or depression) experience more severe psychosocial problems and additional problems (e.g., problematic use of social media) as a result of extensive social media use. The psychosocially poor are motivated to use social media to seek social support and do experience enhanced mood while they are online (Bian & Leung, 2014; Townsend, 2000). This finding can be explained by Caplan's social skill account of problematic Internet use model (Caplan, 2005), which proposes that people who are not comfortable in face-to-face interactions for various reasons (e.g., loneliness, anxiety, depression) would prefer mediated communication to face-to-face interaction. Therefore, social media can be an attractive venue for the psychosocially impaired to feel less intimidated than face-to-face interactions in gratifying their desire to be connected with others. However, if they indulge in social media too much, the psychosocially impaired would have a harder time regulating their excessive use than psychosocially healthier users (LaRose, Kim, & Peng, 2010). They might not be able to improve their preceding problems (e.g., loneliness or depression) or even face additional challenges like problematic use of social media.

Suggestions for Future Research

One area that needs further investigation is the causal association between social media use and well-being. With its rapid integration with our daily lives, however, it is difficult to separate social media's effects from the effects of other factors (e.g., interpersonal relationships, other media influences, users' personalities, etc.) and test its pure causal association with users' well-being. Cross-sectional (correlational) studies cannot answer this question, and longitudinal or experimental studies are necessary.

Another area for further research is to categorize various types of social media and their features in a systematic manner and test their different effects on social media users. This also is a difficult task because of the growing number, types, and functions of social media platforms. Furthermore, examining only the effects of functions and features of social media would not provide valuable information, if not accompanied by examination of individual differences. Therefore, research should examine the interactions between technological composites of social media and individual characteristics of users (e.g., goals, needs, personalities, psychosocial states, etc.)

Additionally, future research on social media and well-being should broaden its scope by comparing the effects of social media with those of other media or social interaction channels (e.g., face-to-face interaction). Even with explosive growth of social media research, few studies have examined real-life settings in which users engage in diverse media and social interactions at the same time. Research should continue to examine the effectiveness of social media in expanding, compensating for, or even replacing people's existing social relationships that are mainly based on face-to-face interactions.

Finally, we need to develop theoretical frameworks that can help explain underlying mechanisms linking social media use and individuals' psychosocial states, going beyond shortsighted and pragmatic descriptions on rapidly evolving social media technologies and features.

Summary

Social media is rapidly permeating into our daily lives and becoming a major influence on well-being. As an effort to provide a systematic and synthesized overview on the exploding research on the association between social media use and well-being, this chapter reviewed existing studies under three subjects: (1) who are using social media and why, (2) the link between social media use and users' psychosocial well-being, and (3) enhancement versus exacerbation effects of social media on users' existing psychosocial challenges.

According to the review of this chapter, both the psychosocially well off and the psychosocially impaired seem to rely on social media, but for different reasons. While the former uses social media to maintain and strengthen the existing relationships, the latter uses social media to compensate for the lacking social support. The association between social media use and well-being can be either positive or negative depending on a number of factors such as the size of networks, self-presentation styles, types and intensity of use, content and formats of communication, and the strength of social ties. A larger number of studies seem to support the social enhancement model (the poor get poorer model) rather than the social compensation model (the poor get richer model). Finally, this chapter suggested research topics that need further investigation.

References

American Psychiatric Association. (2013). *DSM: Diagnostic and statistical manual of mental disorders* (5th ed.). Retrieved from www.psych.org/research/dor/dsm/dsmintro81301. cfm

Andalibi, N., Ozturk, P., & Forte, A. (2015). Depression-related imagery on Instagram. *Proceedings of the 18th ACM Conference Companion on Computer-Supported Cooperative Work and Social Computing (CSCW) Companion, 231–234.*

Argyle, M., & Dean, J. (1965). Eye contact, distance and affiliation. *Sociometry, 28*(3), 289–304.

Best, P., Manktelow, R., & Taylor, B. (2014). Online communication, social media and adolescent wellbeing: A systematic narrative review. *Children and Youth Services Review, 41,* 27–36.

Bian, M., & Leung, L. (2014). Linking loneliness, shyness, smartphone addiction symptoms, and patterns of smartphone use to social capital. *Social Science Computer Review, 33*(1), 61–79.

Blease, C. R. (2015). Too many "friends", too few "likes"? Evolutionary psychology and "Facebook depression". *Review of General Psychology, 19*(1), 1–13.

Boogart, V. (2006). *Uncovering the social impacts of Facebook on a college campus* (Unpublished master's thesis). Kansas State University, Kansas.

boyd, D. M., & Ellison, N. B. (2007). Social network sites: Definition, history, and scholarship. *Journal of Computer-Mediated Communication, 13*(1), 210–230.

Brooks, S. (2015). Does person al social media usage affect efficiency and well-being? *Computers in Human Behavior, 46,* 26–37.

Burgoon, J. K., Buller, D. B., Hale, J. L., & deTurck, M. (1984). Relational messages associated with nonverbal behaviors. *Human Communication Research, 10*(3), 351–378.

Burke, M., Marlow, C., & Lento, T. (2010). Social network activity and social well-being. *ACM CHI '10 Proceedings of the SIGCHI Conference on Human Factors in Computing Systems, 28,* 1909–1912.

Cam, E., & Isbulan, O. (2012). A new addiction for teacher candidates: Social networks. *The Turkish Online Journal of Education Technology: TOJET, 11*(3), 14–19.

Campisi, J., Bynog, P., McGehee, H., Oakland, J. C., Quirk, S., & Taga, C. (2012). Facebook, stress, and incidence of upper respiratory infection in undergraduate college students. *Cyberpsychology, Behavior, & Social Networking, 15,* 675–681.

Caplan, S. E. (2005). A social skill account of problematic Internet use. *Journal of Communication, 55*(4), 721–736.

Carpenter, C. J. (2012). Narcissism on Facebook: Self-promotional and anti-social behavior. *Personality and Individual Differences, 52*(4), 482–486.

Choliz, M. (2010). Mobile phone addiction: A point of issue. *Addiction, 105*(2), 373–374.

Chou, H., & Edge, N. (2012). They are happier and having better lives than I am: The impact of using Facebook on perceptions of others' lives. *Cyberpsychology, Behavior, & Social Networking, 15*(2), 117–121.

Clayton, R. B., Osborne, R. E., Miller, B. K., & Oberie, C. D. (2013). Loneliness, anxiousness, and substance use as predictors of Facebook use. *Computers in Human Behavior, 29*(3), 687–693.

Correa, T., Hinsley, A. W., & de Zúñiga, H. G. (2010). Who interacts on the Web?: The intersection of users' personality and social media use. *Computers in Human Behavior, 26*(2), 247–253.

Denti, L., Barbopuolos, I., Nilsson, I., Holmberg, L., Thulin, M., Wendeblad, M., & Davidsson, E. (2012). Sweden's largest Facebook study. *GRI Rapport, 3,* 1–38.

Diener, E., Emmons, R. A., Larson, R. J., & Griffin, S. (1985). The satisfaction with life scale. *Journal of Personality Assessment, 49*(1), 71–75.

Donath, J., & boyd, D. (2004). Public displays of connection. *BT Technology Journal, 22*(4), 71.

Ellison, N. B., Steinfield, C., & Lampe, C. (2007). The benefits of Facebook "friends": Social capital and college students' use of online social network sites. *Journal of Computer-Mediated Communication, 12*(4), 1143–1168.

Feinstein, B. A., Hershenberg, R., Bhatia, V., Latack, J. A., Meuwly, N. & Davila, J. (2013). Negative social comparison on Facebook and depressive symptoms: Rumination as a mechanism. *Psychology of Popular Media Culture, 2*(3), 161–170.

Gibbs, J. L., Ellison, N. B., & Heino, R. D. (2006). Self-presentation in online personals: The role of anticipated future interaction, self-disclosure, and perceived success in Internet dating. *Communication Research, 33*(2), 1–26.

Granovetter, M. (1983). The strength of weak ties: A network theory revisited. *Sociological Theory, 1,* 201–233.

Grieve, R., Indian, M., Witteveen, K., Tolan, G. A., & Marrington, J. (2013). Face-to-face or Facebook: Can social connectedness be derived online? *Computers in Human Behavior, 29*(3), 604–609.

Han, J.-Y., Kim, J.-H., Shim, M., Yoon, H., McTavish, F., & Gufstafson, D. (2012). Social and psychological determinants of levels of engagement with online breast cancer support group: Posters, lurkers, and non-users. *Journal of Health Communication, 17*(3), 356–371.

Jackson, T., & Ebnet, S. (2006). Appraisal and coping in romantic relationship narratives: Effects of shyness, gender, and connoted affect of relationship events. *Individual Differences Research, 4*(1), 2–15.

Jelenchick, L. A., Eickhoff, J. C., & Moreno, M. A. (2013). "Facebook depression?" Social networking site use and depression in older adolescents. *Journal of Adolescent Health, 52*(1), 128–130.

Jin, B. (2013). How lonely people use and perceive Facebook. *Computers in Human Behavior, 29*(6), 2463–2470.

John, O. P., & Srivastava, S. (1999). The Big-Five trait taxonomy: History, measurement, and theoretical perspectives. In L. A. Pervin & O. P. John (Eds.), *Handbook of personality: Theory and research* (Vol. 2, pp. 102–138). New York: Guilford Press.

Joinson, A. N. (2008). Looking at, looking up or keeping up with people? Motives and use of Facebook. *Proceeding of the Twenty-Sixth Annual SIGCHI Conference on Human Factors in Computing Systems,* 1027–1036.

Jones, W. H. (1982). Loneliness and social behavior. In L. A. Peplau & D. Perlman (Eds.), *Loneliness: A sourcebook of current theory, research and therapy* (pp. 238–252). New York: Wiley.

Karaiskos, D., Tzavellas, E., Balta, G., & Paparrigopoulos, T. (2010). P02–232: Social network addiction: A new clinical disorder? *European Psychiatry, 25*(1), 855.

Kim, J.-H. (2017). Smartphone-mediated communication vs. face-to-face interaction: Two routes to social support and problematic use of smartphone. *Computers in Human Behavior, 67,* 282–291.

Kim, J.-H., LaRose, R., & Peng, W. (2009). Loneliness as the cause and the effect of Internet habits: The relationship between Internet use and psychological well-being. *Cyberpsychology & Behavior, 12*(4), 451–455.

Kim, J.-H., & Lee, J. R. (equal authorship). (2011). The Facebook paths to happiness: Effects of the number of Facebook friends and self-presentation on subjective well-being. *Cyberpsychology, Behavior, and Social Networking, 14*(6), 359–364.

Koc, M., & Gulyagci, S. (2013). Facebook addiction among Turkish college students: The role of psychological health, demographic, and usage characteristics. *Cyberpsychology, Behavior and Social Networking, 16*(4), 279–284.

Kraut, R., Kiesler, S., Boneva, B., Cummings, J., Helgeson, V., & Crawford, A. (2002). The Internet paradox revisited. *Journal of Social Issues, 58*(1), 49–74.

Kross, E., Verduyn, P., Demiralp, E., Park, J., Lee, D. S., Lin, N., Shablack, H., Jonides, J., & Ybarra, O. (2013). Facebook use predicts declines in subjective wellbeing in young adults. *PLoS One, 8*(8), e69841. Retrieved from http://dx.doi.org/10.1371/journal.pone.0069841

LaRose, R., Kim, J.-H., & Peng, W. (2010). Social networking: Addictive, compulsive, problematic, or just another media habit? In Z. Papacharissi (Ed.), *The networked self: Identity, community and culture on social network sites* (pp. 59–81). Routledge: New York.

Lee, D. S., Park, J., & Shablack, H. (2015). Passive Facebook usage undermines affective well-being: Experimental and longitudinal evidence. *Journal of Experimental Psychology, 144*(2), 480–488.

Lee, K., Noh, M., & Koo, D. (2013). Lonely people are no longer lonely on social networking sites: The mediating role of self-disclosure and social support. *Cyberpsychology, Behavior, and Social Networking, 16*(6), 413–418.

Lee-Won, R. J., Herzog, L., & Park, S. (2015). Hooked on Facebook: The role of social anxiety and need for social assurance in problematic use of Facebook. *Cyberpsychology, Behavior, and Social Networking, 18*(10), 567–574.

Lin, R., & Utz, S. (2015). The emotional responses of browsing Facebook: Happiness, envy, and the role. *Computers in Human Behavior, 52*, 29–38.

Liu, C., Ang, R. P., & Lwin, M. O. (2016). Influences of narcissism and parental mediation on adolescents' textual and visual personal information disclosure in Facebook. *Computers in Human Behavior, 58*, 82–88.

Lönnqvist, J., & Itkonen, J. V. A. (2014). It's all about extraversion: Why Facebook friend count doesn't count towards well-being. *Journal of Research in Personality, 53*, 64–67.

Lup, K., Trub, L., & Rosenthal, L. (2015). Instagram #Instasad?: Exploring associations among Instagram use, depressive symptoms, negative social comparison, and strangers followed. *Cyberpsychology, Behavior, and Social Networking, 18*(5), 247–252.

Lyubomirsky, S., & Lepper, H. S. (1999). A measure of subjective happiness: Preliminary reliability and construct validation. *Social Indicators Research, 46*(2), 137–155.

Manago, A. M., Taylor, T., & Greenfield, P. M. (2012). Me and my 400 friends: The anatomy of college students' Facebook networks, their communication patterns, and well-being. *Developmental Psychology, 48*(2), 369–380.

Marlow, C. (2009). *Maintained relationships on Facebook.* Retrieved from http://overstated.net/2009/03/09/maintained-relationshipson-facebook

McKenna, K. Y. A., & Bargh, J. A. (1998). Coming out in the age of the internet: Identity "demarginalization" through virtual group participation. *Journal of Personality and Social Psychology, 75*(3), 681–694.

Merriam-Webster. (2017). *Definition of social media.* Retrieved from www.merriam-webster.com/dictionary/social%20media

Nabi, R. L., Prestin, A., & So, J. (2013). Facebook friends with (health) benefits? Exploring social network site use and perceptions of social support, stress, and well-being. *Cyberpsychology, Behavior, and Social Networking, 16*(10), 721–727.

O'Keeffe, G. S., & Clarke-Pearson, K. (2011). The impact of social media on children, adolescents, and families. *American Academy of Pediatrics*, *127*(4), 800–804.

Park, J., & Lee, D. S. (2016). When perceptions defy reality: The relationships between depression and actual and perceived Facebook social support. *Journal of Affective Disorders*, *200*, 37–44.

Pew Research Center. (2014). Pew Research Center's Internet Project Survey. Retrieved from www.pewresearch.org/fact-tank/2014/02/03/6-new-facts-about-facebook/

Pittman, M., & Reich, B. (2016). Social media and loneliness: Why an Instagram picture may be worth more than a thousand Twitter words. *Computers in Human Behavior*, *62*, 155–167.

Raskin, R., & Terry, H. (1988). A principal-components analysis of the narcissistic personality inventory and further evidence of its construct validity. *Journal of Personality and Social Psychology*, *54*(5), 890–902.

Rice, R. E. (1993). Media appropriateness: Using social presence theory to compare traditional and new organization media. *Human Communication Research*, *19*(4), 451–484.

Ryan, T., Chester, A., Reece, J., & Xenos, S. (2014). The uses and abuse of Facebook: A review of Facebook addiction. *Journal of Behavioral Addiction*, *3*(3), 133–148.

Ryan, T., & Xenos, S. (2011). Who uses Facebook? An investigation into the relationship between the Big Five, shyness, narcissism, loneliness, and Facebook usage. *Computers in Human Behavior*, *27*(5), 1658–1664.

Sagioglou, C., & Greitemeyer, T. (2014). Facebook's emotional consequences: Why Facebook causes a decrease in mood and why people still use it. *Computers in Human Behavior*, *35*, 359–363.

Sampasa-Kanyinga, H., & Lewis, R. F. (2015). Frequent use of social networking sites is associated with poor psychological functioning among children and adolescents. *Cyberpsychology, Behavior, and Social Networking*, *18*(7), 380–385.

Satici, S. A., & Uysal, R. (2015). Well-being and problematic Facebook use. *Computers in Human Behavior*, *49*, 185–190.

Selfhout, M. H., Branje, S. J., Delsing, M., ter Bogt, T. F., & Meeus, W. H. (2009). Different types of Internet use, depression, and social anxiety: The role of perceived friendship quality. *Journal of Adolescence*, *32*(4), 819–833.

Shaw, A. M., Timpano, K. R., Tran, T. B., & Joormann, J. (2015). Correlates of Facebook usages patterns: The relationship between passive Facebook use, social anxiety symptoms, and brooding. *Computers in Human Behavior*, *48*, 575–580.

Short, J. A., Williams, E., & Christie, B. (1976). *The social psychology of telecommunication*. London: Wiley.

Skues, J. L., Williams, B., & Wise, L. (2012). The effects of personality traits, self-esteem, loneliness, and narcissism on Facebook use among university students. *Computers in Human Behavior*, *28*(6), 2414–2419.

Spitzberg, B. H., & Canary, D. J. (1985). Loneliness and relationally competent communication. *Journal of Social and Personal Relationships*, *2*(4), 387–402.

Statista. (2017). *Number of social network users worldwide from 2010 to 2020 (in billions)*. Retrieved from www.statista.com/statistics/278414/number-of-worldwide-social-network-users/

Steele, C. M. (1988). The psychology of self-affirmation: Sustaining the integrity of the self. In L. Berkowitz (Ed.), *Advances in experimental social psychology* (pp. 261–302). San Diego, CA: Academic Press.

Sundar, S. S. (2008). The MAIN model: A heuristic approach to understanding technology effects on credibility. In M. J. Metzger & A. J. Flanagin (Eds.), *Digital media, youth, and credibility* (pp. 73–100). Cambridge, MA: The MIT Press.

Taylor, S., & Armor, D. (1996). Positive illusions and coping with adversity. *Journal of Personality, 64*(4), 873–898.

Taylor, S., & Brown, J. (1988). Illusion and well-being: A social psychological perspective on mental health. *Psychological Bulletin, 103*(2), 193–210.

Tidwell, L., & Walther, J. (2002). Computer-mediated communication effects on disclosure, impressions, and interpersonal evaluations: Getting to know one another a bit at a time. *Human Communication Research, 28*(3), 317–348.

Toma, C. (2010). Affirming the self through online profiles: Beneficial effects of social networking sites. *Proceedings of the 28th International Conference on Human Factors in Computing Systems*, 1749–1752.

Toma, C. (2013). Feeling better but doing worse: Effects of Facebook self-presentation on implicit self esteem and cognitive task performance. *Media Psychology, 16*(2), 199–220.

Toma, C. (2016). Taking the good with the bad: Effects of Facebook self-presentation on emotional well-being. In L. Reinecke & M. B. Oliver (Eds.), *The Routledge handbook of media use and well-being* (pp. 170–182). Routledge: New York.

Toma, C., & Hancock, J. (2013). Self-affirmation underlies Facebook use. *Personality and Social Psychology Bulletin, 39*(3), 321–331.

Townsend, A. M. (2000). Life in the real-time city: Mobile telephones and urban metabolism. *Journal of Urban Technology, 7*(2), 85–104.

Utz, S., & Beukeboom, C. J. (2011). The role of social network sites in romantic relationships: Effects on jealousy and relationship happiness. *Journal of Computer-Mediated Communication, 16*(4), 511–527.

Uysal, R., Satici, S. A., & Akin, A. (2013). Mediating effect of Facebook addiction on the relationship between subjective vitality and subjective happiness. *Psychological Report, 113*(3), 948–953.

Valkenburg, P. M., Peter, J., & Schouten, A. P. (2006). Friend networking sites and their relationship to adolescents' well-being and social self-esteem. *CyberPsychology & Behavior, 9*(5), 584–590.

Veerasamy, V. (2013). *Social networking sites and social media: What's the difference?* Retrieved from www.referralcandy.com/blog/difference-between-social-networks-and-social-media/

Verduyn, P., Lee, D. S., Park, J., Shablack, H., Orvell, A., Bayer, J., Ybarra, O., Jonides, J., & Kross, E. (2015). Passive Facebook usage undermines affective well-being: Experimental and longitudinal evidence. *Journal of Experimental Psychology General, 144*(2), 480–488.

Walters, N. T., & Horton, R. (2015). A diary study of the influence of Facebook use on narcissism among male. *Computers in Human Behavior, 52*, 326–330.

Walther, J. B. (1992). Interpersonal effects in computer-mediated interaction: A relational perspective. *Communication Research, 19*(1), 52–90.

Walther, J. B. (1996). Computer-mediated communication: Impersonal, interpersonal, and hyperpersonal interaction. *Communication Research, 23*(3), 3–44.

Walther, J. B. (2007). Selective self-presentation in computer-mediated communication: Hyperpersonal dimensions of technology, language, and cognition. *Computers in Human Behavior, 23*, 2538–2557.

Wikipedia. (2017). *List of social networking websites*. Retrieved from https://en.wikipedia.org/wiki/List_of_social_networking_websites

Wohn, D. Y., & LaRose, R. (2014). Effects of loneliness and differential usage of Facebook on college adjustment of first-year students. *Computers & Education, 76*, 158–167.

Wright, K. B., Rosenberg, J., Egbert, N., Ploeger, N. A., Bernard, D. R., & King, S. (2013). Communication competence, social support, and depression among college students: A model of Facebook and face-to-face support network influence. *Journal of Health Communication, 18*(1), 41–57.

Yao, M. Z., & Zhong, Z. (2014). Loneliness, social contacts and Internet addiction: A cross-lagged panel study. *Computers in Human Behavior, 30,* 164–170.

Zhao, S., Grasmuck, S., & Martin, J. (2008). Identity construction on Facebook: Digital empowerment in anchored relationships. *Computers in Human Behavior, 24,* 1816–1836.

13

THE SOCIAL PSYCHOLOGY OF EMPLOYEE WELL-BEING

A Needs-Based Perspective

Nathan A. Bowling

Many of the variables that influence a person's psychological well-being originate in the workplace. These variables are diverse: They include qualities of one's work tasks and work roles; the manner in which one is treated by supervisors, coworkers, and subordinates; and pay level (see Brief, 1998; Spector, 1997; Warr, 2007). Unfortunately, most studies have examined one category of predictor of employee well-being without considering the effects of others. As a result of this piecemeal approach, there is a need for a unifying framework that explains the effects of the various predictors of employee well-being. In this chapter I will first discuss the most popular conceptualization of employee well-being and hence the focus of the current chapter: global job satisfaction. I will then propose an integrative framework that invokes the three psychological needs identified by *self-determination theory* (SDT; Deci & Ryan, 2000; Ryan & Deci, 2000)—the needs for autonomy, competence, and relatedness.

Global Job Satisfaction as a Conceptualization of Employee Well-Being

Job satisfaction—an attitude representing the extent to which a person likes or dislikes his or her job—has been examined within thousands of studies (Brief, 1998; Dalal, 2013; Locke, 1976). In fact, job satisfaction is not only the most popular means of conceptualizing employee well-being, but is perhaps the most widely studied topic in the history of industrial and organizational psychology (Judge, Parker, Colbert, Heller, & Ilies, 2001; Spector, 1997).

Researchers have used two basic approaches to measuring job satisfaction: the *facet satisfaction* approach and the *global satisfaction* approach (for discussions of these two approaches, see Brief, 1998; Dalal, 2013; Spector, 1997). The facet satisfaction approach examines employees' attitudes toward *specific aspects* of their jobs. For example, the *Job Descriptive Index* (*JDI*; Smith, Kendall, & Hulin, 1969)— the most widely used measure of facet satisfaction—includes subscales for five distinct facets: (1) satisfaction with work itself, (2) satisfaction with supervision, (3) satisfaction with coworkers, (4) satisfaction with pay, and (5) satisfaction with promotional opportunities. Although researchers have identified additional job satisfaction facets (see Spector, 1985; Weiss, Dawis, England, & Lofquist, 1967), the *JDI* facets have received the most research attention.

The global satisfaction approach examines employees' *overall* attitudes toward their jobs and is exemplified by the *Michigan Organizational Assessment Questionnaire* (Cammann, Fichman, Jenkins, & Klesh, 1979) item "All in all I am satisfied with my job". I will focus on global job satisfaction in the current chapter because it has particularly strong relationships with other conceptualizations of employee well-being (e.g., burnout; see Alarcon, 2011) and with more general forms of psychological well-being (see Bowling, Eschleman, & Wang, 2010). Evidence for global job satisfaction's relevance to general well-being comes from a meta-analysis by Bowling et al., which found that it had stronger relationships with life satisfaction ($\rho = .48$) and happiness ($\rho = .43$) than did any of the *JDI* facets.

The Work Environment's Relationship With Job Satisfaction

Decades of research have identified several environmental factors that are related to job satisfaction, including (but not limited to) (1) the qualities of work tasks, (2) the qualities of work roles, (3) interpersonal treatment at work, and (4) pay level. Table 13.1 summarizes prior meta-analyses linking each of these environmental variables to global job satisfaction.

The Qualities of Work Tasks

Considerable research has found that the nature of work tasks is an important predictor of global job satisfaction. The *Job Characteristics Model* (JCM; Hackman & Oldham, 1975, 1980) has been particularly influential in shaping job satisfaction researchers' understanding of the importance of the qualities of work tasks. The JCM posits that five job characteristics influence global job satisfaction: (1) skill variety (the extent to which a job allows one use many different skills), (2) task identity (the extent to which a job allows one to complete tasks from start to finish), (3) task significance (the extent to which job tasks contribute to the well-being of other people), (4) autonomy (the extent to which a job allows discretion regarding how and when tasks are performed), and (5) task feedback (the extent to which task completion provides workers with information about how effectively they have performed). Although each of these five job characteristics can be treated as distinct variables, researchers often sum them into an overall measure of job complexity or "job scope" (see Fried & Ferris, 1987).

TABLE 13.1 Meta-Analytic Findings for Aspects of the Work Environment as Predictors of Global Job Satisfaction

Global Job Satisfaction Predictors	k	N	Mean r	Mean ρ	Reference to Meta-Analytic Findings
Qualities of work tasks					
Skill variety	22	18,035	.29	.45	Fried and Ferris (1987)
Task identity	19	18,455	.20	.26	Fried and Ferris (1987)
Task significance	16	17,887	.26	.35	Fried and Ferris (1987)
Autonomy	20	7,861	.34	.48	Fried and Ferris (1987)
Task feedback	20	18,561	.29	.43	Fried and Ferris (1987)
Overall job scope	17	5,549	.49	.74	Fried and Ferris (1987)
Organizational constraints	64	17,959	−.33	—	Pindek and Spector (2016)
Qualities of work roles					
Role ambiguity	56	10,489	−.30	−.46	Jackson and Schuler (1985)
Role conflict	37	6,314	−.31	−.48	Jackson and Schuler (1985)
Role overload	97	70,915	−.18	−.22	Bowling, Alarcon, Bragg, and Hartman (2015)
Interpersonal treatment at work					
Social support	46	31,423	.24	.30	Viswesvaran, Sanchez, and Fisher (1999)
Leader consideration	76	11,374	.40	.46	Judge, Piccolo, and Ilies (2004)
Leader initiating structure	72	10,317	.19	.22	Judge et al. (2004)
General abuse	42	19,871	−.32	−.39	Bowling and Beehr (2006)
Abusive supervision	17	6,560	−.31	−.34	Mackey, Frieder, Brees, and Martinko (in press)
Pay level	61	18,460	.14	.15	Judge, Piccolo, Podsakoff, Shaw, and Rich (2010)

Note: k = number of samples; N = total sample size; mean r = average weighted uncorrected correlation coefficient; mean ρ = average weighted correlation coefficient corrected for unreliability in both the predictor and criterion. "—" indicates that the statistic in question was not reported in the cited article.

Meta-analytic evidence reported by Fried and Ferris (1987) indicates that the JCM job characteristics are robust predictors of global job satisfaction (see Table 13.1). Specifically, they found that the corrected correlations (ρs) between the individual job characteristics and job satisfaction ranged from .26 to .48. The ρ for job scope was even stronger (.74) making it among the strongest predictors of global job satisfaction.

The JCM, however, omits some qualities of job tasks that might relate to global job satisfaction (see Campion, 1988). Organizational constraints, which are any characteristic of one's work environment that can interfere with effective job performance, are one such task quality (see Peters & O'Connor, 1980). The content domain of organizational constraints comprises various situations such as having insufficient tools or resources to do one's job, inadequate training, and supervisors or coworkers who habitually interrupt one's work. Rather than treating various constraints as distinct constructs, however, researchers have typically summed workers' responses to items reflecting several distinct types of constraints, thus creating an overall constraints measure (see Spector & Jex's [1998] Organizational Constraints Scale). Meta-analytic evidence indicates that these overall constraints scales are negatively related to global job satisfaction (mean uncorrected $r = -.33$; Pindek & Spector, 2016).

The Qualities of Work Roles

Employees often hold multiple work roles, each of which defines his or her work-related responsibilities and authority. A college professor, for instance, may be expected to simultaneously satisfy the roles of "researcher", "teacher", and "department citizen". Unfortunately, one's work roles can become dysfunctional, which is reflected in three widely studied variables: (1) role ambiguity (the extent to which one's work roles are unclear), (2) role conflict (the extent to which various work roles are incompatible with each other), and (3) role overload (the extent to which one's roles require too much work or require work that is too difficult; see also Bowling & Kirkendall, 2012; King & King, 1990). Meta-analytic evidence indicates that role ambiguity ($\rho = -.46$; Jackson & Schuler, 1985); role conflict ($\rho = -.48$; Jackson & Schuler, 1985); and role overload ($\rho = -.22$; Bowling et al., 2015) are each negatively related to global job satisfaction (see Table 13.1).

Interpersonal Treatment at Work

Researchers have studied several variables that describe the quality of interpersonal treatment experienced by workers (see Bowling, Camus, & Blackmore, 2015; Cohen & Wills, 1985; Hershcovis, 2011; Viswesvaran et al., 1999). Some of these variables reflect good interpersonal treatment; others reflect bad interpersonal treatment. Table 13.1 reports job satisfaction's relationships with thee forms of positive treatment: social support (the extent to which one receives tangible or emotional aid from others at work), leader consideration (the extent to which one's supervisor displays concern for subordinate well-being), and initiating structure (the extent to which one's supervisor emphasizes the effective completion of work tasks). It also reports job satisfaction's relationships with two forms of negative treatment: general abuse (the extent to which one is the target of negative verbal or physical behavior within the workplace) and abusive supervision (the extent to which one is the target of mistreatment perpetrated by his or her supervisor).

These behaviors should be viewed as separate because the extent to which a given worker reports experiencing good treatment is largely independent of the extent to which he or she reports experiencing bad treatment. Duffy, Ganster, and Pagon (2002), for instance, found that the relationship between social support (a form of good treatment) provided by one's supervisor and social undermining (a form of bad treatment) perpetrated by one's supervisor was modest ($r = -.18$, $p < .01$) and that the relationship between social support provided by one's closest coworker and social undermining perpetrated by one's closest coworker was essentially zero ($r = -.03$, n.s.).

Conceptualizations of interpersonal treatment can also vary according to their source. One's supervisor, coworkers, subordinates, or customers, for instance, can each be the origin of either good or bad treatment (see Bowling et al., 2015; Viswesvaran et al., 1999). Meta-analyses, unfortunately, have generally combined the results of studies examining interpersonal treatment from different sources. One exception to this comes from the leader behavior research, which distinguishes between various forms of good and bad treatment supervisors may direct at their subordinates (see Judge et al., 2004; Tepper, 2000).

Meta-analyses have found that good interpersonal treatment is positively related to job satisfaction and that bad interpersonal treatment is negatively related to job satisfaction (see Table 13.1). As a whole, the ρs reported in these meta-analyses have been in the .20s to .40s for good treatment and in the $-.30$s for bad treatment.

Pay Level

Perhaps the most obvious reason people work is to earn money (Paul & Batinic, 2010). The amount workers are paid may contribute to job satisfaction by allowing them to afford both necessities and material comforts. Indeed, meta-analytic evidence suggests a positive relationship between pay level and global job satisfaction ($\rho = .15$; Judge et al., 2010).

Self-Determination Theory and Fundamental Psychological Needs

Might there be a parsimonious set of mechanisms that explains the relationships between the most widely studied environmental variables and global job satisfaction? Self-determination theory (SDT) would suggest that environmental variables are related to global job satisfaction because they either contribute to or thwart the fulfillment of one's fundamental psychological needs. Because it is an ambitious theory that comprises several sub-theories (see Ryan & Deci, 2000; Sheldon, Turban, Brown, Barrick, & Judge, 2003), I will not provide a comprehensive discussion of SDT (for a more comprehensive review of SDT, see Ryan & Deci, 2000; for reviews of SDT's relevance to several work-related topics, see Gagne´ & Deci, 2005; Sheldon et al., 2003). Instead, I will focus on the three fundamental psychological needs identified by SDT—the needs for *autonomy*, *competence*, and *relatedness*—as a framework for interpreting past research on the causes of global job satisfaction.

A "psychological need" is an innate, fundamental nutriment whose fulfillment is a prerequisite to psychological well-being (Baard, Deci, & Ryan, 2004; Deci & Ryan, 2000; Ryan, 1995). Thus, when a person's needs are fulfilled, he or she will display psychological health and growth; when a person's needs are thwarted, he or she will display psychological difficulties and decline. Any supposed need whose fulfillment is unrelated to well-being is not really a "need" (Ryan, 1995). Much of the SDT literature has focused on identifying specific environmental factors that can either facilitate or hinder need fulfillment (Deci & Ryan, 2000; Ryan & Deci, 2000). For instance, people are more likely to achieve need fulfillment when their environments include other people (e.g., parents, teachers, or bosses) who encourage them to behave in internally motivated ways.

SDT is not the first theory to acknowledge the importance of psychological needs. In fact, the history of psychology has seen a proliferation of potential needs (e.g., Maslow, 1943; McClelland, 1965; Murray, 1938). Unlike other needs, however, the needs for autonomy, competence, and relatedness have each been consistently shown to meet Ryan's (1995) requirement that a psychological need must relate to psychological well-being (see Reis, Sheldon, Gable, Roscoe, & Ryan, 2000; Sheldon & Elliot, 1999; Sheldon, Elliot, Kim, & Kasser, 2001).

The Need for Autonomy

People have a fundamental need to feel in control of their own behavior—to believe that their actions originate from themselves and not from some external source (Deci & Ryan, 2000; Ryan, 1995; Ryan & Deci, 2000). For example, consider the following autonomy items form the Work-Related Basic Need Satisfaction measure (W-BNS; Van den Broeck, Vansteenkiste, De Witte, Soenens, & Lens, 2010): "I feel like I can be myself at my job", "The tasks I have to do at work are in line with what I really want to do", and "I feel free to do my job the way I think it could best be done".

The Need for Competence

People need to believe that they have mastery over life's challenges, that they can perform tasks effectively, and have acquired new skills (Deci & Ryan, 2000; Ryan, 1995; Ryan & Deci, 2000). This need is illustrated by the following W-BNS (Van den Broeck et al., 2010) items: "I am good at the things I do in my job", "I feel competent at my job", and "I really master my tasks at my job".

The Need for Relatedness

Finally, people have a need for relatedness (Baumeister & Leary, 1995; Deci & Ryan, 2000; Ryan & Deci, 2000). Psychological health can only be achieved if a person has close interpersonal relationships—that is, if he or she gives and receives affection and support. The following relatedness items from the W-BNS (Van den

Broeck et al., 2010) illustrate the nature of this need: "At work, I feel part of a group", "Some people I work with are close friends of mine", and "At work, I can talk with people about things that really matter to me".

According to SDT, a person's general psychological well-being hinges upon the fulfillment of the needs for autonomy, competence, and relatedness (Deci & Ryan, 2000; Ryan, 1995; Ryan & Deci, 2000). By extension, the fulfillment of these needs is also relevant to various conceptualizations of work-related well-being, such as global job satisfaction (see Baard et al., 2004; Gagne´ & Deci, 2005; Van den Broeck, Ferris, Chang, & Rosen, 2016).

Reinterpreting the Predictors of Global Job Satisfaction: A Needs-Based Perspective

From the perspective of SDT, aspects of the work environment that contribute to the fulfillment of fundamental psychological needs will have a positive effect on global job satisfaction. This basic argument has, in fact, been advanced by other researchers (Alderfer, 1969; Herzberg, 1968; Porter, 1963; Wolf, 1970). Despite this, early need theories have been the target of criticism (Salancik & Pfeffer, 1977) and have largely fallen out of favor among job satisfaction researchers (see Brief, 1998; Spector, 1997). The most critical problem with these early need theories is their lack of empirical support. In light of the accumulated evidence supporting the importance of the needs for autonomy, competence, and relatedness, however, it is appropriate to revisit the idea that need fulfillment contributes to job satisfaction (see Van den Broeck et al., 2016).

Figure 13.1 presents a mediation modeling linking the work environment to global job satisfaction. The model suggests that (1) perceptions of one's work environment mediate the relationship between the objective nature of the work environment and need fulfillment and (2) need fulfillment mediates the relationship between perceptions of one's environment and global job satisfaction.

The Relationship Between the Objective and Perceived Work Environment

Researchers have distinguished between objective measures and subjective measures of the work environment (e.g., Liu, Spector, & Jex, 2005; Spector, Dwyer, & Jex,

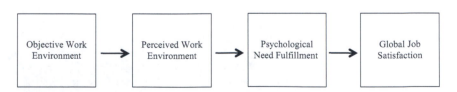

FIGURE 13.1 Needs-Based Model Explaining the Work Environment's Relationship With Global Job Satisfaction

1988; Spector & Jex, 1991). The former is assessed using measures that are independent of participant self-reports (e.g., ratings provided by job analysts) whereas the latter is based upon participant self-reports using questionnaire measures. As an example of an objective measure, researchers have used ratings from trained job analysts to assess the amount of autonomy provided by one's job (Liu et al., 2005). Objective and subjective measures of a given aspect of one's work environment are often only modestly related to each other. Spector and Jex (1991), for example, found that perceived job scope yielded correlations of only .21 and .27 with two objective measures of job scope derived from the *Dictionary of Occupational Titles*.

The weak relationship between the objective work environment and the perceived work environment has important practical implications: It suggests that organizational efforts to improve the objective environment are likely to have weak effects on workers' perceptions of the work environment. This is important because the perceived environment is likely to have stronger effects on job satisfaction than is the objective environment (see Spector & Jex, 1991), whereas the objective environment is more amenable to organizational intervention than is the perceived environment.

The Relationship Between Perceived Work Environment and Need Fulfillment

Not every dimension of the work environment is likely to be related to the fulfillment of all three STD needs; instead, each dimension is likely related only to the fulfillment of those needs with which it shares conceptual similarity.

Dimensions of the Work Environment Conceptually Linked With Autonomy

Job autonomy is the extent to which workers are allowed discretion in how and when their work is performed (Hackman & Oldham, 1975, 1980). This has an obvious conceptual link with the fulfillment of the need for autonomy. Although the two "autonomy" variables may seem very similar, their distinction is clear when viewed from a stimulus-response perspective (see Judge & Larsen, 2001): Job autonomy refers to a quality of one's work environment (a stimulus); the fulfillment of the *need* for autonomy is an internal psychological state (a response). Research supports this distinction. The Van den Broeck et al. (2016) meta-analysis, for instance, reported that job autonomy had a mean ρ of .48 with the fulfillment of the need for autonomy, suggesting that the two variables are distinct.

Dimensions of the Work Environment Conceptually Linked With Competence

The qualities of work tasks (with the exception of autonomy; see the previous subsection), the qualities of work roles, and pay level should primarily influence the fulfillment of the need for competence. Each of these environmental variables provides cues to the worker indicating whether he or she has attained a challenging, worthwhile, and fulfilling job (see Bowling, Eschleman, Wang, Kirkendall, & Alarcon, 2010; Pierce & Gardner, 2004). Workers may, in turn, use these cues to draw inferences about their own general competence. Workers employed in desirable jobs, for instance, may conclude that they are generally competent because they were able to attain positions that others would want.

Dimensions of the Work Environment Conceptually Linked With Relatedness

Interpersonal treatment at work should be an especially strong predictor of the fulfillment of the need for relatedness. Both good and bad treatment can provide employees with implicit and explicit cues regarding how well they are accepted, cared for, and valued by other organizational members. As an example of an implicit cue, an employee whose coworkers put considerable effort into providing social support may infer that others care about him or her—why else would they go through the trouble of providing support? And in the process of providing emotional support, coworkers may tell the employee (explicitly) that he or she is accepted, cared for, and valued. Bad treatment, of course, may provide both implicit and explicit cues suggesting that the targeted employee is rejected, disliked, and unvalued.

As a whole, the ρs reported in Table 13.2 provide limited support for pattern of relationships predicted in the previous paragraphs. The job characteristic autonomy, for instance, predicts the fulfillment of the need for autonomy better than it predicts the fulfillment of either competence or relatedness; however, other environmental variables (e.g., role conflict, general abuse) predicted the fulfillment of the need for autonomy better than does the job characteristic autonomy. Second, many of the environmental variables that I expected to predict the fulfillment of the need for competence are actually better predictors of the fulfillment of the needs for autonomy and relatedness. And although one of the interpersonal treatment variables (social support) produces a pattern of relationships consistent with my expectations, the other interpersonal treatment variable (general abuse) does not. As a result of these findings, more work needs to be done to clarify which aspects of the work environment contribute to the fulfillment of which needs.

The Relationship Between Need Fulfillment and Global Job Satisfaction

SDT predicts that the fulfillment of the needs for autonomy, competence, and relatedness is a prerequisite to psychological health (Deci & Ryan, 2000; Ryan, 1995; Ryan & Deci, 2000). Applied to the work context, this suggests that the fulfillment of each need is related to various conceptualizations of employee well-being, including global job satisfaction. The meta-analysis by Van den Broeck

TABLE 13.2 Needs Corresponding to Each Predictor of Global Job Satisfaction

Predictor of Global Job Satisfaction	Corresponding Needs		
	Mean ρ Autonomy	Mean ρ Competence	Mean ρ Relatedness
Qualities of work tasks			
Skill variety	.49	.25	.32
Task identity	.46	.42	.38
Task significance	.35	.41	.31
Autonomy	.48	.19	.28
Task feedback	.42	.14	.35
Overall job scope	—	—	—
Organizational constraints	—	—	—
Qualities of work roles			
Role ambiguity	−.43	−.43	—
Role conflict	−.64	−.24	—
Role overload	−.19	−.10	−.09
Interpersonal treatment at work			
Social support	.41	.17	.54
Leader consideration	—	—	—
Leader initiating structure	—	—	—
General abuse	−.59	−.38	−.46
Abusive supervision	—	—	—
Pay level	—	—	—

Note: Shading indicates especially strong conceptual links between job environment variables and needs. All meta-analytic results are from Van den Broeck et al. (2016). Mean ρ = average weighted correlation coefficient corrected for unreliability in both the predictor and criterion. "—" indicates that the statistic in question was not reported by Van den Broeck et al.

et al. (2016) provides support for this prediction. Specifically, they found that the fulfillment of the needs for autonomy ($\rho = .69$), competence ($\rho = .50$), and relatedness ($\rho = .52$) were each positively related to job satisfaction. Regression analyses further found that the fulfillment of each need was uniquely related to job satisfaction and that as a set, fulfillment of the three SDT needs explained roughly 50% of the variance in job satisfaction.

Future Research Directions

Are Need Satisfaction and Need Frustration Distinct Constructs?

Throughout this chapter I have treated need fulfillment as a unitary construct. Some research, however, suggests that need fulfillment consists of two sub-dimensions: *need satisfaction* and *need frustration*. Chen et al. (2015), for instance, found that these two sub-dimensions are empirically distinct from each other and are differentially related to various operationalizations of psychological health. Specifically, need satisfaction is a particularly good predictor of psychological health (e.g., life satisfaction), whereas need frustration is a particularly good predictor of psychological illness (e.g., depression). Future research should examine the differential effects of need satisfaction and need frustration on employee well-being.

Are the Effects of Need Fulfillment Linear?

Researchers have generally assumed that the effects of need fulfillment on psychological health are linear—that the more a person's needs are fulfilled, the more psychological health that person will experience. Is it possible, however, that need fulfillment actually has non-linear effects of health? There is indeed evidence that a "too-much-of-a-good-thing effect" (TMGT effect) is present across many research areas (Pierce & Aguinis, 2013). A TMGT effect occurs when variables that have generally been assumed to have desirable linear effects, actually produce non-linear effects.

Consistent with the TMGT effect, research has examined whether various dimensions of the work environment yield non-linear relationship with employee well-being. Much of this research draws from the *vitamin model* (so named because dietary vitamins have non-linear effects on physical health; De Jonge & Schaufeli, 1998; Warr, 1987). According to the vitamin model, dimensions of the work environment that have generally been shown to have positive linear effects on employee well-being (e.g., autonomy, social support) may produce either a *constant effect* or an *additional decrement effect*. The former occurs when an improvement in the job environment beyond a critical level produces no changes in employee well-being; the latter occurs when an improvement in the job environment beyond a critical level produces negative changes in employee well-being. The vitamin model predicts that some dimensions of the work environment produce constant effects (e.g., task significance, pay level), whereas other dimensions produce additional decrement effects (e.g., autonomy, social support). Tests of the vitamin model have provided mixed support for the hypothesized non-linear effects of the work environment on job satisfaction (De Jonge & Schaufeli, 1998). Additional research is needed to examine whether the hypothesized non-linear effects of the work environment can be extended to the effects of need fulfillment. That is, might there be an ideal level of need fulfillment beyond which additional fulfillment produces either no changes or negative changes in employee well-being?

Can Need Fulfillment Within One Domain Compensate for Need Deficits Within Another Domain?

The needs for autonomy, competence, and relatedness are fundamental and thus relevant across life domains (Deci & Ryan, 2000; Ryan, 1995; Ryan & Deci, 2000). Each can be satisfied in a variety of ways. The need for competence, for instance, can be satisfied via several sources—school, hobbies, and the successful performance of job tasks. This raises an important question: Can the fulfillment of a given need within one domain counteract a deficit in that same need originating within another domain? For example, can need fulfillment in the workplace counteract the negative effects of need deficits in a non-work domain (e.g., one's family life)? And can need fulfillment in a non-work domain counteract the negative effects of need deficits in the workplace?

Although need fulfillment in one domain might moderate (i.e., buffer) the effects that need deficits in another domain have on psychological well-being, fulfillment of a given need within one domain is unlikely to be entirely interchangeable with fulfillment of that need in another domain. Having the need for relatedness satisfied by a romantic partner, for example, is likely to differ in important ways from having the same need satisfied by one's supervisor. And indeed, the research examining the relationship between need fulfillment and work-related variables has typically used *work-specific* measures of need fulfillment, such as the Basic Need Satisfaction at Work scale (Deci et al., 2001) and the Work-Related Basic Need Satisfaction measure (Van den Broeck et al., 2010). Further research is needed to understand how work-specific need fulfillment interacts with other forms of domain-specific need fulfillment and with general need fulfillment. Such research could draw from the work-life balance literature, which has found that one's work and non-work life can either undermine (Greenhaus & Beutell, 1985) or enhance (Greenhaus & Powell, 2006) each other.

Do General Need Fulfillment and Domain-Specific Need Fulfillment Predict Different Criteria?

Domain-specific measures of need fulfillment are likely to yield stronger relationship with well-being measures from the same domain than are either general measures of need fulfillment or domain-specific measures of need fulfillment from a different domain (see Bowling & Burns, 2010; Lievens, De Corte, & Schollaert, 2008). The extent to which one's needs are fulfilled by work, for instance, should be a good predictor of job satisfaction; the extent to which one's needs are fulfilled by one's family, on the other hand, should be a good predictor of family satisfaction. Furthermore, general need fulfillment should yield stronger relationships with general indicators of psychological well-being (e.g., life satisfaction) than should domain-specific need fulfillment measures.

How Might Individual Differences Fit into the Proposed Needs-Based Model?

The needs for autonomy, competence, and relatedness have generally been assumed by SDT researchers to be universal (Deci & Ryan, 2000; Ryan, 1995; Ryan & Deci,

2000). That is, each of the three psychological needs are thought to be a necessary prerequisite to psychological health for *all people*—much the same way food and water are prerequisites to physical health for all people. Although individual differences have generally been deemphasized by SDT researchers, research has shown that they play an important role in job satisfaction. For instance, personality traits (e.g., emotional stability and extraversion) have main effects on job satisfaction (Judge, Heller, & Mount, 2002), and individual difference variables moderate the effects of work environment dimensions on job satisfaction (e.g., Fried & Ferris, 1987). Given these findings, individual difference variables could be integrated into the model depicted in Figure 13.1.

First, individual differences could have indirect effects on need fulfillment that are mediated via effects on both the objective and perceived work environment. Personality traits, for instance, could influence the types of objective work environments that people choose, and they could influence peoples' perceptions of their work environments after they've chosen them (see Spector, Zapf, Chen, & Frese, 2000). Individual difference variables might also have direct effects on need fulfillment. People who are low in self-esteem, for instance, may habitually perceive that their need for competence has been left unsatisfied (i.e., because low self-esteem is linked to the tendency to perceive one's own abilities as insufficient; Judge, Erez, Bono, & Thoresen, 2002). Future research should consider these and other possibilities.

Methodological Challenges to Testing the Proposed Needs-Based Model

Methodological challenges to testing the current needs-based model largely stem from the fact that three types of variables depicted in Figure 13.1—the perceived work environment, psychological need fulfillment, and global job satisfaction—are internal psychological states. For this reason, self-report measures likely provide the most effective means of measuring these constructs. Unfortunately, using self-report measures to assess multiple variables makes a study vulnerable to the effects of common-method variance (see Spector, 2006). As a result, researchers should take methodological precautions when testing the needs-based model. For instance, they should consider measuring predictor, mediator, and criterion variables at different time points (Podsakoff & Organ, 1986), and they should consider including measures of marker variables (i.e., self-reported variables that are theoretically unrelated to the self-reported substantive variables included in one's study) in their datasets (Lindell & Whitney, 2001).

A second problem with testing the proposed needs-based model concerns the causal ordering of variables. Although Figure 13.1 predicts *causal* paths from (1) the perceived work environment to psychological need fulfillment and (2) from psychological need fulfillment to global job satisfaction, there are two obstacles to testing these causal effects. First, with the exception of the objective work environment, the variables depicted in Figure 13.1 do not lend themselves to experimental manipulation; instead, researchers must measure these variables as they naturally occur. As a result, researchers will find it difficult to unambiguously test these causal paths. Second, the amount of time needed for the effects depicted in the proposed needs model to unfold is currently unclear. This complicates attempts to use longitudinal designs to test the causal effects predicted by the model because researchers are left without guidance as to when to measure each construct.

Summary

Thousands of studies have examined the causes of global job satisfaction, the most popular conceptualization of employee well-being (Brief, 1998; Judge et al., 2001; Spector, 1997). This research has found that several environmental variables—including qualities of work tasks, qualities of work roles, interpersonal treatment at work, and pay level—are related to global job satisfaction. In the current chapter I argue that these findings can be understood through the lens of SDT (Deci & Ryan, 2000; Ryan, 1995; Ryan & Deci, 2000). Specifically, the fulfillment of the needs for autonomy, competence, and relatedness may provide the mechanisms by which the work environment influences job satisfaction. And indeed, meta-analytic evidence indicates that need fulfillment is related to work environment dimensions and to job satisfaction (Van den Broeck et al., 2016). Given job satisfaction's role as an indicator of employee well-being and its relationships with more general indicators of psychological well-being (e.g., life satisfaction; Bowling et al., 2010), continued research attention should be given to need fulfillment as a cause of job satisfaction.

References

Alarcon, G. M. (2011). A meta-analysis of burnout with job demands, resources, and attitudes. *Journal of Vocational Behavior, 79*, 549–562.

Alderfer, C. P. (1969). An empirical test of a new theory of human needs. *Organizational Behavior and Human Performance, 4*, 142–175.

Baard, P. P., Deci, E. L., & Ryan, R. M. (2004). Intrinsic need satisfaction: A motivational basis of performance and well-being in two work settings. *Journal of Applied Social Psychology, 34*, 2045–2068.

Baumeister, R. F., & Leary, M. R. (1995). The need to belong: Desire for interpersonal attachments as a fundamental human motivation. *Psychological Bulletin, 117*, 497–529.

Bowling, N. A., Alarcon, G. M., Bragg, C., & Hartman, M. (2015). A meta-analytic examination of the potential correlates and consequences of workload. *Work & Stress, 29*, 95–113.

Bowling, N. A., & Beehr, T. A. (2006). Workplace harassment from the victim's perspective: A theoretical model and meta-analysis. *Journal of Applied Psychology, 91*, 998–1012.

Bowling, N. A., & Burns, G. N. (2010). A comparison of work-specific and general personality measures as predictors of work and non-work criteria. *Personality and Individual Differences, 49*, 95–101.

Bowling, N. A., Camus, K. A., & Blackmore, C. E. (2015). Conceptualizing and measuring workplace abuse: Implications for the study of abuse's predictors and consequences. In C. C. Rosen, P. Perrewé, & J. R. B. Halbesleben (Eds.), *Research in occupational stress and well-being: Mistreatment in organizations* (Vol. 13, pp. 225–263). New York: Emerald.

Bowling, N. A., Eschleman, K. J., & Wang, Q. (2010). A meta-analytic examination of the relationship between job satisfaction and subjective well-being. *Journal of Occupational and Organizational Psychology, 83*, 915–934.

Bowling, N. A., Eschleman, K. J., Wang, Q., Kirkendall, C., & Alarcon, G. (2010). A meta-analysis of the predictors and consequences of organization-based self-esteem. *Journal of Occupational and Organizational Psychology, 83*, 601–626.

Bowling, N. A., & Kirkendall, C. (2012). Workload: A review of potential causes, consequences, and interventions. In J. Houdmont, S. Leka, & R. Sinclair (Eds.), *Contemporary occupational health psychology: Global perspectives on research and practice* (Vol. 2, pp. 221–238). Chichester, UK: Wiley-Blackwell.

Brief, A. P. (1998). *Attitudes in and around organizations.* Thousand Oaks, CA: Sage.

Cammann, C., Fichman, M., Jenkins, D., & Klesh, J. (1979). *The Michigan Organizational Assessment Questionnaire* (Unpublished manuscript). University of Michigan, Ann Arbor.

Campion, M. A. (1988). A meta-analysis of burnout with job demands, resources, and attitudes. *Journal of Applied Psychology, 73*, 467–481.

Chen, B., Vansteenkiste, M., Beyers, W., Boone, L., Deci, E. L., Van der Kaap-Deeder, J., . . . Verstuyf, J. (2015). Basic psychological need satisfaction, need frustration, and need strength across four cultures. *Motivation and Emotion, 39*, 216–236.

Cohen, S., & Wills, T. A. (1985). Stress, social support, and the buffering hypothesis. *Psychological Bulletin, 98*, 310–357.

Dalal, R. S. (2013). Job attitudes: Cognition and affect. In I. B. Weiner (Series Ed.) and N. Schmitt & S. Highhouse (Vol. Eds.) *Handbook of psychology, vol. 12: Industrial and organizational psychology* (pp. 341–366). Hoboken, NJ: John Wiley & Sons.

Deci, E. L., & Ryan, R. M. (2000). The "what" and "why" of goal pursuits: Human needs and the self-determination of behavior. *Psychological Inquiry, 11*, 227–268.

Deci, E. L., Ryan, R. M., Gagne´, M., Leone, D. R., Usunov, J., & Kornazheva, B. P. (2001). Need satisfaction, motivation, and well-being in the work organizations of a former Eastern Bloc country. *Personality and Social Psychology Bulletin, 27*, 930–942.

De Jonge, J., & Schaufeli, W. B. (1998). Job characteristics and employee well-being: A test of Warr's vitamin model in health care workers using structural equation modelling. *Journal of Organizational Behavior, 19*, 387–407.

Duffy, M. K., Ganster, D. C., & Pagon, M. (2002). Social undermining at work. *Academy of Management Journal, 45*, 331–351.

Fried, Y., & Ferris, G. R. (1987). The validity of the Job Characteristics Model: A review and meta-analysis. *Personnel Psychology, 40*, 287–322.

Gagné, M., & Deci, E. L. (2005). Self-determination theory and work motivation. *Journal of Organizational Behavior, 26*, 331–362.

Greenhaus, J. H., & Beutell, N. J. (1985). Sources and conflict between work and family roles. *Academy of Management Review, 10*, 76–88.

Greenhaus, J. H., & Powell, G. N. (2006). When work and family are allies: A theory of work-family enrichment. *Academy of Management Review, 31*, 72–92.

Hackman, J. R., & Oldham, G. R. (1975). Development of the Job Diagnostic Survey. *The Journal of Applied Psychology, 60*, 159–170.

Hackman, J. R., & Oldham, G. R. (1980). *Work redesign.* Reading, MA: Addison-Wesley.

Hershcovis, M. S. (2011). "Incivility, social undermining, bullying . . . oh my!": A call to reconcile constructs within workplace aggression research. *Journal of Organizational Behavior, 32,* 499–519.

Herzberg, F. (1968). One more time: How do you motivate employees? *Harvard Business Review, 46,* 53–62.

Jackson, S. E., & Schuler, R. S. (1985). A meta-analysis and conceptual critique of research on role ambiguity and role conflict in work settings. *Organizational Behavior and Human Decision Processes, 36,* 16–78.

Judge, T. A., Erez, A., Bono, J. E., & Thoresen, C. J. (2002). Are measures of self-esteem, neuroticism, locus of control, and generalized self-efficacy indicators of a common core construct? *Journal of Personality and Social Psychology, 83,* 693–710.

Judge, T. A., Heller, D., & Mount, M. K. (2002). Five-factor model of personality and job satisfaction: A meta-analysis. *Journal of Applied Psychology, 87,* 530–541.

Judge, T. A., & Larsen, R. J. (2001). Dispositional affect and job satisfaction: A review and theoretical extension. *Organizational Behavior and Human Decision Processes, 86,* 67–98.

Judge, T. A., Parker, S. K., Colbert, A. E., Heller, D., & Ilies, R. (2001). Job satisfaction: A cross-cultural review. In N. Anderson, D. S. Ones, H. K. Sinangil, & C. Viswesvaran (Eds.), *Handbook of industrial, work, and organizational psychology* (pp. 25–52). London, UK: Sage.

Judge, T. A., Piccolo, R. F., & Ilies, R. (2004). The forgotten ones? The validity of consideration and initiating structure in leadership research. *Journal of Applied Psychology, 89,* 36–51.

Judge, T. A., Piccolo, R. F., Podsakoff, N. P., Shaw, J. C., & Rich B. L. (2010). The relationship between pay and job satisfaction: A meta-analysis of the literature. *Journal of Vocational Behavior, 77,* 157–167.

King, L. A., & King, D. W. (1990). Role conflict and role ambiguity: A critical assessment of construct validity. *Psychological Bulletin, 107,* 48–64.

Lievens, F., De Corte, W., & Schollaert, E. (2008). A closer look at the frame-of-reference effect in personality scale scores and validity. *Journal of Applied Psychology, 93,* 268–279.

Lindell, M. K., & Whitney, D. J. (2001). Accounting for common method variance in cross-sectional research designs. *Journal of Applied Psychology, 86,* 114–121.

Liu, C., Spector, P. E., & Jex, S. M. (2005). The relation of job control with job strains: A comparison of multiple data sources. *Journal of Occupational and Organizational Psychology, 78,* 325–336.

Locke, E. A. (1976). The nature and causes of job satisfaction. In M. D. Dunnette (Ed.), *Handbook of industrial and organizational psychology* (pp. 1297–1349). Chicago: Rand-McNally.

Mackey, J. D., Frieder, R. E., Brees, J. R., & Martinko, M. J. (2017). Abusive supervision: A meta-analysis and empirical review. *Journal of Management, 43,* 1940–1965.

Maslow, A. H. (1943). A theory of human motivation. *Psychological Review, 50,* 370–396.

McClelland, D. C. (1965). N Achievement and entrepreneurship: A longitudinal study. *Journal of Personality and Social Psychology, 14,* 389–392.

Murray, H. A. (1938). *Explorations in personality.* New York: Oxford University Press.

Paul, K. I., & Batinic, B. (2010). The need for work: Jahoda's latent function of employment in a representative sample of the German population. *Journal of Organizational Behavior, 31,* 45–64.

Peters, L. H., & O'Connor, E. J. (1980). Situational constraints and work outcomes: The influences of a frequently overlooked construct. *Academy of Management Review, 5,* 391–397.

Pierce, J. L, & Gardner, D. G. (2004). Self-esteem within the work and organizational context: A review of the organization-based self-esteem literature. *Journal of Management, 30*, 591–622.

Pierce, J. R., & Aguinis, H. (2013). The too-much-of-a-good-thing effect in management. *Journal of Management, 39*, 313–338.

Pindek, S., & Spector, P. E. (2016). Organizational constraints: A meta-analysis of a major stressor. *Work & Stress, 30*, 7–25.

Podsakoff, P. M., & Organ, D. W. (1986). Self-reports in organizational research: Problems and prospects. *Journal of Management, 12*, 531–544.

Porter, L. W. (1963). Job attitudes in management: IV. Perceived deficiencies in need fulfillment as a function of size of company. *Journal of Applied Psychology, 47*, 386–397.

Reis, H. T., Sheldon, K. M., Gable, S. L., Roscoe, J., & Ryan, R. M. (2000). Daily well-being: The role of autonomy, competence, and relatedness. *Personality and Social Psychology Bulletin, 26*, 419–435.

Ryan, R. M. (1995). Psychological needs and the facilitation of integrative processes. *Journal of Personality, 63*, 397–427.

Ryan, R. M., & Deci, E. L. (2000). Self-determination theory and the facilitation of intrinsic motivation, social development, and well-being. *American Psychologist, 55*, 68–78.

Salancik, G. R., & Pfeffer, J. (1977). An examination of need-satisfaction models of job attitudes. *Administrative Science Quarterly, 22*, 427–456.

Sheldon, K. M., & Elliot, A. J. (1999). Goal striving, need satisfaction, and longitudinal well-being: The self-concordance model. *Journal of Personality and Social Psychology, 76*, 482–497.

Sheldon, K. M., Elliot, A. J., Kim, Y., & Kasser, T. (2001). What is satisfying about satisfying events? Testing 10 candidate psychological needs. *Journal of Personality and Social Psychology, 80*, 325–339.

Sheldon, K. M., Turban, D. B., Brown, K. G., Barrick, M. R., & Judge, T. A. (2003). Applying self-determination theory to organizational research. *Research in Personnel and Human Resource Management, 22*, 357–393.

Smith, P. C., Kendall, L. M., & Hulin, C. L. (1969). *Measurement of satisfaction in work and retirement.* Chicago: Rand-McNally.

Spector, P. E. (1985). Measurement of human service staff satisfaction: Development of the job satisfaction survey. *American Journal of Community Psychology, 13*, 693–713.

Spector, P. E. (1997). *Job Satisfaction: Applications, assessment, causes and consequences.* Thousand Oaks, CA: Sage.

Spector, P. E. (2006). Method variance in organizational research: Truth or urban legend? *Organizational Research Methods, 9*, 221–232.

Spector, P. E., Dwyer, D. J., & Jex, S. M. (1988). The relationship of job stressors to affective, health, and performance outcomes: A comparison of multiple data sources. *Journal of Applied Psychology, 73*, 11–19.

Spector, P. E., & Jex, S. M. (1991). Relations of job characteristics from multiple data sources with employee affect, absence, turnover intentions, and health. *Journal of Applied Psychology, 76*, 46–53.

Spector, P. E., & Jex, S. M. (1998). Development of four self-report measures of job stressors and strain: Interpersonal conflict at Work Scale, Organizational Constraints Scale, Qualitative Workload Inventory, and Physical Symptoms Inventory. *Journal of Occupational Health Psychology, 3*, 356–367.

Spector, P. E., Zapf, D., Chen, P. Y., & Frese, M. (2000). Why negative affectivity should not be controlled in job stress research: Don't throw out the baby with the bathwater. *Journal of Organizational Behavior, 21,* 79–95.

Tepper, B. J. (2000). Consequences of abusive supervision. *Academy of Management Journal, 43,* 178–190.

Van den Broeck, A., Ferris, D. L., Chang, C. H., & Rosen, C. C. (2016). A review of self-determination theory's basic psychological needs at work. *Journal of Management, 42,* 1195–1229.

Van den Broeck, A., Vansteenkiste, M., De Witte, H., Soenens, B., & Lens, W. (2010). Capturing autonomy, competence, and relatedness at work: Construction and initial validation of the Work-Related Basic Need Satisfaction Scale. *Journal of Occupational and Organizational Psychology, 83,* 981–1002.

Viswesvaran, C., Sanchez, J. I., & Fisher, J. (1999). The role of social support in the process of work stress: A meta-analysis. *Journal of Vocational Behavior, 54,* 314–334.

Warr, P. (1987). *Work, unemployment, and mental health.* Oxford: Clarendon Press.

Warr, P. B. (2007). *Work, happiness, and unhappiness.* New York: Routledge.

Weiss, D. J., Dawis, R. V., England, G. W., & Lofquist, L. H. (1967). *Manual for the Minnesota Satisfaction Questionnaire.* Minnesota Studies on Vocational Rehabilitation, 22. Minneapolis, MN: University of Minnesota.

Wolf, M. G. (1970). Need gratification theory: A theoretical reformulation of job satisfaction/dissatisfaction and job motivation. *Journal of Applied Psychology, 54,* 87–94.

PART III

Intrapersonal and Self-Related Influences

14

MEANING IN LIFE IN CONTEXT

Samantha J. Heintzelman

Meaning in life is, ultimately, a personal experience. Victor Frankl's (1963/1984) seminal autobiography demonstrated the human ability to derive a sense of personal meaning despite the direst situational factors. Following this tradition, the scientific study of meaning in life has maintained a strong focus on meaning as an *intrapersonal* process. Yet despite the subjective nature of this internal feeling, the experience that one's life is meaningful is intertwined in one's broader external—and often social—world. A growing body of research points to the considerable roles played by social relationships, cultural worldviews, and the stability of one's surroundings in the experience of meaning in life.

In this chapter, I will bring together research from across divergent areas of the meaning in life literature that employs a broadened, situated, view of meaning in life. Then, I will outline the *meaning-as-information* approach as one example to demonstrate how situating feelings of meaning within an external context is crucial in facilitating novel theory building and important advances in the science of meaning in life by approaching age-old questions from a fresh, contextualized, perspective. In order to most completely understand the experience of meaning in life, we must broaden our scope of focus to include such features of the world beyond the person.

What Is Meaning in Life?

Examinations of any particular features of the experience of meaning in life must be built on a foundational understanding of meaning in life more broadly. Psychological science, over the last several decades, has expanded upon centuries of philosophical and theological thinking on this topic, offering empirical insights regarding the human experience of meaning in life.

Broadly, meaning in life is an important feature of psychological well-being (Ryff, 1995), though while related to other aspects of well-being, it remains a distinct construct (e.g., Baumeister, Vohs, Aaker, & Garbinsky, 2013; King, Hicks, Krull, & Del Gaiso, 2006). For example, the Meaning in Life Questionnaire, a widely used measure of meaning in life with the strongest psychometric qualities among other available assessments (Brandstätter, Baumann, Borasio, & Fegg, 2012), shares an $r = .46$ correlation with Diener and colleagues' (1985) Satisfaction with Life Scale (Steger, Frazier, Oishi, & Kaler, 2006). As a feature of healthy psychological functioning, individuals share a general strong motivation to experience the sense that their lives are meaningful (Baumeister, 1991; Frankl, 1963/1984; Klinger, 1977; Maslow, 1968).

In addition to positioning meaning in life within a broader conceptual net of human experience, another essential contribution emerging from the empirical research on this topic is a more precise definition of meaning in life. According to one such definition, "Lives may be experienced as meaningful when they are felt to have a significance beyond the trivial or momentary, to have purpose, or to have a coherence that transcends chaos" (King et al., 2006, p. 180). This definition highlights three central features of the subjective feeling that one's life is meaningful: purpose, significance, and coherence (George & Park, 2016, 2017; Heintzelman & King, 2013, 2014a; Martela & Steger, 2016).

First, *purpose* refers to engagement in goal-directed pursuits: Spending time and effort striving towards personally significant goals is associated with feelings that one's life is more worth living (Battista & Almond, 1973; Emmons, 2003; McGregor & Little, 1998; McKnight & Kashdan, 2009; Vallerand, 2008). Second, *significance* encompasses the degree to which a person feels like his or her life matters—that he or she is making a mark on the world and forming a lasting legacy that transcends the self (George & Park, 2016a). Lastly, *coherence* is the degree to which stimuli, events, and one's life make sense (Battista & Almond, 1973; Baumeister & Vohs, 2002). Coherence can be found, in part, in the comprehensibility of regularities, patterns, and expected associations in one's environment (Antonovsky, 1993; Baumeister, 1991; Heine, Proulx, & Vohs, 2006; Heintzelman, Trent, & King, 2013; Hicks, Cicero, Trent, Burton, & King, 2010).

Meaning in Life in the External World

Among the aspects that characterize a meaningful life are qualities of experience that are essentially embedded in the external world. These include perceptions of significance, which is often gained through relationships that allow a person to feel that he or she matters to others, and coherence, which can stem from the presence of reliabilities in one's external environment. The influence of the outside world on meaning in life is an emerging theme of recent research in this area, to which I will now turn.

Social Relationships

One central source of meaning in life deeply embedded in most people's lives is social relationships. Ryff (1995) included positive relationships as one of six core dimensions of psychological well-being. Similarly, Emmons (2003) pointed out that several lines of work, each utilizing different methodologies and populations, all included relationships/intimacy as a major category of life meaning and suggested that life goals that include maintaining close relationship are among those that influence personal meaning. A growing body of research validates these claims and demonstrates the role of social connections in everyday experiences of meaning in life.

Relationships in Lay Beliefs of Meaning in Life

First, naïve lay beliefs indicate that most people find their relationships to be essential features of a meaningful life. DeBats (1999) classified sources of meaning in life into categories and found relationships to be the most frequently occurring source of meaning (over lifework, personal well-being, self-actualization, service, beliefs, and materiality) in young adult patients with a variety of nonpsychotic psychological symptomologies and non-patient samples. Cultivating descriptions of the characteristics of an ideally meaningful life, Wong (1998) similarly found a strong relational component in lay conceptualizations of the ideal meaning in life as well as in personal profiles of the sources of participants' own sense of meaning in life. Furthermore, when Lambert, Stillman, and colleagues (2010) asked participants to "pick the one thing that makes life most meaningful for you", 82% of the sample selected family, a specific family member, or friends. Similarly, when another sample was provided with a list of potential sources of meaning in life to rank in terms of what gave their lives the most meaning, family was rated as the most important source of meaning in life, with friends ranking third (Lambert, Stillman et al., 2010). Relationships are consistently included in lay conceptualizations of meaning in life.

Relationship Factors in Experienced Meaning in Life

Research examining relationships and feelings of meaning in life suggest that connections with others are, indeed, important features of a meaningful life. In general, feelings of belonging (Lambert et al., 2013) and relatedness need satisfaction (Hicks & King, 2009; Hicks, Schlegel, & King, 2010) are positively related to meaning in life. Furthermore, the Meaning in Life Questionnaire correlates with socially relevant subscales from personality measures (Steger, Kashdan, Sullivan, & Lorentz, 2008) including the Social Closeness subscale of the Multidimensional Personality Questionnaire (Tellegen, 1982) and the Social subscale of the Strong

Interest Inventory (Harmon, Hansen, Borgen, & Hammer, 1994). Similarly, the extent to which participants rate good relationships as an important life goal also associates with higher meaning in life (Martos & Kopp, 2012). More experiential evidence bolsters these findings as well. For instance, a daily diary study spanning 2 weeks found that the occurrence of positive social events in a day positively predicts (and the daily occurrence of negative social events negatively predicts) a person's meaning in life that day (Machell, Kashdan, Short, & Nezlek, 2015). In sum, the association between meaning in life and social functioning assessments is quite robust.

Another lens through which to examine a link between social relationships and meaning in life is *attachment theory*, which posits that people have a general system driven to seek out caring and supportive others (Bowlby, 1980). Shaver and Mikulincer (2012) proposed that the availability of supportive and caring attachment figures should promote a sense of meaning in life. Indeed, empirical findings support this claim. Most directly, securely attached adults report higher meaning in life compared to those with dismissive, preoccupied, and fearful attachment styles (Bodner, Bergman, & Cohen-Fridel, 2014). Furthermore, in one small study, writing about how the statement, "human life is purposeful and meaningful", was *untrue*, led to increased desire for closeness and intimacy, which mirrors attachment-system activation (Shaver & Mikulincer, 2012). In another study, secure attachment primes (i.e., thinking about a supportive other; compared to neutral primes, i.e., thinking about someone with whom no attachment is shared) increased meaning and coherence regardless of dispositional attachment (Mikulincer & Shaver, 2005). Secure attachments are another strong indicator of the relationship between meaning in life and healthy social relationships.

Beyond secure attachments, other features of strong and healthy relationships include forgiveness and gratitude. If meaning in life is associated with quality relationships, then these constituent positive relationship processes ought to also relate to meaning in life. First, forgiveness is an important aspect of healthy relationships (Bono, McCullough, & Root, 2008), and the trait tendency to forgive and features of state forgiveness following the recounting of a past offense are positively related to meaning in life (Van Tongeren et al., 2015). (See also Chapter 7.) Furthermore, the average forgiveness of romantic partners' offenses prospectively predicts meaning in life over 6 months, controlling for baseline meaning in life (Van Tongeren et al., 2015). Second, gratitude is another powerful relationship skill (e.g., Algoe, Gable, & Maisel, 2010; Lambert, Clark, et al., 2010) and also shares a relationship with meaning in life. One study found that participants randomly assigned to a gratitude exercise subsequently reported higher meaning in life compared to controls (Van Tongeren, Green, Davis, Hook, & Hulsey, 2016). (See also Chapter 10.) Forgiveness and gratitude represent features of strong relationships and are, themselves, related to meaning in life.

Research has also examined the role of particular relationships in the experience that life is meaningful, most frequently family relationships. Feelings of closeness to one's family and family social support relate to greater meaning in life (Lambert et al., 2010). Furthermore, Nelson, Kushlev, English, Dunn, & Lyubomirsky (2013) have studied meaning in life in a parenting context. First, they found that parents (both mothers and fathers) report thinking about the meaning and purpose of life more often than non-parents. Next, in an experience sampling study in which surveys were administered 5 times a day for 7 days to more precisely capture momentary experiences, they found that parents reported higher momentary meaning in life than non-parents across these real-time episodes. Finally, utilizing the day reconstruction method, they found that parents experienced a stronger sense of meaning in life while they were taking care of their children than when engaged in any other activity. Parenthood seems to be a meaningful role, and the act of parenting seems to make parents' lives feel more meaningful. Together, these findings clearly support that meaning in life and close relationships are inexorably linked.

Causal Relationships

The work above identifies a consistent correlational association between social relationships and meaning in life. The question remains, however: Do healthy relationships cause meaning in life or does meaning in life lead to stronger relationships? In work teasing apart this relationship, evidence supporting both causal directions has emerged, as is the case with most factors associated with feelings of psychological well-being (e.g., Lyubomirsky, King, & Diener, 2005).

First, relationships seem to make a person's life feel more meaningful. Longitudinal evidence demonstrates that social qualities can subsequently influence feelings of meaning in life. In a study of older adults, anticipated social and emotional support from close others related to a deeper sense of meaning over time (Krause, 2007). Direct experimental evidence manipulating relationship factors provides further evidence for this causal effect. Participants primed with belongingness reported the highest levels of meaning compared to others primed with social value, suggesting that these feelings of connection lead to feelings of meaning in life (Lambert et al., 2013). Taking this a step further, relatedness need satisfaction was more strongly related to meaning in life following a series of relationship primes compared to primes of dessert foods, suggesting that relationships are especially relevant to meaning in life judgments when they are at the forefront of one's current thoughts (Hicks & King, 2009). This work suggests that relationship qualities can, indeed, foster feelings of meaning in life.

Still, additional research offers support for reciprocal causal effects as well; meaning in life also can promote healthier relationships. In one study, participants with high self-ratings of meaning in life were judged to be more likable, and more desirable friends and conversation partners by independent evaluators who watched videos they had created of themselves (Stillman, Lambert, Fincham, & Baumeister, 2011). In addition, in a large-scale longitudinal sample, Stavrova and

Luhmann (2016) found that participants who reported higher meaning in life at baseline were more likely to become a new active member of a voluntary organization 2 years later. In addition, for those respondents who were single at baseline, those who got married in the subsequent 7 years had reported higher meaning in life at baseline compared to those respondents who remained single (Stavrova & Luhmann, 2016).

Together, these findings provide evidence for a bidirectional causal relationship between social thriving and meaning in life. Feeling that one's life is meaningful can enhance relationship outcomes, while at the same time strong relationships and social connections are important sources of meaning in life.

Social Exclusion and Meaning in Life

While the presence of social connections is important for feelings of meaning in life, the absence of these connections, exemplified by loneliness, social exclusion, or ostracism, can be devastating to a sense that one's life is meaningful (see Williams 2007, 2012, for reviews). Even isolated laboratory manipulations of being forgotten (King & Geise, 2011) or receiving rejecting feedback (Stillman et al., 2009) can lead to profound decreases in meaning in life compared to being remembered or given neutral or accepting feedback.

In addition, a body of work has utilized the innovative Cyberball methodology, an interactive computer game in which a participant experiences exclusion when avatars stop tossing the participant a ball gradually over the course of a ball-tossing game. Across a number of studies, participants who are excluded in a game of Cyberball rated their lives as more meaningless and less meaningful compared to those who were included in the game (e.g., Stillman et al., 2009). Interesting extensions of this work have altered the characteristics of the excluders and the situation surrounding the exclusion event. Even when participants are told that their exclusion was being executed randomly by a computer program or by a party restrained by task instructions rather than by a human who had made this choice freely, they still experienced a loss of meaning following the exclusion experience (Zadro, Williams, & Richardson, 2004). Meaning was also lower following exclusion by members of an opposing political party or a despised outgroup (Gonsalkorale & Williams, 2007). Furthermore, even when exclusion was beneficial for monetary gains in a task, it was, nevertheless, associated with lower meaningfulness (van Beest & Williams, 2006). These robust effects of social exclusion on feelings of meaning in life strongly support the importance of social connections for personal meaning.

Why Do Social Relationships Matter for Meaning in Life?

The work I have reviewed thus far clearly supports that social relationships are an important part of meaning in life, despite their position outside the self. Why might relationships with others be so important to feelings of personal meaning?

Writing about social relationships from a terror management theory perspective, Mikulincer, Florian, and Hirschberger (2003) offer one potential answer to this question, suggesting that close relationships serve a deep existential function. They propose that relationships provide a person with a symbolic meaning structure that allows self-transcendence and achievement of symbolic immortality. Essentially, from this perspective, the people left behind following a person's death can carry that person's legacy forward into the future. Therefore, one function of relationships may be to serve to secure and protect one's legacy—the meaningfulness of his or her life—forward into the future. With the burgeoning of research regarding the association between social relationships and meaning in life, an important direction moving forward is to engage in further theoretical and empirical work examining the function of social relationships for feelings of meaning in life.

Making Sense of the External World

The manner with which the external world relates to and influences the experience of meaning in life extends beyond one's interactions with other people. I will now turn to examining the importance of making sense of one's external world for the feeling that one's life is meaningful. First, I will focus on the effects of environmental reliabilities for meaning in life and then will review research regarding the role of cultural worldviews for understanding the world and experiencing life as meaningful.

Environmental Coherence

The extent to which life and the world around us make sense, are characteristically comprehensible, and contain reliable patterns that are essential components of meaning in life (e.g., Baumeister, 1991; Baumeister & Vohs, 2002; Heintzelman & King, 2014a; Reker & Wong, 1988). Experimental research has shown that exposing participants to reliable patterns or implicit associations increased their ratings of meaning in life (Heintzelman et al., 2013). For example, participants shown pictures of trees with four trees depicting each of the four seasons in repeating patterned cycles based on their seasonal content rated their lives as more meaningful compared to controls who saw the same pictures in a random order (Heintzelman et al., 2013). Beyond feelings of meaning, such exposures to environmental structure have been found to spur engagement in purposeful goal-pursuit behaviors as well (Kay, Laurin, Fitzsimons, & Landau, 2014). In fitting with the theoretical inclusion of coherence and comprehensibility as key components of a meaningful life, objective regularities in the external world can influence feelings of meaning in life.

Cultural Worldviews

In addition to benefiting from the presence of objective external coherence, humans also engage in top-down strategies to actively make sense of the world and their experiences. One way the world is organized is through one's cultural worldviews. Worldviews are defined as "sets of beliefs and assumptions that describe reality" (Koltko-Rivera, 2004, p. 3). Cultural worldviews serve as a lens through which the world and one's experiences are perceived, comprehended, and collectively understood (Miller, 1999; Miller & West, 1993). Koltko-Rivera (2004) highlights the importance of worldviews in providing "a sense of coherence to all aspects of life and reality" (p. 20) and describes that cultural worldviews offer a ready framework for interpreting and understanding the vast and varied external world, including the composition of the universe, conceptualizations of human nature, and the meaning of life.

Given the importance of coherence for meaning in life, it is not surprising that worldviews, which promote sense-making, have even been referred to as "unconscious systems of meaning" (Koltko-Rivera, 2004) and even as the "ultimate system of meaning" (Schlegel & Hicks, 2017). Ernest Becker (1971) suggested that individuals participate in cultures to provide a sense that they matter to the world in a lasting way—a key component of a modern psychological view of meaning in life. Similarly, Allport (1961) argued that cultures emerged to assist people in ordering, interpreting, and navigating the "problems of life" including the pursuit of personal welfare and meaning.

Threat Compensation Theories

One area of social psychology that has been interested in cultural worldviews and meaning in life is the threat compensation literature, including work in terror management theory (TMT), uncertainty management theory, and the meaning maintenance model (MMM). These theories emphasize the use of cultural worldviews to maintain a sense of meaning in the face of a threat.

One such threat to life's meaning is the inevitability of one's own mortality. Dilthey (1957/1970) suggested that worldviews work to quell concerns about the meaning of life in the face of death. Subsequently, work within terror management theory has provided evidence to support this notion and has offered further insights regarding the role of cultural worldviews for meaning processes in the context of existential anxiety. Broadly, TMT posits that cultural worldviews function to assuage the existential terror of our inevitable deaths by offering a more secure sense of meaning and permanence (Becker, 1973; Greenberg, Pyszczynski, & Solomon, 1986).

TMT research demonstrates how reminders of one's own death—mortality salience manipulations—lead to reaffirmations of stable sources of meaning drawn from one's cultural belief systems, such as national identity (Arndt, Greenberg, & Cook, 2002) or social structure (Landau et al., 2004), to ameliorate existential anxiety (see Greenberg, Solomon, & Arndt, 2008, for further review). Beyond conceptualizing the defense of one's cultural values and institutions as evidence for meaning buffering in the face of existential threat, more direct tests of the relationship between cultural worldviews and meaning in life have been conducted in the TMT literature as well.

A number of studies have examined various aspects of an overarching model that being reminded of one's own mortality facilitates worldview defense processes aimed at protectively bolstering the sense that one's life is meaningful, which dampens death-related anxiety. First, and crucially, mortality salience increased death anxiety in participants who reported low levels of meaning in life; however, those who reported high levels of meaning in life were buffered from the impact of a mortality salience manipulation on death anxiety (Routledge & Juhl, 2010). This suggests that mortality salience leads to death anxiety to the extent that it threatens a sense of meaning in life.

Next, Simon, Arndt, Greenberg, Pyszczynski, and Solomon (1998) tested the assumption that the function of cultural worldviews in this existential process is to imbue life with meaning. They found that, among mildly depressed participants, those who were reminded of their mortality and then were given an opportunity to defend an important worldview reported higher meaning in life compared to those who were either not exposed to mortality salience or did not have an opportunity to defend a cultural worldview. Following an existential threat, bolstering one's cultural worldviews promotes a sense of meaning in life.

Researchers have also identified alternate meaning-relevant pathways through which the link between mortality salience and meaning in life can be mitigated. First, while mortality salience led participants low in personal need for structure to feel like their lives were less meaningful, this effect was reversed for participants high in personal need for structure who were able to fall back on their stable views of the world in the face of this threat (Vess, Routledge, Landau, & Arndt, 2009). In addition, when the low personal need for structure participants were given an opportunity to explore novel interpretations of their selves and the world—to work to make sense of things—the threat no longer negatively impacted their meaning in life (Vess et al., 2009). Furthermore, the distance from and quick adoption of long-term goals (Vess, Rogers, Routledge, & Hicks, 2017) and the tendency to engage in nostalgic reflection (Routledge, Arndt, Sedikides, & Wildschut, 2008) also function to maintain a sense of meaning in the face of death reminders. Overall, bolstering cultural worldviews, sense of structure, goal orientation, or feelings of significance can mitigate the deleterious effects of existential terror on meaning in life, and this process can even foster a sense that one's life is meaningful.

From the TMT perspective, meaninglessness is threatening because the ability to comprehend the world is crucial for people to "imbue life with death-transcending meaning and significance" (Landau, Greenberg, Solomon, Pyszczynski, & Martens, 2006, p. 887). However, other threat management perspectives argue that threats to meaning don't need to be death-relevant to have implications for cultural worldviews and meaning in life. Cultural worldviews seem to similarly serve to manage meaning threats from personal uncertainty, according to uncertainty management theory (McGregor, Zanna, Holmes, & Spencer, 2001; van den Bos,

Poortvliet, Maas, Miedema, & van den Ham, 2005). Meaning in life has not been the focus of much research in this area, although one study showed that personal certainty threats—goal frustration and goal conflict—led to increases in a motivational search for meaning compared to controls (McGregor, Prentice, & Nash, 2009).

A third threat management model, the MMM (Heine et al., 2006) posits that violations of expectancies, which are often born from aspects of one's cultural worldviews, can also threaten meaning. The MMM predicts that, when expectancies are violated, individuals work to reinforce aspects of their cultural worldviews or identify structure in the environment, ostensibly to maintain a sense of meaning in the face of this threat to understanding. For example, following expectancy violations via perceptual anomalies, participants were more punitive towards a prostitute (Proulx & Heine, 2008) and better at implicitly learning an artificial grammar (Proulx & Heine, 2009). According to MMM, threats to one's expectancies for the world to make sense motivate reactive behaviors that reinforce one's cultural worldviews or sense of coherence. These reactions are thought to combat threats to meaning in life, though direct assessments of meaning in life have not been integrated into this literature.

The threat management theories reviewed diverge in the existential threat of focus (and there has been much discussion regarding the divergence and overlap of these models, e.g., McGregor, 2006; Pyszczynski, Greenberg, Solomon, & Maxfield, 2006; Tritt, Inzlicht, & Harmon-Jones, 2012), yet all share a focus on the manner in which such threats motivate people to defend foundations of meaning. Namely, bolstering aspects of one's cultural worldviews and emphasizing the stability and coherence in one's life seem to be strong factors in maintaining a sense of meaning in life in the face of external threats. Together, these lines of research regarding the effects of environmental coherence and cultural worldviews on meaning in life highlight, again, that feelings of personal meaning are importantly situated in the context of one's outside world.

A Functional Understanding of Meaning in Life

Attending to the ways that feelings of meaning in life are embedded in one's external world, rather than exclusively in one's internal world, affords novel insights regarding longstanding questions about meaning in life. For example, what is the function of meaning in life and why is it adaptive to experience one's life as meaningful? Answering these questions is important for understanding the associations between meaning in life and a host of adaptive outcomes across life domains. For example, meaning in life is associated with better physical health (see Roepke, Jayawickreme, & Riffle, 2014 for review). Self-reports of meaning in life associated, not only with better self-reported health (Krause, 2004; Steger, Mann, Michels, & Cooper, 2009), but also with more objective measures of health such as decreased mortality (Boyle, Barnes, Buchman, & Bennett, 2009;

Hill & Turiano, 2014; Krause, 2009) and decreased risk of heart disease (Kim, Sun, Park, Kubzansky, & Peterson, 2013) and Alzheimer's disease (Boyle, Buchman, Barnes, & Bennett, 2010). Furthermore, meaning in life is associated with lower blood pressure (Holt-Lunstad, Steffen, Sandberg, & Jensen, 2011) and less inflammation (Friedman, Hayney, Love, Singer, & Ryff, 2007) and greater engagement in preventative health measures such as regular health checks (Kim, Strecher, & Ryff, 2014); better sleep (Hamilton, Nelson, Stevens, & Kitzman, 2007; Kim, Hershner, & Strecher, 2015); and more physical activity (Holahan et al., 2011; Hooker & Masters, 2016). The benefits of meaning in life extend to better mental health as well, including decreased suicidal ideation (Heisel & Flett, 2004) and lower incidence of a variety of psychological disorders (Mascaro & Rosen, 2005; Owens, Steger, Whitesell, & Herrera, 2009; Steger & Kashdan, 2009). Clearly, experiencing one's life as meaningful is beneficial. Yet understanding *why* meaning in life relates to these adaptive outcomes has been difficult.

One way to understand why meaning in life is associated with this wide menu of adaptive outcomes is through a focus on the connection of this experience with features of one's external environments, such as those discussed above. The *meaning-as-information* framework (Heintzelman & King, 2014b) does this by drawing on a functional approach to feelings: the *feelings-as-information* hypothesis (e.g., Schwarz, 2012; Schwarz & Clore, 1983, 1996), which suggests that feeling states provide information about one's external world. Individuals can then use this environmental knowledge to think and act in ways that will most adaptively serve them in the circumstances indicated by their feelings. While this approach has been most frequently applied to affective feeling states, Clore (1992) suggested that other feeling states also hold informational value for facilitating optimal functioning and adaptive interactions with one's surrounding world.

The meaning-as-information approach (Heintzelman & King, 2014b) posits that feelings of meaning, like other feeling states, provide us with information about the environment. Specifically, feelings of meaning can provide unique information (not conveyed by affective feelings) about the existence of reliable patterns and coherence in one's environment—whether things are making sense. From this perspective, feelings of meaning ebb and flow in response to present environmental circumstances, and these fluctuations prompt environmentally appropriate cognitive strategies, namely, a reliance on intuitive, rather than more reflective, thought processes.

The first assumption of this model is that meaning in life has a state component that flexibly responds to variations a person's external environment. While the science of meaning in life traditionally focuses on stable trait levels of meaning in life (Steger & Kashdan, 2006), a growing body of work suggests that meaning in life also has a state component and represents a feeling that can fluctuate across time. In a daily diary study, approximately 80% of the variance in meaning in life was found to be within, rather than across, individuals (King et al., 2006). Further daily diary studies have identified transient predictors of daily meaning in life, including daily social and achievement events (Machell et al., 2015), daily experiential avoidance (Machell, Goodman, & Kashdan, 2015), and daily curiosity (Kashdan & Steger, 2007). Finally, as mentioned above, manipulations of pattern and associations in external stimuli influence ratings of meaning in life (Heintzelman et al., 2013). Together, this work highlights that meaning in life contains a momentary and environmentally responsive state component in addition to a state component.

Beyond positing that feelings of meaning respond to conditions in one's external environment, the meaning-as-information approach also suggests that this information is used by the individual to think and behave in a manner that is best-suited for that environment. Specifically, it proposes that feelings of meaning are related to associative, or intuitive, cognitive processes—to trusting one's hunches (Heintzelman & King, 2014b). Indeed, in support of this proposition, meaning in life and the tendency to use and trust one's intuitive thoughts are positively correlated; when meaning in life is low, reflective processing strategies are more likely to be engaged, whereas when meaning in life is high, intuitive cognitive processes are more likely to dominate (Heintzelman & King, 2016).

In linking feelings of meaning to the external world, the meaning-as-information approach can account for the adaptive outcomes associated with feelings of meaning in life: These outcomes are fostered by the same environments that spur feelings that things are making sense, that life itself is meaningful. The meaning-as-information perspective provides an example of how taking an embedded approach to the study of meaning in life, which is traditionally viewed as exclusively intrapersonal, offers crucial insights into the experience and function of feelings of meaning in life.

The research reviewed in this chapter highlights an emergent trend of increasingly acknowledging that feelings of meaning are embedded within a broader context that extends beyond the internal self. Widening the scope in meaning research to include the context of interpersonal relationships and environmental coherence has been essential for recent advances in this area. In order to continue making progress towards a full understanding of meaning in life, we must move beyond the identification of the antecedents and correlates of meaning in life and also begin to explain *why* these relationships exist. An embedded approach to the study of meaning in life is essential for this type of progress.

References

Algoe, S. B., Gable, S. L., & Maisel, N. C. (2010). It's the little things: Everyday gratitude as a booster shot for romantic relationships. *Personal Relationships, 17*, 217–233.

Allport, G. (1961). *Patterns and growth in personality.* New York: Holt, Rinehart, and Winston.

Antonovsky, A. (1993). The structure and properties of the sense of coherence scale. *Social Science & Medicine, 36*, 725–733.

Arndt, J., Greenberg, J., & Cook, A. (2002). Mortality salience and the spreading activation of worldview-relevant constructs: Exploring the cognitive architecture of terror management. *Journal of Experimental Psychology: General, 131*, 307–324.

Battista, J., & Almond, R. (1973). The development of meaning in life. *Psychiatry*, *36*, 409–427.

Baumeister, R. F. (1991). *Meanings of life*. New York, NY: Guilford.

Baumeister, R. F., & Vohs, K. D. (2002). The pursuit of meaningfulness in life. In C. R. Snyder & S. J. Lopez (Eds.), *Handbook of positive psychology* (pp. 608–618). New York, NY: Oxford University Press.

Baumeister, R. F., Vohs, K. D., Aaker, J. L., & Garbinsky, E. N. (2013). Some key differences between a happy life and a meaningful life. *The Journal of Positive Psychology*, *8*, 505–516.

Becker, E. (1971). *The birth and death of meaning* (2nd ed.). New York: Free Press.

Becker, E. (1973). *The denial of death*. New York: Free Press.

Bodner, E., Bergman, Y. S., & Cohen-Fridel, S. (2014). Do attachment styles affect the presence and search for meaning in life? *Journal of Happiness Studies*, *15*, 1041–1059.

Bono, G., McCullough, M. E., & Root, L. (2008). Forgiveness, feeling connected to others, and well-being: Two longitudinal studies. *Personality and Social Psychology Bulletin*, *34*, 182–195.

Bowlby, J. (1980). *Attachment and loss: Volume 3-Loss: Sadness and depression*. New York: Basic Books.

Boyle, P. A., Barnes, L. L., Buchman, A. S., & Bennett, D. A. (2009). Purpose in life is associated with mortality among community-dwelling older persons. *Psychosomatic Medicine*, *71*, 574–579.

Boyle, P. A., Buchman, A. S., Barnes, L. L., & Bennett, D. A. (2010). Effect of a purpose in life on risk of incident Alzheimer disease and mild cognitive impairment in community-dwelling older persons. *Archives of General Psychiatry*, *67*, 304–310.

Brandstätter, M., Baumann, U., Borasio, G. D., & Fegg, M. J. (2012). Systematic review of meaning in life assessment instruments. *Psycho-Oncology*, *21*, 1034–1052.

Clore, G. L. (1992). Cognitive phenomenology: Feelings and the construction of judgment. In L. L. Martin & A. Tesser (Eds.), *The construction of social judgments* (pp. 133–163). Hillsdale, NJ: Lawrence Erlbaum.

Debats, D. L. (1999). Sources of meaning: An investigation of significant commitments in life. *Journal of Humanistic Psychology*, *39*, 30–57.

Diener, E. D., Emmons, R. A., Larsen, R. J., & Griffin, S. (1985). The satisfaction with life scale. *Journal of Personality Assessment*, *49*, 71–75.

Dilthey, W. (1970). Culture and the production of world views. In D. P. Verene (Ed.), *Man and culture* (pp. 103–132). New York: Laurel/Dell. (Reprinted from *Philosophy of existence*, trans. by W. Kluback & M. Weinbaum, 1957, New York: Twayne).

Emmons, R. (2003). Personal goals, life meaning, and virtue: Wellsprings of a positive life. In C. L. M. Keyes & J. Haidt (Eds.), *Flourishing: Positive psychology and the life well-lived* (pp. 105–128). Washington, DC: APA.

Frankl, V. E. (1984). *Man's search for meaning* (3rd ed.). New York, NY: First Washington Square Press. (Original work published 1963).

Friedman, E. M., Hayney, M., Love, G. D., Singer, B. H., & Ryff, C. D. (2007). Plasma interleukin-6 and soluble IL-6 receptors are associated with psychological wellbeing in aging women. *Health Psychology*, *26*, 305–313.

George, L. S., & Park, C. L. (2016a). Meaning in life as comprehension, purpose, and mattering: Toward integration and new research questions. *Review of General Psychology*, *20*, 205–220.

George, L. S., & Park, C. L. (2016b). The multidimensional existential meaning scale: A tripartite approach to measuring meaning in life. *The Journal of Positive Psychology*, *12*, 1–15.

Gonsalkorale, K., & Williams, K. D. (2007). The KKK won't let me play: Ostracism even by a despised outgroup hurts. *European Journal of Social Psychology, 37*, 1176–1186.

Greenberg, J., Pyszczynski, T., & Solomon, S. (1986). The causes and consequences of a need for self-esteem: A terror management theory. In R. Baumeister (Ed.), *Public self and private self* (pp. 189–212). New York: Springer.

Greenberg, J., Solomon, S., & Arndt, J. (2008). A basic but uniquely human motivation: Terror management. In J. Shah & W. Gardner (Eds.), *Handbook of motivation science* (pp. 114–134). New York: Guilford Press.

Hamilton, N. A., Nelson, C. A., Stevens, N., & Kitzman, H. (2007). Sleep and psychological well-being. *Social Indicators Research, 82*, 147–163.

Harmon, L. W., Hansen, J. C., Borgen, F. H., & Hammer, A. L. (1994). *Applications and technical guide for the Strong Interest Inventory*. Palo Alto, CA: Consulting Psychologists Press.

Heine, S. J., Proulx, T., & Vohs, K. D. (2006). The meaning maintenance model: On the coherence of social motivations. *Personality and Social Psychology Review, 10*, 88–110.

Heintzelman, S. J., & King, L. A. (2013). On knowing more than we can tell: Intuitive processes and the experience of meaning. *Journal of Positive Psychology, 8*, 471–482.

Heintzelman, S. J., & King, L. A. (2014a). Life is pretty meaningful. *American Psychologist, 69*, 561–574.

Heintzelman, S. J., & King, L. A. (2014b). (The feeling of) Meaning-as-information. *Personality and Social Psychology Review, 18*, 153–167.

Heintzelman, S. J., & King, L. A. (2016). Meaning in life and intuition. *Journal of Personality and Social Psychology, 110*, 477–492.

Heintzelman, S. J., Trent, J., & King, L. A. (2013). Encounters with objective coherence and the experience of meaning in life. *Psychological Science, 24*, 991–998.

Heisel, M. J., & Flett, G. L. (2004). Purpose in life, satisfaction with life, and suicide ideation in a clinical sample. *Journal of Psychopathology and Behavioral Assessment, 26*, 127–135.

Hicks, J. A., Cicero, D. C., Trent, J., Burton, C. M., & King, L. A. (2010). Positive affect, intuition, and feelings of meaning. *Journal of Personality and Social Psychology, 98*, 967–979.

Hicks, J. A., & King, L. A. (2009). Positive mood and social relatedness as information about meaning in life. *The Journal of Positive Psychology, 4*, 471–482.

Hicks, J. A., Schlegel, R. J., & King, L. A. (2010). Social threats, happiness, and the dynamics of meaning in life judgments. *Personality and Social Psychology Bulletin, 36*, 1305–1317.

Hill, P. L., & Turiano, N. A. (2014). Purpose in life as a predictor of mortality across adulthood. *Psychological Science, 25*, 1482–1486.

Holahan, C. K., Holahan, C. J., Velasquez, K. E., Jung, S., North, R. J., & Pahl, S. A. (2011). Purposiveness and leisure-time physical activity in women in early midlife. *Women & Health, 51*, 661–675.

Holt-Lunstad, J., Steffen, P. R., Sandberg, J., & Jensen, B. (2011). Understanding the connection between spiritual well-being and physical health: An examination of ambulatory blood pressure, inflammation, blood lipids and fasting glucose. *Journal of Behavioral Medicine, 34*, 477–488.

Hooker, S. A., & Masters, K. S. (2016). Purpose in life is associated with physical activity measured by accelerometer. *Journal of Health Psychology, 21*, 962–971.

Kashdan, T. B., & Steger, M. F. (2007). Curiosity and pathways to well-being and meaning in life: Traits, states, and everyday behaviors. *Motivation and Emotion, 31*, 159–173.

Kay, A. C., Laurin, K., Fitzsimons, G. M., & Landau, M. J. (2014). A functional basis for structure-seeking: Exposure to structure promotes willingness to engage in motivated action. *Journal of Experimental Psychology: General, 143*, 486–491.

Kim, E. S., Hershner, S. D., & Strecher, V. J. (2015). Purpose in life and incidence of sleep disturbances. *Journal of Behavioral Medicine, 38,* 590–597.

Kim, E. S., Strecher, V. J., & Ryff, C. D. (2014). Purpose in life and use of preventive health care services. *Proceedings of the National Academy of Sciences, 111,* 16331–16336.

Kim, E. S., Sun, J. K., Park, N., Kubzansky, L. D., & Peterson, C. (2013). Purpose in life and reduced risk of myocardial infarction among older U.S. adults with coronary heart disease: A two-year follow-up. *Journal of Behavioral Medicine, 36,* 124–133.

King, L. A., & Geise, A. C. (2011). Being forgotten: Implications for the experience of meaning in life. *The Journal of Social Psychology, 151,* 696–709.

King, L. A., Hicks, J. A., Krull, J., & Del Gaiso, A. K. (2006). Positive affect and the experience of meaning in life. *Journal of Personality and Social Psychology, 90,* 179–196.

Klinger, E. (1977). *Meaning and void: Inner experience and the incentives in people's lives.* Minneapolis: University of Minnesota Press.

Koltko-Rivera, M. E. (2004). The psychology of worldviews. *Review of General Psychology, 8,* 3–58.

Krause, N. (2004). Stressors arising in highly valued roles, meaning in life, and the physical health status of older adults. *The Journals of Gerontology Series B: Psychological Sciences and Social Sciences, 59B,* S287–S291.

Krause, N. (2007). Longitudinal study of social support and meaning in life. *Psychology and Aging, 22,* 456–469.

Krause, N. (2009). Meaning in life and mortality. *The Journals of Gerontology Series B: Psychological Sciences and Social Sciences, 64B,* 517–527.

Lambert, N. M., Clark, M. S., Durtschi, J., Fincham, F. D., & Graham, S. M. (2010). Benefits of expressing gratitude: Expressing gratitude to a partner changes one's view of the relationship. *Psychological Science, 21,* 574–580.

Lambert, N. M., Stillman, T. F., Baumeister, R. F., Fincham, F. D., Hicks, J. A., & Graham, S. M. (2010). Family as a salient source of meaning in young adulthood. *The Journal of Positive Psychology, 5,* 367–376.

Lambert, N. M., Stillman, T. F., Hicks, J. A., Kamble, S., Baumeister, R. F., & Fincham, F. D. (2013). To belong is to matter sense of belonging enhances meaning in life. *Personality and Social Psychology Bulletin, 39,* 1418–1427.

Landau, M. J., Greenberg, J., Solomon, S., Pyszczynski, T., & Martens, A. (2006). Windows into nothingness: Terror management, meaninglessness, and negative reactions to modern art. *Journal of Personality and Social Psychology, 90,* 879–892.

Landau, M. J., Johns, M., Greenberg, J., Pyszczynski, T., Solomon, S., & Martens, A. (2004). A function of form: Terror management and structuring of the social world. *Journal of Personality and Social Psychology, 87,* 190–210.

Lyubomirsky, S., King, L., & Diener, E. (2005). The benefits of frequent positive affect: Does happiness lead to success? *Psychological Bulletin, 131,* 803–855.

Machell, K. A., Goodman, F. R., & Kashdan, T. B. (2015). Experiential avoidance and well-being: A daily diary analysis. *Cognition and Emotion, 29,* 351–359.

Machell, K. A., Kashdan, T. B., Short, J. L., & Nezlek, J. B. (2015). Relationships between meaning in life, social and achievement events, and positive and negative affect in daily life. *Journal of Personality, 83,* 287–298.

Martela, F., & Steger, M. F. (2016). The three meanings of meaning in life: Distinguishing coherence, purpose, and significance. *Journal of Positive Psychology, 11,* 531–545.

Martos, T., & Kopp, M. S. (2012). Life goals and well-being: Does financial status matter? Evidence from a representative Hungarian sample. *Social Indicators Research, 105,* 561–568.

Mascaro, N., & Rosen, D. H. (2005). Existential meaning's role in the enhancement of hope and prevention of depressive symptoms. *Journal of Personality, 73*, 985–1014.

Maslow, A. H. (1968). *Toward a psychology of being* (2nd ed.). New York, NY: John Wiley.

McGregor, I. (2006). Offensive defensiveness: Toward an integrative neuroscience of compensatory zeal after mortality salience, personal uncertainty, and other poignant self-threats. *Psychological Inquiry, 17*, 299–308.

McGregor, I., & Little, B. R. (1998). Personal projects, happiness, and meaning: On doing well and being yourself. *Journal of Personality and Social Psychology, 74*, 494–512.

McGregor, I., Prentice, M. S., & Nash, K. A. (2009). Personal uncertainty management by reactive approach motivation. *Psychological Inquiry, 20*, 225–229.

McGregor, I., Zanna, M. P., Holmes, J. G., & Spencer, S. J. (2001). Compensatory conviction in the face of personal uncertainty: Going to extremes and being oneself. *Journal of Personality and Social Psychology, 80*, 472–488.

McKnight, P. E., & Kashdan, T. B. (2009). Purpose in life as a system that creates and sustains health and well-being: An integrative, testable theory. *Review of General Psychology, 13*, 242–251.

Mikulincer, M., Florian, V., & Hirschberger, G. (2003). The existential function of close relationships: Introducing death into the science of love. *Personality and Social Psychology Review, 7*, 20–40.

Mikulincer, M., & Shaver, P. R. (2005). Mental representations of attachment security: Theoretical foundation for a positive social psychology. In M. W. Baldwin (Ed.), *Interpersonal cognition* (pp. 233–266). New York: Guilford Press.

Miller, J. G. (1999). Cultural psychology: Implications for basic psychological theory. *Psychological Science, 10*, 85–91.

Miller, M. E., & West, A. N. (1993). Influences of world view on personality, epistemology, and choice of profession. In J. Demick & P. M. Miller (Eds.), *Development in the workplace* (pp. 3–19). Hillsdale, NJ: Erlbaum.

Nelson, S. K., Kushlev, K., English, T., Dunn, E. W., & Lyubomirsky, S. (2013). In defense of parenthood: Children are associated with more joy than misery. *Psychological Science, 24*, 3–10.

Owens, G. P., Steger, M. F., Whitesell, A. A., & Herrera, C. J. (2009). Relationships among posttraumatic stress disorder, guilt, and meaning in life for military veterans. *Journal of Traumatic Stress, 22*, 654–657.

Proulx, T., & Heine, S. J. (2008). The case of the transmogrifying experimenter affirmation of a moral schema following implicit change detection. *Psychological Science, 19*, 1294–1300.

Proulx, T., & Heine, S. J. (2009). Connections from Kafka exposure to meaning threats improves implicit learning of an artificial grammar. *Psychological Science, 20*, 1125–1131.

Pyszczynski, T., Greenberg, J., Solomon, S., & Maxfield, M. (2006). On the unique psychological import of the human awareness of mortality: Theme and variations. *Psychological Inquiry, 17*, 328–356.

Reker, G. T., & Wong, P. T. P. (1988). Aging as an individual process: Toward a theory of personal meaning. In J. E. Birren & V. L. Bengtson (Eds.), *Emergent theories of aging* (pp. 214–246). New York: Springer Publishing Co.

Roepke, A. M., Jayawickreme, E., & Riffle, O. M. (2014). Meaning and health: A systematic review. *Applied Research in Quality of Life, 9*, 1055–1079.

Routledge, C., Arndt, J., Sedikides, C., & Wildschut, T. (2008). A blast from the past: The terror management function of nostalgia. *Journal of Experimental Social Psychology, 44*, 132–140.

Routledge, C., & Juhl, J. (2010). When death thoughts lead to death fears: Mortality salience increases death anxiety for individuals who lack meaning in life. *Cognition and Emotion, 24*, 848–854.

Ryff, C. D. (1995). Psychological well-being in adult life. *Current Directions in Psychological Science, 4*, 99–104.

Schlegel, R. J., & Hicks, J. A. (2017). Reflections on the scientific study of meaning in life. *Journal of Constructivist Psychology, 30*, 26–31.

Schwarz, N. (2012). Feelings-as-information theory. In P. A. M. Van Lange, A. W. Kruglanski, & E. T. Higgins (Eds.), *Handbook of theories in social psychology* (pp. 289–308). Thousand Oaks, CA: Sage.

Schwarz, N., & Clore, G. L. (1983). Mood, misattribution, and judgments of well-being: Informative and directive functions of affective states. *Journal of Personality and Social Psychology, 45*, 513–523.

Schwarz, N., & Clore, G. L. (1996). Feelings as phenomenal experiences. In E. T. Higgins & A. Kruglanski (Eds.), *Social psychology: Handbook of basic principles* (pp. 433–465). New York, NY: Guilford.

Shaver, P. R., & Mikulincer, M. (2012). An attachment perspective on coping with existential concerns. In P. R. Shaver & M. Mikulincer (Eds.), *Meaning, mortality, and choice: The social psychology of existential concerns* (pp. 291–307). Washington, DC: American Psychological Association.

Simon, L., Arndt, J., Greenberg, J., Pyszczynski, T., & Solomon, S. (1998). Terror management and meaning: Evidence that the opportunity to defend the worldview in response to mortality salience increases the meaningfulness of life in the mildly depressed. *Journal of Personality, 66*, 359–382.

Stavrova, O., & Luhmann, M. (2016). Social connectedness as a source and consequence of meaning in life. *The Journal of Positive Psychology, 11*, 470–479.

Steger, M. F., Frazier, P., Oishi, S., & Kaler, M. (2006). The meaning in life questionnaire: Assessing the presence of and search for meaning in life. *Journal of Counseling Psychology, 53*, 80–93.

Steger, M. F., & Kashdan, T. B. (2007). Stability and specificity of meaning in life and life satisfaction over one year. *Journal of Happiness Studies, 8*, 161–179.

Steger, M. F., & Kashdan, T. B. (2009). Depression and everyday social activity, intimacy, and well-being. *Journal of Counseling Psychology, 56*, 289–300.

Steger, M. F., Kashdan, T. B., Sullivan, B. A., & Lorentz, D. (2008). Understanding the search for meaning in life: Personality, cognitive style, and the dynamic between seeking and experiencing meaning. *Journal of Personality, 76*, 199–228.

Steger, M. F., Mann, J. R., Michels, P., & Cooper, T. C. (2009). Meaning in life, anxiety, depression, and general health among smoking cessation patients. *Journal of Psychosomatic Research, 67*, 353–358.

Stillman, T. F., Baumeister, R. F., Lambert, N. M., Crescioni, A. W., DeWall, C. N., & Fincham, F. D. (2009). Alone and without purpose: Life loses meaning following social exclusion. *Journal of Experimental Social Psychology, 45*, 686–694.

Stillman, T. F., Lambert, N. M., Fincham, F. D., & Baumeister, R. F. (2011). Meaning as magnetic force: Evidence that meaning in life promotes interpersonal appeal. *Social Psychological and Personality Science, 2*, 13–20.

Tellegen, A. (1982). Brief manual for the multidimensional personality questionnaire. Unpublished manuscript, University of Minnesota, Minneapolis.

Tritt, S. M., Inzlicht, M., & Harmon-Jones, E. (2012). Toward a biological understanding of mortality salience (and other threat compensation processes). *Social Cognition, 30*, 715–733.

Vallerand, R. J. (2008). On the psychology of passion: In search of what makes people's lives most worth living. *Canadian Psychology, 49*, 1–13.

Van Beest, I., & Williams, K. D. (2006). When inclusion costs and ostracism pays, ostracism still hurts. *Journal of Personality and Social Psychology, 91*, 918–928.

van den Bos, K., Poortvliet, P. M., Maas, M., Miedema, J., & van den Ham, E. (2005). An enquiry concerning the principles of cultural norms and values: The impact of uncertainty and mortality salience on reactions to violations and bolstering of cultural worldviews. *Journal of Experimental Social Psychology, 41*, 91–113.

Van Tongeren, D. R., Green, J. D., Davis, D. E., Hook, J. N., & Hulsey, T. L. (2016). Prosociality enhances meaning in life. *The Journal of Positive Psychology, 11*, 225–236.

Van Tongeren, D. R., Green, J. D., Hook, J. N., Davis, D. E., Davis, J. L., & Ramos, M. (2015). Forgiveness increases meaning in life. *Social Psychological and Personality Science, 6*, 47–55.

Vess, M., Rogers, R., Routledge, C., & Hicks, J. A. (2017). When being far away is good: Exploring how mortality salience, regulatory mode, and goal progress affect judgments of meaning in life. *European Journal of Social Psychology, 46*, 82–91.

Vess, M., Routledge, C., Landau, M. J., & Arndt, J. (2009). The dynamics of death and meaning: The effects of death-relevant cognitions and personal need for structure on perceptions of meaning in life. *Journal of Personality and Social Psychology, 97*, 728–744.

Williams, K. D. (2007). Ostracism. *Annual Review of Psychology, 58*, 425–452.

Williams, K. D. (2012). Ostracism: The impact of being rendered meaningless. In M. Mikulincer & P. R. Shaver (Eds.), *Meaning, mortality, and choice: The social psychology of existential concerns* (pp. 309–323). Washington, DC: American Psychological Association.

Wong, P. T. P. (1998). Implicit theories of meaningful life and the development of the personal meaning profile. In P. T. P. Wong & P. S. Fry (Eds.), *The human quest for meaning: A handbook of psychological research and clinical applications* (pp. 111–140). London: Erlbaum.

Zadro, L., Williams, K. D., & Richardson, R. (2004). How low can you go? Ostracism by a computer is sufficient to lower self-reported levels of belonging, control, self-esteem, and meaningful existence. *Journal of Experimental Social Psychology, 40*, 560–567.

15

THE IMPACT OF A MATERIALISTIC VALUE ORIENTATION ON WELL-BEING

Helga Dittmar and Megan Hurst

If we take a longer look at human well-being, rather than a snapshot, what is most striking is that mental health problems have steadily increased over the last 80 years. Cross-temporal meta-analyses of data from over 75,000 students in the United States collected since 1938 find large generational increases in depression and other forms of psychopathology, with five times as many now scoring above established cut-off points (Twenge et al., 2010). Of course, there are many reasons for this deterioration in mental health, also recorded in other economically developed countries, including the United Kingdom where depression and anxiety in adolescents have increased by 70% since the 1980s (Young Minds at www.youngminds.org.uk). The large-scale US analysis is compelling, not only because it spans such a long time, but also because it tested several factors that may be particularly significant causes of mental ill health. Periods of economic recession and boom were not found to be significant influences, nor changes in stigma attached to reporting, and seeking treatment for, mental health problems. The results best fit a model of cultural shifts towards extrinsic values, such as materialism and status, and away from intrinsic values such as community involvement, meaning in life, and close relationships. Alongside rising psychopathology, the percentage of young adults who reported wealth, expensive possessions, and status as essential long-term life goals increased dramatically, rising from below 30% to over 75%, while the importance of other goals dwindled away.

Taking a historical perspective, the core of Cushman's (1990) seminal analysis of the emergence of an "empty self" as a socio-cultural phenomenon in developed mass consumer societies is that

> the post-World War II empty self . . . is soothed and made cohesive by becoming "filled up" with food, consumer products, and celebrities. . . .

The two professions most responsible for healing the empty self, advertising and psychotherapy, find themselves in a bind: They must treat a psychological symptom without being able to address its historical causes. Both circumvent the bind by employing the life-style solution, a strategy that attempts to heal by covertly filling the empty self with the accoutrements, values, and mannerisms of idealized figures.

(p. 599)

This analysis foreshadows the development of a social psychological perspective on negative self-appraisal linked to a *materialistic value orientation* as a form of psychological imprisonment, a "cage within" where individuals attempt to construct an identity through material goods that ends up as a psychological state where the self is non-authentic:

The impact of the material "Good Life" and "Body Perfect" ideals on individuals' identity and well-being . . . is often negative. Thus, instead of supposedly empowering and liberating people through greater spending power, greater choice of consumer goods, and greater self-expression through consumption, consumer culture also means entrapment, and possibly entrapment of the worst kind, because people tend to be unaware of its pervasive influence . . . the pursuit of these ideals often means damage to their psychological, and even physical, health. In short, consumer culture can become a "cage within," its bars invisible and its power pernicious.

(Dittmar, 2007, p. 23)

In this chapter, our aims are threefold: First, to summarize the psychological frameworks that have theorized why and how a materialistic value orientation, or MVO for short, has an impact on well-being. Second, to review and synthesize the substantial body of research in psychology and closely related disciplines that provides a growing base of evidence for the impact of MVO on personal, social, consumer, and ecological well-being. And last, but not least, to reflect on a future research agenda that is conducive to providing an extended evidence case for improved understanding of how MVO affects adults as well as children, and for aiding in the development of psychological and policy interventions to curb MVO.

Materialistic Value Orientation (MVO)

A materialistic value orientation is a particular, precise, psychological construct and therefore *not* synonymous with materialism in a broader philosophical sense. Materialism refers to a set of complex, contested, and multi-faceted constructs that differ by discipline. For example, in philosophy and political science, we find debates on materialism versus idealism (Hegel, 1807; Marx, 1867), and in sociology and social theory, materialism has been discussed as the satisfaction of human material needs, such as food and shelter, as opposed to post-materialism referring to human needs for self-expression and a sense of belonging (Inglehart, 1990), similar to the hierarchy of needs proposed by Maslow (1943).

Instead, by MVO, we mean a person's "long-term endorsement of values, goals, and associated beliefs that center on the importance of acquiring money and possessions that convey status" (Dittmar, Bond, Hurst, & Kasser, 2014, p. 880). Central to MVO, then, is not only the striving for money and expensive goods, but also an associated set of beliefs about the psychological and social benefits these goals are expected to bring with them, such as image, recognition, status, and greater happiness. MVO can be measured by questionnaire scales that have well-documented face and construct validity as well as excellent psychometric properties. In consumer and marketing research, the scale best reflecting our definition and most widely used is the *Material Values Scale* (Richins & Dawson, 1992; Richins, 2004). In psychology, the *Aspirations Index* has been more prominent, where MVO is the relative importance of wealth, fame, and image as (extrinsic) life goals compared to other (intrinsic) life goals, such as community involvement, personal relationships, and self-development (Kasser & Ryan, 1993; www.selfdeterminationtheory.org). In the Children's Consumer Culture Project, with over 2,000 children in the UK (www.sussex.ac.uk/Psychology/consumercultureproject/), we developed a materialistic value internalization scale based on interviews with children (Wright, Hurst, Dittmar, & Banerjee, 2017) that is suitable for children as young as 8 years, as well as adolescents and adults (Easterbrook, Wright, Dittmar, & Banerjee, 2014).

MVO is one psychological orientation that people have towards money and material goods, but it is certainly not the only possible orientation. Material possessions can, and do, function as an extended part of a person's sense of self and positively help in identity construction and maintenance (Dittmar, 1992). People's accounts of the meanings and functions of treasured personal possessions clearly show how material objects can symbolize landmarks in their personal history (new career, travel mementos, certificates or trophies of achievement); can express and remind them of close personal relationships (photos, gifts, heirlooms); and can make them smile, lift their mood, and/or give reassurance when they look at them or touch them. Such personal possessions help them experience continuity, uniqueness, and connectedness in their sense of self-identity (Dittmar, 2011). Goffman's classic writings (1961, 1968) show how inmates in psychiatric or penal institutions experienced identity loss when stripped of all personal possessions and made to wear a uniform, a technique still used in Guantanamo Bay or Abu Ghraib prisons. Taking particularly important personal possessions with us through major life transitions, such as moving into a new home or emigrating to a different country, is helpful for maintaining a sense of who we are as well as for adjusting to our new circumstances. Compared to people who have to give up their personal possessions when moving into an old age care home, people who can take a selection of what they most treasure with them are happier, feel less helpless, and adapt better to this major life change (Wapner, Demick, & Redondo, 1990).

Thus, there are self-expressive, emotionally reassuring, and socially bonding ways of relating to personal possessions that have a positive impact on well-being. In contrast to MVO, these beneficial orientations often entail objects that have little material value.

Theoretical Explanations of the Link between MVO and Well-Being

MVO is a particular value or life goal that has to be understood in the context of *Value Theory* (Rokeach, 1973). The original definition of a value as "an enduring belief that a specific mode of conduct or end state of existence is personally or socially preferable to an opposite or converse mode of conduct or end state of existence" (p. 5) remains pertinent, and subsequent developments have shown convincingly that values worldwide can be summarized as arranged in a circumplex, with two main axes. Seminal work by Schwartz and colleagues identified ten value types, where values located next to each other on the circle are similar, whereas dissimilar values are located opposite (Schwartz, 1992). The two perpendicular axes represent value types that range from *Self-Enhancement* to *Self-Transcendence*, and from *Conservation* to *Openness to Experience*. Most similar to MVO are power, wealth, and achievement, which are self-enhancing values. These are the opposite of helpfulness, equality, and social justice, representing self-transcendent values. Later work using the life-goal measure described earlier, showed that the MVO values of money, fame, and image are extrinsic and opposite to community and affiliation values (Grouzet et al., 2005). What is important about placing MVO in the context of other values is, first, evidence showing that opposite values are linked in the sense that the more a person endorses one of them, the less the person endorses the opposite value (Maio, 2015) and that experimental priming of a value "crowds out" or reduces the opposite value (Maio, Pakizeh, Cheung, & Rees, 2009). Second, a large body of evidence supports the proposal that some values are good for well-being and some values are bad.

Much of that evidence arises from one of the most important theoretical frameworks for understanding the link of values or goals with psychological well-being: *Self-Determination Theory (SDT)*, developed by Ryan and Deci in the 1990s. This highly influential account, which was central to the development of the Positive Psychology movement, holds that there are three universal, basic human needs that need to be fulfilled for well-being to develop: *agency* (a sense of free will rather than coercion), *competence* (a sense of efficacy and mastery), and *relatedness* (a sense of close relationships with others). Self-transcendent, rather than self-enhancing, values and goals are conducive to fulfilling these needs, thus leading to higher well-being. It is assumed that self-enhancing values are linked with *extrinsic* motivation, which is characterized by a concern with sanctions from others (rewards or punishments) and a sense of having to fulfill standards that others have chosen or imposed. In contrast, *intrinsic* motivation refers to being guided by standards that people have freely chosen for themselves (Ryan & Deci, 2000). MVO involves both self-enhancing goals and extrinsic motivation, and thus is likely to be doubly detrimental to the fulfillment of basic psychological needs.

Work on MVO within a self-determination framework has flourished since the early 1990, starting with a seminal paper on the "dark side of the American dream", showing that strong MVO is linked to less vitality, lower psychological functioning, and stronger symptoms of anxiety (Kasser & Ryan, 1993). Furthermore, MVO is stronger when people grow up in environments that lack nurturance, such as "broken" family homes (Rindfleisch, Burroughs, & Denton, 1997) or, more generally, socio-economic or non-loving familial backgrounds that are less supportive of children's growth, self-expression, and intrinsic needs (Kasser, Ryan, Zax, & Sameroff, 1995). Kasser has developed this work into a framework that sees *psychological insecurity* as a major mechanism that leads individuals to adopt MVO as a coping strategy—one that is culturally sanctioned, but maladaptive (Kasser, 2002, 2016). In a similar vein, a recent systematic review conceptualized buying goods to blunt negative feelings as a materialistic escape from the self (Donnelly, Ksendzova, Howell, Vohs, & Baumeister, 2016). Several experimental studies show that inducing people to feel psychologically insecure leads directly and immediately to a stronger endorsement of MVO and related consumer behaviors (Arndt, Solomon, Kasser, & Sheldon, 2004; Kasser & Sheldon, 2000; Sheldon & Kasser, 2008). Kasser argues that MVO is aligned with the values and profit motive central to free market, capitalist economic systems (Kasser, Cohn, Kanner, & Ryan, 2007). This argument is supported by research showing that culture-level indices of threat, instability, and advertising spend between 1976 and 2007 were linked with changes in MVO in a large sample of over 350,000 US adolescents (Twenge & Kasser, 2013). Societal instability and disconnection (unemployment, divorce) and spending on advertising, which profiles materialistic concerns, had associations with higher levels of MVO, both contemporaneously and over time. The importance of money and of owning expensive material goods increased, peaking in the late 1980s to early 1990s with Generation X (born between the early 1960s and late 1970s) and then staying at high levels for Millennials (born between the early 1980s and late 1990s).

MVO is strongly profiled in the culture of mass consumer societies, particularly in fashion and in advertising. An excellent example is an advert by a UK retail chain screened around Christmas 2011, where rapping kids show each other that they need expensive branded consumer goods to be cool and liked by their peers and tell their parents that they need to buy these goods if they want to be a "lovely, lovely mother"; loan facilities are offered at the same time (www.youtube.com/watch?v=qGIN_SbjtYA). This advert resulted in a large number of complaints to the UK's Advertising Standards Authority (Sweney, 2011), but its contents were not judged to breach any advertising code.

The link between national advertising spending and the strength of cultural-level materialistic values (Kasser, 2011) supports the proposal that advertising is a potent source of materialistic images and messages that become internalized through frequently being exposed to them. At the level of individual socialization, greater media exposure in children is linked to stronger MVO (Opree, Buijzen, & Valkenburg, 2012). Similarly, Dittmar (2018) argues that the consumer culture ideal of materialistic striving has a powerful psychological impact in mass consumer societies. Celebrities, fashion models, media stars, even computer game heroes and toys, influence who young people aspire to be. Having the "right" branded and expensive, consumer goods and an affluent lifestyle has become vital, not so much because of these material goods themselves, but because of hoped-for psychological and social benefits: greater popularity, a more positive sense of identity, social status, and greater happiness. The prominence accorded to the material "good life" as a goal we should strive for is central to MVO, as is the belief that an affluent lifestyle has a transformative power, offering a golden bridge to better self-identity, social status, and greater well-being.

The *Consumer Culture Value Impact Model* (Dittmar, Banerjee, Easterbrook, Hurst, & Wright, 2017, see Figure 15.1) conceptualizes MVO as consisting of materialistic motives and materialistic value internalization (Banerjee & Dittmar, 2008). An example of a materialistic motive is the belief that having money and expensive possessions is important *"because others like you more"*. *"I wish I was rich like the celebrities on TV"* is an example of a materialistic value item that has been internalized as a personal long-term goal (Easterbrook et al., 2014).

MVO leads us to be particularly attentive to materialistic ideals in the media, and when we compare ourselves to unrealistic standards of affluence and owning expensive consumer goods, we typically experience a discrepancy between who we would like to be—a person like the materialistic model we are confronted with—and who we actually are. Such *self-discrepancies* are harmful self-appraisals linked to negative emotions, such as dejection, gloom, and depression (Higgins, 1987; Dittmar, 2007, 2008, 2011). Such self-discrepancy states—a combination of negative self-appraisal and negative emotions—are psychologically painful, and we are motivated to escape them. Here the prominent consumer culture message of *retail therapy* offers a culturally sanctioned coping strategy: It advocates that the

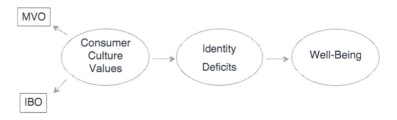

FIGURE 15.1 The Consumer Culture Value Impact Model of a Materialistic Value (MVO) and an Ideal Body Orientation[1] (IBO) as Predictors of Identity Deficits and Well-Being

consumption of desirable goods, and the activity of shopping itself, are effective strategies for alleviating such negative self states. Yet, the behaviors that result may be the exact opposite: Overspending and excessive buying of goods are behavioral manifestations of maladaptive coping strategies that may lead to a brief "high" but are harmful in the longer term to people's personal well-being, leading to negative emotions, negative self-appraisal, and mental health problems. They are also detrimental to ecological well-being because they lead to high rates of consuming and waste. The frameworks discussed so far clearly predict that MVO is toxic for well-being.

Some perspectives, however, propose that MVO can, or should, have positive effects on well-being, at least in certain contexts. From a free market economic perspective, MVO is viewed as a motivational driver for individual effort and achievement, as well as a motor for economic growth, and is thus beneficial for both individuals and countries:

> Our enormously productive economy demands that we make consumption our way of life, that we convert the buying and use of goods into rituals, that we seek our spiritual satisfaction and our ego satisfaction in consumption. We need things consumed, burned up, worn out, replaced and discarded at an ever-increasing rate.
>
> *(Lebow, 1955)*

The wealth of both nations and individuals may be a major moderating influence, but in opposite directions. On the one hand, MVO may be good (or at least not bad) for the wealthy because they have better opportunities to fulfill their materialistic desires than do the poor. On the other hand, MVO may have beneficial effects for the poor because it encourages them to strive more for fulfillment of their basic material needs (see Dittmar et al., 2014, for more detail). The *person-environment congruence hypothesis* states that people derive positive well-being from their values if they are in an environment that explicitly supports those values, which implies that MVO would be good for individuals who work or study in MVO-supportive environments, such as business, marketing, or economics, or who live in societies that are particularly high in MVO as a cultural value (Kasser & Ahuvia, 2002; Sagiv & Schwartz, 2000).

Research on the Link Between MVO and Well-Being

In addition to the diverse sets of single studies that show negative correlates of MVO, meta-analyses provide powerful evidence for the link between MVO and well-being because they assess and evaluate the strength of this link by (1) synthesizing across all available research studies that contain relevant measures, (2) testing whether the strength of the link is influenced by various factors (moderators), and (3) testing mechanisms that have been proposed to explain the link (mediators).

MVO and Personal Well-Being

A wide-ranging meta-analysis focused on the link between MVO and personal well-being examined four different dimensions of well-being (Dittmar et al., 2014): subjective well-being, self-appraisals, psychiatric symptoms and compulsive buying, and physical health. Subjective well-being (SWB) is a person's evaluation of his or her quality of life over time, as well as his or her experience of positive rather than negative emotions. High SWB indicates that one is satisfied with one's life and feels happy more frequently than unhappy (Diener, Suh, Lucas, & Smith, 1999; see also Chapter 1). Self-appraisals are people's evaluations of themselves, which can be positive, such as self-esteem, or negative, such as self-doubt. Symptoms of depression and anxiety, as well as compulsive buying, are indicators of mood-related mental health problems as found in the *Diagnostic and Statistical Manual of Mental Disorders* of the American Psychiatric Association (DSM-IV-TR, 2000). The final category of well-being was physical health: somatic symptoms of ill health and risk behaviors, such as alcohol or drug addiction.

Synthesizing findings from over 250 studies, the core finding of the meta-analysis was a robust and significant link between higher MVO and lower personal well-being.

As shown in Figure 15.2, the strength of this link differs depending on the particular dimension of personal well-being examined, but the most striking finding is that *all* effect sizes are negative and statistically reliable. The valence of negative well-being dimensions was reversed, such that the negative sign of the effect means a worse well-being outcome, for instance, that higher MVO is linked to

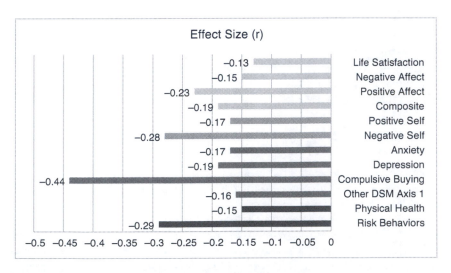

FIGURE 15.2 Effect Sizes of the Link Between MVO and Dimensions of Personal Well-Being

more negative affect. The effect sizes range from .13 for life satisfaction, a small effect, to .44 for compulsive buying, which indicates a large effect.

This core finding documents the weight of the evidence in this entire field of research. However, a meta-analysis can also address further research questions. The meta-analysis examined a range of factors that may influence the strength of the link (moderators) and concluded that the core finding is robust. Most factors tested were not a significant influence on the strength of the link between MVO and personal well-being, often challenging predictions made in the literature, including those made about cultural values, economic systems, and national or individual wealth. In the few instances where the strength of the link differed significantly by moderator, only the size of the link varied, not the direction: Higher levels of MVO were always linked to *lower* well-being. For example, consistent with the person-environment congruence hypothesis, the larger the proportion of the sample studying or working in an environment likely to support MVO (e.g., business students, marketing managers), the weaker the link between individuals' MVO and lower personal well-being, with $r = -.19$ if none of the sample worked in such an environment and $r = -.12$ if the whole sample did. One cultural value moderated the effect, affective autonomy, such that correlations were stronger in nations high on the pursuit of pleasure and an exciting life (e.g., Denmark, $r = -.21$) than in countries which score low on affective autonomy (e.g., Egypt, $r = -.09$). Income and socio-economic status (SES) did not emerge as a significant moderator of the link between MVO and personal well-being. However, few studies reported income or SES data, limiting the robustness of this finding.

Finally, the meta-analysis examined underlying processes proposed to explain this negative link (see section above on theoretical explanations), even though the number of studies in the meta-regression was relatively small. Higher MVO was linked to lower satisfaction of basic needs that, in turn, was linked to lower personal well-being, supporting *SDT*. In addition, MVO was linked to stronger extrinsic motives, which are linked to lower well-being. This finding is consistent with the three theoretical perspectives on MVO discussed earlier.

This meta-analysis also revealed a number of research gaps, including few studies with longitudinal and experimental designs, and few studies involving children. To address the dearth of research linking MVO with young children's well-being, the Children's Consumer Culture Project, which included over 2,000 children in the UK, examined a number of dimensions of well-being: symptoms of depression, subjective well-being, and symptoms of physical ill health. Among a sample of over 500 7- to 11-year-olds, greater endorsement of materialistic motives and materialistic values were significant predictors of lower well-being (Dittmar et al., 2017). The strength of the link was slightly lower than that reported as the average in the meta-analysis with predominantly adult samples but is still statistically reliable already in such young children.

Relationships between MVO and well-being were modeled over three time points. Children's initial well-being and endorsement of MVO were modeled as predictors of each other 8 months later; well-being and MVO from this time point were then modeled to predict one another after a further 8 months (16 months after the start of the project). The resulting model shows a pattern whereby (1) initial MVO significantly predicts lower well-being 8 months later and (2) lower well-being at time 2 is linked significantly with a stronger endorsement of MVO 8 months later. These results suggest a vicious cycle whereby MVO initiates a deterioration of well-being during the following 8 months that, in turn, then leads children to an increased adoption of MVO as a personal goal. These findings are consistent with all three theoretical perspectives outlined in the "Theoretical Explanations" section earlier and support the causal emphasis in the Consumer Culture Value Impact Model and Self-Determination Theory by suggesting that the endorsement of MVO may well be the causal starting point for negative changes in young children's well-being.

Good examples of some of the longitudinal research with adolescents and adults, are several studies reported in a single article (Kasser et al., 2014) that show that adolescents with higher MVO suffered impaired social and psychological functioning 20 years later and that well-being in Iceland, after its economic crash in 2008, increased over time when MVO decreased. This work can go some, but not all, the way towards addressing the question of antecedence, which is a necessary pre-condition for causality.

To address the question of causal direction directly, we need experimental studies. An intervention with groups of adolescents in the US and their parents showed that focusing on less materialistic orientations towards money and material goods, such as saving, led to a reduction in MVO among the adolescents who were initially high in MVO (Study 4 in Kasser et al., 2014). For adults, the sparse experimental evidence supports a bi-directional relationship. Priming MVO led to an immediate reduction in well-being (Bauer, Wilkie, Kim, & Bodenhausen, 2012), and experimental manipulations of psychological insecurity showed that such insecurity leads to an increased endorsement of MVO and related behaviors, such as higher consumption (Sheldon & Kasser, 2008).

MVO and Social Well-Being

A search for personal characteristics likely to impact social well-being that are associated with MVO yields a long list of problematic personality traits, relationship difficulties, anti-social attitudes, and socially harmful behaviors. MVO is higher in people who suffer from psychopathy, Machiavellian, and narcissistic personality disorders (Pilch & Durnik-Durose, 2016), all known to be linked with anti-social or aggressive behaviors. Individuals high in MVO report less satisfaction with their close relationships (Carroll, Dean, Call, & Busby, 2011); hold stronger prejudices against a range of ethnic and racial groups (Duriez, Vansteenkiste, Soenens, & De Witte, 2007); are less likely to be involved in community or charitable activities

(Roberts & Roberts, 2012); and engage more frequently in unethical business behaviors and work practices (Lu & Lu, 2010).

One of the most striking features of contemporary consumer culture is that messages about what is "cool" are deliberately targeted at young children, thus making materialistic norms a significant focus of their socialization experience. Yet, MVO in children younger than 10 years had hardly been explored before the Children's Consumer Culture Project, which examined children age 7 to 14 years, even though parental worry about kids being damaged by materialism is not new (BBC News, 2008). This dearth of research is even more surprising given the fact that they are at a developmental stage where concerns with peer relations are strong and owning "cool things" comes to play a core role in social comparisons, self-presentation, and peer-group acceptance. Norms within their peer culture are very important to children in primary school, aged 7–11 years, a time when peer-group acceptance becomes a dominant social goal (Parker & Gottman, 1989). Material goods and the beliefs associated with them have increasingly become a focus of peer-group interests and activities, as preadolescent children are a market segment that is heavily targeted by advertisers for a range of consumer goods—clothes, accessories, shoes, toys, mobile phones, and electronic items. As a consequence, children see materialistic norms as relevant to peer-group acceptance, and children feel pressured to fit in by adopting this material peer culture.

The first research linking MVO to young children's peer relations developed a new measure of perceived peer culture pressures in 7–11-year-olds and found that material characteristics form an integral part of peer culture, such as feeling under pressure to dress in certain clothes, look older, and like certain types of food or music (Banerjee & Dittmar, 2008). It proposed that beliefs and cultural messages associated with "cool stuff" would generate particular social and extrinsic motives in children, such as wanting fashionable goods because "children like you more if you have 'cool' things". Furthermore, it was expected that children who have troubled relationships with their peers would be most likely to feel under pressure to conform to the surrounding peer material culture and would endorse extrinsic social motives for wanting "cool" things, which, in turn, would predict the extent to which they internalize MVO. The key findings from two surveys support these proposed links: Children rejected by their peers (i.e., most nominated by their classmates as somebody they would "least like to play with") reported stronger perceptions of peer culture pressure, which were associated with stronger extrinsic social motives for wanting "cool" things. These materialistic motives were closely linked with MVO.

The Children's Consumer Culture Project subsequently examined what characteristics of a child predict peer acceptance over time (Banerjee, Dittmar, Easterbrook, Hurst, & Wright, 2017). Sociometric data from children offer an objective (as opposed to self-reported) assessment of peer relations. To measure differences among children in the extent to which they are liked by their peers, sociometric procedures typically require all children in a class to nominate three peers with whom they "most like to play" and "least like to play" (Coie, Dodge, & Coppotelli, 1982). Rejected children are those who receive few "most like to play" nominations and many "least like to play" nominations. The project assessed additional characteristics of children, using an adapted sociometric method. First, children were asked to nominate three peers in their class who are most "cooperative" and most "disruptive", because these characteristics have been identified as strong predictors of peer liking (Mostow, Izard, Fine, & Trentacosta, 2002). Second, it assessed characteristics specific to consumer culture by asking children to nominate three peers who have the most "cool stuff" and the best "good looks". Finally, we asked children to nominate three classmates who are seen as most "popular" in the class.

The existing research illuminates the important distinction between levels of acceptance based on *actual liking* by group members and levels of *perceived popularity* (Parkhurst & Hopmeyer, 1998; La Fontana & Cillessen, 1999). Although these appear similar (popularity after all should mean being well liked), research indicates substantial divergence: Those who are perceived to be popular often exhibit a behavioral profile of social dominance that contrasts with the more affiliative, prosocial, and cooperative behavior of those who are actually well liked (La Fontana & Cillessen, 2002; Lease, Musgrove, & Axelrod, 2002).

We hypothesized that "cool stuff" and "good looks" would be associated with the perception of social status—perceived popularity—more than with actual liking. Modeling of sociometric and self-report data from over 2,000 children over 3 school years revealed cross-lagged associations that show that cooperative behavior was a positive predictor of subsequent liking by peers, whereas a reputation for having the most stuff and looking good—along with disruptive behavior—predicted gains in being perceived as popular. Thus, in contrast to children's strong beliefs that "children like you more when you have 'cool' things", the MVO-related characteristics of having the most stuff and looking good were *unrelated* to actual peer acceptance. Moreover, we found that early peer rejection predicted an increase over time in extrinsic (social status) motivations for pursuing consumer culture ideals. This, in turn, predicted worsening, rather than improving, peer relations. Our results highlight the misconceived and potentially damaging assumption that pursuing consumer culture ideals such as MVO would lead to social "success". Instead, they suggest a vicious cycle in which peer rejection is linked with counterproductive motivations to increase social peer status though MVO. It also demonstrates that the images of social success heavily promoted by consumer culture are social representations of popularity, but do not lead to actual peer acceptance, and maybe have damaging effects on the motivational orientation of children who are experiencing difficulties in their peer relations.

MVO and Consumer Well-Being

Overspending and excessive buying of goods are often maladaptive coping strategies that may lead to a brief "high" but are harmful in the longer term. MVO has been identified as a significant predictor of consumer debt (Watson, 2003; Garðarsdottir & Dittmar, 2012).

Excessive buying of consumer goods central to *compulsive buying* is included in the current *Diagnostic and Statistical Manual* (DSM-V; APA, 2013) under the category of "behavioral addictions", that is, addictions where no substance is consumed (such as drugs or alcohol). Although there is not yet a consensus on the precise definition of compulsive buying, there is agreement on three characteristics: preoccupation with shopping and buying, irresistible impulses to buy as soon as a person sees consumer goods, and continuing with buying despite harmful consequences. A possible fourth characteristic is a search for a better self-identity (see Dittmar, 2004, 2008; Dittmar & Bond, 2010).

Questionnaire surveys on buying in shops and buying online (Dittmar, 2005a, 2005b; Dittmar, Long, & Bond, 2007) and interviews with self-diagnosed compulsive buyers (Dittmar, 2004, Dittmar & Drury, 2000) have revealed that higher MVO is linked to stronger tendencies towards attitudes and behaviors characteristic of compulsive buying. Such compulsive buying tendencies are a gradated continuum with compulsive buying at a clinical level at the extreme upper end. MVO is linked compulsive buying tendencies through motivations for buying that are focused on repairing and improving self-identity, mood, and emotions. There is also substantive evidence that compulsive buying is associated with lower personal well-being; higher mental health problems; such as depression and anxiety, and co-morbidity with impulsive-compulsive psychiatric disorders (Black, 2006; Dittmar, 2004; Maraz, Griffiths, & Demetrovics, 2016). There is also evidence that compulsive buying tendencies are increasing in developed mass consumer societies (Neuner, Raab, & Reisch, 2005), which is reflected in age cohort prevalence figures: Younger consumers report stronger compulsive buying tendencies than older consumers. These tendencies were shown to be due to stronger MVO in a UK study comparing samples of younger and older consumers (Dittmar, 2005b). In the meta-analysis reported earlier, the link between MVO and compulsive buying was the strongest effect found.

We also carried out an experimental study to examine whether exposure to a materialistic role model would have direct and immediate effects on children's behavior (Dittmar, Banerjee et al., 2017). Using a procedure similar to that used in an experiment on children's learning (Ku, Dittmar, & Banerjee, 2014), we showed 8–10-year-olds a "video diary" of a same-sex child talking excitedly about Christmas. In the *extrinsic materialistic prime*, the child in the video talked about getting lots of expensive presents, which would make other children envious, although they would still want to play with the owner of those presents. In the *intrinsic prime*, the child talked about having lots of quality time with friends and family, where they would have fun and enjoy each other's company. A neutral video in which children watched abstract moving shapes (control condition) primed no values at all. As a measure of rudimentary consumer behavior, we gave children photocopied money notes totaling £100 and asked them to distribute this windfall money between three different activities: spending on self, spending on others, and saving. Then, we asked them whether they would like to borrow further money, making it clear that, this time, this would be money that they would need to pay back. Children's borrowing decisions in this task can be seen as a rudimentary consumer behavior that indicates spending money that one does not have—that is, going into debt.

The type of video the children saw had a direct impact on their materialistic motives, which were highest after the extrinsic materialistic video and lowest after the intrinsic video emphasizing close relationships with friends and family; means after the neutral video were in between. Crucially, the type of video also had a strong effect on how much money the children wanted to borrow. In the neutral video condition, the average amount of money children wanted to borrow just over £8, and just below £8 in the intrinsic value condition. In contrast, children wanted to borrow over £17 after having been exposed to materialistic modeling by a peer. Such materialistic peer modeling mirrors closely the advertising typically aimed at children of this age group.

MVO and Environmental Well-Being

MVO appears to be detrimental, not only to individual and interpersonal well-being, but to environmental well-being as well. Many studies have linked the pursuit of economic growth to the erosion of the natural environment, at a global level (e.g., Jackson, 2009): Internationally, the pursuit of economic growth is argued to take a toll on the environment. At a country level, these suggestions appear to hold true: The more citizens of a country endorse MVO, or closely related values from Schwartz's circumplex, such as power and hierarchy, the higher the level of that country's carbon dioxide emissions (Kasser, 2011).

At the level of the individual, considerable cross-sectional research links greater endorsement of MVO to lower environmental concern and more damaging environmental behavior. A comprehensive review of the literature and meta-analysis of 13 independent samples showed that MVO was associated significantly with both lower pro-environmental attitudes ($\bar{p} = -.28$) and environmental behaviors ($\bar{p} = -.32$), representing medium effect sizes (Hurst, Dittmar, Bond, & Kasser, 2013). These links were not moderated by age or gender. However, a number of questions remain that this research cannot answer, which are explored below.

Why Are MVO and the Environment Linked?

One possible explanation for the link between MVO and environmental attitudes and behaviors draws on theoretical work described earlier, relating to value conflict or value opposition. Materialistic values tend to be closely associated with self-enhancement values and are thus inconsistent with self-transcendence values, which focus on benevolence and universalism. Universalism is particularly relevant for environmental concerns as it implies a consideration and value for both protecting the natural environment, as well as equality and fairness among humans (Schwartz, 2012). However, materialistic values' negative association with further other-oriented values, such as benevolence, may also lead to detrimental environmental behaviors. Indeed, some have conceptualized environmental crises as social dilemmas (Hardin, 1968), and research from this perspective provides further support that prosocial behaviors (e.g., those intended to benefit others) and pro-environmental behavior and attitudes are linked (e.g., Kaiser & Byrka, 2011; Van Lange, 1999). If materialistic values suppress prosocial values, they are likely to also suppress pro-environmental values. However, beyond this shared explanation with influences on personal well-being, there are also a number of explanations for the association between a materialistic value orientation and environmental attitudes and behaviors which are specific to these outcomes.

Materialistic values may also be associated with particular worldviews that are detrimental to the environment. Kasser (2002; Khanna & Kasser, 2001) provides evidence that materialists are more likely to objectify other human beings, viewing them as a means to an end, and this appears to extend to the natural world. Individuals who more strongly believe that money is important in their lives have more instrumental views of nature and are more likely to believe that nature exists to be exploited by humanity (Hedlund-de Witt, de Boer, & Boersema, 2014). These anthropocentric views of the environment are typically associated with less environmentally friendly attitudes and behaviors, such as higher emission transport choices and lower levels of recycling (e.g., De Groot & Steg, 2007). Thus, to the extent that MVO promotes this anthropocentric orientation towards the environment, it may also promote other negative environmental attitudes and behaviors.

The two processes above, of value conflict and anthropocentric worldviews, focus primarily on MVO as an indirect influence on environmentalism: MVO is related to environmental behavior via environmental attitudes. However, Brown and Kasser (2005) suggest that MVO has a more direct influence on environmental behavior via its influence on consumer behavior. People higher in MVO are more concerned with material possessions and demonstrating status via these, suggesting that they are likely to consume more, and thus have larger ecological footprints, by using more resources and generating more waste. The findings of the Hurst et al. (2013) meta-analysis provide tentative support for this suggestion: The correlations between MVO and environmental behaviors and attitudes were similar in size, suggesting there are influences of MVO on environmental behaviors which are *not* dependent on its association with attitudes. Future research could consider this link with environmental behavior more specifically by focusing on particular behaviors. Brown and Kasser (2005) suggest that people high in MVO are directly harmful to the environment because they consume more luxury goods, drive more "impressive" but fuel-intense cars, and purchase larger homes. However, a recent analysis of Swedish participants' actual emissions (estimated from objective sources, e.g., energy bills) suggests that this is not the case (Andersson & Nässén,

2016). More materialistic participants *were* responsible for greater greenhouse gas emissions, but this was due primarily to their greater use of air travel. Understanding the particular behaviors people higher in MVO are more likely to engage in may help in designing interventions to combat MVO's negative effects.

A final possibility is that those who are higher in MVO live more in the present: They seem to value the future less than those who are not so driven by money and status. Environmental behavior is, to an extent, an issue of time perspectives: Environmentally damaging behaviors (such as air travel or the consumption of luxury goods) offer immediate rewards in the present, whereas their environmental impact is only visible at a later time. Interestingly, research suggests participants do not sufficiently consider the temporal elements of environmental dilemmas (Messick & McClelland, 1983). Thus, if higher MVO makes individuals focus more on the present, and less likely to adopt a future time perspective in general, then they may be even less likely to engage in pro-environmental behaviors. There is some tentative evidence that those higher in MVO focus even more on the present at the expense of the future than those low in MVO: In a hypothetical consumer situation, where participants gained goods of higher value if they waited longer before receiving them, participants who were higher in MVO required considerably higher values of goods later to consider the delay worthwhile (Dittmar & Bond, 2010). Time perspectives (present and future) also appear to play a critical role in determining MVO's effects on problematic spending behaviors, where a focus on future time perspectives mitigates some of the negative effects of MVO on problematic spending behaviors (Ku, Wu, Lao, & Lam, 2016). Thus the link between MVO and time perspectives may be worth investigating further because it may be a potential intervention target for reducing MVO's impact on the environment.

Clearly there are many ways that MVO may be associated with pro-environmental behaviors and attitudes. These processes are not mutually exclusive; indeed, a number of these processes may be acting simultaneously, and future research should explore how they are interlinked.

Cause or Effect?

A second question that the cross-sectional literature cannot address concerns the direction of the link between MVO and environmental outcomes, including whether this link is causal. However, longitudinal research can examine this question, by assessing whether MVO predicts decreases in pro-environmental behavior over time, or vice versa. In a 2-year longitudinal study with participants in the UK and Chile, Unanue, Vignoles, Dittmar, & Vansteenkiste (2016) found a significant effect of MVO on environmental behavior over time: The more materialistic participants were, the more environmentally damaging their behavior was at the next follow-up, even when controlling for their initial levels of environmental behavior.

Additional support for a causal influence of MVO on environmentalism can be found in the gradually expanding number of experimental studies. Participants primed with intrinsic values recommended smaller ecological footprints for policy targets (specifically the use of public transport, reduced air travel, and reduced home size) and donated more imaginary earnings from an experimental game to an environmental fund or cause (Ku & Zaroff, 2014; Sheldon, Nichols, & Kasser, 2011). In other research, participants who were exposed to images of natural environments and imagined the experience of being in these reported higher levels of intrinsic (and lower levels of extrinsic) values, compared with participants who were exposed to industrial and urban images (Weinstein, Przybylski, & Ryan, 2009). This suggests that the causal influences may run in both directions, rather than simply one. Future research should seek to extend these findings beyond single experimental manipulations and develop interventions based around their principles to further confirm the causal directions suggested here. Such interventions could examine the principles of value priming on a longer-term basis than an individual experiment but could also investigate the effect on values of engagement with nature in a real-world context.

Within- and Between-Country Sampling

The majority of the research relating MVO and environmental attitudes and behaviors comes from samples that are restricted in two key ways. First, there is relatively little variation in the socio-economic status of the samples within countries. For this reason, we can only say that MVO is negatively associated with environmental attitudes and behaviors among relatively affluent, well-educated people. Second, the majority of the samples in the Hurst et al. (2013) meta-analysis come from developed Western countries, and research in other countries has produced mixed findings. Some research suggests that the same negative associations emerge in correlational and longitudinal studies in non-Western and less developed countries (Hong Kong, Ku & Zaroff, 2014; Chile, Unanue et al., 2016), whereas other research suggests that MVO may be less strongly associated with negative environmental attitudes and behaviors outside of developed Western countries (e.g., in developing economies like China; Gatersleben, Jackson, Meadows, Soto, & Yan, 2012) or that its effects may be moderated by factors relating to globalization (e.g., the extent to which individuals see themselves as a citizen of the world; Strizhakova & Coulter, 2013). Andersson and Nässén (2016) argue that materialistic values may be expressed differently in different cultures and will therefore be associated with different behaviors and attitudes across these cultures. Examining these cross-cultural differences in expression may be a fruitful line of research.

What Can We Do to Understand MVO Better and Reduce It?

The limitations of studies on the link between MVO and well-being identified in this chapter set a future research agenda. There is need for integrated longitudinal and experimental research to offer a more detailed understanding of the causal direction between MVO and lower well-being and to investigate in greater depth the underlying processes that mediate the links. Progress may come through the systematic use of multi-method approaches, possibly supported by field experiments and observational studies. This could be further supported through the use of non-reactive measures, such as experience sampling and actual behaviors, in addition to self-report scales and quasi-behavioral measures that tend to focus on hypothetical scenarios. In addition, research could investigate promising strategies for changing values and behaviors.

Because of the power of consumer goods advertising, reducing MVO is like David fighting Goliath. We should not, however, underestimate the power of well-constructed interventions based on sound psychological theory and research. Strategies for change can range from encouraging individual's critical reflection on the contents and aims of media representation of the "good life" and MVO as a value, to group-based interventions, and to local and national advertising policy. We need developments on all of these fronts. Policy change is typically the hardest to achieve, but lasting change is most likely when individual critical thinking extends to change in shared values as general guiding principles for our lives and our behavior and when, in turn, those changes are embedded in, and supported by, a wider context of policy change. Of course, policy change may also lead to changes in social values, so that there is a bi-directional interaction between change at an individual and at a social level.

Critical Reflection on Materialistic Media Contents

Effective treatment of adults suffering from compulsive buying typically includes examining, and critically reflecting on, materialistic modeling and messages in advertising (Benson, 2008; www.stoppingovershopping.com). Advertising messages suggest strongly that buying and consuming material goods is a good strategy for achieving social and personal goals, as well as a successful coping strategy for feeling low and dissatisfied with ourselves (Dittmar, 2008). Coming to understand that these messages are not only untrue, but potentially damaging is effective in helping people resist their excessive buying habits (Benson, 2008, personal communication). Although there do not (yet) seem to be such critical thinking interventions designed specifically to reduce MVO, a large number of such interventions have attempted to reduce the impact of consumer culture ideals closely linked to MVO. These are appearance-focused ideals, such as a thin body for women and a muscular body for men, which lead to higher body dissatisfaction, a potent predictor of unhealthy body-related behaviors, such as disordered eating or taking muscle-enhancing substances (Cafri et al., 2005; Stice, 2002). One example is exposure to the Dove *Evolution* video (www.youtube.com/watch?v=iYhCn0jf46U), which shows the techniques used to create images of idealized women models, as an intervention to protect girls against the negative impact of body perfect models on their body image (Halliwell & Diedrichs, 2014). Other interventions have been developed with the aim to reduce the internalization of body perfect ideals of extreme thinness for girls and women (see meta-analysis by Stice, 2002), a strong predictor of body dissatisfaction (Halliwell & Dittmar, 2004; Hurst, Dittmar, Halliwell, & Diedrichs, 2016).

Interventions to Change Values and Behaviors

In contrast to the lack of MVO-focused critical awareness interventions, there are some studies that have focused on altering materialistic values and related behaviors. Experimental studies that prime intrinsic values (over extrinsic values such as MVO) report increased pro-environmental attitudes or behaviors (e.g., Ku & Zaroff, 2014; Sheldon et al., 2011). However, these have been short term, have been examined primarily in laboratory settings, and have measured imagined outcomes or "recommendations" rather than real behaviors. Interventions have been developed to reduce materialism in other contexts, such as addressing adolescents' spending behavior and personal well-being (e.g., Kasser et al., 2014). An educational video about MVO's negative effects on people and the planet developed by Kasser (www.youtube.com/watch?v=oGab38pKscw) could provide an excellent intervention for reducing MVO and encouraging pro-environmentalism at the same time.

A recent school-based intervention with primary school children in the UK showed that a week of pro-environmental activities and education led, not only to greater environmental knowledge, but also to a significant reduction in the self-enhancing values that are closely linked to MVO (Zamanpour, Dittmar, Döring, Mendese, & Hurst, 2017). We also have preliminary evidence that mindfulness is helpful not only in increasing personal well-being (Grossman, Niemann, Schmidt, & Walach, 2004) but may also be effective in reducing MVO and associated dysfunctional consumer behaviors in young adults (Dittmar, Strauss et al., 2017).

Advertising Spending and Policy

School-based interventions would be strengthened if they did not stand alone. Real, lasting change of values and value-relevant behaviors is much more likely when supported by public recognition of the need for such change, priority on political agendas, and concurrent policy changes at local and national levels. Yet, despite the substantial evidence of the harmful impacts of MVO, policy-makers and politicians do not yet seem to recognize the gravity of these problems. In contrast to MVO, the damaging effects of consumer culture ideals focusing on appearance are on the international policy agenda. Examples are legal changes in France, Spain, Italy, and Israel that enforce that female advertising or cat-walk models need to have a body weight that is categorized as healthy by the World Health Organisation, i.e., a Body Mass Index of at least 18 (see Paxton, 2015, for a full review). In the UK, the Body Confidence campaign by the UK government has led to numerous policy changes (www.gov.uk/government/publications/body-confidence-progress-report-2015), and the first act of London's new mayor Sadiq Khan was to ban advertising on London's public transport that uses ultra-thin women models (www.london.gov.uk/press-releases/mayoral/mayor-in-crackdown-on-body-image-advertisements).

Yet, there are already some examples of policy changes that may be effective in reducing people's endorsement of MVO. For example, Sweden has introduced policies to restrict advertising to children (Olsen, 2007). Furthermore, given evidence that exposure to advertising increases children's MVO (Opree et al., 2012) and that nations' advertising spend predicts cultural prevalence of materialistic values (Kasser, 2011), it is possible that policies which limit advertising on billboards—such as in Grenoble and Sao Paolo—may contribute towards lower levels of MVO. What is needed is the development of local and national advertising policies that explicitly aim to reduce MVO, and scientific evaluation of such interventions.

Interventions at both individual and social levels, as well as collaboration between parents, schools, practitioners in education and health, and policy-makers are crucial for alleviating MVO, a major source of lower well-being in contemporary consumer culture.

Irish philosopher and priest John O'Donohue offers this insightful synopsis:

> Our consumerist culture thrives on the awakening and manipulation of desire. This is how advertising works. It stirs our desire and then cleverly directs it towards products. Advertising is the schooling of false desire and relies on our need to belong, to play a central part in society and not exist merely on the fringes of it. And because awakened desire is full of immediacy, it wants gratification and does not want to be slowed down or wait. It wants no distance to open between it and the object of desire: it wants to have it now. This manipulation of desire accounts for the saturation of our culture with products that we don't need but are made to feel we do. There is no end to false desire. Like the consumption of fast food, it merely deepens and extends the hunger. It satisfies nothing in the end.
>
> *(2014, pp. 43–44)*

Note

1 Consumer culture values include both a materialistic orientation and an idealized body orientation, IBO for short, internalizing a thin (for women) or muscular (for men) body shape ideal as a personal value

References

American Psychiatric Association. (2000). *Diagnostic and statistical manual of mental disorders* (4th ed., text rev.). Washington, DC: Author.

American Psychiatric Association. (2013). *Diagnostic and statistical manual of mental disorders* (5th ed.). Washington, DC: Author.

Andersson, D., & Nässén, J. (2016). Should environmentalists be concerned about materialism? An analysis of attitudes, behaviours and greenhouse gas emissions. *Journal of Environmental Psychology*, *48*, 1–11.

Arndt, J., Solomon, M., Kasser, T., & Sheldon, K. M. (2004). The urge to splurge: A Terror Management account of materialism and consumer behaviour. *Journal of Consumer Psychology*, *14*(3), 198–212. doi: 10.1207/s15327663jcp1403_2

Banerjee, R., & Dittmar, H. (2008). Individual differences in children's materialism: The role of peer relations. *Personality and Social Psychology Bulletin*, *34*(1), 17–31. doi: 10.1177/0146167207309196

Banerjee, R., Dittmar, H., Easterbrook, M., Hurst, M., & Wright, M. (2017). Good looks, cool stuff, and children's "popularity": A cautionary tale. *Child Development*.

Bauer, M. A., Wilkie, J. E. B., Kim, J. K., & Bodenhausen, G. V. (2012). Cuing consumerism: Situational materialism undermines personal and social wellbeing. *Psychological Science*, *23*, 517–523. doi: 10.1177/0956797611429579

BBC News. (2008). *Children "damaged" by materialism.* Last retrieved July 12, 2017 from http://news.bbc.co.uk/1/hi/uk/7262936.stm

Benson, A. (2008). *To buy or not to buy: Why we overshop and how to stop.* Boston, MA: Trumpeter Books.

Black, D. W. (2006). Compulsive shopping. In E. Hollander & D. J. Stein (Eds.), *Clinical manual of impulse-control disorders* (pp. 203–228). Washington, DC: American Psychiatric Publishing.

Brown, K., & Kasser, T. (2005). Are psychological and ecological well-being compatible? The role of values, mindfulness, and lifestyle. *Social Indicators Research*, *74*, 349–368. doi: 10.1007/s11205-004-8207-8

Cafri, G., Thompson, J. K., Riciardelli, M., McCabe, M., Smolak, L., & Yesalis, C., (2005). Pursuit of the muscular ideal: Physical and psychological consequences and putative risk factors. *Clinical Psychology Review*, *25*, 215–239. doi:10.1016/j.cpr.2004.09.003

Carroll, J. S., Dean, L. R., Call, L., & Busby, D. M. (2011). Materialism and marriage: Couple profiles of congruent and incongruent spouses. *Journal of Couple and Relationship Therapy*, *10*(4), 287–308. doi: 10.1080/15332691.2011.613306

Coie, J. D., Dodge, K. A., & Coppotelli, H. (1982). Dimensions and types of social status: A cross-age perspective. *Developmental Psychology*, *18*, 557–570.

Cushman, P. (1990). Why the self is empty: Toward a historically situated psychology. *American Psychologist*, *45*(5), 599–611.

De Groot, J. I. M., & Steg, L. (2007). Value orientations and environmental beliefs in five countries: Validity of an instrument to measure egoistic, altruistic, and biospheric value orientations. *Journal of Cross-Cultural Psychology*, *38*, 318–332. doi: 10.1177/0022022107300278

Diener, E., Suh, E. M., Lucas, R. E., & Smith, H. L. (1999). Subjective well-being: Three decades of progress. *Psychological Bulletin*, *125*, 276–302. doi: 10.1037/0033-2909.125.2.276

Dittmar, H. (1992). *The social psychology of material possessions: To have is to be.* Hemel Hempstead: Harvester Wheatsheaf.

Dittmar, H. (2004). Understanding and diagnosing compulsive buying. In R. H. Coombs (Ed.), *Handbook of addictive disorders: A practical guide to diagnosis and treatment* (pp. 451–494). New York: Wiley.

Dittmar, H. (2005a). A new look at "compulsive buying": Self-discrepancies and materialistic values as predictors of compulsive buying tendency. *Journal of Social and Clinical Psychology*, *24*(6), 806–833. doi: 10.1521/jscp.2005.24.6.832

Dittmar, H. (2005b). Compulsive buying behaviour—a growing concern? An empirical exploration of the role of gender, age, and materialism. *British Journal of Psychology*, *96*(4), 467–491. doi: 10.1348/000712605X53533

Dittmar, H. (2007). The costs of consumer culture and the "cage within": The impact of the material "good life" and "body perfect" ideals on individuals' identity and well-being. *Psychological Inquiry*, *18*(1), 23–31. doi: 10.1080/10478400701389045

Dittmar, H. (2008). *Consumer culture, identity and well-being: The search for the "good life" and the "body perfect"*. Hove, UK: Psychology Press.

Dittmar, H. (2011). Material and consumer identities. In S. J. Schwartz, K. Luyckx, & V. L. Vignoles (Eds.), *Handbook of identity theory and research: Domains and categories* (pp. 745–769). New York: Springer.

Dittmar, H. (2018). *Consumer society, identity, and well-being: The search for the "good life" and the "body perfect"* (2nd rev. ed.). European Monographs in Social Psychology Series (edited by R. Brown). London & New York: Psychology Press.

Dittmar, H., Banerjee, R., Easterbrook, M., Hurst, M., & Wright, M. (2017). Is a materialistic value orientation detrimental to young children's well-being? Cross-sectional, longitudinal, and experimental evidence. *Journal of Personality and Social Psychology*.

Dittmar, H., & Bond, R. (2010). I want it and I want it now: Self-discrepancies and materialistic values as predictors of ordinary and compulsive buyers' temporal discounting of different consumer goods. *British Journal of Psychology*, *101*(4), 751–776. doi: 10.1348/000712609X484658

Dittmar, H., Bond, R., Hurst, M., & Kasser, T. (2014). The relationship between materialism and personal well-being: A meta-analysis. *Journal of Personality and Social Psychology*, *107*(5), 879–924. doi: 10.1037/a0037409

Dittmar, H., & Drury, J. (2000). Self-image—is it in the bag? A qualitative comparison between ordinary and "excessive" consumers. *Journal of Economic Psychology*, *21*(2), 109–142. doi: 10.1016/S0167-4870(99)00039-2

Dittmar, H., Long, K., & Bond, R. (2007). When a better self is only a button click away: Associations between materialistic values, emotional and identity-related buying motives, and compulsive buying tendency online. *Journal of Social and Clinical Psychology*, *26*(3), 334–361. doi: 10.1521/jscp.2007.26.3.334

Dittmar, H., Strauss, C., Cavanagh, K., Costin, V., Koc, Y., Marx, R., . . . Yang, S. (2017). "I meditate, therefore I am, and I am well": Consumer culture values, identity, mindfulness, and well-being. University of Sussex.

Donnelly, G. E., Ksendzova, M., Howell, R. T., Vohs, K. D., & Baumeister, R. F. (2016). Buying to blunt negative feelings: Materialistic escape from the self. *Review of General Psychology*, *20*(3), 272–316.

Duriez, B., Vansteenkiste, M., Soenens, B., & De Witte, J. (2007). The social costs of extrinsic relative to intrinsic goal pursuits: Their relation with social dominance and racial and ethnic prejudice. *Journal of Personality*, *75*(4), 757–782. doi: 10.1111/j.1467-6494.2007.00456.x

Easterbrook, M. J., Wright, M. L., Dittmar, H., & Banerjee, R. (2014). Consumer culture ideals, extrinsic motivations, and well-being in children. *European Journal of Social Psychology*, *44*(4), 349–359. doi: 10.1002/ejsp.2020

Garðarsdottir, R., & Dittmar, H. (2012). The relationship of materialism to debt and financial well-being: The case of Iceland's perceived prosperity. *Journal of Economic Psychology, 33,* 471–481.

Gatersleben, B., Jackson, T., Meadows, J., Soto, E., & Yan, Y. (2012). Materialism and environmentalism: Exploring the views of young adults in the UK, Spain and China. Unpublished manuscript. Guildford, UK: University of Surrey.

Goffman, E. (1961). *Asylums.* New York: Anchor.

Goffman, E. (1968). The inmate world. In C. Gordon & K. J. Gergen (Eds.), *The self in social interaction, vol. 1: Classic and contemporary perspectives* (pp. 115–136). New York: Wiley.

Grossman, P., Niemann, L., Schmidt, S., & Walach, H. (2004). Mindfulness-based stress reduction and health benefits: A meta-analysis. *Journal of Psychosomatic Research, 57,* 35–43.

Grouzet, F. M. E., Ahuvia, A., Kim, Y., Ryan, R. M., Schmuck, P., Kasser, T., . . . Sheldon, K. M. (2005). The structure of goals across 15 cultures. *Journal of Personality and Social Psychology, 89*(5), 800–816. doi: 10.1037/0022-3514.89.5.800

Halliwell, E., & Diedrichs, P. C. (2014). Brief report: Testing a dissonance body image intervention among young girls. *Health Psychology, 33* (2), 201–204. doi: 10.1037/a0032585

Halliwell, E., & Dittmar, H. (2004). Does size matter? The impact of model's body size on advertising effectiveness and women's body-focused anxiety. *Journal of Social and Clinical Psychology, 23,* 105–132.

Hardin, G. (1968). The tragedy of the commons. *Science, 162,* 1243–1248.

Hedlund-de Witt, A., de Boer, J., & Boersema, J. J. (2014). Exploring inner and outer worlds: A quantitative study of worldviews, environmental attitudes, and sustainable lifestyles. *Journal of Environmental Psychology, 37,* 40–54.

Hegel, G. W. F. (1807). *System der Wissenschaft, Erster Teil: Phänomenologie des Geistes.* Bamberg: Goebhart.

Higgins, E. T. (1987). Self-discrepancy: A theory relating self and affect. *Psychological Review, 94,* 319–340.

Hurst, M., Dittmar, H., Bond, R., & Kasser, T. (2013). The relationship between materialistic values and environmental attitudes and behaviors: A meta-analysis. *Journal of Environmental Psychology, 36,* 257–269. doi: 10.1016/j.jenvp.2013.09.003

Hurst, M., Dittmar, H., Halliwell, E., & Diedrichs, P. C. (2016). Does size matter? Media influences and body image. In C. Jansson-Boyd & M. Zawiska (Eds.), *International handbook of consumer psychology.* London: Taylor and Francis.

Inglehart, R. (1990). *Culture shift in advanced industrial society.* Princeton, NJ: Princeton University Press.

Jackson, T. (2009). *Prosperity without growth: Economics for a finite planet.* London: Earthscan.

Kaiser, F. G., & Byrka, K. (2011). Environmentalism as a trait: Gauging people's prosocial personality in terms of environmental engagement. *International Journal of Psychology, 46,* 71–79. doi: 10.1080/00207594.2010.516830

Kasser, T. (2002). *The high price of materialism.* Cambridge, MA: MIT Press.

Kasser, T. (2011). Cultural values and the well-being of future generations: A cross-national study. *Journal of Cross-Cultural Psychology, 42*(2), 206–215.

Kasser, T. (2016). Materialistic values and goals. *Annual Review of Psychology, 67,* 489–514.

Kasser, T., & Ahuvia, A. (2002). Materialistic values and well-being in business students. *European Journal of Social Psychology, 32,* 137–146. doi: 10.1002/ejsp.85

Kasser, T., Cohn, S., Kanner, A. D., & Ryan, R. M. (2007). Some costs of American corporate capitalism: A psychological exploration of value and goal conflicts. *Psychological Inquiry, 18*(1), 1–22.

Kasser, T., Rosenblum, K. L., Sameroff, A. J., Deci, E. L., Niemiec, C. P., Ryan, R. M., . . . Hawks, S. (2014). Changes in materialism, changes in psychological well-being: Evidence from three longitudinal studies and an intervention experiment. *Motivation and Emotion, 38*(1), 1–22. doi: 10.1007/s11031-013-9371-4

Kasser, T., & Ryan, R. M. (1993). A dark side of the American dream: Correlates of financial success as a central life aspiration. *Journal of Personality and Social Psychology, 65*, 410–422. doi: 10.1037/0022-3514.65.2.410

Kasser, T., Ryan, R. M., Zax, M., & Sameroff, A. J. (1995). The relations of maternal and social environments to late adolescents' materialistic and prosocial values. *Developmental Psychology, 31*, 907–914. doi: 10.1037/0012-1649.31.6.907

Kasser, T., & Sheldon, K. M. (2000). Of wealth and death: Materialism, mortality salience, and consumption behavior. *Psychological Science, 11*, 348–351. doi: 10.1111/1467-9280.00269

Khanna, S., & Kasser, T. (2001). Materialism, objectification, and alienation from a cross-cultural perspective. Unpublished manuscript.

Ku, L., Dittmar, H., & Banerjee, R. (2014). To have or to learn? The effects of materialism on British and Chinese children's learning. *Journal of Personality and Social Psychology, 106*(5), 803–821. doi: 10.1037/a0036038

Ku, L., Wu, A. M., Lao, A. K., & Lam, K. I. (2016). "We want the world and we want it now": Materialism, time perspectives and problem spending tendency of Chinese. *International Journal of Psychology*. Online publication. doi: 10.1002/ijop.12391

Ku, L., & Zaroff, C. (2014). How far is your money from your mouth? The effects of intrinsic relative to extrinsic values on willingness to pay and protect the environment. *Journal of Environmental Psychology, 40*, 472–483.

LaFontana, K. M., & Cillessen, A. H. N. (1999). Children's interpersonal perceptions as a function of sociometric and peer-perceived popularity. *Journal of General Psychology, 160*, 225–242.

LaFontana, K. M., & Cillessen, A. H. N. (2002). Children's perceptions of popular and unpopular peers: A multimethod assessment. *Developmental Psychology, 38*, 635–647.

Lease, A. M., Musgrove, K. T., & Axelrod, J. L. (2002). Dimensions of social status in preadolescent peer groups: Likeability, perceived popularity and social dominance. *Social Development, 11*, 508–533.

Lebow, V. (1955). Price competition in 1955. *Journal of Retailing*. Retrieved from hundredgoals.files.wordpress.com/2009/05/journal-of-retailing.pdf

Lu, L. C., & Lu, C. J. (2010). Moral philosophy, materialism, and consumer ethics: An exploratory study in Indonesia. *Journal of Business, 94*(2), 193–210. doi: 10.1007/s10551-009-0256-0

Maio, G. R. (2015). *The psychology of human values. European Monographs in Social Psychology*, series edited by Rupert Brown. London: Psychology Press.

Maio, G. R., Pakizeh, A., Cheung, W., & Rees, K. J. (2009). Changing, priming, and acting on values: Effects via motivational relations in a circular model. *Journal of Personality and Social Psychology, 97*(4), 699–715. doi: 10.1037/a0016420

Maraz, A., Griffiths, M. D., & Demetrovics, Z. (2016). The prevalence of compulsive buying: A meta-analysis. *Addiction, 111*(3), 408–419. doi: 10.1111/add.13223

Marx, K. (1867). *Das Kapital: Kritik der politischen Ökonomie*. Hamburg: Meissner.

Maslow, A. (1943). A theory of human motivation. *Psychological Review, 50*(4), 370–396. doi: 10.1037/h0054346

Messick, D. M., & McClelland, C. L. (1983). Social traps and temporal traps. *Personality and Social Psychology Bulletin*, *9*(1), 105–110.

Mostow, A. J., Izard, C. E., Fine, S., & Trentacosta, C. J. (2002). Modeling emotional, cognitive, and behavioral predictors of peer acceptance. *Child Development*, *73*, 1775–1787. doi: 10.1111/1467-8624.00505

Neuner, M., Raab, G., & Reisch, L. A. (2005). Compulsive buying in maturing consumer societies: An empirical re-inquiry. *Journal of Economic Psychology*, *26*, 509–522. doi: 10.1016/j.joep.2004.08.002

O'Donahue, J. (2014). *Benedictus: A book of blessings*. London: Bantam.

Olsen, L. (2007). Children and advertising. In P. Wahlgren (Ed.), *What is Scandinavian law?* (pp. 436–461). Stockholm: Stockholm Institute for Scandinavian Law.

Opree, S. J., Buijzen, M., & Valkenburg, P. M. (2012). Lower life satisfaction related to materialism in children frequently exposed to advertising. *Pediatrics*, *130*, 486–491.

Parker, J. G., & Gottman, J. M. (1989). Social and emotional development in a relational context: Friendship interaction from early childhood to adolescence. In J. T. Berndt & G. W. Ladd (Eds.), *Peer relationships in child development* (pp. 95–131). Oxford: Wiley.

Parkhurst, J. T., & Hopmeyer, A. (1998). Sociometric popularity and peer-perceived popularity: Two distinct dimensions of peer status. *Journal of Early Adolescence*, *18*, 125–144.

Paxton, S. J. (2015). Social policy and prevention. In M. Levine & L. Smolak (Eds.), *The Wiley-Blackwell handbook of eating disorders* (pp. 655–668). Chichester, UK: Wiley.

Pilch, I., & Durnik-Durose, E. M. (2016). Do we need "dark" traits to explain materialism? The incremental validity of the Dark Triad over the HEXACO domains in predicting materialistic orientation. *Personality and Individual Differences*, *102*, 102–106. doi: 10.1016/j.paid.2016.06.047

Richins, M. L. (2004). The material values scale: Measurement properties and development of a short form. *Journal of Consumer Research*, *31*, 209–219. doi: 10.1086/383436

Richins, M. L., & Dawson, S. (1992). A consumer values orientation for materialism and its measurement: Scale development and validation. *Journal of Consumer Research*, *19*, 303–316. doi: 10.1086/209304

Rindfleisch, A., Burroughs, J. E., & Denton, F. (1997). Family structure, materialism, and compulsive consumption. *Journal of Consumer Research*, *23*, 312–325.

Roberts, J. A., & Roberts, C. R. (2012). Money matters: Does the symbolic presence of money affect charitable giving and attitudes among adolescents? *Young Consumers*, *13*(4), 329–336. doi: 10.1108/17473611211282572

Rokeach, M. (1973). *The nature of human values*. New York: Free Press.

Ryan, R. M., & Deci, E. L. (2000). Self-determination theory and the facilitation of intrinsic motivation, social development, and well-being. *American Psychologist*, *55*(1), 68–78.

Sagiv, L., & Schwartz, S. (2000). Value priorities and subjective well-being: Direct relations and congruity effects. *European Journal of Social Psychology*, *30*(2), 177–198. doi: 10.1002/(SICI)1099-0992(200003/04)

Schwartz, S. H. (1992). Universals in the content and structure of values: Theoretical advances and empirical tests in 20 countries. In M. P. Zanna (Ed.), *Advances in experimental social psychology* (Vol. 25, pp. 1–654). Orlando, FL: Academic Press.

Schwartz, S. H. (2012). An overview of the Schwartz theory of basic values. *Online Readings in Psychology and Culture*, *2*(1), 1–20. doi: 10.9707/2307-0919.1116

Sheldon, K. M., & Kasser, T. (2008). Psychological threat and extrinsic goal striving. *Motivation and Emotion*, *32*, 37–45.

Sheldon, K. M., Nichols, C. P., & Kasser, T. (2011). Americans recommend smaller ecological footprints when reminded of intrinsic American values of self-expression, family, and generosity. *Ecopsychology, 3*, 97–104. doi: 10.1089/eco.2010.0078

Stice, E. (2002). Risk and maintenance factors for eating pathology: A meta-analytic review. *Psychological Bulletin, 128*(5), 825–848.

Strizhakova, Y., & Coulter, R. A. (2013). The "green" side of materialism in emerging BRIC and developed markets: The moderating role of global cultural identity. *International Journal of Research in Marketing, 30*(1), 69–82.

Sweney, M. (2011, November 25). Humbug: Littlewoods Christmas ad causes hundreds to complain to ASA. *Guardian*. Last retrieved March 16, 2017 from www.theguardian.com/media/2011/nov/25/littlewoods-christmas-ad-complaints

Twenge, J. M., Gentile, B., DeWall, C. N., Ma, D. S., Lacefield, K., Schurtz, D. R. (2010). Birth cohort increases in psychopathology among young Americans, 1938–2007: A cross-temporal meta-analysis of the MMPI. *Clinical Psychology Review, 30*, 145–154.

Twenge, J. M., & Kasser, T. (2013). Generational changes in materialism and work centrality, 1976–2007: Associations with temporal changes in societal insecurity and materialistic role modelling. *Social Psychology and Personality Bulletin, 39*(7), 883–897. doi: 10.1177/0146167213484586

Unanue, W., Vignoles, V. L., Dittmar, H., & Vansteenkiste, M. (2016). Life goals predict environmental behavior: Cross-sectional and longitudinal evidence. *Journal of Environmental Psychology, 46*, 10–22. doi: 10.1016/j.jenvp.2016.02.001

Van Lange, P. A. M. (1999). The pursuit of joint outcomes and equality in outcomes: An integrative model of social value orientation. *Journal of Personality and Social Psychology, 77*, 337–349. doi: 10.1037/0022-3514.77.2.337

Wapner, S., Demick, J., & Redondo, J. P. (1990). Cherished possessions and adaption of older people to nursing homes. *International Journal of Aging and Human Development, 31*, 219–235.

Watson, J. J. (2003). The relationship of materialism to spending tendencies, saving, and debt. *Journal of Economic Psychology, 24*, 723–739.

Weinstein, N., Przybylski, A. K., & Ryan, R. M. (2009). Can nature make us more caring? Effects of immersion in nature on intrinsic aspirations and generosity. *Personality and Social Psychology Bulletin, 35*, 1315–1329. doi: 10.1177/0146167209341649

White, M. C. (2014). Here's proof buying more stuff actually makes you miserable. *Time*, 13th March. Retrieved from http://time.com/22257/heres-proof-buying-more-stuff-actually-makes-you-miserable/

Wright, M., Hurst, M., Dittmar, H., & Banerjee (2017). "Having cool stuff" and "looking good": A qualitative study on children's beliefs and motives. MS in preparation, University of Brighton and University of Sussex.

Zamanpour, N., Dittmar, H., Döring, A. K., Mendese, A., & Hurst, M. (2017). Sustainable consumers of the future? A school-based intervention to increase children's pro-environmentalism. *Journal of Environmental Psychology*, under editorial consideration.

16

RELIGION, SPIRITUALITY, AND WELL-BEING

Joshua A. Wilt, Nick Stauner, and Julie J. Exline[1]

Religious and Spiritual Foundations of Well-Being

In *The Varieties of Religious Experience* (James, 1902/1985, p. 59), the classic volume that birthed the psychology of religion/spirituality (R/S), William James asks, "What is human life's chief concern?" and answers, "It is happiness". James details how a lively, engaged R/S life and a healthy, happy temperament can support each other mutually; yet, because spiritual and psychological evils and sicknesses plague humanity, a more melancholy approach to R/S life may actually have greater depth and realism. In the century since this book's publication, psychology has taken great interest in the relationship of R/S to well-being. Enthusiasm for this topic has grown recently; publication has accelerated and spiked over the last two decades, with thousands of new articles every year (Koenig, 2012; Lucchetti & Lucchetti, 2014).

As the body of research on R/S and well-being is extremely large, this chapter is an illustrative review, not an exhaustive one. Its purpose is to give overviews of several areas relevant to R/S and well-being, highlight the latest advances in them, and present novel and exciting theories and empirical work. After a brief primer on definitional and measurement issues, the chapter touches upon the light and shadowy sides of R/S: its potential benefits and costs (Pargament, 2002).

Historically, research has focused on light aspects of R/S: its relations to physical/mental health and well-being. We introduce these areas briefly, then bridge light and shadow with a summary of extensive research on positive and negative religious coping, which also relates to many health and well-being factors. Last, we review the shadowy side, *R/S struggles*: tensions, conflicts, and strains inherent in R/S life (Exline & Rose, 2013). Although most evidence relates R/S struggles to poorer mental health, we end by reviewing preliminary evidence that struggles

might present opportunities for spiritual growth, maturity, and healthy psychosocial functioning.

Definition and Measurement

Theorists have had trouble in defining boundary conditions for the psychology of
R/S since its inception. Pargament, Mahoney, Exline, Jones, and Shafranske (2013)
tracked evolving meanings of R/S over time. Though these terms originally had
broad and similar connotations (James, 1902/1985), their uses in the social sciences
became narrower over time and developed popular yet controversial contrasts.
Many theorists and researchers conceive spirituality as one's internal, personal,
idiosyncratic relation to the divine, sacred, or transcendent, whereas religion more
often refers to external, institutional, normative, and sometimes rigid sets of beliefs
and behaviors. Emerging definitions conceive spirituality as the search for the
sacred or matters of transcendent significance, while religion encompasses institutions meant to support spirituality (Hill & Pargament, 2003; Pargament, 2013). We
adopt this view in our chapter.

Throughout, we attempt to avoid causal language in reviewing R/S's relationships to other characteristics and life outcomes of interest. We defer all authority
for causal claims to works we cite, which may often presume effects of R/S on
certain outcomes. Some such claims may be premature, and some may be errant;
even longitudinal prediction cannot rule out causation by third variables. Yet
some truly, merely predictive *effects* (a technical term) on *outcomes* (or "dependent
variables") in *regression models* (a popular statistical method) may be misinterpreted
as causal when this meaning is sometimes unintended. Thus, we caution readers
against causal interpretations even where they seem explicit. Causal inference is
the purview of experimenters, who face several formidable obstacles within the
psychology of religion (Batson, 1979).

Measurement of R/S constructs has also posed challenges for psychology, such
as the sheer number of scales and R/S dimensions (several hundred). These are
often redundant or lack precise definition and empirical validation (Kapuscinski &
Masters, 2010). Hill (2013) listed scales with strong theoretical bases that had been
employed in highly representative samples and produced evidence of reliability
and validity.

However, we emphasize that measurement of R/S constructs is theoretically
complicated when samples include the nonreligious and nonspiritual (non-R/S),
and when conclusions presume to include them as well. For example, what is the
meaning of a positive or negative god image when an atheist reports it? Coherent
answers may exist (e.g., Bradley, Exline, & Uzdavines, 2015), but simple questionnaires are routinely (perhaps necessarily) insensitive to idiosyncrasies in individuals'
interpretations of words that their designers assumed to hold consensual meaning.
Therefore, one must be sensitive to how awkwardly constrained response options
can seem to those who would explain or qualify their answers. This reality of

standardized survey research may discourage effortful responding among those whose views a measure seems to invalidate, even accidentally. Thus, when a sample includes even a fairly large subsample of non-R/S participants (as increasingly many do; see Pew Research Center, 2015), members of this subpopulation may feel compelled to misrepresent themselves or their views. As with causal claims, implications that claims about R/S might apply equally to people who eschew R/S must be read with reservation. Very little work has been done in resolving non-R/S perspectives with others from within R/S, let alone resolving differences among R/S traditions. We exclude non-R/S populations from our claims except where noted explicitly. Explaining the role of R/S among non-R/S people would exceed the scope of this chapter and, arguably, the evidence.

The next two sections focus on relations of R/S to indicators of physical health and mental health, respectively. We use the term "R/S" throughout to refer to the wide range of measures that include content related to R/S (e.g., religious-ness, spiritual transcendence). These measures vary meaningfully in content, and therefore our decision to group these measures sacrifices precision. However, describing this variation in detail would also go beyond the scope of this chapter.

Physical Health

Several recent reviews cover R/S and physical health. A review of 11 method-ologically and statistically rigorous studies conducted in the in the United States (8 of which relied on nationally representative samples) determined that church attendees had about a 25% lower risk of mortality over the span of 2–31 years after controlling for known risk factors (Powell, Shahabi, & Thoresen, 2003). R/S predicted less cardiovascular disease, although the authors found no evidence that R/S slowed cancer progression or aided recovery from illness. Oman and Thore-sen (2005) focused on the history of research on R/S and physical health and gave robust evidence linking R/S to lower mortality, morbidity, and disease. Mediat-ing factors related to R/S included social support, meditation, forgiveness, and service to others. In a more recent review, Masters and Hooker (2013) concluded that higher R/S involvement (measured in various ways) predicts a 10–40% risk reduction in mortality across several studies of various time frames; has general, positive relationships with cardiovascular health (e.g., myocardial infarction, con-gestive heart failure, hypertension); and predicts fewer risk factors for cancer in general (e.g., drinking alcohol, smoking) and breast cancer in particular (e.g., using oral contraceptives, having a first birth after 30 years of age), but not less risk for cancer *per se*. They encouraged future prospective, longitudinal research to explain these links.

Koenig, King, and Carson (2012) covered many dimensions of physical health (e.g., self-rated health, diet, exercise, sexual behavior, cardiovascular health, demen-tia, immune function, cancer, mortality). A review article condensed the main findings (Koenig, 2012); most of the studies reviewed attested to benefits of R/S for physical health. A theoretical model explained these effects with a causal path flowing from (1) R/S factors (e.g., beliefs, commitment, practices) through (2) psychological traits and virtues (e.g., forgiveness, self-discipline, humility, gratefulness), (3) positive emotions and social connections, (4) physiological functioning, and finally (4) health and longevity: see Figure 16.2 in Koenig (2012) for a schematic representation of this model. In a similar model, Park (2007) described R/S as meaning systems comprising (1) beliefs and goals that (2) support adaptive psychosocial functioning (e.g., meaning in life, social support, optimism), which predicts (3) healthy behaviors and coping mechanisms that predict (4) physical health.

Research on R/S and physical health has expanded rapidly since these reviews, generating some particularly innovative and potent ideas. First, person–culture fit may moderate relations between R/S and health. In one cross-cultural study (Stavrova, 2015), the relation between R/S and self-rated health held for 19 of 59 countries, emerging mostly where R/S is the social norm. Stavrova also found that links from R/S to self-rated health and lower mortality in the United States only held in highly religious regions such as the Southeastern "Bible Belt". Examining R/S and health in understudied populations such as ethnic minorities is crucial to further progress. A nationally representative longitudinal study of African Americans found that religious beliefs and behaviors predicted better physical quality of life over 2.5 years (Roth, Usher, Clark, & Holt, 2016). Another representative sample of from the United States supported a mediational model specifying that attending church predicts self-rated health through engagement in R/S activities, social and emotional support at church, and feeling grateful toward God (Krause, Bruce, Hayward, & Woolever, 2014).

Mental Health

Research on R/S and mental health is even broader than research on physical health (Koenig, 2012). We first summarize some main findings from recent reviews of global measures of R/S. Miller and Kelley (2005) noted that most research on adults has linked R/S to facets of well-being (e.g., happiness, satisfaction with life, meaning in life). Adolescents reporting greater R/S involvement also showed greater psychological well-being, self-esteem, and self-acceptance. Research on R/S and mental health in children was nascent in 2005, and Miller and Kelly encouraged research in the area. Turning to psychopathology, they concluded that R/S associates robustly and negatively with depressive symptoms. Relations with anxiety and obsessive-compulsive symptoms were less clear; some studies found positive associations, and others reported no association. The authors noted that R/S beliefs may increase the expression of R/S delusions and hallucinations but likely has no bearing on the etiology of psychosis, which is mainly biological.

Theories and research linking R/S positively to psychological well-being and negatively to depressive symptoms have depended primarily on Caucasian samples of young adult Christians from the United States, but recent studies have included several demographic, religious, and cultural groups, as Park and Slattery (2013) noted. Though they did not draw strong paths between R/S and anxiety or post-traumatic stress, they suggested that R/S involvement may predict better prognoses in cases of substance abuse. A review of 43 publications on mental disorders and R/S in 1990–2010 largely confirmed these observations and also revealed that higher R/S relates to lower rates of suicide, dementia, and stress disorders (Bonelli & Koenig, 2013). Both reviews noted that the landscape of findings pertaining to R/S and psychotic disorders was mixed and rather complicated; a key issue for future research is to distinguish adaptive R/S beliefs from maladaptive symptoms of disorders (obsessions, delusions, hallucinations) involving R/S content.

Park and Slattery (2013) warned readers to interpret research on R/S and mental health carefully due to the lack of clinical samples (given that such samples are more likely to more fully represent the more troubled end of the general population distribution), experimental designs, and longitudinal research. They encouraged researchers to address these limitations, include lesser-studied R/S traditions (e.g., Buddhism, Islam, Hinduism); consider how nonbelief (e.g., atheism, agnosticism) relates to mental health; and explain relations of R/S to mental health. Their bidirectional model synthesized across several prominent approaches to well-being and specified potential mediators to guide explanatory research. This model stated that R/S may build adaptive psychological functioning through various mechanisms associated with R/S (e.g., social support, forgiveness, R/S practices). Well-being may promote engagement with R/S by increasing personal resources (e.g., vitality) and social resources (access to supportive R/S groups) that facilitate R/S (see also Fredrickson, 2002). They also noted that some aspects of R/S (e.g., maladaptive religious coping methods and R/S struggles, reviewed later) may have negative bidirectional associations with mental health.

Headway has already been made along these lines, most notably the association between R/S and depression. Placing high importance on R/S predicted a roughly 75% reduced risk of depression diagnosis over a 10-year period (Miller et al., 2012). Furthermore, for people who were at increased risk of depression (those with a depressed parent), risk reduction for a depressive episode was about 90%. Frequency of service attendance did not predict risk reduction for depression in this sample. With the same sample, Miller and colleagues (2014) found that thicker cortices in certain brain regions (parietal and occipital, the right mesial frontal lobe, and the left cuneus and precuneus) were positively related to the importance of R/S, particularly in the group at high risk for depression. These correlations suggest potential neuroanatomical mediators of the negative path between R/S and depression risk. As for psychological mediators, one study found that hope for achieving one's goals mediated over 80% of the effects of R/S constructs (religious practices, feeling connected to the divine, seeing life as a sacred journey) on reduced depressive symptoms (Chang et al.,

2016). Finding paths between R/S and depression may be vital. A new 15-year study showed that lower depressive symptoms partially mediated the association of R/S service attendance with less suicide among female nurses in the United States (VanderWeele, Li, Tsai, & Kawachi, 2016). Based on this study, Koenig (2016) encouraged mental health clinicians to obtain a spiritual history at the outset of treatment to help gauge suicide risk.

Research on R/S and depression in understudied populations across cultures is needed to firmly establish any causal role of R/S and its generalizability. One study of African American women with low socioeconomic status found that R/S predicts lower risk of postpartum depression (Cheadle et al., 2015). Research on R/S in military populations is relatively limited, but a cross-sectional study of National Guard soldiers revealed that R/S well-being related to lower lifetime risk of depression and less suicidal ideation during the past year (Ganocy et al., 2016). One cross-cultural longitudinal study, however, found that strongly endorsing R/S worldviews predicted an increased risk of depression (Leurent et al., 2013). Further research is needed to clarify boundary conditions for the predictive role of R/S on depressive symptomology.

Research is also making progress in specifying the relations between R/S and psychological health (as distinct from psychological disorders). Person-culture fit, which moderates relations of R/S and physical health (Stavrova, 2015), also seems to moderate the associations of R/S and well-being. Diener, Tay, and Myers (2011) found that religiosity is more normative in areas of the United States and the world (across 154 nations) that pose adverse circumstances (low education, income, life expectancy, safety, and basic need fulfillment), and religiosity related to subjective well-being more strongly in those areas than in areas in which religiosity is less normative. Social support, feeling respected, and a sense of purpose or meaning in life mediated this relationship. Findings from a cross-cultural study of 29 European countries shed some more light on why R/S may be so important to well-being in difficult circumstances (Joshanloo, 2016). Specifically, this study found that the relations between negative affect and life satisfaction were attenuated in more religious individuals, even when controlling for social support and religious affiliation. Taken together with the findings from Diener et al. (2011), these results suggest that the negative affect arising from harsher life conditions may not matter as much to overall judgments of satisfaction with life for those who put a high value on R/S. This may be due to R/S individuals being better able to find meaning in suffering (Joshanloo, 2016).

Other mechanisms may help explain the relations of R/S to well-being. In two samples (Christian churchgoers in Belgium and university employees in the United States), positive emotions mediated the relation of R/S to life satisfaction (Van Cappellen, Toth-Gauthier, Saroglou, & Fredrickson, 2016). Transcendent emotions (e.g., awe, love) were stronger mediators than others (e.g., pride, amusement). Using Gallup Poll data, Lim (2016) found higher affective well-being (more positive emotions than negative) among churchgoers (religious affiliation was not specified) in the United States than among non-churchgoers, and this association was partially mediated by participation in activities with non-household family members and friends. These results support Park and Slattery's (2013) model that links R/S involvement to life satisfaction and psychological health through social activities and affective well-being, reviewed previously.

Recent work has focused also on identifying groups or classes of persons based on profiles of scores across R/S dimensions and comparing well-being across these groups. Using latent class analysis, Bravo, Pearson, and Stevens (2016) grouped individuals by three orientations to R/S life: *extrinsic* (using R/S to serve other values); *intrinsic* (seeing inherent value in R/S); and *quest* (seeing R/S life as a growing, changing, questioning process). Groups with higher intrinsic motivation had higher autonomy, environmental mastery, personal growth, positive relations, purpose in life, and self-acceptance than groups with higher extrinsic or quest religiosity, suggesting that intrinsic R/S motivation may relate most positively to psychological well-being. Barton and Miller (2015) used latent class analysis to identify groups of younger (ages 18–25) and older adults (age > 25) reporting more spiritual experiences and virtues (e.g., forgiveness, gratitude, optimism, grit, meaning in life); these groups had lower rates of depression and substance abuse than groups that reported lower levels of spiritual experiences. Though these group studies showcase the power of latent class analysis, we caution readers and analysts alike against pure typological thinking, which would risk denying both the individuality of persons within groups and their commonalities with similar others separated by little more than statistically determined group boundaries. As Bravo and colleagues (2016) note, individuals belong to theoretical classes not certainly but probabilistically, and these classes may reflect idiosyncrasies of samples. Changes in data design (e.g., idiographic, qualitative) may serve to focus analysis on persons rather than groups.

Technological advances in time-intensive, experience sampling methodology (Wilt, Condon, & Revelle, 2011) have made it feasible to investigate associations of R/S and well-being within persons over time. With 1,239 daily reports of R/S and psychological well-being, Kashdan and Nezlek (2012) found that daily R/S involvement related positively to daily self-esteem and positive affect, and these relationships were mediated by increased daily experiences of meaning in life. In another within-person study, daily religious activities (e.g., prayer, meditation) positively predicted spiritual experiences (e.g., feeling guided by God), which positively related to moral emotions (e.g., forgiveness, gratitude, empathy; Hardy, Zhang, Skalski, Melling, & Brinton, 2014). These studies made use of multilevel data, that is, when one level of observations (e.g., daily reports) are nested within another level (e.g., individuals). These data are best handled by multilevel modeling techniques, which can separate out between- and within-person variance and estimate relationships more precisely than ordinary regressions (Bliese, Chan, & Ployhart, 2007). These methods may find increasing use in studying within-person (or intraindividual) consequences of R/S.

Several areas related to R/S and psychological health are ripe for progress. Theory in this field is still rudimentary and disorganized (Krause, 2011), but formal, conceptual, data-driven models may be built on moderators and mediators. Advances in theory bring advances in measurement (and vice versa); constructs defined precisely may be assessed precisely. Existing R/S measures often include items relevant to general psychological well-being, conflating it with R/S (Garssen, Visser, & de Jager Meezenbroek, 2016). Theoretical and empirical work should focus on distinguishing these areas to avoid tautology. People often use R/S to define themselves in relation to others and the world, so we should conduct research how R/S relates to identity and self-concept. The *narrative identity framework*, which uses life stories to connect one's present to the remembered past and imagined future (McAdams, 2008), could give insight on how R/S relates to meaning in life (e.g., Hill, Terrell, Arellano, Schuetz, & Nagoshi, 2015). In an interview study, people reported that their involvement with R/S was reflective of their "true self" and core values (Franzese, 2009); therefore, research should continue exploring how R/S relates to feelings of authenticity (e.g., Lenton, Slabu, Sedikides, 2016). This research could test humanistic approaches (e.g., Elkins, Hedstrom, Hughes, Leaf, & Saunders, 1988) that portray R/S as part of the journey to self-actualization and transcendence. Finally, research on R/S and well-being in understudied populations such as Asian cultures (Shiah, Chang, Chiang, Lin, & Tam, 2015); non-Christian religious groups (Aghababaei et al., 2016); the military (Currier, Drescher, Holland, Lisman, & Foy, 2016); and combinations of these groups (Abu-Ras & Hosein, 2015) continues to garner interest.

Religious Coping

Use of R/S to manage stress is termed *religious coping* (Pargament, 1997). This area of research has blossomed over the past 30 years (see Pargament, Falb, Ano, & Wachholtz, 2013). People use R/S to cope in many ways and for many purposes, such as to gain (1) meaning; (2) mastery; control; (3) closeness to God, intimacy with others, comfort; or (4) life transformation. People can turn to religious coping in ways that imply an optimistic, proactive engagement with religion (positive religious coping) or in ways characterized by struggle or distress (negative religious coping). This section bridges light and shadow by reviewing the relations between positive and negative religious coping with well-being.

One of the early breakthroughs in this area was the development of the RCOPE (Pargament, Koenig, & Perez, 2000), a valid measure of ten positive and seven negative religious coping factors. Positive factors include Benevolent Religious Reappraisal (using R/S to reconsider potential benefits of stressors), Collaborative Religious Coping (seeking solutions with God as a partner), Spiritual Connection (aligning with transcendent forces), and Religious Helping (supporting others with R/S). Negative factors include Punishing God Reappraisal (attributing stressors to divine punishment), Passive Religious Deferral (relying entirely on God for solutions), and Interpersonal Religious Discontent (negativity about church or clergy). In general, positive religious coping related to perceived growth whereas negative religious coping related to poorer physical health and greater psychological distress. The shorter Brief RCOPE (Pargament, Smith, Koenig, & Perez, 1998) measures general positive and negative religious coping with seven items each.

Many studies have used positive and negative religious coping to predict various forms of adjustment to stress. A meta-analysis of 105 effect estimates in 49 studies with demographic diversity (e.g., ethnicity, age, education, religious affiliation) linked positive religious coping to positive well-being (e.g., spiritual growth, life satisfaction, happiness, self-esteem, purpose in life) and negative religious coping to negative emotions (guilt, distress, depression, anxiety, anger; Ano & Vasconcelles, 2005). A review of studies using the Brief RCOPE reached nearly identical conclusions (Pargament, Feuille, & Burdzy, 2011). Based on this research, some have concluded that religious coping may be an important mediator in the link between R/S and mental health (Krok, 2014; Park & Slattery, 2013). Additionally, recent work has begun to explore explanations for why religious coping strategies have been linked to psychological health; for example, among people with psychiatric disorders, optimism partially mediated positive and negative religious coping's links to psychological distress and life satisfaction (Warren, Van Eck, Townley, & Kloos, 2015).

Theory on religious coping has demonstrated validity in many understudied populations. One review evaluated the research on religious coping among Christian samples and then compared it to the work done among other faith traditions (Abu-Raiya & Pargament, 2015); the measures developed for Jews, Buddhists, and Hindus largely replicated the key associations between religious coping and well-being shown in earlier studies with Christians. Studies of the elderly (Hayward & Krause, 2015); patients with psychotic disorders (Rosmarin, Bigda-Peyton, Ongur, Pargament, & Bjorgvinsson, 2013); and patients with HIV/AIDS (Trevino et al., 2010) attest to the diversity of populations in which religious coping methods relate to adapting to life stressors.

Religious coping also relates to spiritual transformation. Positive religious coping predicted cancer patients' perceptions of *spiritual growth* (deepening of R/S involvement and commitment) over 9 months (Allmon, Tallman, & Altmaier, 2013). In a sample of university students reporting negativity (e.g., anger, alienation) in their relationship with God, positive religious coping predicted increased spiritual growth and less perceived spiritual decline (stagnation or disenchantment with R/S; Desai & Pargament, 2015). A structural equation model showed that positive religious coping was positively, concurrently related to spiritual growth among Christians with R/S struggles (Exline, Hall, Pargament, & Harriott, 2016). These studies imply that positive religious coping may help even during difficult phases of R/S life.

Religious and Spiritual Struggles

Religious and spiritual struggles involve strain or conflict about R/S issues (Exline & Rose, 2005; Pargament, Murray-Swank, Magyar, & Ano, 2005). At the time of these reviews, research caught up with a wave of interest in the dark side of R/S over the prior decade, likely as an effort to balance the extant research that focused on benefits of R/S (Ellison & Lee, 2010). By the next set of reviews 8 years later (Exline & Rose, 2013; Murray-Swank & Murray-Swank, 2013), the number of articles had more than doubled—"a veritable tidal wave of empirical research" (Exline, 2013, p. 459).

R/S struggles can take many forms, including *divine* (feeling anger at or from God, feeling punished or abandoned by God); *demonic* struggles (feeling tormented or tempted by the devil or evil spirits); *interpersonal* struggles (conflicts in R/S with people or institutions); *doubt* struggles (concerns about beliefs); *moral* struggles (guilt for perceived transgressions); and *ultimate meaning struggles* (concerns around existential meaning, life purpose, or the lack thereof). Divine, demonic, and interpersonal struggles are external conflicts, while moral, doubt, and ultimate meaning struggles are intrapersonal. Only divine and demonic struggles involve supernatural entities by definition, yet even atheists and agnostics may report them (Stauner, Exline, Grubbs, et al., 2016).

Much of the research to date on religious and spiritual struggles has focused on anger toward God and related forms of divine struggle. Though most believers in God feel positively toward God, anger at God is common and often coexists with positive feelings (Exline, Park, Smyth, & Carey, 2011). Anger at God has many forms, such as blaming God for harm to the self or others, viewing God as cruel, and having difficulty finding meaning in negative events. Research on individual differences has found that insecure attachment, neuroticism, and entitlement also predict anger at God and negative attitudes toward God in general (see Exline & Rose, 2013).

Recent reviews have found that, R/S struggles are linked with many indicators of distress, including depression, anxiety, physical complaints, difficulty adjusting to trauma, and suicidal ideation (Exline, 2013; Exline & Rose, 2013). They are also linked with lower levels of well-being (e.g., life satisfaction and meaning). Longitudinal studies indicate that struggles predict poorer outcomes from physical rehabilitation, poorer recovery from disease, and higher risk of death. We refer the interested reader to Exline and Rose (2013) and Exline (2013) for more thorough overviews of research on R/S struggles and mental/physical health, and to Exline and Rose (2005) and Murray-Swank and Murray-Swank (2013) for discussions related to how R/S struggles may be addressed in clinical practice.

As research on R/S struggles is in a relatively early stage, some primary concerns include (1) developing valid measures of struggles (especially brief, cross-culturally valid measures); (2) optimizing latent structural models of concepts that fall in the realm of struggles (e.g., voids of meaning, demonic attributions); and (3) distinguishing struggles from related yet distinct constructs such as religiousness and distress. The Religious and Spiritual Struggles Scale (RSS) measures the six afore-mentioned highly correlated types of struggles (divine, demonic, interpersonal, moral, doubt, ultimate meaning; Exline, Pargament, Grubbs, & Yali, 2014). Each type of struggle has replicable, unique variance that is mostly independent of religiousness and distress, yet all struggles share a general factor that can be modeled in two ways to further distinguish each kind of R/S struggle from religiousness or distress (Stauner, Exline, Grubbs, et al., 2016).

Because R/S struggles cannot be reduced simply to religiousness or distress, their causes and effects deserve further research. Recent work has examined the predictors of struggles more systematically, for struggles in general and across different types of struggles. For example, an exploratory study found that negative appraisals of a stressful situation, insecure attachment to God, and the personality trait neuroticism predicted R/S struggles (Ano & Pargament, 2013). Another study found that neuroticism and low self-esteem predicted all types of struggles, agreeableness and openness predicted interpersonal struggles and doubt struggles, and psychological entitlement predicted divine struggles (Grubbs, Wilt, Stauner, Exline, & Pargament, 2016). Lower levels of self-esteem positively predicted more struggles over 1 year. Perceived addiction to pornography—feeling compelled, making repeated efforts, and associated distress—positively predicted more moral struggles over 1 year (Grubbs, Exline, Pargament, Volk, & Lindberg, 2016). Anxiety positively predicted a higher degree of doubt struggles across three time frames: 2 weeks, a month, and a year (Wilt, Grubbs, Lindberg, Exline, & Pargament, 2016).

Several other areas related to struggles warrant attention. One type of struggle that has received very little attention is demonic struggle (Harriot & Exline, 2017). There is also currently little work on explanations of links between struggles and well-being, but Harris, Erbes, Winskowski, Engdahl, and Nguyen (2014) showed that R/S struggles lead to symptoms of posttraumatic stress through lack of social support. It will also be important to reinforce the incremental validity of R/S struggles as predictors of well-being above and beyond R/S and personality factors (Wilt, Grubbs, Pargament, & Exline, 2017). Additional research is also needed on understudied populations, such as nonbelievers (Bradley, Uzdavines, Pargament, & Exline, 2016); Muslims (Abu Raiya, Exline, Pargament, & Agbaria, 2015; Saritoprak & Exline, in press); Jews (Rosmarin, Pargament, & Flannelly, 2009); Hindus (Tarakeshwar, Pargament, & Mahoney, 2003); Buddhists (Phillips et al., 2009); and other non-Christian groups (e.g., Chinese folk), as well as military veterans (Kopacz & Connery, 2015).

Potential for Growth From Religious/Spiritual Struggles

Although often painful, religious and spiritual struggles are a normal and natural part of life for many people. These struggles may represent turning points in the lives of some individuals: When facing R/S struggles, people may sink deeper into spiritual despair, or they may experience spiritual growth, maturation, and ultimately enhanced well-being (Pargament, 2007). The potential for R/S struggles to engender growth is understudied, though this idea is common across theological traditions (Fitzpatrick et al., 2016) and theories in the philosophy and psychology of R/S (Hall, Langer, & McMartin, 2010; Scrutton, 2015). A chapter written from the Jesuit perspective suggested that spiritual unrest is a call to growth toward the divine (Himes, Pilarski, & McNeill, 2014). Popular perceptions seem to agree: One study found that adults judged people who had navigated moral struggles successfully as morally superior to others who did not struggle at all (Starmans & Bloom, 2016). Some recent empirical research also supports the idea that people often perceive themselves as growing spiritually in response to R/S struggles, especially if they engage in positive religious coping methods such as working together with God (Desai & Pargament, 2015; Exline et al., 2016) and see God as intervening to help them with their struggles (Exline et al., 2016; Wilt, Stauner, Harriott, Exline, & Pargament, 2017). Wilt, Grubbs, Exline, and Pargament (2016) found that people who experienced higher levels of spiritual growth and found greater meaning in religious and spiritual struggles reported higher life satisfaction and self-esteem and lower depression and anxiety.

Conclusion

Although most work on spiritual and religious struggles has focused on ways that religiosity and spirituality related positively to mental and physical health, research on the dark side of R/S is emerging. Many studies show that religious coping strategies are associated with positive and negative outcomes during times of stress and that emotionally painful R/S struggles can pervade the lives of individuals endorsing R/S worldviews. Theoretical and methodological hurdles need to be addressed. The dearth of experimental studies may be the most notable shortcoming, as experiments have the greatest potential to advance evidence for causality. Limits aside, the field is vibrant, diverse, and growing in the right direction. In a sense, private R/S life for many individuals seems to parallel research on R/S and well-being. The personal journey of religion and spirituality can be rewarding and enlightening, but those who take this journey must be prepared to persevere through formidable obstacles along the way (James, 1902/1985); so must the research aimed at understanding the links between R/S and well-being.

Note

1 Author note: We are grateful for funding from the John Templeton Foundation (grants #36094 and 59916).

References

Abu Raiya, H., Exline, J. J., Pargament, K. I., & Agbaria, Q. (2015). Prevalence, predictors, and implications of religions/spiritual struggles among Muslims. *Journal for the Scientific Study of Religion, 54*, 631–648. doi: 10.1111/jssr.12230

Abu-Raiya, H., & Pargament, K. I. (2015). Religious coping among diverse religions: Commonalities and divergences. *Psychology of Religion and Spirituality, 7*, 24–33. doi: 10.1037/a0037652

Abu-Ras, W., & Hosein, S. (2015). Understanding resiliency through vulnerability: Cultural meaning and religious practice among Muslim military personnel. *Psychology of Religion and Spirituality, 7*, 179–191. doi: 10.1037/rel0000017

Aghababaei, N., Sohrabi, F., Eskandari, H., Borjali, A., Farrokhi, N., & Chen, Z. J. (2016). Predicting subjective well-being by religious and scientific attitudes with hope, purpose in life, and death anxiety as mediators. *Personality and Individual Differences, 90*, 93–98. doi: 10.1016/j.paid.2015.10.046

Allmon, A. L., Tallman, B. A., & Altmaier, E. M. (2013). Spiritual growth and decline among patients with cancer. *Oncology Nursing Forum, 40*, 559–565. doi: 10.1188/13. ONF.559-565

Ano, G. G., & Pargament, K. I. (2013). Predictors of spiritual struggles: An exploratory study. *Mental Health, Religion & Culture, 16*, 419–434. doi: 10.1080/13674676.2012.680434

Ano, G. G., & Vasconcelles, E. B. (2005). Religious coping and psychological adjustment to stress: A meta-analysis. *Journal of Clinical Psychology, 61*, 461–480. doi: 10.1002/jclp.20049

Barton, Y. A., & Miller, L. (2015). Spirituality and positive psychology go hand in hand: An investigation of multiple empirically derived profiles and related protective benefits. *Journal of Religion and Health, 54*, 829–843.

Batson, C. D. (1979). Experimentation in psychology of religion: Living with or in a dream? *Journal for the Scientific Study of Religion, 18*(1), 90–93. doi: 10.2307/1385384

Bliese, P. D., Chan, D., & Ployhart, R. E. (2007). Multilevel methods: Future directions in measurement, longitudinal analyses, and nonnormal outcomes. *Organizational Research Methods, 10*, 551–563.

Bonelli, R. M., & Koenig, H. G. (2013). Mental disorders, religion and spirituality 1990 to 2010: A systematic evidence-based review. *Journal of Religion and Health, 52*, 657–673.

Bradley, D. F., Exline, J. J., & Uzdavines, A. (2015). The god of nonbelievers: Characteristics of a hypothetical god. *Science, Religion and Culture, 2*(3), 120–130. doi: 10.17582/journal.src/2015/2.3.120.130

Bradley, D. F., Uzdavines, A., Pargament, K. I., & Exline, J. J. (2016). Counseling atheists who experience religious and spiritual struggles. In A. E. Schmidt, T. S. J. O'Connor, M. Chow, & P. Berendsen (Eds.), *Thriving on the edge: Integrating spiritual practice, theory, and research* (pp. 193–206). Toronto, ON: CASC Southwestern Ontario Region.

Bravo, A. J., Pearson, M. R., & Stevens, L. E. (2016). Making religiosity person-centered: A latent profile analysis of religiosity and psychological health outcomes. *Personality and Individual Differences, 88*, 160–169. doi: 10.1016/j.paid.2015.08.049

Chang, E. C., Jilani, Z., Fowler, E. E., Yu, T., Chia, S. W., Yu, E. A., . . . Hirsch, J. K. (2016). The relationship between multidimensional spirituality and depressive symptoms in college students: Examining hope agency and pathways as potential mediators. *The Journal of Positive Psychology, 11*, 189–198. doi: 10.1080/17439760.2015.1037859

Cheadle, A. C. D., Dunkel Schetter, C., Gaines Lanzi, R., Reed Vance, M., Sahadeo, L. S., Shalowitz, M. U., & Network, T. C. C. H. (2015). Spiritual and religious resources in African American women: Protection from depressive symptoms after childbirth. *Clinical Psychological Science, 3*, 283–291. doi: 10.1177/2167702614531581

Desai, K. M., & Pargament, K. I. (2015). Predictors of growth and decline following spiritual struggles. *International Journal for the Psychology of Religion, 25*, 42–56. doi: 10.1080/10508619.2013.847697

Diener, E., Tay, L., & Myers, D. G. (2011). The religion paradox: If religion makes people happy, why are so many dropping out? *Journal of Personality and Social Psychology, 101,* 1278–1290. doi: 10.1037/a0024402

Elkins, D. N., Hedstrom, L. J., Hughes, L. L., Leaf, J. A., & Saunders, C. (1988). Toward a humanistic-phenomenological spirituality: Definition, description, and measurement. *Journal of Humanistic Psychology, 28,* 5–18. doi: 10.1177/0022167888284002

Ellison, C. G., & Lee, J. (2010). Spiritual struggles and psychological distress: Is there a dark side of religion? *Social Indicators Research, 98,* 501–517. doi: 10.1007/s11205-009-9553-3

Exline, J. J. (2013). Religious and spiritual struggles. In K. I. Pargament, J. J. Exline, & J. W. Jones (Eds.), *APA handbook of psychology, religion, and spirituality (Vol 1): Context, theory, and research* (pp. 459–475). Washington, DC: American Psychological Association.

Exline, J. J., Hall, T. W., Pargament, K. I., & Harriott, V. A. (2016). Predictors of growth from spiritual struggle among Christian undergraduates: Religious coping and perceptions of helpful action by God are both important. *Journal of Positive Psychology, 12,* 501–508. doi: 10.1080/17439760.2016.1228007

Exline, J. J., Pargament, K. I., Grubbs, J. B., & Yali, A. M. (2014). The religious and spiritual struggles scale: Development and initial validation. *Psychology of Religion and Spirituality, 6,* 208–222. doi: 10.1037/a0036465

Exline, J. J., Park, C. L., Smyth, J. M., & Carey, M. P. (2011). Anger toward God: Social-cognitive predictors, prevalence, and links with adjustment to bereavement and cancer. *Journal of Personality and Social Psychology, 100,* 129–148. doi: 10.1037/a0021716

Exline, J. J., & Rose, E. (2005). Religious and spiritual struggles. In R. F. Paloutzian & C. L. Park (Eds.), *Handbook of the psychology of religion and spirituality* (pp. 315–330). New York, NY: Guilford Press.

Exline, J. J., & Rose, E. (2013). Religious and spiritual struggles. In R. F. Paloutzian & C. L. Park (Eds.), *Handbook of the psychology of religion and spirituality* (2nd ed., pp. 380–398). New York, NY: Guilford Press.

Fitzpatrick, S. J., Kerridge, I. H., Jordens, C. F. C., Zoloth, L., Tollefsen, C., Tsomo, K. L., . . . Sarma, D. (2016). Religious perspectives on human suffering: Implications for medicine and bioethics. *Journal of Religion and Health, 55,* 159–173. doi: 10.1007/s10943-015-0014-9

Franzese, A. T. (2009). Authenticity: Perspectives and experiences. In P. Vannini & J. P. Williams (Eds.), *Authenticity in culture, self, and society* (pp. 87–102). Surrey: Ashgate.

Fredrickson, B. L. (2002). How does religion benefit health and well-being? Are positive emotions active ingredients? *Psychological Inquiry, 13,* 209–213.

Ganocy, S. J., Goto, T., Chan, P. K., Cohen, G. H., Sampson, L., Galea, S., . . . Sizemore, J. (2016). Association of spirituality with mental health conditions in Ohio National Guard soldiers. *The Journal of Nervous and Mental Disease, 204,* 524–529. doi: 10.1097/NMD.0000000000000519

Garssen, B., Visser, A., & de Jager Meezenbroek, E. (2016). Examining whether spirituality predicts subjective well-being: How to avoid tautology. *Psychology of Religion and Spirituality, 8,* 141–148. doi: 10.1037/rel0000025

Grubbs, J. B., Exline, J. J., Pargament, K. I., Volk, F., & Lindberg, M. J. (2016). Internet pornography use, perceived addiction, and religious/spiritual struggles. *Archives of Sexual Behavior, 46,* 1733–1745. doi: 10.1007/s10508-016-0772-9

Grubbs, J. B., Wilt, J. A., Stauner, N., Exline, J. J., & Pargament, K. I. (2016). Self, struggle, and soul: Linking personality, self-concept, and religious/spiritual struggle. *Personality and Individual Differences, 101,* 144–152.

Hall, M. E. L., Langer, R., & McMartin, J. (2010). The role of suffering in human flourishing: Contributions from positive psychology, theology, and philosophy. *Journal of Psychology & Theology, 38*, 111–121.

Hardy, S. A., Zhang, Z., Skalski, J. E., Melling, B. S., & Brinton, C. T. (2014). Daily religious involvement, spirituality, and moral emotions. *Psychology of Religion and Spirituality, 6*, 338–348. doi: 10.1037/a0037293

Harriot, V. A., & Exline, J. J. (2017). To light the dark: A review of the literature on demonic attribution. Manuscript in preparation.

Harris, J. I., Erbes, C. R., Winskowski, A. M., Engdahl, B. E., & Nguyen, X. V. (2014). Social support as a mediator in the relationship between religious comforts and strains and trauma symptoms. *Psychology of Religion and Spirituality, 6*, 223–229. doi: 10.1037/a0036421

Hayward, R. D., & Krause, N. (2015). Classes of individual growth trajectories of religious coping in older adulthood: Patterns and predictors. *Research on Aging, 38*, 554–579. doi: 10.1177/0164027515593347

Hill, E., Terrell, H., Arellano, A., Schuetz, B., & Nagoshi, C. (2015). A good story: Using future life narratives to predict present well-being. *Journal of Happiness Studies, 16*, 1615–1634. doi: 10.1007/s10902-014-9581-9

Hill, P. C. (2013). Measurement assessment and issues in the psychology of religion and spirituality. In R. F. Paloutzian & C. L. Park (Eds.), *Handbook of the psychology of religion and spirituality* (2nd ed., pp. 48–74). New York, NY: Guilford Press.

Hill, P. C., & Pargament, K. I. (2003). Advances in the conceptualization and measurement of religion and spirituality: Implications for physical and mental health research. *Psychology of Religion and Spirituality, S*, 3–17. doi: 10.1037/1941-1022.S.1.3

Himes, M. J., Pilarski, J., & McNeill, D. P. (2014). *Doing the truth in love: Conversations about God, relationships, and service.* New York: NY: Paulist Press (Chapter 3).

James, W. (1902/1985). *The varieties of religious experience.* New York, NY: Random House.

Joshanloo, M. (2016). Religiosity moderates the relationship between negative affect and life satisfaction: A study in 29 European countries. *Journal of Research in Personality, 61*, 11–14. doi: 10.1016/j.jrp.2016.01.001

Kapuscinski, A. N., & Masters, K. S. (2010). The current status of measures of spirituality: A critical review of scale development. *Psychology of Religion and Spirituality, 2*, 191–205. doi: 10.1037/a0020498.supp (Supplemental).

Kashdan, T. B., & Nezlek, J. B. (2012). Whether, when, and how is spirituality related to well-being? Moving beyond single occasion questionnaires to understanding daily process. *Personality and Social Psychology Bulletin, 38*, 1523–1535. doi: 10.1177/0146167212454549

Koenig, H. G. (2012). Religion, spirituality, and health: The research and clinical implications. *ISRN Psychiatry 2012.* doi: 10.5402/2012/278730

Koenig, H. G. (2016). Association of religious involvement and suicide. *Jama Psychiatry, 73*, 775–776. doi: 10.1001/jamapsychiatry.2016.1214

Koenig, H. G., King, D., & Carson, V. B. (2012). *Handbook of religion and health.* New York, NY: Oxford University Press.

Kopacz, M. S., & Connery, A. L. (2015). The veteran spiritual struggle. *Spirituality in Clinical Practice, 2*, 61–67. doi: 10.1037/scp0000059

Krause, N. (2011). Religion and health: Making sense of a disheveled literature. *Journal of Religion and Health, 50*, 20–35. doi: 10.1007/s10943-010-9373-4

Krause, N., Bruce, D., Hayward, R. D., & Woolever, C. (2014). Gratitude to God, self-rated health, and depressive symptoms. *Journal for the Scientific Study of Religion, 53*, 341–355. doi: 10.1111/jssr.12110

Krok, D. (2014). The mediating role of coping in the relationships between religiousness and mental health. *Archives of Psychiatry and Psychotherapy, 2,* 5–13.

Lenton, A. P., Slabu, L., & Sedikides, C. (2016). State authenticity in everyday life. *European Journal of Personality, 30,* 64–82. doi: 10.1002/per.2033

Leurent, B., Nazareth, I., Bellón-Saameño, J., Geerlings, M.-I., Maaroos, H., Saldivia, S., . . . King, M. (2013). Spiritual and religious beliefs as risk factors for the onset of major depression: An international cohort study. *Psychological medicine, 43,* 2109–2120.

Lim, C. (2016). Religion, time use, and affective well-being. *Sociological Science, 3,* 685–709.

Lucchetti, G., & Lucchetti, A. L. G. (2014). Spirituality, religion, and health: Over the last 15 years of field research (1999–2013). *The International Journal of Psychiatry in Medicine, 48,* 199–215. doi: 10.2190/PM.48.3.e

Masters, K. S., & Hooker, S. A. (2013). Religion, spirituality, and health. In R. F. Paloutzian & C. L. Park (Eds.), *Handbook of the psychology of religion and spirituality* (2nd ed., pp. 519–539). New York, NY: Guilford Press.

McAdams, D. P. (2008). Personal narratives and the life story. In O. P. John, R. W. Robins, & L. A. Pervin (Eds.), *Handbook of personality: Theory and research* (3rd ed., pp. 242–264). New York, NY: Guilford Press.

Miller, L., Bansal, R., Wickramaratne, P., Hao, X., Tenke, C. E., Weissman, M. M., Peterson, B. S. (2014). Neuroanatomical correlates of religiosity and spirituality: A study in adults at high and low familial risk for depression. *Jama Psychiatry, 71,* 128–135. doi: 10.1001/jamapsychiatry.2013.3067

Miller, L., & Kelley, B. S. (2005). Relationships of religiosity and spirituality with mental health and psychopathology. In R. F. Paloutzian & C. L. Park (Eds.), *Handbook of the psychology of religion and spirituality* (pp. 460–478). New York, NY: Guilford Press.

Miller, L., Wickramaratne, P., Gameroff, M. J., Sage, M., Tenke, C. E., & Weissman, M. M. (2012). Religiosity and major depression in adults at high risk: A ten-year prospective study. *American Journal of Psychiatry, 169,* 89–94.

Murray-Swank, A., & Murray-Swank, N. A. (2013). Spiritual and religious problems: Integrating theory and clinical practice. In R. F. Paloutzian & C. L. Park (Eds.), *Handbook of the psychology of religion and spirituality* (pp. 421–437). New York, NY: Guilford Press.

Oman, D., & Thoresen, C. E. (2005). Do religion and spirituality influence health. In R. F. Paloutzian & C. L. Park (Eds.), *Handbook of the psychology of religion and spirituality* (pp. 435–459). New York, NY: Guilford Press.

Pargament, K. I. (1997). *The psychology of religion and coping: Theory, research, practice.* New York, NY: Guilford Press.

Pargament, K. I. (2002). The bitter and the sweet: An evaluation of the costs and benefits of religiousness. *Psychological Inquiry, 13,* 168–181. doi: 10.2307/1449326

Pargament, K. I. (2007). *Spiritually integrated psychotherapy: Understanding and addressing the sacred.* New York, NY: Guilford Press.

Pargament, K. I. (2013). Spirituality as an irreducible human motivation and process. *International Journal for the Psychology of Religion, 23,* 271–281.

Pargament, K. I., Falb, M. D., Ano, G. G., & Wachholtz, A. B. (2013). The religious dimension of coping: Advances in theory, research, and practice. In R. F. Paloutzian & C. L. Park (Eds.), *Handbook of the psychology of religion and spirituality* (pp. 560–579). New York, NY: Guilford Press.

Pargament, K. I., Feuille, M., & Burdzy, D. (2011). The Brief RCOPE: Current psychometric status of a short measure of religious coping. *Religions, 2,* 51–76.

Pargament, K. I., Koenig, H. G., & Perez, L. M. (2000). The many methods of religious coping: Development and initial validation of the RCOPE. *Journal of Clinical Psychology, 56,* 519–543.

Pargament, K. I., Mahoney, A., Exline, J. J., Jones, J. W., & Shafranske, E. P. (2013). Envisioning an integrative paradigm for the psychology of religion and spirituality: An introduction to the APA handbook of psychology, religion and spirituality. In K. I. Pargament (Editor-in-Chief), J. J. Exline, & J. W. Jones (Associate Eds.), *APA handbook of psychology, religion, and spirituality* (Vol. 1: Context, theory, and research, pp. 3–19). Washington, DC: American Psychological Association.

Pargament, K. I., Murray-Swank, N. A., Magyar, G. M., & Ano, G. G. (2005). Spiritual struggle: A phenomenon of interest to psychology and religion. In W. R. Miller & H. D. Delaney (Eds.), *Judeo-Christian perspectives on psychology: Human nature, motivation, and change* (pp. 245–268). Washington, DC, US: American Psychological Association.

Pargament, K. I., Smith, B. W., Koenig, H. G., & Perez, L. (1998). Patterns of positive and negative religious coping with major life stressors. *Journal for the Scientific Study of Religion, 37,* 710–724. doi: 10.2307/1388152

Park, C. L. (2007). Religiousness/spirituality and health: A meaning systems perspective. *Journal of Behavioral Medicine, 30,* 319–328. doi: 10.1007/s10865-007-9111-x

Park, C. L., & Slattery, J. M. (2013). Religion, spirituality, and mental health. In R. F. Paloutzian & C. L. Park (Eds.), *Handbook of the psychology of religion and spirituality* (2nd ed., pp. 540–559). New York, NY: Guilford Press.

Pew Research Center. (2015, May 12). *America's changing religious landscape.* Retrieved March 1, 2017 from www.pewforum.org/2015/05/12/americas-changing-religious-landscape/

Phillips, R. E. III, Cheng, C. M., Pargament, K. I., Oemig, C., Colvin, S. D., Abarr, A. N., . . . Reed, A. S. (2009). Spiritual coping in American Buddhists: An exploratory study. *The International Journal for the Psychology of Religion, 19*(4), 231–243.

Powell, L. H., Shahabi, L., & Thoresen, C. E. (2003). Religion and spirituality: Linkages to physical health. *American Psychologist, 58,* 36–52. doi: 10.1037/0003-066X.58.1.36

Rosmarin, D. H., Bigda-Peyton, J. S., Ongur, D., Pargament, K. I., & Bjorgvinsson, T. (2013). Religious coping among psychotic patients: Relevance to suicidality and treatment outcomes. *Psychiatry Research, 210,* 182–187. doi: 10.1016/j.psychres.2013.03.023

Rosmarin, D. H., Pargament, K. I., & Flannelly, K. J. (2009). Do spiritual struggles predict poorer physical/mental health among Jews? *The International Journal for the Psychology of Religion, 19*(4), 244–258. doi: 10.1080/10508610903143503

Roth, D. L., Usher, T., Clark, E. M., & Holt, C. L. (2016). Religious involvement and health over time: Predictive effects in a national sample of African American adults. *Journal for the Scientific Study of Religion, 55,* 417–424. doi: 10.1111/JSSR.12269

Saritoprak, S. N., & Exline, J. J. (in press). Spiritual jihad: Implications for struggle and growth. Chapter to appear in C. Y. Al-Karam (Ed.), *Islamic psychology: Research, theory, and practice.* Manuscript submitted for publication.

Scrutton, A. P. (2015). Suffering as potentially transformative: A philosophical and pastoral consideration drawing on Henri Nouwen's experience of depression. *Pastoral Psychology, 64,* 99–109. doi: 10.1007/s11089-013-0589-6

Shiah, Y.-J., Chang, F., Chiang, S.-K., Lin, I.-M., & Tam, W.-C. C. (2015). Religion and health: Anxiety, religiosity, meaning of life and mental health. *Journal of Religion and Health, 54,* 35–45.

Starmans, C., & Bloom, P. (2016). When the spirit is willing, but the flesh is weak: Developmental differences in judgments about inner moral conflict. *Psychological Science, 27,* 1498–1506. doi: 10.1177/0956797616665813

Stauner, N., Exline, J. J., Grubbs, J. B., Pargament, K. I., Bradley, D. F., & Uzdavines, A. (2016). Bifactor models of religions and spiritual struggles: Distinct from religiousness and distress. *Religions, 7,* 68. doi: 10.3390/rel7060068h

Stavrova, O. (2015). Religion, self-rated health, and mortality: Whether religiosity delays death depends on the cultural context. *Social Psychological and Personality Science, 6*, 911–922. doi: 10.1177/1948550615593149

Tarakeshwar, N., Pargament, K. I., & Mahoney, A. (2003). Initial development of a measure of religious coping among Hindus. *Journal of Community Psychology, 31*(6), 607–628.

Trevino, K. M., Pargament, K. I., Cotton, S., Leonard, A. C., Hahn, J., Caprini-Faigin, C. A., & Tsevat, J. (2010). Religious coping and physiological, psychological, social, and spiritual outcomes in patients with HIV/AIDS: Cross-sectional and longitudinal findings. *AIDS and Behavior, 14*, 379–389. doi: 10.1007/s10461-007-9332-6

Van Cappellen, P., Toth-Gauthier, M., Saroglou, V., & Fredrickson, B. (2016). Religion and well-being: The mediating role of positive emotions. *Journal of Happiness Studies, 17*, 485–505. doi: 10.1007/s10902-014-9605-5

VanderWeele, T. J., Li, S., Tsai, A. C., & Kawachi, I. (2016). Association between religious service attendance and lower suicide rates among us women. *Jama Psychiatry, 73*, 845–851. doi: 10.1001/jamapsychiatry.2016.1243

Warren, P., Van Eck, K., Townley, G., & Kloos, B. (2015). Relationships among religious coping, optimism, and outcomes for persons with psychiatric disabilities. *Psychology of Religion and Spirituality, 7*, 91–99. doi: 10.1037/a0038346

Wilt, J. A., Condon, D. M., & Revelle, W. (2011). Telemetrics and online data collection: Collecting data at a distance. In B. Laursen, T. D. Little, & N. A. Card (Eds.), *Handbook of developmental research methods* (pp. 163–180). New York: Guildford Press.

Wilt, J. A., Grubbs, J. B., Exline, J. J., & Pargament, K. I. (2016). Personality, religious and spiritual struggles, and well-being. *Psychology of Religion and Spirituality, 8*, 341–351.

Wilt, J. A., Grubbs, J. B., Lindberg, M. J., Exline, J. J., & Pargament, K. I. (2016). Anxiety predicts increases in struggles with religious/spiritual doubt over two weeks, one month, and one year. *International Journal for the Psychology of Religion, 27*, 26–34. doi: 10.1080/10508619.2015.1098820

Wilt, J. A., Grubbs, J. B., Pargament, K. I., & Exline, J. J. (2017). Religious and spiritual struggles, past and present: Relations to the Big Five and well-being. *International Journal for the Psychology of Religion, 27*, 51–64. doi: 10.1080/10508619.2016.1183251h

Wilt, J. A., Stauner, N., Harriott, V. A., Exline, J. J., & Pargament, K. I. (2017). Religious coping and perceptions of divine intervention predict spiritual transformation during a religious/spiritual struggle. Manuscript in preparation.

17

SELF-PRESENTATION AND SUBJECTIVE WELL-BEING

James M. Tyler, Katherine E. Adams, and Peter Kearns

Bring him into society, and he is immediately provided with a mirror which he wanted before. It is placed in the countenance and behavior of those he lives with. This is the only looking glass by which we can, in some measure, with the eyes of other people, scrutinize the propriety of our own conduct.

Adam Smith (1759)

Considerable evidence underscores the central importance and value of developing and maintaining social attachments. Indeed, many have argued that such concerns are a fundamental aspect of human functioning (Adler, 1930; Maslow, 1968). In their seminal paper, Baumeister and Leary (1995) argued that "human beings have a pervasive drive to form and maintain at least a minimum quantity of lasting, positive, and significant interpersonal relationships, and this desire for acceptance and belonging underlies a great deal of human behavior" (p. 497). Consistent with the proposition that human beings possess a basic need to belong, Leary, Tambor, Terdal, and Downs (1995) developed sociometer theory and proposed that people possess an internal gauge to monitor the social environment for their relational value in the *eyes of others*—relational value signifies how much others value interacting and having a relationship with the individual (Leary, 2001; Leary & Baumeister, 2000). Tooby and Cosmides (1996) also argued, similarly, that "adaptations should be designed to respond to signs of waning affection by increasing the desire to be liked, and mobilizing changes that will bring it about" (p. 139).

The evolution of a gauge to monitor and assess relational value suggests the corresponding development of a process that would aid people in managing how others view them—that is, a process that guides the *expression of one's public self*, which Leary (2002, p. 460) describes as "the behaviors from which other people . . . draw inferences about the person's characteristics, motives, feelings, roles, and other attributes", more typically referred to as self-presentation. Theorists posit that self-presentation patterns and associated behaviors serve to increase the likelihood that one will be included in desired groups and relationships (Leary, 1995; Schlenker, 2003). Or as Leary (2002) states directly, "self-presentation serves as the primary means of maintaining and enhancing one's relational value to other people" (p. 471).

From the standpoint of both sociometer theory and research, we draw a number of plausible suppositions. People's self-presentations are grounded in their motivation to be viewed by others in a favorable manner (Schlenker, 2003), and their efforts are not just for approval per se, but rather to enhance their relational value (Leary, 2004), which increases the odds of being accepted by a desired group or individual (i.e., increased belongingness). This suggests that a central function underlying self-presentational efforts is the satisfaction of people's need to belong (Gere & MacDonald, 2010). In sum, people manage the expression of their public self as a means to enhance their relational value because they are motivated to establish or maintain acceptable levels of belongingness.

In accord with Baumeister and Leary (1995), acceptance and belonging increase access to desired social and material outcomes. For example, abundant evidence consistently suggests a robust positive association between increased belongingness and positive emotions (e.g., happiness, well-being, and contentment), whereas decreased belongingness is linked to a host of negative emotions (e.g., unhappiness and loneliness) (Baumeister & Leary, 1995). People's subjective well-being (SWB[1]) appears to depend on having at least a minimum number of close social connections; social isolation, on the other hand, has been solidly linked to various patterns of unhappiness (Baumeister, 1991; Myers, 1992; Ryan & Deci, 2001; Greenaway et al., 2015).

Although the relationship between belongingness and SWB is robust, the degree to which self-presentation increases belongingness, and as a result increases SWB, is less empirically clear. The current chapter examines only the latter question: Does effectively managing the expression of one's public self positively influence one's SWB?[2] In what follows, we provide a brief overview of sociometer theory and self-presentation, after which we discuss self-presentational efforts within the framework of sociometer theory. We outline the sequential path between self-presentation and SWB, discussing the intentions, goals, and functions of self-presentation and the process by which it unfolds, with the general orienting perspective that people possess a need to belong and are motivated to engage in behaviors to satisfy this need. We then examine the degree to which evidence supports the proposition that effective self-presentations positively influence people's SWB.

Sociometer

The *sociometer*[3] is a self-regulatory process that operates as a monitoring system to alert an individual to social cues (e.g., reactions of others) that reflect the individual's relational value in the eyes of others. For the most part, people know that others' impressions and evaluations of them can significantly impact the degree to which they achieve desirable social and material outcomes (e.g., friendships, social support) (Leary & Allen, 2011; Leary, Allen, & Terry, 2011; Schlenker, 2003). Put simply, when people are relationally valued, it increases the likelihood they will accrue greater life benefits. For this reason, sociometer theory argues that people are highly motivated to maintain high relational value in the eyes of others and are particularly sensitive to and quickly process, often automatically and non-consciously, information that connotes their relational value (Baldwin & Sinclair, 1996; Baldwin, 1994).

During social interactions, people govern the behavioral expressions of their identity to a target, which typically involves people disclosing personal/intimate information[4] about themselves. From these behaviors/disclosures an interaction partner forms an impression of the individual, evaluating his/her behavior to determine whether the partner values a relationship with the person. According to sociometer theory, self-esteem serves as the gauge to monitor the qualitative nature (i.e., relational value) of an individual's interpersonal relationships. When the sociometer indicates an acceptable level of relational value to a group or to a particular individual, people experience greater self-esteem and perceive an increased sense of belongingness. By comparison, when the person interprets social cues as indicating relational devaluation (e.g., person is disliked) feelings of rejection occur, and the sociometer alerts the individual with a cautionary signal, which manifests through feelings of diminished self-esteem (additional sociometer details are provided in later sections) (Leary, 2004). Moreover, the individual is prompted by the sociometer to engage in behaviors to increase his/her relational value in the eyes of the partner. "The resulting behaviors are, in large part, self-presentational efforts to show other people that the individual possesses characteristics, beliefs, motives, and abilities that are valued by others" (Leary, 2002, p. 462).

Self-Presentation

Erving Goffman (1959) described self-presentation as a series of behavioral performances by which people symbolically convey information to demonstrate that they are a particular type of person to a target audience. More formally, self-presentation is the "goal-directed activity in which people communicate identity-images for themselves with audiences by behaving in ways that convey certain roles and personal qualities" (Schlenker, 2003, p. 492). In all, people are motivated to manage their public self, governing the behavioral expression of their identity to others.

Most theorists agree that the overarching goal of self-presentation falls under the umbrella of social influence, in that people's self-presentations are aimed at influencing how others perceive them and behave toward them. This perspective is consistent with how Leary (2002) describes the public self as the observable behaviors that targets use to form impressions and make inferences concerning the self-presenting individual's characteristics, attitudes, motives, and other attributional qualities. Leary and Kowalski (1990) succinctly capture this goal in their characterization of self-presentation as including "all behavioral attempts to create impressions in others' minds" (p. 39).

The dominant components of self-presentation are often described as involving deliberate behaviors, grounded in the implicit or explicit belief that such actions include only conscious efforts that are meant to explicitly influence others' impressions. From this perspective, self-presentation is narrowly characterized as largely occurring only in limited situations in which people are intentionally (consciously) trying to convey a favorable identity-image to others (e.g., job interviews, first dates). As we have argued elsewhere, this characterization is only a smaller slice of how and when people engage in self-presentation (Tyler & Adams, 2017).

A broader perspective argues that self-presentation involves people's non-conscious, automatic, and ongoing efforts to manage the expression of their public self *in the eyes* of others (Leary et al., 2011; Schlenker, 2003; Tyler & Adams, 2017). This typically entails regulating the disclosure of self-oriented information. And recall that people are strongly motivated that others judge such information favorably because they understand that the impressions others hold of them influence a variety of desired life outcomes such as friendships, romantic relationships, and achieving goals that require others' cooperation (Leary et al., 2011; Schlenker, 2003). To meet this aim, people exhibit and/or disclose personal characteristics and traits that highlight desirable and truthful elements of their identity—elements that establish, enhance, or maintain their relational value and facilitate increased acceptance and belonging (Miller, 2002).

Such disclosures unfold casually throughout the course of daily interactions in which people share information about themselves, including personal characteristics, interests, likes, dislikes, beliefs, and attitudes—all in the service of conveying impressions that result in favorable reactions from others (Schlenker, 1980). Moreover, people are judged by the general tenor of their social expressions—are they friendly, are they negative or positive, are they withdrawn, nervous, or excited, and so on—more colloquially, how is the person acting. People are aware that being viewed as friendly (vs. unfriendly), likable (vs. unlikable), and interesting (vs. boring) is nearly always viewed favorably and leads to increased acceptance. As such, people prefer to be perceived as fun, caring, friendly, and sincere rather than arrogant, obnoxious, superficial, boring, and mean—all of which represent characteristic traits that lead others to dislike an individual (Leary et al., 1995). In addition, people's ratings of how they would feel about themselves after engaging in certain behaviors is nearly identical to how they believe others would react to them (i.e., relational value) (Leary et al., 1995).

To foster social acceptance, people learn to demonstrate concrete examples of desirable behaviors that convey a favorable impression[5] to an interaction partner (Leary, 2009; Schlenker, 1986, 2003). Self-disclosures are primarily meant to convince the interaction partner that the individual possesses the attributes associated with an acceptable, if not good, relational partner (i.e., friend, team member, colleague). Although people do this automatically, they are able to convey a favorable, but accurate, representation of their identity—that is, what the individual considers to be relatively true about him or herself (Schlenker, 2003; Leary et al., 2011; Tyler & Adams, 2017). In all, self-presentation is a social influence tactic in which people engage in efforts to convey desired images of themselves to influence the thoughts, feelings, and behaviors of others as applied and related to the self-presenter.

Self-Presentation, Relational Value, Need to Belong, and SWB

Both theory and research provide a compelling case that people possess a basic need to belong and that the satisfaction of this need requires that one is relationally valued and accepted by others. A great deal of what people do to enhance their relational value and develop belongingness involves self-presentational efforts (Leary, 1995; Schlenker, 1980, 2003). In what follows, we briefly outline the relationship between belongingness and SWB, after which we summarize the relationship between self-presentation and SWB.

Belongingness and SWB

People routinely indicate that the key source of their daily happiness and life satisfaction is grounded in the qualitative nature of their interpersonal relationships including romantic partners, family connections, and friendships (Reis, Sheldon, Gable, Roscoe, & Ryan, 2000; Ryan & Deci, 2001; Myers, 1992). For instance, when a marriage partner satisfies one's close relational needs, it results in decreased loneliness and increased happiness (Olson & Wong, 2001). Likewise, those who have a strong motivation for intimacy tend to develop an active social network of friends, and they exhibit greater overall happiness (McAdams, 1985; McAdams & Bryant, 1987). Reis et al. (2000) also showed that daily fluctuations in belongingness (relatedness) are strongly associated to changes in SWB during the same period.

On the flip side, when people lack intimate social connections, they frequently report greater levels of unhappiness and depression (Myers, 1992). In fact, there is an inverse relationship between social depression, relating to the quality of one's social connections, and the extent to which people feel they are included and accepted by others (Leary et al., 1995). People also report greater loneliness when devoid of intimate social relationships (Leary, 1990); in support, Spivey (1990) found that self-reported loneliness and general feelings of inclusion are strongly negatively correlated (−.71). Other work, likewise, shows that losing social support, for example, via divorce, has profound and long-term negative impacts on SWB (Lucas, Clark, Georgellis, & Diener, 2003). Moreover, smaller social networks and limited interactions with family and friends are also associated with increased feelings of loneliness and depression (Dykstra, Van Tilburg, & Gierveld, 2005; Hawkley, Burleson, Berntson, & Cacioppo, 2003; Pinquart & Sörensen, 2003).

Over 30 years of accumulated evidence supports the conclusion that having some intimate social connections is strongly positively related to SWB. By comparison, a lack of close social ties is associated with greater unhappiness and is related to a host of negative emotional consequences (Argyle, 1987; Baumeister, 1991; Myers, 1992). This evidence underscores theorists' argument that the need to belong is a key motivational force that is linked to valued personal and social consequences (e.g., Baumeister & Leary, 1995).

Self-Presentation and SWB

Sociometer theory posits that, during social interactions, people manage the expression of their public self to enhance their relational value and increase their sense of belongingness. We posit that self-presentational efforts largely center on satisfying one's belonging needs and people who are better at managing the expression of their public self should have higher relational value and should experience greater belongingness. Given that belongingness leads to increased SWB, people who are more effective at self-presentation should also experience greater SWB.

Although no work directly examines the relationship between self-presentation and SWB, we reason that there are various factors (e.g., self-monitoring, ambivalent expression, self-esteem, self-enhancement, introversion) with which we may infer that those higher (or lower in some cases) on such measures may be more effective at self-presentation, and therefore should experience greater SWB.[6] We are not claiming that ineffective self-presentations necessarily result, for example, in low self-esteem; rather low self-esteem may diminish one's ability to successfully manage the expression of one's public self in a manner that enhances belongingness and relational value and, as a result, increases SWB.

Self-Presentation, Sociometer, and SWB

According to sociometer theory, the affective signal (i.e., self-esteem[7]) that emerges from the monitoring phase is accompanied by a self-relevant appraisal of what the social experience means in terms of the individual's relational value. We first outline the sequence, consequences, and responses when relational value is high after which we outline the process when relational value is low; for both we note the potential relationship between self-presentation and SWB.

Favorable Relational Value—Effective Self-Presentation

If the sociometer alerts the individual that his/her relational value in the eyes of a target other is favorable, the individual experiences increased self-esteem—an affectively tinged positive self-appraisal—from which the individual infers that his/her self-presentations have been successful, that is, the target other views the individual favorably. Likewise, higher self-esteem (i.e., positive self-appraisal) intimates that the individual's relational value is sufficient and his/her social acceptance level is adequate. Thus, the individual experiences an increased sense of belongingness. As a result, the individual has little motivation to adjust or change his/her self-presentational efforts. Rather, when an individual perceives his/her relational value as satisfactory, the individual continues to automatically and unconsciously manage the behavioral expression of his/her public self, while monitoring for any substantive change in his/her relational value. When self-presentations are effective and successfully influence a target other to view the individual favorably (i.e., enhanced relational value), the individual should have greater SWB.

Unfavorable Relational Value—Minimal Self-Presentation

If the individual detects that his or her relational value has diminished in the eyes of a target, the individual experiences lower self-esteem and appraises this change as an indication that he/she has not been socially accepted, leading the individual to feel that his/her belonging needs have not been satisfactorily met. These diminished levels indicate that the target did not view the individual favorably and perceives him or her as having less relational value. As a result, the individual is motivated to adjust the expression of his/her pubic self; this motivation rests on the individual's desire to repair the unfavorable image and restore his/her diminished relational value (Leary & Downs, 1995; Tooby & Cosmides, 1996). These self-presentation efforts are meant to convince the target that the individual possesses favorable attributes, attitudes, and skills (Leary, 2009). The underlying desire is to increase the extent to which the individual experiences greater belongingness and acceptance.

However, the motivation to *fix* one's diminished relational value does not always lead people to take self-presentational action. In some instances, a person may be motivated to repair an unfavorable view but may simply lack the will or the self-presentational skill to do so. Under these conditions, people continue to monitor their relational value but fail to change or adjust their self-presentation behaviors in ways that might improve their image in the eyes of a target. As a result, the target maintains an unfavorable view of the individual, and the individual's relational value does not substantively improve, and he/she continues to experience decreased belongingness, which likely leads to lower SWB.

Unfavorable Relational Value—Ineffective Self-presentation

Alternatively, the heightened motivation to repair an unfavorable view can lead people to engage in self-presentations to change the target other's view of him/her from an unfavorable perception to a favorable one, ultimately increasing his/her relational value in the eyes of the target. If the individual's self-presentations are still unsuccessful[8] and fail to improve his/her relational value, he/she will continue to experience lower self-esteem. This negative signal indicates that he/she is still viewed by the target other in a less than favorable manner, leading the individual to feel less belongingness. Because the sociometer is a feedback loop, if the individual continues to experience diminished relational value he/she will continue to monitor the social situation and will continue to be motivated to manage the expression of his/her public self. If these continued self-presentation efforts fail to positively influence the target's view of the individual, the individual should exhibit lower SWB. If the individual's diminished relational value represents an occasional state, the person will likely continue his/her self-presentations, making public self adjustments as a means to enhance his/her relational value. However, if relational devaluation (and low self-esteem) continues over a long period of time, the individual may simply *give up* trying to positively impact his/her image in the eyes of others.

Unfavorable Relational Value—Effective Self-Presentation

If self-presentations change the target's perception of the individual to a more favorable view, the individual will experience greater self-esteem, which signals that his/her self-presentations have been effective and successful. The target now views the individual in a favorable manner and his/her relational value is boosted, and the person experiences increased belongingness. As a result, the individual has little motivation to make self-presentational adjustments to his/her public self.[9] When a person perceives that his/her relational value has sufficiently improved, the individual continues to both manage his/her self-presentations and monitor his/her relational value and should experience an increase in SWB.

Overview of Evidence

Effectively managing the expression of one's public self involves social behaviors that are meant to influence others to view the self-presenting individual favorably. These self-presentational efforts are motivated by the desire to establish an acceptable level of relational value. To do so, people exhibit characteristics and behaviors that convey a desirable impression; the intent is to persuade an interaction partner that the individual possesses attributes associated with a good relational partner. Such behaviors typically show that the individual is open, positive, sociable, reliable, trustworthy, likable, interesting, and friendly (Mehrabian, 1969; McAndrew, Gold, Lenney, & Ryckman, 1984; Patterson, 1976).

Although the self-presentation literature is massive, few studies include measurements or manipulations that directly examine the self-presentation—SWB relationship. Thus, evidence for the relationship is primarily inferential, and the preponderance is focused on various factors that are conceptually related to effective self-presentation, such as extraversion, self-esteem, shyness, self-monitoring, and self-disclosure. Managing the expression of one's public self may involve behaviors and skills that are descriptive of some characteristics and abilities associated with these factors. For example, the social behaviors of highly extraverted people or people with high self-esteem strongly resemble the behaviors associated with effective self-presentation. Specifically, extraverts or high self-esteem people are often described as sociable, gregarious, engaging, warm, open, socially skilled, friendly, emotionally expressive, optimistic, generally confident, worry-free, and socially competent and involved (see Costa & McCrae, 1980, 1984)—all positive attributes that should increase relational value. We posit that those who score higher on these factors (or lower in some cases, e.g., shyness) are likely to be more effective and successful at managing the expression of their public self, which should result in greater SWB. This is consistent with Wilson's statement that "happiness is consistently related to *successful involvement* with people" (1967, p. 304). Again, the qualities associated with these factors resemble behaviors related to effective self-presentation and represent characteristics that would likely enhance the ability to develop and maintain social connections, leading to increased belongingness, and, as a result, greater SWB.

This resemblance supports the idea that people higher on these attributes/factors are more effective at managing the expression of their public self. In part, they may have learned how to socially interact in a manner that increases the likelihood of conveying a persona that others perceive favorably, thus enhancing their relational value and belongingness. People higher on these factors often report greater levels of SWB than those who score lower.[10] Although self-presentation skills are not the only reason that people higher on these factors become happier, being a more effective manager of one's public self is likely an important pathway to greater SWB because it *greases the wheels of social connections*. Viewing those who score high on these factors as better managers of their public self offers useful insight into the self-presentation—SWB relationship.

In the following sections, we discuss evidence for the general proposition that the behaviors/skills associated with effectively managing the expression of one's public self increases the likelihood of greater SWB. The evidence is divided into eight sections addressing various research areas ranging from extraversion and self-esteem to self-disclosure and concealment.

Extraversion

Several factors associated with extraversion are akin to various attributes that should increase one's sense of acceptance and belonging. For instance, compared to introverts, extraverts are described as more sociable, talkative, warm, and friendly (Costa & McCrae, 1980, 1984). Moreover, extraverts exhibit high social involvement by actively seeking out and readily participating in social interactions. As noted previously, some of these behavioral tendencies resemble how people might behave to successfully and effectively manage the expression of their public self.

If these tendencies are behavioral indications that extraverts possess self-presentation skills and manage their public self effectively, then they should have greater SWB, a proposition that is strongly supported by research (Brebner, Donaldson, Kirby, & Ward, 1995; Chan & Joseph, 2000; Emmons & Diener, 1986; Lu & Shih, 1997; Wilson, 1967). For instance, DeNeve and Cooper (1998) showed that extraversion reliably predicts SWB in the short term, while Costa and McCrae (1980) showed that it predicts positive affect and happiness, even in the long term, 10 years later. Hotard, McFatter, McWhirter, and Stegall (1989) also replicated the extraversion-happiness effect showing that more socially outgoing and uninhibited college students (i.e., extraverted) experienced greater SWB compared to their more introverted counterparts. However, when introverts had many social relationships, they also experienced SWB at or near the same level as an extravert, but if introverts had few relationships, their SWB was markedly lower.[11]

Other work has produced similar conclusions by correlating dispositional measures of extraversion with overall positive affect. Correlations range as high as .70, and this association remains robust (Hayes & Joseph, 2003; Larsen & Ketelaar, 1991; Lucas, Diener, Grob, Suh, & Shao, 2000; Lucas & Fujita, 2000). Research also shows that individuals report being happier when they behave in a more extraverted (vs. introverted) manner, both when they are randomly assigned to act extraverted (vs. introverted) and when they naturally engage in more extraverted behavior (i.e., using daily diary methods; Fleeson, Malanos, & Achille, 2002); this effect did not change as a function of dispositional extraversion. Moreover, Emmons and Diener (1986) found that it was the sociability rather than the impulsivity aspect of extraversion that was responsible for the positive association between extraversion and SWB. Extraversion also correlates with aspects of eudaimonic well-being such as personal growth, self-acceptance, and autonomy (Keyes, Shmotkin, & Ryff, 2002). Likewise, extraversion is a strong and reliable predictor of various indices of life satisfaction, well-being, and general self-acceptance (Schmutte & Ryff, 1997)

Extraverts do not experience greater happiness simply because they spend more time in social interactions. In fact, evidence shows that extraverts do not spend more time socially interacting than introverts, and even when alone, they show greater happiness than introverts (Pavot, Diener, & Fujita, 1990). Other work also shows that working in social or non-social jobs, living in rural or urban areas, or living alone or with others does not affect the basic finding—extraverts still experience more happiness than introverts (Diener, Sandvik, Pavot, & Fujita, 1992). In all, the trail of evidence largely supports the idea that extravert's may possess a heightened capacity to manage the expression of their public self.

Social Skills and Sociability

Social skills, described as the "emission of behavior that yields positive reactions from others", involve the ability to effectively interact and communicate with others and comprise characteristics that are similar to how people might behave to effectively manage the expression of their public self (Segrin & Taylor, 2007, p. 644; Spitzberg & Hurt, 1987). Effective social skills are critically important to not only healthy social and psychological functioning, but also to developing and maintaining fulfilling relationships (Hollin & Trower, 1986; Riggio & Zimmerman, 1991). For example, such skills increase the likelihood of positive interpersonal experiences, increase people's satisfaction with their social interactions and relationships, and lead to increased perceptions of social support and connections (Segrin & Flora, 1998; Riggio & Watring, 1993; Riggio & Zimmerman, 1991; Segrin & Taylor, 2007). Conversely, a deficit in social skills is related to various negative outcomes including social anxiety, depression, and general loneliness (Segrin, 2000; Wenzel, Graff-Dolezal, Macho, & Brendle, 2005). In all, abundant evidence shows that possessing the social wherewithal to foster and promote favorable relationships results in greater SWB.[12]

Similar to social skills, the degree to which an individual is sociable comprises at least some positive characteristics that would likely aid the person in being a better manager of his/her pubic self. Early theorists, in reviewing the well-being literature, consistently identified a host of social variables, including social activity, social contact, and social interest that were associated with SWB (Diener, 1984; Wilson, 1967). Like the early extraversion work, personality research also found that sociability-oriented constructs were well correlated with people's SWB (Bradburn, 1969; Smith, 1961; Wessman & Ricks, 1966). Recall that it was the sociability aspect of extraversion rather than the impulsivity aspect that was associated with increased happiness; impulsivity was related more to negative affect (Emmons & Diener, 1986). Impulsive individuals ignore the potential consequences of their behavior and tend to blurt out the first thing that comes to mind, which could plausibly lead to less SWB. In addition, measures of global social skills are associated negatively with loneliness and depression and positively with life satisfaction, hope, happiness, and overall quality of life (Riggio, Watring, & Throckmorton, 1993; Segrin & Taylor, 2007; Segrin, Hanzal, Donnerstein, Taylor, & Domschke, 2007). Likewise, people with higher emotional intelligence have a greater capacity to perceive, understand, and manage their emotional life, which helps to foster an increased sense of SWB (Kong, Zhao, & You, 2012a; Mayer & Salovey, 1997;

Mikolajczak, Nelis, Hansenne, & Quoidbach, 2008; Petrides, Perez-Gonzalez, & Furnham, 2007; Salovey, Bedell, Detweiler, & Mayer, 1999). Additional evidence (Mehl, Vazire, Holleran, & Clark, 2010), consistent with prior work (Diener & Seligman, 2002), also demonstrates that SWB is associated with socially oriented efforts. Specifically, people higher in SWB engage in more substantive conversations rather than general small talk; they also spend less time alone and more time talking to others. Although causally ambiguous, Mehl et al. advanced the possibility that more substantive conversations may result in making people happier. Similar to self-disclosure, which serves to increase relationship intimacy, engaging in deeper conversations may increase relational understanding and strengthen social connections.[13]

Social Anxiety, Shyness, and Loneliness

Social anxiety, shyness, and loneliness may emerge, in part, due to social skill deficits, but we will discuss these factors separately from social skills for ease of presentation (Jones & Carpenter, 1986; Riggio, 1986; Wittenberg & Reis, 1986). Theorists describe those high in social anxiety as being overly concerned with how they are perceived by others, whether they are making a good impression, how positive the impression is, the degree to which they are being evaluated, and how well the target other likes them (Leary & Kowalski, 1993; Schlenker & Leary, 1982a). For example, those who score high on the Interaction Anxiousness Scale (Leary, 1983) have less confidence in their self-presentational capacity, expect others to view them less favorably, and hold lower expectations that their social behaviors will lead to desired outcomes (Leary, Kowalski, & Campbell, 1988; Maddux, Norton, & Leary, 1988; Schlenker & Leary, 1982b).

Moreover, those high in social anxiety prefer solitary activities rather than social ones and tend to be taciturn, withdrawn, and wary during social situations, all of which are positively related to lower life satisfaction and SWB (Crozier & Alden, 2001; Leary & Kowalski, 1993; Rapee et al., 2011). Social anxiety is also negatively associated with extraversion, sociability, and a willingness to disclose personal information and positively with unhappiness and depression (Bruch, Kaflowitz, & Pearl, 1988; Leary & Kowalski, 1993). Likewise, prospective studies show that social phobia is negatively associated with SWB, even after controlling for comorbid depression (Stein & Kean, 2000; Stein et al., 2001).

Similar to anxious individuals, lonely people also view social exchanges and interactions as less gratifying and rewarding, and assume they do not have the ability to satisfy their social acceptance needs (Hawkley et al., 2003; Solano, 1987). People who report experiencing greater loneliness behave in ways that are perceived as negatively toned and highly anxious, which results in others holding a less than favorable impression of them (Lau & Gruen, 1992). In fact, lonely people experience less acceptance from others, and as a result are less responsive during social interactions (Anderson & Martin, 1995; Rotenberg &

Kmill, 1992; Wittenberg & Reis, 1986). Both adults' and adolescents' happiness and satisfaction with life is negatively related to loneliness (Neto, 1993; Riggio et al., 1993).

Shy people are also characterized as socially uncomfortable, inhibited, and interpersonally reticent, and they become negatively preoccupied with their identity prior, during, and after social interactions (Jones, Briggs, & Smith, 1986; Zimbardo, 1986, 1990). Likewise, during interactions they have trouble engaging in positive and adaptive coping behaviors (Eisenberg, Fabes, & Murphy, 1995). Shyness is also associated with emotional and interpersonal difficulties including anxiety, depression, negative affect, peer rejection, and social isolation (Findlay, Coplan, & Bowker, 2009; Henderson & Zimbardo, 2010; Twenge, 2002). Shy people also exhibit fearfulness, bitterness, and distrust; they have trouble developing relationships; and their current relationships are marked by increased negativity (Mounts, Valentiner, Anderson, & Boswell, 2006; Nelson et al., 2008; Rubin, Wojslawowicz, Rose-Krasnor, Booth-LaForce, & Burgess, 2006). Not surprisingly, a growing literature shows that shyness is strongly negatively associated with SWB for both adults and children[14] (Eisenberg et al., 1995; Findlay et al., 2009; Gross & John, 2003; Henderson & Zimbardo, 2010; Nelson et al., 2008; Rowsell & Coplan, 2013).

Self-Esteem

Although both low (LSE) and high self-esteem (HSE) individuals consider interpersonal situations important, their social lives are starkly different (Wood & Forest, 2016a). For example, LSEs (vs. HSEs) are excessively vigilant for signals of social exclusion, and they experience rejection as more painful and actually perceive and expect it to occur more frequently (Leary et al., 1995; Sommer & Baumeister, 2002; Murray, Holmes, & Griffin, 2000). Likewise, LSEs are uncertain whether others like them and express grave doubts concerning their social acceptance (Brockner & Lloyd, 1986; Campbell & Fehr, 1990; Wood et al., 2009). Even within romantic relationships, LSEs underestimate how much their partners love them (e.g., Murray et al., 2000). Considerable research also indicates that, when LSEs experience threat in their romantic relationships, they distance themselves from their partner, whereas HSEs increase reconnection efforts (Cavallo, Murray, & Holmes, 2014).

To avoid social rejection, LSEs engage in protective self-presentations, conveying a persona of guardedness, prudence, reserve, and general evasiveness (Baumeister, Tice, & Hutton, 1989; Forest & Wood, 2015d). Because of their self-protectiveness, LSEs (vs. HSEs) hide their weaknesses, engage in more self-handicapping behaviors, initiate fewer relationships, are reluctant to join groups, and approach potential romantic partners very cautiously (Anthony, Wood, & Holmes, 2007; Cameron, Stinson, & Wood, 2013; Tice, 1991). Likewise, LSEs' self-disclosures are more negative and less expressive and revealing compared to

HSEs (DePaulo, Epstein, & Lemay, 1990; Graham, Huang, Clark, & Helgeson, 2008; Gross & John, 1997, 2003). Even the content of LSEs' Facebook posts convey more negative affect, including sadness, anxiety, fear, irritability, boredom, and unhappiness (Forest & Wood, 2012); these findings are consistent with studies using standard experimental designs (e.g., Forest, Kille, Wood, & Holmes, 2015; Forest & Wood, 2015b). As a result of such chronic negativity, others generally behave less positively toward LSEs and report greater dislike for and less intention to be friends with them (Forest & Wood, 2015a).

Both research and theory posit that, even though LSEs desire acceptance as much as HSEs, LSEs may simply not be aware that people respond harshly to others' negativity (Forest & Wood, 2015c). Indeed, LSEs' chronic negativity suggests they are unaware that a cumulative history of negative disclosures adversely affects social relationships. However, to effectively manage the expression of ones' public self requires, in part, that people understand how others respond to negative behaviors, and if LSEs are unaware of how others view negative disclosures, it suggests that LSEs may lack adequate self-presentational skills.

Decades of research indicates that nearly every form of negative emotion correlates negatively with self-esteem including anxiety, depression, and sadness (Leary & MacDonald, 2003; Rosenberg, 1985; Watson & Clark, 1984). Compared to HSEs, LSEs experience more unpleasant emotions, and they are less motivated to repair their moods when unhappy (Heimpel, Wood, Marshall, & Brown, 2002; Wood, Heimpel, Manwell, & Whittington, 2009). LSEs (vs. HSEs) are also less content and satisfied with their social lives (Campbell, 1981). Moreover, LSEs (vs. HSEs) are less happy in their romantic relationships, feel less loved by specific individuals, and perceive less inclusion and acceptance in general, and their romantic relationships are less successful (Denissen, Penke, Schmitt, & van Aken, 2008; Leary & MacDonald, 2003; Wood et al., 2009). Self-esteem also correlates positively with overall life satisfaction, as well as both eudaimonic and subjective well-being (Diener, Emmons, Larsen, & Griffin, 1985; Diener, Suh, Lucas, & Smith 1999; Ryff, 1989). Although the causal direction remains uncertain, the general conclusion is not—HSEs are typically happier than LSEs (Baumeister, Campbell, Krueger, & Vohs, 2003; Wood & Forest, 2016b).

Self-Monitoring

Self-monitoring refers to how people regulate their expressive and self-presentation behaviors during social interactions. Some people, more than others, harbor greater concerns that their self-presentations are appropriate to a given situation. As a result, people high (vs. low) in self-monitoring (heretofore referred to as HSM and LSM) are more strongly motivated to attend to their behavioral expressions and to adjust their self-presentations to convey a desired identity. And for the most part, HSMs possess greater skill at controlling the images they present, and they frequently make use of these skills (Fuglestad & Snyder, 2009).

Research on self-monitoring has covered a host of topics, including attitudes, persuasion, deception, romantic relationships, consumer products, and organizational behavior. To the best of our knowledge, however, no studies directly link self-monitoring to measures of SWB. However, given their skills at managing the expression of their public self, HSMs should experience greater life satisfaction.

As noted, HSMs are particularly sensitive to and rely on socially oriented information to guide their self-presentations (Bain, Baxter, & Ballantyne, 2007; DeBono & Rubin, 1995). For example, compared to LSMs, HSMs are more likely to recall personal information about an upcoming interaction partner, are better able to judge emotional displays, are more skilled at decoding nonverbal behaviors, are more accurate at judging deceptive actions, show better performance on interpersonal perception tasks, and are more focused on their interaction partners, and they seek out and consider more information about an audience when trying to convey a particular identity (Ambady, Hallahan, & Rosenthal, 1995; Berscheid, Graziano, Monson, & Dermer, 1976; Costanzo & Archer, 1989; Ickes, Reidhead, & Patterson, 1986).

Compared to LSMs, HSMs also have more elaborate mental representations of social information, exhibit more extensive repertoires and more sophisticated understanding of social interaction scripts, have greater cognitive access to more richly developed self-presentation concepts, and make use of this information more often (Danheiser & Graziano, 1982; Douglas, 1983, 1984; Tyler, McIntyre, Graziano, & Sands, 2015). For instance, high self-monitors more frequently draw on relevant social scripts when describing interpersonal situations, are able to use social information to fashion and guide expressive behaviors that are deemed more situationally appropriate, and demonstrate greater linguistic competence, in part because they have a broader knowledge of social scripts related to contextually appropriate interactions. As Douglas (1983) notes, this "enhanced social acuity may be expected to invest HSMs with considerably more social knowledge than is possessed by LSMs" (p. 82).

In addition, Turnley and Bolino (2001) found, consistent with prior work, that HSMs (vs. LSMs) are more effective and skilled at expressing emotions, at engaging in social communications, and at conveying desirable identity-images; HSMs are also perceived as more likable and approachable when engaging in such efforts (Anderson, 1990; Caldwell & O'Reilly, 1982; Lippa, 1976; Snyder, 1974; Zaccaro, Foti, & Kenny, 1991). HSMs' social acuity also provides them the skills to perform better in *boundary spanning* positions that require employees to socially interact and communicate with groups inside and outside an organization and thus call for the individual to adapt to new social situations and changing group norms (Caldwell & O'Reilly, 1982).

Although no work directly shows that HSMs have greater SWB, their well-documented skill at navigating social interactions and managing their public image may allow them to more easily develop social bonds (Gabrenya & Arkin, 1980). This heightened ability to develop social connections likely fosters greater relational value and enhances belongingness. In turn, the satisfaction of one's belonging needs should subsequently lead to greater SWB.

Ambivalent, Inaccurate, or Inconsistent Expressive Behaviors

For the most part, people's efforts to manage the expression of their public self involve truthful claims (Schlenker, 2003). At times, however, people's public expressions can be less than accurate or overly enhancing, and in some cases, people simply conceal information about themselves. In this section, we discuss ambivalent, inaccurate, and inconsistent expressions; in the second section, we discuss self-enhancement, self-evaluative bias, and capitalization (e.g., the tendency to share positive events with others), and in the last section, we address disclosure and concealment.

When people's social behaviors are confusing, ambivalent, or difficult to interpret, they experience relational difficulty. Theorists following a social-functional perspective (Keltner & Haidt, 1999) posit that emotions function to guide people's social interactions. Specifically, positive emotions convey one's intention to form a social bond and prompt others to experience positive emotions, which then fosters short- and long-term social connections (Anderson, Keltner, & John, 2003; Frijda & Mesquita, 1994; Keltner & Haidt, 1999; King, 2000; Reis & Patrick, 1996). However, whether positive emotions lead to adaptive relational effects hinges on how accurately they are communicated (Buck, 1994; Keltner & Kring, 1998). When one's emotional state corresponds to the actual expression of one's emotions, social communication improves, but if behavioral expressions are disconnected from one's emotional state, communications suffer, diminishing the overall quality of one's social interactions (Bonanno et al., 2007; Boone & Buck, 2003; Keltner & Kring, 1998; Wubben, De Cremer, & Van Dijk, 2009).

Theorists argue that, when emotional states and behavioral expressions are dissociated, others perceive the individual as confused, as withholding key aspects of the self, as less trustworthy, and as less authentic (Bonanno et al., 2007; Boone & Buck, 2003; English & John, 2013). These characteristics suggest that the individual would be less effective at managing the expression of his/her public self, which may lead to decrements in SWB. In support, Mauss et al. (2011) found that, when positive experience and behavior were dissociated, people experienced increased depression and lower levels of SWB, even 6 months later.

Likewise, people who exhibit ambivalence concerning their expressive behaviors are less self-disclosing and experience increased depression and anxiety (Katz & Campbell, 1994; King & Emmons, 1990, 1991). Similarly, those who display a fear of intimacy are less likely to express intimate feelings or disclose personal information (Descutner & Thelen, 1991). Not surprisingly, well-being measures are negatively correlated with both ambivalence and fear of intimacy (Emmons & King, 1988; King & Emmons, 1990; King & Emmons, 1991). In addition, people who suppress expressive behaviors experience interpersonal communication problems (English & John, 2013; Gross & John, 2003; Srivastava, Tamir, McGonigal, John, & Gross, 2009). For example, they have difficulties expressing empathy, developing complex self and other representations, and they tend to lack assertiveness, all of which diminishes the quality of their social relationships and leads to lower SWB (Bonanno & Singer, 1990; Emmons, 1991; Lane & Schwartz, 1987; Weinberger, 1990).

Other work shows that people who exhibit greater consistency (less variability) in personality trait profiles (i.e., the Big Five) across different role contexts are viewed as more authentic and score higher on various indices of SWB (Donahue, Robins, Roberts, & John, 1993; Sheldon, Ryan, Rawsthorne, & Ilardi, 1997). Research examining Facebook identities has produced similar results (Ellison, Steinfield, & Lampe, 2007; Michikyan, Dennis, & Subrahmanyam, 2015). Such findings are consistent with Grieve and Watkinson's (2016) analysis in which they posited that expressive behaviors that are more authentic, consistent, and believable are positively related to greater SWB. When one's expressive behaviors are confusing, ambivalent, difficult to interpret, or inconsistent others have difficulty trusting the individual, which in turn damages social connections and reduces SWB.

Self-Enhancement, Self-Evaluative Bias, and Capitalization

Self-enhancement is characterized as people's efforts to convey personal behaviors, tendencies, events, and even situations in a relatively positive fashion. People with greater SWB construe the same life events and social encounters as more favorable and positive than do people with lower SWB (Lyubomirsky & Ross, 1999; Lyubomirsky & Tucker, 1998). Theorists posit that happier people's attributional tendency to view their life circumstances positively adds to the general stability of their SWB (Ryan & Deci, 2001).

Additional work also provides evidence for a linear relationship between self-enhancement and a host of beneficial outcomes. For example, friends describe high (compared to low) self-enhancers as more psychologically adjusted and mentally healthy, and as having minimal disappointments concerning life accomplishments. High (vs. low) self-enhancers also make a more favorable impression on others and are characterized as more confident, having a more positive life attitude, having an easier time maintaining relationships, and their friends view them more positively and like them better (Taylor, Lerner, Sherman, Sage, & McDowell, 2003). Self-enhancement also leads to more social connections and increased SWB (Taylor et al., 2013). Likewise, positively oriented self-presentations, which are akin to self-enhancement, are also positively related to SWB (Kim & Roselyn, 2011). In addition, people who describe both themselves and others in more positive terms (positive evaluative bias) also exhibit greater SWB (Kim, Schimmack, & Oishi, 2012; Wood, Harms, & Vazire, 2010).

Capitalization—the tendency to share positive and enhancing events with others—also fosters relational connections and strengthens social relationships (Gable & Reis, 2001). For example, on days that people communicate positive life episodes to others, they experience greater positive affect, life satisfaction, and SWB, regardless of the importance or frequency of these events (Gable, Reis, Impett, & Asher, 2004). Moreover, couples who demonstrate support and enthusiasm for positive (vs. negative) spousal events exhibit increased well-being across both self-report data and coded observations, and this effect holds even 2 months later (Gable, Gonzaga, & Strachman, 2006).

Disclosure and Concealment

Self-disclosure is a complicated social exchange that requires self-management and control and should entail the capacity to effectively manage the expression of one's public self. Although research indicates that self-disclosure leads to deeper, more meaningful relationships, little research has explored the relationship between self-disclosure and life satisfaction (Berg, & Wright-Buckley, 1988; Reis & Shaver, 1988). However, from Pennebaker and colleague's work, we know that people's psychological health and SWB typically improve after they engage in written emotional self-disclosures (Pennebaker, 1985; Pennebaker, 1990; Pennebaker & Beall, 1986; Pennebaker, Colder, & Sharp, 1990). More recent work also indicates that the disclosure of emotional information is associated with increased life satisfaction (Butzel & Ryan 1997; for review, see Ryan & Deci, 2001). For example, spurning opportunities to engage in disclosure or being unresponsive to a friend's disclosure diminishes social connections and is negatively associated with well-being indices (Bevan, Gomez, & Sparks, 2014). In contrast, when bloggers share what they are thinking, feeling, and experiencing via self-disclosures, they report increased social connectedness and SWB (Ko & Kuo, 2009). Likewise, people who self-disclose more to their romantic partners are more tender and loving, experience greater relationship satisfaction, and are more likely to remain in the relationship (Sprecher & Hendrick, 2004).

Theorists posit that people with ecosystem motivations consider the impact that self-disclosures have on the self and others; they also consider the extent to which a disclosure promotes positive social outcomes (Crocker, Garcia, & Nuer, 2008). People with such motivations disclose with the clear understanding that it will impact their interaction partner. Those with greater ecosystem motivations experience reduced fear of disclosure, engage in more disclosures, and as a result exhibit greater positive affect and SWB (Chaudoir & Quinn, 2010; Garcia & Crocker, 2008).

In addition, people who are skilled at getting others to disclose information about themselves—referred to as *openers*, find it easier to prompt others to interact with them (Miller, Berg, & Archer, 1983). Their social behaviors tend to overlap with effective self-presentational efforts. Specifically, high (vs. low) openers enjoy social interactions, are interpersonally comfortable and socially agreeable, and their facial expressions are more attentive and engaging (Colvin & Longueuil, 2001; Shaffer, Ruammake, & Pegalis, 1990; Purvis, Dabbs, & Hopper, 1984). Moreover, people like high openers better than low openers because their behaviors foster social and affiliative connections, which subsequently leads to greater SWB for high openers (Miller, Berg, & Archer, 1983).

The counterpart to self-disclosure involves efforts to conceal or withhold emotional disclosures, which negatively impacts people's psychological health (King & Pennebaker, 1998; Ryan & Deci, 2001). High concealers are notably concerned with social evaluation, and concealment is positively correlated with evaluative constructs ranging from fear of negative evaluation and social reticence to loss of face concerns and perfectionism (DeRosa, 2000; DiBartolo, Li, & Frost, 2008; Hewitt et al., 2003; Larson, Chastain, Hoyt, & Ayzenberg, 2015; Leventhal, 2009). People high in concealment avoid risk, keep life events secret, withhold key information from therapists, fear intimate disclosures, and are afforded less social support, and the relationships they develop are often not secure (Cruddas, Gilbert, & McEwan, 2012; Cramer, Gallant, & Langlois, 2005; Fedde, 2009; Lopez & Rice, 2006; Kelly & Achter, 1995; Mohr & Kendra, 2011; Murphy, Shevlin, Adamson, Cruddas, & Houston, 2012; Reyome, Ward, & Witkiewitz, 2010). High concealers are also ambivalent about and effortfully inhibit and control the expression of their emotions (Barr, Kahn, & Schneider, 2008; King, Emmons, & Woodley, 1992; Zayco, 2008).

High (vs. low) concealers also experience more anxiety, depression, and loneliness (Kahn & Hessling, 2001; King et al., 1992). Likewise, concealment is negatively associated with SWB; in fact, SWB decreases on the days that people conceal aspects of the self from others (DeNeve & Cooper, 1998; Uysal, Lin, & Knee, 2010). A growing consensus also negatively links concealment to well-being within romantic relationships; for example, high concealers report greater marital dissatisfaction, less trust in their partner, and increased marital conflicts (Finkenauer & Hazam, 2000; Finkenauer, Kerkhof, Righetti, & Branje, 2009; Uysal, Lin, Knee, & Bush, 2012; Wickham & Knee, 2013).

Finally, research indicates that people high in perfectionism typically conceal and avoid admitting to less-than-perfect behaviors. They also keep errors and self-oriented information secret, even if sharing their problems has distinct advantages (Hewitt, Habke, Lee-Baggley, Sherry, & Flett, 2008; Kawamura & Frost, 2004). As a result of such concealment, people high on perfectionism also report lower SWB (Hewitt & Flett, 2002; Mackinnon & Sherry, 2012).

General Discussion

Considerable evidence has accumulated to support the idea that people have a basic need to belong. The satisfaction of this need requires that others perceive an individual in a relatively positive fashion and deem him/her as relationally valued and socially acceptable. Therefore, people are highly motivated to exhibit personal characteristics and behaviors that align with socially accepted attributes and convey a desirable impression. To do so, people engage in self-presentation—they manage the behavioral expression of their public self (Leary, 1995; Schlenker, 1980, 2003). People also monitor the degree to which their self-presentations successfully influence their relational value; if effective, they experience a greater sense of belongingness and greater SWB.

Managing the expression of one's public self involves efforts to demonstrate that one possesses the positive qualities (e.g., open, confident, positive, sociable, reliable, trustworthy, likable, interesting, and friendly) considered necessary for a good relational partner. These behavioral qualities resemble some of the characteristics and attributes associated with the factors we discussed in the evidence section (e.g., extraversion, self-esteem, shyness). Moreover, the behavioral qualities (e.g., sociable, gregarious, engaging, warm, open, socially skilled, friendly, emotionally expressive, optimistic, confident, worry-free) of people who score higher on these factors (e.g., HSE) illustrate how we would typically characterize the behaviors of people who are more effective at managing the expression of their public self, which should enhance social connections and increase SWB. This description is consistent with Diener et al.'s (1995) general statement that the "happy individual is one who is extraverted, generally optimistic, and worry-free" (p. 282; see also Wilson, 1967). By comparison, the behavioral qualities (e.g., less warm and friendly, closed, emotionally suppressive, ambivalent, shy) of people who score lower on these factors (e.g., LSE) are similar to the characteristics of people who are less effective at managing the expression of their pubic self, which makes it more difficult for them to develop relationships and likely results in lower SWB.

To reiterate, we are not claiming that self-presentational skill is the only pathway to happiness, rather we posit simply that being an effective manager of one's public self makes the pathway to SWB smoother. Skillful self-presenters are better able to effectively manage the expression of their public self in a fashion that conveys a favorable and relationally valuable impression. From the descriptions of the factors in the evidence section, it would appear that some people (e.g., extraverts) possess more rather than less of these particular skills. To be sure, we are not claiming, for example, that introverts or socially anxious people are miserable, just that they find it more socially difficult to successfully navigate a smooth path to happiness.

One may wonder whether the behavioral qualities associated with the various factors (e.g., extravert) represent efforts to manage the expression of one's public self, or are these qualities simply representative of one's *true* personality traits. Although these options may seem mutually exclusive, they are not; just because one's expressive behaviors are a truthful rendition of one's identity should *not* be interpreted as meaning people are *not* managing the expression of their public self. Truth-telling does not indicate the absence of self-presentation, in fact, we, along with many theorists assert that the vast majority of self-presentations fall within the boundaries of truth (DePaulo, 1992; Schlenker, 2003). This latter position is consistent with the wider theoretical perspective that self-presentation involves non-conscious, automatic, and ongoing efforts to manage the expression of one's public self (Leary & Kowalski, 1990; Schlenker, 2003; Tyler, 2012; Tyler & Adams, 2017). The disclosures involved in such efforts rarely involve outright falsehoods; rather, they typically include somewhat enriched statements that highlight and illustrate one's interests, likes, dislikes, beliefs, and attitudes, as well as more broadly, the tone, nature, and general essence of one's behavioral expressions.

Beginning early in life, people learn to publically express their identity to others, and while these self-presentations are partially constrained by stable personality characteristics (i.e., genetics), they are not immutable. People can learn and adopt various ways to socially express themselves that go beyond their dispositional tendencies. In effect, they can learn how to behaviorally express themselves in a socially acceptable and favorable manner; however, these efforts nonetheless, remain grounded in their *true* personality—they are not lies. With that in mind, it is not a giant leap to imagine that the skills and behaviors associated with effectively managing the expression of one's public self can be learned, practiced, and improved upon at any point in one's life, with the underlying precept that even marginally improving self-presentational abilities can increase the likelihood of developing valued social connections, leading subsequently to greater SWB.

Not everyone possesses the same intrinsic capacity to smoothly navigate social relationships. However, just as we learn the fundamentals of mathematics, learning basic interpersonal skills (e.g., express less negativity) to optimize the likelihood of greater SWB represents an outcome that most people desire. We posit that the overwhelming evidence showing that relational connections and increased belongingness nearly always result in greater SWB is reason enough to better learn how to navigate one's social relationships. However, we are not encouraging people to simply *fake* social behaviors—it is not our intent to suggest that a shy person will magically learn how to be the most socially outgoing person in the room. Nonetheless, we are proposing that an ample number of the negative social behaviors we outlined are, in part, learned, and as such, are open to improvement via increased learning and continued practice.

The majority of the research we summarized concerning the self-presentation—SWB relationship was indirect and inferential. As we speculated previously, the path underlying this relationship is likely mediated by the ability to establish social connections and increased belongingness. However, no research has directly measured or manipulated self-presentational efforts within this conceptual frame, nor has any tried to empirically link SWB to self-presentation. Thus, future research would do well to examine if and when this relationship may involve a direct path or is such a path necessarily mediated by increased social connections and belongingness. Such examinations would require measuring self-presentations with more behavioral specificity than has typically been done in the past (see Leary et al., 2011).

Conclusion

From the evidence presented, it would seem safe to say that some people have more of an important and desired resource than others—namely, SWB. Given the manifest importance of establishing and maintaining satisfying social connections and relationships (i.e., belongingness), it stands to reason that people who have more rather than less skill at effectively managing the expression of their public self should also exhibit greater SWB. It is not much of a stretch to claim that it is psychologically healthier to possess more of these expressive qualities than less— from our perspective, the majority of evidence strongly suggests that those who do are more likely to be part of a valued *tribe* and report greater happiness than those who exhibit less of these qualities. By their inherently social nature, people desire positive social relationships and self-presentational skills may represent a key mechanism by which people acquire such relationships, and when quality relationships emerge, clear indications of positive psychological health, in the guise of greater SWB, are abundantly evident. In all, the preponderance of evidence supports the proposition that possessing better skills at managing the expression of one's public self results in increased SWB. We hope that our chapter encourages research designed to better understand the sequential process running from self-presentation to relational value to belongingness to increased SWB.

Notes

1 We examine the relationship between self-presentation and people's overall sense of well-being, with the acknowledgment that as a general term, well-being can encompass a variety of different outcomes. For example, well-being can include objective mental and physical health indicators, feelings of personal growth and autonomy (i.e., psychological well-being; Ryff, 1989), or one's general sense of happiness and satisfaction with life (Diener & Lucas, 1999; Ryan & Deci, 2001; Ryff, 1989). An in-depth discussion of these facets is beyond the scope of the current chapter. Our discussion primarily (though not exclusively) focuses on individuals' subjective sense of happiness and life satisfaction, that is, their subjective well-being (SWB). SWB has a long history in the positive psychology literature and has been widely studied using well-defined and validated instruments (Diener & Lucas, 1999). SWB is also correlated with several aspects of well-being, such as feelings of personal growth and autonomy (e.g., Sheldon & Niemiec, 2006; see Biswas-Diener, Kashdan, & King, 2009, for an overview); thus, SWB might also serve as a multidimensional "proxy" for other key facets of well-being. Our focus on SWB, however, should not be taken as a statement on the relative importance of the different well-being outcomes and measures.
2 We note that, while it is certainly important to examine the degree to which belongingness mediates the association between self-presentation and SWB, this question lies outside the scope of the current chapter.
3 We do not view the sociometer as a device inside a person but simply use it as a convenient shorthand term for a complex interpersonal process that people engage in automatically.
4 One's outer appearance also provides some degree of personal information.
5 In some cases, the favorable impression is associated with negative characteristics (e.g., behaving aggressively).

6 With little doubt, being rejected or excluded diminishes one's sense of belongingness (DeWall & Richman, 2011). However, while there is some evidence that under certain conditions (i.e., prospect of social acceptance) people may increase self-presentations (e.g., behave cooperatively, prosocially) as a result of rejection, to the best of our knowledge, there is no work that directly examines, links, or measures SWB within this context.

7 For the sake of clarity, we discuss self-esteem in a categorical frame as being either high or low.

8 Although self-presentations to adjust the public self may more or less successfully improve one's relational value, for the sake of simplicity, we discuss the potential outcomes in discrete terms of being successful or not successful.

9 This situation is similar to the initial context described earlier in which the individual is viewed favorably from the outset of a particular social interaction.

10 This is not to say, of course, that all introverted people or people with low self-esteem, for example, are unhappy.

11 The finding associated with the frequency of social relationships supports the idea that belongingness may mediate the self-presentation-SWB relationship.

12 We cannot express *why* any more clearly than Segrin and Taylor (2007): It is understandable why people with good social skills would experience positive relations with others. People who are capable of accurately reading other people's emotional states, clearly communicating their ideas and feelings, and effectively managing their own emotional states in social situations will, by and large, leave a positive impression on other people. These positive experiences become the building blocks of successful relationships with other people. Positive relations with others are so essential to virtually any theory of social skills that the social skills construct would be rendered virtually meaningless if it could not be shown that it was associated with these positive interpersonal outcomes (p. 644).

13 There is also evidence indicating that belongingness partially mediates the relationship between social skills and SWB (Riggio et al., 1993; Segrin & Taylor, 2007).

14 Certainly not all shy people experience social adjustment problems; evidence with children suggests that stable relationships with key others (i.e., parents, teachers) can attenuate the frequency of negative outcomes (e.g., anxiety, depression) while promoting SWB (Rubin, Coplan, & Bowker, 2009).

References

Adler, A. (1930). Individual psychology. In C. Murchison (Ed.), *Psychologies of 1930* (pp. 395–405). Worcester, MA: Clark University Press.

Ambady, N., Hallahan, M., & Rosenthal, R. (1995). On judging and being judged accurately in zero-acquaintance situations. *Journal of Personality and Social Psychology, 69*(3), 518–529.

Anderson, C., Keltner, D., & John, O. P. (2003). Emotional convergence between people over time. *Journal of Personality and Social Psychology, 84*, 1054–1068. doi: 10.1037/0022–3514.84.5.1054

Anderson, C. M., & Martin, M. M. (1995). The effects of communication motives, interaction involvement, and loneliness on satisfaction: A model of small groups. *Small Group Research, 26*(1), 118–137.

Anderson, L. R. (1990). Toward a two-track model of leadership training: Suggestions from self-monitoring theory. *Small Group Research, 21*(2), 147–167.

Anthony, D. B., Wood, J. V., & Holmes, J. G. (2007). Testing sociometer theory: Self-esteem and the importance of acceptance for social decision-making. *Journal of Experimental Social Psychology, 43*, 425–432.

Argyle, M. (1987). *The psychology of happiness*. London: Routledge.

Bain, S. A., Baxter, J. S., & Ballantyne, K. (2007). Self-monitoring style and levels of interrogative suggestibility. *Personality and Individual Differences, 42*(4), 623–630.

Baldwin, M. W. (1992). Relational schemas and the processing of social information. *Psychological Bulletin, 112,* 461–484.

Baldwin, M. W. (1994). Primed relational schemas as a source of self-evaluative reactions. *Journal of Social and Clinical Psychology, 13,* 380–403.

Baldwin, M. W., & Sinclair, L. (1996). Self-esteem and "if . . . then" contingencies of interpersonal acceptance. *Journal of Personality and Social Psychology, 71,* 1130–1141.

Barr, L. K., Kahn, J. H., & Schneider, W. J. (2008). Individual differences in emotion expression: Hierarchical structure and relations with psychological distress. *Journal of Social and Clinical Psychology, 27*(10), 1045–1077.

Baumeister, R. F. (1991). *Meanings of life*. New York: Guilford Press.

Baumeister, R. F., Campbell, J. D., Krueger, J. I., & Vohs, K. D. (2003). Does high self-esteem cause better performance, interpersonal success, happiness, or healthier lifestyles? *Psychological Science in the Public Interest, 4,* 1–44.

Baumeister, R. F., & Leary, M. R. (1995). The need to belong: Desire for interpersonal attachments as a fundamental human motivation. *Psychological Bulletin, 117,* 497–529.

Baumeister, R. F., Tice, D. M., & Hutton, D. G. (1989). Self-presentational motivations and personality differences in self-esteem. *Journal of Personality, 57,* 547–579.

Berg, J. H., & Wright-Buckley, C. (1988). Effects of racial similarity and interviewer intimacy in a peer counseling analogue. *Journal of Counseling Psychology, 35*(4), 377–384.

Berscheid, E., Graziano, W., Monson, T. C., & Dermer, M. (1976). Outcome dependency: Attention, attribution, and attraction. *Journal of Personality and Social Psychology, 34,* 978–989. doi: 10.1037/0022–3514.34.5.978

Bevan, J. L., Gomez, R., & Sparks, L. (2014). Disclosures about important life events on Facebook: Relationships with stress and quality of life. *Computers in Human Behavior, 39,* 246–253.

Biswas-Diener, R., Kashdan, T. B., & King, L. A. (2009). Two traditions of happiness research, not two distinct types of happiness. *The Journal of Positive Psychology, 4*(3), 208–211.

Bonanno, G. A., Colak, D. M., Keltner, D., Shiota, M. N., Papa, A., Noll, J. G., . . . Trickett, P. K. (2007). Context matters: The benefits and costs of expressing positive emotion among survivors of childhood sexual abuse. *Emotion, 7,* 824–837. doi: 10.1037/1528–3542.7.4.824

Bonanno, G. A., & Singer, J. L. (1990). Repressive personality style: Theoretical and methodological implications for health and pathology. In J. L. Singer (Ed.), *Repression and dissociation: Implications for personality theory, psychopathology, and health* (pp. 435–470). Chicago, IL: University of Chicago Press.

Boone, R. T., & Buck, R. (2003). Emotional expressivity and trustworthiness: The role of nonverbal behavior in the evolution of cooperation. *Journal of Nonverbal Behavior, 27*(3), 163–182.

Bradburn, N. M. (1969). *The structure of psychological well-being*. Oxford: Aldine.

Brebner, J., Donaldson, J., Kirby, N., & Ward, L. (1995). Relationships between happiness and personality. *Personality and Individual Differences, 19*(2), 251–258.

Brockner, J., & Lloyd, K. (1986). Self-esteem and likability: Separating fact from fantasy. *Journal of Research in Personality, 20,* 496–508.

Bruch, M. A., Kaflowitz, N. G., & Pearl, L. (1988). Mediated and nonmediated relationships of personality components to loneliness. *Journal of Social and Clinical Psychology, 6*(3–4), 346–355.

Buck, R. (1994). Social and emotional functions in facial expression and communication: The readout hypothesis. *Biological Psychology, 38*(2), 95–115.

Butzel, J. S., & Ryan, R. M. (1997). The dynamics of volitional reliance. In G. R. Pierce, B. Lakey, I. G. Sarason, & B. R. Sarason (Eds.), *Sourcebook of social support and personality* (pp. 49–67). Boston, MA: Springer.

Caldwell, D. F., & O'Reilly, C. A. (1982). Boundary spanning and individual performance: The impact of self-monitoring. *Journal of Applied Psychology, 67*(1), 124.

Cameron, J. J., Stinson, D. A., & Wood, J. V. (2013). The bold and the bashful: Self-esteem, gender, and relationship initiation. *Social Psychological and Personality Science, 4*, 685–691.

Campbell, A. (1981). *The sense of well-being in America: Recent patterns and trends.* New York: McGraw-Hill.

Campbell, J. D., & Fehr, B. (1990). Self-esteem and perceptions of conveyed impressions: Is negative affectivity associated with greater realism? *Journal of Personality and Social Psychology, 58*, 122–133.

Cavallo, J. V., Murray, S. L., & Holmes, J. G. (2014). Risk regulation in close relationships. In M. Mikulincer & P. R. Shaver (Eds.), *The Herzliya series on personality and social psychology: Mechanisms of social connection: From brain to group* (pp. 237–254). Washington, DC: American Psychological Association.

Chan, R., & Joseph, S. (2000). Dimensions of personality, domains of aspiration, and subjective well-being. *Personality and Individual Differences, 28*(2), 347–354.

Chaudoir, S. R., & Quinn, D. M. (2010). Revealing concealable stigmatized identities: The impact of disclosure motivations and positive first-disclosure experiences on fear of disclosure and well-being. *Journal of Social Issues, 66*(3), 570–584.

Colvin, C. R., & Longueuil, D. (2001). Eliciting self-disclosure: The personality and behavioral correlates of the opener scale. *Journal of Research in Personality, 35*(2), 238–246.

Costa, P. T., & McCrae, R. R. (1980). Influence of extraversion and neuroticism on subjective well-being: Happy and unhappy people. *Journal of Personality and Social Psychology, 38*, 668–678.

Costa, P. T., & McCrae, R. R. (1984). Personality as a lifelong determinant of well-being. In C. Z. Malatesta and C. E. Izzard (Eds.), *Emotion in adult development* (pp. 141–157). Beverly Hills, CA: Sage.

Costanzo, M., & Archer, D. (1989). Interpreting the expressive behavior of others: The interpersonal perception task. *Journal of Nonverbal Behavior, 13*(4), 225–245.

Cramer, K. M., Gallant, M. D., & Langlois, M. W. (2005). Self-silencing and depression in women and men: Comparative structural equation models. *Personality and Individual Differences, 39*(3), 581–592.

Crocker, J., Garcia, J. A., & Nuer, N. (2008). From egosystem to ecosystem in intergroup interactions: Implications for intergroup reconciliation. In A. Nadler, T. Molloy & J. D. Fisher (Eds.), *The social psychology of intergroup reconciliation* (pp. 171–194). New York: McGraw-Hill.

Crozier, W. R., & Alden, L. E. (2001). The social nature of social anxiety. In W. R. Crozier & L. E. Alden (Eds.), *International handbook of social anxiety: Concepts, research and interventions relating to the self and shyness* (pp. 1–20). New York: Wiley.

Cruddas, S., Gilbert, P., & McEwan, K. (2012). The relationship between self-concealment and disclosure, early experiences, attachment, and social comparison. *International Journal of Cognitive Therapy, 5*, 28–37. doi: 10.1521/ijct.2012.5.1.28

Danheiser, P. R., & Graziano, W. G. (1982). Self-monitoring and cooperation as a self-presentational strategy. *Journal of Personality and Social Psychology, 42*, 469–497. doi: 10.1037/0022–3514.42.3.497

DeBono, K. G., & Rubin, K. (1995). Country of origin and perceptions of product quality: An individual difference perspective. *Basic and Applied Social Psychology, 17*(1–2), 239–247.

DeNeve, K. M., & Cooper, H. (1998). The happy personality: A meta-analysis of 137 personality traits and subjective well-being. *Psychological Bulletin, 124,* 197–229.

Denissen, J. J., Penke, L., Schmitt, D. P., & Van Aken, M. A. (2008). Self-esteem reactions to social interactions: Evidence for sociometer mechanisms across days, people, and nations. *Journal of Personality and Social Psychology, 95*(1), 181–196.

DePaulo, B. M. (1992). Nonverbal behavior and self-presentation. *Psychological Bulletin, 111*(2), 203–243.

DePaulo, B. M., Epstein, J. A., & Lemay, C. S. (1990). Responses of the socially anxious to the prospect of interpersonal evaluation. *Journal of Personality, 58,* 623–640.

DeRosa, T. (2000). Personality, help-seeking attitudes, and depression in adolescents (Doctoral thesis). University of Toronto, Toronto, Canada. Retrieved from https://tspace.library.utoronto.ca/bitstream/1807/14074/1/NQ49894.pdf

Descutner, C. J., & Thelen, M. H. (1991). Development and validation of a fear-of-intimacy scale. *Psychological Assessment: A Journal of Consulting and Clinical Psychology, 3*(2), 218–225.

DeWall, C. N., & Richman, S. B. (2011). Social exclusion and the desire to reconnect. *Social and Personality Psychology Compass, 5*(11), 919–932.

DiBartolo, P. M., Li, C. Y., & Frost, R. O. (2008). How do the dimensions of perfectionism relate to mental health? *Cognitive Therapy and Research, 32*(3), 401–417.

Diener, E. (1984). Subjective well-being. *Psychological Bulletin, 95,* 542–575.

Diener, E., Emmons, R. A., Larsen, R. J., & Griffin, S. (1985). The satisfaction with life scale. *Journal of Personality Assessment, 49,* 71–75.

Diener, E., & Lucas, R. (1999). Personality, and subjective well-being. In Kahneman, D., Diener, E. & Schwarz, N. (Eds.) *Well-being: The foundations of hedonic psychology* (pp. 213–229). New York: Russell Sage Foundation.

Diener, E., Sandvik, E., Pavot, W., & Fujita, F. (1992). Extraversion and subjective well-being in a U.S. national probability sample. *Journal of Research in Personality, 26,* 205–215.

Diener, E., & Seligman, M. E. (2002). Very happy people. *Psychological Science, 13*(1), 81–84.

Diener, E., Suh, E. M., Lucas, R. E., & Smith, H. L. (1999). Subjective well-being: Three decades of progress. *Psychological Bulletin, 125*(2), 276–302.

Donahue, E. M., Robins, R. W., Roberts, B. W., & John, O. P. (1993). The divided self: Concurrent and longitudinal effects of psychological adjustment and social roles on self-concept differentiation. *Journal of Personality and Social Psychology, 64*(5), 834–846.

Douglas, W. (1983). Scripts and self-monitoring: When does being a high self-monitor really make a difference? *Human Communication Research, 10,* 81–96. doi: 10.1111/j.1468–2958.1983.tb00005.x

Douglas, W. (1984). Initial interaction scripts: When knowing is behaving. *Human Communication Research, 11,* 203–219. doi: 10.1111/j.1468–2958.1984.tb00045.x

Dykstra, P. A., Van Tilburg, T. G., & Gierveld, J. D. J. (2005). Changes in older adult loneliness: Results from a seven-year longitudinal study. *Research on Aging, 27*(6), 725–747.

Eisenberg, N., Fabes, R. A., & Murphy, B. (1995). The relations of shyness and low sociability to regulation and emotionality. *Journal of Personality and Social Psychology, 68,* 505–517.

Eisenberg, N., Fabes, R. A., Murphy, B., Maszk, P., Smith, M., & Karbon, M. (1995). The role of emotionality and regulation in children's social functioning: A longitudinal study. *Child Development, 66,* 1360–1384.

Ellison, N. B., Steinfield, C., & Lampe, C. (2007). The benefits of Facebook "friends": Social capital and college students' use of online social network sites. *Journal of Computer-Mediated Communication, 12*(4), 1143–1168.

Emmons, R. (1991). Personal strivings, daily life events, and psychological and physical well-being. *Journal of Personality, 59*, 453–472.

Emmons, R. A., & Diener, E. (1986). An interactional approach to the study of personality and emotion. *Journal of Personality, 54*, 371–384.

Emmons, R. A., & King, L. A. (1988). Conflict among personal strivings: Immediate and long-term implications for psychological and physical well-being. *Journal of Personality and Social Psychology, 54*, 1040–1048.

English, T., & John, O. P. (2013). Understanding the social effects of emotion regulation: The mediating role of authenticity for individual differences in suppression. *Emotion, 13*(2), 314–329.

Fedde, F. (2009). *Secret keeping and working alliance: The impact of concealment on the therapeutic process and the development of a solid client -therapist relationship* (Order No. 3400158). Available from ProQuest Dissertations & Theses Global. (304925391). Retrieved from https://search.proquest.com/docview/304925391?accountid=13360

Findlay, L. C., Coplan, R. J., & Bowker, A. (2009). Keeping it all inside: Shyness, internalizing coping strategies and socio-emotional adjustment in middle childhood. *International Journal of Behavioral Development, 33*(1), 47–54.

Finkenauer, C., & Hazam, H. (2000). Disclosure and secrecy in marriage: Do both contribute to marital satisfaction? *Journal of Social and Personal Relationships, 17*(2), 245–263.

Finkenauer, C., Kerkhof, P., Righetti, F., & Branje, S. (2009). Living together apart: Perceived concealment as a signal of exclusion in marital relationships. *Personality and Social Psychology Bulletin, 35*(10), 1410–1422.

Fleeson, W., Malanos, A. B., & Achille, N. M. (2002). An intraindividual process approach to the relationship between extraversion and positive affect: Is acting extraverted as "good" as being extraverted? *Journal of Personality and Social Psychology, 83*(6), 1409–1422.

Forest, A. L., Kille, D. R., Wood, J. V., & Holmes, J. G. (2014). Discount and disengage: How chronic negative expressivity undermines partner responsiveness to negative disclosures. *Journal of Personality and Social Psychology, 107*, 1013–1032.

Forest, A. L., Kille, D. R., Wood, J. V., & Holmes, J. G. (2015). Reasons for expressing positivity and negativity to romantic partners. Unpublished raw data. Cited in Wood, J. V., & Forest, A. L. (2016). Self-protective yet self-defeating: The paradox of low self-esteem people's self-disclosures. In J. M. Olson & M. P. Zanna (Eds.), *Advances in experimental social psychology* (Vol. 53, pp. 131–181). Cambridge, MA: Academic Press.

Forest, A. L., & Wood, J. V. (2012). When social networking is not working: Individuals with low self-esteem recognize but do not reap the benefits of self-disclosure on Facebook. *Psychological Science, 23*, 295–302.

Forest, A. L., & Wood, J. V. (2015a). Expressivity and relationship development between college roommates. Unpublished raw data. Cited in Wood, J. V., & Forest, A. L. (2016). Self-protective yet self-defeating: The paradox of low self-esteem people's self-disclosures. In J. M. Olson & M. P. Zanna (Eds.), *Advances in experimental social psychology* (Vol. 53, pp. 131–181). Cambridge, MA: Academic Press.

Forest, A. L., & Wood, J. V. (2015b). Expressivity in friend dyads. Unpublished raw data. Cited in Wood, J. V., & Forest, A. L. (2016). Self-protective yet self-defeating: The paradox of low self-esteem people's self-disclosures. In J. M. Olson & M. P. Zanna

(Eds.), *Advances in experimental social psychology* (Vol. 53, pp. 131–181). Cambridge, MA: Academic Press.

Forest, A. L., & Wood, J. V. (2015c). Perceptions of others' Facebook posts. Unpublished raw data. Cited in Wood, J. V., & Forest, A. L. (2016). Self-protective yet self-defeating: The paradox of low self-esteem people's self-disclosures. In J. M. Olson & M. P. Zanna (Eds.), *Advances in experimental social psychology* (Vol. 53, pp. 131–181). Cambridge, MA: Academic Press.

Forest, A. L., & Wood, J. V. (2015d). Self-protection, self-esteem-boosting, and unburdened reward pursuit: How self-esteem-related motives affect behavior in interpersonal relationships. Cited in Wood, J. V., & Forest, A. L. (2016). Self-protective yet self-defeating: The paradox of low self-esteem people's self-disclosures. In J. M. Olson & M. P. Zanna (Eds.), *Advances in experimental social psychology* (Vol. 53, pp. 131–181). Cambridge, MA: Academic Press.

Frijda, N. H., & Mesquita, B. (1994). The social roles and functions of emotions. In S. Kitayama & H. R. Markus (Eds.), *Emotion and culture: Empirical studies of mutual influence* (pp. 51–87). Washington, DC: American Psychological Association.

Fuglestad, P. T., & Snyder, M. (2009). Self-monitoring: Appraisal and reappraisal. In M. R. Leary & R. H. Hoyle (Eds.), *Handbook of individual differences in social behavior* (pp. 574–591). New York, NY: Guilford Press.

Gable, S. L., Gonzaga, G. C., & Strachman, A. (2006). Will you be there for me when things go right? Supportive responses to positive event disclosures. *Journal of Personality and Social Psychology, 91*(5), 904–917.

Gable, S. L., & Reis, H. T. (2001). Appetitive and aversive social interaction. In J. Harvey & A. Wenzel (Eds.), *Close romantic relationships: Maintenance and enhancement* (pp. 169–194). Mahwah, NJ: Lawrence Erlbaum Associates.

Gable, S. L., Reis, H. T., Impett, E. A., & Asher, E. R. (2004). What do you do when things go right? The intrapersonal and interpersonal benefits of sharing positive events. *Journal of Personality and Social Psychology, 87*(2), 228–245.

Gabrenya, Jr., W. K., & Arkin, R. M. (1980). Self-monitoring scale: Factor structure and correlates. *Personality and Social Psychology Bulletin, 6*(1), 13–22.

Garcia, J. A., & Crocker, J. (2008). Reasons for disclosing depression matter: The consequences of having egosystem and ecosystem goals. *Social Science & Medicine, 67*(3), 453–462.

Gere, J., & MacDonald, G. (2010). An update of the empirical case for the need to belong. *Journal of Individual Psychology, 66*(1), 93–115.

Goffman, E. (1959). *The presentation of self in everyday life*. Garden City, NY: Doubleday/Anchor Books.

Graham, S. M., Huang, J. Y., Clark, M. S., & Helgeson, V. S. (2008). The positives of negative emotions: Willingness to express negative emotions promotes relationships. *Personality and Social Psychology Bulletin, 34*, 394–406.

Greenaway, K. H., Haslam, S. A., Cruwys, T., Branscombe, N. R., Ysseldyk, R., & Heldreth, C. (2015). From "we" to "me": Group identification enhances perceived personal control with consequences for health and well-being. *Journal of Personality and Social Psychology, 109*, 53–64.

Grieve, R., & Watkinson, J. (2016). The psychological benefits of being authentic on Facebook. *Cyberpsychology, Behavior, and Social Networking, 19*(7), 420–425.

Gross, J. J., & John, O. P. (1997). Revealing feelings: Facets of emotional expressivity in self reports, peer ratings, and behavior. *Journal of Personality and Social Psychology, 72*, 435–448.

Gross, J. J., & John, O. P. (2003). Individual differences in two emotion regulation processes: Implications for affect, relationships, and well-being. *Journal of Personality and Social Psychology*, *85*, 348–362.

Hawkley, L. C., Burleson, M. H., Berntson, G. G., & Cacioppo, J. T. (2003). Loneliness in everyday life: Cardiovascular activity, psychosocial context, and health behaviors. *Journal of Personality and Social Psychology*, *85*(1), 105–120.

Hayes, N., & Joseph, S. (2003). Big 5 correlates of three measures of subjective well-being. *Personality and Individual Differences*, *34*(4), 723–727.

Heimpel, S. A., Wood, J. V., Marshall, M. A., & Brown, J. D. (2002). Do people with low self-esteem really want to feel better? Self-esteem differences in motivation to repair negative moods. *Journal of Personality and Social Psychology*, *82*, 128–147.

Henderson, L., & Zimbardo, P. (2010). Shyness, social anxiety, and social anxiety disorder. *Social Anxiety: Clinical, Developmental, and Social Perspectives*, *2*, 65–92.

Hewitt, P. L., & Flett, G. L. (2002). Perfectionism and stress processes in psychopathology. In G. L. Flett & P. L. Hewitt (Eds.), *Perfectionism: Theory, research, and treatment* (pp. 255–284). Washington, DC: American Psychological Association.

Hewitt, P. L., Flett, G. L., Sherry, S. B., Habke, M., Parkin, M., Lam, R. W., . . . Stein, M. B. (2003). The interpersonal expression of perfection: Perfectionistic self-presentation and psychological distress. *Journal of Personality and Social Psychology*, *84*, 1303–1325. doi: 10.1037/0022–3514.84.6.1303

Hewitt, P. L., Habke, A., Lee-Baggley, D. L., Sherry, S. B., & Flett, G. L. (2008). The impact of perfectionistic self-presentation on the cognitive, affective, and physiological experience of a clinical interview. *Psychiatry: Interpersonal and Biological Processes*, *71*, 93–122. doi: 10.1521/psyc.2008.71.2.93

Hollin, C. R., & Trower, P. (1986). Social skills training: Critique and future development. In P. Trower & C. R. Hollin (Eds.), *Handbook of social skills training: Clinical applications and new directions* (Vol. 2, pp. 237–257). Oxford: Pergamon.

Hotard, S. R., McFatter, R. M., McWhirter, R. M., & Stegall, M. E. (1989). Interactive effects of extraversion, neuroticism, and social relationships on subjective well-being. *Journal of Personality and Social Psychology*, *57*(2), 321–331.

Ickes, W., Reidhead, S., & Patterson, M. (1986). Machiavellianism and self-monitoring: As different as "me" and "you". *Social Cognition*, *4*(1), 58–74.

Jones, W. H., Briggs, S. R., & Smith, T. G. (1986). Shyness: Conceptualization and measurement. *Journal of Personality and Social Psychology*, *51*(3), 629–639.

Jones, W. H., & Carpenter, B. N. (1986). Shyness, social behavior, and relationships. In W. H. Jones, J. M. Cheek, & S. R. Briggs (Eds.), *Shyness: Perspectives on researcher and treatment* (pp. 227–238). New York: Plenum.

Kahn, J. H., & Hessling, R. M. (2001). Measuring the tendency to conceal versus disclose psychological distress. *Journal of Social and Clinical Psychology*, *20*, 41–65.

Katz, I. M., & Campbell, J. D. (1994). Ambivalence over emotional expression and well-being: Nomothetic and idiographic tests of the stress-buffering hypothesis. *Journal of Personality and Social Psychology*, *67*(3), 513–524.

Kawamura, K. Y., & Frost, R. O. (2004). Self-concealment as a mediator in the relationship between perfectionism and psychological distress. *Cognitive Therapy and Research*, *28*(2), 183–191.

Kelly, A. E., & Achter, J. A. (1995). Self-concealment and attitudes toward counseling in university students. *Journal of Counseling Psychology*, *42*(1), 40–46.

Keltner, D., & Haidt, J. (1999). Social functions of emotions at four levels of analysis. *Cognition & Emotion*, *13*(5), 505–521.

Keltner, D., & Kring, A. M. (1998). Emotion, social function, and psychopathology. *Review of General Psychology*, *2*(3), 320–342.

Keyes, C. L., Shmotkin, D., & Ryff, C. D. (2002). Optimizing well-being: The empirical encounter of two traditions. *Journal of Personality and Social Psychology*, *82*(6), 1007–1022.

Kim, H., Schimmack, U., & Oishi, S. (2012). Cultural differences in self-and other-evaluations and well-being: A study of European and Asian Canadians. *Journal of Personality and Social Psychology*, *102*(4), 856.

Kim, J. & Roselyn, J. L. (2011). The Facebook paths to happiness: effects of the number of Facebook friends and self-presentation on subjective well-being. *Cyberpsychology, Behavior, and Social Networking*, *6*, 359–364.

King, L. A. (2000). Why happiness is good for you: A commentary on Fredrickson. *Prevention & Treatment*, *3*(1), 1–4.

King, L. A., & Emmons, R. A. (1990). Conflict over emotional expression: Psychological and physical correlates. *Journal of Personality and Social Psychology*, *58*(5), 864.

King, L. A., & Emmons, R. A. (1991). Psychological, physical, and interpersonal correlates of emotional expressiveness, conflict, and control. *European Journal of Personality*, *5*(2), 131–150.

King, L. A., Emmons, R. A., & Woodley, S. (1992). The structure of inhibition. *Journal of Research in Personality*, *26*, 85–102.

King, L. A., & Pennebaker, J. W. (1998). What's so great about feeling good? *Psychological Inquiry*, *9*, 53–56.

Ko, H. C., & Kuo, F. Y. (2009). Can blogging enhance subjective well-being through self-disclosure? *CyberPsychology & Behavior*, *12*(1), 75–79.

Kong, F., Zhao, J., & You, X. (2012a). Self-esteem as mediator and moderator of the relationship between social support and subjective well-being among Chinese university students. *Social Indicators Research*, *112*, 151–161. doi: 10.1007/s11205-012-0044-6

Kong, F., Zhao, J., & You, X. (2012b). Social support mediates the impact of emotional intelligence on mental distress and life satisfaction in Chinese young adults. *Personality and Individual Differences*, *53*, 513–517.

Lane, R. D., & Schwartz, G. E. (1987). Levels of emotional awareness: A cognitive-developmental theory and its application to psychopathology. *The American Journal of Psychiatry*, *144*, 133–143.

Larsen, R. J., & Ketelaar, T. (1991). Personality and susceptibility to positive and negative emotional states. *Journal of Personality and Social Psychology*, *61*, 132–140.

Larson, D. G., Chastain, R. L., Hoyt, W. T., & Ayzenberg, R. (2015). Self-concealment: Integrative review and working model. *Journal of Social and Clinical Psychology*, *34*(8), e705–e774.

Lau, S., & Gruen, G. E. (1992). The social stigma of loneliness: Effect of target person's and perceiver's sex. *Personality and Social Psychology Bulletin*, *18*(2), 182–189.

Leary, M. R. (1983). *Understanding social anxiety: Social, personality, and clinical perspectives*. Beverly Hills, CA: Sage.

Leary, M. R. (1990). Social anxiety, shyness, and related constructs. In J. Robinson, P. Shaver, & L. Wrightsman (Eds.), *Measures of personality and social psychological attitudes* (pp. 161–194). New York: Academic Press.

Leary, M. R. (1995). *Self-presentation: Impression management and interpersonal behavior*. Boulder: Westview.

Leary, M. R. (2001). The self we know and the self we show: Self-esteem, self-presentation, and the maintenance of interpersonal relationships. In G. J. O. Fletcher & M. Clark

(Eds.), *Blackwell handbook of social psychology: Interpersonal processes* (pp. 457–477). Malden, MA: Blackwell.

Leary, M. R. (2002). The self as a source of relational difficulties. *Self and Identity, 1*, 137–142.

Leary, M. R. (2004). The sociometer, self-esteem, and the regulation of interpersonal behavior. In R. F. Baumeister & K. D. Vohs (Eds.), *Handbook of self-regulation: Research, theory, and applications* (pp. 373–391). New York: Guilford Press.

Leary, M. R. (2009). Affiliation, acceptance, and belonging: The pursuit of interpersonal connection. In S. Fiske, D. Gilbert, & G. Lindzey (Eds.), *Handbook of social psychology* (4th ed., pp. 864–897). New York: McGraw-Hill.

Leary, M. R., & Allen, A. B. (2011). Self-presentational persona: Simultaneous management of multiple impressions. *Journal of Personality and Social Psychology, 101*, 1033–1049.

Leary, M. R., Allen, A. B., & Terry, M. L. (2011). Managing social images in naturalistic versus laboratory settings: Implications for understanding and studying self-presentation. *European Journal of Social Psychology, 23*, 3448–3455.

Leary, M. R., & Baumeister, R. F. (2000). The nature and function of self-esteem: Sociometer theory. In M. P. Zanna (Ed.), *Advances in experimental social psychology* (Vol. 32, pp. 1–62). San Diego, CA: Academic Press.

Leary, M. R., & Downs, D. L. (1995). Interpersonal functions of the self-esteem motive: The self-esteem system as a sociometer. In M. Kernis (Ed.), *Efficacy, agency, and self-esteem* (pp. 123–144). New York: Plenum.

Leary, M. R., & Kowalski, R. M. (1990). Impression management: A literature review and two-component model. *Psychological Bulletin, 107*, 34–47.

Leary, M. R., & Kowalski, R. M. (1993). The interaction anxiousness scale: Construct and criterion-related validity. *Journal of Personality Assessment, 61*, 136–146.

Leary, M. R., Kowalski, R. M., & Campbell, C. (1988). Self-presentational concerns and social anxiety: The role of generalized impression expectancies. *Journal of Research in Personality, 22*, 308–321.

Leary, M. R., & MacDonald, G. (2003). Individual differences in self-esteem: A review and theoretical integration. In M. R. Leary & J. P. Tangney (Eds.), *Handbook of self and identity* (pp. 401–418). New York, NY: Guilford Press.

Leary, M. R., Nezlek, J. B., Downs, D. L., Radford-Davenport, J., Martin, J., & McMullen, A. (1994). Self-presentation in everyday interactions. *Journal of Personality and Social Psychology, 67*, 664–673.

Leary, M. R., Tambor, E. S., Terdal, S. K., & Downs, D. L. (1995). Self-esteem as an interpersonal monitor: The sociometer hypothesis. *Journal of Personality and Social Psychology, 68*, 518–530.

Leventhal, N. (2009). Perfectionism, self-concealment, and attitudes toward mental health treatment. *Dissertation Abstracts International, 69*, 6421.

Lippa, R. (1976). Expressive control and the leakage of dispositional introversion-extraversion during role-played teaching. *Journal of Personality, 44*(4), 541–559.

Lopez, F. G., & Rice, K. G. (2006). Preliminary development and validation of a measure of relationship authenticity. *Journal of Counseling Psychology, 53*(3), 362.

Lu, L., & Shih, J. B. (1997). Sources of happiness: A qualitative approach. *The Journal of Social Psychology, 137*(2), 181–187.

Lucas, R. E., Clark, A. E., Georgellis, Y., & Diener, E. (2003). Reexamining adaptation and the set point model of happiness: Reactions to changes in marital status. *Journal of Personality and Social Psychology, 84*(3), 527.

Lucas, R. E., Diener, E., Grob, A., Suh, E. M., & Shao, L. (2000). Cross-cultural evidence for the fundamental features of extroversion. *Journal of Personality and Social Psychology, 79*, 452–468.

Lucas, R. E., & Fujita, F. (2000). Factors influencing the relation between extraversion and pleasant affect. *Journal of Personality and Social Psychology, 79*(6), 1039–1056.

Lyubomirsky, S., & Ross, L. (1999). Changes in attractiveness of elected, rejected, and precluded alternatives: A comparison of happy and unhappy individuals. *Journal of Personality and Social Psychology, 76*, 988–1007.

Lyubomirsky, S., & Tucker, K. L. (1998). Implications of individual differences in subjective happiness for perceiving, interpreting, and thinking about life events. *Motivation and Emotion, 22*, 155–186.

Mackinnon, S. P., & Sherry, S. B. (2012). Perfectionistic self-presentation mediates the relationship between perfectionistic concerns and subjective well-being: A three-wave longitudinal study. *Personality and Individual Differences, 53*(1), 22–28.

Maddux, J. E., Norton, L. W., & Leary, M. R. (1988). Cognitive components of social anxiety: An investigation of the integration of self-presentation theory and self-efficacy theory. *Journal of Social and Clinical Psychology, 6*(2), 180–190.

Maslow, A. (1968). Some educational implications of the humanistic psychologies. *Harvard Educational Review, 38*, 685–696.

Mauss, I. B., Shallcross, A. J., Troy, A. S., John, O. P., Ferrer, E., Wilhelm, F. H., & Gross, J. J. (2011). Don't hide your happiness! Positive emotion dissociation, social connectedness, and psychological functioning. *Journal of Personality and Social Psychology, 100*, 738–751.

Mayer, J. D., & Salovey, P. (1997). Chapter 1: What is emotional intelligence. In P. Salovey & D. J. Sluyter (Eds.), *Emotional development and emotional intelligence: Education implications* (pp. 3–34). New York: Harper Collins.

McAdams, D. P. (1985). *Power, intimacy, and the life story*. Homewood, IL: Dorsey, pp. 11–32.

McAdams, D. P., & Bryant, F. B. (1987). Intimacy motivation and subjective mental health in a nationwide sample. *Journal of Personality, 55*(3), 395–413.

McAndrew, F. T., Gold, J. A., Lenney, E., & Ryckman, R. M. (1984). Explorations in immediacy: The nonverbal system and its relationship to affective and situational factors. *Journal of Nonverbal Behavior, 8*(3), 210–228.

Mehl, M. R., Vazire, S., Holleran, S. E., & Clark, C. S. (2010). Eavesdropping on happiness: Well-being is related to having less small talk and more substantive conversations. *Psychological Science, 21*(4), 539–541.

Mehrabian, A. (1969). Significance of posture and position in the communication of attitude and status relationships. *Psychological Bulletin, 71*(5), 359.

Michikyan, M., Dennis, J., & Subrahmanyam, K. (2015). Can you guess who I am? Real, ideal, and false self-presentation on Facebook among emerging adults. *Emerging Adulthood, 3*(1), 55–64.

Mikolajczak, M., Nelis, D., Hansenne, M., & Quoidbach, J. (2008). If you can regulate sadness, you can probably regulate shame: Associations between trait emotional intelligence, emotion regulation and coping efficiency across discrete emotions. *Personality and Individual Differences, 44*, 1356–1368.

Miller, L. C., Berg, J. H., & Archer, R. L. (1983). Openers: Individuals who elicit intimate self-disclosure. *Journal of Personality and Social Psychology, 44*(6), 1234.

Miller, N. (2002). Personalization and the promise of contact theory. *Journal of Social Issues, 58*(2), 387–410.

Mohr, J. J., & Kendra, M. S. (2011). Revision and extension of a multidimensional measure of sexual minority identity: The lesbian, gay, and bisexual identity scale. *Journal of Counseling Psychology, 58*(2), 234.

Mounts, N. S., Valentiner, D. P., Anderson, K. L., & Boswell, M. K. (2006). Shyness, sociability, and parental support for the college transition: Relation to adolescents' adjustment. *Journal of Youth and Adolescence, 35*(1), 68–77.

Murphy, J., Shevlin, M., Adamson, G., Cruddas, S., & Houston, J. (2012). Memories of childhood threat, fear of disclosure and paranoid ideation: A mediation analysis using a nonclinical sample. *Journal of Aggression, Maltreatment & Trauma, 21,* 459–476. doi: 10.1080/10926771.2012.667521

Murray, S. L., Holmes, J. G., & Griffin, D. W. (2000). Self-esteem and the quest for felt security: How perceived regard regulates attachment processes. *Journal of Personality and Social Psychology, 78,* 478–498.

Myers, D. G. (1992). *The pursuit of happiness.* New York: William Morrow.

Nelson, L. J., Padilla-Walker, L. M., Badger, S., McNamara, B. C., Carroll, J. S., & Madsen, S. D. (2008). Associations between shyness and internalizing behaviors, externalizing behaviors, and relationships during emerging adulthood. *Journal of Youth and Adolescence, 37,* 605–615. doi: 10.1007/s10964-007-9203-5

Neto, F. (1993). The satisfaction with life scale: Psychometrics properties in an adolescent sample. *Journal of Youth and Adolescence, 22*(2), 125–134.

Olson, K. L., & Wong, E. H. (2001). Loneliness in marriage. *Family Therapy, 28*(2), 105.

Patterson, M. L. (1976). An arousal model of interpersonal intimacy. *Psychological Review, 3,* 235–245.

Pavot, W., Diener, E., & Fujita, F. (1990). Extraversion and happiness. *Personality and Individual Differences, 11,* 1299–1306.

Pennebaker, J. W. (1985). Traumatic experience and psychosomatic disease: Exploring the roles of behavioural inhibition, obsession, and confiding. *Canadian Psychology, 26,* 82–91.

Pennebaker, J. W. (1990). *Opening up: The healing power of confiding in others.* New York: William Morrow.

Pennebaker, J. W., & Beall, S. K. (1986). Confronting a traumatic event: Toward an understanding of inhibition and disease. *Journal of Abnormal Psychology, 95,* 274–284.

Pennebaker, J. W., Colder, M., & Sharp, L. K. (1990). Accelerating the coping process. *Journal of Personality and Social Psychology, 58,* 528–541.

Petrides, K. V., Perez-Gonzalez, J. C., & Furnham, A. (2007). On the criterion and incremental validity of trait emotional intelligence. *Cognition and Emotion, 21,* 26–55.

Pinquart, M., & Sörensen, S. (2003). Associations of stressors and uplifts of caregiving with caregiver burden and depressive mood: A meta-analysis. *The Journals of Gerontology Series B: Psychological Sciences and Social Sciences, 58*(2), 112–128.

Purvis, J. A., Dabbs, Jr., J. M., & Hopper, C. H. (1984). The "opener" skilled user of facial expression and speech pattern. *Personality and Social Psychology Bulletin, 10*(1), 61–66.

Rapee, R. M., Kim, J., Wang, J., Liu, X., Hofmann, S. G., Chen, J., . . . Alden, L. E. (2011). Perceived impact of socially anxious behaviors on individuals' lives in Western and East Asian countries. *Behavior Therapy, 42,* 485–492.

Reis, H. T., & Patrick, B. C. (1996). Attachment and intimacy: Component processes. In E. T. Higgins & A. Kruglanski (Eds.), *Social psychology: Handbook of basic principles* (pp. 523–563). New York: Guilford Press.

Reis, H. T., & Shaver, P. (1988). Intimacy as an interpersonal process. In S. Duck (Ed.), *Handbook of personal relationships* (pp. 367–389). Chichester, UK: John Wiley and Sons, Ltd.

Reis, H. T., Sheldon, K. M., Gable, S. L., Roscoe, J., & Ryan, R. M. (2000). Daily well-being: The role of autonomy, competence, and relatedness. *Personality and Social Psychology Bulletin, 26,* 419–435.

Reyome, N. D., Ward, K. S., & Witkiewitz, K. (2010). Psychosocial variables as mediators of the relationship between childhood history of emotional maltreatment, codependency, and self-silencing. *Journal of Aggression, Maltreatment & Trauma, 19*(2), 159–179.

Riggio, R. E. (1986). Assessment of basic social skills. *Journal of Personality and Social Psychology, 51,* 649–660.

Riggio, R. E., & Watring, K. P. (1993). Social skills, social support, and psychosocial adjustment. *Personality and Individual Differences, 15,* 275–280.

Riggio, R. E., Watring, K. P., & Throckmorton, B. (1993). Social skills, social support, and psychosocial adjustment. *Personality and Individual Differences, 15*(3), 275–280.

Riggio, R. E., & Zimmerman, J. (1991). Social skills and interpersonal relationships: Influences on social support and support seeking. In W. H. Jones & D. Perlman (Eds.), *Advances in personal relationships* (Vol. 2, pp. 133–155). London: Jessica Kingsley.

Rosenberg, M. (1985). Self-concept and psychological well-being in adolescence. In R. L. Leary (Ed.), *The development of the self* (pp. 205–246). New York: Academic Press.

Rotenberg, K. J., & Kmill, J. (1992). Perception of lonely and non-lonely persons as a function of individual differences in loneliness. *Journal of Social and Personal Relationships, 9*(2), 325–330.

Rowsell, H. C., & Coplan, R. J. (2013). Exploring links between shyness, romantic relationship quality, and well-being. *Canadian Journal of Behavioural Science/Revue canadienne des sciences du comportement, 45*(4), 287.

Rubin, K. H., Coplan, R. J., & Bowker, J. C. (2009). Social withdrawal in childhood. *Annual Review of Psychology, 60,* 141–171.

Rubin, K. H., Wojslawowicz, J. C., Rose-Krasnor, L., Booth-LaForce, C., & Burgess, K. B. (2006). The best friendships of shy/withdrawn children: Prevalence, stability, and relationship quality. *Journal of Abnormal Child Psychology, 34,* 143–157.

Ryan, R. M., & Deci, E. L. (2001). On happiness and human potentials: A review of research on hedonic and eudaimonic well-being. *Annual Review of Psychology, 52*(1), 141–166.

Ryff, C. D. (1989). Happiness is everything, or is it? Explorations on the meaning of psychological well-being. *Journal of Personality and Social Psychology, 57,* 1069–1081.

Salovey, P., Bedell, B., Detweiler, J. B., & Mayer, J. (1999). Coping intelligently: Emotional intelligence and the coping process. In C. R. Snyder (Ed.), *Coping: The psychology of what works* (pp. 141–164). New York: Oxford University Press.

Schlenker, B. R. (1980). *Impression management: The self-concept, social identity, and interpersonal relations.* Monterey, CA: Brooks/Cole.

Schlenker, B. R. (1986). Self-identification: Toward an integration of the private and public self. In R. Baumeister (Ed.), *Public self and private self* (pp. 21–62). New York: Springer-Verlag.

Schlenker, B. R. (2003). Self-presentation. In M. R. Leary & J. P. Tangney (Eds.), *Handbook of self and identity* (pp. 492–518). New York: Guilford Press.

Schlenker, B. R., & Leary, M. R. (1982a). Audiences' reactions to self-enhancing, self-denigrating, accurate, and modest self-presentations. *Journal of Experimental Social Psychology, 18,* 89–104.

Schlenker, B. R., & Leary, M. R. (1982b). Social anxiety and self-presentation: A conceptualization model. *Psychological Bulletin, 92*, 641–669.

Schmutte, P. S., & Ryff, C. D. (1997). Personality and well-being: Reexamining methods and meanings. *Journal of Personality and Social Psychology, 73*(3), 549.

Segrin, C. (2000). Social skills deficits associated with depression. *Clinical Psychology Review, 20*, 379–403.

Segrin, C., & Flora, J. (1998). Depression and verbal behavior in conversations with friends and strangers. *Journal of Language and Social Psychology, 17*(4), 492–503.

Segrin, C., Hanzal, A., Donnerstein, C., Taylor, M., & Domschke, T. J. (2007). Social skills, psychological well-being, and the mediating role of perceived stress. *Anxiety, Stress, and Coping, 20*(3), 321–329.

Segrin, C., & Taylor, M. (2007). Positive interpersonal relationships mediate the association between social skills and psychological well-being. *Personality and Individual Differences, 43*(4), 637–646.

Shaffer, D. R., Ruammake, C., & Pegalis, L. J. (1990). The "opener" highly skilled as interviewer or interviewee. *Personality and Social Psychology Bulletin, 16*(3), 511–520.

Sheldon, K. M., & Niemiec, C. P. (2006). It's not just the amount that counts: balanced need satisfaction also affects well-being. *Journal of Personality and Social Psychology, 91*, 231–341.

Sheldon, K. M., Ryan, R. M., Rawsthorne, L. J., & Ilardi, B. (1997). Trait self and true self: Cross-role variation in the Big-Five personality traits and its relations with psychological authenticity and subjective well-being. *Journal of Personality and Social Psychology, 73*(6), 1380.

Smith, A. (1759). *A theory of moral sentiments.* London: A. Miller.

Smith, H. C. (1961). *Personality adjustment.* New York: McGraw-Hill.

Snyder, M. (1974). Self-monitoring of expressive behavior. *Journal of Personality and Social Psychology, 30*, 526–537. doi: 10.1037/h0037039

Solano, C. H. (1987). Loneliness and perceptions of control: General traits versus specific attributions. *Journal of Social Behavior and Personality, 2*(2), 201.

Sommer, K. L., & Baumeister, R. F. (2002). Self-evaluation, persistence, and performance following implicit rejection: The role of trait self-esteem. *Personality and Social Psychology Bulletin, 28*, 926–938. doi: 10.1177/01467202028007006

Spitzberg, B. H., & Hurt, H. T. (1987). The measurement of interpersonal skills in instructional contexts. *Communication Education, 36*(1), 28–45.

Spivey, E. (1990). *Social exclusion as a common factor in social anxiety, loneliness, jealousy, and social depression: Testing an integrative model* (Doctoral dissertation). Winston-Salem, NC: Wake Forest University. Department of Psychology.

Sprecher, S., & Hendrick, S. S. (2004). Self-disclosure in intimate relationships: Associations with individual and relationship characteristics over time. *Journal of Social and Clinical Psychology, 23*, 857–877.

Srivastava, S., Tamir, M., McGonigal, K. M., John, O. P., & Gross, J. J. (2009). The social costs of emotional suppression: A prospective study of the transition to college. *Journal of Personality and Social Psychology, 96*(4), 883.

Stein, M. B., Fuetsch, M., Müller, N., Höfler, M., Lieb, R., & Wittchen, H. U. (2001). Social anxiety disorder and the risk of depression: A prospective community study of adolescents and young adults. *Archives of General Psychiatry, 58*, 251–256.

Stein, M. B., & Kean, Y. M. (2000). Disability and quality of life in social phobia: Epidemiologic findings. *American Journal of Psychiatry, 157*(10), 1606–1613.

Taylor, S. E., Lerner, J. S., Sherman, D. K., Sage, R. M., & McDowell, N. K. (2003). Portrait of the self-enhancer: Well adjusted and well liked or maladjusted and friendless? *Journal of Personality and Social Psychology, 84*(1), 165.

Tice, D. M. (1991). Esteem protection or enhancement? Self-handicapping motives and attributions differ by trait self-esteem. *Journal of Personality and Social Psychology, 60,* 711–723.

Tooby, J., & Cosmides, L. (1996). Friendship and the banker's paradox: Other pathways to the evolution of adaptations for altruism. In W.G. Runciman, J. Maynard Smith, and R.I.M. Dunbar (Eds.), *Proceedings-British Academy* (Vol. 88, pp. 119–144). Oxford: Oxford University Press.

Turnley, W. H., & Bolino, M. C. (2001). Achieving desired images while avoiding undesired images: Exploring the role of self-monitoring in impression management. *Journal of Applied Psychology, 86*(2), 351.

Twenge, J. M. (2002). *Birth cohort, social change, and personality: The interplay of dysphoria and individualism in the 20th century.* New York: Guilford Press.

Tyler, J. M. (2012). Triggering self-presentation efforts outside of people's conscious awareness. *Personality and Social Psychology Bulletin, 38,* 619–627.

Tyler, J. M., & Adams, K. E. (2017). Impression management. In K. D. Williams & S. G. Harkins (Eds.), *The Oxford handbook of social influence* (pp. 219–235). New York: Oxford Press.

Tyler, J. M., McIntyre, M. M., Graziano, W. G., & Sands, K. J. (2015). High self-monitor's cognitive access to self-presentation related information. *British Journal of Social Psychology, 54,* 205–219. doi: 10.1111/bjso.12085

Uysal, A., Lin, H. L., & Knee, C. R. (2010). The role of need satisfaction in self-concealment and well-being. *Personality and Social Psychology Bulletin, 36*(2), 187–199.

Uysal, A., Lin, H. L., Knee, C. R., & Bush, A. L. (2012). The association between self-concealment from one's partner and relationship well-being. *Personality and Social Psychology Bulletin, 38*(1), 39–51.

Watson, D., & Clark, L. A. (1984). Negative affectivity: The disposition to experience aversive emotional states. *Psychological Bulletin, 96,* 465–490.

Weinberger, D. A. (1990). The construct validity of the repressive coping style. In J. L. Singer (Ed.), *Repression and dissociation: Implications for personality theory, psychopathology, and health* (pp. 337–386). Chicago: University of Chicago Press.

Wenzel, A., Graff-Dolezal, J., Macho, M., & Brendle, J. R. (2005). Communication and social skills in socially anxious and nonanxious individuals in the context of romantic relationships. *Behaviour Research and Therapy, 43*(4), 505–519.

Wessman, A. E., & Ricks, D. F. (1966). *Mood and personality.* New York: Holt, Rinehart, and Wilson,

Wickham, R. E., & Knee, C. R. (2013). Examining temporal processes in diary studies. *Personality and Social Psychology Bulletin, 39*(9), 1184–1198.

Wilson, W. (1967). Correlates of avowed happiness. *Psychological Bulletin, 67,* 294–306.

Wittenberg, M. T., & Reis, H. T. (1986). Loneliness, social skills, and social perception. *Personality and Social Psychology Bulletin, 12*(1), 121–130.

Wood, D., Harms, P., & Vazire, S. (2010). Perceiver effects as projective tests: What your perceptions of others say about you. *Journal of Personality and Social Psychology, 99*(1), 174.

Wood, J. V., & Forest, A. L. (2016a). Chapter three-self-protective yet self-defeating: The paradox of low self-esteem people's self-disclosures. *Advances in Experimental Social Psychology, 53,* 131–188.

Wood, J. V., & Forest, A. L. (2016b). Self-protective yet self-defeating: The paradox of low self-esteem people's self-disclosures. In J. M. Olson & M. P. Zanna (Eds.), *Advances in experimental social psychology* (Vol. 53, pp. 131–181). Cambridge, MA: Academic Press.

Wood, J. V., Heimpel, S. A., Manwell, L. A., & Whittington, E. J. (2009). This mood is familiar and I don't deserve to feel better anyway: Mechanisms underlying self-esteem differences in motivation to repair sad moods. *Journal of Personality and Social Psychology, 96*, 363–380.

Wubben, M. J., De Cremer, D., & Van Dijk, E. (2009). How emotion communication guides reciprocity: Establishing cooperation through disappointment and anger. *Journal of Experimental Social Psychology, 45*(4), 987–990.

Zaccaro, S. J., Foti, R. J., & Kenny, D. A. (1991). Self-monitoring and trait-based variance in leadership: An investigation of leader flexibility across multiple group situations. *Journal of Applied Psychology, 76*, 308–315.

Zayco, R. A. (2008). *Asian American cultural values, loss of face, and self-concealment as predictors of attitudes toward seeking professional psychological help* (Doctoral dissertation). Rutgers University, NJ.

Zimbardo, P. G. (1986). The Stanford shyness project. In W. H. Jones, J. M. Cheek, & S.R. Briggs (Eds.), *Shyness* (pp. 17–25). New York: Springer.

Zimbardo, P. G. (1990). *Shyness: What it is, what to do about it.* Cambridge, MA: Da Capo Press.

18

SELF-AWARENESS, HYPO-EGOICISM, AND PSYCHOLOGICAL WELL-BEING

Mark R. Leary[1]

The English language lacks a word to describe things that simultaneously have both highly positive and highly negative consequences. We might use metaphors to refer to something as a "mixed blessing" or a "double-edged sword", or say that something "cuts both ways", but no single word clearly expresses the fact that precisely the same feature of an object, event, or process is both very good and very bad. This shortcoming is relevant here because such a word would provide an apt and useful description of self-awareness: The same features of self-relevant thought that are absolutely essential for human well-being are precisely the same features of self-relevant thought that are also fundamental causes of unhappiness, dysfunctional behavior, interpersonal problems, and certain forms of psychopathology. The uniquely human capacity to think consciously about oneself vastly enhances human welfare yet is also the source of deep dysfunction and suffering.

Historically, psychologists have emphasized the beneficial aspects of self-awareness for self-regulation, foresight and planning, behaving consistently with one's values and standards, understanding other people, the inhibition of antisocial impulses, identity development, and other behaviors that are advantageous to oneself or others. Furthermore, the major accomplishments of human civilization—philosophy, religion, science, government, education, health care, and innumerable technological innovations—stem from the human ability to self-reflect; without abstract self-awareness, human beings would be just another species of intelligent ape. Yet, as I will discuss, most of the behavioral problems that compromise human well-being, undermine the quality of life, and foster conflict among people would not arise if people did not have the ability to self-reflect (Leary, 2004).

This chapter examines the two-sided nature of self-awareness and speculates why a cognitive ability that presumably evolved because it conveyed adaptive advantages is a primary cause of unhappiness and maladjustment. Drawing upon theory and research in social, personality, evolutionary, and clinical psychology, I will explore source of this self-reflection paradox and consider ways in which people may enhance their well-being by reducing the maladaptive aspects of self-awareness and cultivating beneficial ways of thinking about themselves.

Basic Self-Reflective Operations

Although theorists often talk about self-awareness as if it is a single, unitary process, the ability to think consciously about oneself involves a number of distinct, though interrelated, cognitive processes. Although self-reflection is involved in all of them, different types of self-relevant thought seem to involve different cognitive operations. For example, the capacity to imagine oneself in other places and times involves somewhat different cognitive operations than those involved in introspecting on one's internal states, which differs from those involved in evaluating oneself according to arbitrary standards or thinking about how one is viewed by other people (Neisser, 1988). For purposes of this chapter, we will find it useful to distinguish among four basic cognitive operations that involve self-reflection.

Temporal Self-Reflection

Although the evidence is circumstantial, the first advanced feature of self-reflection to appear during evolution may have been the ability to think consciously about oneself in the future. Modern chimpanzees and bonobos are able to think ahead a short time (Mulcahy & Call, 2006), suggesting that rudiments of this ability might have been present in the common ancestor that they shared with human beings more than 7 million years ago (White et al., 2009). Furthermore, archeological evidence reveals that, by 1.5 million years ago, *Homo habilis* carried crude stone tools as they moved, which suggests that *habilis* could imagine the possibility of needing a sharp rock in the future (Leary & Buttermore, 2004; Potts, 1984).

Although people could not function fully without being able to think about themselves in past and future, temporal self-reflection has some notable liabilities. In general, people spend far more time thinking about, planning for, and worrying about future events than needed to deal with future contingencies. When future-directed self-thoughts might lead to action—in planning a course of action, avoiding a threat, or preparing to cope with upcoming challenges—they are quite functional. However, most of people's future-oriented thoughts are not only unnecessary in dealing with upcoming events but are decidedly problematic in that they make people anxious and unhappy at the moment and undermine psychological well-being more generally (Borkovec, 2002; Leary, 2004; Watkins, 2008).

Among other things, thinking about the future distracts people from immediate situations that need their attention, fuels anxiety that serves no useful purpose, results in maladaptive behaviors to reduce uncertainty and anxiety, and disrupts sleep (Leary, 2004). Yet, the human brain regularly cogitates about other times and places when it is not already occupied (Mason et al., 2007), and people often engage in abstract thoughts about past and future even while they are doing other things (Hyman, Sarb, & Wise-Swanson, 2014). To make matters worse, in most cases, people who are gripped by anxiety about the future cannot currently take concrete actions to avert imagined threats, negating the benefits of fretting about them at the moment. And even when people's future thoughts deal with positive, desired outcomes, they can be dysfunctional in focusing people on distal outcomes that they believe must be attained in order to be satisfied and happy.

Introspection

Although other animals experience emotions, they do not seem to think consciously about their inner states or later revisit those thoughts, feelings, and experiences in their minds. In contrast, people often introspect on their thoughts and subjective experiences. The adaptive significance of introspection is not clear, although one function may be to allow people to double-check and, if necessary, override their inclinations. People often respond to situations with little or no conscious deliberation (Bargh & Chartrand, 1999), and the ability to introspect on one's goals, motives, feelings, and other internal states may allow people to confirm their initial impulses. Of course, introspection is not possible for reactions that are not consciously mediated, so it is limited to thoughts, feelings, and motives of which people are aware (Wilson, 2002).

Although people are often encouraged to introspect, reflect, and ponder, some researchers have raised questions about the usefulness of introspection (Engelbert & Carruthers, 2010). Introspection can be beneficial under certain circumstances (Hixon & Swann, 1993; McAdams, 2008; Pennebaker, 1993; Schooler & Schreiber, 2004), but it can also lower the quality of people's decisions (Wilson & Schooler, 1991) because thinking consciously about one's reactions can interfere with systematic processing of information that is important to decision quality (Tordesillas & Chaiken, 1999; Tversky & Kahneman, 1974).

Moreover, people put far greater credence on the accuracy of the conclusions that they draw from introspection than is warranted (Pronin, 2009). Contrary to how it seems, introspection does not involve accessing the deep contents of one's psyche but rather is an inference in which people construct a reasonable interpretation or explanation for what they feel or how they behaved (McLean, 2008; Wilson, 2002; Wilson & Dunn, 2004). By its nature, people can introspect only mental contents that are available to conscious awareness, so introspection is blind to many, if not most, of the processes that affect behavior and emotion (Kahneman, 2011). Despite the fact that introspection is partially informative at best and entirely inaccurate and disruptive at worst, people demonstrate an "introspection illusion" in which they place undue faith in their introspections (Pronin, 2009; Wilson, 2002).

Self-Conceptualization and Self-Evaluation

Other animals possess mechanisms that permit them to assess their efficacy at completing certain actions, such as when a squirrel judges whether it can leap far enough to land on a particular branch, but nonhuman animals do not appear to evaluate themselves in abstract and symbolic ways. In contrast, human beings conceptualize and evaluate themselves in broad, abstract, and symbolic ways that go far beyond the assessment of particular behaviors. Indeed, at least since the oracle at Delphi admonished ancient Greeks to "Know thyself", self-knowledge has been widely regarded as a valued attribute that plays an important role in well-being, and people have been explicitly encouraged to figure out who they are, what they are like, and how they relate to other people and the world.

Understanding one's capabilities, characteristics, preferences, motives, and values is exceptionally beneficial in helping people to choose environments and actions that are congruent with their abilities and inclinations. Yet, again, the search for self-knowledge has drawbacks. Many of people's self-beliefs and their corresponding self-evaluations are overgeneralizations that go far beyond objective, concrete judgments of particular attributes or abilities. Yet, once people have formed broad, abstract representations of what they are like, those self-views can constrain their decisions and choices, often leading them in less than optimal directions. By believing themselves to be a certain sort of person with particular abilities, interests, and inclinations, people may seek certain activities and avoid others, thereby limiting their opportunities to try new things and inhibiting personal growth (Ibarra, 2015). Once people reify a self-belief based on faulty information and overgeneralizations, that belief can misdirect their behavior in ways that lead to struggle, stress, and unhappiness.

Mind-Reading and Reflected Appraisals

Self-awareness is necessarily involved whenever people think about what other people might be thinking and feeling, including when people think about others' thoughts and feelings about them. In order to infer what another person might be thinking, people extrapolate from what they believe they themselves might think and feel if they were in the other person's position, adjusting for what they know about the other individual (Humphrey, 1986). Like the other three self-reflective operations, the ability to imagine the world, including oneself, through the eyes of other people can be an exceptionally beneficial skill. Yet, the ability to consider how one is viewed by others—the ability to form "reflected appraisals"—can also create problems.

One such problem is that many people are chronically concerned with how they are viewed by other people, even when other people's impressions of them do not matter in a particular situation and even when their efforts to make desired impressions leads to actions that hurt themselves or other people (Leary, 1995,

2004). When other people's impressions of them have implications for important outcomes, people must monitor and manage their impressions in ways that facilitate their attainment of desired goals. But many people are pervasively and excessively concerned with what other people think of them when others' views do not matter in any practical way.

Concerns with others' impressions lie at the core of social anxiety and a host of other problems in which excessive concerns with other people's evaluations is a feature. Momentary bouts of social anxiety are functional in leading people to attend to others' impressions and evaluations of them, but a chronic concern with one's impressions is a source of debilitating distress and maladaptive behavior, one that fosters not only recurrent anxiety but that also fuels interpersonal reticence, inhibition, avoidance, conformity, and downstream interpersonal problems (Leary & Jongman-Sereno, 2014).

The Central Problem With Self-Awareness

Each of these four self-reflective operations—thinking about oneself in past and future, introspection, self-conceptualization and -evaluation, and forming reflected appraisals—can be both exceptionally beneficial and exceptionally detrimental to people's well-being. This state of affairs obviously puts all of us in a terrible bind. We are equipped with an indispensable cognitive apparatus that nonetheless compromises our well-being on a regular basis.

The central difficulty with self-awareness is that people think consciously about themselves much more frequently than needed to meet the challenges of daily living, and they do so in situations in which conscious self-reflection is not needed or, worse, is unnecessarily distressing or behaviorally maladaptive (Leary, 2004). Elsewhere, I have characterized the self-focused mindset in which people typically operate as highly *egoic* in the sense that people think almost incessantly about themselves and their concerns, interpret and evaluate events in terms of their personal relevance, and focus more than needed on satisfying their own goals and desires, often with little consideration of their effects on others.[2]

Egoicism is, in one sense, perfectly normal. Natural selection would have favored organisms that focused on their own needs and concerns, so human beings naturally think mostly about themselves and put themselves (and, often, their kin) first. The problem is not that people are fundamentally egoic but rather that they are much more egoic than they need to be to function optimally, and their unnecessarily high level of egoicism frequently works against their well-being. The central question, then, is why do people respond more egoically than they need to, particularly given that obsessive egoicism creates emotional, behavioral, and interpersonal problems on a regular basis? Why did the human brain evolve in this way?

The answer to this question is a matter of speculation, but one possibility is that the cognitive mechanisms that underlie the four self-reflective operations evolved under conditions that were so dramatically different from those in which people live today that self-reflection is not calibrated for life in agricultural or industrial circumstances. As a result, the conditions of modern life evoke much more egoic, self-focused thought than would have been the case for most of human history (and prehistory). To see how this might be the case, let's consider the conditions under which each of the self-reflective operations evolved.

The ability to think about oneself in other times and places was presumably an exceptionally beneficial evolutionary adaptation. Being able to consider what one might encounter in the future would have given our prehistoric ancestors a notable advantage over animals that could think only about the immediate situation or, at most, a minute or two ahead. Yet, *Homo habilis* (the first species for which evidence of forethought is available; Leary & Buttermore, 2004) and the prehistoric species that followed had no reason to look further than a few hours or perhaps a day into the future. For nomadic hunter-gatherers, the critical demands of daily living—acquiring food, avoiding predators, interacting with mates and offspring, and managing intragroup relationships—play out over very short periods of time. People without property, possessions, or permanent residences have no reason to plan for the accumulation of resources and, thus, no long-term goals. In Martin's (1999) terminology, our ancestors lived for millions of years in an immediate-return environment in which the outcomes of their efforts to meet life's challenges were more-or-less immediate and concerns about the future were minimal. According to Turnbull (1983), people who live in immediate-return societies seem to live by the motto "If it is not here and now, what does it matter where (or when) it is?" (p. 122).

Contrast the immediate-return environment of our Paleolithic ancestors with contemporary societies in which much of people's attention, effort, and daily activity are aimed toward outcomes that lie in the future—educational degrees, paychecks, promotions, new jobs, new houses, special events (such as holidays, trips, visits from other people), children's developmental milestones, retirement, and so on. In a delayed-return environment, people devote much of their daily activity toward outcomes that lie in the future and receive little ongoing feedback that their efforts today will pay off in the long run. Most of the important life goals that dominate people's attention lie weeks, months, or years in the future.

According to Martin (1999), human beings began a transition from millions of years of living in an immediate-return to a delayed-return environment only about 10,000 years ago with the agricultural revolution. Whereas hunter-gatherers receive ongoing, daily feedback regarding their progress at meeting the challenges of living, in agricultural societies, people's important outcomes lie in the future, and people can rarely be certain that their work in the fields today is going to pay off weeks or months from now at harvest time. As a result, farmers—and all of the people who depend on them—have many reasons to think about, plan for, work toward, and worry about the future. And, because people in agricultural and industrial societies have permanent residences and personal property, they are also oriented toward accumulating and protecting their possessions. If Martin is correct, the ability to think about the future evolved because it allowed our prehistoric ancestors to see a short distance into the future, but virtually nothing beyond that short time horizon drew their attention. In contrast, modern people obsess about the future because they live in a delayed-return environment. In essence, a cognitive process that evolved to look a short time ahead has been pressed into the service of considering threats and challenges that may lie weeks, months, or years in the future, and we can't turn it off.

The problems associated with temporal self-reflection are compounded in modern life by the fact that, for most of human evolution, the majority of threatening events were physically present, and people could usually take immediate actions in an effort to deal with them. Their actions might not have always been successful, but they could almost always respond in the moment. Today, however, most events that evoke anxiety lie in the future, and often, people can do little at the present time to deal with the threat. So we worry about the medical test that we must have next week, the fact that our teenager is late getting home, the presentation we must give next month, or whether we will have enough money to retire in 10 years, with no way to take meaningful action in the current moment. Yet, the cognitive system that mediates mental time travel continues to churn out future-related self-thoughts.

A similar case can be made for the problems associated with introspection. Modern people typically introspect on their thoughts, feelings, and motives to decide what course of action to take, analyze retrospectively why they reacted to an event as they did, clarify their goals and values, or simply "find themselves". Yet, figuring out who one is, what one is like, and what one wants to do in life are relatively modern concerns.

Prehistoric people didn't have many choices about what they were going to do on a given day, much less with their lives. The daily tasks of living were well specified and ongoing, and our ancestors would not have considered the possibility that they could be something other than what they already were. And, they presumably would not have struggled with issues of personal identity and meaning, which Baumeister (1987) suggested did not become prevalent until the late Middle Ages. Prehistoric people might have occasionally found it useful to introspect when making choices, but reasons to look inward were limited.

Today, however, people in contemporary societies are confronted with a staggering array of options, both in the moment and in life more generally, and they often consider their values, goals, motives, feelings, and personal characteristics to make choices among them. More broadly, many people struggle to figure out who they are and what they should do with their lives, trying to ascertain what they value and where their priorities lie. At the extreme, many people confront identity crises either because they have difficulty establishing their goals and values or because they have multiple identities that prescribe conflicting behaviors (Baumeister, Shapiro, & Tice, 1985). Our ancestors began confronting these issues only a few hundred years ago (Baumeister, 1987).

As prehistoric people gained the ability to self-reflect, they would have naturally started conceptualizing and evaluating themselves, perhaps concluding that they were a particularly good tool-maker or an unusually bad hunter. But, the dimensions on which they evaluated themselves were quite limited compared with those on which people evaluate themselves today. Until hominids developed the capacity for abstract and symbolic self-thought (which may have occurred only in the last 100,000 years; Leary & Buttermore, 2004), the central characteristics on which individuals evaluated themselves were probably concrete and functional in the sense that they were relevant to their ability to accomplish vital tasks or to their role in the group (see MacIntyre, 1981). Today, however, many—perhaps most—of people's self-evaluations do not involve functional characteristics that serve as guides for their actions. Moreover, many of the values promulgated in modern Western societies—values that emphasize individualism, status, power, self-promotion, and success (Markus & Kitayama, 1991)—promote attention to characteristics that are not always intrinsically beneficial to either oneself or others.

In addition, rather than comparing themselves to 30 to 50 individuals in their clan, only a small number of whom were age- and sex-appropriate comparisons, people today can see how they compare not only to large numbers of people with whom they associate personally but also potentially thousands more who they glimpse on television and the Internet. In a small clan, social comparisons on important dimensions provided information with immediate implications for how one should behave, but the social comparison processes that functioned well in a Paleolithic band are often dysfunctional when the comparisons are virtually endless and not relevant to one's daily behavior.

As I noted, being able to infer how one is viewed by other people is important for achieving one's goals and managing one's relationships with other people (Leary, 1995). Failing to be perceived in desired ways can result in undesirable consequences such as low status, limited relational opportunities, inadequate social support, punishment, and ostracism, so people must know how others view them in terms of their competence, social attributes, and other valued characteristics. But, it's one thing to be concerned about the impressions one makes on important dimensions to a few dozen members of one's clan, most of whom one has known since birth, and something else to monitor how one is viewed by dozens, if not hundreds of people, many of whom one does not know personally. Our prehistoric ancestors presumably had ongoing, supportive relationships with most of the people with whom they regularly interacted, so the self-presentational demands were far less daunting than having to establish and maintain a desired image in the eyes of a large, unfamiliar, and frequently changing cast of people (Leary & Jongman-Sereno, 2014).

The Hypo-Egoic Solution

I devoted so much time speculating about differences between the worlds of our Paleolithic hunter-gatherer ancestors and people today to help us appreciate the excessively egoic nature of modern life, provide a possible explanation for why self-relevant thought has such negative effects in contemporary society, and guide us toward possible solutions. As I noted, the problem is that the cognitive processes that mediate self-reflection evolved under a set of adaptive pressures that were quite unlike those that people live under today. As a result, the cognitive systems that mediate self-reflection are activated too frequently, for unnecessarily long periods of time, and under circumstances in which self-reflection is not useful. As a result, people ruminate about the past and future, introspect, self-evaluate, and worry about what others think of them far more than necessary.

Understanding the source of our egoic problems may lead our search for solutions in directions that might not otherwise be obvious. If excessive egoicism compromises well-being, the solution is to find ways to attenuate the degree to which life in the modern world evokes self-relevant thought so that people are not unnecessarily preoccupied by egoic concerns. This in no way suggests that people should not be self-interested or personally invested in their outcomes. And, it certainly does not imply that people should somehow be "selfless", if indeed such a thing is even possible. Rather, the goal is to lower unnecessary self-thought under conditions that naturally elicit it—to raise the threshold at which self-relevant thought is engaged so that people operate less frequently in an egoic mindset than they typically do.

The challenge is more complicated than merely lowering "self-awareness" because, as we have seen, different self-reflective operations serve different functions and are elicited in different contexts. Furthermore, people can be self-aware in *hypo-egoic* ways in which their self-attention is not commandeered by unnecessary future-oriented thoughts, introspection, abstract self-evaluation, or concerns regarding social evaluation (Leary & Diebels, 2013). Thus, from the standpoint of promoting well-being, the primary goal is to lower egoicism rather than to reduce self-awareness *per se*. By lowering the degree to which people think about past and future, introspect, think about and evaluate themselves in generalized, abstract ways, and think about other people's impressions and evaluations of them, people can lower the detrimental impact of excessive egoicism and enhance their well-being (Leary & Diebels, 2013; Leary & Terry, 2012).

Routes Toward a Hypo-Egoic Mindset

Despite the fact that a large number of philosophers, sages, religious functionaries, psychologists, and self-help gurus have discussed the problems associated with excessive self-absorption for at least 3,000 years, most people do not seem to have considered the possibility that a large portion of their unhappiness, dissatisfaction, and dysfunctional behavior stem from egoic self-preoccupation. Thus, the first step in promoting a hypo-egoic orientation involves leading people to realize the myriad downsides of being excessively egoic.

In discussing these ideas, I have found that many people resist this notion at first, fearing that devoting less attention to themselves and their self-interests will decrease their motivation, compromise their ability to self-regulate, hinder self-improvement, reduce their probability of success, allow others to take advantage of them, or result in other undesired outcomes. These concerns may be reduced by encouraging people to distinguish between functional and dysfunctional self-preoccupation and by assuring them that the likelihood that any normal person will lower egoism to the point that it becomes maladaptive is virtually nil.

Once they recognize the benefits of becoming more hypo-egoic, people can learn to ask, "Are my current self-relevant thoughts likely to increase or decrease my well-being and the likelihood of achieving my goals? Are my self-relevant thoughts functional or dysfunctional?" When people detect that egoism is getting in the way of their goals and well-being, they can employ tactics that steer them in a hypo-egoic direction. Specific ways of achieving these ends fall into four broad categories.

Readers who are familiar with mindfulness and other forms of meditation will recognize that certain contemplative practices provide a powerful mechanism for reducing egoic thought. Many meditative approaches not only reduce internal, self-chatter in general (Brown, Ryan, & Creswell, 2007) but also focus specifically on maintaining one's attention on the present moment; experiencing sensations, thoughts, and feelings with minimal internal commentary or judgment; and focusing on concrete behaviors rather than abstract, conceptual thoughts about them. Thus, mindfulness and related practices explicitly address three of the four self-reflective operations, and evidence suggests that social-evaluative concerns may be lowered as well (Brown, Weinstein, & Creswell, 2012).

A second set of tactics involve cognitive self-regulation. Once people learn to discriminate functional self-attention and self-interest from dysfunctional self-preoccupation, they may be able to control excessively egoic thoughts that arise by either merely stopping them or substituting hypo-egoic ones. Cognitive-based psychological treatments, such as cognitive-behavioral therapy, have used such approaches for many years, and newer psychotherapies such as acceptance and commitment therapy (Hayes & Strosahl, 2005) and dialectical behavior therapy (Linehan, 2014) have extended such techniques in hypo-egoic directions. Of course, most people are unlikely to need formal psychotherapy, but elements of these approaches could be used to change the egoic manner in which people think about themselves and their lives. In addition, work on cognitive self-regulation suggests strategies that can be used to stop or modify unwanted and dysfunctional thoughts (Bakker, 2009). Some advocates of hypo-egoicism, including many meditation teachers, reject the idea that people should resist their thoughts directly (as opposed to letting them come and go with only passing attention), and efforts to suppress thoughts directly can backfire (Wegner, 1994). Even so, the possibility remains that the judicious use of cognitive self-regulation strategies may be useful in reducing egoic thought.

Third, although direct research on this possibility does not exist, egoic thought can probably be reduced by changing people's values, existential beliefs, or views of themselves. Philosophies, beliefs, and perspectives that deemphasize the importance of the individual or highlight the importance of people and things beyond oneself may lower egoic self-preoccupation. For example, promoting the idea that all people are connected or interdependent, that people everywhere share the same fundamental desires and problems, or that everything that exists is part of the same fundamental thing (e.g., God, the Tao, the cosmos, cosmic consciousness) may fuel the realization that one's personal concerns are not unique and, thereby, lower self-preoccupation (Leary, Tipsord, & Tate, 2008). Similarly, emphasizing values that focus on the well-being of other people, such as benevolence and universalism (Schwartz, 1992), may reduce egoicism.

Fourth, and perhaps most provocatively, creating conditions that coincide with the environment in which human self-awareness evolved might diminish egoicism by allowing people to rely on evolved strategies that reduce the need for deliberate, conscious self-thought. Given that people are probably predisposed to function optimally under the conditions in which our prehistoric ancestors lived (Marlowe, 2005), living in contexts that are structurally similar to Paleolithic conditions may allow people to respond with less conscious thought (Schreier & Evans, 2003). Hypo-egoic functioning may be easier and more natural the more one's environment resembles the ancestral environment of the Paleolithic (Martin et al., 2016; Ryan & Hawley, 2016). This does not suggest that we should live as nomadic hunter-gathers or sacrifice the comforts of modern life. Rather, Martin et al. (2016) reviewed literature suggesting that structuring one's life to mimic conditions that exist in hunter-gatherer societies may lower egoicism and provide psychological benefits. Martin et al. suggested, for example, that people could immerse themselves in nature (whether by spending more time outside or putting plants in their office), foster the kinds of egalitarian and interdependent relationships found in hunter-gatherer communities, and structure their lives in ways that provide them with as much ongoing feedback as possible to mimic an immediate-return environment.

The Psychological and Social Effects of Hypo-Egoicism

Most theorists and researchers who have written about phenomena that are characterized by a hypo-egoic mindset assume that lowering egoic self-preoccupation is generally beneficial (for reviews, see Brown & Leary, 2016). Yet, the evidence is largely circumstantial, and work is needed to examine the effects of hypo-egoicism directly.

At present, the evidence is strongest for effects on emotion. Given that a great deal of distress is engendered by unnecessary thoughts about past and future, ruminative introspection, overgeneralized self-beliefs, and nonproductive concerns with what other people think, reducing egoic thought should lower the frequency and duration of negative affect. In addition to lowering self-relevant thought in general, hypo-egoicism seems to be associated with a style of responding to undesired events that is less judgmental, personalized, and defensive than egoic thought (Brown, Berry, & Quaglia, 2016). For example, people who are less egoic seem less likely to internalize failures, catastrophize negative events, and overreact when they are questioned, corrected, or criticized by others, resulting in lower reactivity and greater equanimity (Brown, Ryan, Cresswell, & Niemiec, 2008; Kesebir, 2014; Lakey, Kernis, Heppner, & Lance, 2008; Sahdra, Shaver, & Brown, 2010).

Hypo-egoicism may also have positive effects on people's interpersonal interactions and close relationships (Brown et al., 2016). The most direct effect is that people in a hypo-egoic state are more present, attentive, and undistracted in social encounters, which should foster higher-quality interactions (Nichols, 2009; Parker, Nelson, Epel, & Siegel, 2015). They should also be less likely to dominate conversations, display intellectual arrogance, or interact in a self-centered manner.

Lower self-preoccupation may also allow people to take the perspectives of other people more easily, increasing empathy and perhaps prosocial behavior (Cialdini, Brown, Lewis, Luce, & Neuberg, 1997). However, whether hypo-egoicism naturally causes people to be more other-focused, empathic, and prosocial remains an open question. Although one might assume that decreasing attention on oneself should increase attentiveness to other people and their needs (Crocker, Olivier, & Nuer, 2009; Crocker & Canevello, 2016; Wayment & Bauer, 2008a), a person operating in a hypo-egoic mindset might conceivably be inattentive to others. However, given that people often mistreat others when they put their own interests too far above those of other people, hypo-egoicism should lower the probability of behaving in unkind, inconsiderate, selfish, and antisocial ways (Jonason, & Webster, 2010; Weigel, Hessing, & Elffers, 1999). Research is needed that explicitly examines the nature of the relationship between hypo-egoic states and a positive, prosocial orientation toward other people.

Reducing egoic thought might also improve the quality of people's decisions. Because egoic thought is inherently egocentric, people who are less preoccupied with themselves may naturally consider other perspectives, which should lead to better decisions (Ardelt, 2008; Levenson, Aldwin, & Cupertino, 2001; Webster, 2003). Furthermore, cognitive resources that are freed from unnecessary self-reflection can be deployed to focus on the demands of the immediate situation. As a result, people operating in a hypo-egoic manner may be more attentive to situational cues that promote discernment, judicious decisions, and effective action (Brown et al., 2007; Troyer, Tost, Yoshimura, LaFontaine, & Mabie, 2012).

A final consequence of promoting a hypo-egoic mindset is an increase in the likelihood that people will experience psychological states that are otherwise hindered by excessive self-attention, many of which are pleasurable and beneficial. People who function more often in a hypo-egoic mindset should be more likely experience states that occur under conditions of low self-awareness and egoism, such as flow (Nakamura & Roberts, 2016), so-called self-transcendent emotions such as awe and elevation (Van Cappellen, Saroglou, Iweins, Piovesana, & Fredrickson, 2013), and mystical experiences (Hood, 2016), each of which involves a reduction of conceptual self-thought. They might also experience greater gratitude, which itself is a strong predictor of well-being (Chapter 10). Furthermore, the more often that people have these kinds of experiences, the more likely they may be to seek activities and contexts in which such states arise (e.g., meditation, the flow arts, spending time in nature), which may further reduce their general level of egoicism.

Most researchers who have studied hypo-egoic phenomena have assumed that people who operate hypo-egoically generally fare better than those who are more egoic. Indeed, many of the characteristics that are associated with hypo-egoicism—such as present-focused attention, experiential processing, and equanimity—are linked to psychological well-being and the quality of people's relationships (Brown et al., 2007; Brown et al., 2016; Chambers, Gullone, & Allen, 2009; Chiesa & Serretti, 2009; Leary, Brown, & Diebels, 2016; Sedlmeier et al., 2012; Weyment & Bauer, 2008a). Even so, the research literature is neither large nor varied enough to conclude that hypo-egoic people are uniformly better-off than egoic individuals or that being hypo-egoic does not have unrecognized liabilities. We also do not know for certain whether the benefits of hypo-egoicism are due solely to the reduction in problems that are fueled by excessive egoicism or whether hypo-egoic states have positive effects in their own right. Even so, all signs point to the idea that hypo-egoic functioning is associated with less personal distress, lower psychological dysfunction, fewer interpersonal problems, and higher well-being.

Conclusion

The premise on which this chapter is based—that people are excessively egoic because the conditions of modern life evoke far more self-reflection than the human mind evolved to manage—is admittedly speculative and difficult to test. Even so, it provides a framework for thinking about the paradoxical effects of self-awareness, the problems associated with egoic self-thought, and ways of enhancing well-being through the promotion of hypo-egoicism. Understanding the nature of egoic thought and the problems that it causes can help people to harness self-reflection to work for, rather than against, their interests and well-being.

Aside from the burgeoning literature on mindfulness (Brown et al., 2007), research on the nature and effects of hypo-egoicism is quite limited. Fortunately, speculations regarding hypo-egoic phenomena are in ample supply (Brown & Leary, 2016; Weyment & Bauer, 2008b), offering a large array of hypotheses that call out for researchers' attention.

Notes

1 I thank Kate Diebels for her exceptionally helpful feedback on an earlier version of this chapter.

2 To be clear, egoicism (adjective: egoic) refers to the degree to which a person is self-centered in the sense of being self-absorbed, egocentric, and preoccupied with his or her personal concerns. Egoicism should be distinguished from both *egotism* (the tendency to perceive oneself in excessively favorable ways) and *egoism* (being motivated by self-interest).

References

Ardelt, M. (2008). Self-development through selflessness: The paradoxical process of growing wiser. In H. A. Wayment & J. J. Bauer (Eds.), *Transcending self-interest: Psychological explorations of the quiet ego* (pp. 221–233). Washington, DC: American Psychological Association.

Bakker, G. M. (2009). In defense of thought stopping. *Clinical Psychologist, 13*, 59–68.

Bargh, J. A., & Chartrand, T. L. (1999). The unbearable automaticity of being. *American Psychologist, 54*, 462–479.

Baumeister, R. F. (1987). How the self became a problem: A psychological review of historical research. *Journal of Personality and Social Psychology, 52*, 163–176.

Baumeister, R. F., Shapiro, J. P., & Tice, D. M. (1985). Two kinds of identity crisis. *Journal of Personality, 53*, 407–424.

Borkovec, T. D. (2002). Life in the future versus life in the present. *Clinical Psychology: Science and Practice, 9*, 76–80.

Brown, K. W., Berry, D. R., & Quaglia, J. T. (2016). The hypo-egoic expression of mindfulness in social life. In K. W. Brown & M. R. Leary (Eds.), *Oxford handbook of hypo-egoic phenomena* (pp. 147–159). New York: Oxford University Press.

Brown, K. W., & Leary, M. R. (Eds.). (2016). *Oxford handbook of hypo-egoic phenomena.* New York: Oxford University Press.

Brown, K. W., Ryan, R. M., & Creswell, J. D. (2007). Mindfulness: Theoretical foundations and evidence for its salutary effects. *Psychological Inquiry, 18*, 211–237.

Brown, K. W., Ryan, R. M., Creswell, J. D., & Niemiec, C. P. (2008). Beyond me: Mindful responses to social threat. In H. A. Wayment & J. J. Bauer (Eds.), *Transcending self-interest: Psychological explorations of the quiet ego* (pp. 75–84). Washington, DC: American Psychological Association.

Brown, K. W., Weinstein, N., & Creswell, J. D. (2012). Trait mindfulness modulates neuroendocrine and affective responses to social evaluative threat. *Psychoneuroendocrinology, 37*, 2037–2041.

Chambers, R., Gullone, E., & Allen, N. B. (2009). Mindful emotion regulation: An integrative review. *Clinical Psychology Review, 29*, 560–572.

Chiesa, A., & Serretti, A. (2009). Mindfulness-based stress reduction for stress management in healthy people: A review and meta-analysis. *Journal of Alternative and Complementary Medicine, 15*, 593–600.

Cialdini, R., Brown, S., Lewis, B., Luce, C., & Neuberg, S. (1997). Reinterpreting the empathy–altruism relationship: When one into one equals oneness. *Journal of Personality and Social Psychology, 73*, 481–494.

Crocker, J., & Canevello, A. (2016). Egosystem and ecosystem: Motivational orientations of the self in relation to others. In K. W. Brown & M. R. Leary (Eds.), *Oxford handbook of hypo-egoic phenomena* (pp. 271–283). New York: Oxford University Press.

Crocker, J., Olivier, M. A., & Nuer, N. (2009). Self-image goals and compassionate goals: Costs and benefits. *Self and Identity, 8*, 251–269.

Engelbert, M., & Carruthers, P. (2010). Introspection. *Wiley Integrative Reviews: Cognitive Science, 1,* 245–253.

Hayes, S. C., & Strosahl, K. D. (2005). *A practical guide to acceptance and commitment therapy.* New York: Springer-Verlag.

Hixon, J. G., & Swann, W. (1993). When does introspection bear fruit? Self-reflection, self-insight, and interpersonal choices. *Journal of Personality and Social Psychology, 64,* 35–43.

Hood, Jr., R. W. (2016). Mysticism and hypo-egoicism. In K. W. Brown & M. R. Leary (Eds.), *Oxford handbook of hypo-egoic phenom*ena (pp. 285–296). New York: Oxford University Press.

Humphrey, N. (1986). *The inner eye.* London: Faber & Faber.

Hyman, I. E., Sarb, B. A., & Wise-Swanson, B. M. (2014). Failure to see money on a tree: Inattentional blindness for objects that guided behavior. *Frontiers in Psychology, 5,* 1–7.

Ibarra, H. (2015). The authenticity paradox. *Harvard Business Review, 93,* 54–59.

Jonason, P. K., & Webster, G. D. (2010). The dirty dozen: A concise measure of the dark triad. *Psychological Assessment, 22,* 420–432.

Kahneman, D. (2011). *Thinking, fast and slow.* New York: Farrar, Straus and Giroux.

Kesebir, P. (2014). A quiet ego quiets death anxiety: Humility as an existential anxiety buffer. *Journal of Personality and Social Psychology, I,* 610–623.

Lakey, C. E., Kernis, M. H., Heppner, W. L., & Lance, C. E. (2008). Individual differences in authenticity and mindfulness as predictors of verbal defensiveness. *Journal of Research in Personality, 42,* 230–238.

Leary, M. R. (1995). *Self-presentation: Impression management and interpersonal behavior.* Boulder: Westview.

Leary, M. R. (2004). *The curse of the self: Self-awareness, egotism, and the quality of life.* New York: Oxford University Press.

Leary, M. R., Brown, K. W., & Diebels, K. J. (2016). Dispositional hypo-egoicism: Insights into the hypo-egoic person. In K. W. Brown & M. R. Leary (Eds.), *Oxford handbook of hypo-egoic phenomena* (pp. 297–311). New York: Oxford University Press.

Leary, M. R., & Buttermore, N. (2004). The evolution of the human self: Tracing the natural history of self-awareness. *Journal for the Theory of Social Behaviour, 33,* 365–404.

Leary, M. R., & Diebels, K. J. (2013). Hypo-egoic states: Features and developmental processes. In D. M. McInerney, H. W. Marsh, R. G. Craven, & F. Guay (Eds.), *Theory driving research: New wave perspectives on self-processes and human development* (pp. 31–52). Charlotte, NC: Information Age Publishing.

Leary, M. R., & Jongman-Sereno, K. (2014). Social anxiety as an early warning system: A refinement and extension of the self-presentational theory of social anxiety. In S. G. Hofman & P. M. DiBartolo (Eds.), *Social anxiety: Clinical, developmental, and social perspectives* (3rd ed., pp. 579–597). New York: Elsevier.

Leary, M. R., & Terry, M. L. (2012). Hypo-egoic mindsets: Antecedents and implications of quieting the self. In M. R. Leary & J. P. Tangney (Eds.), *Handbook of self and identity* (2nd ed., pp. 268–288). New York: Guilford Press.

Leary, M. R., Tipsord, J., & Tate, E. B. (2008). Allo-inclusive identity: Incorporating the natural and social worlds into one's sense of self. In H. Wayment & J. Bauer (Eds.), *Transcending self-interest: Psychological explorations of the quiet ego* (pp. 137–148). Washington, DC: American Psychological Association.

Levenson, M. R, Aldwin, C. M., & Cupertino, A. P. (2001). Transcending the self: Towards a liberative model of adult development. In A. L. Neri (Ed.), *Maturidode & Velhice: Um enfoque multidisciplinary* (pp. 99–116). Sao Paulo, Brazil: Papirus.

Linehan, M. M. (2014). *DBT skills training manual* (2nd ed.). New York: Guilford Press.

MacIntyre, A. (1981). *After virtue.* Notre Dame, IN: University of Notre Dame Press.

Markus, H. R., & Kitayama, S. (1991). Culture and the self: Implications for cognition, emotion, and motivation. *Psychological Review, 98,* 224–253.

Marlowe, F. (2005). Hunter-gatherers and human evolution. *Evolutionary Anthropology, 14,* 54–67.

Martin, L. L. (1999). ID compensation theory: Some implications of trying to satisfy immediate-return needs in a delayed-return culture. *Psychological Inquiry, 10,* 195–208.

Martin, L. L., Kulkarni, A., Anderson, W. C., Sanders, M. A., Newbold, J. A., & Knowles, J. (2017). Hypo-egoicism and cultural evolution. In K. W. Brown & M. R. Leary (Eds.), *Oxford handbook of hypo-egoic phenomena* (pp. 63–77). New York: Oxford University Press.

Mason, M. F., Norton, M. I., Van Horn, J. D., Wegner, D. M., Grafton, S. T., & Macrae, C. N. (2007). Wandering minds: The default network and stimulus-independent thought. *Science, 315,* 393–395.

McAdams, D. P. (2008). Personal narratives and the life story. In O. John, R. Robins, & L. A. Pervin (Eds.), *Handbook of personality: Theory and research* (3rd ed., pp. 241–261). New York: Guilford Press.

McLean, K. C. (2008). The emergence of narrative identity. *Social and Personality Psychology Compass, 2,* 1685–1702.

Mulcahy, N. J., & Call, J. (2006). Apes save tools for future use. *Science, 312,* 1038–1040.

Nakamura, J., & Roberts, A. (2016). The hypo-egoic component of flow. In K. W. Brown & M. R. Leary (Eds.), *Oxford handbook of hypo-egoic phenomena* (pp. 133–146). New York: Oxford University Press.

Neisser, U. (1988). Five kinds of self-knowledge. *Philosophical Psychology, 1,* 35–59.

Nichols, M. (2009). *The lost art of listening* (2nd ed.). New York: Guilford Press.

Parker, S. C., Nelson, B. W., Epel, E. S., & Siegel, D. J. (2015). The science of presence: A central mediator of the interpersonal benefits of mindfulness. In K. W. Brown, J. D. Creswell, & R. M. Ryan (Eds.), *Handbook of mindfulness: Theory, research, and practice* (pp. 225–244). New York: Guilford Press.

Pennebaker, J. W. (1993). Putting stress into words: Health, linguistic, and therapeutic implications. *Behaviour Research and Therapy, 31,* 539–548.

Potts, R. (1984). Home bases and early hominids. *American Scientist, 72,* 338–347.

Pronin, E. (2009). The introspection illusion. *Advances in Experimental Social Psychology, 41,* 1–68.

Ryan, R. M., & Hawley, P. (2016). Naturally good? Basic psychological needs and the proximal and evolutionary bases of human benevolence. In K. W. Brown & M. R. Leary (Eds.), *Oxford handbook of hypo-egoic phenomena* (pp. 205–221). New York: Oxford University Press.

Sahdra B. K., Shaver P. R., Brown K. W. (2010). A scale to measure nonattachment: A Buddhist complement to Western research on attachment and adaptive functioning. *Journal of Personality Assessment, 92,* 116–127.

Schooler, J. W., & Schreiber, C. A. (2004). Experience, meta-consciousness, and the paradox of introspection. *Journal of Consciousness Studies, 11,* 17–39.

Schreier, A., & Evans, G. W. (2003). Adrenal cortical response of young children to modern and ancient stressors. *Current Anthropology, 44,* 306–309.

Schwartz, S. H. (1992). Universals in the content and structure of values: Theory and empirical tests in 20 countries. In M. Zanna (Ed.), *Advances in experimental social psychology* (Vol. 25, pp. 1–65). New York: Academic Press.

Sedlmeier, P., Eberth, J., Schwarz, M., Zimmermann, D., Haarig, F., Jaeger, S., & Kunze, S. (2012). The psychological effects of meditation: A meta-analysis. *Psychological Bulletin, 138*, 1139–1171.

Tordesillas, R. S., & Chaiken, S. (1999). Thinking too much of too little? The effects of introspection on the decision-making process. *Personality and Social Psychology Bulletin, 25*, 623–629.

Troyer, J. A., Tost, J. A., Yoshimura, M., LaFontaine, S. D., & Mabie, A. R. (2012). Teaching students how to meditate can improve level of consciousness and problem solving ability. *Procedia—Social and Behavioral Sciences, 69*, 153–161.

Turnbull, C. M. (1983). *The Mbuti pygmies: Change and adaptation.* New York: Holt, Rinehart Winston.

Tversky, A., & Kahneman, D. (1974). Judgment under uncertainty: Heuristics and biases. *Science, 185*, 1124–1131.

Van Cappellen, P., Saroglou, V., Iweins, C., Piovesana, M., & Fredrickson, B. L. (2013). Self-transcendent positive emotions increase spirituality through basic world assumptions. *Cognition and Emotion, 27*, 1378–1394.

Watkins, E. R. (2008). Constructive and unconstructive repetitive thought. *Psychological Bulletin, 134*, 163–206.

Wayment, H. A., & Bauer, J. J. (2008a). The psychology of the quiet ego. In H. Wayment & J. Bauer (Eds.), *Transcending self-interest: Psychological explorations of the quiet ego* (pp. 7–19). Washington, DC: American Psychological Association.

Wayment, H. A., & Bauer, J. J. (2008b). *Transcending self-interest: Psychological explorations of the quiet ego.* Washington, DC: American Psychological Association.

Webster, J. D. (2003). An exploratory analysis of a self-assessed wisdom scale. *Journal of Adult Development, 10*, 13–22.

Wegner, D. M. (1994). Ironic processes of mental control. *Psychological Review, 101*, 34–52.

Weigel, R. H., Hessing, D. J., & Elffers, H. (1999). Egoism: Concept, measurement and implications for deviance. *Psychology, Crime & Law, 5*, 349–378.

White, T. D., Asfaw, B., Beyene, Y., Haile-Selassie, Y., Lovejoy, C.O., Suwa, G., & Wolde-Gabriel, G. (2009). Ardipithecus ramidus and the paleobiology of early hominids. *Science, 326*(5949), 75–86.

Wilson, T. D. (2002). *Strangers to ourselves: Discovering the adaptive unconscious.* Cambridge, MA: Harvard University Press.

Wilson, T. D., & Dunn, E. W. (2004). Self-knowledge: Its limits, value, and potential for improvement. *Annual Review of Psychology, 55*, 493–518.

Wilson, T. D., & Schooler, J. W. (1991). Thinking too much: Introspection can reduce the quality of preferences and decisions. *Journal of Personality and Social Psychology, 60*, 181–192.

19

SEXUAL ORIENTATION AND WELL-BEING

Adam W. Fingerhut[1]

Sexual Orientation and Well-Being

In line with psychological research in general, psychological research related to sexual orientation has focused on pathology (Vaughan & Rodriguez, 2014). In the early days, such research, often based on non-representative samples of sexual minority individuals undergoing psychiatric treatment, served to corroborate societal notions of homosexuals as deviants. Even as the gay rights era emerged following the Stonewall riots[2] in 1969 and the removal of homosexuality as a mental disorder in the *Diagnostic and Statistical Manual of Mental Disorders* in 1973, researchers still focused on difference and illness, now demonstrating that sexual minorities were subject to great stressors that served to elevate psychological disorders such as depression and anxiety (Meyer & Frost, 2013; Herek & Garnets, 2007). Referring to research related specifically to sexual minority youth, Savin-Williams (2008) commented on this focus on pathology stating the following: "It is as if same-sex oriented populations are only interesting to the extent that they differ in the negative. Indeed, reading the clinical literature, one would be amazed that any same-sex oriented child or adolescent survives into adulthood!" (p. 137).

Only within the past decade or so have researchers begun to assess well-being among sexual minority individuals. This has likely been guided by the growth of the positive psychology movement, which has brought with it increasing awareness that the absence of a negative is not the same as the presence of a positive. Corroborating this point and thus demonstrating the necessity for researchers to include well-being in the study of sexual minorities, Bariola, Lyons, and Lucke (2016) showed that, though positive mental health and mental disorders were related in a sample of LGB individuals, they did not perfectly overlap. Of specific interest were the 22.7% of the sample that did not evidence mental disorders but that also did not demonstrate the presence of well-being, again highlighting the distinct nature of these two constructs. Moe (2016) reported similar findings in a meta-analysis of 25 studies including measures of both well-being and psychological distress. Results revealed a small to medium association between the constructs (average $r = .39$).

I imagine that a move to include measures of well-being among researchers of sexual minority populations also stems from the fact that examples of well-being kept appearing in datasets, even in studies focused on pathology (Russell, 2000). As an example of this, Meyer, Ouellette, Haile, and McFarlane (2011) found that adult sexual minority participants responded to the question "What do you think your life would be like without homophobia, racism, and sexism?" in ways that suggested a positive connection to their marginalized identity. For example, some participants discussed ways in which a minority identity helped them not only be different but also better. As an example, one White lesbian participant stated the following: "in some ways, I'm almost grateful that I am lesbian, because it was sort of the only thing that saved me, you know, from a life of [a] pretty, pretty limited world view" (p. 210). Others in this sample noted how a marginalized identity allowed them to connect with others, either with those who possess the same identity or with others who possess a different identity but who might be similarly marginalized. In work that I conducted in relation to the fight against California's Proposition 8 banning same-sex marriage (Maisel & Fingerhut, 2011), participants reported many negative experiences and emotions but also reported feeling increased connection with community, a sense of pride, and social support from both close others and society at large.

The purpose of this chapter is to review research linking sexual orientation with well-being. The chapter begins by examining work that has included measures of well-being (i.e., the presence of positive indicators of mental health as opposed to as the absence of negative indicators). Next, the chapter reviews research investigating resilience among sexual minority individuals. Though most of this work assesses constructs such as depression and anxiety (or the lack thereof), it simultaneously examines factors that predict effective coping and the overcoming of pathology, thus making it important in a discussion of well-being. The chapter ends with a consideration of future research as well as a discussion of implications for both policy and practice. Throughout, the work presented focuses on samples of individuals who identify as lesbian, gay, or bisexual or who engage in same-sex sexual behavior; given a very limited pool of research linking gender identity and well-being (see Fredriksen-Goldsen et al., 2014; Riggle, Rostosky, McCants, & Pascale-Hague, 2011), issues related to transgender identity will not be covered in this chapter.

Though burgeoning, research linking sexual orientation and well-being is still in its nascent stage. In a recent content analysis, Vaughan et al. (2014) examined peer reviewed articles assessing strengths such as positive subjective experiences and virtues among sexual minority populations between 1973 and 2011. Within these nearly 4 decades, only 339 articles were found, with almost 90% of the articles appearing after the year 2000. Furthermore, of the 339 articles, only about half (55%) were empirical in nature, with the others reporting personal narratives and case studies or making a theoretical or conceptual argument. Speaking to this issue, Meyer (2015) noted that though resilience is a key part of his minority stress model, research on resilience among sexual minority individuals has not "progressed in lockstep" (p. 209) with research on minority stress in general.

Research Directly Assessing Well-Being Constructs

Research directly assessing well-being among sexual minorities can be categorized as falling into two camps: (1) studies that compare sexual minorities with heterosexuals on indicators of well-being; and (2) studies that compare sexual minority individuals to one another to examine factors that predict higher levels of well-being.

Comparisons Between LGB and Heterosexual Individuals

To date, studies examining differences between LGB and heterosexuals on indicators of well-being are quite rare. This is likely a consequence of the longstanding failure to include measures of well-being in studies of LGB individuals as well as the lack of demographic questions allowing identification of sexual minorities in large-scale studies that include both heterosexual and sexual minority individuals. A recent study by Thomeer and Reczek (2016) is representative of this camp of research and of the type of research that is needed as the field moves forward. Based on data from the General Social Survey, which includes a nationally representative sample, the researchers assessed sexual orientation differences in happiness. Sexual orientation was assessed in two ways: via a self-report measure of same-sex sexual behavior and via a measure of sexual orientation identity. Happiness was measured using a single item.

Results showed no statistical differences in happiness between those who reported having only same-sex sexual partners and those reporting having only different-sex sexual partners. However, those with sexual partners of both sexes were significantly more likely to say that they were "not too happy" and significantly less likely to say that they were "very happy" compared to those with only different-sex sexual partners. Across all three of the groups, the most common response to the question "Would you say that you are very happy, pretty happy, or not too happy?" was "pretty happy". There were no differences in self-reported happiness among those who identified as heterosexual, gay/lesbian, or bisexual. Again among all three groups, the most common response was "pretty happy". This general lack of group differences highlights the orthogonality of pathology and well-being, as these results stand in contrast to the literature examining between-group differences in psychological pathology, which consistently shows that sexual minorities report higher levels of disorders such as anxiety and depression than do heterosexuals.

Cochran, Mays, Corliss, Smith, and Turner (2009) similarly used population-based data from the General Social Survey, examining differences in empathic concern and altruistic values among individuals who have engaged in same-sex sexual behavior versus those who have not. The data for the women paralleled the results from Thomeer and Reczek (2016), showing no differences based on sexual behavior. For men, however, those who engaged in same-sex sexual behavior reported significantly higher levels of altruistic values than did those who had not, though there were no differences in empathic concern. The researchers highlighted the general lack of differences based on sexual orientation, again suggesting far more similarities than are often presented in studies focused on pathology.

Comparisons Among Sexual Minority Individuals

A second line of research that has included assessments of well-being consists of studies sampling only sexual minorities and investigating within group differences in well-being based on some other predictor variable. Borrowing from the broader literature examining predictors of well-being in the general population (Keyes, 1998), researchers have been particularly interested in the role of social integration, including strength of LGB identity and LGB community involvement, in the well-being of sexual minority individuals (Moe, Dupuy, & Laux, 2008; Ramirez-Valles, Fergus, Reisen, Poppen, & Zea, 2005). With a sample of LGB individuals, Luhtanen (2002) examined positive LGB identity and friendship and interactions with other LGB individuals as predictors of both well-being and pathology, using self-esteem and life satisfaction to measure the former and depression to measure the latter. Higher levels of positive LGB identity were associated with higher levels of self-esteem and life satisfaction, and this was true for both sexual minority men and women. Furthermore, higher levels of positive identity were associated with lower levels of depression, suggesting that this variable may have important roles in terms of both well-being and mental health. Interestingly, friendship and interactions with LGB others predicted only sexual minority women's life satisfaction scores, and had no relation with self-esteem and depression for the women and no relation with any of the outcomes for the men.

Kertzner, Meyer, Frost, and Stirratt (2009) similarly investigated connections between a positive sense of sexual minority identity and connection to LGB community and psychological well-being. Corroborating Luhtanen's (2002) work, positive identity was positively related to psychological well-being and negatively related to depression. Also, connection to LGB community, conceived as an affective and/or cognitive sense of positivity about and closeness to LGBT community, was unrelated to depression. Finally, though there was a significant correlation between connection to LGB community and psychological well-being, it was small ($r = .17$). This work is particularly important in that, whereas Luhtanen's sample was overwhelmingly White (92%), Kertzner and colleagues' sample was ethnically diverse, allowing tests of group differences based on ethnicity. In contrast to what they predicted based on a model of multiple disadvantages, there were no differences in personal well-being based on ethnicity (see the "Future Research" section below for a larger discussion of ethnicity as it potentially relates to well-being for LGB individuals).

In contrast to research operationalizing identity as a sense of connectedness with LGB others and/or positive views of one's minority sexual orientation, some research has used outness, or degree of disclosure of one's minority sexual orientation, as a proxy variable. Jordan and Deluty (1998) demonstrated in a sample of lesbian women that degree of disclosure was positively related to reports of positive affect. Riggle, Rostosky, Black, and Rosenkrantz (2016) used a more nuanced operationalization of identity disclosure, simultaneously considering *authenticity* (i.e., a sense of honesty about one's LGB identity); level of *outness* (i.e., whether one was out to certain constituencies such as family, friends, and coworkers, and the percentage of people within these groups one was out to); and *concealment* (i.e., the degree to which one hides aspects of their LGB identity from others). Though outness and concealment are related constructs, they are conceptualized as distinct from one another. Whereas outness refers to the number or percentage of specific people that a person is out to, concealment refers to a general tendency or desire to withhold information about one's sexual orientation from others. Concealment was positively associated with depression and negatively associated with well-being, whereas authenticity was negatively associated with depression and positively associated with well-being. Outness was related to the outcome variables in ways not predicted by the researchers. Specifically, outness did not predict well-being and was positively associated with depression (i.e., higher levels of outness were associated with more rather than less depression). The authors speculated that outness might be related to depression because being out might increase one's exposure to acts of discrimination and rejection, ultimately leading to poorer mental health. More research is needed, however, to fully understand the mediating mechanisms linking outness and depression and to better understand the lack of a role that outness might play in well-being.

Other constructs unrelated to identity have also been investigated as potential predictors of within-group differences in well-being for LGB individuals. Among these is self-compassion, or a sense of kindness and caring toward oneself (Neff, 2003). In a study of gay men, Jennings and Tan (2014) showed that self-compassion was positively related to life satisfaction, even after controlling for age, income, and outness. Using attachment theory, Greene and Britton (2015) expanded on this work, proposing that self-compassion serves as a mediator in the link between childhood attachment and happiness later in life. In a sample of LGBT participants, results confirmed that happiness was positively related to perceptions of childhood warmth and safety, self-compassion, and personal mastery, or a sense that one has control over their own life outcomes (Pearlin & Schooler, 1978). Additionally, the link between warmth and safety and happiness was mediated by self-compassion and personal mastery. Of course these data are correlational and based on retrospective reports of childhood, and thus any conclusions, particularly causal conclusions, should be viewed cautiously. At the same time, researchers and practitioners should take heed of the notion that individual differences in well-being among sexual minorities exist, can be predicted, and perhaps can be molded via interventions targeted at constructs that are malleable, such as self-compassion.

Research Assessing Resilience

Resilience involves successful coping in the face of challenge and, as such, requires the presence of adversity in one's life. Given this, resilience is potentially debatable as a positive psychology or well-being construct. The construct of resilience is further complicated by varying conceptualizations (Hill & Gunderson, 2015). Squarely in the realm of the study of well-being is a definition of resilience focused on how individuals not only survive adversity but ultimately experience positive outcomes because of it. Research on post-traumatic growth, for example, suggests that being faced with hardship can lead some individuals to find meaning in life, improve social relationships, and change perceptions of oneself as strong and self-assured (Tedeschi & Calhoun, 1996). Other research views resilience as a return to baseline and/or as the absence of adverse outcomes in the face of hardship (O'Leary & Ickovics, 1995) and, as such, may be less aligned with psychologists' operationalizations of well-being. Where possible, the research presented below will highlight resilience from the former perspective rather than the latter. However, given that most of the research on resilience within LGB communities has focused on factors that contribute to the absence of pathology in the face of stress, the research presented below necessarily includes measures that are more likely aligned with mental health disorders than with well-being.

Minority Stress Model and Coping

In the past two decades, much of the psychological study of LGB individuals has focused on the existence and seeming persistence of heightened mental health problems among sexual minorities in contrast to heterosexuals (Cochran & Mays, 2013; King et al., 2008). Though such disparities were once used as evidence that homosexuality was itself a pathology (D'Emilio, 1998), more recent work has suggested and demonstrated that these sexual orientation differences in mental health result from a unique set of stress experiences that sexual minorities experience as part of a stigmatized group. Central to this explanation is the minority stress model proposed by Meyer (1995, 2003). As part of the model, two distinct forms of stressors are presented. On one hand are stressors that are considered proximal to the individual, or that emanate from within the individual, such as perceptions of stigma, internalized homophobia, and disclosure of one's sexual minority identity. On the other hand are stressors considered distal to the individual, or that emanate from outside the individual, such as experiences of discrimination where one is called a derogatory name or is physically assaulted on account of being LGB.

Research on the minority stress model shows that stressors in the lives of sexual minorities are ubiquitous and linked with deleterious health outcomes. Studies using biased sampling methods (i.e., samples of LGB individuals recruited from LGB organizations and LGB social networks; Fingerhut, Peplau, & Gable, 2010; Meyer, 1995) and representative sampling methods (i.e., random digit telephone dialing; Mays & Cochran, 2001) converge on these points. Despite this, research also makes it clear that most sexual minority individuals are doing just fine in terms of psychological health (Cochran & Mays, 2013; Herek & Garnets, 2007). How do we make sense of the following paradox: (1) Most LGB individuals report prejudice and discrimination in their lifetime, *and* (2) such experiences are clearly linked with poor psychological outcomes, *but* (3) most LGB individuals report psychological health on par with their heterosexual counterparts? Research on coping and resilience provides the most likely answer.

Resilience as Applied to LGB Experience

Borrowing from more general models of resilience (Davydov, Stewart, Ritchie, & Chaudieu, 2010), several scholars have applied resiliency concepts to the experiences of LGB individuals (Herrick, Friedman, & Stall, 2013; Hill & Gunderson, 2015; Kwon, 2013; Meyer, 2003). In fact, built into the overall model of minority stress (Meyer, 2003) is the concept of resilience, leading Meyer (2015) to state that "resilience is an essential part of minority stress" (p. 209). A theme that consistently emerges in work related to LGB resilience is the presence of both personal and community resources that individuals tap into as a way to effectively (and sometimes ineffectively) cope with minority stress related to their LGB identity. In discussing these ideas, Meyer (2003) highlighted the importance of both person-level resources, such as hardiness and mastery, as well as community-level resources, such as community cohesiveness and affirming community values and social structures. Tied into Meyer's ideas concerning community-level resources, Herrick et al. (2013) presented a model of cultural resilience. As part of this model, they suggested that the sexual minority community has placed pride as a central tenet of community values, which then serves as buffer in the face of adversity. Similarly, Mereish and Poteat (2015) argued that resilience for individuals in general and for sexual minority individuals in particular is more interpersonal than it is intrapersonal. At the center of their theory are growth-fostering relationships that provide support and empowerment in the face of adversity.

Reviewing a broad range of sources on resilience, Hill and Gunderson (2015) presented a variety of personal characteristics and social environmental factors that aid resilience in sexual minorities. Examples of personal characteristics include hope and optimism, positive LGB identity, and the personality trait of openness. Examples of social environmental factors include LGB community norms and attitudes and social support as well as local, state, and federal policies protecting LGB rights. Taking all of these ideas together, the following sections will present two distinct lines of research regarding resilience in LGB populations: The first will examine intrapersonal resources, and the second will examine interpersonal and community resources. Most of the studies presented include only sexual minority individuals and look at moderators altering the link between experiences of minority stress and health and well-being for these individuals. This section will conclude with a discussion of work examining the positive aspects of LGB identity, many of which reflect resilience as they arise from the experience of marginalization.

Intrapersonal Resources

A small handful of intrapersonal characteristics or traits have been examined as potential stress buffers for sexual minorities, including such constructs as hope (Kwon & Hugelshofer, 2010) and life meaning (Szymanski & Mikorski, 2016). Smith and Gray (2009) suggested that hardiness, or a capacity to persevere and maintain belief in one's goals in the face of setbacks, may be a key stress buffer for sexual minorities, stating that it may be least "likely to be influenced by external contexts, and therefore the [characteristic] most likely to have the greatest relevance for LGBT individuals" (p. 76). The researchers operationalize the construct in a way that is particularly relevant for sexual minorities, defining it specifically as the *courage to challenge* or "the courage to challenge negative social messages about one's sexual orientation or gender expression" (p. 77). Though the authors present a validation study of a measure they created to assess LGB hardiness, they do not present data demonstrating its predictive validity as a stress buffer, nor does it seem that other published studies have used this scale as a moderating variable.

Figueroa and Zoccola (2015) more directly investigated the moderating role that hardiness plays in the stress processes of LGB individuals by examining the interaction between hardiness and minority stress in predicting mental and physical health in a sample of LGB adults. They defined minority stress as *stigma consciousness*, a type of proximal minority stressor which involves persistent awareness of one's stigmatized identity and the potential for rejection based on that identity. Additionally, these researchers considered hardiness to be multifaceted, consisting of a confluence of a sense of control, engagement and interest in life, and a view that hardships can be overcome and that something can be gained from them. Supporting the minority stress model, the direct effects showed that stigma consciousness was associated with lower overall mental health, higher reports of specific physical health symptoms such as headaches or back pain, and lower self-reported overall physical health. Those high in hardiness were protected against the potentially damaging effects of stigma consciousness with regard to physical health symptoms; more specifically, for those high in hardiness, there were no differences in reports of physical health symptoms between those high versus low in stigma consciousness. In contrast for those low in hardiness, those high in stigma consciousness reported significantly more symptoms than those low in stigma consciousness. In contrast to prediction, however, hardiness did not moderate links between stigma consciousness and mental health (as measured by the Brief Symptom Inventory) or self-reported physical health level.

In research that I have conducted, I have examined the role that gay identity plays in LGB resilience. As mentioned above, strength of identity and sense of connectedness to a community are directly related to well-being. Building on this idea and on work examining the stress-buffering properties of identity in other marginalized communities (Sellers, Caldwell, Schmeelk-Cone, & Zimmerman, 2003), I investigated the extent to which strength of identity could simultaneously buffer LGB individuals against the deleterious consequences of minority stress. In a sample of self-identified gay men and lesbian women, we examined links among gay identity (operationalized as a sense of belonging to the LGBT community), discrimination, perceived stigma, and depressive symptoms (Fingerhut et al., 2010). Though gay identity did not alter links between discrimination and mental health, it did alter links between perceived stigma and mental health. For those high in gay identity, there were no differences in depressive symptoms based on whether they reported low versus high levels of perceived stigma. In contrast, those low in gay identity reported higher levels of depressive symptoms if they reported high levels of perceived stigma than did those who reported low levels of stigma.

These data suggest that a sense of belonging to one's minority community can ameliorate the negative consequences that can arise from minority stress. Of course, more research is needed to better explicate the conditions under which identity serves this function. For example, though identity as assessed via a sense of belonging did not moderate the link between discrimination and mental health, other components of identity such as a sense of affirmation or actual participation in the community may moderate this particular stress–health link. An additional issue is the extent to which identity protects well-being in the face of stress, regardless of its role in protecting against pathology

Interpersonal and Community Resources

Social support has been presented as an important resource protecting individuals in the face of stress (Cohen & Wills, 1985; Feeney & Collins, 2014; Thoits, 2011). Research with LGB participants, however, is currently inconclusive about the effectiveness of social support as a stress buffer, with some studies demonstrating a moderating role for social support (e.g., Graham & Barnow, 2013; Hershberger & D'Augelli, 1995) and others failing to reveal such a role (e.g., Graham & Barnow, 2013; Szymanski, 2009). Rather than indicating that social support plays no role in the stress-buffering process, these conflicting findings may instead reveal the complexities in defining and measuring constructs such as social support and stress. For example, in research by Szymanski (2009), social support was assessed globally as a measure of the number of supportive individuals a person reported having. Additionally, stress was assessed as the frequency with which an individual experienced rejection, discrimination, and harassment based on sexual orientation. In contrast, in research by Hershberger and D'Augelli (1995), social support was operationalized much more narrowly—as family support for one's minority sexual orientation—and stress as three levels of attacks ranging from verbal attacks on one end to physical assaults at the other. That the former study found no buffering effect and the latter did may reflect these different operationalizations and the nuances that may be part of the minority stress process for LGB individuals.

The role of social support is particularly complex for LGB individuals, many who receive support from families of choice, or close others that one commits to even though they are not biologically or legally related (Weeks, Heaphy, & Donovan, 2001), as opposed to the families into which they were born. In line with this, in a short-term longitudinal study I conducted with a sample of Caucasian gay men, I examined separately the role of support from family and friends in moderating the stress-mental health link (Fingerhut, 2017). At the start of the study, participants completed a measure assessing perceived social support from family and friends; then at the end of each day for 14 consecutive days, they reported on their affect and on their exposure that day to minority stress. Friend support, but not family support, served a protective function against the negative mental health outcomes generally associated with stress exposure. Specifically, those with low levels of friend support reported increases in negative affect from days with average levels of minority stress to days with above-average levels of minority stress. In contrast, those with high levels of friend support did not experience increased negative affect on above-average stress days. Interestingly, recent research by Frost, Meyer, and Schwartz (2016) indicated that, while gay men may receive support more from friends than family, the same may not be true for lesbian women. This suggests that, if my sample included lesbian women, a very different pattern of results may have been obtained. More work is needed to catalogue the ways in which various facets of stress and social support, as well as mental health and well-being, correlate, and research is needed to better understand the mechanisms underlying the different patterns that emerge when these constructs are linked.

Social support is often construed and operationalized as connection to other individuals; for many with marginalized identities, another important source of support comes from connection to the marginalized community (Hobfoll, Jackson, Hobfoll, Pierce, & Young, 2002). In line with this idea, several scholars examining stress buffering among LGB individuals have pointed to the construct of group-level coping. Meyer (2003) referred to this construct as *minority coping* and defined it as a "group-level resource, related to the group's ability to mount self-enhancing structures to counteract stigma" (p. 7). In subsequent work,

Meyer (2015) further elucidated the construct, explaining that it consists of tangible resources such as access to LGBT focused centers and role models, and also intangible resources such as values, norms, and goals. Unfortunately, empirical tests of hypotheses regarding group-level coping in sexual minority individuals are sparse (i.e., the author could only find two) and fail to support predictions about its moderating effect. In a sample of German gay men, Sattler, Wagner, and Christiansen (2016) found that group-level coping, including gay rights support and activism, did not moderate links between minority stressors (e.g., victimization, internalized homophobia) and mental health. Additionally, Szymanski and Owens (2009) found no interaction between group-level coping with regard to sexual orientation and heterosexism in predicting psychological distress. However, they did find that group-level coping with regard to gender did interact with sexism in predicting distress, showing that such coping protected women in the face of sexist events. This finding suggests then that group-level coping has potential impacts but that it may function differently with regard to sexual orientation than with regard to other social identities.

Coming Out Growth and the Positive Aspects of LGB Identity

One of the stressors in Meyer's (2003) minority stress model is coming out, or disclosing a sexual minority identity. Research confirms this conceptualization, demonstrating that the coming out process is experienced as stressful for many LGB individuals (Pew Research Center, 2013). At the same time, many report growing from the experience, a phenomenon closely aligned with theories of resilience emphasizing thriving in the face of adversity and growth as a result of trauma (Tedeschi & Calhoun, 1996). In line with this, Vaughan and Waehler (2009) coined the term "coming out growth" (COG) to highlight the fact that many individuals report positive outcomes as a result of the difficult process of reconciling a sexual minority identity and coming out. In work creating and validating a scale to measure COG, these researchers discovered two overarching domains where participants reported growth as a result of coming out. The first was labeled "Individualistic Growth" and involved an improved understanding and sense of self, better well-being, and also deeper relationships with others. The second domain was labeled "Collectivistic Growth" and involved improved connection with LGB others and community, increased interest in advocacy, and more critical thinking about societal expectations.

In research cataloguing the positive aspects of LGB identity, Riggle, Rostosky, and colleagues have reached similar conclusions about thriving in the face of sexual minority stress (Riggle & Rostosky, 2012; Riggle, Whitman, Olson, Rostosky, & Strong, 2008; Riggle, Mohr, Rostosky, Fingerhut, & Balsam, 2014; Rostosky, Riggle, Pascale-Hague, & McCants, 2010). In perhaps the first study of its kind, Riggle et al. (2008) used qualitative methods to examine the positive aspects of lesbian or gay identity. Via an online survey, over 550 self-labeled lesbian and gay men responded to the question: "Please tell us what you think the positive things are about being a [gay man/lesbian or man-loving-man/woman-loving-woman]?"

Three themes emerged from participant's responses that were clear indicators of growth in the face of stress: disclosure and social support, insight into and empathy for self and other, and freedom from societal definitions or roles. For example, with regard to support and community, participants indicated that their minority sexual orientation permitted them to have *stronger* connections with others than if they were heterosexual. One participant, a gay man, wrote the following: "Living outside of many of society's expectations for male-female interactions, gay men are free to have closer, nonsexual friendships with women (lesbian or heterosexual)" (p. 213). With regard to insight and empathy, participants wrote about how coming to terms with a minority identity and "coming out" increased a feeling of authenticity and also facilitated a deeper understanding of the self, free from societal expectations. This self-understanding was also tied to a better understanding for others and to a desire to fight for justice for everyone, illustrated in such comments as "I am more concerned with social justice, not only for LGBT issues, but any minority, the disabled, children, and so on" (p. 214). Subsequent work with bisexual individuals (Rostosky et al., 2010) and transgender individuals (Riggle et al., 2011) revealed similar themes regarding growth amidst the stress associated with marginalized sexual and gender identities.

Future Research

One of the clear limitations of much of the research involving LGB samples is the lack of diversity in those samples, many containing predominantly White, educated, adults in the United States. This obviously fails to capture the experiences of the broader population of LGB individuals (Gates & Ost, 2004) and fails to consider the ways in which various identities might intersect to produce unique outcomes. As research on the link between sexual orientation and well-being grows, it will be essential to examine how these associations generalize to subpopulations of sexual minority individuals. Further research needs to examine cross-cultural differences and the role of culture in LGB well-being, gender identity and transgender populations, and more fine-grained comparisons between various sexual orientation groups (e.g., gay men vs. bisexual men vs. lesbian women).

As with the general body of research in psychology and the more narrow body of research on LGB individuals, research on LGB people of color has been largely negative in its orientation, focusing on deficits and pathologies. For example, a content analysis of 228 empirical psychological articles related to LGB people of color published between 1998 and 2007 found that the top five topics, in order, were: AIDS/HIV, high-risk sexual behavior, alcohol and drug abuse, psychological symptoms, and condom use (Huang et al., 2010). Though studies of resilience within ethnic minority LGB individuals have been conducted (e.g., Bowleg,

Craig, & Burkholder, 2004; Zea, Reisen, & Poppen, 1999), studies directly examining well-being constructs are difficult to find (for an exception, see Kertzner et al., 2009).

Though research at the intersection of sexual orientation and ethnicity is needed, predictions about the moderating role of ethnicity are difficult to make. For example, in the world of research on mental health disparities, Moradi et al. (2010) discussed potentially contradictory hypotheses with regard to LGB people of color and their experiences in the world. On one hand, in line with a risk hypothesis, Moradi et al (2010) predicted that these individuals would experience increased stigma because they possess multiple minority identities and because their sexual and ethnic identities are at odds with one another. On the other hand, in line with a resilience hypothesis, they predicted that LGB individuals of color would be better equipped to rise above marginalization because of the coping strategies they may have been exposed to early on to handle racism and because of community-level resources that communities of color may possess such as communalism and spirituality.

Adding to the complication, data for each hypothesis, again potentially conflicting as they are, are not consistent. For example, with regard to the risk hypothesis, Meyer, Schwartz, and Frost (2008) found that LGB people of color did in fact report higher levels of minority stress than LGB White people and that this difference was the result of differences in exposure to racism but not heterosexism. However, failing to support a risk hypothesis, Meyer, Dietrich, and Schwartz (2008) found that LGB people of color do not evidence higher levels of psychological disorders than LGB White individuals. Furthermore, research with LGB African Americans has found that internalized heterosexism, but not internalized racism, predicts psychological distress, again contradicting a risk or double jeopardy model (Szymanski & Gupta, 2009; Szymanski & Meyer, 2008). Contradicting what the resilience hypothesis might suggest, Frost et al. (2016) found that LGB people of color reported receiving everyday support along fewer dimensions (e.g., help with decision making, someone to discuss worries with, someone to do activities with) than did LGB White people. Additionally, in contexts where major support was needed, race/ethnicity did not emerge as a strong predictor of who individuals turned to for support, though gender did. Specifically, LGB women of all races tended to indicate a preference for family over non-family as a source of major support, whereas LGB men of all races tended to indicate a preference for non-family over family.

Meyer (2010) acknowledged the important role of subgroup identities among LGB people and simultaneously warned against potential exaggeration of cultural and ethnic differences, which may be more reflective of stereotypes than actuality. He also noted the problematic way in which researchers assess intersectional identities—having participants complete separate measures of identity for each of their "subidentities". This potentially sets up a dynamic where identities are seen by participants as competing, when in fact they may not be. An artifact of this approach may be an overstatement of difference between subgroups of LGB individuals (e.g., Black versus White gay men). This is not to say that real differences among LGB people based on race and ethnicity do not exist, but rather to say that as scholars further develop lines of research examining well-being among LGB people of color, they should pay attention to methodological innovations in assessing intersectional identities (e.g., Narváez, Meyer, Kertzner, Ouellette, & Gordon, 2009) and be aware of the potential for both similarities and differences among LGB subgroups.

Researchers have also pointed to the need to examine subpopulations based on age. Working from a lifespan developmental perspective, researchers interested in sexual minority populations have made clear that LGB individuals face unique challenges at each end of the life course. Sexual minority youth not only experience the typical developmental challenges faced by everyone else, but they also experience a growing recognition of being different from others, often including one's immediate family (Troiden, 1989; Wright & Perry, 2006). These heightened and unique stress experiences put sexual minority youth at greater risk for mental health problems and suicidal behaviors than their heterosexual counterparts. A growing body of evidence has documented these disparities (Becker, Cortina, Tsai, & Eccles, 2014). At the same time, as in the adult population of sexual minorities, LGB youth also find positivity in their minority identity and even in their marginalization (Horne, Puckett, Apter, & Levitt, 2014). Research, however, has been slow to capture these positive experiences

Only a handful of studies including samples of LGB youth have assessed positive well-being as opposed to psychopathology (Detrie & Lease, 2007; Diamond & Lucas, 2004; Rieger & Savin-Williams, 2012), and more often, though the term "well-being" is used, mental health problems such as anxiety and depression (or the lack thereof) are assessed (Kosciw, Greytak, Diaz, & Bartkiewicz, 2010; Vanden Berghe, Dewaele, Cox, & Vincke, 2010). Furthermore, most of the studies examining well-being in LGB youth are descriptive studies using qualitative methods with very small, unrepresentative samples (Abes & Jones, 2004; Harper, Brodsky, & Bruce, 2012; Higa et al., 2014). With this type of research in mind, Herrick, Egan, Coulter, Friedman, and Stall (2014) concluded the following: "We have reached the end of the era during which descriptive research was the most valuable approach to studying health among [sexual minority youth]" (p. 208). With this, there is a call for research testing predictions and examining links among various predictors as well as potential interventions to enhance well-being in LGB youth.

The other end of the developmental spectrum also needs to be studied. Again, research on well-being in older LGB adults is severely lacking, though some scholars have hypothesized that these individuals may in fact be more resilient to the transition to older age than their heterosexual counterparts (Fredriksen-Goldsen & Muraco, 2010). Kimmel (1978) made predictions about this increased resilience for LGB older adults suggesting that the skill set that they developed navigating marginalization due to their minority sexual orientation aids them in dealing with the marginalization that comes with older age. Unfortunately, research testing this hypothesis is limited, and the results from this research are not consistent.

Whitford (1997) sampled gay men 50 years and older and assessed constructs such as life satisfaction and feelings about the aging process. Though the measure of life satisfaction was not clearly described, 75% of participants scored above the midpoint on the scale, with 37.5% scoring in the top quartile of the scale. Furthermore, over 75% indicated that they were either "very accepting" or "somewhat accepting" of the aging process, with almost 45% of the sample indicating that their minority sexual orientation helped them in the aging process. Though limited in ways that make it difficult to draw a conclusion (including the lack of a comparison group), the data suggest that older LGB adults may have adequate levels of well-being—in contrast to stereotypes of them as lonely, isolated, and depressed (Pugh, 2005)—and may find that their minority sexual identity serves as a source of resilience in the aging process.

More recent research with nationally representative data provides comparisons across sexual orientation groups. Kertzner, Meyer, and Dolezal (2003) tested predictions consistent with the "crisis competence" conceptualization, examining (among a variety of hypotheses) whether older gay/bisexual men (above 40) would have higher levels of personal autonomy than their heterosexual peers. However, the pattern that emerged from the interaction combining age and sexual orientation suggests a counter to the resilience model. Specifically, it appears that the interaction was driven by significantly *lower* scores for personal autonomy among the older gay/bisexual men compared to the other groups (older heterosexual men, and younger and older gay/bisexual men).

Given the lack of data concerning well-being across the life course for sexual minorities, a first step is simply to begin collecting these data, including more research with samples of both younger and older individuals and research that assesses well-being alongside such cousins as depression and anxiety. Furthermore, such research needs to consider cohort effects in addition to general developmental phenomena. For lesbians and gay men currently in their mid-60s and above, coming of age and the potential realization of a minority sexual orientation occurred amidst a backdrop of deep pathologizing of homosexuality. In contrast, lesbian and gay youth of today are coming out in a context in which marriage for same-sex couples is currently legal in the US and in which representations of happy, productive, healthy gay and lesbian individuals are easy to come across in popular media and potentially in day-to-day interactions. These vastly different contexts likely have consequences for the well-being of individuals across the life course and must therefore be considered alongside age.

In addition to a focus on individual well-being, future research should attend to relationship outcomes and to well-being among same-sex couples. Generally, research has shown that same-sex couples report levels of relationship satisfaction on par with their heterosexual counterparts and that the factors that predict relationship quality are similar across relationship types (Fingerhut & Peplau, 2013), despite the minority stressors that LGB individuals and same-sex couples face and the links we know exist between stress exposure and well-being. More research is needed to better understand resilience in same-sex couples and processes that allow for high levels of satisfaction even in the face of marginalization. As part of this effort, research exploring strengths unique to same-sex couples should be conducted. For example, previous research has shown that same-sex couples report a more equitable division of household labor than do different-sex couples (Fingerhut & Peplau, 2013) and that gay and lesbian couples are more likely than different-sex couples to use humor and other positive emotions during conflict resolution (Gottman et al., 2003).

Implications for Practice and Policy

In as much as research needs to attend more to well-being and to move away from focusing solely on reducing pathology, policy and practice need to do the same (Vaughan & Rodriguez, 2014). Bariola et al. (2016) pointed out that the presence of flourishing may be more important to psychosocial functioning than the absence of mental health problems, suggesting that any real attempt to eliminate sexual orientation mental health disparities must attend to well-being. Furthermore, even in work aimed at reducing psychopathology among LGB individuals, more can be done to attend to resilience rather than only working toward the elimination of minority stressors (Herrick et al., 2013). In addition, more needs to be done to incorporate interventions that identify and build strengths that may be unique to sexual minority individuals. Speaking to this in regard to HIV interventions targeting men who have sex with men, Herrick et al. (2011) wrote about creating a "Theory of Resilience" that could be crafted by examining "naturally occurring strengths and resiliencies that exist within both individuals and communities" (p. 27).

As interventions focus more on well-being and on resilience, attention must be given not only to individual-level variables, but also to community-level variables as well. Scholars interested in resilience among LGB individuals have already heeded a warning that paying attention to only individual strengths is not only narrow but may also lead to victim blaming and to leading people to believe that they cannot overcome adversity because they do not possess certain personal characteristics (Herrick et al., 2013; Meyer, 2015). Referring back to Meyer's (2015) ideas regarding minority coping, interventions focused on community-level resilience should consider both tangible and intangible resources. A tangible resource could consist of spaces where community members can gather such as an LGBT Community Center or a Gay Straight Alliance in a school. Policies and laws that protect LGB rights and that provide equal access to resources also serve a tangible function. Intangible resources consist of social norms and values that may exist both within LGB communities and the larger society.

Considerations of intangible resources deserve special attention as LGB individuals gain more and more acceptance in society and more access to rights and perhaps, as a result, become more assimilated into the larger culture. A paradox potentially exists for those working toward thriving among LGB individuals. Although increased social acceptance and reduced prejudice and discrimination are good for well-being, much strength, meaning, and growth occur as a result of outsider status and marginalization. For this reason, it will be important for those in LGB communities and those working with LGB individuals to think about what strengths are unique to LGB populations and to find ways to maintain those strengths and perhaps reframe them in a context where sexual minorities are more welcome in society than they have been in the past.

As an example, we can consider pride as a central value or strength in LGB communities. LGB pride arose out of reactance to continual shaming, silencing, and criminalizing of homosexuality. Following the Stonewall riots, which are often marked as the birth of the gay rights movement, a proposal was put forth among organizations working toward LGB equality to host an annual pride parade. The proposal stated that such an event could "encompass the ideas and ideals of the larger struggle in which we are engaged, that of our fundamental human rights" (Bruce, 2016, p. 45). Pride parades still occur today, but many have questioned their meaning in the modern era (Savage, 1999). Assuming equality can and does happen for LGB individuals, pride should not be abandoned simply because it was framed in the context of a struggle. Instead, pride needs to be thought about truly in the affirmative, as an acknowledgment of unique strengths, perspectives, histories, and contributions. In this way, LGB well-being is benefited by increased acceptance and, at the same time, by maintenance of those community characteristics that allow for resilience when struggle is encountered.

Notes

1 The author thanks his research assistants, Siham Ayoub and Hannah Champagne, for their help gathering sources for this article.
2 The Stonewall riots consisted of violent protests and demonstrations by members of the LGBT community in response to a police raid of the Stonewall Inn, a Greenwich Village bar frequented by gay patrons. At the time, police raids in establishments with gay patrons were common, and individuals who were dressed in clothes deemed appropriate for the other gender were often arrested, and others identified as gay or lesbian were often harassed and beaten. The Stonewall riots mark one of the first acts of resistance on the part of the gay community and are often noted as the start of the LGBT civil rights movement (Faderman, 2015).

References

Abes, E. S., & Jones, S. R. (2004). Meaning-making capacity and the dynamics of lesbian college students' multiple dimensions of identity. *Journal of College Student Development*, *45*, 612–632.

Bariola, E., Lyons, A., & Lucke, J. (2016, November 21). Flourishing among sexual minority individuals: Application of the Dual Continuum Model of mental health in a sample of lesbians and gay men. *Psychology of Sexual Orientation and Gender Diversity*. Advance online publication. http://dx.doi.org/10.1037/sgd0000210

Becker, M., Cortina, K. S., Tsai, Y.-M., & Eccles, J. S. (2014). Sexual orientation, psychological well-being, and mental health: A longitudinal analysis from adolescence to young adulthood. *Psychology of Sexual Orientation and Gender Diversity, 1*, 132–145.

Bowleg, L., Craig, M. L., & Burkholder, G. (2004). Rising and surviving: A conceptual model of active coping among Black lesbians. *Cultural Diversity and Ethnic Minority Psychology, 10*, 229–240.

Bruce, K. M. (2016). *Pride parades: How a parade changed the world.* New York, NY: New York University Press.

Cochran, S. D., & Mays, V. M. (2013). Sexual orientation and mental health. In C. J. Patterson & A. R. D'Augelli (Eds.), *Handbook of psychology and sexual orientation* (pp. 204–222). New York: Oxford University Press.

Cochran, S. D., Mays, V. M., Corliss, H., Smith, T. W., & Turner, J. (2009). Self-reported altruistic and reciprocal behaviors among homosexually and heterosexually experienced adults: Implications for HIV/AIDS service organizations. *AIDS Care, 21*, 675–682.

Cohen, S., & Wills, T. A. (1985). Stress, social support, and the buffering hypothesis. *Psychological Bulletin, 98*, 310–357.

Davydov, D. M., Stewart, R., Ritchie, K., & Chaudieu, I. (2010). Resilience and mental health. *Clinical Psychology Review, 30*, 479–495.

D'Emilio, J. (1998). *Sexual politics, sexual communities: The making of a homosexual minority in the United States, 1940–1970.* Chicago, IL: University of Chicago Press.

Detrie, P. M., & Lease, S. H. (2007). The relation of social support, connectedness, and collective self-esteem to the psychological well-being of lesbian, gay, and bisexual youth. *Journal of Homosexuality, 53*, 173–199.

Diamond, L. M., & Lucas, S. (2004). Sexual-minority and heterosexual youths' peer relationships: Experiences, expectations, and implications for well-being. *Journal of Research on Adolescence, 14*, 313–340.

Faderman, L. (2015). *The gay revolution: The story of the struggle.* New York, NY: Simon & Schuster.

Feeney, B. C., & Collins, N. L. (2014). A new look at social support: A theoretical perspective on thriving through relationships. *Personality and Social Psychology Review, 19*, 113–147.

Figueroa, W. S., & Zoccola, P. M. (2015). Individual differences in risk and resiliency on sexual minority health: The roles of stigma consciousness and psychological hardiness. *Psychology of Sexual Orientation and Gender Diversity, 2*, 329–338.

Fingerhut, A. W. (2017). *Minority stress and well-being: The role of social support and social identity* (Unpublished manuscript). Department of Psychology, Loyola Marymount University, Los Angeles, CA, US.

Fingerhut, A. W., & Peplau, L. A. (2013). Same-sex romantic relationships. In C. J. Patterson & A. R. D'Augelli (Eds.), *Handbook of psychology and sexual orientation* (pp. 165–178). New York: Oxford University Press.

Fingerhut, A. W., Peplau, L. A., & Gable, S. L. (2010). Identity, minority stress and psychological well-being among gay men and lesbians. *Psychology & Sexuality, 1*, 101–114.

Fredriksen-Goldsen, K. I., & Muraco, A. (2010). Aging and sexual orientation: A 25-year review of the literature. *Research on Aging, 32*, 372–413.

Fredriksen-Goldsen, K. I., Cook-Daniels, L., Kim, H. J., Erosheva, E. A., Emlet, C. A., Hoy-Ellis, C. P., Goldsen, J, & Muraco, A. (2014). Physical and mental health of transgender older adults: An at-risk and underserved population. *The Gerontologist, 54,* 488–500. http://dx.doi.org/10.1093/geront/gnt021

Frost, D. M., Meyer, I. H., & Schwartz, S. (2016). Social support networks among diverse sexual minority populations. *American Journal of Orthopsychiatry, 86,* 91–102.

Gates, G. J., & Ost, J. (2004). *The gay and lesbian atlas.* Washington, DC: Urban Institute Press.

Gottman J. M., Levenson, R. W., Swanson, C., Swanson, K., Tyson, R., & Yoshimoto, D. (2003). Observing gay, lesbian and heterosexual couples' relationships: Mathematical modeling of conflict interaction. *Journal of Homosexuality, 45,* 65–91.

Graham, J., & Barnow, Z. (2013). Stress and social support in gay, lesbian, and heterosexual couples: Direct effects and buffering models. *Journal of Family Psychology, 27,* 569–578.

Greene, D. C., & Britton, P. J. (2015). Predicting adult LGBTQ happiness: Impact of childhood affirmation, self-compassion, and personal mastery. *Journal of LGBT Issues in Counseling, 9,* 158–179.

Harper, G. W., Brodsky, A., & Bruce, D. (2012). What's good about being gay? Perspectives from youth. *Journal of LGBT Youth, 9,* 22–41.

Herek, G. M., & Garnets, L. D. (2007). Sexual orientation and mental health. *Annual Review of Clinical Psychology, 3,* 353–375.

Herrick, A. L., Egan, J. E., Coulter, R. W., Friedman, M. R., & Stall, R. (2014). Raising sexual minority youths' health levels by incorporating resiliencies into health promotion efforts. *American Journal of Public Health, 104,* 206–210.

Herrick, A. L., Friedman, M. S., & Stall, R. (2013). Gay men's health and the theory of cultural resilience. In C. J. Patterson & A. R. D'Augelli (Eds.), *Handbook of psychology and sexual orientation* (pp. 191–203). New York, NY: Oxford University Press.

Herrick, A. L., Lim, S. H., Wei, C., Smith, H., Guadamuz, T., Friedman, M. S., & Stall, R. (2011). Resilience as an untapped resource in behavioral intervention design for gay men. *AIDS and Behavior, 15*(Suppl 1), S25–S29. doi:10.1007/s10461-011-9895-0

Hershberger, S. L., & D'Augelli, A. R. (1995). The impact of victimization on the mental health and suicidality of lesbian, gay, and bisexual youth. *Developmental Psychology, 31,* 65–74.

Higa, D., Hoppe, M. J., Lindhorst, T., Mincer, S., Beadnell, B., Morrison, D. M., . . . Mountz, S. (2014). Negative and positive factors associated with the well-being of lesbian, gay, bisexual, transgender, queer, and questioning (LGBTQ) youth. *Youth & Society, 46,* 663–687.

Hill, C. A., & Gunderson, C. J. (2015). Resilience of lesbian, gay, and bisexual individuals in relation to social environment, personal characteristics, and emotion regulation strategies. *Psychology of Sexual Orientation and Gender Diversity, 2,* 232–252.

Hobfoll, S. E., Jackson, A., Hobfoll, I., Pierce, C. A., & Young, S. (2002). The impact of communal-mastery versus self-mastery on emotional outcomes during stressful conditions: A prospective study of Native American women. *American Journal of Community Psychology, 30,* 853–871.

Horne, S. G., Puckett, J. A., Apter, R., & Levitt, H. M. (2014). Positive psychology and LGBTQ populations. In J. Teramota Pedrotti & L. Edwards (Eds.), *Perspectives on the intersection of positive psychology and multiculturalism* (pp. 189–204). New York, NY: Springer Publishing.

Huang, Y., Brewster, M. E., Moradi, B., Goodman, M. B., Wiseman, M. C., & Martin, A. (2010). Content analysis of literature about LGB people of color: 1998–2007. *The Counseling Psychologist, 38,* 363–396.

Jennings, L. K., & Tan, P. P. (2014). Self-compassion and life satisfaction in gay men. *Psychological Reports, 115,* 888–895.

Jordan, K. M., & Deluty, R. (1998). Coming out for lesbian women: Its relations to anxiety, positive affectivity, self-esteem, and social support. *Journal of Homosexuality, 35,* 41–63.

Kertzner, R. M., Meyer, I. H., & Dolezal, C. (2003). Psychological well-being in midlife and older gay men. In G. Herdt & B. de Vries (Eds.), *Gay and lesbian aging: Research and future directions* (pp. 97–116). New York, NY: Springer Publishing.

Kertzner, R. M., Meyer, I. H., Frost, D. M., & Stirratt, M. J. (2009). Social and psychological well-being in lesbians, gay men, and bisexuals: The effects of race, gender, age, and sexual identity. *American Journal of Orthopsychiatry, 79,* 500–510.

Keyes, C. L. M. (1998). Social well-being. *Social Psychology Quarterly, 61,* 121–140.

Kimmel, D. (1978). Adult development and aging: A gay perspective. *Journal of Social Issues, 34,* 113–130.

King, M., Semlyen, J., Tai, S. S., Killaspy, H., Osborn, D., Popelyuk, D., & Nazareth, I. (2008). A systematic review of mental disorder, suicide, and deliberate self harm in lesbian, gay and bisexual people. *BMC Psychiatry, 8.*

Kosciw, J. G., Greytak, E. A., Diaz, E. M., & Bartkiewicz, M. J. (2010). *The 2009 national school climate survey: The experiences of lesbian, gay, bisexual and transgender youth in our nation's schools.* New York, NY: GLSEN.

Kwon, P. (2013). Resilience in lesbian, gay, and bisexual individuals. *Personality and Social Psychology Review, 17,* 371–383.

Kwon, P., & Hugelshofer, D. S. (2010). The protective role of hope for lesbian, gay, and bisexual individuals facing a hostile workplace climate. *Journal of Gay & Lesbian Mental Health, 14,* 3–18.

Luhtanen, R. K. (2002). Identity, stigma management, and well-being. *Journal of Lesbian Studies, 7,* 85–100.

Maisel, N. C., & Fingerhut, A. W. (2011). California's ban on same-sex marriage: The campaign and its effects on gay, lesbian, and bisexual individuals. *Journal of Social Issues, 67,* 242–263.

Mays, V. M., & Cochran, S. D. (2001). Mental health correlates of perceived discrimination among lesbian, gay, and bisexual adults in the United States. *American Journal of Public Health, 91,* 1869–1876.

Mereish, E. H., & Poteat, V. P. (2015). The conditions under which growth-fostering relationships promote resilience and alleviate psychological distress among sexual minorities: Applications of relational cultural theory. *Psychology of Sexual Orientation and Gender Diversity, 2,* 339–344.

Meyer, I. H. (1995). Minority stress and mental health in gay men. *Journal of Health and Social Behavior, 36,* 38–56.

Meyer, I. H. (2003). Prejudice, social stress, and mental health in lesbian, gay, bisexual populations: Conceptual issues and research evidence. *Psychological Bulletin, 129,* 674–697.

Meyer, I. H. (2010). Identity, stress, and resilience in lesbians, gay men, and bisexuals of color. *The Counseling Psychologist, 38,* 442–454.

Meyer, I. H. (2015). Resilience in the study of minority stress and health of sexual and gender minorities. *Psychology of Sexual Orientation and Gender Diversity, 2,* 209–213.

Meyer, I. H., Dietrich, J. D., & Schwartz, S. (2008). Lifetime prevalence of mental disorders in diverse lesbian, gay, and bisexual populations. *American Journal of Public Health, 98,* 1004–1006.

Meyer, I. H., & Frost, D. M. (2013). Minority stress and the health of sexual minorities. In C. J. Patterson & A. R. D'Augelli (Eds.), *Handbook of psychology and sexual orientation* (pp. 252–266). New York, NY: Oxford University Press.

Meyer, I. H., Ouellette, S. C., Haile, R., & McFarlane, T. A. (2011). "We'd be free": Narratives of life without homophobia, racism, or sexism. *Sexuality Research & Social Policy, 8,* 204–214.

Meyer, I. H., Schwartz, S., & Frost, D. M. (2008). Social patterning of stress and coping: Does disadvantaged social statuses confer more stress and fewer coping resources? *Social Science & Medicine, 67,* 368–379.

Moe, J. L. (2016). Wellness and distress in LGBTQ populations: A meta-analysis. *Journal of LGBT Issues in Counseling, 10,* 112–129.

Moe, J. L., Dupuy, P. J., & Laux, J. M. (2008). The relationship between LGBQ identity development and hope, optimism, and life engagement. *Journal of LGBT Issues in Counseling, 2,* 199–215.

Moradi, B., Wiseman, M. C., DeBlaere, C., Goodman, M. B., Sarkees, A., Brewster, M. E., & Huang, Y. (2010). LGB of color and white individuals' perceptions of heterosexist stigma, internalized homophobia, and outness: Comparisons of levels and links. *The Counseling Psychologist, 38,* 397–424.

Narváez, R. F., Meyer, I. H., Kertzner, R. M., Ouellette, S. C., & Gordon, A. R. (2009). A qualitative approach to the intersection of sexual, ethnic, and gender identities. *Identity, 9,* 63–86.

Neff, K. D. (2003). The development and validation of a scale to measure self-compassion. *Self and Identity, 2,* 223–250.

O'Leary, V. E., & Ickovics, I. R. (1995). Resilience and thriving in response to challenge: An opportunity for a paradigm shift in women's health. *Women's Health, 1,* 121–142.

Pearlin, L. I., & Schooler, C. (1978). The structure of coping. *Journal of Health and Social Behavior, 19,* 2–21.

Pew Research Center. (2013, June 13). *A survey of LGBT Americans: Attitudes, experiences and values in changing times.* Washington, DC: Author.

Pugh, S. (2005). Assessing the cultural needs of older lesbians and gay men: Implications for practice. *Practice, 17,* 207–218.

Ramirez-Valles, J., Fergus, S., Reisen, C. A., Poppen, P. J., & Zea, M. C. (2005). Confronting stigma: Community involvement and psychological well-being among HIV-positive Latino gay men. *Hispanic Journal of Behavioral Sciences, 27,* 101–119. doi: 10.1177/0739986304270232

Rieger, G., & Savin-Williams, R. C. (2012). Gender nonconformity, sexual orientation, and psychological well-being. *Archives of Sexual Behavior, 41,* 611–621.

Riggle, E. D. B., Mohr, J. J., Rostosky, S. S., Fingerhut, A. W., & Balsam, K. F. (2014). A multifactor lesbian, gay, and bisexual positive identity measure (LGBPIM). *Psychology of Sexual Orientation and Gender Diversity, 1,* 398–411.

Riggle, E. D. B., & Rostosky, S. S. (2012). *A positive view of LBGTQ: Embracing identity and cultivating well-being.* Lanham, MD: Rowman & Littlefield.

Riggle, E. D. B., Rostosky, S. S., Black, W. W., & Rosenkrantz, D. E. (2016, September 22). Outness, concealment, and authenticity: Associations with LGB individuals' psychological distress and well-being. *Psychology of Sexual Orientation and Gender Diversity.* Advance online publication. http://dx.doi.org/10.1037/sgd0000202

Riggle, E. D. B., Rostosky, S. S., McCants, L. E., & Pascale-Hague, D. (2011). The positive aspects of a transgender self-identification. *Psychology and Sexuality, 2,* 147–158.

Riggle, E. D. B., Whitman, J. S., Olson, A., Rostosky, S. S., & Strong, S. (2008). The positive aspects of being a lesbian or gay man. *Professional Psychology: Research and Practice, 39,* 210–217.

Rostosky, S. S., Riggle, E. D. B., Pascale-Hague, D., & McCants, L. E. (2010). The positive aspects of a bisexual self-identification. *Psychology and Sexuality, 1,* 131–144.

Russell, G. M. (2000). *Voted out: The psychological consequences of anti-gay politics.* New York, NY: New York University Press.

Sattler, F. A., Wagner, U., & Christiansen, H. (2016). The effect of minority stress, group level coping, and social support on mental health of German gay men. *PLoS One, 11,* 1–14.

Savage, D. (1999). Pride. *The Stranger, 8*(39). Retrieved from www.thestranger.com/seattle/pride/Content?oid=1313

Savin-Williams, R. C. (2008). Then and now: Recruitment, definition, diversity, and positive attributes of same-sex populations. *Developmental Psychology, 44,* 135–138.

Sellers, R. M., Caldwell, C. H., Schmeelk-Cone, K., & Zimmerman, M. A. (2003). The role of racial identity and racial discrimination in the mental health of African American young adults. *Journal of Health and Social Behavior, 44,* 302–317.

Smith, M. S., & Gray, S. W. (2009). The courage to challenge: A new measure of hardiness in LGBT adults. *Journal of Gay & Lesbian Social Services, 21,* 73–89.

Szymanski, D. M. (2009). Examining potential moderators of the link between heterosexist events and gay and bisexual men's psychological distress. *Journal of Counseling Psychology, 56,* 142–151.

Szymanski, D. M., & Gupta, A. (2009). Examining the relationship between multiple internalized oppressions and African American lesbian, gay, bisexual, and questioning persons' self-esteem and psychological distress. *Journal of Counseling Psychology, 56,* 110–118.

Szymanski, D. M., & Meyer, D. (2008). Racism and heterosexism as correlates of psychological distress in African American sexual minority women. *Journal of LGBT Issues in Counseling, 2,* 94–108.

Szymanski, D. M., & Mikorski, R. (2016). External and internalized heterosexism, meaning in life, and psychological distress. *Psychology of Sexual Orientation and Gender Diversity, 3,* 265–274.

Szymanski, D. M., & Owens, G. P. (2009). Group-level coping as a moderator between heterosexism and sexism and psychological distress in sexual minority women. *Psychology of Women Quarterly, 33,* 197–205.

Tedeschi, R. G., & Calhoun, L. G. (1996). The posttraumatic growth inventory: Measuring the positive legacy of trauma. *Journal of Traumatic Stress, 9,* 455–472.

Thoits, P. A. (2011). Mechanisms linking social ties and support to physical and mental health. *Journal of Health and Social Behavior, 52,* 145–161.

Thomeer, M. B., & Reczek, C. (2016). Happiness and sexual minority status. *Archives of Sexual Behavior, 45,* 1745–1758.

Troiden, R. R. (1989). The formation of homosexual identities. *Journal of Homosexuality, 17,* 43–73.

Van Den Berghe, W., Dewaele, A., Cox, N., & Vincke, J. (2010). Minority-specific determinants of mental well-being among lesbian, gay and bisexual youth. *Journal of Applied Social Psychology, 40,* 153–166.

Vaughan, M. D., Miles, J., Parent, M. C., Lee, H. S., Tilghman, J. D., & Prokhorets, S. (2014). A content analysis of LGBT-themed positive psychology articles. *Psychology of Sexual Orientation and Gender Diversity, 1*, 313–324.

Vaughan, M. D., & Rodriguez, E. M. (2014). LGBT strengths: Incorporating positive psychology into theory, research, training, and practice. *Psychology of Sexual Orientation and Gender Diversity, 1*, 325–334.

Vaughan, M. D., & Waehler, C. A. (2009). Coming out growth: Conceptualizing and measuring stress related growth associated with coming out to others as a sexual minority. *Journal of Adult Development, 17*, 94–109.

Weeks, J., Heaphy, B., & Donovan, C. (2001). *Same-sex intimacies: Families of choice and other life experiments.* London: Routledge.

Whitford, G. S. (1997). Realities and hopes for older gay males. *Journal of Gay and Lesbian Social Services, 6*, 79–95.

Wright, E., & Perry, B. (2006). Sexual identity distress, social support, and the health of gay, lesbian and bisexual youth. *Journal of Homosexuality, 51*, 81–110.

Zea, M. C., Reisen, C. A., & Poppen, P. J. (1999). Psychological well-being among Latino lesbians and gay men. *Cultural Diversity and Ethnic Minority Psychology, 5*, 371–379.

20

MOTIVES, GOALS, AND WELL-BEING THROUGHOUT THE LIFESPAN

Jutta Heckhausen and Joseph S. Kay

Across the lifespan, motivation, goal pursuits and achievements, and subjective well-being influence one another directly and indirectly in a process that can promote and optimize development and maintenance of skills and abilities. Differences in well-being call attention to opportunities available and a person's potential for control over his or her goals, as well as of success in approaching goals. Conversely, poor well-being can result from and call attention to a lack of opportunities or control over goals or slower than expected progress. Motivation also indirectly influences well-being through the effect it has on goal achievement. Therefore, well-being can be viewed as both a primary and secondary outcome of motivation and, in turn, a cause or driver of motivation.

In this chapter, we take a lifespan approach to describing the interactions between motivation, opportunities, goals and their pursuits, and well-being. First, we describe the Motivational Theory of Lifespan Development (MTD) as it relates to changes in motivation over the lifespan. We then describe how motivation predicts well-being, with a specific emphasis on the importance of perceptions of control. Next, we describe ways in which well-being influences motivation and the goals we pursue. Last, we highlight how implicit motives are distinct from explicit goals. In this final section, we discuss the functional relationship between implicit motives and explicit goals, how well-being is influenced by our goal achievement (or failure to achieve our goal), and how this depends on the goal and its congruence with implicit motives.

Motivational Theory of Lifespan Development

The Motivational Theory of Lifespan Development (MTD; Heckhausen & Schulz, 1993; Heckhausen, Wrosch, & Schulz, 2010) focuses on humans as active agents in promoting their development throughout the lifespan. At any given time, most individuals have multiple potential goals in different domains of life that they can choose to pursue. Since an individual can only invest effort into a single goal at any given time, he or she is forced to choose which goal to pursue. For example, a young adult may need to decide whether to invest effort into education or into career, and pursuing one may have negative repercussions on the other. Similarly, an adult in midlife who decides to focus on family relationships may harm his or her career progress. In order to optimize development and maintenance of skills and capacities across the lifespan, the decision of which goal to pursue at any time should be made based on which goal is developmentally appropriate given the opportunities and constraints present. To make the best decisions to promote long-term development of skills and capacities, individuals must consider the potential long-term beneficial and harmful effects that pursuing each goal may have, both within that domain of life and across other domains, and must keep in mind that investing effort and achieving success in one domain of life may come at the expense of opportunities in other domains of life. Although well-being influences the goals people pursue (discussed below), MTD proposes that choosing goals in order to maximize the amount of primary control one can exert over the environment and life course will lead to optimal development and maintenance of skills and capacities throughout the lifespan. Several affective and action-regulatory modules favor such an orientation in human motivational functioning (Heckhausen et al., 2010). Human motivational functioning does not serve to promote well-being per se but serves to maximize primary control, with changes to well-being resulting from such successes or failures.

MTD describes three distinct phases of goal pursuits, the transitions between which are discrete and discontinuous. The first is the *pre-decisional phase*, when the individual must decide between multiple goals. During this stage, it is adaptive to accurately evaluate the possible goals given the opportunities and constraints present (Gollwitzer, 1990; Gollwitzer, Heckhausen, & Steller, 1990), as well as the likelihood of attaining each goal and the effect that goal attainment would have within and across different domains of life (Beckman & Gollwitzer, 1987). Selecting a goal according to these criteria leads to greater goal engagement (Wrosch & Schulz, 2008) and allows the individual to develop or maintain skills and capacities, without harming the chances of later development in other areas of life (Heckhausen et al., 2010).

Once a goal has been selected, the individual shifts from a deliberative to an implemental mindset (Gollwitzer et al., 1990) and enters the *goal engagement* phase. In order to focus fully on and pursue the chosen goal, the individual no longer evaluates that goal and its alternatives in an unbiased way but instead perceives greater levels of control over the chosen goal (Achtziger & Gollwitzer, 2010). To pursue the goal, the individual uses *primary control* and *secondary control* strategies, depending on the difficulty of the goal (Heckhausen et al., 2010; Rothbaum,

Weisz, & Snyder, 1982). Primary control strategies are aimed at directly effecting change in the world to bring about that goal (e.g., investing time and effort into the goal or using external supports such as enlisting help to achieve the goal) and are the first strategies used when pursuing a goal. When the goal is difficult and primary control strategies are insufficient to attain it, the individual should also use secondary control strategies to pursue the goal. These are motivational strategies that boost the effectiveness of the primary control strategies (e.g., by enhancing the value of the goal or diminishing the value of the alternatives) and contribute to goal attainment (Hamm et al., 2013; Heckhausen et al., 2010; McQuillen, Licht, & Licht, 2003). By using the appropriate motivational strategies, people increase the likelihood of attaining their goals while also avoiding wasting effort by investing more than necessary.

The third phase described by MTD is the *goal disengagement phase*, which occurs when the opportunity to attain a goal has passed, either because the person was successful and attained it, or because attaining it no longer seems possible. Once a goal has been attained, it is most adaptive for long-term successful life-course development of desired skills and capacities to shift back to a deliberative mindset and re-enter the pre-decision phase of goal pursuits. In order to promote positive development, deliberation should begin on the next goal to pursue rather than dwelling on the success of attaining the previous goal because pursuing goals that are no longer attainable is maladaptive and has negative effects on well-being (Heckhausen, Wrosch, & Fleeson, 2001; Wrosch, Scheier, Carver, & Schulz, 2003). To avoid wasting effort, individuals reduce their engagement levels as soon as a goal is no longer attainable (Heckhausen, 2000). During the goal disengagement stage, the individual uses compensatory secondary control strategies to disengage from the chosen goal by devaluing the prior goal and promoting re-engagement with other goals (Heckhausen et al., 2010). This disengagement is self-protective because it reduces the negative consequences associated with failure to attain a goal (Heckhausen, 1999; Heckhausen et al., 2001). Furthermore, re-engagement with other goals allows for further development in other domains of life and limits the long-term harm that may come from failure to achieve a goal (Wrosch et al., 2003).

Humans' capacity for primary and secondary control change over the lifespan based on abilities, skills and knowledge, and societal opportunities and constraints. Primary control capacity follows an inverted U shape (Heckhausen, 1999; Wrosch, Heckhausen, & Lachman, 2000) that peaks in midlife. Children's primary control capacities are low due to lack of abilities and opportunities. Primary control capacity rises into mid-adulthood, individuals gain skills and knowledge, and opportunities in society increase, thus providing greater freedom to select and pursue goals. Primary control capacity then declines again in old age, as skills and functioning decline and societal constraints (e.g., required retirement) arise. Secondary control capacity follows a different trajectory, increasing throughout the lifespan as individuals become better able to self-regulate (Heckhausen, 1999;

Wrosch et al., 2000). Older adults are better able to use self-motivational strategies and disengage from unattainable goals. Because control is important for well-being, these trajectories have important implications for well-being across the lifespan.

Importance of Motivation and Perceived Control for Well-Being

The perception of personal control over one's environment, in addition to actual opportunities for control, is a critical aspect of motivation related to well-being. Perceptions of control predict well-being on both a daily basis and more broadly across the lifespan (Lang & Heckhausen, 2001; Sheldon, Ryan, & Reis, 1996). For example, participants in a daily diary study reported that on days in which they felt more competent and autonomous, they also felt greater well-being (Sheldon et al., 1996). More broadly, cross-sectional research shows that while there are international differences in mean levels of perceived personal control and well-being in adults, there are consistently strong correlations between the two across Eastern and Western, developed and developing, countries (Spector et al., 2001). There are also strong correlations between perceived control over one's own goal attainment and development and subjective well-being, although in a study of adults aged 20–90, age mediated these relationships such that correlations were stronger as age increased (Lang & Heckhausen, 2001).

Despite changing capacities and opportunities across the lifespan, well-being largely remains stable until near the end of life (Diener, Lucas, & Scollon, 2006; Gerstorf et al., 2010; Scheibe & Carstensen, 2010). Early research suggested that people are on a "hedonic treadmill", responding positively or negatively to good or bad events but returning quickly to a neutral baseline emotional state (Brickman & Campbell, 1971). According to this early theorizing, there may be minor fluctuations in affect and well-being on a day-to-day basis, and life events may positively or negatively influence well-being, but the affective system adjusts and ultimately returns back to its original neutral levels (Brickman & Campbell, 1971). More recent research shows that the baseline levels of well-being and affective states are not always neutral and vary between people (e.g., Biswas-Diener, Vitterso, & Diener, 2005; Diener et al., 2006). Furthermore, the impact that significant life events such as the death of a spouse or unemployment have on affect and well-being can persist for several years (Lucas, 2007), although affect and well-being still tend to return toward the initial baseline levels over time (Luhmann, Hofmann, Eid, & Lucas, 2012). Additionally, older adults experience similar levels of positive affect as younger adults and less negative affect (Charles & Carstensen, 2010). These positive and negative affective states are aspects of but do not reflect the entirety of well-being. Positive and negative affect varies more over time than measures that also include domain-specific life satisfaction (e.g., satisfaction with work, family, etc.) and domain-general measures of life satisfaction (e.g., satisfaction with current life and with expectations for the future) (Diener et al., 2006; Diener, Suh, Lucas, & Smith, 1999). Because of their more flexible variation with situational conditions and with the degree of progress towards an anticipated goal, affective states more than more general life satisfaction indicators are more useful for helping individuals assess the feasibility of their goal pursuits, and for prompting upward or downward adjustments in goal aspiration.

At first glance, the relative stability of well-being into old age (Diener et al., 2006; Scheibe & Carstensen, 2010) may seem to conflict with the actual opportunities for control that are available to older adults. This stability in well-being despite increasing declines in functioning and social losses has been referred to as the "well-being paradox" (Kunzmann, Little, & Smith, 2000). However, researchers have found that health functioning, as opposed to age, is related to well-being and that age predicts declines in well-being only if it leads to changes in functional capacity or impairments (Kunzmann et al., 2000). Indeed, declines in well-being in older adults come largely during terminal declines in functioning 3–5 years prior to death, largely independent of age (Gerstorf et al., 2010), as well as in the very old and those who are institutionalized due to poor health and poor functioning (Smith, Borchelt, Maier, & Jopp, 2002). This research suggests that although declines in functioning increase in old age, they only impact well-being at the latest stages of old age or illness.

One reason why minor functional impairments in old age may not impact well-being is because older adults are better able to use secondary control strategies (Heckhausen, 1997; Lachman & Firth, 2004), which may allow them to overcome their functional impairments. For example, older adults with vision impairments who are better able to use compensatory control strategies are more likely to use assistive devices 1 year later (Becker, Wahl, Schilling, & Burmedi, 2005), which may prevent declines in well-being by enabling longer-term independence. Older adults who perceive they have control may be more active in taking steps to avoid the risks or may be better than younger adults at managing the negative psychological effects of impairments by using strategies to avoid negative or distressing situations (e.g., Charles, 2010).

Indeed, maintaining perceptions of control by effectively using primary and secondary control strategies in the face of limitations is critical. Perceived control buffers against the steep declines in well-being that typically occur in late-life independent of disability status, socioeconomic status, and age (Gerstorf et al., 2014), and optimism regarding one's relative health risk compared to others is associated with higher well-being only when combined with perceptions of control over one's health outcomes, though optimism and perceived control are independent of one another (Ruthig, Chipperfield, Perry, Newall, & Swift, 2007). These perceptions of control may be valuable too, since those who perceive greater levels of personal control over their aging processes report higher levels of engagement and lower levels of disengagement from their goals (Tomasik & Silbereisen, 2013), and those who are more engaged in their goals report they are better able to cope with stressors and have better psychological and physical well-being (Haynes, Heckhausen, Chipperfield, Perry, & Newall, 2009; Wrosch & Schulz, 2008).

There is also strong evidence that perceiving one has control over one's environment is beneficial in a wide range of situations and populations and is not limited to older adults. For example, although older adults were found to rely more on control strategies than younger adults, across adulthood, use of primary or secondary control strategies was related to psychological well-being, and these associations are present when facing both health and financial stressors (Wrosch et al., 2000). Similarly, university students who struggle with their academics and use both primary and secondary control strategies report lower levels of perceived academic stress, more positive and fewer negative course-related emotions, than those do not use both strategies (Hall, Perry, Ruthig, Hladkyj, & Chipperfield, 2006). These findings extend beyond academics into the transition to work. Goal engagement is generally beneficial for well-being during this transition when occupational prospects are favorable (Haase, Heckhausen, & Köller, 2008; Haase, Heckhausen, & Silbereisen, 2012), and goal disengagement is beneficial for well-being when occupational prospects are unfavorable (Haase et al., 2012). This research indicates that perceiving some form of control over one's goals is beneficial, although whether the most beneficial way control is expressed is through goal engagement or disengagement depends on the opportunities present.

Fit Between Opportunities and Control

Perceiving control, by itself, is not enough to promote well-being. Rather, the use of appropriate goal engagement and disengagement strategies according to the actual opportunities for control is critical. Although disengaging from attainable goals prevents their attainment, remaining engaged in goals after they are no longer attainable is maladaptive and results in diminished well-being (Heckhausen et al., 2010). Loss of control is associated with diminished positive affect, but these negative effects can be avoided by disengaging from the uncontrollable or unattainable goal. Disengagement from unattainable goals allows for re-engagement with new, more attainable goals (Wrosch, Bauer, & Scheier, 2005; Wrosch et al., 2003). That is, when opportunities for control are high, goal engagement is beneficial for affective well-being, and the negative effects of low levels of perceived control on well-being can be reduced by using goal disengagement strategies to re-engage with more controllable goals.

In the work domain, disengagement from goals can buffer the negative effects of low opportunities for control, for example when living in a region with limited job opportunities (Tomasik, Silbereisen, & Heckhausen, 2010) or when the individual perceives they have low levels of control (Grumer, Silbereisen, & Heckhausen, 2013). Specifically, in German regions where career opportunities are high, disengagement is associated with reduced well-being, but in regions where career opportunities are low, disengagement has positive effects on well-being (Tomasik et al., 2010). On an individual level, the negative effects of perceived work demands can be buffered by using appropriate goal engagement strategies when demands are perceived to be controllable and disengagement strategies when perceived to be uncontrollable (Grumer et al., 2013). Conversely, the negative effects of low opportunities or work demands may be compounded if the individual continues to use goal engagement strategies.

The ability to disengage from unattainable goals may be particularly important for well-being in older adults, whose opportunities for control decline as functional impairments grow. Older adults who persist with their goals experience positive effects for their psychological and physical well-being. Those who do not persist but modify their goals or find alternate approaches to their goals and also use self-protective secondary control strategies to reduce the negative impact of failing to achieve their goals also experience these same positive effects (Haynes et al., 2009). However, those older adults who accept a lack of control over their goals and those who modify their goals but do not re-engage with the modified goals experience declines in well-being (Haynes et al., 2009). Similarly, in older adults with serious health problems, being engaged in health goals is beneficial for both health and well-being when health problems are acute and controllable (e.g., acute vascular events like heart attacks, the effects of which may be controlled by careful monitoring and treatment) (Hall, Chipperfield, Heckhausen, & Perry, 2010). This is in contrast to those with chronic and uncontrollable conditions (e.g., arthritis), for whom engagement with health goals is harmful and disengagement beneficial for well-being, health, and survival (Hall et al., 2010). The ability to recognize when goals are controllable and adjust goal engagement and disengagement strategies accordingly is important for health and well-being.

These findings suggest that, when trying to manage health threats, older adults should adopt "lines of defense" as a way to maintain functioning and avoid wasted effort or striving for unattainable health goals when facing functional declines (Heckhausen, Wrosch, & Schulz, 2013). When healthy, it is most adaptive for older adults to be fully engaged in preserving their functioning and avoiding illness by engaging in health-promoting behaviors and preventative health measures. If a disease arises, it becomes adaptive to accept the disease and work to prevent disease progression or to revert the effects of the disease. As the disease progresses, individuals may need to withdraw from the goal of remaining disease-free and instead work toward maintaining functioning and preventing decline, including accepting the need to alter the environment (Becker et al., 2005); request help from others (Berg & Upchurch, 2007); or replace activities that are no longer possible because of reduced functioning with other meaningful activities (Zimmer, Hickey, & Searle, 1997). Finally, among individuals with terminal illnesses, psychological well-being is highest among those who withdraw from health goals altogether and instead focus on what is actually controllable (Gerstorf et al., 2014). By following these lines of defense, individuals can focus on health and other life goals that are attainable to promote or preserve functioning as long as possible and avoid the negative psychological effects of striving for unattainable goals.

Influence of Well-Being on Goals and Action

Affect and well-being influence the goals we select and our engagement with those goals. According to Frijda's (1988) Laws of Emotion, emotions arise from individual's appraisals of events or situations that are important to their goals, motives, or concerns based on their perceptions or expectations of the short- or long-term consequences of the events or situations. However, there is an asymmetry between the situations that cause positive and negative affect. According to Frijda, positive emotions are only elicited by favorable changes in circumstances (i.e., changes that make goals more likely to be attained), whereas negative emotions are elicited both by unfavorable changes as well as by persistent unfavorable circumstances (i.e., when goals become less likely to be attained, or when they are persistently unlikely to be attained). One implication is that positive affect results from achieving a goal or making progress towards the goal, but diminishes quickly because only the positive changes result in positive affect, prompting new goal setting and pursuit. Unlike positive affect, negative affect that results from goal failures or struggles continues over time, promoting goal persistence and striving to overcome these failures or difficulties.

The prediction that positive affect leads to new goal pursuits and negative affect leads to continued perseverance is supported by research showing that affect is associated with types of cognitive processing. Positive affect leads to broader attentional focus and increased task-switching (Dreisbach & Goschke, 2004; Fredrickson & Branigan, 2005). This broader attentional focus is also related to higher levels of creativity and flexibility and with an increased use of heuristics and intuition as opposed to reason and deep processing when problem-solving (Lyubomirsky, King, & Diener, 2005). Overall, this positive affect leads to faster and more efficient decision-making but may come at the expense of deep processing and evaluation when making decisions or pursuing goals (Lyubomirsky et al., 2005), although these negative effects may be reduced when the task is particularly meaningful and important to the individual (Isen, 2001). The cognitive effects of well-being and affect may allow individuals to attempt to solve problems quickly and then switch their focus to other issues or goals. Struggling to reach one's goals leads to less positive and more negative affect, which in turn causes the individual to slow down, narrow their focus, and persevere, which can be adaptive when the goals are attainable (although it may be maladaptive when goals are unattainable).

Positive affect results from goal achievement and also leads to behaviors that result in success (Lyubomirsky et al., 2005). Lyubomirsky and colleagues' meta-analysis found that longitudinal research shows that positive affect precedes success and behaviors that lead to success and that experimental studies show causal relationships between positive affect and success. Experimental studies, although fewer in number than cross-sectional and longitudinal observational studies, show that inducing positive affect leads people to have higher energy levels and exert more willpower and self-control over unhealthy desires (e.g., are more likely to resist the desire to smoke), and seek more social contact and work on collaboration as opposed to conflict.

Negative affect is also valuable for long-term success. In a longitudinal study of adolescents, depressive symptoms predicted growth in the capacity to disengage from goals (Wrosch & Miller, 2009). This is beneficial as goal disengagement can be self-protective and the capacity for goal disengagement can help to protect against the negative implications of failure when goals are unattainable (Wrosch et al., 2003; Wrosch, Scheier, & Miller, 2013); goal disengagement is also associated with lower levels of negative affect and increased well-being when goals are difficult or impossible to achieve (Dunne, Wrosch, & Miller, 2011; Wrosch & Miller, 2009). Negative affect resulting from failures, then, helps to develop long-term capacities to help reduce the negative psychological impact that would arise from future failures, although these capacities may reduce perseverance and the likelihood of attaining difficult but not impossible goals.

Influence of Goals and Achievement on Well-Being

In addition to well-being and affect influencing goal selection, perseverance, and success at achieving goals, well-being also results from successes or failures at making adequate progress toward goals. Carver and Scheier (1990) argue that one way to determine the adequacy of progress toward goals is through positive and negative affect that result from our progress. That is, affect serves as a signal of progress toward goals and discrepancies between expected goal progress and actual goal progress. Negative affect signals slower than expected progress creating a negative feedback loop where we increase our efforts toward the goal in order to reduce this discrepancy (and the negative affect). Positive affect that results from the perception of making greater than expected progress toward a goal also creates a negative feedback loop by promoting broader attentional focus and task-switching. When perceived actual progress toward a goal is equal to expected progress toward a goal, little affective response is produced, since positive affect would signal that it is appropriate to reduce goal pursuit behaviors. Neutral or no affective response results in continued goal pursuit at the same level, in order to maintain progress.

Although goal achievement is beneficial for well-being, the relationship between our achievements and our well-being depends on stage in the lifespan and on the specific content of the goals. According to the Socioemotional Selectivity Theory (SST) (Carstensen, 1992; Carstensen, Isaacowitz, & Charles, 1999), the importance of the emotional content of a goal varies depending on our perception of the time available to us. Younger individuals and those who perceive time to be open-ended select future-oriented goals with the aim of building knowledge and long-term abilities, while older individuals and those who perceive time to be limited (e.g., due to terminal illness or approaching a transition point like graduating from college) select more present-oriented goals aimed at increasing emotional well-being and satisfaction. That is, as individuals age, they become more motivated to pursue emotion-related goals and less motivated to pursue knowledge-related goals (Carstensen, Fung, & Charles, 2003). For example, older adults narrow their social goals to include fewer but more emotionally meaningful relationships rather than having a greater number of less emotionally meaningful relationships found among younger adults (Carstensen, 1992). In addition, older adults are less inclined to pursue goals that are unpleasant but beneficial in the long term than are younger adults (Lockenhoff & Carstensen, 2004). These differences indicate that the goal content (i.e., the types of the goals people pursue) and their perceived level of success in pursuing goals are both important in understanding the impact of goals on well-being.

Implicit Motives, Goal Pursuits, and Well-Being

Thus far, the discussion of goals and motivation has focused on explicit goals and the motivational strategies people use to pursue them. These explicit goals are objectives that the individual consciously pursues in order to bring about a desirable outcome or avoid an undesirable outcome. However, individuals differ in their implicit motives, which are their affective or hedonic responses to certain types of situations. The study of implicit motives has focused on the *achievement motive*, which is a positive affective response to achieving excellence or learning or developing new skills and proficiencies (McClelland, 1976; Pang, 2010), the power motive, which is a positive affective response to being in positions of control or influence over other people or the world (Fodor, 2010), and the *affiliation motive*, which is a positive affective response to building and maintaining close social relationships (Weinberger, Cotler, & Fishman, 2010). People have varying levels of achievement, power, and affiliation motives (i.e., some are more driven by achievement, others by power, and others by affiliation). These motives are unconscious, so people are generally unaware of them, and are relatively stable across the lifespan (Brunstein & Maier, 2005; Schultheiss, Rösch, Rawolle, Kordik, & Graham, 2010). In addition, well-being is related to the pursuit of these goals, as well as the strategies needed to achieve them.

Explicit goals vary in the degree to which they reflect implicit motivation. For example, many individuals pursue explicit goals that are achievement-oriented (e.g., the pursuit of a university degree), but they vary on their levels of implicit achievement motivation. Goal pursuits that are congruent with implicit motivations require less effortful control and self-regulation to pursue because they are reinforced by affective rewards (Kehr, 2004b). The pursuit of these goals is inherently rewarding, and results in improvements in well-being, and people whose goals are congruent with their motives put more effort into their goals (Schüler, Job, Fröhlich, & Brandstätter, 2008). These effects are likely due to the impact that congruence has on the goal pursuit process and the resultant changes in affect and well-being. Pursuing goals that are congruent with implicit motivation and making progress towards achieving those goals are associated with improvements in well-being, both on a daily basis and over the course of a several months, while pursuit of or progress towards goals that are incongruent with implicit motivation is associated with limited positive or negative changes in well-being (Brunstein, Schultheiss, & Grassmann, 1998).

Pursuing goals that are not consistent with implicit motivations requires greater volitional control and is more taxing (Kehr, 2004a, 2004b). Successful pursuit of these goals requires greater effort and use of volitional control strategies in order to make up for the lack of hedonic rewards (Kehr, 2004b). This results in two separate goal pursuit pathways. Schultheiss and colleagues (2008) describe the pursuit of *affectively rewarding goals* (i.e., those which are congruent with implicit motivation) as a *hot* goal pursuit, and pursuit of *non-affectively rewarding goals* (i.e., those which are not reinforced by, or are incongruent with, implicit motivation) as a *cold* goal pursuit. Both types of goals can be valuable for long-term development of skills or capacities (e.g., it is valuable to complete a university degree even for an individual who does not have high implicit achievement motivation). However, those that are congruent with implicit motives are easier to pursue and result in greater improvements in well-being.

Conclusion

Throughout the lifespan, motivation, goal pursuits, and their successes or failures influence and are influenced by well-being and affect in ways that vary with time and life stage. Specifically, perceptions of control lead to greater well-being in ways that may be particularly important for older adults facing functional deficits. At the same time, well-being remains relatively stable across the lifespan, despite declines in control in later life. This can be explained by older adults' greater ability to use motivational strategies to maintain control or prevent the negative implications of losing control. Additionally, the impact of control on well-being depends on the fit between goal selection and the opportunities available. When appropriately attainable and adaptive goals are selected and control strategies accordingly activated, well-being is increased. In contrast, choosing unattainable goals leads to diminished well-being. Well-being and affect also influence goals and action; positive affect leads to broader attentional focus and more task-switching and generally greater success and goal achievement, and negative affect promotes narrower attentional focus. Goal achievement also leads to increased well-being, but this may depend on the specific content of the goal. Older adults focus more on emotional goals, and younger adults focus more on goals that build knowledge and skills. Goal pursuit and achievement also leads to well-being when the goals are congruent with implicit or unconscious motivations. These effects promote development and maintenance of skills and capacities throughout the lifespan, as they lead individuals to move on from successes quickly to strive for additional goals but also encourage greater focus and increased perseverance when striving for more difficult goals.

References

Achtziger, A., & Gollwitzer, P. M. (2010). Motivation and volition in the course of action. In J. Heckhausen & H. Heckhausen (Eds.), *Motivation and action* (pp. 275–299). New York: Cambridge University Press.

Becker, S., Wahl, H., Schilling, O., & Burmedi, D. (2005). Assistive device use in visually impaired older adults: Role of control beliefs. *The Gerontologist, 45*(6), 739–746. doi: 10.1093/geront/45.6.739

Beckman, J., & Gollwitzer, P. M. (1987). Deliberative versus implemental states of mind: The issue of impartiality in predecisional and postdecisional information processing. *Social Cognition, 5*(3), 259–249. doi: 10.1521/soco.1987.5.3.259

Berg, C. A., & Upchurch, R. (2007). A developmental-contextual model of couples coping with chronic illness across the adult life span. *Psychological Bulletin, 133*(6), 920–954. doi: 10.1037/0033–2909.133.6.920

Biswas-Diener, R., Vittersø, J., & Diener, E. (2005). Most people are pretty happy, but there is cultural variation: The Inughuit, the Amish, and the Maasai. *Journal of Happiness Studies, 6*(3), 205–226. doi: 10.1007/s10902-005-5683-8

Brickman, P., & Campbell, D. T. (1971). Hedonic relativism and planning the good society. In M. H. Appley (Ed.), *Adaptation level theory: A symposium* (pp. 287–302). New York: Academic Press.

Brunstein, J. C., & Maier, G. W. (2005). Implicit and self-attributed motives to achieve: Two separate but interacting needs. *Journal of Personality and Social Psychology, 89*(2), 205–222. doi: 10.1037/0022–3514.89.2.205

Brunstein, J. C., Schultheiss, O. C., & Grassmann, R. (1998). Personal goals and emotional well-being: The moderating role of motive dispositions. *Journal of Personality and Social Psychology, 75*(2), 494–508. doi: 10.1037//0022–3514.75.2.494

Carstensen, L. L. (1992). Social and emotional patterns in adulthood: Support for socioemotional selectivity theory. *Psychology and Aging, 7*(3), 331–338. doi: 10.1037/0882–7974.7.3.331

Carstensen, L. L., Fung, H. H., & Charles, S. T. (2003). Socioemotional selectivity theory and emotion regulation in the second half of life. *Motivation and Emotion, 27*(2), 103–123. doi: 0146–7239/03/0600–0103/0

Carstensen, L. L., Isaacowitz, D. M., & Charles, S. T. (1999). Taking time seriously: A theory of socioemotional selectivity. *American Psychologist, 54*(3), 165–181. doi: 10.1037/0003–066X.54.3.165

Carver, C. S., & Scheier, M. F. (1990). Origins and functions of positive and negative affect: A control-process view. *Psychological Review, 97*(1), 19–35. doi: 10.1037/0033–295X.97.1.19

Charles, S. T. (2010). Strength and Vulnerability Integration (SAVI): A model of emotional well-being across adulthood. *Psychological Bulletin, 136*(6), 1068–1091. doi: 10.1037/a0021232.Strength

Charles, S. T., & Carstensen, L. L. (2010). Social and emotional aging. *Annual Review of Psychology, 61*, 383–409. doi: 10.1146/annurev.psych.093008.100448.Social

Diener, E., Lucas, R. E., & Scollon, C. N. (2006). Beyond the hedonic treadmill: Revising the adaptation theory of well-being. *The American Psychologist, 61*(4), 305–314. doi: 10.1037/0003–066X.61.4.305

Diener, E., Suh, E. M., Lucas, R. E., & Smith, H. L. (1999). Subjective well-being: Three decades of progress. *Psychological Bulletin, 125*(2), 276–302. doi: 10.1037/0033–2909. 125.2.276

Dreisbach, G., & Goschke, T. (2004). How positive affect modulates cognitive control: Reduced perseveration at the cost of increased distractibility. *Journal of Experimental Psychology, 30*(2), 343–353. doi: 10.1037/0278–7393.30.2.343

Dunne, E., Wrosch, C., & Miller, G. E. (2011). Goal disengagement, functional disability, and depressive symptoms in old age. *Health Psychology, 30*(6), 763–770. doi: 10.1037/a0024019

Fodor, E. M. (2010). Power motivation. In O. C. Schultheiss & J. C. Brunstein (Eds.), *Implicit motives* (pp. 3–29). Oxford: Oxford University Press.

Fredrickson, B. L., & Branigan, C. (2005). Positive emotions broaden the scope of attention and thought-action repertoires. *Cognition & Emotion, 19*(3), 313–332. doi: 10.1080/02699930441000238

Frijda, N. H. (1988). The laws of emotion. *American Psychologist, 43*(5), 349–358. doi: 10.5465/AMR.2007.25275690

Gerstorf, D., Heckhausen, J., Ram, N., Infurna, F. J., Schupp, J., & Wagner, G. G. (2014). Perceived personal control buffers terminal decline in well-being. *Psychology and Aging, 29*(3), 612–625. doi: 10.1037/a0037227

Gerstorf, D., Ram, N., Mayraz, G., Hidajat, M., Lindenberger, U., Wagner, G. G., & Schupp, J. (2010). Late-life decline in well-being across adulthood in Germany, the UK, and the US: Something is seriously wrong at the end of life. *Psychology and Aging, 25*(2), 477–485. doi: 10.1037/a0017543

Gollwitzer, P. M. (1990). Action phases and mind-sets. In E. T. Higgins & R. M. Sorrentino (Eds.), *The handbook of motivation and cognition: Foundations of social behavior* (Vol. 2, pp. 53–92). New York: Guilford Press.

Gollwitzer, P. M., Heckhausen, H., & Steller, B. (1990). Deliberative and implemental mind-sets: Cognitive tuning toward congruous thoughts and information. *Journal of Personality and Social Psychology, 59*(6), 1119–1127. doi: 10.1037//0022–3514.59.6.1119

Grumer, S., Silbereisen, R. K., & Heckhausen, J. (2013). Subjective well-being in times of social change: Congruence of control strategies and perceived control. *International Journal of Psychology, 48*(6), 1267–1283. doi: 10.1080/00207594.2012.744839

Haase, C. M., Heckhausen, J., & Köller, O. (2008). Goal engagement during the school-work transition: Beneficial for all, particularly for girls. *Journal of Research on Adolescence, 18*(4), 671–698. doi: 10.1111/j.1532–7795.2008.00576.x

Haase, C. M., Heckhausen, J., & Silbereisen, R. K. (2012). The interplay of occupational motivation and well-being during the transition from university to work. *Developmental Psychology, 48*(6), 1739–1751. doi: 10.1037/a0026641

Hall, N. C., Chipperfield, J. G., Heckhausen, J., & Perry, R. P. (2010). Control striving in older adults with serious health problems: A 9-year longitudinal study of survival, health, and well-being. *Psychology and Aging, 25*(2), 432–445. doi: 10.1037/a0019278

Hall, N. C., Perry, R. P., Ruthig, J. C., Hladkyj, S., & Chipperfield, J. G. (2006). Primary and secondary control in achievement settings: A longitudinal field study of academic motivation, emotions, and performance. *Journal of Applied Social Psychology, 36*(6), 1430–1470. doi: 10.1111/j.0021–9029.2006.00067.x

Hamm, J. M., Stewart, T. L., Perry, R. P., Clifton, R. A., Chipperfield, J. G., & Heckhausen, J. (2013). Sustaining primary control striving for achievement goals during challenging developmental transitions: The role of secondary control strategies. *Basic and Applied Social Psychology, 35*(3), 286–297. doi: 10.1080/01973533.2013.785404

Haynes, T. L., Heckhausen, J., Chipperfield, J. G., Perry, R. P., & Newall, N. E. (2009). Primary and secondary control strategies: Implications for health and well-being among older adults. *Journal of Social and Clinical Psychology, 28*(2), 165–197. doi: 10.1521/jscp.2009.28.2.165

Heckhausen, J. (1997). Developmental regulation across adulthood: Primary and secondary control of age-related challenges. *Developmental Psychology, 33*(1), 176–187. doi: 10.1037//0012–1649.33.1.176

Heckhausen, J. (1999). *Developmental regulation in adulthood: Age-normative and sociostructural constraints as adaptive challenges.* New York: Cambridge University Press.

Heckhausen, J. (2000). Developmental regulation across the life span: An action-phase model of engagement and disengagement with developmental goals. In J. Heckhausen (Ed.), *Motivational psychology of human development: Developing motivation and motivating development* (pp. 213–232). Amsterdam: Elsevier.

Heckhausen, J., & Schulz, R. (1993). Optimisation by selection and compensation: Balancing primary and secondary control in life span development. *International Journal of Behavioral Development, 16*(2), 287–303. doi: 10.1177/016502549301600210

Heckhausen, J., Wrosch, C., & Fleeson, W. (2001). Developmental regulation before and after a developmental deadline: The sample case of "biological clock" for childbearing. *Psychology and Aging, 16*(3), 400–413. doi: 10.1037//0882–7974.16.3.400

Heckhausen, J., Wrosch, C., & Schulz, R. (2010). A motivational theory of life-span development. *Psychological Review, 117*(1), 1–53. doi: 10.1037/a0017668.A

Heckhausen, J., Wrosch, C., & Schulz, R. (2013). A lines-of-defense model for managing health threats: A review. *Gerontology, 7085.* doi: 10.1159/000351269

Isen, A. M. (2001). An influence of positive affect on decision making in complex situations: Theoretical issues with practical implications. *Journal of Consumer Psychology, 11*(2), 75–85. doi: 10.1207/S15327663JCP1102_01

Kehr, H. M. (2004a). Implicit/explicit motive discrepancies and volitional depletion among managers. *Personality & Social Psychology Bulletin, 30*(3), 315–327. doi: 10.1177/0146167203256967

Kehr, H. M. (2004b). Integrating implicit motives, explicit motives, and perceived abilities: The compensatory model of work motivation and volition. *The Academy of Management Review, 29*(3), 479–499. doi: 10.2307/20159055

Kunzmann, U., Little, T. D., & Smith, J. (2000). Is age-related stability of subjective well-being a paradox? Cross-sectional and longitudinal evidence from the Berlin Aging Study. *Psychology and Aging, 15*(3), 511–526. doi: 10.1037//0882–7974.15.3.511

Lachman, M. E., & Firth, K. M. P. (2004). The adaptive value of feeling in control during midlife. In O. Brim, C. D. Ryff, & R. C. Kessler (Eds.), *How healthy are we? A national study of well-being at midlife* (pp. 320–349). Chicago: The University of Chicago Press.

Lang, F. R., & Heckhausen, J. (2001). Perceived control over development and subjective well-being: Differential benefits across adulthood. *Journal of Personality and Social Psychology, 81*(3), 509–523. doi: 10.1037/0022–3514.81.3.509

Lockenhoff, C. E., & Carstensen, L. L. (2004). Socioemotionol selectivity theory, aging, and health: The increasingly delicate balance between regulating emotions and making tough choices. *Journal of Personality, 72*(6), 1395–1424. doi:10.1111/j.1467–6494.2004.00301.x

Lucas, R. E. (2007). Adaptation and the set-point model of subjective well-being. *Current Directions in Psychological Science, 16*(2), 75–79. doi: 10.1111/j.1467–8721.2007.00479.x

Luhmann, M., Hofmann, W., Eid, M., & Lucas, R. E. (2012). Subjective well-being and adaptation to life events: A meta-analysis on differences between cognitive and affective well-being. *Journal of Personality and Social Psychology, 102*(3), 592–615. doi: 10.1037/a0025948

Lyubomirsky, S., King, L., & Diener, E. (2005). The benefits of frequent positive affect: Does happiness lead to success? *Psychological Bulletin, 131*(6), 803–855. doi: 10.1037/0033–2909.131.6.803

McClelland, D. C. (1976). *The achievement motive*. New York: Irvington Publishers.

McQuillen, A. D., Licht, M. H., & Licht, B. G. (2003). Contributions of disease severity and perceptions of primary and secondary control to the prediction of psychosocial adjustment to Parkinson's disease. *Health Psychology, 22*(5), 504–512. doi: 10.1037/0278–6133.22.5.504

Pang, J. S. (2010). The Achievement Motive: A review of theory and assessment of n achievement, hope of success, and fear of failure. In O. C. Schultheiss & J. C. Brunstein (Eds.), *Implicit motives* (pp. 30–70). Oxford: Oxford University Press.

Rothbaum, F., Weisz, J. R., & Snyder, S. S. (1982). Changing the world and changing the self: A two-process model of perceived control. *Journal of Personality and Social Psychology, 42*(1), 5–37. doi: 10.1037//0022–3514.42.1.5

Ruthig, J. C., Chipperfield, J. G., Perry, R. P., Newall, N. E., & Swift, A. (2007). Comparative risk and perceived control: Implications for psychological and physical well-being among older adults. *The Journal of Social Psychology, 147*(4), 345–370. doi: 10.3200/SOCP.147.4.345–370

Scheibe, S., & Carstensen, L. L. (2010). Emotional aging: Recent findings and future trends. *Journal of Gerontology: Psychological Sciences, 65B*, 135–144. doi: 10.1093/geronb/gbp132

Schüler, J., Job, V., Fröhlich, S. M., & Brandstätter, V. (2008). A high implicit affiliation motive does not always make you happy: A corresponding explicit motive and corresponding behavior are further needed. *Motivation and Emotion, 32*(3), 231–242. doi: 10.1007/s11031–008–9096-y

Schultheiss, O. C., Jones, N. M., Davis, A. Q., & Kley, C. (2008). The role of implicit motivation in hot and cold goal pursuit: Effects on goal progress, goal rumination, and emotional well-being. *Journal of Research in Personality, 42*(4), 971–987. doi: 10.1016/j.jrp.2007.12.009

Schultheiss, O. C., Rösch, A. G., Rawolle, M., Kordik, A., & Graham, S. (2010). Implicit motives: Current topics and future directions. In T. C. Urdan & S. A. Karabenick (Eds.), *Advances in motivation and achievement* (16 Part A, pp. 199–233). Bingley: Emerald Group Publishing Limited. doi: 10.1108/S0749–7423(2010)000016A009

Sheldon, K. M., Ryan, R. M., & Reis, H. T. (1996). What makes for a good day? Competence and autonomy in the day and in the person. *Personality and Social Psychology Bulletin 22*, 1270–1279. doi: 10.1177/01461672962212007

Smith, J., Borchelt, M., Maier, H., & Jopp, D. (2002). Health and well-being in the young old and oldest old. *Journal of Social Issues, 58*(4), 715–732. doi: 10.1111/1540–4560.00286

Spector, P. E., Cooper, C. L., Sanchez, J. I., Michael, O., Sparks, K., Bernin, P., . . . Yu, S. (2001). Do national levels of individualism and internal locus of control relate to well-being: An ecological level international study. *Journal of Organizational Behavior, 22,* 815–832. doi: 10.1002/job.118

Tomasik, M. J., & Silbereisen, R. K. (2013). Negotiating the demands of active ageing: Longitudinal findings from Germany. *Ageing and Society, 34*(5), 790–819. doi: 10.1017/S0144686X12001304

Tomasik, M. J., Silbereisen, R. K., & Heckhausen, J. (2010). Is it adaptive to disengage from demands of social change? Adjustment to developmental barriers in opportunity-deprived regions. *Motivation and Emotion, 34*(4), 384–398. doi: 10.1007/s11031-010-9177-6

Weinberger, J., Cotler, T., & Fishman, D. (2010). The duality of affiliation motive. In O. C. Schultheiss & J. C. Brunstein (Eds.), *Implicit motives* (pp. 71–88). Oxford: Oxford University Press.

Wrosch, C., Bauer, I., & Scheier, M. F. (2005). Regret and quality of life across the adult life span: The influence of disengagement and available future goals. *Psychology and Aging, 20*(4), 657–670. doi: 10.1037/0882–7974.20.4.657

Wrosch, C., Heckhausen, J., & Lachman, M. E. (2000). Primary and secondary control strategies for managing health and financial stress across adulthood. *Psychology and Aging, 15*(3), 387–399. doi: 10.1037/0882–7974.15.3.387

Wrosch, C., & Miller, G. E. (2009). Depressive symptoms can be useful: Self-regulatory and emotional benefits of dysphoric mood in adolescence. *Journal of Personality and Social Psychology, 96*(6), 1181–1190. doi: 10.1037/a0015172

Wrosch, C., Scheier, M. F., Carver, C. S., & Schulz, R. (2003). The importance of goal disengagement in adaptive self-regulation: When giving up is beneficial. *Self and Identity, 2*(1), 1–20. doi: 10.1080/15298860309021

Wrosch, C., Scheier, M. F., & Miller, G. E. (2013). Goal adjustment capacities, subjective well-being, and physical health. *Social and Personality Psychology Compass, 7*(12), 847–860. doi: 10.1111/spc3.12074

Wrosch, C., & Schulz, R. (2008). Health-engagement control strategies and 2-year changes in older adults' physical health. *Psychological Science, 19*(6), 537–541. doi: 10.1111/j.1467–9280.2008.02120.x

Zimmer, Z., Hickey, T., & Searle, M. S. (1997). The pattern of change in leisure activity behavior among older adults with arthritis. *The Gerontologist, 37*(3), 384–393. doi: 10.1093/geront/37.3.384

PART IV

Strategies for Enhancing Subjective Well-Being and Life Satisfaction

21

POSITIVE ACTIVITY INTERVENTIONS TO ENHANCE WELL-BEING

Looking Through a Social Psychological Lens

Julia Revord, Lisa C. Walsh, and Sonja Lyubomirsky

The desire for happiness is widespread, from people's day-to-day strivings for money, fame, and fortune to fairy tales that end with the oft-quoted word "and they lived happily ever after". Most people say they want to be happy (Diener, 2000), and most parents report that they want their children to be happy (Diener & Lucas, 2004). These findings are hardly surprising given the wildly flourishing self-improvement industry, which some estimates indicate is worth almost $10 billion a year (Marketdata Enterprises, 2012). Despite this widespread focus on seeking happiness, actually attaining it is not guaranteed. According to the World Health Organization, an estimated 350 million people worldwide—almost 5% of the world's population—suffer from depression, and the burden of depression is increasing ("Depression", 2017).

Aside from obvious circumstantial impediments, such as dire economic factors, strife, and unsafe living conditions, one universal barrier to achieving durable happiness may be a phenomenon called *hedonic adaptation*—namely, when people become accustomed to changes in their circumstances and no longer derive the same joy or misery from them. When good or bad events happen, such as winning the lottery or losing a loved one, people tend to react with strong positive or negative emotions. Hedonic adaptation occurs over time, when an individual adapts to the target event and ceases to react with the same level of emotion (Frederick & Loewenstein, 1999; Kahneman, 1999). Indeed, people may have a genetically influenced set range for happiness to which they return after experiencing tumultuous life events (Fritz, Walsh, & Lyubomirsky, in press; Lyubomirsky, Sheldon, & Schkade, 2005).

In light of these findings, is it possible for humans to maximize their happiness and, if yes, how? Evolutionary theory suggests that one path to lasting happiness may be regularly engaging in behaviors that would have universally led to increased fitness on the ancestral plain. "On the positive side", states David Buss (2000) in an article called "The Evolution of Happiness", "people also possess evolved mechanisms that produce deep sources of happiness: those for mating bonds, deep friendship, close kinship, and cooperative coalitions". The position is striking: Buss' theorized sources of happiness are all based on the creation and maintenance of social bonds. Indeed, in the literature on hedonic adaptation, for certain people, social relationships are at least somewhat resistant to adaptation (Lucas, Clark, Georgellis, & Diener, 2003; Lyubomirsky, 2011). In addition, evidence from multiple fields suggests that humans have evolved to be social (Alexander, 1974). The biological signature of humans—our large brains and intelligence—likely evolved to help us navigate our complex social worlds (Herrmann, Call, Hernández-Lloreda, Hare, & Tomasello, 2007). Furthermore, one of the most complex features of our species, language, exists to communicate with others and aid bonding (Dunbar, 1993).

In the quest for well-being, individuals need to increase positive emotions and decrease negative emotions over time. It is worth noting that the majority of positive and negative emotions are inherently social—either in their antecedents or their consequences (Keltner & Haidt, 1999). For example, compassion may have emerged to enable humans to become better caregivers for their vulnerable offspring, cooperate with non-kin, and attract and form better mate pair bonds (Goetz, Keltner, & Simon-Thomas, 2010). From an emotion perspective, it seems that Buss is right; social bonds, when correctly tended to, are a potential source of positive emotions.

In this chapter, we argue that social connections are central to achieving lasting happiness by offering emotional security, resources in times of stress, and a source of identity, as well as by providing an arena in which to demonstrate one's competence and autonomy. First, we will describe the link between social relationships and well-being, and then we will present a framework to discuss how existing interventions in well-being science inherently harness social ties to increase happiness.

Social Relationships and Well-Being

The desire to form and maintain strong social relationships is considered a fundamental part of the human psyche, and a lack of such relationships is associated with ill effects on health, adjustment, and well-being (Baumeister & Leary, 1995). Social ties are key to well-being (Diener & Oishi, 2005). In a classic study, for example, the happiest individuals all reported strongly positive interpersonal relationships (Diener & Seligman, 2002).

Both number and quality of social relationships matter. In one study of 4,775 adults, a simple count of social ties (e.g., marriage, contact with extended friends and family, church membership, and other formal and informal group affiliations) predicted reduced mortality (Berkman & Syme, 1979). Quality of relationships with family and friends, however, appears to be an even stronger predictor of life satisfaction than frequency of contact (O'Connor, 1995). A meta-analysis of 286 studies revealed that quality of social contacts was more strongly associated with subjective well-being than the quantity of such contacts (Pinquart & Sörensen, 2000).

One critical element of interpersonal relationships is perceived social support, defined as individuals' reports of the resources intended to aid them in coping with stress (via instrumental, informational, and emotional support; Cohen, 2004). According to the World Happiness Report, across over 150 countries, perceived social support correlates with positive life evaluation at 0.29, with positive affect at 0.43, and with negative affect at 0.35, even after controlling for income, health, education, perceptions of freedom, perceptions of widespread business and government corruption, and divorce (Helliwell & Wang, 2012).

The perceived lack of social support can also be detrimental. Time-lapse analyses of the US General Social Survey suggest that the decline in happiness over the last few decades in the US is predicted by declines in reported social support (Bartolini, Bilancini, & Pugno, 2013). Loneliness (a perceived lack of social support) is a unique risk factor for depression and mortality, even when controlling for a variety of other potentially causal factors, including demographics, marital status, actual social support, hostility, and perceived stress; current loneliness is also a predictor of future depression (Antonucci, Lansford, & Akiyama, 2001; Cacioppo, Hughes, Waite, Hawkley, & Thisted, 2006; Luo, Hawkley, Waite, & Cacioppo, 2012).

Another pathway by which social relationships contribute to health is *social integration*, which is engagement in a wide range of social activities or relationships (Cohen, 2004). For example, sociometric status—a form of social status that is defined by the respect and admiration individuals obtain from their face-to-face groups (e.g., neighbors, co-workers, or classmates)—is also an important predictor of subjective well-being (Anderson, Kraus, Galinsky, & Keltner, 2012). People's social identities contribute to health and well-being in multiple areas of their lives, including symptom appraisal, health behavior, coping, and mental health outcomes (Haslam, Jetten, Postmes, & Haslam, 2009). In the 2008 Survey of Midlife Development in Japan, the perception that one matters to close others significantly predicted the frequency of positive affect. Additionally, the relationship between friendship quality and the frequency of positive affect was significantly mediated by perceptions of positive relations with others and partially mediated by self-acceptance (Taniguchi, 2015), which supports the idea that friendships shape both feelings of belonging and a positive self-image, which in turn leads to greater happiness.

Social Psychology Applied to Positive Activity Interventions

Durable long-term boosts in well-being can be difficult to obtain. Clues into how to successfully accomplish this are suggested by the idea that humans have evolved to experience positive emotions in response to adaptive behavior, specifically behavior that historically aided in survival and reproduction. The modern environment in which humans live is drastically different from their environment of evolutionary adaptation of roughly about 200,000 years ago (Foley, 1995). Some mismatches between the modern and adaptive environment have led to dysfunction—for example, readily available high-sugar and high-fat foods in the modern environment now contribute to shorter lifespans rather than longer ones. However, social relationships have continued to remain rewarding despite drastic changes in the external environment throughout human history. Although the specifics of social interactions may change through the centuries, relationships with others still provide much positive affect and are still relatively similar in form to relationships on the ancestral plain. Thus, not surprisingly, an important pathway to happiness suggested by evolutionary theorists is nurturing social relationships. Indeed, as described above, correlational evidence strongly supports the link between strong social relationships and greater well-being. With this background in mind, we review existing positive activity interventions (PAIs), which encompass a broad range of activities that increase personal well-being (for more comprehensive reviews, see Layous & Lyubomirsky, 2014; Lyubomirsky, 2008).

We view these interventions through a social psychological lens, meaning that we consider the impact of the real, imagined, or implied presence of others on the efficacy of PAIs. Classic social psychological research asks the question of how individual behavior is changed by others—for example, how the real, imagined, or implied presence of others shifts how likely participants are to intervene in the case of an emergency, cause others harm, adopt various roles, and form opinions about the world around them (e.g., Darley & Latane, 1968; Milgram, 1963; Sherif, 1961; Asch, 1956). We apply this same question about the impact of the presence of others to yet another situation: positive activity interventions.

For each intervention, we ask: Who is the *actor* performing the action, who is the *target* receiving the action, and who is the person whose outcome we are focusing on? (See Table 21.1.) Every social interaction consists of different parties who each have different experiences of the situation. For example, an act of kindness potentially affects three possible figures—the actor, the target, or a non-involved witness. Although they share the same objective reality, the subjective experience of these three individuals can range widely. Many studies on positive activity interventions selectively report the effects of an intervention on a single party, without testing or acknowledging the effects on the other parties. We refer to the person whose outcome is measured as the "self". Another way to conceptualize the self is as the participant in the study, or the one who provides a self-report about his or her subjective experience of being an actor, target, or witness.

To illustrate this distinction, consider the act of buying flowers. If a woman buys flowers for herself, and then reports how this affects her, she is the actor, target, and self. If she were instructed to buy flowers for herself as part of a positive activity intervention, such an intervention would be classified by self as actor (buyer) and self as target (receiver; see upper-left-hand quadrant of Table 21.1). Because both the person who performed the action and the person who is the target of the action is the same person, and that person is the one reporting on their subjective experience—i.e., is the self—this action fits into the self-self quadrant. In each of the quadrants, the person whose well-being outcomes are being tested is always the self; in this scenario, the self is both actor and target.

Now imagine instead that the woman was prompted to purchase the flowers for her romantic partner. In this case, three different research questions could be asked about this intervention. First, researchers could investigate the effects of the act of giving flowers on the well-being of the woman (the buyer) herself. The woman whose well-being is assessed is also the actor, so this would be an example of self-as-actor, other-as-target (see lower-left-hand [self-other] quadrant of Table 21.1). Second, researchers could investigate the effects of receiving flowers on the recipient's well-being. Investigating this effect would be an example of other-as-actor, self-as-target, because the person whose well-being is assessed (the partner) was the target of another's kindness (see upper-right-hand [other-self] quadrant of Table 21.1). Finally, researchers could investigate the effects on the well-being of a friend at work who hears about or observes the gift of flowers. Because the friend reporting his reaction is the self, and is neither the actor nor the target, this would be an example of other-as-actor, other-as-target (see lower-right-hand [other-other] quadrant of Table 21.1).

TABLE 21.1 Examples of Interventions in Each of the Four Quadrants

		Actor	
		Self	Other
Target	Self	Self-Self Quadrant • Testing the effect on a woman buying flowers for herself • Testing the effect on a person doing an act of kindness for himself	Other-Self Quadrant • Testing the effect on a partner of receiving flowers from his significant other • Testing the effect on students who write about their gratitude to their parents for a kind act
	Other	Self-Other Quadrant • Testing the effect on a woman of buying flowers for her partner • Testing the effect on a person who does three acts of kindness for someone else	Other-Other Quadrant • Testing the effect on a friend of hearing about a woman buying flowers for her partner • Testing the effect on a bystander watching kids helping a homeless man

Thus, the same interaction can be viewed in multiple ways, depending on whose well-being is being measured. In this way, our taxonomy is akin to observing an interaction in a store and asking, "In that transaction, was something being bought or sold?" The answer, of course, is "both", but the answer depends on whether the customer or the sales clerk is being asked. In the same way that the experiences of buying and selling are unique and carry their own benefits and costs, the experience of being an actor, a target, and an observer of a prosocial act can have different outcomes. We believe that it is helpful to consider this taxonomy when designing new interventions or measuring the effects of existing ones.

Rather than being an exhaustive review of all interventions that fit within the four-quadrant framework, this chapter instead presents several examples within each quadrant. We offer here an introduction to the theoretical implications of perceiving interventions through a social psychological lens—that is, the beginning of an examination of the impact of the real, imagined, or implied presence of others. Overall, we argue that the most effective interventions strengthen real or perceived social ties.

Self as Actor, Other as Target

The first quadrant involves how doing something to benefit another person affects the doer (actor). Of the grid's four quadrants, the effects of this category of (prosocial) acts on people's well-being are perhaps best supported in the positive activity literature, likely because the interventions represented by the self-other quadrant meet all three basic psychological needs proposed by self-determination theory (Deci & Ryan, 1985; Ryan & Deci, 2000)—competence, autonomy, and connectedness.

The most prominent interventions represented by this quadrant are prosocial behaviors—actions intended to benefit one or more people other than oneself (Batson & Powell, 2003). Engaging in prosocial behavior has been shown to promote better mental health outcomes in multiple samples, including college students (Crocker, Canevello, Breines, & Flynn, 2010) and high school students (Yinon & Landau, 1987). A classic real-world example of prosocial behavior directed at others is volunteering, which has consistently been correlated with indicators of higher well-being (Wheeler, Gorey, & Greenblatt, 1998).

Acts of Kindness

Correlational studies suggesting benefits of prosocial behavior are inherently limited, as the results could be due to reverse causality (i.e., if those with higher well-being choose to volunteer more) or third variables (i.e., if those with more leisure time both volunteer more and have higher well-being). Fortunately, the effects of doing prosocial behavior on well-being and related outcomes have been tested experimentally. For example, in a growing number of tests of prosocial behavior interventions, participants are randomly assigned to complete acts of kindness for other people in their lives and report on their emotional state before and after (e.g., Nelson et al., 2015; Sheldon, Boehm, & Lyubomirsky, 2012). Because the actor (or kindness doer) is the one whose well-being is assessed, acts of kindness interventions epitomize the self-as-actor quadrant. Doing kindness for others has been shown to yield benefits for the actor even when compared to active control activities that may be positive but not inherently prosocial, such as engaging in a novel act every day (Buchanan & Bardi, 2010) or keeping track of different locations visited (Layous, Lee, Choi, & Lyubomirsky, 2013). Additionally, engaging in prosocial behavior has recently been shown even to change gene expression in a way that decreases pro-inflammatory genetic markers in the bloodstream (Nelson-Coffey, Fritz, Lyubomirsky, & Cole, 2017). Taken together, these studies provide support that experimentally manipulated prosocial behavior can increase the well-being of the actor.

Prosocial Spending

Prosocial spending is another type of other-directed helping that benefits the self. Charitable behavior has long been linked to happiness in a bidirectional way, such that happiness leads to increased giving behavior, and giving promotes happiness (Aknin, Dunn, & Norton, 2012). Spending on others activates reward systems in the brain (Harbaugh, Mayr, & Burghart, 2007) and increases happiness (Dunn, Aknin, & Norton, 2008). For example, in an oft-cited study, students were given an envelope with either $5 or $20 and instructed to spend the money either on themselves or on others. Students who spent money on others reported greater happiness at the end of the day than students who spent the same amount of money on themselves (Dunn et al., 2008). Overall, prosocial spending, like doing acts of kindness for others or volunteering, promotes increases in well-being.

Why Giving Support May Be Good

In sum, giving emotional, financial, or even imagined support to others has been shown to bring many emotional and physical health benefits. There are multiple possible pathways by which giving support may benefit the well-being of the giver (or actor). The most obvious pathway is that giving to others strengthens perceptions of one's social connectedness with friends and family. Because humans evolved to be social beings who live in communities and share resources for long periods of time, they may feel positive emotions because helping others aids in their survival (Trivers, 1971, 2005). Specifically, giving others support may be akin to putting money into a social bank account that can later be withdrawn in a time of need.

Acts of kindness may also serve to strengthen one's place in a social network. In one study, children who performed acts of kindness experienced larger increases in peer acceptance than children who performed an alternative positive activity (Layous, Nelson, Oberle, Schonert-Reichl, & Lyubomirsky, 2012). Furthermore, gratitude directed from self to other increases the perceived communal strength and willingness to sacrifice for the relationship (Lambert, Clark, Durtschi, Fincham, & Graham, 2010). Additionally, helping others—whether in person or anonymously—may also serve as a positive signal about one's own identity. A person who helps others may feel that she is competent and autonomous, in addition to feeling good and sensing that she is in a position to help. Finally, giving to others may be valuable to individuals because it lessens self-focus. Self-focus has been shown to have adverse effects across a variety of domains (Ingram, 1990; Mor & Winquist, 2002; Nolen-Hoeksema, Wisco, & Lyubomirsky, 2008; see also Chapter 18). By contrast, helping others may distract people from their own problems and increase their focus on others.

Others as Actor, Self as Target

The other-self quadrant involves activities in which another person is the prosocial actor and the person being assessed (the self) is the receiver or target. The other-self quadrant is relatively under-studied compared to the others.

Gratitude

Gratitude is the positive activity intervention that has received the most attention in the other-self quadrant. Gratitude has been defined as a state that requires an individual to endorse (1) that they have acquired a positive outcome and (2) that positive outcome came from an external source (Emmons & McCullough, 2003). As such, expressing gratitude requires recognizing that another individual (the benefactor, or actor) has engaged in prosocial behavior towards the self (the target). Thus, interventions that prompt participants to express gratitude for others' kindness and support fall within the other-self quadrant. Another, less oft-studied way in which gratitude falls into the other-self quadrant involves individuals sharing their gratitude with their benefactor. When this occurs, the individual sharing his gratitude becomes the actor and the benefactor becomes the target.

Expressing Gratitude

There are two primary positive activity interventions designed to increase gratitude in the expresser and, in turn, well-being. The first type of intervention involves participants "counting their blessings"—an example of general appreciation for one's own good fortune, not necessarily coming from a specific other. The second type of intervention asks participants to write a gratitude letter directly to someone (e.g., a parent, teacher, or friend) who has done something to help them for which they are extremely grateful (Boehm, Lyubomirsky, & Sheldon, 2011; Layous et al., 2012; Layous & Lyubomirsky, 2014). Because gratitude letters depend on an interpersonal context—being addressed directly to another person and deeply considering how that person has had an important impact on the participant's life—such letters may provide relatively large boosts in social connectedness and, in turn, well-being.

The benefits of expressing gratitude are numerous and well documented. Expressing gratitude has been found to increase psychological well-being (Boehm et al., 2011; Kashdan, Uswatte, & Julian, 2006; Seligman, Steen, Park, & Peterson, 2005; Watkins, 2004) and physical well-being (Bono & McCullough, 2006; Emmons & McCullough, 2003; Wood, Joseph, Lloyd, & Atkins, 2009) and may strengthen social bonds in relationships and communities (Lambert et al., 2010; Fredrickson, 2004). Gratitude has also been linked with superior mental health (Nelson & Lyubomirsky, 2014), and associated with greater perceived social support and less stress and depression during a life transition (Wood et al., 2008). A recent meta-analysis found that expressing gratitude (e.g., via gratitude letters) had an effect size $d = .20$, outperforming measurement-only control conditions and alternative-activity conditions in enhancing well-being, and performing as well as other psychologically active conditions (Davis et al., 2016).

Receiving Gratitude

Another way in which gratitude falls into the other-self quadrant involves individuals sharing their gratitude with their benefactor. Few studies, however, investigate the impact of receiving gratitude. One exception is a series of experiments showing that those who received small gratitude expressions (e.g., "Thank you so much! I am really grateful".) after helping someone were more likely to aid the same person, a different person, or an organization a second time; furthermore, perceptions of social worth, or feeling valued by the thanker, mediated these effects (Grant & Gino, 2010).

Other relevant studies on receiving gratitude have focused on romantic relationships. For example, when partners were assigned to express and receive gratitude to and from one another in a laboratory paradigm, perceived responsiveness (e.g., "my partner understood me", "my partner expressed liking and encouragement of me") was significantly associated with benefactors' relationship satisfaction (Algoe, Fredrickson, & Gable, 2013). Expressing and receiving gratitude within romantic bonds has also been shown to promote relationship development (Algoe, Haidt, & Gable, 2008), maintenance (Gordon, Impett, Kogan, Oveis, & Keltner, 2012; Lambert & Fincham, 2011), and satisfaction (Algoe et al., 2013). However, many of these studies focus on the dynamic process in which two individuals in a couple express and receive expressions of gratitude—conflating expressing and receiving. A notable exception is a study that randomly assigned one member of a romantic couple to express gratitude during a video-recorded laboratory session, and found that, when expressers used more other-praising behavior, gratitude recipients perceived them as more responsive and felt more general positive emotions and love toward the expresser (Algoe, Kurtz, & Hilaire, 2016; see Chapter 10 for a more detailed discussion of the research on gratitude and well-being).

Receiving Acts of Kindness

Much of the research on performing acts of kindness has focused on givers (i.e., actors) more than receivers (i.e., targets). This may be because performing prosocial acts benefits the actor more than the target (Schwartz, Meisenhelder, Ma, & Reed, 2003). Yet research has demonstrated that the targets of kindness can benefit emotionally, as well as tangibly, from the receipt of a kind act (e.g., receiving some much-needed help from a co-worker). In a study conducted in Spain, Coca-Cola employees were randomly assigned to be givers, receivers, or observers of kind acts; with givers practicing acts of kindness for a personalized list of receivers (unbeknownst to those on the list) over 4 weeks. Receivers performed more prosocial acts and experienced increases in happiness, autonomy, intrinsic motivation, and flow, but surprisingly not stronger feelings of connectedness (Chancellor, Jacobs Bao, & Lyubomirsky, 2014).

In another study tracking both givers and receivers of kindness, receivers of kindness smiled more than controls (Pressman, Kraft, & Cross, 2015). On a subsequent follow-up survey, receivers also reported that they had either already paid it forward or were highly likely to do so in the future. Altogether, the research suggests that receiving kindness can benefit the recipients.

Self as Actor, Self as Target

A third quadrant of the grid falls at the intersection where the self is both actor and target. This quadrant involves positive activities in which individuals act upon themselves to increase their own well-being (e.g., a woman buys flowers for herself; see Table 21.1). Although many positive activity interventions presumably involve the self acting on the self (e.g., savoring, positive reminiscence, visualizing best possible selves), we focus specifically on studies of PAIs that ask the participant to act kindly toward herself. Examples of positive activities that fall within this quadrant include self-directed kindness, self-spending, and self-compassion. The effects of these interventions on well-being are mixed, with some self-oriented exercises failing to produce well-being benefits when compared to prosocial or other-oriented activities. This may be because human beings are innately social creatures, and the critical mechanism underlying the success of many positive activities appears to be connecting with others.

Self-Directed Kindness

Prosocial behavior typically refers to actions intended to benefit others. But can prosocial behavior be effectively directed at the self to increase well-being? Such intrapersonal prosocial behavior (or self-directed kindness) may seem like an oxymoron, yet common cultural wisdom in the secular West suggests that individuals need to put themselves before others. However, the doctrine of "treat yourself" is not substantiated by science, especially when compared to more powerful prosocial interventions.

The two juxtaposing paths to happiness—"treat yourself" and "do unto others" with kindness—fundamentally conflict. Materialist culture whispers "treat yourself", while a wealth of empirical literature suggests that one becomes happier by engaging in other-focused prosocial behavior (Chancellor, Margolis, Jacobs Bao, & Lyubomirsky, 2017; Pressman et al., 2015; Aknin, Hamlin, & Dunn, 2012; see Chapter 15 for a detailed discussion of the negative effects of materialism on well-being). A recent study (Nelson, Layous, Cole, & Lyubomirsky, 2016) investigated these contrasting pathways in a 6-week longitudinal experiment that instructed participants to perform (1) acts of kindness for others (e.g., buying a cup of coffee for a co-worker or helping a friend move); (2) acts of kindness for the world (e.g., picking up litter on a beach or donating money to cancer research); and (3) acts of kindness for the self (e.g., enjoying a favorite meal or getting a massage). Relative to a neutral activity control condition, acts of kindness to the self were not associated with shifts in positive or negative emotions, and led to a slight decline in psychological flourishing, followed by a return to baseline levels (Nelson et al., 2016).

Self-Directed Spending

People looking to buy happiness by procuring the things that they desire most are also likely to be disappointed, possibly because such behavior undermines well-being via reductions in social connectedness. Although people often forecast that spending money on themselves will make them happier than spending money on other people (Dunn et al., 2008), research suggests that prosocial spending is much more beneficial than spending on oneself. In one study, participants assigned to recall spending money on themselves were significantly less happy than those assigned to recall spending money on another person, and this effect was stable across smaller ($20) and larger ($100) purchases (Aknin Dunn, & Norton, 2012). In another study, undergraduate students who gave less (versus more) money away to an anonymous partner (up to $10) reported lower levels of positive affect, higher levels of negative affect, and more shame (Dunn, Ashton-James, Hanson, & Aknin, 2010). Finally, spending less of one's income on gifts for others and donations to charity predicted less happiness in a US nationally representative survey, and undergraduate students randomly assigned to spend more money on themselves were less happy than those assigned to spend money on others (Dunn et al., 2008).

Even if an individual is able to boost his happiness by spending money on himself, the lift is likely to be temporary. Human beings are remarkably adept at adapting to positive changes in their lives (Lyubomirsky, 2011), and the hedonic adaptation is much more rapid for changes in circumstances (e.g., a material gain) than changes in activities (e.g., helping others) (Sheldon & Lyubomirsky, 2006). For example, the joy that may follow even a large personal purchase, like treating oneself to a new car, usually fades with time. A new BMW Series 3 may make one happier in the beginning, but adaptation occurs as the new owner enjoys fewer and fewer positive experiences (e.g., receiving compliments from friends, driving the car to new places) and positive emotions (e.g., appreciation, pride, and joy) from the new car over time, and her aspirations rise (Sheldon & Lyubomirsky, 2012).

Fortunately, research on how to stave off hedonic adaptation suggests a number of strategies that people can use to boost the well-benefits of self-spending. For example, one way that spending on the self may improve happiness is when people invest in their experiences. Anticipating experiential purchases (e.g., a vacation in California) is associated with higher levels of happiness, pleasure, and excitement than is waiting for material objects (e.g., a bigger flat screen TV) (e.g., Kumar, Killingsworth, & Gilovich, 2014). The reasons for this finding are that consumers adapt to experiential purchases at a slower rate than they do to material purchases (Nicolao, Irwin, & Goodman, 2009), and experiential purchases are more open to positive reinterpretation with the passage of time, are a more meaningful part of an individual's identity, and facilitate fulfilling social relationships (Van Boven & Gilovich, 2003).

Because hedonic adaptation occurs in the context of repeating or static events, another approach to thwarting it involves fostering variety (Fritz Walsh, & Lyubomirsky, 2017). Studies suggest that, when individuals spend money on themselves, they will obtain more happiness by investing in a variety of frequent, small pleasures rather than fewer, larger purchases (Dunn, Gilbert, & Wilson, 2011).

Self-Compassion

Notably, many of the self-self-quadrant positive activities that reliably and lastingly boost happiness via self-oriented action are those that instruct an individual to treat herself as she might treat an "other". One example of such activities is self-compassion. Self-compassion has been defined as the experience of being kind toward oneself when one is in pain or after having failed at something; when one is construing one's experiences as part of a larger human whole; and when one's awareness of aversive feelings and negative thoughts are in balance (Neff, Rude, & Kirkpatrick, 2007). Self-compassion is positively and strongly correlated with life satisfaction, happiness, optimism, and positive affect and negatively correlated with negative affect (Neff, 2003; Neff et al., 2007).

In one study, female undergraduates were assigned for 3 weeks to either a self-compassion intervention (e.g., keeping a "self-compassion journal" and considering one's behavior from the perspective of an unconditionally accepting friend) or a time management control group (e.g., writing down a detailed overview of their daily activities of the past week; Smeets, Neff, Alberts, & Peters, 2014). Compared to the time management control group, the self-compassion intervention group experienced significantly greater gains in self-compassion and optimism, as well as reductions in rumination (Smeets et al., 2014).

Other studies also provide evidence that self-compassion—an activity that falls within the self-self quadrant—can enhance well-being (e.g., Breines & Chen, 2012; Leary, Tate, Adams, Allen, & Hancock, 2007). Although self-compassion interventions direct the self to act upon the self, they are doing so through the borrowed perspective of an "other"—that is, instead of simply directing kindness toward oneself, individuals picture another's kindness first and then direct this same kindness at themselves. Thus, the self-kindness in self-compassion actually has a prosocial quality to it. For example, Leary and colleagues (2007) directed participants to write a paragraph expressing understanding, kindness, and concern for themselves in the same way that they might express concern for a friend and found that self-compassion buffered negative reactions to negative and ambivalent self-relevant events (Leary et al., 2007). Smeets and colleagues (2014) directed participants to write a self-compassionate letter from the perspective of an unconditionally kind, accepting, and compassionate imaginary friend (Smeets et al., 2014). In order to produce effects on well-being, self-compassion exercises often borrow the perspective of "a friend" or direct participants to view themselves within the scope of a greater, shared humanity. In other words, connectedness and an imagined other are still present, and this may be one important key to the efficacy of self-compassion interventions.

Others as Actor, Others as Target

There are very few interventions in which a person observes another person acting on behalf of someone else. The most relevant research is that focusing on a distinct emotional experience referred to as *elevation*, which stems from observing another person coming to the aid of someone else.

Elevation and Related Interventions

Elevation is the most frequently empirically studied reaction to watching someone help another person. Along with gratitude and admiration, elevation is one of three "other-praising" emotions. Although all three involve recognizing someone else for a particular behavior, elevation is the result of witnessing moral beauty or "morally virtuous" actions (Algoe & Haidt, 2009; Haidt, 2003). Elevation is the positive emotion of being moved by witnessing someone else doing "an act of charity, gratitude, fidelity, generosity, or any other strong display of virtue" (Algoe & Haidt, 2009). Therefore, elevation is a positive reaction to acts that are prosocial (i.e., not mere admiration) and directed at another (i.e., not gratitude).

Elevation is associated with many positive feelings, such as awe, admiration, warmth (Algoe & Haidt, 2009), inspiration, and optimism about humanity (Aquino, McFerran, & Laven, 2011). Additionally, elevation is a prosocial emotion; it drives individuals to feel and behave more prosocially (Thomson & Siegel, 2013; Vianello, Galliani, & Haidt, 2010). Elevated participants are more likely to volunteer for an unpaid study and to give more help to an experimenter (Schnall, Roper, & Fessler, 2010). Additionally, people are more likely to donate to a moral charity after recalling an elevating act than after recalling a gratitude-inducing generous act (Siegel et al., 2014).

Other-to-other prosocial acts have mainly been documented within the elevation literature. However, a great deal more exploration of such effects is needed to fully establish in which situations witnessing others' generosity is most likely to boost well-being.

Summary

Our review suggests that social interactions are a critical mechanism underlying the well-being boosting effects of positive activity interventions. Prosocial behavior from the self to other people, embodied in the first quadrant, seems to be the most effective in enhancing well-being, because it fulfills the three basic human psychological needs of competence, autonomy, and connectedness proposed by self-determination theory (Deci & Ryan, 1985). Additionally, in a reciprocal relationship, the belief that "people will help me in a time of need" is important to well-being. For this reason, doing kindness for others may indicate that the recipients of kind acts will be indebted and likely to help the kindness provider in the future. Second, interventions that mainly involve another person acting prosocially toward the self can increase perceptions of connectedness and positive affect by deepening social ties, in part because receiving kindnesses from others signals that the benefactors are likely to help again. Third, many of the positive effects of self-self interventions seem to involve an imagined prosocial component (such as when cultivating self-compassion by imagining a sympathetic friend sending kind thoughts one's way). Finally, the other-as-actor, other-as-target quadrant describes situations (i.e., moral virtue) that have been shown to induce elevation, which can have many benefits.

The review of research presented here is not exhaustive, but is meant to illustrate the importance of other people in positive activity interventions that enhance well-being. Our proposed four-quadrant framework can be used to design future studies that ask questions in novel and important ways. For example, within quadrants, which interventions have the most durable impact on well-being? Another question, which applies to the prosocial interpersonal quadrants, is the extent to which the benefits (or costs) to well-being may differ when one is helping or being helped by a stranger versus a friend versus a family member.

Our four-quadrant framework also raises a question about which individual difference characteristics might moderate the effectiveness of different quadrants for different people. That is, do activities in different quadrants represent a better "person-activity fit" for particular individuals (Lyubomirsky, 2008; Lyubomirsky et al., 2005; Parks, Della Porta, Pierce, Zilca, & Lyubomirsky, 2012; Sin, Della Porta, & Lyubomirsky, 2011) and thus might be associated with greater benefit for those individuals? For example, someone with a low sense of autonomy may benefit more than someone with high autonomy from engaging in behaviors characterized by self as actor, whereas someone low in connectedness may benefit more than someone high in connectedness from activities within both interpersonal quadrants.

Conclusion

Humans exist almost exclusively in social settings, and it is nearly impossible to divorce the study of humans from the study of the social relationships and cultures that encompass them. Unlike many other species, humans are born into cultures and willfully stay near others of the same species for almost their entire lives. In this review of interventions, we focus on this critical medium and highlight the importance of human interaction to well-being as a moderator that deserves a great deal more empirical attention.

References

Aknin, L. B., Dunn, E. W., & Norton, M. I. (2012). Happiness runs in a circular motion: Evidence for a positive feedback loop between prosocial spending and happiness. *Journal of Happiness Studies*, *13*(2), 347–355. https://doi.org/10.1007/s10902-011-9267-5

Aknin, L. B., Hamlin, J. K., & Dunn, E. W. (2012). Giving leads to happiness in young children. *PLoS One*, *7*(6), e39211. https://doi.org/10.1371/journal.pone.0039211

Alexander, R. D. (1974). The evolution of social behavior. *Annual Review of Ecology and Systematics*, *5*(1), 325–383.

Algoe, S. B., Fredrickson, B. L., & Gable, S. L. (2013). The social functions of the emotion of gratitude via expression. *Emotion*, *13*(4), 605–609. https://doi.org/10.1037/a0032701

Algoe, S. B., & Haidt, J. (2009). Witnessing excellence in action: The "other-praising" emotions of elevation, gratitude, and admiration. *The Journal of Positive Psychology*, *4*(2), 105–127. https://doi.org/10.1080/17439760802650519

Algoe, S. B., Haidt, J., & Gable, S. L. (2008). Beyond reciprocity: Gratitude and relationships in everyday life. *Emotion*, *8*(3), 425–429. https://doi.org/10.1037/1528-3542.8.3.425

Algoe, S. B., Kurtz, L. E., & Hilaire, N. M. (2016). Putting the "you" in "thank you". *Social Psychological and Personality Science*, *7*(7), 658–666. https://doi.org/10.1177/1948550616651681

Anderson, C., Kraus, M. W., Galinsky, A. D., & Keltner, D. (2012). The local-ladder effect: Social status and subjective well-being. *Psychological Science, 23*(7), 764–771. https://doi.org/10.1177/0956797611434537

Antonucci, T. C., Lansford, J. E., & Akiyama, H. (2001). Impact of positive and negative aspects of marital relationships and friendships on well-being of older adults. *Applied Developmental Science, 5*(2), 68–75. https://doi.org/10.1207/S1532480XADS0502_2

Aquino, K., McFerran, B., & Laven, M. (2011). Moral identity and the experience of moral elevation in response to acts of uncommon goodness. *Journal of Personality and Social Psychology, 100*(4), 703–718. https://doi.org/10.1037/a0022540

Asch, S. E. (1956). Studies of independence and conformity: A minority of one against a unanimous majority. *Psychological Monographs: General and Applied, 70*(9), 1–70. https://doi.org/10.1037/h0093718

Bartolini, S., Bilancini, E., & Pugno, M. (2013). Did the decline in social connections depress Americans' happiness? *Social Indicators Research, 110*(3), 1033–1059. https://doi.org/10.1007/s11205-011-9971-x

Batson, C. D., & Powell, A. A. (2003). Altruism and prosocial behavior. In T. Millon & M. J. Lerner (Eds.), *Handbook of psychology, volume 5: Personality and social psychology* (pp. 463–484). Hoboken, NJ: Wiley.

Baumeister, R. F., & Leary, M. R. (1995). The need to belong: Desire for interpersonal attachments as a fundamental human motivation. *Psychological Bulletin, 117*(3), 497–529. https://doi.org/10.1037/0033-2909.117.3.497

Berkman, L. F., & Syme, S. L. (1979). Social networks, host resistance, and mortality: A nine-year follow-up study of Alameda County residents. *American Journal of Epidemiology, 109*(2), 186–204. https://doi.org/10.1093/oxfordjournals.aje.a112674

Boehm, J. K., Lyubomirsky, S., & Sheldon, K. M. (2011). A longitudinal experimental study comparing the effectiveness of happiness-enhancing strategies in Anglo Americans and Asian Americans. *Cognition & Emotion, 25*(7), 1263–1272. https://doi.org/10.1080/02699931.2010.541227

Bono, G., & McCullough, M. E. (2006). Positive responses to benefit and harm: Bringing forgiveness and gratitude into cognitive psychotherapy. *Journal of Cognitive Psychotherapy, 20*(2), 147–158. https://doi.org/10.1891/jcop.20.2.147

Breines, J. G., & Chen, S. (2012). Self-compassion increases self-improvement motivation. *Personality and Social Psychology Bulletin, 38*(9), 1133–1143. https://doi.org/10.1177/0146167212445599

Buchanan, K. E., & Bardi, A. (2010). Acts of kindness and acts of novelty affect life satisfaction. *The Journal of Social Psychology, 150*(3), 235–237. https://doi.org/10.1080/00224540903365554

Buss, D. M. (2000). The evolution of happiness. *American Psychologist, 55*(1), 15–23. https://doi.org/10.1037//0003-066x.55.1.15

Cacioppo, J. T., Hughes, M. E., Waite, L. J., Hawkley, L. C., & Thisted, R. A. (2006). Loneliness as a specific risk factor for depressive symptoms: Cross-sectional and longitudinal analyses. *Psychology and Aging, 21*(1), 140–151. https://doi.org/10.1037/0882-7974.21.1.140

Chancellor, J., Jacobs Bao, K., & Lyubomirsky, S. (2014). *The ripples of generosity in the workplace* (Unpublished data). Department of Psychology, University of California, Riverside.

Chancellor, J., Margolis, S. M., Jacobs Bao, K., & Lyubomirsky, S. (2017). *Everyday Prosociality in the Workplace: The Reinforcing Benefits of Giving, Getting, and Glimpsing.* doi:10.1037/emo0000321

Cohen, S. (2004). Social relationships and health. *American Psychologist, 59*(8), 676–684. https://doi.org/10.1037/0003-066x.59.8.676

Cohen-Charash, Y., & Mueller, J. S. (2007). Does perceived unfairness exacerbate or mitigate interpersonal counterproductive work behaviors related to envy? *Journal of Applied Psychology, 92*(3), 666–680. https://doi.org/10.1037/0021-9010.92.3.666

Crocker, J., Canevello, A., Breines, J. G., & Flynn, H. (2010). Interpersonal goals and change in anxiety and dysphoria in first-semester college students. *Journal of Personality and Social Psychology, 98*(6), 1009–1024. https://doi.org/10.1037/a0019400

Darley, J. M., & Latane, B. (1968). Bystander intervention in emergencies: Diffusion of responsibility. *Journal of Personality and Social Psychology, 8*(4), 377–383. https://doi.org/10.1037/h0025589

Davis, D. E., Choe, E., Meyers, J., Wade, N., Varjas, K., Gifford, A., Quinn, A., Hook, J. N., Van Tongeren, D. R., Griffin, B. J., & Worthington, Jr., E. L. (2016). Thankful for the little things: A meta-analysis of gratitude interventions. *Journal of Counseling Psychology, 63*(1). https://doi.org/10.1037/cou0000107

Deci, E. L., & Ryan, R. M. (1985). *Intrinsic motivation and self-determination in human behavior.* New York: Plenum.

Depression. (2017, February). Retrieved from www.who.int/mediacentre/factsheets/fs369/en/

Diener, E. (2000). Subjective well-being: The science of happiness and a proposal for a national index. *American Psychologist, 55*(1), 34–43. https://doi.org/10.1037//0003-066X.55.1.34

Diener, E., & Oishi, S. (2005). The nonobvious social psychology of happiness. *Psychological Inquiry, 16*(4), 162–167. https://doi.org/10.1207/s15327965pli1604_04

Diener, E., & Seligman, M. E. (2002). Very happy people. *Psychological Science, 13*(1), 81–84. https://doi.org/10.1111/1467-9280.00415

Diener, M. L., & Lucas, R. E. (2004). Adults' desires for children's emotions across 48 countries: Associations with individual and national characteristics. *Journal of Cross-Cultural Psychology, 35*(5), 525–547. https://.doi.org/10.1177/0022022104268387

Dunbar, R. I. (1993). Coevolution of neocortical size, group size and language in humans. *Behavioral and Brain Sciences, 16*(04), 681–694. ttps://doi.org/10.1017/s0140525x00032325

Dunn, E. W., Aknin, L. B., & Norton, M. I. (2008). Spending money on others promotes happiness. *Science, 319*(5870), 1687–1688. https://doi.org/10.1126/science.1150952

Dunn, E. W., Ashton-James, C. E., Hanson, M. D., & Aknin, L. B. (2010). On the costs of self-interested economic behavior how does stinginess get under the skin? *Journal of Health Psychology, 15*(4), 627–633. https://doi.org/10.1177/1359105309356366

Dunn, E. W., Gilbert, D. T., & Wilson, T. D. (2011). If money doesn't make you happy, then you probably aren't spending it right. *Journal of Consumer Psychology, 21*(2), 115–125. https://doi.org/10.1016/j.jcps.2011.02.002

Emmons, R. A., & McCullough, M. E. (2003). Counting blessings versus burdens: An experimental investigation of gratitude and subjective well-being in daily life. *Journal of Personality and Social Psychology, 84*(2), 377–389. https://doi.org/10.1037/0022-3514.84.2.377

Foley, R. (1995). The adaptive legacy of human evolution: A search for the environment of evolutionary adaptedness. *Evolutionary Anthropology: Issues, News, and Reviews, 4*(6), 194–203.

Frederick, S., & Loewenstein, G. (1999). Hedonic adaptation. In D. Kahneman, E. Diener, & N. Schwarz (Eds.), *Well-being: The foundations of hedonic psychology.* New York: Russel Sage Foundation.

Fredrickson, B. L. (2004). The broaden-and-build theory of positive emotions. *Philosophical Transactions-Royal Society of London Series B Biological Sciences,* 1367–1378. https://doi.org/10.1098/rstb.2004.1512

Fritz, M., Walsh, L. C., & Lyubomirsky, S. (2017). Staying happier. In M. D. Robinson & M. Eid (Eds.), *The happy mind: Cognitive contributions to well-being.* New York: Springer.

Goetz, J. L., Keltner, D., & Simon-Thomas, E. (2010). Compassion: An evolutionary analysis and empirical review. *Psychological Bulletin, 136*(3), 351–374. https://doi.org/10.1037/a0018807

Gordon, A. M., Impett, E. A., Kogan, A., Oveis, C., & Keltner, D. (2012). To have and to hold: Gratitude promotes relationship maintenance in intimate bonds. *Journal of Personality and Social Psychology, 103*(2), 257–274. https://doi.org/10.1037/a0028723

Grant, A. M., & Gino, F. (2010). A little thanks goes a long way: Explaining why gratitude expressions motivate prosocial behavior. *Journal of Personality and Social Psychology, 98*(6), 946–955. https://doi.org/10.1037/a0017935

Haidt, J. (2003). Elevation and the positive psychology of morality. *Flourishing: Positive Psychology and the Life Well-Lived, 275,* 289. https://doi.org/10.1037/10594-012

Harbaugh, W. T., Mayr, U., & Burghart, D. R. (2007). Neural responses to taxation and voluntary giving reveal motives for charitable donations. *Science, 316*(5831), 1622–1625. https://doi.org/10.1126/science.1140738

Haslam, S. A., Jetten, J., Postmes, T., & Haslam, C. (2009). Social identity, health and well-being: An emerging agenda for applied psychology. *Applied Psychology, 58*(1), 1–23. https://doi.org/10.1111/j.1464-0597.2008.00379.x

Helliwell, J. F., & Wang, S. (2012). The state of world happiness. *World Happiness Report,* 10–57.

Herrmann, E., Call, J., Hernández-Lloreda, M. V., Hare, B., & Tomasello, M. (2007). Humans have evolved specialized skills of social cognition: The cultural intelligence hypothesis. *Science, 317*(5843), 1360–1366. https://doi.org/ 10.1126/science.1146282

Ingram, R. E. (1990). Self-focused attention in clinical disorders: Review and a conceptual model. *Psychological bulletin, 107*(2), 156.

Kahneman, D. (1999). Objective happiness. In D. Kahneman, E. Diener, & N. Schwarz (Eds.), *Well-being: The foundations of hedonic psychology.* New York: Russel Sage Foundation.

Kashdan, T. B., Uswatte, G., & Julian, T. (2006). Gratitude and hedonic and eudaimonic well-being in Vietnam War veterans. *Behaviour Research and Therapy, 44*(2), 177–199. https://doi.org/10.1016/j.brat.2005.01.005

Keltner, D., & Haidt, J. (1999). Social functions of emotions at four levels of analysis. *Cognition & Emotion, 13*(5), 505–521. https://doi.org/10.1080/026999399379168

Kumar, A., Killingsworth, M. A., & Gilovich, T. (2014). Waiting for merlot: Anticipatory consumption of experiential and material purchases. *Psychological Science, 25*(10), 1924–1931. https://doi.org/10.1177/0956797614546556

Lambert, N. M., Clark, M. S., Durtschi, J., Fincham, F. D., & Graham, S. M. (2010). Benefits of expressing gratitude: Expressing gratitude to a partner changes one's view of the relationship. *Psychological Science, 21*(4), 574–580. https://doi.org/10.1177/0956797610364003

Lambert, N. M., & Fincham, F. D. (2011). Expressing gratitude to a partner leads to more relationship maintenance behavior. *Emotion, 11*(1), 52–60. https://doi.org/10.1037/a0021557

Layous, K., Lee, H., Choi, I., & Lyubomirsky, S. (2013). Culture matters when designing a successful happiness-increasing activity: A comparison of the United States and South Korea. *Journal of Cross-Cultural Psychology, 44*(8), 1294–1303. https://doi.org/10.1177/0022022113487591

Layous, K., & Lyubomirsky, S. (2014). The how, why, what, when, and who of happiness: Mechanisms underlying the success of positive interventions. In J. Gruber &

J. Moscowitz (Eds.), *Positive emotion: Integrating the light sides and dark sides* (pp. 473–495). New York: Oxford University Press.

Layous, K., Nelson, S. K., Oberle, E., Schonert-Reichl, K. A., & Lyubomirsky, S. (2012). Kindness counts: Prompting prosocial behavior in preadolescents boosts peer acceptance and well-being. *PLoS One*, 7(12). https://doi.org/10.1371/journal.pone.0051380

Leary, M. R., Tate, E. B., Adams, C. E., Batts Allen, A., & Hancock, J. (2007). Self-compassion and reactions to unpleasant self-relevant events: The implications of treating oneself kindly. *Journal of Personality and Social Psychology*, 92(5), 887–904. https://doi.org/10.1037/0022-3514.92.5.887

Lucas, R. E., Clark, A. E., Georgellis, Y., & Diener, E. (2003). Reexamining adaptation and the set point model of happiness: Reactions to changes in marital status. *Journal of Personality and Social Psychology*, 84(3), 527–539. https://doi.org/10.1037/0022-3514.84.3.527

Luo, Y., Hawkley, L. C., Waite, L. J., & Cacioppo, J. T. (2012). Loneliness, health, and mortality in old age: A national longitudinal study. *Social Science & Medicine*, 74(6), 907–914. https://doi.org/10.1016/j.socscimed.2011.11.028

Lyubomirsky, S. (2008). *The how of happiness: A scientific approach to getting the life you want.* New York: Penguin Press.

Lyubomirsky, S. (2011). Hedonic adaptation to positive and negative experiences. In S. Folkman (Ed.), *Oxford handbook of stress, health, and coping* (pp. 200–224). New York, NY: Oxford University Press.

Lyubomirsky, S., Sheldon, K. M., & Schkade, D. (2005). Pursuing happiness: The architecture of sustainable change. *Review of General Psychology*, 9(2), 111. https://doi.org/10.1037/1089-2680.9.2.111

Marketdata Enterprises. (2012). *Internet bigger factor in $10.4 billion self-improvement market business holds up well, despite scandals and recession* [Press release]. Retrieved from www.marketdataenterprises.com

Milgram, S. (1963). Behavioral study of obedience. *The Journal of Abnormal and Social Psychology*, 67(4), 371–378. https://doi.org/10.1037/h0040525

Mor, N., & Winquist, J. (2002). Self-focused attention and negative affect: A meta-analysis. *Psychological Bulletin*, 28(4), 638–662. https://doi.org/10.1037//0033-2909.128.4.638

Neff, K. (2003). Self-compassion: An alternative conceptualization of a healthy attitude toward oneself. *Self and Identity*, 2, 85–101. https://doi.org/10.1080/15298860309032

Neff, K. D., Rude, S. S., & Kirkpatrick, K. L. (2007). An examination of self-compassion in relation to positive psychological functioning and personality traits. *Journal of Research in Personality*, 41(4), 908–916. https://doi.org/10.1016/j.jrp.2006.08.002

Nelson, S. K., Della Porta, M. D., Jacobs Bao, K., Lee, H. C., Choi, I., & Lyubomirsky, S. (2015). "It's up to you": Experimentally manipulated autonomy support for prosocial behavior improves well-being in two cultures over six weeks. *The Journal of Positive Psychology*, 10(5), 463–476. https://doi.org/10.1080/17439760.2014.983959

Nelson, S. K., Layous, K., Cole, S. W., & Lyubomirsky, S. (2016). Do unto others or treat yourself? The effects of prosocial and self-focused behavior on psychological flourishing. *Emotion*, 16(6), 850–861. https://doi.org/10.1037/emo0000178

Nelson, S. K., & Lyubomirsky, S. (2014). Finding happiness: Tailoring positive activities for optimal well-being benefits. In M. Tugade, M, Shiota, & L. Kirby (Eds.), *Handbook of positive emotions* (pp. 275–293). New York: Guilford Press.

Nelson-Coffey, S. K., Fritz, M., Lyubomirsky, S., & Cole, S. (2017). Kindness in the blood: A randomized controlled trial of the gene regulatory impact of prosocial behavior. *Psychoneuroendocrinology*, 81, 8–13. https://doi.org/10.1016/j.psyneuen.2017.03.025

Nicolao, L., Irwin, J. R., & Goodman, J. K. (2009). Happiness for sale: Do experiential purchases make consumers happier than material purchases? *Journal of Consumer Research, 36*(2), 188–198. https://doi.org/10.1086/597049

Nolen-Hoeksema, S., Wisco, B. E., & Lyubomirsky, S. (2008). Rethinking rumination. *Perspectives on Psychological Science, 3*, 400–424. https://doi.org/10.1111/j.1745-6924.2008.00088.x

O'Connor, B. P. (1995). Family and friend relationships among older and younger adults: Interaction motivation, mood, and quality. *The International Journal of Aging and Human Development, 40*(1), 9–29. https://doi.org/10.2190/B37N-K317-KY8Q-0TNW

Parks, A. C., Della Porta, M. D., Pierce, R. S., Zilca, R., & Lyubomirsky, S. (2012). Pursuing happiness in everyday life: The characteristics and behaviors of online happiness seekers. *Emotion, 12*(6), 1222. https://doi.org/ 10.1037/a0028587

Pinquart, M., & Sörensen, S. (2000). Influences of socioeconomic status, social network, and competence on subjective well-being in later life: A meta-analysis. *Psychology and Aging, 15*(2), 187–224. https://doi.org/10.1037/0882-7974.15.2.187

Pressman, S. D., Kraft, T. L., & Cross, M. P. (2015). It's good to do good and receive good: The impact of a "pay it forward" style kindness intervention on giver and receiver well-being. *The Journal of Positive Psychology, 10*(4), 293–302. https://doi.org/10.1080/174 39760.2014.965269

Ryan, R. M., & Deci, E. L. (2000). Self-determination theory and the facilitation of intrinsic motivation, social development, and well-being. *American Psychologist, 55*(1), 68–78. https://doi.org/10.1037//0003-066x.55.1.68

Schnall, S., Roper, J., & Fessler, D. M. T. (2010). Elevation leads to altruistic behavior. *Psychological Science, 21*(3), 315–320. https://doi.org/10.1177/0956797609359882

Schwartz, C., Meisenhelder, J. B., Ma, Y., & Reed, G. (2003). Altruistic social interest behaviors are associated with better mental health. *Psychosomatic Medicine, 65*(5), 778–785. https://doi.org/10.1097/01.psy.0000079378.39062.d4

Seligman, M. E. P., Steen, T. A., Park, N., & Peterson, C. (2005). Positive psychology progress: Empirical validation of interventions. *American Psychologist, 60*(5), 410–421. https://doi.org/10.1037/0003-066X.60.5.410

Sheldon, K. M., Boehm, J. K., & Lyubomirsky, S. (2012). Variety is the spice of happiness: The hedonic adaptation prevention (hap) model. In I. Boniwell & S. David (Eds.), *Oxford handbook of happiness* (pp. 901–914). Oxford: Oxford University Press.

Sheldon, K. M., & Lyubomirsky, S. (2006). Achieving sustainable gains in happiness: Change your actions, not your circumstances. *Journal of Happiness Studies, 7*, 55–86.

Sheldon, K. M., & Lyubomirsky, S. (2012). The challenge of staying happier testing the hedonic adaptation prevention model. *Personality and Social Psychology Bulletin, 38*(5), 670–680. https://doi.org/10.1177/0146167212436400

Sherif, M. (1961). *Intergroup conflict and cooperation: The robbers cave experiment* (Vol. 10, pp. 150–198). Norman, OK: University Book Exchange.

Siegel, J. T., Thomson, A. L., & Navarro, M. A. (2014). Experimentally distinguishing elevation from gratitude: Oh, the morality. *The Journal of Positive Psychology, 9*(5), 414–427.

Sin, N. L., Della Porta, M. D., & Lyubomirsky, S. (2011). Tailoring positive psychology interventions to treat depressed individuals. *Applied positive psychology: Improving Everyday Life, Health, Schools, Work, and Society*, 79–96.

Smeets, E., Neff, K., Alberts, H., & Peters, M. (2014). Meeting suffering with kindness: Effects of a brief self-compassion intervention for female college students: Self-compassion intervention for students. *Journal of Clinical Psychology, 70*(9), 794–807. https://doi.org/10.1002/jclp.22076

Taniguchi, H. (2015). Interpersonal mattering in friendship as a predictor of happiness in Japan: The case of Tokyoites. *Journal of Happiness Studies, 16*(6), 1475–1491. https://doi.org/10.1007/s10902-014-9570-z

Thomson, A. L., & Siegel, J. T. (2013). A moral act, elevation, and prosocial behavior: Moderators of morality. *The Journal of Positive Psychology, 8*(1), 50–64. https://doi.org/10.1080/17439760.2012.754926

Trivers, R. L. (1971). The evolution of reciprocal altruism. *The Quarterly Review of Biology, 46*(1), 35–57. https://doi.org/10.1086/406755

Trivers, R. L. (2005). Reciprocal altruism: 30 years later. In C. P. van Schaik & P. M. Kappeler (Eds.), *Cooperation in primates and humans: Mechanisms and evolution* (pp. 67–83). Berlin: Springer-Verlag.

Van Boven, L., & Gilovich, T. (2003). To do or to have? That is the question. *Journal of Personality and Social Psychology, 85*(6), 1193. https://doi.org/10.1037/0022-3514.85.6.1193

Vianello, M., Galliani, E. M., & Haidt, J. (2010). Elevation at work: The effects of leaders' moral excellence. *The Journal of Positive Psychology, 5*(5), 390–411. https://doi.org/10.1080/17439760.2010.516764

Watkins, P. C. (2004). Gratitude and subjective well-being. In R. A. Emmons & M. E. McCullough (Eds.), *The psychology of gratitude* (pp. 167–192). New York, NY: Oxford University Press.

Wheeler, J. A., Gorey, K. M., & Greenblatt, B. (1998). The beneficial effects of volunteering for older volunteers and the people they serve: A meta-analysis. *The International Journal of Aging and Human Development, 47*(1), 69–79. https://doi.org/10.2190/vump-xcmf-fqyu-v0jh

Wood, A. M., Maltby, J., Gillett, R., Linley, P. A., & Joseph, S. (2008). The role of gratitude in the development of social support, stress, and depression: Two longitudinal studies. *Journal of Research in Personality, 42*, 854–871. http://doi.org/10.1016/j.jrp.2007.11.003

Wood, A. M., Joseph, S., Lloyd, J., & Atkins, S. (2009). Gratitude influences sleep through the mechanism of pre-sleep cognitions. *Journal of Psychosomatic Research, 66*(1), 43–48. https://doi.org/10.1016/j.jpsychores.2008.09.002

Yinon, Y., & Landau, M. O. (1987). On the reinforcing value of helping behavior in a positive mood. *Motivation and Emotion, 11*(1), 83–93. https://doi.org/10.1007/bf00992215

INDEX

acquisitive friendship style 106
advertising 329–330
Affect Balance Scale 19
Affectometer 2 19
agency 314
agreeableness 13–14
Algoe's Find, Remind, and Bind theory of gratitude 210, 217–219, 224–225
altruistic motivation 193, 198
ambivalent/inaccurate/inconsistent expressions 370–371
anterior cingulate cortex (ACC) 41–42
anthropocentric worldviews 325–326
anxiety 255, 366–367
attachment theory 296
attention restoration theory 136–137
autonomy 277, 279
autonomy support 118

behavioral processes 82, 86–87
beliefs 53–54
belongingness 356, 359–360
better-than-average (BTA) effect 237
big-fish-little-pond effect 236
biological processes 82, 84–86
boundary spanning 369
Bradburn Scale of Psychological Well-Being 19
brain 15, 36–43
broaden-and-build theory of positive emotions 233–235

Cantril's ladder 21
capitalization 371–372
causal relationships 297–298
coherence 294
collectivism 52–53, 56–57, 198–199
collectivistic motivation 198–199
"coming out growth" (COG) 419–420
compassion fatigue 203
competence 277, 279–280, 314
composite model 18
compulsive buying 323
concealment 371–372
configuration model 18
confirmatory factor analysis (CFA) 62
conscientious 13–14
conservation 314
Consumer Culture Value Impact Model 316
consumer well-being 322–324
contradiction 54
control: fit between opportunities and 437–439; perceiving 435–437; strategies 433–437
correlational studies 22–23
couple relationships 174–175; see also romantic relationships
cultural differences: collectivist values 52–53, 56–57; in correlation between PA and NA 54–56; dialectical beliefs 54, 57–58; identifying mechanisms underlying 63–65; individualist values

52–53, 56–57, 64; in life satisfaction 54–58; relational beliefs 53; self-construals 53, 57; in SWB 54–67
cultural humility 175–176
cultural identity 9
cultural worldviews 299–300
"cycles of virtue" 223–224

dark triad traits 176
day reconstruction method (DRM) 20
decay curve 162
decision to forgive 150–151
default network 15, 35–36
demonic struggles 346
depression 39–40, 60, 255–256, 342
dialectical beliefs 54, 57–58
diffusion tensor imaging (DTI) 34, 38
discerning friendship style 106
disclosure 371–372
dispositional/construal theories 13–17, 23–24
divine struggles 346
domain-specific satisfaction 18–19
doubt struggles 346
downward contrast 231–236, 239, 240, 245
downward identification 231–235
dyadic models: future research directions and considerations 94–96; of partner influence 87–96; romantic relationships and health 79–82

Easterners 11–12, 57–58, 60, 63–65
economic well-being 4–5
egoistic motivation 196–197
electroencephalography (EEG) 33
elevation 463–464
emotional forgiveness 150–151
emotional security 107
emotion regulation 43–44, 60, 63, 439
empathic distress fatigue 203
empathy-altruism model 193
empathy burnout 203–204
employee well-being 272–285
enduring mental health 15
Enright's process theory of forgiveness 156
environmental coherence 299
environmental well-being 324–327
envy 239
eudaimonic well-being: conceptions of 7–12, 23–24, 148–149, 170; correlates of hedonic well-being and 149–150;

empirical research on differences between hedonia and 149
evolutionary theories 15–16
evolutionary theory of forgiveness 157–158
experience sampling method (ESM), 20
explicit regulation 43
exposure theory of forgiveness 160–163
extraversion 13–14, 364–365

facet satisfaction approach 272
factor analytic methods 61–62
Fordyce Happiness Measure 19
forgiveness: definition of 150–151; Enright's process theory of forgiveness 156; evolutionary theory of 157–158; exposure theory of 160–163; interpersonal theory of 156–157; occupational well-being and 154; physical well-being and 152; psychological well-being and 152–153; relational well-being and 153–154; romantic relationships and 153–154; spirituality/religion theory of relational 158–159; spiritual/religious well-being and 154–155; stress-and-coping theory of 155–156; theories 155–164; types of 150–151; virtue theory of 159–160; well-being and 151–155
Friendship Autonomy Support Questionnaire 118
friendships: benefits 117–118; cognitive variables 116–117; composition 105; expectations 108; experts' definitions of 107–108; as function of culture 112–113; as function of sex and gender 110–112; functions 107–108, 111, 117–118; health outcomes 121–123; "heterosexist bias" of researchers 111; ideal standards 108; individual-level variables 115–116; laypeople's definitions of friendship 108–110; macro-level definitions of 104–106; micro-level definitions of 106–110; networks 105–106, 120–123; online 113–115, 124; relational definitions of 106–107; rewards 117–118; role in well-being 115–118; rules 107–108; satisfaction with life/subjective well-being 119–121; satisfying 115–118; social variables 116; strength of social tie 105; styles 106
functional connectivity 34
functional neuroimaging (fMRI) 33, 37

gender 110–112
genetic predisposition 13
global satisfaction approach 272
goal disengagement phase 434
goal engagement phase 433
goals: influence of well-being on achievement and 440–441; influence of well-being on action and 439–440; pursuits 441–442
gratitude: Algoe's Find, Remind, and Bind theory of gratitude 210; cognitive mechanisms of gratitude and well-being relationship 213–216; "cycles of virtue" and 223–224; definition of 211–212; expressing 458–459; interventions 214–216, 222, 458–460; receiving 459–460; social and personal consequences of expressing 221–223; social consequences of experiencing 217–221; social mechanisms of the gratitude and well-being relationship 216–224; SWB and 212–213; well-being 213–225
Gratitude Questionnaire (GQ-6) 211
Gratitude, Resentment, and Appreciation Test (GRAT) 211–212
"gross national happiness" 5

happiness 9, 61, 64, 66
health: actor behavioral processes 82, 86–87; actor biological processes 82, 83–84; actor psychological processes 82, 84–86; benefits of close relationships on well-being and 78–79; dyadic models of romantic relationships and 79–82; humility-health hypothesis 176–177; impact of partner characteristics on actor 80–81; impact of relationship on actor 81; processes underlying effects of romantic relationships on 82–83; religious/spiritual well-being and 339–344; role of friendships 121–123; social comparisons and 240–241, 245–246; social relationships and 453; see also mental health
heart-rate variability 15
hedonic adaptation 451, 461–462
hedonic treadmill 16
hedonic well-being: conceptions of 7–12, 23–24, 148–149, 170; correlates of eudaimonic well-being and 149–150; empirical research on differences between eudaimonia and 149

helping: altruistic motivation for well-being and 193, 198; collectivistic motivation for well-being and 198–199; costs of 193–195; defining helping behavior 184–185; egoistic motivation for well-being and 196–197; evidence of negative association between well-being and 190–191; evidence of positive association between well-being and 187–190; experimental induction of 188–190; in friendships 107; longevity and 187–188; mental health and 187–188; promoting and undermining the effects of helping on well-being 200–205; resolving empirical discrepancies 200–202; strain-satisfaction theoretical framework 193–200; theories of positive effect of helping on well-being 191–193; theories on negative association between informal caregiving and well-being 191–193; types of motivations 195–199; well-being and 184–205
heterosexual individuals 411–412
hierarchical construct model 18
humility: couple relationships and 174–175; cultural 175–176; definition of 168–170; humility-health hypothesis 176–177; key unresolved questions 178–180; other-oriented virtues and 174; physical well-being and 176–177; psychological well-being and 176; religious/spiritual well-being and 171–173; social/relational well-being 173–176; trust and 174–175; types of 169–170; well-being and 168–180
hypo-egoicism: benefits of 401, 403–404; functioning 402; psychological and social effects of 402–404; routes toward mindset 400–402; self-regulation and 401; solution 399–400

identification-contrast model 232–233, 237, 240
implicit motives 441–442
implicit regulation 43
impression management theory 140
independent friendship style 106
individualism 52–53, 56–57, 64
informant reports 20
injustice gap 150
interpersonal relationships 77
interpersonal theory of forgiveness 156–157
interpersonal treatment 275–276

interventions: acts of kindness 456–457, 458, 460; aimed at improving well-being 51; to change values and behaviors 329; elevation 463–464; employee well-being 279; to enhance well-being in LGB youth 422; gratitude 214–216, 222, 458–460; humility 174, 179; mindful-based 139–140; MVO 312, 320, 326–330; positive activity 453–465; to promote forgiveness 148, 156, 160–161; prosocial behavior/action 453–465; prosocial spending 457; self-compassion 462–463; self-directed kindness 461; self-directed spending 461–462; for sexual minority individuals 424; social comparisons 231, 233, 244–246; social support 457–458
intimacy 107
introspection 394, 398
introversion 137–139
invariance 62–63

Job Descriptive Index (JDI) 273
job satisfaction: approaches to measuring 272–273; dimensions of work environment conceptually liked with autonomy 279; dimensions of work environment conceptually liked with competence 279–280; future research directions 281–285; global job satisfaction as a conceptualization of employee well-being 272–273, 285; interpersonal treatment at work 275–276; methodological challenges to testing proposed needs-based model 284–285; need for autonomy 277; need for competence 277; need for relatedness 277–278; pay level 276; qualities of work roles 275; qualities of work tasks 273–275; reinterpreting predictors of global job satisfaction 278–281; relationship between need fulfillment and global job satisfaction 280–281; relationship between objective and perceived work environment 278–279; relationship between perceived work environment and need fulfillment 279–280; work environment's relationship with 273–276

kindness 456–457, 458, 460, 461

learning disabilities 245
LGB individuals 411–412

life circumstance theories 12–13, 24
life meaningfulness 9
life satisfaction: cultural differences in 54–58, 62–63, 67; domain-specific 18–19; measures of 20–21; overall 18–19; role of friendships 119–121; sexual orientation and 423; and well-being in face of adversity 239–242
Life Satisfaction Index A 21
Life Satisfaction Index B 21
Life Satisfaction Rating 21
Life Satisfaction Scale 21
linear dose-response relationship 161–162
loneliness 42–43, 129, 255, 366–367
longevity 187–188
low self-esteem 38–39

materialistic value orientation (MVO): advertising spending and policy 329–330; conceptions of 312–314; consumer well-being and 322–324; critical reflection on materialistic media contents 328–329; environmental well-being and 324–327; future research agenda 327–330; interventions to change values and behaviors 329; personal well-being and 318–320; research on link between well-being and 317–327; social well-being and 320–322; theoretical explanations of the link between well-being and 314–317
McGill Friendship Questionnaire-Friend's Functions 117–118, 119
meaning-as-information approach 293, 303–304
meaning in life: causal relationships 297–298; cultural worldviews 299–300; definition of 293–294; environmental coherence 299; in external world 294–302; features 294; functional understanding of 302–304; making sense of external world 299–302; relationship factors in experienced 295–297; relationships in lay beliefs of 295; social exclusion and 298; social relationships 295–299; threat compensation theories 300–302
Meaning in Life Questionnaire 295
meaning maintenance model (MMM) 300–302
measures: of affect and happiness 19–20; approaches for job satisfaction 272–273; confirmatory factor analysis 62; of

eudaimonic well-being 21; factor analytic methods 61; of happiness 9; invariance 62; issues 61–63; lack of common measurement protocol 22; of life meaningfulness 9; of life satisfaction 20–21; need fulfillment 282–283; overreliance on correlational studies 22–23; overreliance on self-report measures 22; problems in measurement of SWB 22; reification 23; religious/ spiritual well-being 338–339; response styles 61; tripartite model of hedonic 17–19; of well-being 186
media 328–329
medial prefrontal cortex (mPFC) 37–43
mediated moderation 63
meditation 139
mental health: enduring 15; forgiveness and 148, 152–153, 155, 157, 160; friendships and 121, 123; helping and 187–188; humility-health hypothesis and 177; life circumstance and 12; life satisfaction and 5–6; partner relationships and 84–85; relationship between well-being and 13; religious/spiritual well-being and 340–344; self-regulation and 43; *see also* health
Mental Health Continuum 21
mentalizing 40–41
metric invariance 62–63
Michigan Organizational Assessment Questionnaire 273
mindfulness 139
mind-reading 395–396
minority individuals 412–414
mirroring 40
moral struggles 346
motivation: factor in dyadic model of partner influence 95–96; helping 192, 195–199; importance of and perceived control for well-being 435–437; social comparisons 239; strain-satisfaction theoretical framework 193–200
motivational strain 194–195
Motivational Theory of Lifespan Development (MTD) 432–435
Multidimensional Personality Questionnaire 295
Multidimensional Students' Life Satisfaction Scale (MSLSS) 21

naïve dialecticism 54
narcissism 255

nature 136–137
need deficits 282–283
need frustration 281–282
need fulfillment: domain-specific measures of 283; effects of 282; need deficits and 282–283; needs-based model 283–285; relationship between global job satisfaction and 280–281; relationship between perceived work environment and 279–280; sub-dimensions 281–285; work-specific measures of 282–283
need satisfaction 281–282
negative affect (NA) 54–56, 60, 240, 435
networks 15, 35–36
neuroticism 13–14, 255
noncontradiction 54

occupational well-being 154
online friendships 113–115, 124
openness to experience 13–14, 314
other-directed motivation 192–193
otherish motivation 192
other-oriented virtues 174
overall life satisfaction 18–19
overlapping selves 237
Oxford Happiness Inventory (OHI) 21
Oxford Happiness Questionnaire 21

partner influence: on actor's behavior 92–94; dyadic model of 87–96; future research directions and considerations 94–96; impact of partner health beliefs on actor health beliefs 88–89; impact of partner's use of influence strategies on actor health beliefs 89–91; through actor's psychological processes 88–91
pathological helping 191
pay level 276
peers 131, 133–134
personal expressiveness 9
personality 13–14
Personally Expressive Activities Questionnaire 21
personal well-being 318–320
person-environment congruence hypothesis 317
physical well-being 152, 176–177, 339–340
positive affect (PA) 54–56, 64, 233–235, 435
Positive and Negative Affective Schedule (PANAS) 19
Positive and Negative Affect Scales (PANAS-X) 211

"positive education" movement 4–5
positive self-image 235–239
positron emission tomography (PET) 37
power curve 162
pre-decisional phase 433
primary control strategies 433–434, 436
principlistic motivation 199
prosocial behavior/action 184, 453–465
prosocial emotion 464
prosocial spending 457
psychological constructs 3–4, 10–11
psychological insecurity 315
psychological processes 82, 84–86
psychological well-being (PWB) 77,
    152–153, 170, 176, 194, 294
psychophysiological interaction (PPI)
    34, 38
purpose 294

Questionnaire for Eudaimonic Well-
    Being 21

reflected appraisals 395–396
reification 23
relatedness 277–278, 280, 314
relational spirituality 158–159
relational well-being 153–154, 173–176
relationship harmony 59, 63, 153–154
reliable alliance 107
religious/spiritual well-being: definition
    of 338–339; forgiveness and 154–155;
    foundations of 337–338; humility and
    171–173; influence of religion on well-
    being 67; measures 338–339; mental
    health and 340–344; physical health and
    340–344; potential for growth from
    religious/spiritual struggles 347–348;
    religious and spiritual struggles 346–
    347; religious coping 344–345; spiritual
    growth 346
resilience 414–420
resting-state functional connectivity
    (rsfMRI) 34
reward for application 67
romantic relationships: actor behavioral
    processes 82, 86–87; actor biological
    processes 82, 83–84; actor psychological
    processes 82, 84–86; dyadic model of
    partner influence 87–96; dyadic models
    of health and 79–82; forgiveness and
    153–154; humility and 174–175; impact
    of partner characteristics on actor
    health 80–81; impact on actor health

81; partner influence through actor's
    psychological processes 88–91; processes
    underlying effects on health 82–83
rumination 39–40
Ryff 's Scales of Psychological Well-Being
    8, 9

Santa Monica Well-Being Project 5
Satisfaction with Life Scale (SWLS) 20
scalar invariance 62–63
Scales of Psychological Well-Being
    (SPWB) 21
secondary control strategies 433–434, 436
selective-investment theory (SIT) 192–193
selectively acquisitive friendship style 106
selective tenderness and nurturance
    diffused (STAND) 193
self affect 38–39
self-appraisals 318
self-awareness: basic self-reflective
    operations 393–396; beneficial aspects
    of 392; central problem with 396–
    399; hypo-egoic solution 399–404;
    introspection 394, 398; mind-reading
    395–396; reflected appraisals 395–396;
    self-conceptualization and 395, 399;
    self-evaluation and 395, 399; temporal
    self-reflection 393–394, 398
self-compassion 462–463
self-conceptualization 395, 399
self-consistency 59–60
self-construals 53, 57, 64
self-determination theory (SDT) 137, 272,
    276–278, 285, 314–315
self-directed kindness 461
self-directed motivation 192
self-directed spending 461–462
self-discrepancies 316–317
self-enhancement 231, 232, 237–238, 314,
    371–372
self-esteem 38–39, 58–59, 63–64, 236, 238,
    255, 367–368
self-evaluation 395, 399
self-evaluative bias 371–372
self-improvement 231, 238
selfish motivation 192
self-knowledge 36
self-monitoring 368–370
self-presentation: ambivalent/inaccurate/
    inconsistent expressions and
    370–371; belongingness and 356,
    359–360; capitalization and 371–372;
    concealment and 372–373; definition

of 357–359; disclosure and 372–373; effective 361; extraversion and 364–365; function underlying 356; ineffective 362; loneliness and 366–367; minimal 361–362; self-enhancement and 371–372; self-esteem and 367–368; self-evaluative bias and 371–372; self-monitoring and 368–370; shyness and 366–367; sociability and 365–366; social anxiety and 366–367; social skills and 365–366; sociometer theory and 356–357; styles 258–259; SWB and 360–376
self-projection 40
self-regulation 43–44, 368–370, 401
self-report measures 22, 170
self-transcendence 314
self-validation 107
separate components model 18
sexual identity 111–112
sexuality 110–112
sexual orientation: "coming out growth" 419–420; comparisons among sexual minority individuals 412–414; comparisons between LGB and heterosexual individuals 411–412; future research 420–424; interpersonal and community resources 417–419; intrapersonal resources 416–417; minority stress model and coping 414–415; positive aspects of LGB identity 419–420; research assessing resilience 414–420; research directly assessing well-being constructs 411–414; research implications for practice and policy 424–425; resilience as applied to LGB experience 415–420; well-being and 409–425
shared attention 136
shyness 366–367
significance 294
simulation 40
sociability 365–366
social anhedonia 132
social anxiety 132, 366–367
social belonging 41–43
social bond hypothesis 174
social brain 36–37
social comparison orientation (SCO), 242–244
social comparisons: downward 231–235; health and 240–241, 245–246; individual differences that affect the

relation between well-being and 242–244; interventions that may increase well-being 244–246; mood-enhancing pattern of 235; positive affective responses 233–235; positive self-image and 235–239; social media 259–260; theory on 230–231; types of 231–233; upward 231–235
social compensation model 263–264
social connections 363
social constructionism 10–11
social cynicism 67
social enhancement model 263–264
social facilitation 136
social integration 453
social interaction 133–135, 465
social media: associations between well-being and 256–262; causal relationship between well-being and 262–263; enhancement versus compensation 263–264; negative associations 259–262; online friendships 113–115; passive use and well-being 259–260; positive associations 256–259, 261–262; problematic use and well-being 260–261; self-presentation styles and well-being 258–259; versus social network sites 254–255; social network size and well-being 257–258; suggestions for future research 264–265; users 255–256; well-being and 253–263
social network sites 254–255, 257–258
social neuroscience: key assumptions of 14–15, 32–33; of mentalizing 40–41; methods of 33–35; of the self 37–38; of self-regulation 43–44; of threat detection and social belonging 41–43
social relationships 134–135, 295–299, 452–453
social skills 365–366
social support 453, 457–458
social tie 105
social well-being 173–176, 320–322
sociometer theory 356–357, 360–362
solitary play 131
solitude: active ingredient of 141; alone across the lifespan 139; alone in the now 139–140; benefits of 129, 136–139; conceptual and methodological approaches 130–132, 140–141; creatively alone 140; damaging effects of 129; definition of 130; effect of dosage 141; electronic communications and

131; impact on well-being 132, 141; internal and external sources of 132; introversion and 137–139; potential consequences of 132; promising places to further explore benefits of 139–140; as restorative haven 136–137; as state of being 131; as state of mind 131
spirituality *see* religious/spiritual well-being
state humility 169–170
stimulating companionship 107
strain-satisfaction theoretical framework 193–200
stress-and-coping theory of forgiveness 155–156
structural connectivity 34
subjective well-being (SWB): ambivalent/ inaccurate/inconsistent expressions and 370–371; : associations between social media use and 256–262; belongingness and 356, 359–360; benefits of close relationships on health and 78–79; capitalization and 371–372; causal relationship between social media use and 262–263; cognitive mechanisms of gratitude and well-being relationship 213–216; combining life circumstance and dispositional/construal theories 16–17; components of 52; concealment and 372–373; conceptions of 6–8, 51–52, 148–149, 170, 185–186; correlates of 58–59; cultural differences in 54–67; default network 15, 35–36; definition of 3–4; disclosure and 372–373; dispositional/construal theories 13–17; Eastern conceptions of 11–12, 65; emotion regulation and 43–44, 60, 63; eudaimonic conception of 7–12; evidence of negative association between helping and 190–191; evidence of positive association between helping and 187–190; evolutionary theories of 15–16; extraversion and 364–365; forgiveness and 151–155; goal pursuits and 441–442; gratitude and 212–225; hedonic conception of 7–12; helping and 184–205; humility and 168–180; identifying mechanisms underlying cultural differences in 63–65; impact of a MVO on 311–330; impact of solitude on 132, 141; implicit motives and 441–442; importance of motivation and perceived control for 435–437;

individual differences that affect the relation between social comparison and 242–244; influence of goals and achievement on 440–441; influence of religion on 67; influence on goals and action 439–440; life circumstance theories 12–13, 16–17; and life satisfaction in face of adversity 239–242; loneliness and 366–367; mean levels of 56–58; measures of 4–5, 17–23, 61–63; MVO and consumer 322–324; MVO and environmental 324–327; MVO and personal well-being 318–320; MVO and social 320–322; passive use of social media and 259–260; potential mediators between humility and aspects of 177–178; problematic use of social media and 260–261; promoting and undermining the effects of helping on 200–205; public policy and 4–5; relationship harmony and 59, 63; religious/spiritual 67, 154–155, 171, 337–348; research on link between MVO and 317–327; role of friendships in 103–124; scientific study of 5–6; self-consistency and 59–60; self-construals and 57, 64–65; self-enhancement and 371–372; self-esteem and 38–39, 58–59, 63, 367–368; self-evaluative bias and 371–372; self-monitoring and 368–370; self-presentation and 355–376; self-presentation styles and 258–259; set point 13; sexual orientation and 409–425; shyness and 366–367; social comparison-based interventions that may increase 244–246; social anxiety and 366–367; social brain and 36–37; sociability and 365–366; social mechanisms of the gratitude and well-being relationship 216–224; social media and 253–263; social network size and 257–258; social psychology of employee 272–285; social relationships and 452–453; social skills and 365–366; stability in 436; structure of 54–56; theoretical explanations of the link between MVO and 314–317; theories of 12–17, 23–24; theories of positive effect of helping on 191–193; theories on negative association between informal caregiving and well-being 191–193; threats to helping that enhances 203–205; ways to promote helping that

enhances 202–203; Western conceptions of 11–12, 65
suppression 60

Taoism 54
Temporal Satisfaction with Life Scale (TSWLS) 20
temporal self-reflection 393–394, 398
terror management theory 299, 300–302
theories: Algoe's Find, Remind, and Bind theory of gratitude 210; attachment 296; attention restoration 136–137; broaden-and-build theory of positive emotions 233–235; combining life circumstance and dispositional/ construal 16–17; of constructs 6–7; dispositional/construal 13–17, 23–24; Enright's process theory of forgiveness 156; evolutionary theory of forgiveness 157–158; exposure theory of forgiveness 160–163; of forgiveness 155–164; interpersonal theory of forgiveness 156–157; life circumstance 12–13, 16–17, 24; meaning maintenance model 300–302; on negative association between informal caregiving and well-being 191–193; of positive effect of helping on well-being 191–193; selective-investment 192–193; self-determination 137, 272, 314; social comparisons 230–231; sociometer 356–357, 360–362; spirituality/religion theory of relational forgiveness 158–159; strain-satisfaction theoretical framework 193–200; stress-and-coping theory of forgiveness 155–156; terror management 299, 300–302; theoretical explanations of the link between well-being and MVO

314–317; threat compensation 300–302; uncertainty management 300–302; value 314; virtue theory of forgiveness 159–160; voluntary settlement 56
threat compensation theories 300–302
threat detection 41–43
"too-much-of-a-good-thing effect" (TMGT effect) 282
tripartite model of hedonic well-being 7, 17–19, 170
trust 174–175

U-index (U = unpleasant or undesirable) 20
ultimate meaning struggles 346
ultimate satisfaction hypothesis 176
uncertainty management theory 300–302
unconditionally acquisitive friendship style 106
upward contrast 231–235, 239, 241
upward identification 231–235, 241–242, 244

Values in Action Scale (VIA) 212
value theory 314
virtue: "cycles of virtue" 223–224; theory of forgiveness 159–160; virtue and vice hypothesis 176
vitamin model 282
voluntary settlement theory 56
volunteerism 192

well-being *see* subjective well-being (SWB)
Westerners 11–12, 57–58, 60, 63–65
work roles 275
work tasks 273–275

Yerkes-Dodson law 141

Taylor & Francis eBooks

Helping you to choose the right eBooks for your Library

Add Routledge titles to your library's digital collection today. Taylor and Francis ebooks contains over 50,000 titles in the Humanities, Social Sciences, Behavioural Sciences, Built Environment and Law.

Choose from a range of subject packages or create your own!

Benefits for you

» Free MARC records
» COUNTER-compliant usage statistics
» Flexible purchase and pricing options
» All titles DRM-free.

Benefits for your user

» Off-site, anytime access via Athens or referring URL
» Print or copy pages or chapters
» Full content search
» Bookmark, highlight and annotate text
» Access to thousands of pages of quality research at the click of a button.

> **REQUEST YOUR FREE INSTITUTIONAL TRIAL TODAY**
>
> **Free Trials Available**
> We offer free trials to qualifying academic, corporate and government customers.

eCollections – Choose from over 30 subject eCollections, including:

Archaeology	Language Learning
Architecture	Law
Asian Studies	Literature
Business & Management	Media & Communication
Classical Studies	Middle East Studies
Construction	Music
Creative & Media Arts	Philosophy
Criminology & Criminal Justice	Planning
Economics	Politics
Education	Psychology & Mental Health
Energy	Religion
Engineering	Security
English Language & Linguistics	Social Work
Environment & Sustainability	Sociology
Geography	Sport
Health Studies	Theatre & Performance
History	Tourism, Hospitality & Events

For more information, pricing enquiries or to order a free trial, please contact your local sales team: www.tandfebooks.com/page/sales

 **Routledge** Taylor & Francis Group | The home of Routledge books

www.tandfebooks.com